THE
DELPHIC
ORACLE

... ἔνθα ἄναξ τεκμήρατο Φοῖβος Ἀπόλλων
νηὸν ποιησάσθαι ἐπήρατον εἶπέ τε μῦθον·
   Ἐνθάδε δὴ φρονέω τεύξειν περικαλλέα νηὸν
ἔμμεναι ἀνθρώποις χρηστήριον οἵ τέ μοι αἰεὶ
ἐνθάδ' ἀγινήσουσι τεληέσσας ἑκατόμβας,
ἠμὲν ὅσοι Πελοπόννησον πίειραν ἔχουσιν,
ἠδ' ὅσοι Εὐρώπην τε καὶ ἀμφιρύτους κατὰ νήσους,
χρησόμενοι· τοῖσιν δ' ἄρ' ἐγὼ νημερτέα βουλὴν
πᾶσι θεμιστεύοιμι χρέων ἐνὶ πίονι νηῷ.
   —Homeric Hymn to Apollo 285–293.

The oracles are dumb,
No voice or hideous hum
   Runs through the archèd roof in words deceiving,
Apollo from his shrine
Can no more divine,
   With hollow shriek the steep of Delphos leaving.
No nightly trance or breathèd spell
Inspires the pale-eyed priest from the prophetic cell.
   —John Milton, *On the Morning of Christ's Nativity* xix.

THE
DELPHIC
ORACLE

Its Responses and Operations

with a Catalogue of Responses

JOSEPH FONTENROSE

UNIVERSITY OF CALIFORNIA PRESS

Berkeley · Los Angeles · London

University of California Press
Berkeley and Los Angeles, California
University of California Press, Ltd.
London, England

Copyright © 1978 by The Regents of the University of California

First Paperback Printing, 1981
ISBN 0-520-04359-6
Library of Congress Catalog Card Number: 76-47969
Printed in the United States of America
Designed by Jim Mennick

1 2 3 4 5 6 7 8 9

In Memory of
IVAN M. LINFORTH
My teacher and friend, a great Hellenist,

καλὸς κἀγαθὸς ἀνήρ

View of the Pleistos Valley and Mount Kirphis from Apollo's Temenos at Delphi.

Contents

Illustrations

Addenda

P. 9. In saying that Historical responses are commonplace pronouncements I mean simply that none is extraordinary. Not one is an unqualified prediction of an actual event, and not one is ambiguous or unclear. There are no conditioned commands or predictions as defined in modes B and F. It is true that some are important, in the sense that the consultation concerned a significant matter and that the response was historically important. For example, those that Thucydides attests for his own lifetime, H4–8, are important in this sense, but they are not like the Croesus oracles (Q99–103) or those spoken to Sparta on Tegea (Q88–90). Q5 is essentially a direction to Sparta to go to war with Athens (probably a sanction, as the question indicates) telling her to fight with all her strength in order to have victory; and this is followed by a statement of future intention.

P. 284, Q47. The inscription of Cyrene (fourth century B.C.), cited under NP, Indirect, purports to reproduce the text of the seventh-century compact between Thera and the colonists under Battos. The quoted compact is not likely to be authentic. The receiver of the response is called Battos, although that was probably not his Theraean name; and the response is merely "Found Cyrene" (indirect). The colony would not have had that name until its foundation; or if Apollo is supposed to have ordained the name, he didn't tell Battos where to go; cf. Herod. 4.150.3, 4.155.3. The response is introduced with *Apollôn automatixen*, taken as

"Apollo spoke spontaneously." But, according to Herodotos, Battos asked a question about his speech. No other source indicates spontaneous response. The inscription may mean that Apollo spoke in his own person (according to Herodotos the Pythia spoke); but who is going to believe that really happened? In any case, this inscription does not confirm Herodotos' verse-oracle. If authentic, it would be no more than a simple direction or sanction and would go to show that Delphi had something to do with colonization.

P. 429, after Didyma response 50. Add the following to the Catalogue of Responses of Didyma.

51 Historical, c. 130 B.C.
C. Miletos.
Occ. Building of Apollo's temple.
R. Complete the building of the temple (?).
Mode A1, Topic 1a
Testimony—DI 47, lines 10–12.

52 Historical, later second century B.C.
C. Andronikos Potamon's son.
Occ. and Q. Not stated.
R. Propitiate Poseidon Asphaleos with sacrifices at this sign (?) and ask him to be propitious and to preserve the order of your city in tranquillity. For he favors you. You must worship him and pray to him, so that hereafter you may come to old age without harm.
Mode A1, Topic 1a
Direct, Verse—DI 132, lines 2–7.

53 Historical, second century A.D. (?)
C. Hermias.
Occ. and Q. Not stated.
R. Make a thank-offering to Zeus Hypsistos.
Mode A1, Topic 1b
Testimony—DI 129.

54 Historical, third century A.D.
C. Titus Flavius Ulpianus.
Occ. Apparently concern with sacrifices and altars.
Q. (A) On this matter.
R. (A) Like a broad tree you have thriving roots, and you pasture thick-wooled sheep. And so it is right that I respond again to your question. Having obeyed my oracles, augmenting your pious purpose through former ordinances and oracles, you have set your mind upon altars for sacrifice.
Mode D1, Topic 1b

Q. (B) Where shall he place the holy table?

R. (B) Missing.

Direct, Verse (A)—*DI* 277, lines 13–20.

Testimony (B)—*ibid.*, lines 21–22.

Comment: Apparently Ulpianus received several oracles, some perhaps in dreams or visions and perhaps to the same effect.

Preface

It was in the spring of 1934, over forty years ago, when I was teaching in Eugene at the University of Oregon, that I first thought of writing a book on the Delphic Oracle. Just a few months earlier I had completed my dissertation on the cults of Didyma, most of which was necessarily devoted to the cult and Oracle of Apollo Didymeus. It occurred to me that before I reworked my dissertation for publication I should make the same thorough study of Delphi. I planned to cover everything—Oracle, cults of all Delphic gods, myths, town, Amphictiony, history of Oracle and town—and to include a corpus of all responses either spoken at Delphi or attributed to Delphi. Not until I began gathering material, reading the numerous literary sources and inscriptions, did I realize the magnitude of the task. What I could do in under two years for Didyma would take many years for Delphi. Often did I falter on the way, and often did I turn aside to another subject. I became deeply interested in mythology and gave much attention to mythical subjects. This interest was not without relevance to Delphi: my book *Python* deals thoroughly with Delphic myth and fulfills that phase of my project. Myth is also relevant to the present work, as will become evident. In the meantime I have also written a monograph, *The Cult and Myth of Pyrros at Delphi*, and several articles and reviews dealing with Delphic subjects. H. W. Parke's *A History of the Delphic Oracle* (1939; revised in 1956) has relieved me of the historical part of my task; and with D. E. W. Wormell he has compiled a corpus of Delphic oracular texts; hence for this book a Catalogue of Delphic responses is sufficient.

Here at last is the core of my Delphic studies, what I had chiefly in mind when I started upon them, a book upon Apollo's oracular utterances—genuine, spurious, legendary: all that are preserved in literature and inscriptions. It attempts to determine just what kind of business the Delphic Oracle did, what kind of responses were actually spoken there—in short, what sort of institution the Oracle really was—and to distinguish the actual Oracle of history from the Oracle of legend and traditional story. The making of this determination and distinction has demanded a close study of the Oracle and responses as they appear in history and legend. Though it has taken a long time to complete this work, I am sure that time has improved it: I now see farther and deeper in Delphic matters than twenty or more years ago.

In this book I discredit several cherished beliefs about the Delphic Oracle. I expect therefore that my conclusions will meet with objections; for I have encountered a kind of Delphic piety: there are persons who want to believe in the Delphic Oracle as conventionally presented in modern literature (but not in ancient literature, as we shall see). They want to believe in toxic gases or vapors rising from a chasm (their nonexistence was demonstrated over seventy years ago), a frenzied or drugged Pythia talking incoherently, cleverly ambiguous prophecies and remarkable predictions that prophets or attendant bards expressed in dactylic hexameter. I am aware that my argument, however well-founded, will not prevail against the will to believe. Probably two centuries from now readers will pick up a new book or article that will tell them about the toxic gases, the chasm, the frenzy, and the ambiguities. We shall never get rid of the "mephitic vapors," whatever geology has to say. One hundred and fifty years ago Karl Otfried Müller showed that Apollo was not the Greek sun god; but you can still find in recent handbooks, and even in works of classical scholars, the statement that Apollo was a sun god. All that I can ask the reader to do concerning my conclusions is to look at the evidence.

I hope that the reader will enjoy reading these pages as much as I have enjoyed writing them. It has been a hard, time-consuming job, but satisfying. Most of the writing has been done in the last few years; chapters written earlier have been completely rewritten. This I consider the second volume of a Delphic trilogy, the first being *Python* on the myth; the third will be on the cults of Delphi.

As in *Python* I directly transliterate most Greek names; but I keep the familiar Latin form of well-known names, e.g., *Aeschylus*, *Thucydides*, which look strange to readers in their transliterated forms. And the god of Delphi must be *Apollo* rather than *Apollon*, except when the name is joined to an epithet like *Pythios*, since "Apollo Pythios" would be a hybrid form. For *ov* I use *u* (sometimes *û*) in proper names, as in German practice, since *upsilon* is represented by *y*; hence *Lykurgos* must not be considered a hybrid form. But in the transliteration of Greek words and phrases I represent the digraph with *ou*, since there a *u* alone looks strange. For citations in the Catalogue and notes, however, I generally adopt the Latin titles of Greek works that are familiar to scholars, e.g., *Aves*, *Nubes*, of Aristophanes. This seems the most convenient practice and makes for greater consistency: the Greek titles are unfamiliar to many readers, and so are English titles for many minor works (but in the text I generally use English titles). Likewise, in some instances where the initial letter of a Greek author's name would be changed by transliteration, as *Kallimachos* for *Callimachus*, I keep the Latin form, since that is what readers will find in library catalogues.

I owe a debt of gratitude to many friends and several institutions for invaluable help over these many years. First of all I want to thank Raphael Sealey, Ronald Stroud, and Marcia Dobson for reading the manuscript and for their valuable comments and suggestions on it; they have given me references, especially on historical matters, that otherwise I would have missed. Ivan M. Linforth, at the age of ninety-five, also read the manuscript; and his name appeared with the three just mentioned in the Preface of the manuscript that I submitted to the Press. His recent death is a great loss to all of us; I owe him a debt of gratitude for much help and kindness. I must also thank Pierre Amandry, Director of the École Française d'Athènes, most gratefully for granting me permission to reproduce the map of Apollo's Delphic sanctuary (fig. 1). I must also acknowledge my indebtedness to his *La mantique Apollinienne à Delphes*; it has been for me the most valuable book yet written on the Delphic Oracle. To his predecessor too, Georges Daux, I owe thanks for encouragement and help. And my debt is also great to H. W. Parke of Trinity College, Dublin, for information, offprints of articles, and above all for his gift to me of *The Delphic Oracle*, which with Amandry's book has been my greatest aid; it has been a great advantage in particular to have the Parke-Wormell corpus of oracles in volume 2 constantly at hand.

To the American Council of Learned Societies I am indebted for the grant of a fellowship (1935/36) which allowed me to make my first trip to Greece and to visit Delphi three times; also to the John Simon Guggenheim Memorial Foundation for the grant of a fellowship (1958/59) for study of the cults of Delphi; and to the University of California Humanities Institute for an award (1966/67) that allowed me to visit Delphi three more times and also to visit Didyma for the first time, a wonderful experience. It would be possible to write on the Delphic Oracle from study of the literary works, inscriptions, and excavation reports alone; but I am sure that this book would not be the same if I had not visited Delphi twelve times in all and become familiar with its topography and monuments. I am also indebted to Yale University Graduate School for a Sterling Fellowship (1936/37), which enabled me to spend nine months on my earliest Delphic researches; and to the University of California, Berkeley, for several research grants.

My Delphian friends need a word of thanks for unfailing help and hospitality, especially Nikolaos Galatos, *phylax* of the Delphi Museum, whom I met on my first visit to Delphi in October, 1935. He has truly been my Delphic *proxenos*.

He is no longer with us, but I owe thanks also to H. R. W. Smith for interest, help, and encouragement over the years. He was the photographer of the frontispiece.

I especially owe thanks to Stephen Hart, editor of the manuscript, and to several members of the editorial staff of the University Press—Susan Peters, Mary Lamprech, and Phyllis Killen—for pleasant association and careful attention to every stage in the production of this book. Above all, I want to express my gratitude to August Frugé, Director of the University Press to the end of 1976, for his interest in the book from the submission and acceptance of the manuscript.

These have been my principal benefactors. I also want to thank many other friends who have helped me along the way.

JOSEPH FONTENROSE
Berkeley

Abbreviations

H Historical.

ID Inscriptions de Délos. Académie des Inscriptions et Belles Lettres. 6 vols. Paris: Champion, 1926–1950.

IG Inscriptiones Graecae, Academia Litterarum Borussica.

IM Die Inschriften von Magnesia am Maeander, edited by Otto Kern. Berlin, 1900.

J Felix Jacoby, editor, Die Fragmente der griechischen Historiker. 3 vols. in 14. Berlin: Weidmann; Leiden: Brill, 1923–1958.

L Legendary.

LSJ H. G. Liddell, R. Scott, H. S. Jones, A Greek-English Lexicon. 9th edition. Oxford: Clarendon Press, 1940.

LM Ausführliches Lexikon der griechischen und römischen Mythologie, edited by W. H. Roscher. 6 vols. in 9. Leipzig: Teubner, 1884–1937.

M C. and Th. Mueller, editors, Fragmenta Historicorum Graecorum. 5 vols. Paris, 1868–1883.

Michel Charles Michel, Recueil d'Inscriptions Grecques. Paris, 1900.

MIFL Motif-Index of Folk-Literature, compiled by Stith Thompson. 2d edition. 6 vols. Bloomington: Indiana University Press, 1955–1958.

Milet Milet: Ergebnisse der Ausgrabungen und Untersuchungen seit dem Jahre 1899, edited by Theodor Wiegand and others. 4 vols. in several parts each. Berlin: Reimer, 1906– .

OCD Oxford Classical Dictionary. 2d edition, 1970.

PW H. W. Parke, D. E. W. Wormell, The Delphic Oracle II: The Oracular Responses. Oxford: Blackwell, 1956.

Q Quasi-Historical.

RE Real-Encyclopädie der classischen Altertumswissenschaft (Pauly-Wissowa).

SEG Supplementum Epigraphicum Graecum.

SIG Sylloge Inscriptionum Graecarum, edited by W. Dittenberger. 3d edition. 4 vols. in 5. Leipzig: Hirzel, 1915–1924.

TGF Tragicorum Graecorum Fragmenta, edited by August Nauck. 2d edition. Leipzig, 1889.

NOTE: For abbreviations of inscription collections not listed here (cited only in the Catalogue) see Index A, Inscriptions.

Introduction

The Delphic Oracle has captured the imagination of ancients and moderns alike. From the sixth century B.C. it was the most popular of Greek Oracles, attracting clients from all Hellas and beyond. Such was its prestige that most Hellenes after 500 B.C. placed its foundation in the earliest days of the world: before Apollo took possession, they said, Ge (Earth) and her daughter Themis had spoken oracles at Pytho.[1] Such has been the strength of the tradition that many historians and others have accepted as historical fact the ancient statement that Ge and Themis spoke oracles at Delphi before it became Apollo's establishment. Yet nothing but the myth supports this statement. In the earliest account that we have of the Delphic Oracle's beginnings, the story found in the Homeric Hymn to Apollo (281–374), there was no Oracle before Apollo came and killed the great she-dragon, Pytho's only inhabitant. This was apparently the Delphic myth of the sixth century.[2]

Whatever Delphic origin myth a Hellene accepted, he firmly believed

---

1 Aesch. *Eum.* 1–8; Eur. *IT* 1259–1269; Aristonoos *Hymn*, *FD* 3.2.191.15–20; Plut. *Mor.* 421c; Apollod. 1.4.1; Paus. 10.5.5–6; Ael. *VH* 3.1; Men. Rhet. 1.3.2, p. 362 Sp. See Parke 1956: 3–8; Roux 1976: 19–34. In the following pages I shall use the word "oracle" to mean either an oracular establishment or an oracular response. For clarity I shall capitalize it (Oracle) when it refers to oracular establishments or institutions, such as the Delphic Oracle; in lower case (oracle) it will be used interchangeably with "response."

2 See Amandry 1950: 201–203. In *Eum.* 4–8 Aeschylus introduces Phoibe between Themis and Apollo, probably to fill the gap between the Titans' fall and Apollo's acquisition of Delphi; see Amandry 201 note 2; D. S. Robertson, "The Delphian Succession in the

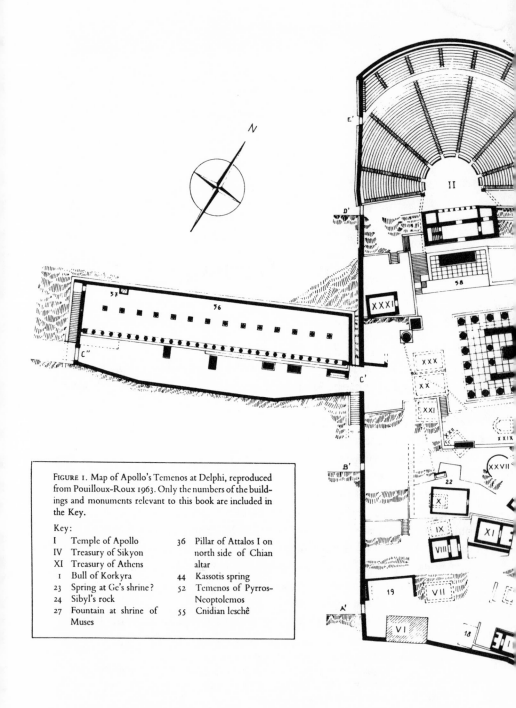

FIGURE 1. Map of Apollo's Temenos at Delphi, reproduced from Pouilloux-Roux 1963. Only the numbers of the buildings and monuments relevant to this book are included in the Key.

Key:

I	Temple of Apollo	36	Pillar of Attalos I on
IV	Treasury of Sikyon		north side of Chian
XI	Treasury of Athens		altar
1	Bull of Korkyra	44	Kassotis spring
23	Spring at Ge's shrine?	52	Temenos of Pyrros-
24	Sibyl's rock		Neoptolemos
27	Fountain at shrine of	55	Cnidian leschê
	Muses		

0   10   50   100 m.

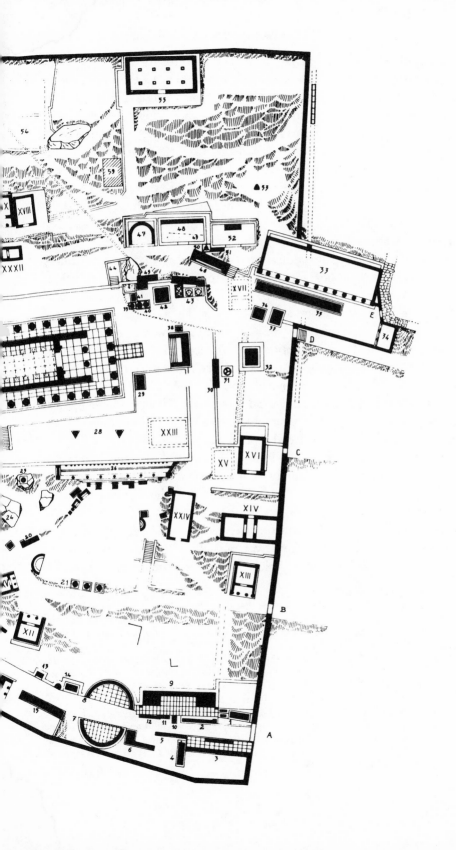

that the Oracle had been active in the later Bronze Age. Already in the Odyssey the bard Demodokos brings Agamemnon to Pytho to consult about the prospects of war against Troy (see the Catalogue, L1). According to the tradition current in historical times the Delphic Oracle played a part in not only the Trojan War, but also in the Theban War and the fortunes of the Theban royal house (e.g., L17, 18), in the Argonautic voyage, and in the deeds of Herakles and Theseus. It is unlikely, however, that Bronze Age Pytho had any such institution, or even a cult of Apollo. Nor does it appear to have had any fame or wealth: the remains show only a modest village and no cult likely to be known beyond the vicinity. Mycenaean remains have been found in the eastern part of Apollo's sanctuary, but there is no indication of a shrine at that time; certainly there was no temple nor apparently any other structure on the site of Apollo's historical temples. The principal settlement of Mycenaean and Dark Age times lay about a kilometre to the southeast, around the temenos of Athena Pronaia, occupying the terrace which runs from that sanctuary to the Castalian spring.[3] A goddess was worshipped there, presumably she who became Athena Pronaia in historical times. There is no indication that she was an oracular goddess—Athena Pronaia was not —or that she had more than a local reputation. Though this deity was probably a mother-goddess, it would be reckless to identify her with Ge and to suppose that she preceded Apollo as oracle-speaker.[4]

If there was an Oracle at Pytho or in its neighborhood before the eighth century B.C. it was a purely local institution which has left no trace. Pottery, bronzes, and other finds indicate that the Pythian Apollo's sanctuary was established on its historical site in the eighth century, perhaps after 750. The first structure, temple or Oracle house, was probably made of wood; there was possibly a succession of wooden structures, reflected in the mythical first three temples of bay wood,

---

Opening of the *Eumenides*," *CR* 55 (1941) 70. For a shrine of Ge (and a shrine of the Muses) by a spring south of the temple in historical times see Plut. *Mor.* 402cd. On the Homeric Hymn see Franz Dornseiff, *Die archaische Mythenerzählung* (Berlin, Leipzig: de Gruyter, 1933); Fontenrose 1969b. See the Bibliography for titles and facts of publication of those works cited only by author's surname and date.

3 On Mycenaean and Dark-Age Pytho see Amandry 1950: 204–211, 231–232; Defradas 1954: 22–27; Lerat 1961: 321, 352–366. On early Delphi and the origins of the Oracle see the varying accounts of Hiller von Gaertringen 1899: 2525–2547; Poulsen 1920: 11–20; Delcourt 1955: 29–38; Parke 1956: 3–13; Roux 1976: 35–51.

4 My suggestion in *Python* (1959: 409–419) that an Oracle at the Corycian Cave, when the Delphoi lived at Lykoreia (Strabo 9.3.3, p. 418), preceded the Oracle at Pytho must apparently be given up, since recent excavations show the cave unused between Mycenaean times and the sixth century B.C. For excavation reports see *BCH* 95 (1971) 771–776, 96 (1972) 906–911, 97 (1973) 528–535.

beeswax and feathers, and bronze. The first stone temple, that of which Agamedes and Trophonios were the legendary architects, was built in the seventh century.[5] This temple was destroyed by fire in 548/7 and was replaced by the so-called Alkmeonid temple, a much larger structure, which in turn was destroyed by earthquake in 373. The temple whose foundations and remains can still be seen was constructed in the fourth century (see Map, fig. 1).

Whatever the origin of the Oracle it soon began to acquire fame and prestige and to attract powerful and wealthy clients from distant parts of Greece. Cities as well as individuals began to consult it. It had acquired some pan-Hellenic reputation by 700; Sparta brought constitutional reforms to Delphi for approval (Q8) perhaps in the early seventh century. The period of Delphi's greatest prestige lasted from approximately 580, following the Amphictionic takeover as a result of the First Sacred War, to 320, around the time of Alexander's death. There is no good evidence that Delphi's reputation sank after 480 because of Medizing pronouncements during the Persian Wars. Delphi's supposed Medism is questionable; it is a modern construction, built up from Herodotos' Delphic oracles on Xerxes' invasion. As we shall see, the authenticity of these oracles is subject to question.

The Delphic Oracle's real decline in prestige and wealth began after Alexander's time and continued through the Hellenistic and Roman periods. The decline runs parallel to the decline of the Greek *polis*. Both cities and individuals continued to patronize Delphi, though in fewer numbers. Some late writers refer to periods of inactivity or to a cessation of operations at various times after about 50 B.C.[6] But their testimony is not very trustworthy; and we know that responses were spoken at Delphi at least down to the third quarter of the third century A.D. There are responses reported for the fourth century, such as two addressed to the Emperor Julian (Q262, 263), but they are either spurious or questionable. It may well be that the Delphic Oracle continued operations until 391, when Theodosius' edict closed all Oracles and forbade divination of any kind.[7] Surely before 400 the Delphic Oracle had disappeared.

---

5 For the temple legends see Homeric Hymn 3.294–299; Paus. 10.5.9–13. On the seventh-century temple see Courby 1921: 190–199.

6 Lucan BC 5.69–70, 111–114, 120–123, 131–140, with Schol. on 5.113; Dion Cass. 62.14.2; Lucian Nero 10; Sopater Prol. in Aristid. Or. 13, p. 740 Dind.; Juvenal 6.553–556; Clem. Alex. Protr. 2.1, 10P.

7 Cod. Theodos. 16.10.9; Cod. Justin. 1.11.2. See Cod. Theodos. 16.10.13 for the edict of Honorius and Arcadius in 400 closing all pagan temples and forbidding sacrifices. Yet pagan worship survived in the empire until well along in the sixth century.

For over a thousand years the Delphic Oracle was a going concern. In all that time the incumbent Pythia spoke oracles to consultants. We are likely to suppose that she always spoke the kind of oracles that Herodotos quotes, those spoken to Croesus or to the Spartans on Tegea or to the Greek states at the time of the Persian Wars, for those oracles are the foundation on which the prevailing modern conception of Delphic responses has been built. If the Pythia could speak prophecies like these, marvelous indeed was her prophetic skill, so marvelous that even yet scholars have recourse to occult powers as the only possible explanation of the phenomenon.[8] I do not believe that we need that hypothesis, as Laplace might have said; as I hope to make clear, we need not step beyond the bounds of the credible or even of the commonplace.

Yet, though we may rule out the supernatural and occult, the usual "rational" explanation of the Delphic Oracle's operation and activity, of its success in giving satisfactory answers to consultants, is almost as incredible: the rationalists' belief is about as strange as their unbelief. The usual contemporary explanation is in substance that the Pythia entered into a mantic frenzy or state of trance, in which she uttered unintelligible sounds, "the confused and disjointed remarks of a hypnotized woman," as Parke puts it; and that the attendant priests interpreted these sounds, giving the inquirer a coherent, more or less ambiguous reply usually expressed in dactylic-hexameter verse. The priests' interpretations (so the hypothesis continues) were slanted and colored by their devotion to Delphic interests and by the unexampled knowledge of Greek affairs and of Mediterranean lands which they picked up from the numerous visitors who came to Delphi from the whole Greek world. Through a combination of judicious interpretations, ambiguities, coincidences, and lucky guesses, the Delphic priesthood managed to keep its many clients satisfied from some preclassical date to the fourth century A.D.[9]

Such is the explanation that we are most likely to read or hear today. It is wonderful if true. We are asked to believe that without divine or demonic aid the Pythia spoke, or the priests produced, a prophecy, albeit often ambiguous, that always suited the occasion; and to believe in an extraordinary skill, sagacity, and knowledge, never failing (or seldom),

---

8 See Myers 1883: 16–17; Dempsey 1918: 71–74; Dodds 1951: 70–75; E. R. Dodds, "Telepathy and Clairvoyance in Classical Antiquity," *Greek Poetry and Life, Essays Presented to Gilbert Murray* (Oxford: Clarendon Press, 1936) 374–377; W. F. J. Knight, *Elysion* (London: Rider, 1970) 67, 71.

9 See Legrand 1898: 53–66; Farnell 1907: 186–197; Parke 1956: 30–40. Cf. Delcourt 1955: 10, 52–55.

which tax our credulity almost as much as do demonic possession, telepathy, and clairvoyance. I am convinced that supernatural and rationalistic explanations are alike based upon a misconception of the kind of
response that was really spoken at Delphi in historical times. The questions
asked about Delphic operations and the answers given are grounded in
false assumptions. Our task in this book is to find out just what sort of
response was verifiably spoken at Delphi. Hence a careful examination of the whole corpus of extant Delphic responses is called for.

Parke and Wormell have gathered a corpus of 615 responses culled
from Greek and Latin literature and inscriptions—authentic, spurious,
legendary, and dubious. They arrange the responses chronologically
in nine periods of the Oracle's history (plus an "Uncertain Date" section);
and for each period divide the responses into two groups, historical and
fictitious (the latter supposedly spoken in earlier times, but invented,
they believe, in the periods under which they list them). But Parke
and Wormell do not consider all their "historical" responses genuine;
and their "fictitious" category includes legendary, pseudo-historical, and
invented oracles (those composed for a literary work). Their judgements
of genuine and non-genuine are likely to be subjective.

In this study I attempt a more objective division of the responses.
It is a fourfold division into Historical, Quasi-Historical, Legendary, and
Fictional responses. I have prepared a Catalogue that suits the require-
ments of this study (see pp. 244–416). The responses of each group are
numbered separately from the others, and each response is referred to
in the following pages by Catalogue number preceded by H, Q, L, or F
according to its classification. The PW number will be found immediately
following the Catalogue number. Appendix A contains the correspondence of PW numbers to Catalogue designations.

1. By *Historical* responses I mean those which appear in contemporary
records; that is, the accepted probable date of the response fell within the
lifetime of the writer who attests it, or of the earliest writer when several
attest it, or not long before the date of the inscription which records it.
Obviously, most of these responses are genuine; but contemporaneity is
not an absolute guarantee of genuineness, since men may be mistaken
about what has happened in their own lifetimes or may put trust in false
reports. Most certainly genuine are those reported or inscribed by the
consultants themselves or by persons close to them. Less certainly genuine
are those that the reporter has received by hearsay, reportedly spoken in

an earlier period of his life, perhaps twenty to fifty years back.[10] Surely a Delphic oracle did not become known to all inhabitants of Hellas soon after it was spoken. An oracle given to a city-state might soon become known to most of its citizen body. But other oracles commonly became known to few besides the receivers and persons close to them. The oracle which Chairephon received on Socrates' wisdom (H3) did not come to most Athenians' knowledge until Socrates' trial, probably more than thirty years after utterance. For in the *Apology* (20e–21a) Socrates is plainly informing the dicasts of an event of which they had not known and which would surprise them. Hence "Historical" does not mean "genuine"; it is simply an objective classification according to the definition given. It is true that later writers generally depend upon earlier; but to avoid uncertain and subjective judgements about sources, I demand that the later writer name his authority before classifying the response "Historical." I make only one exception: Ephoros' history is so surely Diodoros' source for events between 400 and 340 that I have included five fourth-century responses (H14–16, 20, 73) from Diodoros' *Bibliotheca* in the Historical group. Part I of the Catalogue lists 75 Historical responses.

2. By *Quasi-Historical* responses I mean those which were allegedly spoken within historical times, i.e., after the legendary period, but which are, to our knowledge, first attested by a writer whose lifetime was later than the accepted or supposed date of the response. The writers who record them considered them to be events of Greek history that took place after the first Olympiad (776 B.C.) or not more than a few years earlier, 800 B.C. at the earliest; this means that none is dated earlier (or more than a few years earlier) than the foundation of the Delphic Oracle. The prefix *Quasi* must be given its exact Latin meaning: it means that these responses are recorded *as if* spoken in historical times (i.e., after 800); it is not intended to reflect in any way on the authenticity of these responses. Some are obviously authentic; others are obviously not; many others are questionable, and it is the question of how to determine their authenticity or lack of it that will occupy us in many of the following pages. Part II of the Catalogue lists 268 Quasi-Historical responses.

3. By *Legendary* responses I mean (a) those which belong to admittedly legendary narratives, i.e., the traditional tales of events which were supposed to have taken place in the dim past, sometime before the eighth century B.C.,

---

10 A question arises about an oracle dated in the reporter's infancy: should it be called Historical or Quasi-Historical? There is no certain instance of this; but Herodotos reports responses for 481–479, when he may have been an infant. These I have called Quasi-Historical.

and (b) those which belong to timeless folktales and fables. Here I include the responses supposedly spoken to Homer and Hesiod, since the tales in which they appear are entirely legendary, and the Hellenes traditionally placed these poets in the tenth or ninth century. Three oracles on the beginnings of Macedon and Rome (L50, 51, 123), which could be referred to the eighth century, so plainly belong to legend that I include them in this group. In distinguishing between legendary and historical times, and in setting 800 B.C. as a dividing line between them, we must realize that the distinction is ours and that the Greeks considered the tales about Bronze Age and Dark Age events to be just as true as narratives of more recent events. And, as we shall see, some narratives told of later times are as unhistorical as the legends of earlier times. Part III of the Catalogue lists 176 Legendary responses.

4. By *Fictional* responses I mean those invented by poets, dramatists, and romancers to serve their creative purposes. The inventors did not intend that anybody think them authentic; their audience or readers were not likely to believe them genuine. These responses are important only in so far as they reveal ancient conceptions of Delphic oracles. Part IV of the Catalogue lists 16 Fictional responses.

1. In the first chapter I determine the characteristics of Historical and Legendary responses, discovering that Historical responses are commonplace pronouncements, mostly clear commands and sanctions on religious matters, occasionally on public or private affairs. None has the spectacular quality of Legendary responses, among which one finds extraordinary predictions, warnings, and commands, often ambiguously expressed. When the Quasi-Historical responses are analysed in the same manner, many of them turn out to have the characteristics of Legendary responses: many that are usually considered authentic are extraordinary, often ambiguous, predictions and commands.

2. In the second chapter we see that many Quasi-Historical responses conform in theme and expression to the oracles and prophecies of folktale and legend; others, though not extraordinary in themselves, are integral constituents of narratives, which, though told as historical, have a legendary character; still others turn out to be riddles and proverbs given an oracular origin in tradition.

3. Prophecies of narrative, at first anonymous or spoken by a seer, became attributed to the Delphic Oracle either occasionally or consistently in the course of oral or written transmission. If an oracular story had its inception after the eighth century its oracle might have been called

Delphic from the start. Or a Delphic response was introduced into narratives that had no oracle to begin with. These narrative oracles may or may not have a verse form; some were always indirectly expressed.

4. A number of famous responses, quoted by Herodotos and later writers and usually considered authentic, prove on examination in chapter 4 to be unauthentic or dubious.

5. Many Quasi-Historical responses came from the collections of chresmologues, who often represented their oracles as pronouncements of Apollo at Delphi. Some oracles originally attributed to Bakis or the Sibyl were ascribed to Delphi in the course of transmission.

6. Quasi-Historical and Legendary verse oracles generally have the same structure and formulae as chresmologic and narrative oracles; i.e., they manifest the conventions of traditional oracles. Few genuine Delphic responses are expressed in verse; most of these belong to the early Christian centuries and do not conform to the conventions of traditional verse oracles.

7. A close study of all reliable evidence for Delphic mantic procedures reveals no chasm or vapors, no frenzy of the Pythia, no incoherent cries interpreted by priests. The Pythia spoke clearly, coherently, and directly to the consultant in response to his question.

Although the office of Pythia is nearly unique, paralleled only at other Apolline Oracles, a survey of other Oracles, ancient and modern, confirms my conclusions about the responses and operations of the Delphic Oracle. As conventionally pictured the Delphic Oracle has no resemblance to any real Oracle, ancient or modern.

In the Catalogue a final judgement is made on the authenticity of Quasi-Historical responses.

The Characteristics of Recorded Oracles

Our knowledge of Delphic oracular texts depends wholly upon the accidents which have preserved for us the literary works and inscriptions which record or notice them. Consequently the state of each text depends upon the nature and number of its sources: we have excellent knowledge of one text because several writers, whose works have survived, quoted it in full; we have just a hint of the content of another because it receives a single brief notice in one surviving document. Quotations of responses, direct and indirect, complete and incomplete, and allusions to them, more or less informative, are found in histories and orations, in lyric and dramatic poetry, in philosophic and didactic works, in lexica and commentaries, and in both public and private inscriptions of every kind.

The choice of oracle to be quoted or cited and the manner in which it is quoted or cited depend wholly upon the nature of the document and the author's purpose. And the nature and purpose of the document may also affect our confidence in the authenticity of an oracular response, though they are not the only grounds upon which we may judge authenticity. We are sure to consider the oracles of epic and tragedy unauthentic; for others, however, we look to the reliability of the source, to historical probability, and to the credibility both of the narrative which accompanies the response and of the response itself. Most of the oracles which I label

Historical, those which appear in records composed soon after the event, we are likely to judge authentic, though at least two certainly are not. Those which I label Legendary we are likely to consider wholly fictitious, though a few may have roots in authentic responses of historical times. Upon the responses of these two groups most of us can agree; the problem of authenticity becomes more urgent when we consider the Quasi-Historical responses, those which ancient writers set down as historical events occurring in historical times (i.e., after approximately 800 B.C.), but earlier than the earliest reporter's own lifetime.

Some scholars accept most Quasi-Historical responses as genuine pronouncements from the Pythia's mouth (or the priests' pens); a few others are more sceptical and will accept few without reservation. Parke (1939, 1956) steers a middle course, accepting as genuine, or as derived from genuine, responses somewhat over half of those which I class as Quasi-Historical. So far judgements about the authenticity of responses have generally been subjective and tentative, dependent upon a scholar's estimate of the source or sources in each instance and of the source's probable source, if not upon his degree of credulity and sense of probability.

It is plain, therefore that a more objective criterion should be found. May we not find one in a comparative analysis of the Historical and Legendary responses? We have 75 responses attested by contemporaries and 176 which are admittedly Legendary, enough for valid results. If among Historical responses we find formulae and content that are markedly different from those which we find among Legendary responses, we have already made a significant finding, however we interpret it. We have learned at least the characteristics of those responses which by common consent are most probably authentic.

Then we can divide Quasi-Historical responses according to their conformity or lack of conformity with the Historical characteristics; and we may suppose that those which conform to the Historical group are more likely to be authentic than those which resemble Legendary responses. I have said "more likely to be authentic," anticipating the objection that a forger of oracles will copy the pattern of genuine oracles if he wants the forgery to be taken as genuine. It is true that we cannot call a response genuine simply because it has the characteristics of Historical responses: some Legendary responses show these characteristics, yet cannot be considered genuine. But the objection is really irrelevant: forgery is not a question that will come before us. It will soon be evident that there was no need to forge the sort of response which we find in the

Historical group; it would have been quite useless to do so. Forgery, moreover, is a misleading term for Legendary and pseudo-historical responses. A forged response should be an oracular composition that someone has invented with intent to deceive. But the composers of Legendary and other unauthentic oracles had no wish to deceive anybody; in general their oracular compositions served their narrative purposes.[1]

If conformity with the characteristics of Historical responses is no guarantee of genuineness, we can say more confidently that a response which shows Legendary characteristics is dubious, if not unauthentic. In the following analyses we discover the patterns of Historical and Legendary responses and the differences between them.

MODES OF EXPRESSION IN HISTORICAL AND LEGENDARY RESPONSES

The modes of expression I classify under six major heads, four of which have subdivisions, so that there are twelve classes altogether. Some complex responses (e.g., L7, 11, 17, 41) offer difficulties to the classifier: command, prediction, statement of present fact, may occur together in a single pronouncement. Hence initially I classify responses under only the mode of the central message—the kernel of the oracle, the real answer to the consultant's question or the essential message that the god or his representative wishes to convey. When a response is known only from a single indirect statement or testimony which may report it imperfectly, I classify it under the mode which appears to me to be most probably indicated. In every instance, it must be understood, in this and the following analyses, I adhere strictly to the oracular texts as we find them in the sources, or, when there is no text, to the information that the sources give us.

A. Simple Commands and Instructions

The mode which occurs most often in the records which we have is a simple command or instruction, expressed in one of two ways: (1) a command to perform a certain act in order to have success or to avoid misfortune; (2) a statement that if the consultant performs a certain act, he will have success or avoid misfortune. That is, the oracle's instruction may be spoken in the imperative or equivalent mood or in a conditional clause

---

1 Delphians and story-tellers often attributed traditional oracles to Delphi. Such attributions have nothing to do with fraud, deliberate or unconscious; the question of fraud (e.g., bribery of the Pythia) concerns only the mantic procedure and the actual delivery of oracles.

(or equivalent, e.g., conditional participle). In some instances the indirect versions of the response vary between one form and the other: e.g., Apollodoros expresses the command of L45 with an infinitive which stands for an original imperative (give Minos the satisfaction that he asks; then you will escape famine and plague); but Diodoros uses a conditional clause (if you give Minos the satisfaction that he asks, you will escape).[2] In L46 Apollodoros (cf. Clement) uses a conditional clause (you will escape the drought if you have Aiakos make prayers in your behalf); whereas Diodoros shows the imperative form indirectly (go to Aiakos and ask him to make prayers for you).

A1. Clear Commands. In the main subdivision of mode A the oracle's instructions are expressed clearly, either in plain prose or in poetic language that is lucid enough to allow little or no possibility of misunderstanding; in no instance does the inquirer misunderstand. In this subdivision I place 90 Legendary and 20 Historical responses.[3]

A2. Sanctions. These are formally clear commands or instructions, but are in fact no more than the Delphic Oracle's sanction of a plan or enterprise or of legislation which has been virtually decided upon beforehand. The Oracle's direction is not expressed in the imperative mood or a conditional clause, but in the formula λῷον καὶ ἄμεινόν ἐστι (or a variation thereon; literally "it is better and more good"), as in H19, the response made to Philip and the Chalcidians when they submitted their treaty to the Delphic Apollo for his approval. The inscriptional record of H26 does not show the usual phrase, but the response plainly sanctions a long cult-statute already adopted in Cyrene. Several other Historical responses almost certainly are sanctions, although we do not know the exact wording. In H4 the Epidamnians, planning to put their city under Corinth's protection, ask Delphi whether they should do so, and Delphi answers that they should. In H6 the Spartans, after deciding to establish a colony in Trachis, ask for and receive Delphi's approval. H41–43, 46, 71, concerning grants of asylum to certain cities and shrines, are obviously in the same class as H45 and H47, which show the conventional formula that was used for grants of asylum. Several Historical responses that I have placed under A1 may really belong to A2.

---

2 The passages of Apollodoros and Diodoros are cited in the Catalogue of Delphic Responses under L45. In general when referring to the sources of a response under discussion I shall refer to authors' names only; the exact citation will be found in the Catalogue under the indicated response number. In text and notes I shall make full citations only when necessary for clarity, or when an author refers to a response in two or more passages.

3 See Appendix B for listings of the particular responses that I have classified under each of the modes, topics, question formulae, and occasions of this chapter.

This is a rather prosaic sort of oracular response, not as likely to appear among Legendary as among Historical responses. Yet a few Legendary responses may be classified as sanctions of a proposal or enterprise, although the notices may be brief and summary, not clearly indicating a sanction of the Historical kind. L113, addressed to Herakles on sending a colony under Iolaos to Sardinia, is indirectly expressed in the words συμφέρειν ... ἀποικίαν εἰς Σαρδὼ πέμψαι ("that it is advantageous to send a colony to Sardinia"). For L137 Pausanias reports that the Delphic god told the Heraklids that it was better for them (ἄμεινον εἶναί σφισιν) to bury Alkmene in Megara. A2: 4 L, 37 H.

A3. Ambiguous and Obscure Commands and Instructions. These are commands which do not differ formally from those listed under A1, but the command is either obscurely expressed or, if seemingly clear, so phrased that the consultant misunderstands and either does the wrong thing or is in danger of doing so. As examples of obscure Legendary oracles observe L40: Alkmaion is told to go to a land that did not exist at the time when he killed his mother; L65: the Heraklids are told to take a three-eyed guide. In both instances the consultants discovered the right meaning. The ambiguous oracle that misleads the consultant appears in L61, wherein the Heraklids are told to await the third harvest before they invade the Peloponnesos; they take "harvest" literally and meet defeat: the god meant the third generation. In L62 the Heraklids are told to invade through the narrows; they try to go through the Isthmos and are defeated; the god meant the strait at the entrance to the Gulf of Corinth. L118 is the well-known response to Deukalion on casting "mother's bones." There are no Historical responses of this kind.[4] A3: 9 L, 0 H.

B. Conditioned Commands

In a considerable number of Legendary responses the oracular command is made contingent upon a future event: the inquirer must act when such and such happens or is met or is seen—often something surprising or seemingly impossible; or, if not surprising, a person or object of a designated class first encountered. The first-met theme is seen in L2: Manto

---

4 The exiled Dion Chrysostomos received a response to do as he was doing (wandering in exile) until he reached earth's end (H62). He says that this was a strange response and hard to understand. He means that it was difficult for him to see why the oracle instructed him to remain in exile; the command was plain enough, and he did not misunderstand it. H67 is expressed in poetic periphrasis in the manner of late responses; but its meaning was perfectly plain to the recipients, who recognized readily enough the locality defined by the old men's baths, the girls' dancing place, and the halls of the womanish man.

should marry the first man she meets; L82: Kephalos should have intercourse with the first female he meets; L128: a prince of Haliartos, asking
for water for his parched land, is told to kill the first person he meets on
his return—as with Jephthah (Judges 11.30–40), this turned out to be his
own child. Similar is L11, the oracle spoken to Kadmos, who must follow
a cow (in some versions the first cow that he will meet, or a cow that is
marked in a distinctive way) until she lies down, and there build his city
(see also L50, 51, 78).

Several colonization and migration oracles show the other formula
mentioned: i.e., settle where such and such, something surprising or
unusual, occurs or is found. Athamas should settle in the place where he
will be entertained by wild beasts (L33), Lokros where a wooden dog will
bite him (L83), Cretan colonists where the earthborn will make war on
them (L116). The same theme occurs in responses on other subjects: the
Heraklids, Eurysthenes and Prokles, are told to marry in the land where
they see the wildest beast carrying the tamest (L127); Chalkinos and
Daitos, wishing to return to Athens, are instructed to make sacrifice to
Apollo where they see a trireme running on land (L132).

A variety of the mode is "Be first to do A when B (a strange or
obscurely stated event) happens in order to have C." When, after King
Kodros' death, the brothers Medon and Neileus were told that whichever
was first to make sacrifice (or pour a libation) when *sialos* rubbed *sialos*
(L68) should become king of Athens, Neileus waited to see one pig rub
against another; but Medon realised that the condition was fulfilled when
he saw one olive tree rub against another. The only Historical response
which might be considered like this is H15: the citizens of Klazomenai
and Kyme were told that the disputed town of Leuke would belong to the
city whose citizens, starting from their city at sunrise of a fixed day,
should be the first to make sacrifice at Leuke. But this hardly fits the
formula: the Pythia simply sets a contest; therefore I place H15 among
simple clear commands. B: 24 L, o H.

C. Prohibitions and Warnings

A warning has a different form from a prohibition and is sometimes
expressed as a statement, but has essentially the same meaning: "Beware
of doing X" is much the same as "Don't do X."

C1. Clear Prohibitions and Warnings. L17 is in one version a prohibition followed by a warning: Laios is told not to impregnate his wife,

because if she should bear a son, that son will kill him.[5] L49 warns Sparta against killing Kodros, the Athenian king. L22 is a little difficult to classify, but its principal message seems to be that Theseus must not be too much troubled at heart when making plans for his city. L141 is the Pythia's refusal to speak to the young man who deserted his friend: she forbids him to remain in the temple.

Among Historical responses H21 must be considered a prohibition of the working of the Eleusinian *orgas* (sacred land), though the Pythia did no more than indicate the urn which contained this message. In H55 the Romans are forbidden to proceed further in Greece, else dire consequences will come upon them. In H75 the Athenians are refused any response until they pay the assessed Olympic fine. C1: 4 L, 3 H.

C2. Ambiguous and Obscure Prohibitions and Warnings. Aigeus did not understand the response which told him not to open the projecting neck of the wineskin until he reached Athens (L4). The Heraklids, who had a good deal of trouble with oracles, were told not to make war on their table companions (L67); the Arcadian king sent men ahead to traffic with the Heraklid van and to eat something with them, whereupon he pointed out that the terms of the oracle were fulfilled. See also L12, 41. There are no Historical responses of this kind. C2: 5 L, 0 H.

D. Statements of Past or Present Fact

So far modes have been imperative or equivalent. Many responses are statements about past, present, or future. The future statements belong to modes E and F.

D1. Commonplace Statements of Past or Present Fact. These are truths known to everyone, as proverbs, or they are statements of actual or alleged fact that anyone might make. To Chairephon's question whether anyone was wiser than Socrates, the Pythia replied that nobody was wiser (H3). In 387 Agesipolis asked whether he might consistently with piety reject the truce proclaimed by the Argives for celebration of the Carneian festival, since the Argives were unfairly proclaiming the truce every time the Spartans were about to invade their territory; and he received the same reply that he had already received from Zeus at Olympia,

---

5 This seems to be the earlier version. Aeschylus certainly knew the response to Laios as prohibition or warning: Laios should have no son, if he wished to save Thebes. A second version is a prediction that Laios will have a son who will kill him. Sophocles' words (*OT* 713–714, 854, 1176) may be interpreted either way.

that he could lawfully reject a truce that was unrighteously proclaimed (H13).[6] The Emperor Hadrian, desiring to find the answer to a vexed question, asked where Homer was born and who were his parents, and received the reply that Homer was an Ithacan, son of Telemachos and Epikaste Nestor's daughter (H65). This cannot be considered an extraordinary statement of hidden knowledge, since at this time the Delphians could name whom they pleased as Homer's parents and any place as his birthplace without fear of being proved wrong; it was certainly not an expression of superhuman knowledge about Homer's true parents and birthplace.

Among Legendary responses we find Delphi's self-justification made to the Heraklids (L63) and statements about the pleasing offering (L57–59). Proverbs are spoken as response in L87 and L105. L99 is formally a question, wherein the Pythia expresses the paradox that she perceives in the joint consultation of Menelaos and Paris on children and marriage. D1: 15 L, 8 H.

D2. Extraordinary and Obscure Statements of Past or Present Fact. These are revelations, perhaps obscure, of hidden knowledge, events and facts that the speaker could not know without clairvoyant or other superhuman powers. Homer himself was troubled about his birthplace and parents and was told at Delphi that he was born on Ios (L80). This is not on the same footing as H65: for L80 belongs to the world of legend, in terms of which Apollo was revealing through the Pythia a truth that no mortal man was likely to know. In L90 Apollo knows about Kydippe's oath, though no mortal person besides Kydippe herself and Akontios is aware of it. See also L76, 89. There are no Historical responses of this kind. D2: 4 L, 0 H.

---

6 Xenophon's report of Agesipolis' consultation (*Hell.* 4.7.2) has, I think, been misunderstood. After reporting the consultation at Olympia, Xenophon says that Agesipolis then went to Delphi, where ἐπήρετο αὖ τὸν Ἀπόλλω εἰ κἀκείνῳ δοκοίη περὶ τῶν σπονδῶν καθάπερ τῷ πατρί. ὁ δὲ ἀπεκρίνατο καὶ μάλα κατὰ ταὐτά. Xenophon means to say no more than that Agesipolis asked at Delphi the same question that he had asked at Olympia, and received much the same response. But Aristotle and later writers understood Xenophon's *ei*-clause as Agesipolis' actual question rather than as Xenophon's paraphrase; since then many commentators and historians have seen in Agesipolis' question a humor or audacity that was not really present. The Spartans' consultation at Delphi after consulting Olympia was due to their religious fear of breaking the Carneian truce, even when it was wrongly proclaimed. To violate a proclaimed religious truce was in their eyes too serious a step to take without certainty that the gods approved; hence it behooved them to make sure that neither Zeus nor Apollo would be offended. Notice Hyper. *Or.* 3.15: the suggestion of a speaker that an oracle of Amphiaraos be verified by asking the same question at Delphi. H13 may in reality be a sanction; but since Xenophon's indirect report indicates a general statement, we must for the present adhere strictly to the text as we have it.

E. Simple Statements of Future Events

Statements foretelling future events are what we usually think of as oracles. Sometimes the prediction is conditioned as in mode F. But more often the response (or its central message) is a flat statement that a certain event will take place at some future time or that something will be true in the future.

Eɪ. Non-Predictive Future Assertions. Not all statements about the future are really predictions. Some are promises or statements of intention or the like expressed in the future tense: e.g., Apollo's statement to Agamedes and Trophonios in L9 that he will pay them on the third or seventh day, or his statement in L121 that he will deal with Krios' son and then go to Crete for purification. There are two Historical examples. In H18 the exiled Kallistratos is told that he will meet with the laws on his return to Athens. H17 is merely the god's ᾿Εμοὶ μελήσει ("It will be my concern") in the face of Jason of Pherai's threat to Delphi. Eɪ: 2 L, 2 H.

E2. Clear Predictions. Unambiguous predictions occur with fair frequency among Legendary responses. For example, the Achaeans learn that they will take Troy in ten years (L122); Akrisios learns that Danae's son will kill him (L23), Aipytos that Euadne's son will become a great mantis (L10). Among Historical responses only H34 and H70 can be placed in this category. The text of H34 is mostly lost, but appears to predict the birth of a child; and the prediction was apparently fulfilled in the birth of a daughter.[7] H70 is exceptional and certainly not genuine: it is Claudian's statement that the Delphic Oracle broke its silence at Honorius' birth to proclaim the future emperor's greatness. It is no more than

---

7 See W. H. D. Rouse, *Greek Votive Offerings* (Cambridge, 1902) 240–245; Otto Weinreich, "Eine delphische Mirakel-Inschrift und die antiken Haarwunder," *Sitzb. Akad. Heidelberg* (1925) no. 7. We know so little about this response from the present state of the inscribed epigram that it is quite possible that it is no more than a clear command (A1) to the inquirer to make certain sacrifices or offerings as a favorable precondition to his wife's bearing a child. But the only command mentioned in the surviving text is to make an offering of the child's hair, which could only be done after the birth. We need see no miracle, as Weinreich does, in either the newborn daughter's full head of hair or an eleven-month pregnancy, since both phenomena are known to occur; but that the whole interval of eleven months between response and birth was a gestation period is a conclusion which the inscription does not force upon us; moreover it probably means the eleventh month, i.e., after ten months had passed. What we learn from the remains of the epigram is that a husband inquired about his wife's chances of bearing a child. After a gap we read, "Phoibos granted progeny with his oracles, heeding my prayer, and he instructed me to make a hair-offering." The god was commanding the usual offering of a child's hair after birth. Eleven months thereafter a girl was born with a full head of hair, and the father at once assumed that the god had foreseen this in his instruction. More remarkable is the fulfillment of the prediction, if it was made, that a child would be born. But probably the Oracle made the prediction contingent upon sacrifices or votive offerings.

poetic hyperbole; but under the definition given I must class it as Histori-cal, since Honorius was born about fourteen years before this poem was written. E2: 10 L, 2 H.

E3. Ambiguous and Obscure Predictions. Predictions may be ex-pressed in obscure terms, or, if seemingly clear, they may intend something other than what they appear to say and so mislead the recipients. Herakles was told that he would receive his death from the dead (L119), an obscure prophecy of his death from Nessos and the Hydra's poison. L48 is an ob-scure prediction that the Black (Melanthos) would take Blacks (Melainai) by killing the Fair (Xanthos). Oedipus was told that if he went back to his native land (see Apollodoros), he would kill his father and marry his mother (L18). Though the prediction is clearly stated and means what it says, it intentionally and understandably misled Oedipus, who, as Apollo was aware, did not know his true country and parents. Though Delphic oracles are popularly supposed to be obscure and ambiguous predictions, we find only three Legendary responses that have this character, and no Historical responses. E3: 3 L, 0 H.

F. *Conditioned Predictions*

Corresponding to conditioned commands are predictions made contingent on some future occurrence or upon the consultant's encoun-tering a specified object or situation: e.g., the consultant will have victory when such and such an event occurs or such and such a situation is met with—something that may be unusual, surprising, or incredible; or ful-fillment will come with the first met. Agamemnon is told that his army will be victorious when the best Achaeans quarrel (L1). The Boeotians will not lose Arne until white ravens appear (L75), a condition fulfilled when some drunk men painted ravens white. Oedipus will die and find his tomb when he comes to the shrine of the *semnai theai*, which signs from Zeus will reveal to him (L20). Here too I include L28, the statement to Xuthos that the man who will meet him as he leaves the temple is his son, since the condition will be fulfilled in the future, though the man must be already Xuthos' son. There are no Historical responses of this kind. F: 6 L, 0 H.

We know so little about the content of H22, 72, 73, that we cannot perceive the mode used in them; hence 72 Historical and 176 Legendary responses enter into the analysis of modes. Table I shows the numbers and percentages of each mode as it appears among the extant Historical and

TABLE I

MODES OF LEGENDARY AND HISTORICAL RESPONSES

	Legendary (176) Number	Pct	Historical (72) Number	Pct
A. Simple Commands	103	58.5	57	79.2
A1. Clear Commands	90	51.1	20	27.8
A2. Sanctions	4	2.3	37	51.4
A3. Ambiguous Commands	9	5.1	0	0
B. Conditioned Commands	24	13.6	0	0
C. Prohibitions and Warnings	9	5.1	3	4.2
C1. Clear Prohibitions	4	2.3	3	4.2
C2. Ambiguous Prohibitions	5	2.8	0	0
D. Statements on Past or Present	19	10.8	8	11.1
D1. Commonplace statements	15	8.5	8	11.1
D2. Extraordinary Statements	4	2.3	0	0
E. Simple Future Statements	15	8.5	4	5.6
E1. Non-Predictive Statements	2	1.1	2	2.8
E2. Clear Predictions	10	5.7	2	2.8
E3. Ambiguous Predictions	3	1.7	0	0
F. Conditioned Predictions	6	3.4	0	0

Legendary responses. It may be that another person would classify some of the responses differently; but those that do not fall clearly under one mode or another are not numerous enough, I believe, to make a significant difference in the results of my analysis and in the conclusions that I draw from them. The statistical analysis yields the following results.

1. While simple commands have a majority in both the Historical and Legendary groups, they comprise four-fifths of the Historical responses; and over half the remainder are statements of past or present fact.

2. Not one of the simple commands in the Historical group is ambiguous or unclear, whereas 9 in 103 of the Legendary simple commands may be so described.

3. Nearly two-thirds of the Historical simple commands, one-half of all Historical responses, are sanctions, mere approvals of previously formed plans and enterprises. Not more than 5, I believe, whose modes of expression cannot be ascertained with certainty, could be removed from A2 to A1. But even if 10 were reclassified, three-eighths of all Historical responses would still be sanctions. Furthermore the uncertain instances are

balanced by those responses now classified A1 which might on further evidence be revealed as sanctions. On the other hand, the indicated 2.3 percent of Legendary oracles classified as sanctions is the maximum possible, since all reasonably doubtful instances have been so classified.

4. The Historical responses include no ambiguous, unclear, or conditioned commands, no ambiguous prohibitions or warnings, no extraordinary statements about past or present, no ambiguous or conditioned predictions, and only 2 clear predictions, modes generally assumed to be typical of Delphic responses. But 61 Legendary responses show these modes, over one-third of the total.

The Historical responses, therefore, lend no support to the view that the Pythia spoke or that the Delphic priests composed extraordinary responses, marvelous and clever prophecies or directions, often ambiguous. Rather we find simple commands and statements, none requiring uncommon foresight or cleverness. Many are merely approvals of cult laws, treaties, claims to asylum, proposals of cult foundation, and the like, as will be evident from analysis of response topics in the next section.

The conclusions that I draw from my analysis of modes and from the analyses that follow will run counter to prevailing views about the Delphic Oracle. Hence I may expect objections to my method of analysis, in particular to my reduction of each response to a single mode, when many are complex in form and content. Perhaps the advantage of having the numbers of each mode add up to 176 L and 72 H, and the percentages add up to 100, was gained at too great a cost, that of oversimplifying or falsifying the responses. So I shall make an analysis which takes account of subordinate modes, among which I include variant modes (when one source reports a response differently from another) and alternative modes (allowing for different judgements about the principal mode of responses). We may then see whether the extended analysis essentially alters the results gained from the simplified analysis.

A1. Clear command, is subordinate in 7 L, 2 H: 7 + 90 = 97 L; 2 + 20 = 22 H.

A3. Ambiguous or obscure command: 1 + 9 = 10 L.

Since L65 (A3) and H19 (A2) have already been classified as simple commands, the 103 Legendary responses and 57 Historical responses assigned to mode A must be augmented by 7 L and 1 H, so that 110 L and 58 H can be considered simple commands in whole or in part.

B. Conditioned command: 1 + 24 = 25 L.

C1. Clear prohibition or warning: 13 + 4 = 17 L; 1 + 3 = 4 H.

C2. Ambiguous prohibition or warning: 2 + 5 = 7 L.

Total for C, prohibitions and warnings: 15 + 9 = 24 L; 1 + 3 = 4 H.

D1. Commonplace statement of past or present fact: 8 + 15 = 23 L.
D2. Extraordinary statement of past or present fact: 4 + 4 = 8 L.
No Historical response shows D as a subordinate mode.
Total for D, statements of past or present fact: 12 + 19 = 31 L; 8 H.
E1. Non-predictive future statement: 3 + 2 = 5 L; 4 + 2 = 6 H.
E2. Clear prediction: 14 + 10 = 24 L.
Total for E, simple future statements: 17 + 15 = 32 L; 4 + 4 = 8 H.
F. Conditioned prediction: 4 + 6 = 10 L.

The analysis is tabulated in Table I-A. The results of this extended analysis, which takes the complexity of responses into account, not only leave our previous results essentially unchanged, but emphatically reinforce them.

1. Though simple commands appear in five-eighths of all L responses, they amount to over four-fifths of H responses.

2. No H simple command, whether principal mode or subordinate, is ambiguous or unclear, whereas 10 in 110, nearly ten percent of all L simple commands, are ambiguous or unclear.

TABLE I-A

PRINCIPAL AND SUBORDINATE MODES
OF LEGENDARY AND HISTORICAL RESPONSES

	Legendary (176)		Historical (72)	
	Number	Pct	Number	Pct
A. Simple Commands	110*	62.5	58*	80.6
A1. Clear Commands	97	55.1	22	30.6
A2. Sanctions	4	2.3	37	51.4
A3. Ambiguous Commands	10	5.7	0	0
B. Conditioned Commands	25	14.2	0	0
C. Prohibitions and Warnings	24	13.6	4	5.6
C1. Clear Prohibitions	17	9.7	4	5.6
C2. Ambiguous Prohibitions	7	4.0	0	0
D. Statements on Past or Present	31	17.6	8	11.1
D1. Commonplace Statements	23	13.1	8	11.1
D2. Extraordinary Statements	8	4.5	0	0
E. Simple Future Statements	32	18.2	8	11.1
E1. Non-Predictive Statements	5	2.8	6	8.3
E2. Clear Predictions	24	13.6	2	2.8
E3. Ambiguous Predictions	3	1.7	0	0
F. Conditioned Predictions	10	5.7	0	0

* The total eliminates one instance of duplication.

3. The great difference between Historical and Legendary responses in numbers of sanctions remains unchanged.

4. The modes A3, B, C2, D2, E3, and F still make no appearance among H responses. But among L responses all these modes have increased in number and percentage, D2 and F rather spectacularly. Altogether 63 L responses, above one-third of the total, show one or more of these non-H modes. And the number of clear predictions (E2) has more than doubled among L responses, whereas no more appear among H responses, which show only an increase of E1, non-predictive future statements.

5. Finally we should notice that Historical responses are seldom complex: only 7 show a second mode, fewer than 1 in 10. No H response has more than two modes, whereas 45 L responses—just over one-fourth of the total—show two or more modes. Of the 45 L complex responses, 9 have three modes and 1 (L80) has four.

The Topics of Historical and Legendary Responses

We must now see what the Delphic god told Historical and Legendary inquirers, so that we may discover what differences, if any, there are between Legendary and Historical responses in content. This inquiry concerns the kinds of activity which the god prescribed or prohibited in order that the consultant prosper or avoid misfortune, the kinds of events which he predicted or said were happening or had happened, and the kinds of general statement that he made—in short the topics or themes of his answers to consultants' questions. The topics of responses may be conveniently classified under three general heads, each with several subdivisions: (1) *Res Divinae*, directions and statements of religious content; (2) *Res Publicae* (including *res militares*), directions and statements of political and military content; (3) *Res Domesticae et Profanae*, directions and statements of private or secular content. In classifying a response I take the words employed at their face value, ignoring the meaning which the outcome imposes. How would the average Greek understand the speech if it were not oracular? We must bear in mind too that the topic of the response is not necessarily the topic of the question. And, as in the study of the modes, we are limited to what the documents report. For the present we must adhere strictly to the oracular texts as we have them, no matter how incomplete or fragmentary or indirect some of them may be. Though another person might classify a few differently with respect to topic, the results of the analysis would not be seriously affected: the trend of the evidence will, I am sure, be unmistakable.

1. Res Divinae

1a. Cult Foundations. Cities or individuals are instructed to found cults, festivals, or temples of gods, daimones, or heroes in 22 Legendary, 15 Historical responses.

1b. Sacrifices, Offerings. Cities or individuals are instructed to make sacrifices (not human), offerings, or prayers to specified gods, daimones, or heroes. 16 L, 23 H.[8]

1c. Human Sacrifices. Cities or their rulers are instructed to sacrifice human beings to gods or daimones in 10 Legendary responses. No Historical response contains such an instruction. 10 L, 0 H.

1d. Religious Laws, Customs, etc. Several responses are pronouncements on such subjects as ritual ordinances, rights of sanctuary (asylia) and immunity, patron deities of cities, ritual customs, and the like. 3 L, 16 H.

2. Res Publicae

2a. Rulership. Commands or statements on rulers and rulership, e.g., on who should be king. 4 L, 2 H.

2b. Legislation, Civic Welfare. Advice upon or approval of non-religious legislation, statements on established laws. 1 L, 3 H.

2c. City and Colony Foundations. Commands to found a city or colony; indications of times of migration, circumstances of settlement, leaders to be chosen. 16 L, 2 H.

2d. Interstate Relations. Pronouncements on alliances, truces, or dealings with other states or peoples. 1 L, 4 H.

2e. War. Commands to make war, directions on means of victory, predictions of victory or defeat or time of victory. 6 L, 3 H.

3. Res Domesticae et Profanae

3a. Birth and Origin. H65 is an answer to Hadrian's question on Homer's birthplace and parents; H34 appears to be a prediction of a child's birth; L28 informs Xuthos about his son. 1 L, 2 H.

3b. Marriage and Sex Relations. Directions on whom to marry or lie with, whom to marry one's daughter(s) to, where to marry. 5 L, 0 H.

3c. Death and Burial. Commands, warnings, or statements on the

---

8 It is not always easy to decide whether a response instructs the establishment of a new cult or the worship of a god already established in cult. But the decision one way or the other in any instance makes little difference in the results, since, in fact, 1a and 1b are similar in character and will often be combined in the discussion.

place, means, or agent of the consultant's or another person's death; funeral and burial prescriptions. The only Historical response anything like these is H69, spoken to Amelios on Plotinos' fate after death. 13 L, 1 H.

3d. Careers and Professions. 1 Legendary response (L10) makes a prophecy about a child's career, and 1 Historical response (H62) gives advice on the consultant's course of life. 1 L, 1 H.

3e. Actions and Events. Some responses order an action or speak of an event that is not religious or political and which is not a vital event of the 3a–3d kind. 10 L, 0 H.[9]

3f. Rewards and Punishments. Commands, or statements on rewards to, or penalties, punishments, trials, or acquittals of individuals. 13 L, 0 H.

3g. Persons, Agents. Some responses name the person who will bring fulfillment of the consultant's purpose or who caused his difficulty or whose identity provides the answer to the question asked; excluded from 3g are the gods, kings, and colony founders of topics 1 and 2. 5 L, 0 H.

3h. Means and Signs. Indications of the means of fulfillment or the sign which the consultant will recognize as the time of action or fulfill-ment. 26 L, 0 H.

3i. Places, Lands. Indications of the country, city, or other place to which the consultant should go for residence or fulfillment, or the naming of which answers the question asked; excluded are indications of sites for colonies (except in L73, which has the same text as L74). If the response indicates a locality without mentioning settlement the topic is 3i rather than 2c. 9 L, 0 H.

3j. Gnomic utterances. Some responses are proverbs, *sententiae*, metaphors of gnomic meaning, ethical commands or statements, all of which are clearly separable from 3e, 3g, 3h, for example. Only here can we place H3, that no man is wiser than Socrates. 14 L, 2 H.

Since the topic of H72 is completely unknown, 74 Historical and 176 Legendary responses enter into the analysis of topics. Table II is a tabula-tion of the foregoing analysis, which yields the following results.

1. Most striking is the fact that nearly three-fourths of Historical responses belong to Res Divinae, whereas under three-tenths of Legendary responses can be so classified; and one-fifth of these are prescriptions of human sacrifice (1c), not found among Historical responses. The figures,

---

9 I include L18 here. Oedipus' incest and patricide are the consequences of returning to his native land (as Apollodoros reports it, and this is implied at *OT* 794–797), his future actions; therefore I classify the topic as 3e.

TABLE II
Topics of Legendary and Historical Responses

	Legendary (176)		Historical (74)	
	Number	Pct	Number	Pct
1. *Res Divinae*	51	29	54	73
1a. Cult Foundations	22	12.5	15	20.3
1b. Sacrifices, Offerings	16	9.1	23	31.1
1c. Human Sacrifice	10	5.7	0	0
1d. Religious Laws, Customs	3	1.7	16	21.6
2. *Res Publicae*	28	15.9	14	18.9
2a. Rulership	4	2.3	2	2.7
2b. Legislation	1	0.6	3	4.1
2c. City/Colony Foundations	16	9.1	2	2.7
2d. Interstate Relations	1	0.6	4	5.4
2e. War	6	3.4	3	4.1
3. *Res Domesticae et Profanae*	97	55.1	6	8.1
3a. Birth, Origin	1	0.6	2	2.7
3b. Marriage, etc.	5	2.8	0	0
3c. Death, Burial	13	7.4	1	1.4
3d. Careers, Professions	1	0.6	1	1.4
3e. Actions, Events	10	5.7	0	0
3f. Rewards, Punishments	13	7.4	0	0
3g. Persons, Agents	5	2.8	0	0
3h. Means, Signs	26	14.8	0	0
3i. Places, Lands	9	5.1	0	0
3j. Gnomic Utterances	14	8.0	2	2.7

moreover, are conservative. I have excluded from Res Divinae some responses (e.g., H19, 34) which could be so classified. Therefore hardly more than a fourth of known Historical oracles are non-religious pronouncements, whereas over seventy percent of Legendary responses are spoken on non-religious subjects.

2. Most of the non-religious Historical responses—over two-thirds of them, under one-fifth of the total—are pronouncements on public affairs. Res Publicae account for about one-sixth of Legendary responses, not a significantly smaller proportion, but greatly concentrated on city foundations; whereas interstate relations and legislation appear more prominently among Historical responses. The rarity of directions for founding colonies among Historical responses is probably due to the fact

that none of the 75 Historical oracles is earlier than the fifth century, before which the great period of colonization had ended.

3. Considerably over one-half of Legendary responses point to a fulfillment in non-religious and non-political terms, whereas about one-twelfth of Historical responses do so. This does not mean that Historical consultants seldom asked questions on personal affairs; it means only that a question on any subject was likely to receive a religious answer.

4. There are no direct and explicit Historical pronouncements on marriage, journeys, and rewards or punishments, and none in which non-religious and non-political actions, events, agents, means, and places are prescribed or designated. We may suppose that such topics were spoken on, but they do not appear among the 75 Historical responses known to us.

For the topics as for the modes we must now inquire whether the foregoing analysis, which reduces each response to a single topic, misrepresents the actual content of responses by failing to take account of the complexity of many; for some responses are complex in topic as in mode.

1. Res Divinae
1a. Cult foundation: 2 + 22 = 24 L.
1b. Sacrifice or offering: 8 + 16 = 24 L; 2 + 23 = 25 H.
1d. Religious law or custom: 12 + 3 = 15 L; 1 + 16 = 17 H.
Altogether 73 L responses (22 + 51) have Res Divinae as major or minor topic.
   Although 3 H responses show minor religious topics, 1 (H45) already has 1a as principal topic, so that 56 H (2 + 54) have religious content.

2. Res Publicae
2a. Rulership: 1 + 4 = 5 L.
2b. Legislation: 1 + 1 = 2 L.
2c. City foundation: 14 + 16 = 30 L.
2d. Interstate relations: 2 + 4 = 6 H.
2e. War: 7 + 6 = 13 L; 1 + 3 = 4 H.
L69, whose principal topic is in this division, must be subtracted; therefore the total for 2, Res Publicae, is 22 + 28 = 50 L; 3 + 14 = 17 H.

3. Res Domesticae et Profanae
3a. Birth and origin: 5 + 1 = 6 L.
3b. Marriage and sex relations: 3 + 5 = 8 L.
3c. Death and burial: 16 + 13 = 29 L.
3e. Action or event: 6 + 10 = 16 L.
3f. Reward or punishment: 6 + 13 = 19 L.
3g. Person or agent: 5 + 5 = 10 L; 1 + 0 = 1 H.

3h. Means or sign: 9 + 26 = 35 L.

3i. Place: 1 + 9 = 10 L.

3j. Gnomic utterance: 2 + 14 = 16 L; 4 + 2 = 6 H.

Although Res Domesticae et Profanae appear 53 times as subordinate topics among L responses, 32 instances occur in responses whose principal topics also fall within this division, or which have a second subordinate topic of this class. One such duplication occurs among the 5 instances of H subordinate topics of class 3. Hence the total for 3, Res Domesticae et Profanae, is 21 + 97 = 118 L; 4 + 6 = 10 H. The above analysis is tabulated in Table II-A.

TABLE II-A

PRINCIPAL AND SUBORDINATE TOPICS
OF LEGENDARY AND HISTORICAL RESPONSES

	Legendary (176)		Historical (74)	
	Number	Pct	Number	Pct
1. *Res Divinae*	73	41.5	56*	75.7
1a. Cult Foundations	24	13.6	15	20.3
1b. Sacrifices, Offerings	24	13.6	25	33.8
1c. Human Sacrifice	10	5.7	0	0
1d. Religious Laws, Customs	15	8.5	17	23
2. *Res Publicae*	50*	28.4	17	23
2a. Rulership	5	2.8	2	2.7
2b. Legislation	2	1.1	3	4.1
2c. City Foundations	30	17.0	2	2.7
2d. Interstate Relations	1	0.6	6	8.1
2e. War	13	7.4	4	5.4
3. *Res Domesticae et Profanae*	118*	67	10*	13.5
3a. Birth, Origin	6	3.4	2	2.7
3b. Marriage, etc.	8	4.5	0	0
3c. Death, Burial	29	16.5	1	1.4
3d. Careers, Professions	1	0.6	1	1.4
3e. Actions, Events	16	9.1	0	0
3f. Rewards, Punishments	19	10.8	0	0
3g. Persons, Agents	10	5.7	1	1.4
3h. Means, Signs	35	19.9	0	0
3i. Places, Lands	10	5.7	0	0
3j. Gnomic Utterances	16	9.1	6	8.1

* The discrepancy in the total for the division is due to duplication when principal and subordinate topics fall within the same division.

The inclusive survey of the topics as that of the modes confirms the results of the simple analysis.

1. Three-fourths of all known H responses are pronouncements, in whole or in part, on religious topics. The number of L responses on this topic amount to 41.5 percent. This, we must realize, is the maximum number of L responses that can possibly be classified under this head; we must also remember that the L total includes 10 commands to make human sacrifice.

2. The L responses on Res Publicae remain concentrated on foundations of cities and colonies (about one-sixth of all L responses); the remainder are concentrated on war (over one-fourteenth). There is still but one L response on interstate relations, whereas this topic enters into nearly one-twelfth of all Historical responses.

TABLE III
CORRELATION OF MODES AND TOPICS IN LEGENDARY AND HISTORICAL RESPONSES

Legendary Responses

Mode / Topic	A1	A2	A3	B	C1	C2	D1	D2	E1	E2	E3	F	Total
1a	21			1									22
1b	12			1			3						16
1c	10												10
1d	2					1							3
2a	4												4
2b			1										1
2c	12	1		1								2	16
2d						1							1
2e	2		1		1				1	1			6
3a												1	1
3b	1			2				2					5
3c	3	1			1	1				4	2	1	13
3d										1			1
3e	4	1	1		1		1	1			1		10
3f	8	1						1	1	2			13
3g	2		1							2			5
3h			2	19	1	1	1					2	26
3i	7		1					1					9
3j	2		2		1	1	8						14
Total	90	4	9	24	4	5	15	4	2	10	3	6	176

TABLE III (continued)

Historical Responses

Mode Topic	A1	A2	C1	D1	E1	E2	X	Total
1a	7	6	1					14
1b	10	14						24
1d		10	2	3	1			16
2a	1					1		2
2b		2			1			3
2c		2						2
2d		3					1	4
2e	1		1				1	3
3a				1		1		2
3c				1				1
3d	1							1
3j				2				2
Total	20	37	3	8	2	2	2	74

Note: X = Mode unknown.

3. Each of the three main categories of topic is found in from over one-fourth to two-thirds of all L responses, whereas category 3 (Res Domesticae et Profanae) appears in less than one-seventh of H responses, and category 2 (Res Publicae) in a little under one-fourth. Only 18 H, just under one-fourth, so far as we know their texts, make no mention of religious matters. But 103 L responses, nearly three-fifths, have no religious content.

4. Only 10 H responses, in so far as we know their texts, have more than one topic. But 81 L responses, 46 percent of the total, contain two or more topics; 15 have three, about one-twelfth; and one has four (L11).

Most Historical responses are either unambiguous simple commands (A1) or sanctions (A2) which have religious content. The correlation of modes with topics, presented in Table III, shows that among Historical responses, 17 out of 20 clear commands (A1) are religious directions and that 30 out of 37 sanctions (A2) approve religious proposals—over 80 percent of the total for each mode and for both together. At least 47 of 74 Historical oracles, 63.5 percent of the total, are clear commands or sanctions on religious subjects. Among the Legendary responses, 45 out of 90 clear commands, exactly one-half, are religious directions, but 10 of these are commands to make human sacrifice. Thus 35 out of 94 clear commands and sanctions, one-fifth of all Legendary responses, have the same kinds of mode and topic as more than five-eighths of Historical responses.

Res Domesticae et Profanae, topics which rarely or never make up the principal content of Historical oracles, decidedly tend towards the modes that are absent or rare among Historical responses: 61 out of 97 have modes A3, B, C2, D2, E2, E3, F, so that nearly 35 percent of all Legendary oracles have a form and content which are either absent or rare among Historical oracles. Again 85 Legendary oracles, close to one-half, have either a mode or topic that is not found among Historical responses (only 3g appears as topic of the spurious verse form of H3); and if we add 6 E2 responses which have topics attested for the Historical group, we have 91 Legendary responses (over one-half) of essentially non-Historical character.

More than one-half of Legendary responses are clear commands or sanctions: under 30 percent have a religious subject as principal content (three-sevenths have some religious content). Yet we must be aware that our classifying of modes and topics into a few categories is likely to obscure the individual and unique characteristics of the response classified. To group a number of Legendary and a number of Historical responses as clear commands can be misleading if we do not keep in mind the general and classificatory nature of the terms. In fact, the lumping of 90 Legendary and 20 Historical responses together as clear commands (A1) does not inform us that the 20 Historical responses lack the dramatic quality of most of the 90 Legendary responses, which are so framed as to be the integral part of a story. Hence we find prescriptions to avenge and kill (e.g., L7, 19, 25), to make human sacrifice, to banish someone from the land (L6). Even the Legendary prescriptions of cult and sacrifice are usually colorful: e.g., Orestes is sent to fetch the image of the Tauric Artemis so that it may become an Athenian cult image (L29); the frivolous Tirynthians are told to carry a sacrifice through without laughing (L86). Sometimes the command is accompanied by a threat: do it or else (L6, 7).

With few exceptions the corresponding Historical commands are dull prescriptions of cult-foundations or sacrifices, no matter what the question was. Even where we know little of the oracle's actual words, we must suppose that the style and content were much the same as in the responses whose text we know better. Can we suppose, for instance, that H12, concerning which we know only that Xenophon built a temple to Artemis in the place which the god chose, was expressed very differently from the simple direction of H23, which tells the people of Halieis to establish a sanctuary and image of Asklepios? Or from H29, which directs the Athenians to make sacrifice to a number of gods? The only approach to color in H23 is the command to keep in Halieis the Epidaurian snake that had traveled unnoticed in a wagon from Epidauros to Halieis; but the response is much less interesting than the precedent event. An apparent exception to the prevailing dull quality of Historical oracles is H7, which has a "do it or else" formula and expresses the threat in figurative language; but this exceptional quality helps to confirm the accusations, recorded by Thucydides, that Pleistoanax and his brother had bribed the Pythia to speak this response. H67 is expressed in poetic periphrasis, a late attempt at a verse oracle. H5 is the oracle spoken to the Spartans on their proposed war with Athens. This I might have classified as a prediction of the future, but the main response is not a positive prediction of victory. The god says, "If you fight as hard as you can, you will win," which means, "Fight as hard as you can and you will win," so that the formula is that variation of A1 in which the command is expressed in conditional form (a conditional participle in Thucydides' indirect report): in effect the god directs Sparta to make war on Athens; he does little more than sanction Sparta's declaration of war. However we classify H5, we must notice that the prediction of victory depends on a requisite that must be fulfilled. Though Apollo adds a promise of personal aid to Sparta, his assistance could no more be supposed to assure Sparta of victory than it had assured Troy of victory long before.

One of the two Historical prohibitions, H55, is expressed in language that is very similar to that of Legendary responses. It is put into verse in epic language and contains a threat to the Romans if they should ignore the god's warning. But this response, like H70, must be judged spurious, though Phlegon quotes it from Antisthenes the Peripatetic, a contemporary of the events of 191 to which it is assigned. If we should accept this response as authentic, we should also have to accept the occasion for the consultation: a certain Bûplagos, a hipparch in Antiochos' army, rose from the dead on the battlefield and spoke a warning to the Roman camp; and we should also have to accept the subsequent episode: the severed head of Publius spoke an oracle of twelve verses. We can in fact believe nothing of this story except the opening historical statement that Glabrio defeated Antiochos at Thermopylai.[10]

---

10 Square brackets will henceforth enclose the designations H55 and H70 to mark their spurious character, though they fit the definition of Historical response as given on pp. 7–8.

The analysis of modes and topics points to a conclusion that from the fifth century onward, whatever may have happened earlier, the Delphic Oracle's responses were mostly, if not entirely, (1) commonplace sanctions of sacred laws and occasionally of other sorts of legislation, of cult-foundations, proposed festivals, changes in cult practices, and sometimes of colonization, war, or other enterprise; (2) commonplace prescriptions of cult-foundations, sacrifices, or offerings, usually when the question was something other than a request for approval; (3) a residue of safe statements about the past, present, or future, in answer to specific questions.

There remain two statements of present fact that need consideration. One is H3, the response to Chairephon on the wisdom of Socrates, an oracle which was already misunderstood in antiquity. Chairephon, as Plato makes clear (*Apol.* 21a), asked whether any man was wiser than Socrates; and the Pythia replied that nobody was wiser—not, as in a later version, that Socrates was the wisest of men (and as Socrates himself first understood the response, *Apol.* 21b). As the Pythia expressed it, other men could be as wise, and this is the conclusion to which Socrates comes. Though Xenophon (*Apol.* 14) differs from Plato and does not report Chairephon's question, he preserves the negative form of the response: nobody is freer or juster or more sensible than Socrates. In either Plato's or Xenophon's form the response is safe enough and is clearly expressed, though one cannot be sure just what the Pythia had in mind, and one would like to know exactly how Chairephon put his question. In fact, I confess to some doubts about this response. Apparently it must be dated earlier than 430, i.e., before Plato's birth and perhaps before Xenophon's. I have classed it as Historical because both authors show Socrates himself as reporter. But the discrepancy between Plato and Xenophon is serious enough to raise questions. Is Xenophon less trustworthy than Plato? Hardly anyone would say so. But can we doubt Plato? Which version is nearer the truth? Or could this response be a pious fiction of the Socratic circle? That is not impossible, though perhaps incredible. These questions, however, arise from other considerations than the form and content of H3, which require no special mantic powers in the speaker and are not inconsistent with other Historical oracles.

H69 is a long-winded oracle of fifty-one verses, spoken after Plotinos' death in answer to Amelios' question on the destination of the master's soul, and reported by Porphyry, Plotinos' disciple and Amelios' friend. The response, when boiled down, informs one that Plotinos' soul is in paradise enjoying the company of his peers, Plato and Pythagoras. The statement is safe enough: how could anyone prove or disprove it? But the length, language, and content are not only unusual for an Historical response, but are also exceptional in the corpus as a whole. So strange, in fact, is this response as to arouse suspicions. In the first place, we cannot be certain that it is assigned to Delphi. It is attributed to the god who spoke the famous oracles of Croesus and Socrates; but this may mean only that Apollo spoke it, not necessarily the Delphic Apollo. Judging from Oinomaos' treatise on oracles, one would have said that Oinomaos received his own disappointing responses from Apollo at Delphi, if Eusebios' extracts from the work had not included the information that it was the Clarian Apollo who spoke to him. In the second place, it is unlikely that the Pythia (or any other oracle-speaker) would deliver herself of fifty verses of neo-Platonic verbiage, unless the text had been delivered to her beforehand. The poem looks less like an oracle than a disciple's pious labor, a hymn in Plotinos' honor. I would conjecture that Amelios sought approval of his own poem, just as Isyllos and Philodamos had done (H25, 32).

Therefore the apparent exceptions to my conclusion, that the Historical responses are unspectacular in form and content, are either not authentic or fail to give evidence that the Delphic priests and Pythia possessed extraordinary powers or talents, whether divine or human. If after 450 B.C. any responses of a truly extraordinary kind were spoken, they have left no trace in contemporary records. This is a fact worth observing, however we may explain it. If for the last eight centuries of the Delphic Oracle we accept as authentic any response that shows Legendary rather than Historical traits, as I have defined these terms, we must have a cogent reason for doing so.

The Question Formulae of
Historical and Legendary Consultations

We must now inquire whether there is any difference between Legendary and Historical consultations in the form and nature of the questions asked. Unfortunately for no more than 81 Legendary and 34 Historical responses do we have some kind of knowledge about the form of the question. For 3 other Legendary and 2 other Historical oracles the god or Pythia spoke without being questioned (L8, 41, 81; H20, [70]). For the present analysis I shall accept the form and content of questions exactly as the sources report them; and when sources differ, I shall follow the better authority. Several formulae can be distinguished as follows.

1. Shall I do X?, a question expressed usually in the first person singular or plural, future or subjunctive, but sometimes impersonally: e.g., Τὴν ἀνάθεσιν ποιησώμεθα; Μετάλλατόν τι; 5 L, 2 H (see Appendix B).

2. How shall I do X?, expressed by pôs or equivalent and a first-person or impersonal verb, expecting information on the means of carrying out a contemplated action: e.g., Πῶς τιμωρήσομαί τινα; Πῶς ἂν κατέλθοιμεν; 8 L, o H.

3. How shall I have X (or become X)? All questions in this formula ask how to have children or become a parent. The question is usually put in the third person of gignesthai or einai with the dative of the first-person pronoun: e.g., Πῶς ἐμοὶ ἔσονται παῖδες; 5 L, o H.

4. What shall/should I do? How shall/should I act? This is expressed by ti or pôs or equivalent with a first-person or impersonal verb expecting information on how to meet an emergency or problem, or how to meet a danger; e.g., Τί χρὴ πράττειν; Πῶς ἂν ἀπαλλαγείην; 18 L, 5 H.

5. What should I do or say to please the gods? This kind of question should be distinguished from formula 4. L6 seems to show the usual form: Τί χρὴ δρῶντ᾽ ἢ λέγοντα δαίμοσιν πράσσειν φίλα;, which is probably paraphrased in Πῶς ἂν ἱλασαίμην ὑμᾶς;, L64 (Oinomaos). 2 L, 1 H.

6. Who or what is the cause of X? For example, Διὰ τί γίνεται; Τίς ἐμποδίζει; 3 L, o H.

7. Who were X?, which is always "Who were my (or another's) parents?" In each Legendary instance the consultant wants to know who his own parents were: Τίς εἰμι καὶ τίνος υἱός; (L18). Τίνων τ᾽ εἰμὶ γονέων καὶ πόθεν; (L80). In the only Historical example Hadrian reversed the latter question when he asked whence was Homer and whose son (H65). 2 L, 1 H.

8. Whom shall I (we) choose? Who should or will be chosen?, expressed by the proper form of tis or poteros and the future or equivalent of a verb like krinein, lambanein, poieisthai: e.g., Τίνας ποιησόμεθα συμμάχους; Πότερος λήψεται ...; 6 L, 1 H.

9. Where shall I go or find or settle?, expressed by pou or poi with a first-person or impersonal verb: e.g., Ποῦ κατοικήσω; Ποῦ δεῖ πλεῖν; 17 L, 1 H.

10. Shall I succeed in X? Only one Legendary question has this form (L49): Ληψόμεθα τὰς Ἀθήνας; 1 L, o H.

11. What is the truth about X? Under this general formula I place questions in which information about persons, events, or principles is sought: Is it X or Y? How is X valued? For example, Ἔστι τις

σοφώτερος; (H3), Ποῦ κεχώρηκεν; (H69), Πῶς εἰ προσδεδεγμένος τὰ παρ᾽ ἐμοῦ δῶρα; (L59), Πότερόν τι ἔμπνουν ἔχω μετὰ χεῖρας ἢ ἄπνουν; (L155). 2 L, 4 H.

12. Requests. Sometimes, it seems, the Legendary consultant addressed the god with a request or prayer rather than with a question. This kind of address is proper to L9, when Trophonios and Agamedes asked Apollo for their pay. For L93 Statius (*Thebaid* 1.658–661: proinde move pharetras . . . sed illum . . . dispelle globum) shows a request in direct form that Koroibos made. In L121 the Delphians supplicate Apollo. For four other responses the only evidence of question formula is expressed by a form of *aitein* (or Latin *petere*) with an object, which may be simply the source's paraphrase of a truly interrogative formula: e.g., for L17 Dion Chrysostomos shows a form of question which I have classified under 3 above (Laios asks how he may have sons); but the god himself in one version of his reply restates the question with παίδων γένος αἰτεῖς (Argumentum 3 of Sophocles *OT*). Since I am confining myself to just what the sources tell us, I classify those consultations for which no source indicates anything besides a request under *Requests*. 11 L, 0 H.

13. Statements. A number of Legendary responses are double: that is, after the god has responded to the consultant's question, the latter speaks again and the god speaks again. In most instances the consultant asks a second question; but in L63 King Temenos follows the god's response with a statement. In L64 Temenos first addresses the god with what appears to be a statement, a complaint like that of Croesus in Q103. After the god's reply Temenos asks a question. For each response I take the principal question formula from the query, 2 for L63(A), 5 for L64(B), and consider the statements of L63(B) and L64(A) as subordinate. A statement as question formula appears a few times among Quasi-Historical responses. (2 L), 0 H.

14. Is it better for me to do X? The usual form is Λῷον καὶ ἄμεινόν ἐστι ἐμοὶ (ἡμῖν) ποιοῦντι (ποιεῖν) κτλ.;, the two comparatives in the neuter, always in this order, followed by the dative singular or plural of the first-person pronoun, which in turn is followed by either a present participle in agreement with the pronoun or an infinitive to indicate the desired action. Sometimes the future *estai* takes the place of present *estin*. Thucydides' indirect quotation of the question for H5 shows only *ameinon*, but probably the complete formula was actually used as in H21, 25, 33. As H25 shows, the response to this question was likely to repeat the words of the formula; hence there can be little doubt that responses which

begin with *Lôion kai ameinon* were answers to questions so expressed. This is plainly the form of request for a sanction. Just one Legendary question shows this formula imperfectly. 1 L, 14 H.

15. What is better for me to do? This is similar to formula 14, as H36, Τί ἂν ἐμοὶ ... εἴη λῷον καὶ ἄμεινον (ποιοῦντι); though it appears to ask for information rather than a sanction. H54 begins with "Is it better to ...?", but has disjunctive form, "to do X or Y?", and so also appears to ask for information. 0 L, 2 H.

16. To what god(s) shall I sacrifice (and pray)? Τίνι θεῷ(θεῶν) θύων καὶ εὐχόμενος κάλλιστα καὶ ἄριστα ποιήσω; Τίνι ἂν θεῷ θύοντι ἢ εὐχομένῳ εἴη ἐπὶ τὸ ἄμεινον; 0 L, 3 H.

17. No question asked. Three Legendary responses are the god's spontaneous utterances, spoken before the consultant could ask his question. Two Historical responses may be so regarded, but one is the spurious [H70] and the other, H20, is not strictly a response: Philomelos seized upon the Pythia's chance remark, that he had the power to do as he wished, as the god's response, and went off without asking his question. Though the absence of a question can hardly be called a question formula, the appearance of spontaneous responses demands that we treat "no question" as if it were a question and assign it a formula number. 3 L, 2 H.

From Table IV, which tabulates the question formulae, it is evident that over half of the Historical questions show formulae 14, 15, 16; and that only one Legendary question shows a formula in this group. With four exceptions the Legendary questions show formulae 1–12, for which only 15 Historical questions appear (95 pct L, 42 pct H). And 3 of the remaining 4 Legendary consultations show no question. In general the Legendary questions are simple and to the point. The Historical questions tend to fall into prescribed formulae (14–16); when they do not we may suspect inexact paraphrase. The 15 Historical questions showing formulae 1–12 are mostly found indirectly quoted in literary rather than epigraphic sources. H4 (formula 1) was probably expressed in the *lôion kai ameinon* of formula 14. H17 and H23 were probably expressed in formula 15. Formula 5 is the narrative representative of 16; e.g., H48. The alternative form of question, which Amandry and Delcourt emphasize, may be seen in H15, 21, 23, 54, 56 (and in L68, 75, 155).[11] They believe that all actual questions were either expressed in alternatives or according to formula 16; that is, that 14 and 15 were always expressed alternatively. It is true that

---

11 Amandry 1950: 155–159; Delcourt 1955: 11, 114–115, 118–120.

TABLE IV
FORMULAE OF LEGENDARY AND HISTORICAL QUESTIONS

Formula of Question	Legendary	Historical
1. Shall I do X?	5	2
2. How shall I do X?	8	0
3. How may I become a parent?	5	0
4. What shall I do?	18	5
5. What can I do or say to please the gods?	2	1
6. Who or what caused X?	3	0
7. Who were the parents?	2	1
8. Whom or what shall we choose?	6	1
9. Where shall I go or find or settle?	17	1
10. Shall I succeed?	1	0
11. What is the truth about X?	2	4
12. Requests	11	0
13. Statements	(2)*	0
14. Is it better to do X?	1	14
15. What is better to do?	0	2
16. To what god shall I sacrifice?	0	3
17. No question asked	3	2
	84	36

* Not the main question; see p. 37.

all such questions imply an alternative, which may be simply "or not"; but it was probably not always expressed in words.

Non-interrogative formulae, requests (12) and statements (13), do not appear among Historical consultations, nor does spontaneous response (17) really appear among them: H20 and [H70] do not establish spontaneous response as an Historical occurrence.

THE OCCASIONS OF CONSULTATION

Though the records preserve only a relatively small number of consultants' questions, they grant us more information about the occasions or problems which caused the consultants to go to Delphi for a response. For 150 Legendary and 55 Historical oracles we have some knowledge of the reason why the Delphic god was consulted.[12]

---

12 The 150 L include L153(A) and 153(B), for which the occasions differ, and therefore represent 149 responses in the Legendary Catalogue.

i. Plague, famine, drought, catastrophe. 41 L, 1 H.

ii. Sickness of an individual. 9 L, 0 H.

iii. Exile, loss of country, captivity, need to change residence. 16 L, 2 H.

iv. Crime of others. 4 L, 0 H.

v. Crime of self. 7 L, 1 H.

vi. War or *casus belli*. 20 L, 6 H.

vii. Portents, prodigies. 7 L, 3 H.

viii. Problems of rulership. 6 L, 1 H.

ix. Welfare of city or state. 2 L, 3 H.

x. Desire or plan to found a city or colony. 11 L, 2 H.

xi. Lack of children, desire for progeny. 7 L, 1 H.

xii. Desire to marry. 2 L, 0 H.

xiii. Wife or other woman's pregnancy, desire of knowing child's future. 1 L, 0 H.

xiv. Wish to know origin, who one's parents were. 3 L, 1 H.

xv. Death of kin or friends. 1 L, 1 H.

xvi. Disappearance, loss. 2 L, 0 H.

xvii. Contemplated enterprise or career. 3 L, 1 H.

xviii. Desire for reward. 2 L, 0 H.

xix. Test of Oracle. 1 L, 0 H.

xx. Worship of the gods, desire to honor and please them. 5 L, 15 H.

xxi. Religious problems, e.g., whether to open sacred lands to cultivation (H21), how to preserve the sanctity of shrines, etc. 0 L, 9 H.

xxii. Interstate relations. 0 L, 6 H.

xxiii. Desire for information. 0 L, 1 H.

xxiv. Family welfare. 0 L, 1 H.

The analysis of occasions is presented in tabular form in Table V. Though plague, famine, and other catastrophes (i) account for 41 Legendary consultations and the maladies of individuals (ii) for 9 more, only one Historical consultation is said to have been made for such a reason. There are no Historical occasions ii, iv, xii, xiii, xvi, xviii, xix, and no Legendary occasions xxi–xxiv. Occasions i, iii, v, viii, xi, occur relatively few times among Historical consultations; occasion xx is relatively rare among Legendary. The two groups have roughly similar proportions among occasions vi (war), as we might expect, vii (portents), and xiv (origin unknown). Well above half (88/150) of Legendary occasions are concentrated upon occasions i, vi, iii, and x in that order: catastrophes, war, exile, and city foundations, whereas just one fifth (11/55) of Historical

TABLE V

OCCASIONS OF LEGENDARY AND HISTORICAL CONSULTATIONS

Occasion	Legendary (150) Number	Pct	Historical (55) Number	Pct
i. Plague, famine, etc.	41	27.3	1	1.8
ii. Sickness	9	6.0	0	0
iii. Exile, etc.	16	10.7	2	3.6
iv. Crime of others	4	2.7	0	0
v. Crime of self	7	4.7	1	1.8
vi. War	20	13.3	6	10.9
vii. Portents	7	4.7	3	5.5
viii. Rulership	6	4.0	1	1.8
ix. Civic welfare	2	1.3	3	5.5
x. City foundations	11	7.3	2	3.6
xi. Lack of children	7	4.7	1	1.8
xii. Marriage	2	1.3	0	0
xiii. Pregnancy	1	0.7	0	0
xiv. Origin unknown	3	2.0	1	1.8
xv. Death	1	0.7	1	1.8
xvi. Disappearance, loss	2	1.3	0	0
xvii. Enterprise	3	2.0	1	1.8
xviii. Desire for reward	2	1.3	0	0
xix. Test of Oracle	1	0.7	0	0
xx. Worship	5	3.3	15	27.3
xxi. Religious questions	0	0	9	16.4
xxii. Interstate relations	0	0	6	10.9
xxiii. Information	0	0	1	1.8
xxiv. Family welfare	0	0	1	1.8

consultations arise from these occasions. More than half (30/55) of Historical occasions are concentrated on xx, xxi, xxii, in that order: the motives of consultations are mainly religious or political; and about half of the remainder are concentrated on vi, vii, and ix, of which vi and ix are political in nature. But the occasions that occur most often for Historical responses account for under 23 percent of Legendary occasions (mostly vi). Religious occasions xx and xxi precede nearly half (24/55) of Historical responses, but only one thirtieth (5/150) of Legendary responses; and 3 of these belong to variants of the widow's-mite tale, in which rich men ask who made the most pleasing offering.

OBSERVATIONS

The Historical responses that survive tend to show not only that the Delphic shrine's pronouncements, from 450 B.C. at latest, were pretty much confined to sanctions of laws and proposals, particularly on religious subjects, and to prescriptions of cult acts; and that exceptions, if any, were safe statements which anybody could make; but also that the response often had the same form as the question, which was expressed in one of two or three stereotyped forms. Not one can be considered an extraordinary utterance. That a good many of the shrine's transactions were of this character could hardly escape the notice of such scholars as H. W. Parke (1956: 320–323) who have looked closely at the Delphic Oracle. Yet they have believed either that these commonplace responses were a phenomenon of the shrine's decline in postclassical times, or that they were few in number, the appropriate answers to a particular kind of question, and that, in general, the Pythia spoke oracles of the kind with which tradition has made us familiar.

In my earliest study of the Delphic Oracle, when I was still gathering the records of consultations and responses from literature and inscriptions, I soon observed a wide disparity between the responses which I found in contemporary records and the familiar responses of literature and tradition. In my review of Parke's *History of the Delphic Oracle* (1939) I had reached in essentials the conclusions which I express in this book. Then I said:

> My rejection of these oracles that Professor Parke accepts is based upon a comparison of the certainly genuine oracles, those found in inscriptions and contemporary historians, with those that are certainly fictitious, the oracles that are set in the dim legendary past. Only in this way can criteria be established whereby to determine the genuineness of all other records. Many oracles that Professor Parke accepts are exactly like the legendary oracles and not at all like the certainly genuine group. The latter, in fact, show the oracle's business to have been largely a cut-and-dried affair. There were no clever ambiguities, no revelations of the future in difficult language, no motives of the "first to be met" and "this will happen when such and such happens." No matter what the question, the oracle prescribed the foundation of a cult to states, the making of certain sacrifices to individuals; or it merely ratified plans already decided upon.[13]

Since then Amandry, Delcourt, and Crahay have perceived and emphasized the difference between the responses which were inscribed on stone

---

13 Fontenrose 1942b: 475; see also my review (1952: 446) of Amandry 1950.

or otherwise recorded soon after the pronouncement and the bulk of responses which we know from the texts of Greek and Latin historians and poets.[14] They have, in fact, approached the position which I take here. The validity of these scholars' perceptions, as well as the genuineness of individual oracles, can only be determined by a close study of the whole corpus of responses and of all evidence upon the operation of the oracular shrine.

Since the largest part of the responses either command or sanction cult acts and cult laws it would seem that the matters which the Platonic Socrates would have his ideal state refer to the Delphic Apollo were in fact those upon which he usually spoke, and which the Greek states and their citizens did refer to him, "foundation of cults, sacrifices, and other worship of gods, daimones, and heroes."[15] Apollo would be the supreme exegete of the Republic, as he was of Athens (cf. H1, 10).

That consultants expected this sort of response is plain from the questions usually asked. When Xenophon was considering whether he should accept Proxenos' invitation to accompany him on Cyrus the Younger's expedition, he consulted Delphi and asked τίνι ἂν θεῶν θύων καὶ εὐχόμενος κάλλιστα καὶ ἄριστα ἔλθοι τὴν ὁδὸν ἣν ἐπινοεῖ καὶ καλῶς πράξας σωθείη. καὶ ἀνεῖλεν αὐτῷ ὁ Ἀπόλλων θεοῖς οἷς ἔδει θύειν: "to what god should he sacrifice and pray to make his intended journey successful, to fare well upon it, and to return in safety; and Apollo told him to what gods he should sacrifice" (H11). Socrates found fault with Xenophon's question, saying that he should have asked whether it was better to go or stay: πότερον λῷον εἴη αὐτῷ πορεύεσθαι ἢ μένειν. This story makes plain that Xenophon's form of question was usual and conventional: a man asked what ritual acts he should perform in order to prosper in his enterprise. But Socrates' form of alternative question was also common: it comes very close to question formula 14. In H54 Timotheos asks whether it is better for him (πότερον αὐτῷ λῷον καὶ ἄμεινόν ἐστιν) to request from the city a place in the sanctuary of Apollo Asgelatas on which to build a temple of Aphrodite, or a place in the sanctuary of Asklepios. In H21 the two parts of the question on the working of the Eleusinian orgas are each expressed with the lôion kai ameinon formula. Notice too that Sparta's question about making war on Athens (H5) was expressed in Socrates' formula, except that it mentioned no alternative.

The 75 Historical responses, from which we must subtract two as

---

14 Amandry 1950: 149–168, 232; Delcourt 1955: 10–13, 55–60, 91–100, 114–120; Crahay 1956: 6–11, 343–344. For criticism of these writers see Nilsson 1958: 241–247.

15 Plato Rep. 427b; see also Leg. 738bc, 828a; Xen. Mem. 1.3.1.

spurious, are a tiny fraction of all the responses that must have been spoken at Delphi in the last 800 years of the Oracle's activity. So it may be argued that spectacular responses, ambiguous and predictive, were spoken then, as the Quasi-Historical list attests, but do not happen to appear in any contemporary record extant. This is essentially an *argumentum ex silentio*. If it is the spectacular responses that are likely to be remembered and recorded, as the argument goes, then we should expect to find some in contemporary records; but we do not.

The Characteristics of Quasi-Historical Responses

In analysing the Quasi-Historical responses we must keep in mind that ambiguous and obscure commands or prohibitions, conditioned commands and predictions, and extraordinary future predictions are characteristic of Legendary oracles, and are not found among Historical oracles.

We shall now determine which Quasi-Historical responses (as I have defined the term, p. 8) are similar in mode and content to Historical responses. Tables VI-X will suffice to present the analysis of them, since the modes, topics, question formulae, and occasions have been defined. In long or complex responses the kernel of the message determines the principal mode and topic, as in the analysis of Historical and Legendary responses.[16]

Modes

Table VI shows the number of Quasi-Historical responses that represent each mode along with the percentage figure; the third and fourth columns show the corresponding Legendary and Historical percentages from Table I for comparison. In a body of responses which are presumably divided between genuine and spurious utterances one would expect the percentages of most modes to fall somewhere between Legendary and Historical percentages. In fact, this is seldom the case; it is true only of Quasi-Historical clear commands (A1), commonplace statements (D1), and non-predictive future statements (E1), if we leave out of account

---

16 As in dealing with the Legendary and Historical responses I determine the mode and content of Quasi-Historical responses from the available record, which may be only a brief indirect quotation or a statement of what was done in consequence of the oracle received. It is possible, therefore, in some instances to be in error about the mode or topic that was actually used (in fact or in narrative). But the instances where we are really in doubt are few, and any changes in classification that might be made necessary by further knowledge will not affect the results and conclusions of this study.

TABLE VI
MODES OF QUASI-HISTORICAL RESPONSES

	Number (267)	Pct	Legendary Pct	Historical Pct
A. Simple Commands	133	49.8	58.5	79.2
A1. Clear Commands	104	39.0	51.1	27.8
A2. Sanctions	5	1.9	2.3	51.4
A3. Ambiguous Commands	24	9.0	5.1	0
B. Conditioned Commands	9	3.4	13.6	0
C. Prohibitions and Warnings	28	10.5	5.1	4.2
C1. Clear Prohibitions	19	7.1	2.3	4.2
C2. Ambiguous Prohibitions	9	3.4	2.8	0
D. Statements on Past or Present	35	13.1	10.8	11.1
D1. Commonplace Statements	24	9.0	8.5	11.1
D2. Extraordinary Statements	11	4.1	2.3	0
E. Simple Future Statements	42	15.7	8.5	5.8
E1. Non-Predictive Statements	5	1.9	1.1	2.8
E2. Clear Predictions	16	6.0	5.7	2.8
E3. Ambiguous Predictions	21	7.9	1.7	0
F. Conditioned Predictions	20	7.5	3.4	0

those modes in which Historical responses do not appear at all; and for D1 the Quasi-Historical percentage is very close to the Legendary. The class of past and present statements as a whole (D) is the only major division that is fairly evenly represented among the three groups, the Quasi-Historical being a little ahead of the others; such statements number a little more than one-ninth of all responses.

In both absolute and proportionate numbers the Quasi-Historical responses exceed the Legendary in nearly every mode that is non-Historical: in ambiguous commands (A3), ambiguous prohibitions (C2), extraordinary statements (D2), ambiguous predictions (E3), and conditioned predictions (F). In all except C2 the Quasi-Historical ratio greatly exceeds the Legendary figure. Among non-Historical modes only conditioned commands (B) are rare among Quasi-Historical responses in comparison with Legendary responses. In clear predictions (E2), which are rare and questionable among Historical responses, the Quasi-Historical outnumber the Legendary. Proportionately there are almost twice as many Quasi-Historical simple future statements (E) as Legendary. Noteworthy too is the comparatively large number of Quasi-Historical prohibitions (C), clear or obscure, in relation to Legendary and Historical prohibitions.

There are proportionately fewer sanctions (A2) among Quasi-Historical than among Legendary responses. We would expect more, seeing that half of Historical responses are sanctions. There are only 5 Quasi-Historical as against the Legendary 4; and the figure is reached by counting as a sanction every response that can possibly be so classified. In simple commands (A) as a whole the Quasi-Historical percentage is lower than the Legendary and very much below the Historical (the ratio is 5Q/8H).

Earlier in the chapter we found that the more detailed analysis of Legendary and Historical responses which took account of the complexity of many responses did not invalidate the results of the simplified analysis limited to principal modes; that, in fact, the detailed analysis confirmed the results. We should now give attention to the complex Quasi-Historical responses, taking subordinate and variant modes into account, to see whether the results will differ significantly from those of the simpler analysis. The following summary indicates the subordinate modes that occur among Quasi-Historical responses.

A1. Clear Commands: $17 + 104 = 121$.
A3. Ambiguous and Obscure Commands: $2 + 24 = 26$.
When 3 duplications are deducted the total of simple commands (A) is $16 + 133 = 149$.
C1. Clear Prohibitions and Warnings: $14 + 19 = 33$.
The total of prohibitions and warnings (C) is $14 + 28 = 42$.
D1. Commonplace Statements on Past or Present: $20 + 24 = 44$.
D2. Extraordinary Statements on Past or Present: $5 + 11 = 16$.
The total of past and present statements (D) is $25 + 35 = 60$.
E1. Non-Predictive Future Statements: $7 + 5 = 12$.
E2. Clear Predictions: $17 + 16 = 33$.
E3. Ambiguous and Obscure Predictions: $3 + 21 = 24$.
When one duplication is subtracted the total of simple future statements is $26 + 42 = 68$.
F. Conditioned Predictions: $2 + 20 = 22$.

In Table VI-A these figures are tabulated together with the corresponding Legendary and Historical percentages from Table I-A. Here too the inclusive analysis confirms the conclusions drawn from the simple analysis. Most categories remain relatively the same.

1. Clear commands (A1), non-predictive future statements (E1), and clear predictions (E2) are the only categories in which Q falls between L and H, where all three are represented. Q has fallen behind L in E2, but is still very close.

TABLE VI-A
Principal and Subordinate Modes of
Quasi-Historical Responses

	Number (267)	Pct	Legendary Pct	Historical Pct
A. Simple Commands	149*	55.9	62.5	80.6
A1. Clear Commands	121	45.3	55.1	30.6
A2. Sanctions	5	1.9	2.3	51.4
A3. Ambiguous Commands	26	9.7	5.7	0
B. Conditioned Commands	9	3.4	14.2	0
C. Prohibitions and Warnings	42	15.7	13.6	5.6
C1. Clear Prohibitions	33	12.4	9.7	5.6
C2. Ambiguous Prohibitions	9	3.4	4.0	0
D. Statements on Past or Present	60	22.5	17.6	11.1
D1. Commonplace Statements	44	16.5	13.1	11.1
D2. Extraordinary Statements	16	6.0	4.5	0
E. Simple Future Statements	68*	25.5	18.2	11.1
E1. Non-Predictive Statements	12	4.5	2.8	8.3
E2. Clear Predictions	33	12.4	13.6	2.8
E3. Ambiguous Predictions	24	9.0	1.7	0
F. Conditioned Predictions	22	8.2	5.7	0

* Discrepancies in totals for divisions are due to duplications.

2. The number of Q clear commands (A1) and sanctions (A2), taken together, remains considerably lower than L; they are fewer than one-half of all Q responses, whereas over four-fifths of all H responses show these modes.

3. Nearly thirty percent of all Q responses contain predictions (E2, E3, F), and one-fifth contain simple predictions.

4. 125 out of 267 Q responses have a non-H mode (A3, B, C2, D2, E3, F) or E2 in either principal or subordinate content, about 47 percent of the total; rather more than the approximately 41 percent (73/176) of L responses in the same categories.

5. 74 (27.7 pct) of Q responses have two or three modes, a little above the approximately one-fourth (25.6 pct) of L responses that are complex. Of these Q responses 13 have three modes.

Topics

The analysis of Quasi-Historical topics is presented in Table VII, which includes the Legendary and Historical percentages from Table II

TABLE VII
TOPICS OF QUASI-HISTORICAL RESPONSES

	Number (267)	Pct	Legendary Pct	Historical Pct
1. *Res Divinae*	*81*	*30.3*	*29*	*73*
1a. Cult Foundations	41	15.4	12.5	20.3
1b. Sacrifices, Offerings	25	9.4	9.1	31.1
1c. Human Sacrifices	2	0.7	5.7	0
1d. Religious Laws, Customs	13	4.9	1.7	21.6
2. *Res Publicae*	*66*	*24.7*	*15.9*	*18.9*
2a. Rulership	10	3.7	2.3	2.7
2b. Legislation	7	2.6	0.6	4.1
2c. City/Colony Foundations	21	7.9	9.1	2.7
2d. Interstate Relations	2	0.7	0.6	5.4
2e. War	26	9.7	3.4	4.1
3. *Res Domesticae et Profanae*	*120*	*44.9*	*55.1*	*8.1*
3a. Birth, Origin	8	3.0	0.6	2.7
3b. Marriage, etc.	1	0.4	2.8	0
3c. Death, Burial	2	0.7	7.4	1.4
3d. Careers, Professions	4	1.5	0.6	1.4
3e. Actions, Events	16	6.0	5.7	0
3f. Rewards, Punishments	6	2.2	7.4	0
3g. Persons, Agents	16	6.0	2.8	0
3h. Means, Signs	39	14.6	14.8	0
3i. Places	6	2.2	5.1	0
3j. Gnomic Utterances	22	8.2	8.0	2.7

for comparison. Among Quasi-Historical responses Res Divinae have just about the same frequency as among Legendary responses, approximately 30 percent. Res Publicae occur much more frequently than among either Legendary or Historical responses. The large number is mostly due to the prominence of oracles on colony foundation assigned to the period 750–500 and of oracles on war. Res Domesticae et Profanae fall not far below the Legendary proportion; they have the largest number of the three divisions, approaching half of the total.

In 11 of the 19 subdivisions the Quasi-Historical percentage falls between the Legendary and Historical percentages. Among non-H topics Q exceeds L in 3e (actions, events) and 3g (persons, agents), and has almost the same figure as L for 3h (means, signs).

We should now take account of subordinate Quasi-Historical topics.

1. Res Divinae
1a. Cult Foundations: 2 + 41 = 43.
1b. Sacrifices, Offerings: 12 + 25 = 37.
1d. Religious Laws, Customs: 10 + 13 = 23.
When 3 duplications are subtracted the total for Res Divinae is 21 + 81 = 102.

2. Res Publicae.
2a. Rulership: 11 + 10 = 21.
2b. Legislation, Civic Welfare: 6 + 7 = 13.
2c. City and Colony Foundations: 9 + 21 = 30.
2d. Interstate Relations: 2 + 2 = 4.
2e. War: 28 + 26 = 54.
There are 6 duplications, so that the total for Res Publicae is 50 + 66 = 116.

3. Res Domesticae et Profanae.
3a. Birth, Origin: 3 + 8 = 11.
3c. Death, Burial: 12 + 2 = 14.
3d. Careers, Professions: 2 + 4 = 6.
3e. Actions, Events: 5 + 16 = 21.
3f. Rewards, Punishments: 7 + 6 = 13.
3g. Persons, Agents: 5 + 16 = 21.
3h. Means, Signs: 8 + 39 = 47.
3i. Places: 4 + 6 = 10.
3j. Gnomic Utterances: 15 + 22 = 37.
There are 31 duplications, so that the total for this division is 30 + 120 = 150.

The above figures are tabulated in Table VII-A, where the percentages of Legendary and Historical responses are also presented from Table II-A. The inclusion of the minor topics, as of the minor modes, makes no essential difference. The preponderance of Res Divinae in H is hardly reduced: H is nearly double Q or L, which remain fairly close proportionately. Q responses on Res Domesticae et Profanae still lean heavily to the L side. Few changes have to be made in the relative positions of the three classes in each topic. Q now exceeds L or H in 3j, is nearer to L in 3a, and a little above H in 2b. War (2e) and death (3c) are notably frequent as subtopics; Q greatly predominates in 2e and is between L and H in 3c.

One hundred and fifteen Q responses have one or more subtopics, i.e., 43 percent of the total, relatively close to the L percentage (46). Of these 21 have two or three subtopics, about one-twelfth, also close to the proportion in L.

Table VIII presents the correlation of modes and topics of Quasi-Historical responses. Out of 104 clear commands (A1) 56 are religious directions, of which one prescribes human sacrifice (1c). Out of 5 sanctions

TABLE VII-A
Principal and Subordinate Topics of
Quasi-Historical Responses

	Number (267)	Pct	Legendary Pct	Historical Pct
1. Res Divinae	102*	38.2	41.5	75.7
1a. Cult Foundations	43	16.1	13.6	20.3
1b. Sacrifices, Offerings	37	13.9	13.6	33.8
1c. Human Sacrifices	2	0.7	5.7	0
1d. Religious Laws, Customs	23	8.6	8.5	23
2. Res Publicae	116*	43.4	28.4	23
2a. Rulership	21	7.9	2.8	2.7
2b. Legislation	13	4.9	1.1	4.1
2c. City/Colony Foundations	30	11.2	17.0	2.7
2d. Interstate Relations	4	1.5	0.6	8.1
2e. War	54	20.2	7.4	5.4
3. Res Domesticae et Profanae	150*	56.2	67	13.5
3a. Birth, Origin	11	4.1	3.4	2.7
3b. Marriage, etc.	1	0.4	4.5	0
3c. Death, Burial	14	5.2	16.5	1.4
3d. Careers, Professions	6	2.2	0.6	1.4
3e. Actions, Events	21	7.9	9.1	0
3f. Rewards, Punishments	13	4.9	10.8	0
3g. Persons, Agents	21	7.9	5.7	1.4
3h. Means, Signs	47	17.6	19.9	0
3i. Places	10	3.7	5.7	0
3j. Gnomic Utterances	37	13.9	9.1	8.1

* Discrepancies in totals for divisions are due to duplication.

4 are spoken on religious topics. That is, 55 percent of clear commands and sanctions have a religious content, a figure much closer to the nearly 50 percent among Legendary responses than to the 82 percent among Historical responses. If one subtracts the prescription of human sacrifice then 59 clear commands and sanctions, well under one-fourth of all Quasi-Historical responses, have the same kinds of mode and topic as five-eighths of Historical responses; the Legendary proportion is one-fifth.

Of the 120 Quasi-Historical responses spoken on Res Domesticae et Profanae 72, three-fifths, have modes A3, B, C2, D2, E2, E3, or F, so that well over one-fourth of all Quasi-Historical oracles have both a mode and

TABLE VIII
Correlation of Modes and Topics of Quasi-Historical Responses

Topic \ Mode	A1	A2	A3	B	C1	C2	D1	D2	E1	E2	E3	F	Total
1a	35	2	2				2						41
1b	17	1	1		1	2					1	2	25
1c	1		1										2
1d	3	1		1	5		1	1	1				13
2a	1					1	3			4	1		10
2b	4	1	1		1								7
2c	14		3		1				2	1			21
2d	2												2
2e	5		4		4		1			3	7	2	26
3a	1						1	1		3	2		8
3b	1												1
3c		1					1						2
3d	3											1	4
3e	8		2					1		2	3		16
3f	2				3		1						6
3g	3		1				4	1		2	2	3	16
3h	1		3	8	1	7	1	4		1	1	12	39
3i						1	2		1		2		6
3j	3		5		3		7	1	1		2		22
Total	104	5	24	9	19	9	24	11	5	16	21	20	267

a topic that are absent or rare among Historical oracles. The Legendary figures are 51 out of 97, a little over one-half, and nearly three-tenths of the total. 139 Quasi-Historical oracles, over one-half, have a mode or content that is never found among the Historical responses or the mode E2, just about the same proportion as the 91 Legendary responses of the same character.

The statistical analysis of Quasi-Historical responses in terms of modes and topics indicates, therefore, that they are as a group much more like the Legendary responses in these features than like Historical responses.

Question Formulae

For 131 Quasi-Historical responses we have information on the question asked; eight others are responses without a question. Table IX presents the analysis of Quasi-Historical questions, along with the corresponding numbers of Legendary and Historical question formulae in each category as shown in Table IV.

We notice that Quasi-Historical questions are represented for all but one (3) of the question formulae which appear as only Legendary in Table IV (2, 3, 6, 10, 12, 13), and that the numbers are fairly close to the Legendary figures in three of these, in considerable excess in two (10, 13). The three formulae 14, 15, 16, which appear exclusively or nearly so among Historical questions in Table IV are poorly represented in the Quasi-Historical column, 5 only, confined to 14 and 16. In formulae 1, 8, and 11, which appear rarely among Historical questions, much more frequently among Legendary, the Quasi-Historical number greatly exceeds the Legendary. It is noteworthy that 8 of the 29 under formula 11 are questions about the future, expecting a prediction for answer (Q101, 114, 122, 139, 221, 249, 256, 257). There are no instances of such questions

TABLE IX

QUESTION FORMULAE OF QUASI-HISTORICAL RESPONSES

	Q	L	H
1. Shall I do X?	20	5	2
2. How shall I do X?	7	8	0
3. How may I become a parent?	0	5	0
4. What shall I do?	20	18	5
5. What can I say or do to please the gods?	0	2	1
6. Who or what caused X?	5	3	0
7. Who were the parents?	1	2	1
8. Whom or what shall we choose?	12	6	1
9. Where shall I go or find or settle?	11	17	1
10. Shall I succeed?	6	1	0
11. What is the truth about X?	29	2	4
12. Requests	11	11	0
13. Statements	4	(2)	0
14. Is it better to do X?	4	1	14
15. What is better to do?	0	0	2
16. To what god shall I sacrifice?	1	0	3
17. No question asked	8	3	2
	139	84	36

among Historical and Legendary inquiries, where all examples of formula 11 concern past or present. For this reason I have subsumed the question "What will happen?" under this head. The question often asked of fortune-tellers and soothsayers appears very rarely in the Delphic tradition.

In at least 14 Quasi-Historical responses, as we learn from the accounts preserved, the god either did not answer the question asked, but spoke a command or statement on a different subject, or did not wait for the question: Q7, 41, 45, 47, 58, 59, 61, 124, 138, 146, 160, 216, 245, 268. This sort of thing never occurs in the Historical records, unless we count H20 as a response without a question (we can disregard [H70]). Only Q124 has a good claim to authenticity; according to the charge made, the Alkmeonids bribed the Pythia to say the same thing, "Free Athens," to every Spartan consultant, no matter what his business was; and probably this command concluded whatever answer the Pythia gave to the question asked.

Occasions

For 228 Quasi-Historical responses the sources provide information about the occasion or motive which led the consultant to make inquiry at Delphi. The analysis appears in Table X, which also shows for comparison the corresponding Legendary and Historical percentage figures from Table V.

Approximately 56 percent of Quasi-Historical consultations resulted from occasions i, vi, vii, x, more than the approximately 53 percent of Legendary consultations thus motivated; the Historical percentage is about 22. Only 8 percent of Quasi-Historical responses resulted from occasions xx-xxii, which account for nearly 55 percent of Historical consultations. The Quasi-Historical occasions are fewer than the Legendary in i and ii, but are nevertheless well represented in them. In vi-ix the Quasi-Historical exceed either the Legendary or Historical; and almost a quarter of the total are occasions of war (vi), where the Quasi-Historical proportion is almost equal to the Legendary and Historical together.

We may now apply the results of the foregoing analysis to the body of Quasi-Historical oracles in order to judge which responses are acceptable in terms of the analysis and which are not: i.e., which have modes, topics, and preliminary circumstances of the kinds which are attested among Historical responses and which have not. They may be separated into five divisions, ranging from those that are most like Historical responses to those that are most unlike them.

TABLE X

OCCASIONS OF QUASI-HISTORICAL CONSULTATIONS

Occasion	Number (228)	Pct	Legendary (149) Pct	Historical (55) Pct
i. Plague, famine, etc.	37	16.2	27.3	1.8
ii. Sickness, misfortune	9	3.9	6.0	0
iii. Exile	6	2.6	10.7	3.6
iv. Crime of others	3	1.3	2.7	0
v. Crime of self	3	1.3	4.7	1.8
vi. War	53	23.2	13.3	10.9
vii. Portents, prodigies	18	7.9	4.7	5.5
viii. Rulership	14	6.1	4.0	1.8
ix. Civic welfare	18	7.9	1.3	5.5
x. City/colony foundation	20	8.8	7.3	3.6
xi. Desire for children	4	1.8	4.7	1.8
xii. Marriage	1	0.4	1.3	0
xiii. Pregnancy	1	0.4	0.7	0
xiv. Parents unknown	1	0.4	2.0	1.8
xv. Death	2	0.9	0.7	1.8
xvi. Disappearance, loss	6	2.6	1.3	0
xvii. Enterprise, career	6	2.6	2.0	1.8
xviii. Desire for reward	2	0.9	1.3	0
xix. Test of Oracle	2	0.9	0.7	0
xx. Worship	11	4.8	3.3	27.3
xxi. Religious questions	7	3.1	0	16.4
xxii. Interstate relations	0	0	0	10.9
xxiii. Desire for information	3	1.3	0	1.8
xxiv. Family welfare	1	0.4	0	1.8

1. Thirty responses show not only a general but also a specific likeness to the Historical responses in mode, topic, and circumstances of consultation, in so far as the sources inform us about them. To these may be added Q244, though we lack its content, so that 31 responses may be placed in this first division: Q8, 11, 22, 52, 65, 69, 70, 89, 111, 115, 124, 125, 142, 148, 154, 156, 157, 167, 169, 178, 181, 187, 189, 190, 205, 222, 237, 241, 244, 266, 267. About some of these a doubt may be raised either because of the early date at which it must have been spoken or because of the lateness or untrustworthiness of the source. Hence not all responses of this group can be declared authentic without qualification at this point.

2. Many other responses have modes and topics found among

Historical responses. They are therefore acceptable on these general grounds; but for one or more reasons each remains suspect. In many the specific content raises grave doubts, since it is not the kind of direction or statement that is likely to occur among Historical responses. Many are complex in mode or topic, containing one or more subordinate elements, one or more of which may be non-Historical. Many are in verse—and most verse oracles raise doubts. For some the accompanying narrative is questionable: it may be more legend than history. The occasion or question may be of a kind unattested among Historical consultations. Many are assigned to the period 800–500, a time much earlier than the earliest extant record. There are 98 responses in this division, rather too many to list here. It comprises all Quasi-Historical responses not listed in the other four divisions.

3. Some responses conform in mode but not in topic to the Historical responses; that is, the topic belongs to one of the classes (1c, 3b, 3e–3i) not attested among the 75 known Historical oracles. In other respects they are like the responses of the second division. Since nonconformity of topic does not raise such serious doubts about the authenticity of a response (see p. 28) as does nonconformity of mode, we may put the responses of this group on nearly the same level as those of division 2. There are 30 responses in this division: Q14, 21, 24, 27, 31, 49, 53, 54, 58, 75, 76, 86, 92, 94, 97, 102, 106, 123, 128, 143, 161, 162, 196, 233, 257–261, 264.

4. Much more questionable are the responses which have non-Historical modes (including E2) along with an Historical topic. There are 54 such responses: Q6, 15, 17, 37, 38, 41, 43, 55, 56, 59–62, 66, 77, 78, 80, 93, 100, 104, 105, 116, 117, 121, 127, 130, 136, 137, 140, 144, 147, 150, 152, 155, 159, 163, 168, 170, 174, 180, 191, 202, 203, 206, 213, 224, 230, 235, 236, 245, 254, 255, 262, 263.

5. Most questionable are the responses that are non-Historical in both mode and topic, most of which are questionable in other respects too. Aside from being assigned to historical times and persons, they are quite like Legendary oracles. There are 55 responses of this kind: Q16, 20, 25, 33, 34, 36, 39, 44, 64, 71–73, 81, 84, 87, 88, 90, 99, 101, 103, 109, 114, 119, 122, 129, 134, 138, 139, 160, 171, 185, 186, 193–195, 199, 201, 204, 207, 210, 212, 214, 215, 217, 219–221, 225, 238–240, 249, 251, 256, 268.

At this point we shall reject no Quasi-Historical response, though we shall consider those in divisions 4 and 5 highly suspect. We can accept most oracles of the first division as authentic, but must test those in the other divisions on other grounds in the following chapters.

ADDENDUM

It is probable that some readers will object that my definition of Historical response is too narrow. It allows only 75 responses in the Historical group, of which we do not know the mode of three and the topic of one. They may say that the Historical responses should include any that is assigned to the generation or two before the birth of our earliest authority for it. This writer, they will say, would have known and talked to older men who were alive and mature at the time when the response was allegedly spoken, and these informants would have been in most instances reliable. So let us glance at those Quasi-Historical responses spoken within sixty years preceding the birth of the earliest reporter. There are 41 such responses, which have the following modes.

A1. Clear commands: Q113, 124, 131, 148, 153, 161, 165, 175, 223, 257 (10).
A2. Sanctions: Q8 (1).
A3. Ambiguous commands: Q130, 144, 174 (3).
C1. Clear prohibitions: Q143, 146, 149, 181 (4).
C2. Ambiguous prohibitions and warnings: Q114, 119, 251 (3).
D1. Commonplace statements on past or present: Q75, 145, 157, 177, 259, 264 (6).
D2. Extraordinary statements: Q137, 263 (2).
E2. Clear predictions: Q121, 150, 155 (3).
E3. Ambiguous predictions: Q136, 147, 160, 230, 239, 249, 262 (7).
F. Conditioned predictions: Q134, 152 (2).

All the non-Historical modes appear except B. Striking are the 7 ambiguous predictions (E3), one-third of the Q total for this mode. If these 40 responses should be added to H and subtracted from Q, then the number of hitherto absent modes plus E2 for H would amount to nearly 20 percent, still far below approximately 40 percent Q and 35 percent L. But, of course, this result would be entirely due to the inclusion of these 40 non-contemporary responses. Twenty-five of the 40 come from Herodotos for the period 540–479; and as Crahay (1956) has shown, and as we shall see in following chapters, most of Herodotos' oracles are of very questionable authenticity. Only Q8, 124, 137, 148, and 157 are likely to be authentic.

The 40 responses include Q262 and Q263, supposedly spoken to Julian or to his envoy. These are attested respectively by Theodoretos (born 393) and Philostorgios (born 368). Neither is likely to be authentic. These responses also include Q230, the famous oracle supposedly spoken to Pyrros of Epeiros, for which Ennius (born 239 B.C.) is our earliest source. Others equally dubious are Q239, 249, 251.

A review of the topics of these 40 responses shows 13 more appearances of war (2e), mostly in those that Herodotos cites or quotes for the Persian War period; and more topics in Res Domesticae et Profanae, including some that do not appear among the Historical responses. This is not a serious objection to accepting these as Historical, since it is probable that the Delphic Oracle spoke occasionally on such topics. More questionable is the way in which many express this content.

What this survey shows is that responses reported for the period just before the reporter's lifetime are no different in character from those reported for periods farther back. Those that Herodotos reports for the 540–480 period closely resemble those that he reports for earlier times (roughly 1200–540). In those times when oral transmission was almost the only means of conveying news, reports, and narratives of past events, pseudo-historical traditions could grow up very quickly. As we shall see later there were many oracles in circulation, some of which attached themselves to events.

CHAPTER

Oracles of Folkloric Origin

In many responses, both Legendary and Quasi-Historical, the terms used or the asserted condition of fulfillment mislead the receiver, falsely reassuring or discouraging him, because they are obscure or because words are not employed in their ordinary meanings. Prophecies like these occur frequently in the legends and folktales of many peoples. Some of these oracles are enigmatic in expression, and many appear to be riddles in origin. Other responses are popular proverbs. Still others, though unambiguous in themselves, are constituents of traditional tales.

Jerusalem Chamber

Several Quasi-Historical oracles are predictions or warnings of disaster at a certain place or from a certain kind of person, creature, or instrument, or when a certain event occurs. Either they tell the consultant to avoid the place, person, creature, or instrument, or they assure him that his life, power, or prosperity will endure until the condition that marks his doom is fulfilled. Either the indicated agent or sign of doom appears to be easily avoidable, as the receiver interprets the message, and he carefully avoids it—at any rate, he seems to have an assurance of how or when he will meet his doom—only to find at last that the oracle meant something or someone quite different from what he had supposed; or the indicated instrument or event seems incredible, something that he believes cannot possibly occur or appear—at least it is very unlikely to happen—so that he believes that his prosperity or power is secure or permanent, only to find that the condition which seemed unlikely or impossible has a very simple fulfillment.

For example, Epaminondas of Thebes was told to beware of *pelagos* (Q207). He naturally supposed, as anybody would, that he should stay away from the sea; and so he never embarked on ship or boat. But the god meant the wood called Pelagos on the battlefield of Mantinea. King Archidamos of Sparta was told to beware of Sikelia (Q195), and so he took care not to go to Sicily, supposing that the god could mean nothing else. But Apollo meant a hill in Attica, and there Archidamos lost his life in battle.[1]

These two responses, except for being quoted in verse, differ in no essential respect from the central message of L41, which warned Hesiod against the grove of Zeus Nemeios, for there he was fated to die; consequently Hesiod avoided the well-known sanctuary of Zeus at Nemea; but he stayed in the house of Phegeus' sons at Oinoe in Lokris, unaware that the place was called *hieron* of Zeus Nemeios, and there his hosts killed him.

The theme appears frequently in Greek folklore or pseudohistory. Just after Pausanias tells the story of Epaminondas and Pelagos, he tells a similar story about Hannibal; Plutarch also knew the story and quotes the response in verse.[2] Ammon's oracle told Hannibal that Libyan soil (*Libyssa bôlos*) would cover his body, whereupon he thought that he was fated to die and receive burial in his native land, probably after reaching old age. But he was killed in Bithynia at a village called Libyssa. Likewise Kambyses had heard from the Oracle at Buto in Egypt that he would end his life in Agbatana. He supposed that he would die, an old man, in Media's capital city amidst his family and possessions; but having wounded himself accidentally in a Syrian town, he asked the name of the place and was told that it was Agbatana; and there he died a few days later.[3]

---

1 The Suda, the only source for Q195, says that the recipient was Agesilaos' son, who should be Archidamos III, killed in battle in southern Italy in 338. Perhaps he has been confused with Archidamos II, invader of Attica, though the latter was not killed in the invasions. There seems to have been a hill called Sichelia near Athens (*RE* s.v.). According to Pausanias (8.11.12; see Dion Chrys. 17.17), an oracle from Dodona instructed the Athenians to settle Sikelia, and so Athens was led to undertake the disastrous Sicilian expedition; whereas Zeus had meant that they should settle the Attic hill.

2 Paus. 8.11.10–11; Plut. *Titus* 20.

3 Herod. 3.64.3–5. See Aly 1921: 98; Crahay 1956: 217. There was no village called Agbatana in Syria. See Zonaras *Hist.* 13.13, Julian's dream that he would die in Phrygia, which turned out to be a village in Mesopotamia. See also Strabo 6.1.5, p. 256; Steph. Byz. 499

These five prophecies illustrate the Jerusalem Chamber motif; for we may name it after the most widely known example of it, that which appears in Shakespeare's *Henry IV*, part II:

> K. Hen. Doth any name particular belong
> Unto the lodging where I first did swound?
> War. 'Tis call'd Jerusalem, my noble lord.
> K. Hen. Laud be to God! even there my life must end.
> It hath been prophesied to me many years
> I should not die but in Jerusalem,
> Which vainly I suppos'd the Holy Land.
> But bear me to that chamber; there I'll lie:
> In that Jerusalem shall Harry die.
>
> [IV.v.231–239]

The story is earlier told of Gerbert, who became Pope Sylvester II: a phantom told him that he would live until he celebrated mass in Jerusalem. He celebrated mass at a Roman church whose name he learned too late was Jerusalem.[4]

Not very different from the Jerusalem Chamber prophecies are those which predict death or misfortune from a particular instrument, which turns out not to be the object generally known by the term which the prophet has used. A good example is that which the Delphic Oracle (as Valerius Maximus tells the story) gave to Philip of Macedon, that he should guard himself against death from a chariot (Q214).[5] So Philip had all chariots in his realm dismantled (very unlikely for a warlord), but in vain: for the sword with which the young Pausanias struck him down had a figure of a chariot upon the hilt. Similarly the interesting character called Daphidas of Telmessos, a sophist, received a response that he should beware of the *thôrax* (breastplate) (Q240). He was crucified on a hill called Thorax near Magnesia-on-Maeander. Only Strabo alludes to this version of Daphidas' death and does not name the Delphic Oracle; better attested is the story in which the hill or cliff was called Hippos. Daphidas, wanting

---

Mein.: Dodona's warning to Alexander of Epeiros against the Acherusian water; and Josephus *Ant. Jud.* 13.311–313 on the murder of the Maccabee Antigonos at Straton's Tower.

4 Walter Map *Nugae Curialium* 4.11; Andrew of Wyntoun *Chron.* 6.12.999–1054 Cott.; *De fantastica deceptione Gilberti*, in Felix Liebrecht, *Zur Volkskunde* (Heilbronn 1879) 47–48. Compare the Irish legend of Lóegaire, told that he would die between Erin and Alba, which turned out to be two hills beside the Liffey; *The Conversion of Lóegaire and His Death, Rev. Celt.* 6 (1883) 165, 168. For other examples of this motif see *MIFL* M341.3, 3.1, 3.2; Tom Peete Cross, *Motif-Index of Early Irish Literature* (Bloomington: Indiana Univ., 1952) 396.

5 Ael. *VH* 3.45 attributes Q214 to Trophonios. The uncertainty of attribution is itself an indication of the folkloric nature of this story. Cf. Q212, 213, 215. See *MIFL* M341.2.

to make the Delphic Apollo look ridiculous, asked the god whether he would find his horse, although he had neither lost a horse nor owned one. The god replied that he would find his *hippos*, but, as one version adds, would be thrown from it and die (Q239). So Daphidas thought that he had tricked the Delphic god; but soon afterwards King Attalos of Pergamon had him thrown from a cliff called Hippos.[6]

To this kind of prophecy we can assign Q119, spoken to Arkesilaos of Cyrene just before his return from exile. He was told to rule peacefully on his return, and "if you find the oven full of jars, do not bake them, but send them on their way. But if you bake them, avoid the seagirt; otherwise you and the prize bull will die together." Arkesilaos, however, made reprisals upon his political opponents on recovering the throne; and when some of them took refuge in a large tower, he had wood piled up around the structure and kindled, thus destroying the men within. When the deed was done, the meaning of the oracle came to him, and he fled to Barca, seeking the protection of King Alazeir, his father-in-law; soon afterwards a band of Cyrenaean exiles killed both Arkesilaos and Alazeir in the marketplace at Barca. Arkesilaos had understood the god's words literally. But the god was speaking symbolically, making use of the familiar metaphor, pot = man; and the fired tower was obviously an oven. The intent of "seagirt" and "bull" is not clear; but the point is that Arkesilaos, taking care not to flee to an island or peninsula, unwittingly went to a place that for some reason could be called seagirt in the company of a man who could be called *tauros kallisteuôn*.

Similar are the prophecies which the consultant understands to warn him against a certain kind of creature or person; but, it turns out, the oracular term means either another sort of creature than the consultant has supposed, or not a living creature at all, but an inanimate object: in any case the god has employed the term in an obscure and unknown meaning. Lysander was warned against "a shouting hoplite and a snake (*drakôn*), earth's deceitful son, coming behind" (Q199). A military man like Lysander could hardly keep away from shouting hoplites; but the oracle spoke of both a hoplite and a snake, so that whenever he had a hoplite before him and a snake behind, he could expect his death. He fell at Haliartos near a stream called Hoplites, struck down by a soldier whose shield bore a serpent device.

As the Jerusalem Chamber kind of prophecy is found in Greek legend

---

6 See Fontenrose 1960b. PW 359–360 place these two oracles among historical responses of the 300–190 period, but grant that they have a legendary character; see Parke 1956: 390–391.

and folktale without reference to the Delphic Oracle, so is the misleading prophecy of death from a certain object, creature, or person. A good example is the tale of the prophecies which came to two Scythian princes (Diodoros 20.26.1–2). Satyros was told to beware of death from the mouse. Apparently knowing the ways of oracles, Satyros not only guarded himself against actual mice in his houses, but also would allow no man named Mys to come near him. He failed to notice that in Greek a muscle of the body is called *mys* (cf. Latin *musculus*), so that naturally he died after being wounded in a muscle of his arm. His brother Eumelos fared no better in guarding himself against a moving house. Needless to say he never entered a tent; and he never went into a house without first sending his sons inside to inspect the roof and foundations; but he died when he leapt from a runaway chariot which carried a canopy (*skênê*, which is of course an *oikia*). This kind of oracle is called *avertissement incompris*; but the term implies a fault in the recipient, as if he had misunderstood or failed to understand that which was difficult and obscure, yet comprehensible if only his wit were greater. But the gods and manteis of these stories do not intend that the oracle receiver shall understand, no matter how wise or prudent he may be. It is in fact an *avertissement égarant, trompant*.[7] Kambyses, for instance, could not possibly have understood *Smerdis* to mean anybody but his brother, when in a dream a messenger came to him and said that Smerdis sat on the royal throne. This dream led him to kill his brother; but near the end of his life a messenger came to him at Syrian Agbatana with the report that Smerdis had usurped the throne: this was a magus, brother of Kambyses' palace steward.[8]

MACDUFF AND BIRNAM WOOD

The prophecies, Delphic and non-Delphic, which I have discussed in the preceding pages, make use of homonymy. The recipient understands

7 See Crahay 1956: 50: Un des types les mieux représentés de l'équivoque oraculaire est celui où un grand personnage, souvent un roi, reçoit le conseil d'éviter un endroit, de se méfier de quelqu'un, de s'abstenir de telle action. Il se soumet à ce conseil, mais n'échappe pas à la mort ou à la catastrophe parce que l'oracle se réalise d'une manière inattendue, souvent par une homonymie.

8 Herod. 3.62–64. I consider neither the story of Kambyses' dream nor any other story told in this chapter as true history, although I often find it convenient in narrating and discussing a story to take the storyteller's point of view and speak as if it really happened. I do not believe either that Kambyses had such a dream or that he killed his brother Smerdis; I believe that the real Smerdis took the throne and that the false-Smerdis story was concocted by Darius and his fellow-conspirators. See A. T. Olmstead, *History of the Persian Empire* (Chicago: Univ. of Chicago Press, 1948) 109. Herodotos' stories of the prophecies about Agbatana and Smerdis conform closely to the folktale type of *avertissement incompris*. See Aly 1921: 97–98; Crahay 1956: 215–216.

a name or word in its familiar and accepted sense; but it has an unexpected or obscure meaning. Still, there is nothing impossible or incredible about the indicated agent, instrument, place, or time of death, according to the recipient's understanding of the prophecy: in fact, he is led into a false sense of security for that very reason, since he believes that he can guard himself against the foretold danger. In other prophecies, however, the recipient is told that his power or prosperity will endure until something that seems impossible or incredible happens: he takes this to be a prediction of lifelong and long-lasting power or prosperity; but very soon, it may be, his prosperity or reign comes to an end, and perhaps his life too. Most famous of ancient oracles of this kind is that which the Delphic Oracle spoke to King Croesus of Lydia when he asked whether his reign would be long (Q101). The Pythia said,

> ’Αλλ’ ὅταν ἡμίονος βασιλεὺς Μήδοισι γένηται
> καὶ τότε Λυδὲ ποδαβρὲ πολυψήφιδα παρ’ Ἕρμον
> φεύγειν μηδὲ μένειν μηδ’ αἰδεῖσθαι κακὸς εἶναι.⁹

Croesus rejoiced to hear this, thinking, as Herodotos tells us, that a mule could never become king of the Medes. But the predicted sign of doom had already appeared: Cyrus, half Persian and half Mede, and therefore (in oracular reckoning) a mule. All is fair in folktale prophecy, although we would hardly consider the child of a Persian father and a Median mother to be a hybrid in any sense of the term—two peoples could hardly be more closely related than the Medes and Persians—or the parents' marriage to be miscegenation. In the terms of this story anybody who has parents from different peoples is a mule.¹⁰ This particular example of prophetic *pseudadynaton* illustrates what we shall call the Macduff theme, since Shakespeare has made us familiar with the prophecy which the Weird Sisters' Apparition spoke to Macbeth:

> Be bloody, bold, and resolute; laugh to scorn
> The power of man, for none of woman born
> Shall harm Macbeth.
>
> [*Macbeth* IV.i.79–81]

Yet "Macduff was from his mother's womb untimely ripp'd" and was

---

9 For translation of Delphic responses quoted in this chapter see the Catalogue.

10 This prophecy, of course, depends upon the story that Cyrus' mother was a daughter of King Astyages of Media, whose child was ordered put to death by King Astyages in consequence of a dream. To me, as to some other scholars, this story is patently a fiction designed to establish the legitimacy of the Persian usurper Cyrus as monarch of all Iran.

the killer of Macbeth.[11] Thus Macbeth was as unfairly treated by supernatural powers as was Croesus, for Macduff was hardly less born of woman than Cyrus was of homogeneous parents; he was in fact deliberately deceived when the Spirit told him to "laugh to scorn the power of man,"
since Macduff was, after all, just a man. The Croesus oracle and the Macbeth prophecy are on all fours with respect to content, theme, and historical verifiability; each is absurd history though colorful fiction. Yet many
scholars and historians have accepted Q101 (along with the other Croesus
oracles, Q99–103) as a genuine pronouncement of the Delphic Oracle).[12]

We can hardly mention Macduff without being reminded also of
Birnam Wood and the prophecy that

> Macbeth shall never vanquish'd be until
> Great Birnam wood to high Dunsinane hill
> Shall come against him.
>   *Macb.* That will never be:
> Who can impress the forest, bid the tree
> Unfix his earth-bound root? Sweet bodements! good!
> Rebellion's head, rise never till the wood
> Of Birnam rise, and our high-plac'd Macbeth
> Shall live the lease of nature, pay his breath
> To time and mortal custom.
>
>   [*Macbeth* IV.i.92–100]

And we may use the name Birnam Wood for this kind of prophetic
theme, similar to the Macduff theme, but distinguishable in that the
announced term of power or prosperity is an event that seemingly defies
the laws of nature; whereas in the other it is a creature that seems to be not
only unnatural but impossible.

The Birnam Wood theme appears among "Delphic" oracles in a
response that pertains to the First Sacred War (Q71). As reported by
Diodoros and Pausanias, it was given to the Amphictions: they could not
take Krisa until Amphitrite's wave should wash against Apollo's temenos.
As reported by Polyainos, it was spoken to the Crisaeans (Cirrhaeans),
and on hearing it they felt secure, since the temenos at Pytho was four
miles from the nearest shore and 1800 feet above sea level. In any case,
the Amphictions had knowledge of this oracle. Discouraged at first, they

---

11 Macbeth V.vii.44–45. See Andrew of Wyntoun *Chron.* 6.18. 2202–2242 Cott.;
Holinshed *Chron.* 5 (London, 1808) 274–277.

12 E.g., Dempsey 1918: 69–72; Poulsen 1920: 27; D. G. Hogarth, *The Ancient East*
(New York, London, n.d.) 164; Charles Seltman, *The Twelve Olympians and Their Guests*
(London: Parrish, 1956) 116–117. For the Macduff theme see also Q138.

finally realized that the condition could be fulfilled simply by consecrating the whole Crisaean plain to Apollo, thus joining it to his temenos at Pytho.

A similar oracle concerns the Etruscan city of Veii (Q202); and this story too is told differently by different authors. The people of Veii were sure that the Romans could never take their city, since they had received a prophecy, apparently from local soothsayers, that as long as the waters of the Alban Lake should reach the sea when they overflowed, Veii could not be taken. The Romans learned this prophecy either from a Veientine or from the Delphic Apollo; and they constructed a tunnel that drained the waters of the lake into the plain below so that they did not reach the sea. Probably the Delphic shrine did not enter the original story; the Veientine soothsayers were enough. Cicero (*Div.* 1.44.100) tells the story without mentioning Delphi.

Herodotos' story of a Delphic oracle spoken to the Siphnians (Q114) is similar. When in the sixth century the Siphnians had become very rich from their gold and silver mines they asked at Delphi whether their prosperity could last a long time. The Pythia replied,

Ἀλλ' ὅταν ἐν Σίφνῳ πρυτανήια λευκὰ γένηται
λεύκοφρύς τ' ἀγορή, τότε δὴ δεῖ φράδμονος ἀνδρὸς
φράσσασθαι ξύλινόν τε λόχον κήρυκά τ' ἐρυθρόν.

According to Herodotos the prytaneion and agora buildings were already constructed of or faced with Parian marble at the time of this response, so that the first condition was fulfilled. The Siphnians, however, could not understand the last line of the response. One day a red-painted ship came into the harbor bearing Samian envoys, who asked the Siphnians to lend the Samians ten talents; when the Siphnians refused, a Samian force attacked the island and took it, thus bringing an end to Siphnian prosperity. The ship was both the wooden *lochos* (company) and the red herald.

Responses of the Macduff and Birnam Wood kinds are found among Legendary responses, as we might expect. Herakles was told by Zeus, according to Sophocles (*Trach.* 1159–1172), or by both Zeus and Pythian Apollo (L119), according to Seneca, that he would not be killed by any living man, but by a man who was already dead. The dead man was Nessos, whose infected blood poisoned the robe which Deianeira gave to Herakles. See also L77.

EQUIVOCAL PREDICTIONS OF DEATH OR FORTUNE

A similar kind of prophecy is that which promises a peaceful life, escape from present troubles in a certain place or at a certain time. In this kind of prophecy the trick is not about the place or time: it lies in the meaning or the implication of whatever word or phrase is used for peace or escape. Such prophecies appear among Quasi-Historical responses, for example, Q249, in which Appius Claudius was told that he would escape the civil war and find peace in the hollows of Euboea. So he went to Euboea, where he died soon after. This has been accepted as a genuine response of the Delphic Oracle.[13] But aside from being told about an historical person who died in Euboea, the story has an obviously folkloristic complexion.

Similar is Q81, which has also been taken as authentic (Parke 1956: 122–123). Prokles, tyrant of Epidauros, killed and robbed a certain Timarchos, an Athenian guest in his house, and instructed Kleandros, an Aeginetan, to put the body in a basket and sink it in the sea. Nobody except Prokles and Kleandros knew about the deed; but later, when civil strife in Epidauros had seriously endangered Prokles' position and life, he sent his brother Kleotimos to Delphi to ask the god for escape and change of residence. Apollo replied that he granted Prokles escape and change of residence where Prokles had bid the Aeginetan put the basket down or where the stag casts his horn. Then the tyrant, understanding the god to mean that he should either drown or bury himself, stayed in Epidauros until events forced him to leave. Soon thereafter Timarchos' friends seized Prokles, killed him, and cast his body into the sea. Either Plutarch or his source, I believe, has confused the story and transferred the solution of the oracular riddle from the end of the story to Prokles' reception of the oracular message.

Probably in the earliest story of Q81, which we may suppose became current before 500 B.C., six hundred years before Plutarch's time, Prokles understood the god's words to mean that he could find a safe refuge either at that place on the coast where Kleandros had thrown Timarchos' body or at some place in the forest where stags were wont to cast their horns. He went to the coast and there came upon a party of his enemies, who

---

13 Parke 1956: 283, 408, who says "The words of the Pythia may have been a bow drawn at a venture; the death of Appius conveniently gave them an intensity of meaning which otherwise they need never have possessed" and "after his death a deeper meaning was read into the Pythia's words." It is possible that Appius asked Delphic sanction of a plan to occupy a position in Euboea and was granted it; but would a Roman commander seek a Delphic sanction for his movements? See Hugh J. Mason, Malcolm Wallace, "Appius Claudius Pulcher and the Hollows of Euboea," *Hesperia* 41 (1972) 128–140. But that would not be the response which Valerius Maximus and Lucan report. If the story were true, Cicero would certainly have mentioned it in *Div.*, in which he mentions Appius Claudius, since he wrote this essay only three or four years after Appius' death; he would hardly have overlooked a recent example of truthful prophecy concerning *meus amicus Appius* (*Tusc.* 1.16.37).

killed him and fulfilled the oracle by casting his body into the sea. The oracular equivocation in *phygê* (escape) and especially the ambiguity of *metastasis*, either "change of residence" or "departure" in the sense of "death," are nearly lost as Plutarch tells the tale.[14] These ambiguities have no effect on his story, in which Prokles understands what the god means at once.

Philip of Macedon, about to attack Persia, asked the Pythia whether he would defeat the Persian king, and received the reply, "The bull is garlanded; he comes to an end; the sacrificer is at hand" (Q213). Philip understood this to predict his victory: the Persian king would be slaughtered like a sacrificial victim. Philip assumed that Apollo was speaking in metaphor, whereas for once the god was fairly literal in speech. The assassin Pausanias struck Philip down at a sacrifice. In the response the equivocal meanings of "bull" (*tauros*), "end" (*telos*), and "the sacrificer" (*ho thysôn*) can easily be perceived.

The response spoken to Philip (Q213) has the same kind of ambiguity as has the famous oracle spoken to Croesus, that if he crossed the Halys River (or if he marched against the Persians), he would destroy a great kingdom (Q100). Each is an equivocal prediction of doom, so expressed that the recipient, if he studied the words carefully, would realize that the doom might be his own. Yet without reflecting he supposes that the god's words are favorable to himself. In oracular tales of this kind the god's meaning is always unfavorable to the recipient; that is what makes the story.[15]

Another well-known example of this kind of deceptive oracle is Q230, spoken, we are told, to King Pyrros of Epeiros on his Italian campaign: Aio te Aeacida Romanos vincere posse ("I say that you the Romans can defeat"). A response in Latin was unprecedented; and strangely Pyrros did not realize that *Romanos* was as likely as *te* to be the subject of *posse*. He thought that he would defeat the Romans and they defeated him.[16] The same kind of oracle deceived Julian the Apostate (Q262), who, like Croesus, undertook a disastrous Persian campaign. He consulted the

---

14 For *metastasis* as "departure from life" see LSJ s.v. IIb. Though Q81 is certainly an ambiguous prediction and in implication a command, I have classified it as F, a conditioned prediction: "When you come to the place where the Aeginetan lowered the basket, or where the stag casts his horn, there you will find refuge and change of residence."

15 On Q100 see Crahay 1956: 198; Delcourt 1955: 105; Parke 1956: 133–134. On Q213 see Parke 238, who considers it genuine, saying, "a new meaning was given to it by the assassination of Philip." It is possible, and it seems that such reinterpretation of a commonplace oracle occurred for H18; but I do not believe that the Delphic Oracle would have spoken cult instructions in such a form.

16 Dion Cassius attributes this response to Dodona. See Parke 1956: 247–248, who grants that this response is spurious; Delcourt 1955: 105.

Delphic Oracle, as the story goes, concerning his chances of success; and Apollo told him that the gods had already begun to carry trophies to the River Beast (*Thêr*, the Tigris); but as usual Apollo neglected to say whose victory the trophies would celebrate.

Another equivocal oracle is Q64, given to Kylon concerning his attempt to seize Athens, a response that has generally been considered a genuine pronouncement of the Delphic shrine. Kylon was told to seize the Athenian acropolis at Zeus's greatest festival. So he seized it at the time of the Olympic festival at Olympia, thinking that Apollo meant the greatest Zeus festival in Hellas. But the god meant the Diasia, the greatest in Athens; and consequently Kylon's attempt ended in failure and in exile for himself, death for many of his fellow conspirators. See also Q88, 116, 121.

Such misleading prophecy is widespread in folktale and legend. One example will suffice. A witch told Llewellyn II of Wales that "he should ride crowned through the midst of Cheap." He was captured and beheaded by the English; then his head, crowned in mockery, went in a carriage through Westcheap to the Tower.[17]

Similar is a deceptive kind of prophecy that employs the Jerusalem Chamber theme—the ambiguity resides in homonymous names, one being known to everyone, the other to hardly anybody—but whereas a Jerusalem Chamber prophecy such as Q195 and Q207 is a deceptive warning of death, this is a promise of victory or conquest. Such is L62, already noticed in chapter I, in which "the narrows" deceived the Heraklids and caused them an initial defeat. Not very different is the Heraklid oracle of "the third harvest" (L61). A Quasi-Historical oracle of this kind is Q93, in which the Delphic Oracle told the Phocaeans τὸν Κύρνον κτίσαι ("found Kyrnos"). So a colony of Phocaeans founded the city of Alalia on the island of Kyrnos (Corsica), but had to abandon it later. The god meant that they should found a cult of the hero Kyrnos.[18]

King Kleomenes of Sparta was told that he would take Argos (Q136), and he invaded the Argolid. There after an initial victory he burned down a grove of trees into which some Argives had fled for refuge. When he learned that this was the grove of Argos the hero, he led his army back to Sparta on the ground that he had fulfilled the oracular prediction. Like the magi whom Astyages consulted (Herodotos 1.120.3),

---

17 G. L. Kittredge, *Witchcraft in Old and New England* (New York: Russell, 1956) 226–227.

18 See Parke 1956: 142, who accepts the response as genuine and again has recourse to Delphic reinterpretation after the oracular directions had turned out badly.

he knew that prophecies sometimes have trivial fulfillments. If a prophecy has been fulfilled literally, according to some meaning of the words used, though in an unexpected and disappointing way, the recipient can expect no better thereafter—that is a rule of the game. The story is improbable, since, though the Spartans were superstitious, we may doubt that Kleomenes would have abandoned his campaign after winning a battle so decisively.[19]

Most of the prophecies thus far discussed in this chapter illustrate the widespread folktale theme of deception by equivocation. The promise or oath or decision which is equivocally interpreted to someone's disadvantage is replaced by the oracular response that deceives the recipient. But there is pleasant equivocation as well as cruelly deceptive equivocation. In several responses the Jerusalem Chamber or Macduff or Birnam Wood theme works to the consultant's advantage: he fulfills in an unexpected and easy way what seemed to be a difficult or impossible requirement; or he fulfills quickly a condition which literally understood would have required more time; or having failed because he took the god's words in their usual meaning, he succeeds when he interprets them otherwise. For example, Q36 occurs in a story told about Phalanthos, the founder of Tarentum, or in a less reliable source, about Myskellos, the founder of Croton. Phalanthos was told to found his city on that site where he should see rain fall under a clear sky (*hypo aithrâi*). This seemed an impossible event, but he went to Italy and sought a place to settle. Once as he sat feeling discouraged, his wife wept out of sympathy for him as she loused his hair; and her tears fell on his head. He realized then that rain had fallen on him from Aithra, whose name means Clear Sky, and there he founded Tarentum.[20]

Parmeniskos of Metapontum, a philosopher, lost the ability to laugh after consulting the Oracle of Trophonios in Lebadeia. He went to Delphi to seek a remedy for this strange malady. The Pythia said, "Mother will give it to you at home" (Q185). Supposing that this meant his own

---

19 I should make clear that I believe the story of the oracle and its fulfillment to be pure legend; but this does not mean that I consider Kleomenes' attack on Argos to be unhistorical. Here as elsewhere legend has entered into historical narrative; and this is not the only legend that attached itself to Kleomenes' Argive war (see also Q134–135). On Q136 see Parke 1956: 159–160; also Aly 1921: 157–158, who sees little but folktale motifs in this story. That in reality Kleomenes may not have wanted to take Argos is irrelevant to the oracle story, in which he intended to take it.

20 Or in the Myskellos version, in which the condition was that rain fall on him from a clear sky, his unnamed concubine sat beside him and wept, letting tears fall upon him, apparently under a clear sky.

mother, he thought that the god had deceived him when on his return home he failed to laugh. Then he happened to wander into Leto's temple on Delos, where, catching sight of the goddess's ungainly image, he burst out laughing. The oracle meant Apollo's mother at home in her temple.[21]

The well-known Cynic Diogenes was told at Delphi, Παραχάραξον τό νόμισμα (Q201), which he took literally to be an instruction to counterfeit or debase the currency. So interpreted, this is a dangerous though not impossible instruction; and, as the story goes, Diogenes carried it out, only to be forced to flee his city when detected. Then he realized the true meaning of the response, "Revalue (restamp) custom"; namely, he should reject the false customs and opinions of his society and adopt a different way of life and thought; hence his devotion to philosophy and an eccentric manner of life.[22]

DISTINCTIVE SIGN

Another group of responses resembles the foregoing in that they set a condition of fulfillment, usually a sign indicating the place or person or object desired or feared. But the consultant does not misinterpret the response, which may be perfectly clear; or if it is ambiguous or enigmatic, he usually suffers no misfortune from not understanding it: he goes his way until he meets with the thing or event that fulfills the condition. In Q34 the distinctive sign is the goat that dips his beard in the sea (cf. Q20); in Q33 it is the female that marries the male. These are riddles and will be considered later.

In Q134 the Argives were told that when the female vanquished the male and won glory among the Argives, then many Argive women would mourn and men would say that the serpent, symbol of Argos, had perished by the spear. This looks like the sort of deceptive prophecy that would give the Argives a false feeling of security in the belief that a victory in battle of women over men was unlikely, if not impossible. Herodotos connects the oracle with the battle of the Sepia, wherein the Argives suffered a disastrous defeat from the Spartans under Kleomenes, when Kleomenes did not follow up the victory and withdrew from the Argolid (see Q136). Herodotos does not explain the sign, the victory of

---

21 See Q139 and L118 for plays on "mother."

22 See Parke 1956: 406, who rejects the oracle and believes that the story has its origin in the fact that Diogenes' father supervised the mint in Sinope. But he includes the response among historical oracles (PW 180). See Ronald Stroud, "An Athenian Law on Silver Coinage" *Hesperia* 43 (1974) 165. For other examples of equivocal oracles with happy outcomes see Q72, 160, 191.

female over male. Pausanias and other late authors interpret the oracle from the story of Telesilla the poetess: after the Argive defeat at the Sepia she armed the Argive women and saved the city. In this interpretation the mourning precedes the female victory.

In Q33 and Q134 the distinctive sign is expressed in the formula, "When A does X to B," in which A and B may be opposites and X is usually a paradoxical action. In L132 Chalkinos and Daitos, Athenian heroes, were told to make sacrifice to Apollo when they should see a trireme running on land: at Mount Poikilon they saw a snake hurrying into its hole; this snake was the trireme and the condition was fulfilled. It is not clear why the snake should be interpreted as the trireme of the response; but undoubtedly we have here another instance of "spiral twist," the term that Mark Twain's uncle gave to the subject of Biblical exegesis, which he had briefly studied at a theological seminary.[23]

The spiral twist is in essence a forced interpretation of a text: words are not taken in their plain meaning, and the forced interpretation rather than the obvious is authoritative and "right." We have already noticed several examples of spiral twist: it appears among both Legendary and Quasi-Historical responses. L158 and Q37 are nearly identical in content and interpretation: the twist is given to the word "majority." In L158 Aisymnos of Megara was told that the Megarians would prosper if they should deliberate with the majority. This looks like a recommendation of democracy, but the Megarians built their council house around a tomb of heroes, considering the dead to be more numerous than the living. In Q37 the colonists who founded Tarentum were told that they should make their settlement with the majority; and so they placed their graveyard inside the city walls. The spiral twist may also be seen in Q130: the Thebans, wanting to defeat Athens, were told to refer the matter to the many-voiced (*polyphêmon*) and ask the nearest (*tôn anchista*) to help them. They interpreted "many-voiced" straightforwardly enough as the popular assembly; but "the nearest" turned out to be not the nearest cities, but the Aeginetans, since Aigina was sister of Thebe as daughter of Asopos.[24]

Usually the distinctive sign is not expressed in terms of opposites or incompatibles. The inquirer is simply told that when he sees a certain

---

23 Samuel Clemens (Mark Twain), *Christian Science* (New York, London, 1907) 196 with note 1, which explains spiral twist: "That is a technicality—that phrase. I got it of an uncle of mine. He had once studied in a theological cemetery, he said, and he called the Department of Biblical Exegesis the Spiral Twist 'for short.' He said it was always difficult to drive a straight text through an unaccommodating cork, but that if you twisted it it would go."

24 See Q44: Megarian colonists should settle where fish and deer grazed the same pasture; they founded Byzantion on the Golden Horn (*Keras*).

thing, or when a certain event occurs, he will have come to the place or time or object desired. The thing or event, as indicated in oracular language, may or may not be extraordinary; it may sound familiar, even commonplace, and really be so. The response may or may not be a riddle; there may or may not be a spiral twist. There is usually no mistake or difficulty about carrying through the oracle's instructions.

Only those responses in which the Pythia plainly indicates the sign that the consultant must look for could have been received at an oracular shrine. Nevertheless in most instances response and attendant story have legendary or folktale touches. The Pythia would be gifted with clair-voyance, or at least extraordinary knowledge, if she knew that the sign was to be found where it was found; or that it really could be a condition precedent to fulfillment; or it is a sign that the recipient might not encounter for a long time—he might, in fact, miss it altogether—and yet he soon finds it in exactly the right place for his purpose. No Historical response contains such a direction.

Q25 directed Hegesistratos of Ephesos to settle where he saw olive-crowned peasants dancing. He found them on the site of Elaiûs, which took its name from the prophetic sign. Q94 told Megarian and Boeotian colonists to build their city around a certain wild-olive tree that grew from the hero Idmon's tomb in far-off Pontos. See also Q23.

The distinctive sign is frequent in oracles of legend, Delphic and other. In some the sign is indicated metaphorically or enigmatically, so that it seems to be something strange or improbable; in others it is stated plainly without equivocation of any kind. In the former class is L27: Adrastos was told to marry his daughters to a lion and boar that he would see fighting at his doors: Tydeus with a boar device on his shield and Polyneikes with a lion device were the fighters. The sign is clearly indicated in the oracle spoken to Kadmos (L11): the first cow that he met, or which was marked in a certain way, would guide him to the site of his city. Goats are the sign that will mark the site in L50 and L51. Pelias must beware of a man wearing one sandal (L12), a condition that may have seemed unlikely, but nevertheless was expressed plainly and fulfilled literally.[25]

---

[25] The distinctive sign is also present in L1, 20, 33, 54, 70, 78, 79, 80, 83, 93, 102, 116, 120, 124, 135; Q6, 204, 217, 221; and in many legendary responses not attributed to Delphi: e.g., Apollod. 3.12.3; Serv. *Aen.* 4.377 (cf. Plut. *Pyrr.* 32.4–5; Paus. 2.19.3–4); Conon 25; Steph. Byz. 319 Mein.; Schol. vet. on Theokr. *Prolegomena* Ba; PW 593, 594 (among the Delphic Pseudepigrapha).

TRADITIONAL THEMES IN ORACULAR TALES

The foregoing responses are folkloric in themselves; nothing like them was ever spoken at an actual oracular shrine so far as any reliable evidence shows. There are other responses which in themselves may have Historical modes and content and may seem acceptable on that account, but appear in narratives that on examination reveal characteristic traits of myth, legend, and folktale, though the story may be told as history and may embody historical facts. I have dealt elsewhere (1968) with the hero-athlete tale and the Delphic oracles (Q52, 160, 166–171, 221) that appear in its variant forms. Many other oracular narratives contain folktale themes.

The Animal Guide

The legend of Hesiod's death resembles the hero-athlete tale: Hesiod as victor over Homer in a bardic contest at funeral games replaces the athlete. It also illustrates the theme of animal guide. After his hosts killed him in Lokris (see L41) and the culprits were punished with death, plague came upon Boeotian Orchomenos. The city received a Delphic oracle (L42) telling them that the remedy was to bring Hesiod's bones from Naupaktos to their city; and when the envoys asked where in Naupaktos they would find the poet's remains the Pythia replied that a crow would show them. When they went to Naupaktos they saw a crow perched on a rock and found Hesiod's bones in a hollow of the rock.[26]

Q191 is like L42: Delian exiles, instructed to find the place where Apollo was born, having supposed that Apollo was born on their island, were then told that a crow would show them. When at Chaironeia they overheard some men who were conversing with the innkeeper about the Oracle at Tegyra call her Korone (Crow), they realized that Apollo meant Tegyra.

Q164 has a similar second response. The Athenians, directed to bring the bones of Theseus from Skyros, asked where to find the bones and were told that the god was sending them a guide. On Skyros they saw an eagle fly down and begin to claw the earth, and in him they recognized the appointed guide.[27] Plutarch, Pausanias, and a Scholiast on Aristeides

---

26 *Cert. Hom. Hes.* 215–254 Allen; Plut. *Mor.* 162c–f, 969e, 984d; Paus. 9.38.3–4. The story also has animal helpers in the dolphins that carried Hesiod's body to shore and in Hesiod's dog whose barking revealed the culprits.

27 Only the Scholiast on Aristeides 46.172 has this second reply. According to Plutarch (*Kimon* 8, *Theseus* 36), Kimon saw an eagle scratching the earth and recognized the place.

(46.241) associate this response with Kimon's taking of Skyros in 476/5. Other sources allow the reader to suppose that plague or famine came upon Athens after Lykomedes' murder of Theseus and that they received this response in consequence; and if we had only these sources we would classify Q164 as Legendary. Diodoros (4.62.4), who mentions no oracle, appears to place the fetching of Theseus' bones and the founding of Theseus' isotheic cult in prehistoric times. Athens had a Theseion in Peisistratos' time (Aristotle *Ath. Pol.* 15), though a new temple was constructed in 475, with which the Kimon story probably has something to do as foundation legend.[28]

The eagle guide appears in Q23 too. When the Heraklid line in Argos failed, the Argives consulted Delphi on choosing a new king and were told that an eagle would show them. A few days later an eagle lighted on Aigon's house.

The animal guide (or indicator) enters into several legends of city foundation, as in the story of Kadmos (L11). See also L33, 50, 51, 54, 75, 78, 83, 116.[29]

The Hero Helper

The story of Theseus' bones is one of several about a city's recovery of a hero's bones as a talisman of victory or security. Pausanias (3.3.7)

---

28 If the Theseus cult had been long established, how do we explain the Kimon story? It may be that Kimon invoked the old legend of Lykomedes' murder of Theseus on Skyros to further his purpose of taking Skyros from the Dolopian pirates by arousing the Athenians' wrath against the island. He may have asserted that Theseus' bones were still there and not in Athens (saying that Athens had a cenotaph?), and he may have cited the legendary oracle as an unfulfilled divine command. This conjecture seems dubious, though consistent with Kimon's character and policies; but the difficulties of accepting Plutarch's story as historical truth are even greater. We might suppose a simple Delphic command or sanction to move Theseus' bones from Skyros to Athens; but to do so requires that something identified as Theseus' bones was really present on Skyros. Only Plutarch attributes this response to Delphi. Furthermore the sources disagree on the occasion of the response and report its content in various ways. Thuc. 1.98.2 does not mention Theseus' bones in his report of Kimon's taking of Skyros. See A. J. Podlecki, "Cimon, Skyros, and 'Theseus' Bones,'" *JHS* 91 (1971) 141–143; John P. Barron, "New Light on Old Walls: The Murals of the Theseion," *JHS* 92 (1972) 20–22.

29 Cf. Q217. The theme of the animal that guides to or marks the spot of settlement is widespread. It is found in America, as in the Aztec foundation legend, according to which an oracle told the Aztecs that the site of their future city would be marked by a royal eagle of great size and beauty that would be perched on a prickly pear, holding a snake in his talons and spreading his wings to the rising sun. They saw the sight on a rock beside a lake and there founded Tenochtitlán (Mexico City). See W. H. Prescott, *History of the Conquest of Mexico* (New York: Modern Library, n.d.) 15–16; J. N. Leonard and Editors of Time-Life Books, *Ancient America* (New York: Time Inc., 1967) 63–64. For animal guides see *MIFL* B155 and its subdivisions; see also B143.0.8, prophetic crow, and B435, helpful animals.

couples Athens' recovery of Theseus' bones with Sparta's recovery of Orestes' bones (Q89–90; see pp. 123–124). The Spartans were also instructed in a Delphic oracle (Q91) to bring the bones of Orestes' son Tisamenos from Achaean Helike to Sparta. Pausanias, who reports this response, says nothing about the circumstances; but we may suppose that Tisamenos as an Achaean hero was protector of Helike and that in some story of war between the Achaeans and Lakedaimon the bones of Tisamenos played the same part as Orestes' bones in the tale of war between Tegea and Lakedaimon.³⁰ Behind these stories lies a basic tale of the protecting hero's grave. (1) A city is secure as long as it possesses a hero's bones. (2) Therefore the city rulers keep the hero's grave secret and no one else knows where it is.³¹ (3) An enemy city learns that it must get possession of the hero's bones in order to take the city. (4) The enemy city succeeds in finding the grave and removing the bones to bury in its own soil; it both defeats the other city and thereafter possesses the security that possession of the hero's bones affords. The bones protect whatever city or land they lie in. Such is the meaning of the issue over Oedipus' grave in Sophocles' *Oedipus at Kolonos* (L20–21), or the meaning of Eurystheus' grave that would protect Athens from the Heraklids (L24).

In the story of Q188, which told the Athenians who wanted to found a colony at Ennea Hodoi on the Strymon River in Thrace that they should find the remains of Resos in Troy and restore them to their native land, the hero's bones do not lie in the land to be taken. The Athenians had to restore him to his birthplace and keep possession of his grave, whence he would protect the new city Amphipolis for whoever possessed it. Resos was like Theseus in that he died in a foreign land, where he lay until he was restored to his own country (and Orestes may be considered to be at home in Sparta).

---

30 On Tisamenos see Paus. 2.18.6–8, 7.1.8; Apollod.2.8.2–3; Hyg. *Fab.* 124; D. M. Leahy, "The Bones of Tisamenus," *Historia* 4 (1955) 26–38. Orestes = Tisamenos: Anecd. Cramer 2.321. As a tradition develops two names of a hero may become distinguished as two persons, father-son or brothers; e.g., Achilles and Neoptolemos, Fontenrose 1960a: 207–209.

31 In the Q89–90 story, as Herodotos tells it, it may appear that the rulers of Tegea did not know about the bones of Orestes. But all we are told is that the smith did not know the secret of the bones he had found. We should notice that he had apparently told nobody in Tegea about the bones, revealing his secret only to Liches, a total stranger; then he was reluctant to rent the shop to him. The original story may be that Liches guessed the riddle of Q90, rented the smithy, and dug for the bones. It may be that in some variants of the type the possessors of a talisman are unaware of its properties; notice the stories of Resos (Q188) and Phalanthos (Q38).

Offended Gods

The Sybarites killed a citharode who had been participating in contests at Hera's festival and had fled in his professional dress to Hera's altar. Thereupon a spring of blood arose in Hera's temple. The Sybarites sent envoys to Delphi to find out the meaning of this prodigy, and the Pythia turned them away, saying that they had killed the Muses' servant at Hera's altar (Q123). Soon afterwards the Crotoniates destroyed Sybaris.[32] In a related tale Crotoniates, Sybarites, and Metapontines killed fifty young men of Siris who were clinging to Athena's image; and they also killed Athena's priest. Plague and civil war came on the three offending cities. Croton consulted Delphi and was told to appease Athena and the spirits of the dead (Q126). The Crotoniates made images of Athena and the young men; but the Metapontines, having heard about the oracle, anticipated the Crotoniates in producing images of the youths and offering loaves to Athena (Pompeius Trogus/Justin 20.2.3–8). Q122 also concerns Sybaris and its destruction: the Sybarites were told that they would be prosperous until they honored a mortal before a god. This occurred when a man flogged his slave in a god's temple whither the slave had fled, but desisted when the slave sought sanctuary at the tomb of the flogger's father. Thereafter Sybaris fell.

The tyrant Pythagoras of Ephesos killed his political opponents, the Basilids, who had fled to the gods' temples, and he left their bodies unburied. He spared a Basilid girl, but kept her confined in the temple without food, so that she hanged herself to escape starvation. Plague and famine struck Ephesos, and a Delphic oracle told Pythagoras to erect a temple and bury the dead (Q82).[33] Probably the new temple is meant to be that of Artemis Ephesia, built in the sixth century. The maiden is the goddess herself, the hanged Artemis, for in another Ephesian tale Artemis associated the hanged woman with herself.[34] This was the wife

---

32 For a variant story in which dream replaces oracle see Phylarchos 81.45J and Herakl. Pont. *ap.* Ath. 12. 521d–f: the Sybarites killed fifty envoys from Croton at the gods' altars.

33 Parke 1956: 123 accepts Q82 as authentic, though it has poor authority. He says, "The incident is so simple, that it can be taken as authentic and unvarnished." That is, around 569 the Pythia at Delphi or the priesthood was aware of details of events that had happened several months earlier in Ephesos, hundreds of miles away across the sea, and connected these events with the afflictions, though the Ephesians had not. And we must suppose that the bodies of the girl and the other Basilids were unburied all this time. And why should Ephesos in the sixth century consult Delphi on this matter rather than nearby Klaros or Didyma? There is no indication that Delphi then had a greater reputation in Ionian cities than they.

34 With the Basilid girl compare Charila, L140; see Fontenrose 1959: 458–460. For the hanged Artemis of Kaphyai see L91. On Erigone, who hanged herself and whose story is *aition* of the Attic Aiora festival, see L133.

of Ephesos, the city's eponym; she cast Artemis out of the house when Ephesos was entertaining her. The goddess turned her into a bitch and then in pity restored her to human shape. Then the woman hanged herself, and Artemis dressed her in her own apparel and called her Hekate. Here the woman herself was guilty of offensive conduct; but in another story the hanged woman is innocent, like the Basilid girl, and is associated with Artemis after her death, like Ephesos' wife. Tartaros, tyrant of Melite in Phthia, had his men bring him beautiful maidens for his pleasure. He sent them to fetch the beautiful Aspalis, but she anticipated them by hanging herself. Her brother dressed himself in her garments and killed Tartaros. When the people looked for Aspalis' body they found instead an image (*xoanon*) beside that of Artemis and named it Aspalis Ameilêtê Hekaergê. *Hekaergê* is an epithet of Artemis and a variant of *Hekatê*.

The Greeks had many tales of offended gods, many of which have no oracle (e.g., the two last cited). The oracular tales of this kind show the following pattern. (1) Someone offends a god by desecrating his temple or altar or by leaving the dead unburied. (2) The god sends plague, famine, other calamity, or an ominous sign to the offender's city or land. (3) The people seek an oracle, which directs recompense or restitution of some kind (or, as in Q123, rejects the oracle-seekers). (4) The offending people either make amends or come to grief.[35]

It is true that Greeks really did sometimes leave the bodies of enemies or traitors unburied; that some men or governments desecrated temples and committed sacrilege; and that if a plague or other misfortune befell the offenders, an oracle might attribute it to that cause. But in these narratives the offense uniformly produces an immediate calamity; the Pythia knows about the offense, which may be an obscure event, and proposes amendment; and the proposed act always brings an immediate end to affliction. Such narratives belong to legend and folktale, and the oracles in them cannot be genuine.

King's death for his city

According to Herodotos (7.220.3–4) the Spartans received Q152 early in the second Persian War. In seven hexameter verses they were told in essence that they must lose either their country or one of their kings to the Persians. Because of this oracle Leonidas decided upon death at Thermopylai.

This is surely a *post eventum* composition (Parke 1956: 167–168;

---

35 See also L26, 35, 92–93; Q24, 58, 83, 107, 113, 133, 174.

PW, p. 44), and it repeats the theme of L49. In war between Sparta and Athens, the Spartans were told either that they would win if they did not kill the king of Athens, or that the city that lost its king would win. King Kodros of Athens, having heard about this oracle, went out in woodcutter's garb and picked a quarrel with Spartan soldiers, who killed him and thus unwittingly preserved his city. The heroic death of Leonidas and his small company at Thermopylai recalled the old legend: Leonidas, like Kodros, had willingly died to save his city. So Q152 was composed as the oracle needed to fit Leonidas' heroism to the Kodros legend.

Minos and Skylla

Herodotos (6.134–135) recounts a Parian version of Miltiades' siege of Paros in 489. A captive Parian woman, Timo, underpriestess (*hypoza-koros*) of the chthonian gods, came to Miltiades and told him how to go over the city walls easily. Miltiades entered the town at the indicated point, leaping into the temenos of Demeter Thesmophoros, but through some religious fear did not carry out his move, and soon after gave up the siege. The Parians asked at Delphi whether they should put Timo to death for betraying her city and for showing the sacred things of Demeter to a man. The Pythia replied that they should not; for Timo was but the divine agent of Miltiades' doom: he was fated to come to a bad end (Q143). Herodotos does not tell us Timo's motive for directing Miltiades into the town; she simply volunteered the information. But it is probable that the Parians framed the story of Timo and Miltiades upon the pattern that appears in several Greek legends, notably that of Skylla, who betrayed Megara to Minos for love of him by cutting off her father Nisos' lock of purple hair that held the fate of the city. Similar is the story of Komaitho's betrayal of Taphos for love of Amphitryon.[36] In the Parian story, perhaps, Demeter's sacred objects replace the lock of hair; but the actual outcome of the siege determined the conclusion: Miltiades did not take Paros.

Wounder as Healer

Q128 directed Leonymos of Croton to the White Island to seek healing, for his malignant breast wound, from the ghost of the lesser Aias, whom the Locrians had called to their aid in the battle: since Aias had wounded Leonymos, only he could cure him. Leonymos was in the same

---

36 Skylla: Apollod. 3.15.8; Aesch. *Ch.* 613–622; Ovid *Met.* 8.6–151; Hyg. *Fab.* 198. Komaitho: Apollod. 2.4.7; Schol. on Theokr. 24.4 (Theocr. Papyri, p. 50). According to Ps.-Aristotle *Mir. ausc.* 834b, a woman guided Herakles when he took Elis in accordance with an oracle.

plight as Telephos, whom Apollo told to find healing from the wounder (L34); and so Telephos went to Achilles, who applied rust from the wounding spear to the wound and healed it. Similar is L120, which instructed Herakles, suffering from the Hydra's bites, to apply an herb that resembled the hydra to his wound.

Leonymos was probably wounded in the battle of the Sagra, in which his fellow-citizen, Phormion, also received an unhealing wound. An oracle, not specified as Delphic, told him to go to Sparta, where his healer would be the first person who invited him to dinner (Q129). As soon as he reached Sparta a young man invited him to dinner; and when his host learned why he had come, he applied scrapings from his spear to the wound. When after the meal Phormion was about to mount his cart, he found that he had taken hold of his house door in Croton. The young host in Sparta was none other than one of the Dioskuroi, who had helped the Locrians at the battle of the Sagra (see Q127): the wounder is the healer.37

RIDDLES

Alike in ancient and in modern times Delphic oracles have been called enigmatic.38 It was not chance or mere convenience that prompted the compiler of the Palatine Anthology to place riddles alongside oracles in the fourteenth book: he saw two species of one genus. In 14.32 we find the following:

Κτανθεὶς τὸν κτείναντα κατέκτανον· ἀλλ᾿ ὁ μὲν οὐδ᾿ ὣς
ἤλυθεν εἰς Ἅιδην· αὐτὰρ ἔγωγ᾿ ἔθανον.39

Though killed I killed the killer; but even so he didn't go to Hades; it was I who died.

The solution is "Nessos." We simply have to change the first person verbs and pronouns to the third, the third to the second, and the past

---

37 The Crotoniate Phormion is the same as the Spartan Phormion who entertained the Dioskuroi in their native house, now his residence, to which they had come from Cyrene; and in their birth room they left images of themselves and a table with silphion on it; see Paus. 3.16.2–3; Plut. Mor.1103a.

38 On oracular riddles see Schultz 1909: 65–81, and s.v. Rätsel, RE 1A.97–98, 108; Ohlert 1912: 135–145. See also Crahay 1956: 54–56.

39 See Anth. Pal. 14.33, a variant of the same riddle:

Τόν με κατακτείναντα κατέκτανον, οὐδέ μοι ἦδος.
θῆκε γὰρ ἀθάνατον τὸν κτάμενον θάνατος.

"I killed my killer and had no pleasure: for death made the slain deathless." See Schultz 1909:54, nos. 53, 54; Ohlert 1912: 180–181.

tense to future (and disregard metrical fit) in order to convert this riddle
into a version of L119. The riddle is already apparent in the prophecy as
Herakles expresses it in Sophocles' *Trachiniai*:

> ἐμοὶ γὰρ ἦν πρόφαντον ἐκ πατρὸς πάλαι
> πρὸς τῶν πνεόντων μηδενὸς θανεῖν ποτε,
> ἀλλ᾽ ὅστις ᾿Αιδου φθίμενος οἰκήτωρ πέλοι.

[1159–1161]

My father foretold to me that I would never be killed by anyone living, but
by a dead man, resident of Hades.

If we suppose that the Nessos riddle was already current in the fifth
century B.C. in either or both of the forms in which we find it in the
Anthology (see note 39), we may conclude that the riddle has affected
the prophecy which Sophocles introduces. It is a riddle that aptly expresses
the Macduff theme.

The affinity between L119 and a popular riddle of ancient Greece
suggests that other oracle texts, both Legendary and Quasi-Historical,
were not enigmatically phrased simply for the sake of the narratives in
which they occur, but were really riddles to begin with. The deceptively
ambiguous prophecy of legend and folktale does not need a fixed text: in
the earliest story it may be stated indirectly in prose. Then in the course
of transmission someone gives the prophecy an exact text, whether in
prose or verse; and if he knows a riddle that suits the ambiguity upon
which the whole story hinges he adapts it to serve as the prophetic text.
In some instances perhaps the riddle itself suggested the story and the
prophecy. And in some stories almost any ambiguity will do, and so
almost any riddle can fill the breach. For example, in the legend of
Medon and Neileus concerning which brother should become king of
Athens, there seems to be no compelling reason why the place where
sialos rubs *sialos* (L68) should decide the issue rather than the place where
the *tragos* dips his beard in the water (or drinks the water; Q20, 34).
Probably L68 had as antecedent a popular riddle pretty much as follows:
"'Pig' rubs 'pig' in the breeze. What is it? Answer: an olive bough";
and this riddle served the narrator's purpose well enough.

Q33 seems to be derived from a riddle: "What is the female that
takes the male to wife? Answer: the vine (*hē ampelos*) that embraces the
wild fig tree (*ton erineon*)".[40] A riddle on this theme, making use of the

---

40 See Schultz 1909: 79, no. 122; 1912: 107; Ohlert 1912: 139.

vine's marriage to the tree, is found in an ancient collection of riddles, Symphosius' *Aenigmata*:[41]

Nolo toro jungi, quamvis placet esse maritam.
nolo virum thalamo: per me mea nata propago est.
nolo sepulcra pati: scio me submergere terrae.

[53]

I don't want to be joined in marriage, though I am pleased to be married. I don't want a husband for my bed: I produce my children myself. I don't want to suffer burial: I know how to put myself underground.

The answer is *vitis* (vine).

Q34 (cf. Q20) is the riddle "What is the 'goat' that dips his beard in the water? Answer: a wild fig tree (*tragos*) whose boughs dip down into the sea (or a stream)."[42] Q186 is the riddle "Where can one drink water in measure and eat bread without measure? Answer: where water comes out of a *medimnos* [a grain measure and a kind of pipe] and bread does not." And the first three lines of Q90, as quoted by Herodotos, are pure riddle as they stand, except that *Arkadiês Tegeê* might be replaced by any suitable name or term: "There is a certain place on level ground where two winds blow, etc. What is it? Answer: a smithy."[43] The last two lines of Q90 make an oracular response out of the riddle; the enigmatically defined smithy is the place where the Spartans will find Orestes' remains. Q101 expresses the Macduff theme in riddling terms: "What mule sat on the throne of Persia? Answer: Cyrus, who was half Mede and half Persian."[44] Thus we see that the riddle is an excellent device of the story-teller for fashioning a prophecy that refers obscurely to the place where something is to be found or to be established, or to the distinctive sign of fulfillment or doom.

A riddle could change its meaning on becoming an oracular response in a narrative. For example, Ἐν τιμῇ τὸν ἄτιμον ἔχων τότε γαῖαν ἀρώσεις (Q168), as part of the story in which it appears, means that the Epizephyrian Locrians, in order to end the famine which afflicted them, should honor the athlete Euthykles, whose image they had maltreated. The response is phrased in contrary terms, "holding the unhonored in honor you will plow land," and for this reason one suspects that it is really a

41 See R. T. Ohl, *The Enigmas of Symphosius* (Philadelphia: Ph.D. thesis, Univ. of Pennysylvania, 1928) 84–85, for the riddle and for citations concerning the symbol.
42 See Schultz 1909: 77–78, no. 118; Ohlert 1912: 137–138.
43 See Schultz 1909: 72–73, no. 111; 1912: 111; Ohlert 1912: 143–145; Crahay 1956: 156.
44 See Schultz 1909: 70–71, nos 108, 109; Crahay 1956: 55–56.

riddle current in the folklore of some part of the Greek world (possibly south Italy); for expression in contrary or contradictory terms is a frequent riddling device.[45] Then one suspects that the answer was not "Euthykles"; one wants someone or something more familiar than a semi-legendary hero-athlete. The answer must be a masculine noun; it must be something ordinarily unhonored or unvalued, but which must be held in honor or value if one is going to get his field plowed or the benefits that plowing a field brings. I suggest *ponos*, "work," as the answer to the implied riddling question, "What that is unhonored must be honored to plow your field?" Upper-class Greeks, who in general established the prevailing values of ancient Greek society, considered manual work beneath them, fit only for slaves or for low-class freemen. This at any rate was their attitude in post-Homeric times, as we learn from Herodotos, Aristotle, and others.[46] Thus, I believe, was the original riddle solved: a man will not plow his land, i.e., earn his living, unless he undertakes (i.e., esteems) generally disesteemed work.

Q220 looks like another example of diverted and reinterpreted riddle. According to the story that Diodoros tells (17.10), three months before Alexander destroyed Thebes a huge spider web with a rainbow image upon it was seen in Demeter's temple in Thebes. When the Thebans referred the portent to Delphi, they received this response:

Σημεῖον τόδε πᾶσι θεοὶ φαίνουσι βροτοῖσι
Βοιωτοῖς δὲ μάλιστα καὶ οἳ περιναιετάουσι.

They also referred the portent to their own oracular shrine of Apollo Ismenios and were told, Ἱστὸς ὑφαινόμενος ἄλλῳ κακὸν ἄλλῳ ἄμεινον. The Delphic response says nothing about the meaning of the sign; and one should notice that it tells the Thebans nothing; they had to interpret the sign for themselves. The Ismenian Apollo does not say what the sign means for the Thebans, only that it portends good for one, bad for another. The manner of expression suggests that these verses were not originally intended to be oracles. The first verse of the Delphic response looks like the first line of a riddle; the Ismenian response looks like the second line,

---

45 See Archer Taylor, *English Riddles from Oral Tradition* (Berkeley, Los Angeles: Univ. of California Press, 1951) 672–676, nos 1681–1703.

46 Herod. 2.167.1, 5.6.2; Aristotle *Pol.* 1278a, 1326a, 1331a. On the Greek attitude to work see H. Michel, *The Economics of Ancient Greece*, 2d ed., (Cambridge: Heffer, 1957) 10–17. The answer to the riddle could be τὸν ἐργάτην (cf. Herod. 5.6.2) or a synonym; ἐν τιμῇ ἔχων, then, may refer to the plowman's hire. It would then be a riddle for the landowning Greek who did not put his own hand to the plow: "If you want to plow your land, you must hire a plowman." With either solution, *ponos* or *ergatēs*, this may not seem a very good riddle, but it is certainly no worse than many which appear in riddle collections.

if the nominative case be changed to accusative: "The gods show this sign to all mortals, a loom weaving bad for one, better for another," or "a warp being woven (which is) bad for one, better for another," the solution being "spider web" (bad for a fly, better for a spider).[47] So, if I am right, the riddle answered by "spider web" became an oracular response which a spider web motivated. When the riddle was made into an oracle for the tale of Thebes' destruction, a line was added for the sake of the story, indicating that the sign was given especially to the Boeotians.

Some responses may not be riddles in the strict sense of Archer Taylor's definition of riddles as "descriptions of objects in terms intended to suggest something entirely different."[48] Those that require a knowledge of legend or history in order to be solved (e.g., Q59, 60, 101; L119) are puzzles or clever problems rather than true riddles. It matters little for our purpose: every kind of enigmatic question is current in folklore and in the literary genres that are derived from folk traditions. The distinctions that are important to the folklorist are unknown to the folk and even to the amateur collector of riddles and puzzling questions. One kind of popular puzzle is as likely as another to have become an enigmatic oracle in folktale, legend, and pseudohistory. The sort of puzzle called *griphos* may be seen in Q230, the Pyrros oracle: Aio te Aeacida Romanos vincere posse (see p. 67), which has the same sort of verbal play as Πεντήκοντ' ἀνδρῶν ἑκατὸν λίπε δῖος Ἀχιλλεύς: Quinquaginta ubi erant centum inde occidit Achilles.[49]

PROVERBS

As riddles and related puzzles express the intellectual and verbal ingenuity of the folk, so proverbs express the folk's practical wisdom.[50]

---

47 One may object that the word *histos* would give the answer away; but it was seldom used in the meaning "web" and then only for woven cloth, not for a spider web (*arachnion*). See Schultz 1909: 66, 81, no. 125; Ohlert 1912: 143.

48 Taylor, *English Riddles* 1; also see Aristotle *Poet.* 1458a.

49 Ohlert 1912: 6–7. The best that can be done in English is "A hundred where there were fifty Achilles killed (or left)." For other oracular riddles see Q119, 213; L4, 5, 48, 76. L80, spoken to Homer is not itself a riddle, but warns the poet that "the riddle of the young men" will be the sign of his life's end. The riddle, spoken by returning fishermen, was "What we caught we threw away; what we didn't catch we carry with us," the answer being "lice." See *Cert. Hom. Hes.* 328 Allen; Schultz 1909: 65–67, nos 101, 102; Ohlert 1912: 30–31; Archer Taylor, *The Literary Riddle Before 1600* (Berkeley, Los Angeles: Univ. of California Press, 1948) 647–648, nos. 1591, 1592.

50 I do not deny that many riddles and proverbs have a learned or upper-class origin. But once they circulate among the folk they have become part of folklore. See Archer Taylor, *The Proverb* (Cambridge, Mass.: Harvard Univ. Press, 1931) 3: "Let us be content with recognizing that a proverb is a saying current among the folk."

Both riddles and proverbs use a great deal of figurative language. Charlotte Burne aptly expressed the difference between proverb and riddle as follows: "While the proverb states a fact or expresses a thought in vivid metaphor, the riddle describes a person or thing in more obscure metaphor, calculated to exercise the intellectual skill of any who attempt to solve it."[51] Nevertheless a proverbial metaphor may become obscure for several reasons: men of another region or of a later generation unfamiliar with the customs and modes of life which gave birth to the proverb, or with the expressions employed, may not understand the metaphor though they may continue to use the proverb; e.g., why do we say "The game isn't worth the candle" or "as dead as a doornail"? Some proverbial expressions have their origin in riddles: "All the king's horses and all the king's men" (can't do it). Hence we cannot be sure in some instances whether an ancient saying, obscure to us, is a riddle or a proverb. We may also feel uncertainty about a few Legendary and Quasi-Historical responses, since proverbs as well as riddles have contributed to their contents. For example, Q168, on holding the unhonored in honor, might be considered a proverb.

As many as nineteen Quasi-Historical responses and eleven Legendary responses appear in whole or in part in the ancient collections of proverbs that have survived under the names of Zenobios, Plutarch, Diogenianos, and others.[52] One paroemiographer may attribute an oracular origin to a proverb; another may list it simply as a proverb or give it a different *aition*. This means that the proverb collections of Didymos, Lucillus of Tarra, and others—the sources of the extant collections—differed from one another concerning the origin of proverbs: some did not recognize a proverb as originally an oracular response. Moreover the oracular *aitia* have the earmarks of legend or folktale, whether we call the supposed oracle Legendary or Quasi-Historical. Commonly the proverb-oracle is anonymous in a paroemiographer's entry; occasionally Delphi or Apollo is mentioned.

Several statements or commands called oracles by some ancient writers are aphorisms or maxims, stated in plain, unmetaphorical language: they are rules of conduct, formulae of behavior or success, statements of popular philosophy. An example is Q10, 'Α φιλοχρηματία Σπάρταν ἕλοι (ὀλεῖ), ἄλλο δὲ οὐδέν: "Love of money and nothing else will destroy Sparta." According to Diodoros, the Pythia spoke this

---

51 Charlotte S. Burne, *The Handbook of Folk-Lore* (London: Folklore Society, Sidgwick and Jackson, 1914) 284.

52 Q10, 26, 30, 34, 53, 77, 80, 88, 105, 116, 162, 180, 183, 186, 201, 215, 231, 242, 247; L5, 22, 34, 73, 74, 77, 78, 87, 105, 110, 176.

oracle to Lykurgos, the Spartan lawgiver, when he sought from Delphi a new constitution for Sparta. But Pausanias, Plutarch, Scholiasts, and paroemiographers say merely that this was an oracle given to the Spartans; god and oracular shrine are not named. Of these writers Zenobios and a Scholiast cite Aristotle's *Constitution of Lakedaimon* as their source; and this may mean that Aristotle was no more specific than they about the speaker of this response. It was a well-known proverb before Aristotle's time; Aristophanes (*Peace* 622–623) and Euripides (*Andromache* 451) allude to it. It looks as if a proverb about Spartan greed attained popularly the dignity of an oracular statement (cf. Plutarch *Agis* 9); then, as often happened, the unattached or vaguely ascribed oracle picked up a Delphic attribution as it moved about. No doubt the proverb was confused with the tradition that the Lycurgan laws, including their monetary and sumptuary provisions, had been dictated by the Delphic Apollo (Q8); the proverb, men thought, was part of the god-given code.

Q80, Ἄκρον λάβε καὶ μέσον ἕξεις, "Take the top and you will have the middle," is found only in proverb collections and the Suda (A1011), although the Bodleian codex of Zenobios cites as authority the Delphian Anaxandrides; only there do we find a complete hexameter given a Delphic origin. The Suda and the Vindobonensis codex of Diogenianos (1.27) simply list the proverb without mention of an oracle.

The metaphorical aphorism which, literally applicable to a particular situation, becomes the analogue of others to which it does not literally apply (e.g., "A stitch in time saves nine") is also found among responses reputedly spoken at Delphi or elsewhere. For example, Q183, Μὴ κίνει Καμάριναν, ἀκίνητος γὰρ ἀμείνων, "Don't move Camarina; it is better unmoved"—of which only the first three words are commonly quoted—refers, as usually interpreted, to a marshy lake next to Camarina in Sicily; but the words are used metaphorically as a warning against any undertaking that was likely to turn out badly, or that was better not begun. As the story went, Camarina drained the lake in the fifth century, despite being forbidden to do so. Afterward enemies were able to attack and take the city from that side. Nobody definitely says that this oracle was spoken at Delphi, and only the Virgilian commentators say that Apollo spoke it. Callimachus, Lucian, and Stephanos quote the saying simply as a proverb.[53] In the Palatine Anthology it appears, accompanied by a second line, among *Epigrammata demonstrativa*, not among *Oracula*.[54] Plainly it is a

---

53 Callim. *Ait.* 3.64.1–2 Pf.; Lucian *Pseudol.* 32; Steph. Byz. 351 Mein.

54 Anth. Pal. 9.685. The second line is μή ποτε κινήσας τὴν μείονα μείζονα θείης: "lest by moving it you make matters worse." Since no indication is given that this epigram was an oracle, PW 127 are hardly justified in quoting both lines as the oracular response,

well-known proverb that acquired an oracular *aition*; the story of Camarina is very unlikely to be true history.

Q242, Εὐδαίμων ὁ Κόρινθος, ἐγὼ δ' εἴην Τενεάτης, "Blessed is Corinth, but I would be a Teneate," was, according to Strabo's anonymous authority, an oracle spoken to a man from Asia who wanted to move to Corinth. The provenance is not mentioned. The paroemiographers and the Suda quote the verse only as a proverb.[55] Surely the saying has only a tenuous claim to be considered an oracle at all, much less a Delphic response. It is a proverb that urges contentment with a moderate or humble station.[56]

The popular aphorism, simple or metaphorical, with ethical content, is one kind of proverb. Another kind is the conventional phrase, usually figurative, which expresses an analogue of the actual situation. It may be a complete sentence or incomplete; it is usually short and not always precisely fixed in form. It is often allusive, a phrase from a poem or speech, from a school book or the theatre.[57] A number of such proverbial expressions appear among "Delphic" oracles, most of them found in the proverb collections. We have already looked at Q34 as an example both of distinctive sign and of oracular riddle. The first verse is Καλόν τοι τὸ μεταξὺ Κορίνθου καὶ Σικυῶνος, "Fair is the land between Corinth and Sikyon." According to another story Aesop (or someone else, says Athenaios) asked "the god" how he might become rich, and received the mocking reply, "If you should acquire the land between Corinth and Sikyon."[58] Thus there are two oracular *aitia* for the proverb. In a sense there is a third: the chresmologue (*chrêsmologos alazôn*) of Aristophanes' *Birds* (967–968) quotes an oracle, which he attributes to Bakis, that includes τὸ μεταξὺ Κορίνθου καὶ Σικυῶνος.

Q162, Πάντα λίθον κίνει, is said to be an oracular response in the entries of some paroemiographers and lexicographers under this phrase. They tell the story of a certain Polykrates of Athens or Thebes, who, trusting a rumor that Mardonios had buried a treasure in the earth

---

which is always quoted as the first line or half-line. An alternative explanation of the proverb appears in Zen. 5.18: an evil-smelling plant called *kamarina* made a worse smell when waved: "The more you stir it, the worse it stinks."

55 Zen. 3.96; Ps.-Plut. *Prov.* 1.4; Suda *E*3408; Apost.-Arsen. 8.6d.

56 Strabo tells us remarkably little. The response might have been classified as Legendary, since there is no indication of date. I have supposed that those who told the story placed it somewhere in historical times, since the consultant was an Asian who wanted to move to Corinth and who, if we assume that Q242 is Delphic, consulted Apollo at Delphi.

57 See Taylor, *The Proverb* 129–132.

58 Ath. 5.219a. For the proverb see Zen. 3.57; Diog. Vind. 2.60; Makar. 3.58; Eust. *Il.* 2.572, p. 291.

beneath his tent at Plataia, bought the site and dug for the treasure; finding none, he asked Delphi (according to Zenobios and the Suda only) how he could find the treasure, and received the reply, "Turn every stone." Other paroemiographers list the proverb without mentioning either Polykrates or an oracle.[59] In two of these entries the proverb is explained exactly as we explain "to leave no stone unturned." It is a proverb that has had a life of at least 2500 years; for we find it used by Euripides simply as a proverbial phrase.[60] The proverb certainly precedes the story of Polykrates, which seems to be a fable, the moral of which is a warning against greed or credulity.[61]

In all instances cited a proverb has been provided with an oracular *aition*. Might not the Pythia have made use of proverbs in composing responses? For granted that about one in ten Quasi-Historical oracles contains this sort of material, it is not incredible or impossible that a consultant was sometimes answered with a proverb. But it almost certainly did not happen. The mere possibility that it could have happened is outweighed by the trend of historical evidence: no historical response has a proverbial character.[62]

---

59 Diogen. 7.42; Greg. Cypr. 3.54; Makar. 7.4; Mant. Prov. 2.48.

60 *Herakleidai* 1002; see also Pliny Jun. *Epist.* 1.20.15.

61 For other oracles of proverbial character not listed by paroemiographers see Q43, 68, 215. Q177 and L81 are gnomic epigrams.

62 H7 ends with the phrase "plow with a silver plowshare." This phrase is not found in any proverb collection; moreover H7 was a suborned response and as such might show unusual phrasing. For H17 the Athos manuscript of Zenobios gives the trimeter of Q231; but Aelian probably has the correct form of H17. Xenophon has merely "It will be my concern" in indirect form, which can hardly be considered more than ordinary idiom of the Greek language ('Εμοὶ μελήσει). H63 is an epigram in trimeter and has been considered a proverb by Flacelière 1937: 170 note 75; Parke 1956: 359; Crahay 1956: 52; but it is not found in any proverb collection.

The Transmission and Attribution of Narrative Oracles

What does one include in a corpus of Delphic oracles? If the compiler limits his collection to genuine and probably genuine pronouncements of the Pythia, as determined in this study, his corpus will not contain many more than a hundred responses: out of 75 Historical responses 2 must be rejected as spurious; out of 268 Quasi-Historical responses about 30 appear to be genuine, including some that are not certainly so. If one should add a few rather doubtful responses, the corpus would have about 110 entries. Parke and Wormell have a corpus of 615 entries, to which 15 should be added, and a few subtracted. Of these they include 256 in their "historical" sections; but they do not consider all these genuine (although in general they are lenient in acceptance).

There remains the body of legendary and pseudo-historical responses. Here are oracles that the Pythia never spoke, and perhaps no one else outside of the narrative. Do they belong to a corpus of Delphic oracles at all? We may answer the question affirmatively with the argument that the legendary and spurious responses tell us what views and conceptions Greeks and others had of the Delphic Oracle and its responses, what powers and knowledge they attributed to the Delphic Apollo, and what esteem the god held among them. But once we have answered this question we still face a question of what to include and what to exclude.

We may decide to include all responses labeled Delphic by at least one writer who quotes or notices the response, mentioning Delphi or Pytho as the place where it was spoken, or the Pythian Apollo or the Pythia as the speaker of it (or using some recognizably equivalent term for place or speaker). But this practice will admit a number of false ascriptions; for example PW 595, spoken at Dodona according to Strabo, Livy, and Justin, is called a Pythian oracle by Aelian (frag. 329). Again the principle of demanding an explicit ascription to Delphi may lead us to exclude some oracles that were probably considered Delphic in the tradition, although no surviving document says more than that Apollo or "the god" (*ho theos*) spoke them. Parke and Wormell, in fact, include a good number of such unspecific oracles in their corpus, and I have admitted some to the Catalogue.

The role of oracles is the same in legends of the prehistoric past and in pseudo-historical narratives, which are historicized legends (and we must remember that the Greeks considered both equally historical: what I call legends were for them earlier history). These two groups of narratives however, have a different relation to Delphi. Some of the legends were perhaps begun and developed within historical times, but most go back to the Bronze Age or to the Greek Dark Age—though they may have changed a good deal in oral transmission over the centuries— and therefore to times before the Delphic Oracle was established or had acquired fame. So if these early legends contained a prophecy or divine command, it could not have been called Delphic at first; and if classical or post-classical sources call it Delphic, then it became so labeled in later transmission, probably not before 700 at the earliest. But a narrative formed after the eighth century may introduce a Delphic oracle from its inception, though it may also introduce a non-Delphic oracle, and we should not assume that if an oracle contained in it is called Delphic in surviving sources it was originally or universally so ascribed.

In the preceding chapter we have observed the narrative character of many "Delphic" oracles that have been believed genuine in both ancient and modern times. We must therefore consider the processes by which narrative oracles acquired a Delphic ascription. This means that we must look at the employment of oracles in narratives from our earliest literary records down to post-classical times.

PROPHECY IN LEGEND AND EPIC

The Homeric epics illustrate how the future was foretold and how divine commands were spoken in early legends. The heroes and others most often received forecasts and warnings from omens—chance sights, usually of the flights and behavior of birds, and occasionally chance sounds, such as thunder and spoken words.[1] Ordinarily these signs appeared without the perceiver's asking for them, sometimes after a prayer or a reference to Zeus's intentions. Odysseus, however, asked Zeus for a *phêmê* from inside the house and a *teras* from outside (Odyssey 20.98–101); and Zeus obliged him with thunder from on high and the words of a servant woman from within the house as she interpreted the omen in a prayer to Zeus (cf. Iliad 24.308–313). Ordinarily the receiver could interpret the omen for himself, but occasionally he needed a mantis or diviner to translate the sign into a prediction. Thus Kalchas interpreted the omen of the snake and sparrows to the Achaeans gathered at Aulis (Iliad 2.322–332; cf. Odyssey 2.157–170, 15.529–534).

Homeric men also received forecasts, divine instruction, and knowledge of hidden things from dreams. The gods sent dream phantoms in the shape of a friend or kinsman to the sleeper, as when Penelope dreamed that she saw and spoke with her sister Iphthime, who predicted Telemachos' safe return (Odyssey 4.795–841). Or Athena herself took the form of Dymas' daughter to appear in Nausikaa's dream and instruct her (Odyssey 6.20–40). To Agamemnon Zeus sent a dream spirit (*oneiros*) in Nestor's shape with a false prophecy (Iliad 2.5–71).

Occasionally seers spoke predictions or reported the gods' desires, apparently from divine inspiration, if not from a clairvoyant faculty. Thus Helenos, the mantis among Priam's sons, perceived in spirit Apollo's wish as expressed to Athena for a single combat between Hector and an Achaean champion (Iliad 7.44–45). At Achilles' request Kalchas revealed that Apollo's anger at Agamemnon's treatment of Chryses had brought plague upon the Achaean host (Iliad 1.92–100), a knowledge that he may have acquired from past observation of birds: he was best of *oiônopoloi*, but his mantic powers went beyond such divinatory arts; for he knew past, present, and future, and guided the Achaean army with the *mantosynê* that came to him from Apollo (Iliad 1.69–72). Likewise Halitherses, Telemos, and Theoklymenos, great-grandson of Melampûs, made prophetic speeches that appear to be expressions of prophetic knowledge rather than conclusions derived from past observations and divinations.[2] Kalchas, Helenos, and perhaps the other manteis mentioned were gifted in both kinds of divination that Quintus Cicero distinguished: quorum

---

1 Sights: Il. 2.301–332, 8.247–250, 12.200–229, 24.287–321; Od. 2. 146–170, 15.525–534, 19.535–558. Sounds: Il. 7.478–479; Od. 20.97–121.

2 Od. 2.171–176, 9.507–512, 20.350–357, 363–370; cf. 17.151–161.

alterum artis est, alterum naturae (Cicero *Div.* 1.6.11), "one is artful, the other natural."

It is also a feature of legend, as expressed in epic, that gods make their wishes known directly in epiphanies to mortal men, as when Athena appeared to Achilles, though to no one else in the Achaean assembly, to prevent his attacking Agamemnon and to advise him (Iliad 1.194–214). It is most often Athena who thus appears, but Apollo appears to Patroklos on the battlefield to forbid his attacking the city wall, telling him that he is not fated to take Troy (Iliad 16.700–711).

As in dreams, so in real life a god may take on the form of a friend or kinsman or of some other person when he appears to a man that he wants to instruct. Poseidon entered the Achaean host in the shape of Kalchas (Iliad 13.43–45, 68–72). Athena first came to Telemachos in the form of Mentes, ruler of the Taphians (Odyssey 1.103–105, 180–181), then took the form of Telemachos to gather a crew of Ithacans for his voyage (Odyssey 2.382–387), and, soon after, the form of Mentor, an Ithacan elder, to advise and accompany Telemachos (Odyssey 2.399–406; cf. 10.277–306).

Usually the human recipient of divine revelation has not sought it; the gods present him with it (although occasionally someone asks for an omen). And sometimes a person goes to a seer or to an oracular shrine seeking knowledge. Odysseus unwillingly, but at Circe's command went to Hades' realm to consult Teiresias about his home return (Odyssey 11.90–151). Menelaos, instructed by Eidothea, consulted Proteus, the Old Man of the Sea (*halios gerôn*), on the reason for the lack of winds that kept him marooned on Pharos, and also learned about past events unknown to himself (Odyssey 4.384–569). Disguised as a Cretan adventurer Odysseus told Eumaios of a report that Odysseus had gone to consult Zeus at Dodona about his return.[3] At the beginning of the Trojan War, according to a song of Demodokos, Agamemnon went to consult Apollo at Pytho, who told him that a quarrel between the noblest Achaeans would be the sign of victory over Troy (L1, Odyssey 8.75–82). The mention of the Pythian Oracle indicates that this episode cannot have been composed before the eighth century.

Early Greek legend, then, as represented in Homeric epic, shows divine revelation from omens, signs, dream visions, pronouncements of seers, and statements that the gods make directly to mortal men. Not

---

3 Od. 14.327–330. See Il. 16.233–248, where Achilles addresses his prayer to Zeus Dodonaios Pelasgikos.

more than twice does anyone visit an oracular shrine. Greek legends do not differ in these respects from the legends and folktales of other lands. There is only one convention of narrative prophecy-speaking absent from the Homeric poems that is frequent in the orally transmitted prose legends of the Greek and other peoples. That is the anonymous prophecy: a character knows what is destined to happen; how he knows this we are not informed. Sometimes it may be said that he has heard a prophecy; but the speaker is not mentioned or is anonymous and indefinite. In Grimm 29, "Der Teufel mit den drei goldenen Haaren," a poor woman bore a son who had a caul, and "so war ihm geweissagt, es werde im vierzehnten Jahr die Tochter des Königs zur Frau haben." A Swedish variant is a little more specific: a rich merchant consulted astrologers on his daughter's marriage and learned from them that she would marry the miller's son.[4]

In some ancient Greek tales there are introduced prophecies that no extant version attributes to a named speaker or oracular site. In the legend of the Cretan patricide Althaimenes either the father Katreus (Apollodoros 3.2.1) or the son (Diodoros 5.59.1) received an oracle that the son was fated to kill his father; it is another story of how fate cannot be circumvented. Diodoros says no more than that Althaimenes, seeking an oracle somewhere on other matters received this *chrêsmos*; Apollodoros says that the god (*ho theos*) spoke it to Katreus, but does not name the god or inform us where Katreus went to inquire about his life's end. In the same legend Althaimenes planned to leave Crete in order to avoid his destiny and received a *chrêsmos*, not identified (Conon 47), that he should betake himself to Zeus and Helios and ask them for land to settle in. Probably the oracles of this legend were never given a definite speaker.

The oracle is a device that one storyteller needs and another does not. In the tale of Telephos' birth, as Apollodoros tells it (3.9.1), Auge hid her infant son in Athena's temenos and the land became barren; then *chrêsmoi* revealed that there was sacrilege in Athena's temenos. But in Diodoros' version (4.33.8) Aleos noticed Auge's pregnant condition, and there was no crop failure. Only Apollodoros' version of the Nisos-Skylla story tells us that Nisos knew a *chrêsmos* according to which he would die if the purple lock on his head should be shorn (3.15.8). No other version

---

4 Stith Thompson, ed., *One Hundred Favorite Folktales* (Bloomington, London: Indiana Univ. Press, 1968), tale 32, "The Rich Man and His Son-in-Law," p. 137. This is Aarne-Thompson type 461 (cf. 930). In an English tale, "Osmotherly," a mother hears a prophecy that her son will be drowned by gypsies; Katharine M. Briggs, *A Dictionary of British Folk-Tales in the English Language*, part B: *Folk Legends* (London: Routledge & Kegan Paul, 1971) 2.294. The bare "it was prophesied" in one variant of a tale may in another become the prediction of anonymous astrologers or soothsayers.

mentions such an oracle; Pausanias (1.19.4) has only the remark that Nisos was bound (*chrênai*) to die if his purple lock was shorn. The life-index theme needs no oracle: the power of the object is known without that. In the story of Meleager, however, the Moirai appeared soon after his birth, as in modern Greek folktales, and informed Althaia that the child would live only as long as the brand burning in the hearth (Apollodoros 1.8.2).

The cited legends go back to the prehistoric period and to early popular tradition. Some of the stories that Herodotos tells as historical, sometimes with reservations, and which we may call pseudo-historical or legendary, contain anonymous oracular commands and prophecies, though he usually attributes oracles to the god of an established oracular shrine, as to Apollo at Delphi, or to some famous seer; or he may introduce dreams and omens as Homer had done. In his Egyptian tale of the succession to King Sethos, the twelve kings received an oracle at the commencement of their reigns that the king who would pour libation from a golden bowl in Hephaistos' temple would become king of all Egypt.[5] Herodotos attributes other Egyptian oracles to Buto, but this he leaves unidentified, probably as he received the tale. His Greek tales too may have unidentified responses. The Aigeids of Sparta, having lost their children, established a sanctuary of the Erinyes of Laios and Oedipus in compliance with an oracular response (*ek theopropiou*, 4.149.2). It happened often enough that particular tribes or families established sanctuaries in obedience to an oracle, but the legendary nature of this story fragment is indicated by the calamity that affected nobody but the members of a single family, and affected all of them. Since Herodotos generally tells us who spoke an oracle or where it was spoken, the absence of such ascription appears to indicate that he heard none from his source, and that these stories were told without naming an oracle-speaker (see 5.114.2).

THE CITATION AND QUOTATION OF NARRATIVE ORACLES

Numerous were the legends and folktales that floated about Greek lands in the eighth century B.C. when the Delphic Oracle was probably established; and in many of them prophecies and other revelations of divine purpose were favorite motives. It was likely then that as Delphi's fame increased, and especially after Delphi had surpassed other Oracles in prestige, some storytellers would say that Apollo at Delphi had made

---

5 Herod. 2.147.4. Diod. 1.66.10 says only that the rulers received a *chrêsmos*.

the revelation in question. So some versions of a tale acquired a Delphic response; others did not. The version that a poet or logographer or myth collector took from the oral tradition might or might not be that in which the response was called Delphic. The Catalogue of Responses shows varying specifications for many Legendary and Quasi-Historical oracles. One or more writers may say that the Pythian Apollo spoke a response; others may say only that Apollo spoke it; others may say that "the god" (*ho theos*) spoke it; and still others may be even less definite with just the mention of a *chrêsmos* or equivalent term.

The literary tradition may move either way, to more or less specific attribution of oracular statements. The anonymous oracle may become attributed to the Delphic Apollo, or perhaps just to Apollo; but an oracle called Delphic in the primary literary source may be less definitely attributed in later sources whose authors drew directly or indirectly upon the primary source: they may content themselves with "Apollo" or "the god" or an unspecified *chrêsmos*. For example, Herodotos tells about Sparta's war on Tegea not much more than a century after the event, and responses Q88–90 are central features of his story. All later writers depend upon Herodotos for the story and the responses. Introducing Q88 Herodotos says that the Pythia spoke this response to the Spartan consultants, and Pausanias and the Anthology are equally specific. Yet Dion Chrysostomos and the Scholiast on Aristeides (46.172) say no more than that "the god" spoke this response; Diodoros, Polyainos, and others refer only to a *chrêsmos* or *logion* that the Spartans received. For Q90 Diodoros, Pausanias, Lepidus (or Stephanos of Byzantion), and the Anthology report Herodotos' Delphic attribution; Aeneas of Gaza says that Apollo spoke it; the Scholiast on Aristeides attributes this too to "the god"; others are content with a reference to an oracle. Differences among several sources in presenting an oracular response—some ascribing it to Delphi, others not—do not necessarily mean that an originally non-Delphic or anonymous response has acquired a Delphic attribution in some versions of the narrative in which it appears. Each response has to be studied in its own tradition, as far as one can discover it.

The manner of quoting an oracle also varies in the course of narrative transmission and development. The narrator of a folktale commonly expresses a prophecy in indirect form as in Grimm 29 or in many a Greek legend. Such prophecies never had a direct form and never acquired one; the story demands only that the content be known. Often enough, however, the narrator expresses the prophecy in direct prose, having introduced the speaker, as in modern Greek folktales in which the Moires speak a newborn infant's fate.[6] Occasionally a prose tale has a prophecy in verse, but usually the tale has gone into folk poetry, folk song, or epic before it receives a verse expression.[7] Or the prophecy that began as an indirect expression may acquire a direct form in prose or verse in the course of oral transmission or in later literary development. Again an oracle in verse or direct prose may be quoted indirectly by a later narrator or writer.

NARRATIVE ORACLES ORIGINALLY NON-DELPHIC

The Theban legend-cycle of Laios, Oedipus, and the Theban War had taken shape before the eighth century. The Iliad, Odyssey, and Hesiod mention Oedipus or the Theban war; and the Cyclic epics included an *Oidipodeia*, a *Thebais*, and an *Epigonoi*.[8] It is certain that the early legend already contained prophecies and oracles, which were either anonymous or, more likely, ascribed to a Theban seer, probably Teiresias, or to the Ismenian Apollo, if his Oracle was already established. The famous oracles which Laios and Oedipus received (L17, 18) belong to this legend-cycle, and so does the well-known oracle spoken to King Adrastos of Argos on the marriage of his daughters.

Adrastos' Oracle on Lion and Boar (L27).

Although scholars (e.g., Parke 1956: 311) often tell us that Adrastos received a Delphic oracle, we discover on reviewing all sources that not one firmly attaches L27 to Delphi. The only fairly sure evidence of Delphic attribution is the Euripidean Scholiast's quotation of the verse response from Mnaseas, and we know that Mnaseas compiled a collection of Delphic oracles. It is true that in three plays of Euripides—*Phoenician Women, Suppliants, Hypsipyle*—the speaker is Apollo, and that the Apollo who speaks oracles in Euripides' plays is generally meant to be the Apollo of Delphi; and it may be that in the lost *Hypsipyle* Euripides was more specific. But as far as we know, he named only Apollo, who was recognized as the source of prophecy in general; and it may be that in the version of the legend known to Euripides a mantis brought Apollo's message to Adrastos— there is some reason to suppose so—or that Apollo

---

6 See the four Greek tales in Archer Taylor, "The Predestined Wife (Mt. 930*)," *Fabula* 2 (1958) 54–55, 66–67; R. M. Dawkins, *Modern Greek Folktales* (Oxford: Clarendon Press, 1953) 341.

7 In Grimm 47 and 96 birds make revelations in verse; in Grimm 53, "Snow White," the mirror on the wall speaks sooth in verse.

8 Il. 23.679–680; Od. 11.271–280; Cyclic fragments, pp. 111–116 Allen.

appeared to Adrastos in person. Apollodoros says that a mantis had told Adrastos to yoke his daughters to a boar and a lion, and this unnamed mantis is surely the earliest form of oracle speaker in this story.

Only Mnaseas, as quoted by the Scholiast, offers a verse form of L27, three hexameter lines. The first verse contains the whole message given in all other sources (except perhaps Statius *Theb.* 1.397), including Euripides' tragedies, that Adrastos should marry his daughters to a boar and a lion; the other two verses add that Adrastos will see them on the porch of his house as they come from Apollo's shrine (in Argos); and that Adrastos should make no mistake. Are we to suppose that this verse response, or at least the first line of it, belongs to the legend known to Euripides, and that his trimeters (*Suppl.* 140, *Phoen.* 411) are restatements of the first hexameter line? That is possible, but Euripides' trimeters are almost exactly like the prose forms of Apollodoros, Zenobios, and others: Adrastos should simply give or yoke his daughters to a boar and a lion; whereas in the hexameters Adrastos is told, "Yoke your daughters' marriages to a boar and a lion"—not significantly different, but this phrasing recurs in no other source.[9] It appears, then, that in this legend, as commonly told, the oracle was expressed in indirect form; and either no speaker was designated or he was said to be a mantis, whether named or unnamed. The oracle was seldom called Delphic in classical or later times. At some point someone composed hexameter verses for it, which Mnaseas received as Delphic. Since he collected Delphic oracles it may be that the Delphic priesthood had made an effort to claim this response; but it was apparently a feeble effort.

Laios and His Son (L17)

The best-known prophecy from Theban legend is L17, spoken to Laios on the consequences of begetting a son. No Legendary response has been so closely associated with Delphi; and for scholars and readers in general it has been the typical example of a Delphic oracle in legend. So it is surprising to realize that neither Sophocles nor Euripides says that the Apollo of Delphi spoke this oracle. Probably because Delphi is prominent in *Oedipus the King* as the shrine to which Oedipus sent Kreon to inquire

---

9 Euripides differs from other sources in interpretation of the response: Adrastos found Tydeus and Polyneikes fighting like wild beasts, and that was enough for him to recognize fulfillment of the oracle. According to the Scholiast, who quotes Mnaseas, either the combatants had boar (Tydeus, Calydonian boar) and lion (Polyneikes, Sphinx) devices on their shields, or they wore boar and lion skins. These interpretations appear also in Apollodoros, Zenobios, Statius, Hyginus, and the Homeric commentators, so that they cannot be dependent on Euripides for the story.

about the plague at Thebes (L19), and where Oedipus received a response (L18), readers generally assume that Laios received his response there too. But Sophocles indicates only Apollo as speaker.

Nor does Euripides say more in the *Suppliants* and *Phoenician Women* than that it was Apollo who warned Laios against begetting a son, and we cannot be sure that he means the Pythian Apollo. We notice from the citations in the Catalogue that the sources of L17 which do not specify Delphi are considerably more numerous than those that do. A little more than half of those that do not mention Delphi name Apollo as speaker, as we might expect in view of the influence of Sophocles and Euripides on all later writers. But for Apollodoros the speaker is only "the god," and eight sources are content with reference to an anonymous oracle.[10] Pindar and Aeschylus, our earliest authorities for L17, attribute it to the Delphic Oracle, but their attribution means no more than that Delphi was firmly established in the legend by the early fifth century. It could not have had a place in the original Oedipus legend, since that must have been told long before the Delphic Oracle came into being. Homer knew the legend, but did not tell the story, so that his lack of reference to an oracle in Odyssey 11.271–280, where he alludes to Epikaste and her son Oedipus, is not significant. The story, as we have it from Sophocles and later writers, demands a prophecy or some statement of destiny: it is built upon the proposition that the decrees of fate cannot be circumvented. The Oedipus legend is based on an old folktale; the tale has become attached to Theban legendary history, and the father and son have become Theban kings. In the folktale, if we can judge from modern Greek tales, it was the Moirai who appeared on the day when the child was born or a few days later and predicted his destiny to the parents. Once this folktale had taken the form of the Oedipus legend, a supposed event in the early history of Thebes, the speaker of destiny became a mantis. And this mantis was surely Teiresias, as Carl Robert has concluded.[11] In Sophocles' Theban plays the role of Teiresias is crucial. In all Theban legend from Kadmos and Pentheus down to the Epigonoi, Teiresias is the great seer to whom the Thebans appeal in time of crisis. He is sufficient for any soothsaying needed in the Oedipus story, and Delphi is superfluous. As Robert asks, why should Laios have made the journey to consult Apollo, when he

---

10 It may well be that Chrysippos made a more specific indication of speaker than Eus. *PE* 4.3, citing his remarks on Laios' oracle, allows him. Notice that Anth. Pal. 14.67 does not list L17 among Pythian oracles, but labels it *Chrêsmos* among unidentified oracles.

11 Carl Robert, *Oidipus: Geschichte eines poetischen Stoffs im griechischen Altertum* (Berlin: Weidmann, 1915) 64–70.

could have consulted Apollo Ismenios in Thebes? Since the Ismenian Apollo, as far as the sources inform us, is entirely absent from the Oedipus legend, in which the only oracular shrine that appears is the Pythian Apollo's, we may reasonably conclude that Apollo enters the story as the god of Delphi, and that the original speaker of the prophecy was not Apollo (except that any mantis may be supposed to receive inspiration from Apollo).

Sophocles' version of the prophecy as spoken indirectly by Jocasta reflects the prophecy that was spoken in both folktale and early legend. The first line, ὡς αὐτὸν ἕξοι μοῖρα πρὸς παιδὸς θανεῖν (OT 713), "it was his destiny to be killed by his son," suggests the Moirai's pronouncement at the child's birth, "You are fated to be killed by the boy just born." Jocasta's next words, ὅστις γένοιτ' ἐμοῦ τε κἀκείνου πάρα, "who would be born to us," suggests what Teiresias would have to say in addition as speaker of the prophecy before the child was conceived or born.

In another version of the legend the prophecy is replaced by the curse that Pelops put on Laios for abducting his son Chrysippos, that he should have no son, or, if he did, he should be killed by him.[12] The five-verse hexameter version of L17 alludes to Pelops' curse, saying that Zeus has given heed to it. But clearly both curse and response are not needed. The curse version is probably early (though not earliest); for Euripides' trimeters (Phoen. 17–20) express the oracle in the words of Pelops' curse, though Euripides makes no mention of Chrysippos or Pelops; Jocasta bears no child, and Laios asks Apollo's advice.[13]

It is clear, therefore, that the Oedipus legend was developed and told in several versions before the Delphic Oracle entered the story. It may have been around 600 when a Delphic version first appeared. The Delphic attribution may have been due to a growing tendency to attribute oracles of legend to the Pythian Apollo; or, it may be, the Delphic priesthood itself made an effort to claim this famous oracle as its own. As we shall see, L18 was probably Delphic from the start; but apparently a Delphic attribution of L17 was never universally accepted. Throughout antiquity the story was often told without reference to Delphi at all.

It is unlikely that L17 had a verse form before the fifth century. In the old folktale and the Theban legend the prophecy was expressed indirectly or in direct prose. Aeschylus and Sophocles use only an indirect form in

---

12 See Arg. Eur. Phoen., Codex Vaticanus 909.

13 See Robert, Oidipus 400–414 and his fig. 54, the Cista Barberini, which connects Laios' consultation of Apollo with the rape of Chrysippos (Mon. Inst. 8.30). For Apulian vase-paintings see figs. 55–56, p. 405.

trimeters simply expressing in dramatic verse the prose oracle known to them. Euripides quotes the oracle directly in trimeters, which are his own composition, not intended to be the actual words of the god. Verse oracles were expected to be spoken in hexameters, and the very few examples in other meters, which purport to be actual pronouncements of the Delphic god or some other, are all surely drawn from a drama or other poetic composition. Nobody in Euripides' audience would suppose that his Jocasta was quoting the very words that Apollo had spoken to Laios. Yet some later writers appear to quote Euripides' trimeters, or at least one of them, as the genuine response. Of those who quote them, ten in number, Oinomaos alone acknowledges Euripides' authorship, though Lucian was certainly aware of it. Others may have received the verses indirectly and taken them to be the traditional response. Alexander of Aphrodisias and the Scholiasts on Pindar and Aeschylus attribute the trimeters explicitly to the Pythian Apollo, although Euripides' Jocasta says no more than that Apollo spoke them.

The five-verse hexameter version is probably late. We can only say that it had been composed before Mnaseas' time (about 200 B.C.). It is probable that Mnaseas had the hexameter response in his collection (or at least the first three verses, ending with *eneusa* [as Anth. Pal. 14.67] instead of *eneuse*); but the Scholiast on Pindar (*Ol.* 2.42), citing Mnaseas, quotes only one verse: he begins the first verse as we find it elsewhere, but concludes it differently. The full text of the hexameter oracle appears only in Argumenta.

Sophocles, as I have indicated, probably has the original form of the prophecy as spoken in the Theban legend, "If a son is born to you and Jocasta, you will perish at his hand." Pindar has the earliest known notice of L17 (*Ol.* 2.42–44), but only hints at the content. Aeschylus' notice is nearly as early (*Seven* 748–749), and as he expressed the message Apollo told Laios three times to preserve his city by dying without issue. This is probably not still another version of the response, but Aeschylus' own recasting of a traditional version in which he looks ahead to the war of the Seven. It suggests Euripides' version expressed in prohibitory form: "Do not beget a son, for if you do, he will kill you, and your whole house will walk in blood." The hexameter response is neither prohibitory nor conditional: Laios will have a son, but he is fated to die at his son's hands; for thus Zeus carries out Pelops' curse.

In these three versions only the father murder is predicted. But Nicolaus of Damascus, who reports the hexameter verson indirectly, adds a prediction of the future son's marriage with his mother. Malalas,

Kedrenos, and the Suda have the incestuous marriage as the sole content of the oracle spoken to Laios. These writers have probably confused L17 with L18: for in the ancient legend Laios received only a warning of his own death.

The Heraklids (L60–67)

The legend of the Heraklids' return may seem to lie on the border of history, since the Heraklids' legendary occupation of the Peloponnesos has been identified with the Dorian invasion. There is, however, little or no history in the story that Apollodoros and others tell, whatever the truth may be about the historicity of the Dorian invasion. Apollodoros has four oracles in his narrative (2.8.2–3), which appears to have the same source, perhaps Ephoros, as that used by Oinomaos and the Scholiast on Aristeides (46.215), each of whom reports three of these four (but Oinomaos has L64 instead of L65).

Pindar has the earliest reference to the oracles of the Heraklid legend, saying that Apollo as oracular god settled the descendants of Herakles and Aigimios in Lakedaimon, Argos, and Pylos. This seems to be an allusion to L60, but it could be to the whole series. In the fourth century Isokrates appears to have known a version of the Heraklid legend that had only one oracle (L60), which directed the Heraklids to go to their fatherland; and, finding that Argos was their ancestral country, they invaded the Peloponnesos and took it over. In this account the Heraklids had no trouble with oracles; but the version which Isokrates' contemporary Ephoros appears to have reported (PW, p. 117) contains several oracles, which gave the Heraklids much trouble and even caused them misfortunes, since they consistently misunderstood them. In this story the Heraklids invaded the Peloponnesos soon after Eurystheus' death and took over the whole peninsula. This invasion may have been in obedience to L60 in the version of the legend known to Ephoros, but Apollodoros and the Scholiast on Aristeides do not mention L60. After the Heraklids had spent one year in the Peloponnesos a plague came over the whole land; and from an unidentified oracle the Heraklids learned that they had returned too soon. Then Hyllos consulted Apollo at Delphi and received L61, on the third harvest, which he misinterpreted. Then follow L62, 63, and 64/65. It is a tale of *avertissements incompris* (see pp. 62, 148).

The Heraklid legend began as a charter of Dorian supremacy in the Peloponnesos; it was devised to legitimate their dominion by identifying the Dorians with the descendants of Aigimios and their rulers with the Heraklids as the people who had an hereditary right to the land. The original legend surely included the command or sanction of gods. The fully developed legend contained several prophecies, as narrators improved the story by introducing vicissitudes and mishaps before final success. A complete legend was current by 750, according to Gerhard Vitalis.[14]

If the legend was current in the early or middle eighth century, it is unlikely that its oracles were called Delphic at that time. And the legend itself, as Apollodoros and others tell it, betrays the actual state of affairs. An important figure is the mantis Karnos. After Apollo in L63 revealed the right meaning of L61 and L62 to the Heraklids, they still suffered a disaster, when their transport fleet was wrecked at the narrows of the Corinthian Gulf; then they learned from Apollo that Hippotes, a Heraklid, had killed Karnos, an Apolline seer, who had come speaking prophecies to the Heraklid camp at Naupaktos. Apollo instructed them to expel the slayer and to take the three-eyed as guide (L65), or to worship Apollo Karneios (L64). The Theocritean Scholiast informs us that Karnos spoke obscure (asêma) prophecies to the Heraklids, and so they thought him to be an agent of the Peloponnesians (Apollodoros 2.8.3; Theopompos 321GH). Conon (26) calls Karnos a phasma (phantom) of Apollo. Theopompos tells about the murder of Karnos and consequent famine, and no mention is made of the Delphic Oracle in the scholium that cites him.[15] He tells us that Karnos gave oracles to the Heraklids, and that Zeus and Hegetor, as well as Apollo, received the name Karneios from the Argives because Karnos guided the Heraklid host. From this evidence we can perceive the nature of the prophetic role in the early legend: Karnos was mantis of the Heraklids and spokesman of Apollo or Zeus.[16] He it was who spoke L61 and L62 to the Heraklids: these were the asêma that he spoke; and when the Heraklids suffered disasters on account of them (or their misunderstanding of them) they put him to death as an agent of the enemy. Then misfortunes overtook the Heraklids once more, whereupon they propitiated Karnos. Since he was a daimon or phasma the Heraklids continued to consult him in their need.

It may be that Karnos was but one mantis who spoke oracles to the Heraklids in the early legend. According to Apollodoros, portents—toad,

---

14 G. Vitalis, Die Entwicklung der Sage der Rückkehr des Herakliden (Greifswald: Adler, Panzig, 1930) 45–46. On the Heraklid oracles see Nilsson 1951: 70–72.

15 This is a different scholium from that which quotes L64 and which does not cite Theopompos as authority (although PW 292 think that this scholium was taken from Theopompos too): neither Grenfell and Hunt nor Jacoby (115.357) include it in the Theopompos fragment.

16 Theopompos' sentence, as the Scholiast expresses it, may be taken to mean that Karnos was also called Zeus and Hegetor, which is an epithet of Zeus.

snake, fox—appeared upon the altars that the Heraklids erected for making sacrifices to Zeus Patroos when they cast lots for the three conquered provinces of the Peloponnesos, and it was the Heraklid manteis who interpreted the creatures as representing Argos, Lakedaimon, and Messene respectively.

It seems, therefore, that the narratives which we have from late sources reveal the original oracle-speakers of the legend. In Ephoros' version the Delphic Apollo had become the speaker, but he may not have appeared at all in Theopompos' version. We also find that in the early legend the original direction to the Heraklids, telling them to return to their fatherland, came from Herakles and not from Apollo. According to a story that Pausanias reports (3.1.6), Apollo killed Aristodemos, Heraklid leader, with his arrow because he had not come to Apollo's *manteion*, but had learned from Herakles that the Dorians would return to the Peloponnesos (Apollodoros 2.8.2 says that a thunderbolt killed Aristodemos). But in another story, which Pausanias favored, the sons of Pylades and Elektra killed him to avenge the Heraklids' killing of their cousin Tisamenos, Orestes' son. It is likely that in the earliest legend Herakles, man or god, told the Heraklids to take the Peloponnesos; and that Pylades' sons killed Aristodemos as an event of the invasion. Herakles' command was thereafter so firmly fixed in the legend that the makers of the Delphic version had to introduce the Delphic Apollo by having him punish Aristodemos for not consulting him at Delphi about his plans for his people's return; and this feature brought with it the misfortunes which followed the Heraklids' successful first invasion.

That was the only invasion in the earliest legend, when Herakles gave the direction. Then the Karnos episode was introduced and several ambiguous prophecies with it. Finally the Delphic Oracle moved into the multiple-oracle version and also into the one-oracle version (L60); but it did not take them over completely. The sources of L60–67 more often lack attribution to Delphi than make it. Theopompos and Pausanias (3.13) make no mention of these oracles in connection with the Heraklids (that part of Diodoros' seventh book which dealt with the Heraklids is lost).

Apparently few of these eight responses were ever put into verse. The narrators generally expressed the prophecies and divine commands in indirect form, varying this at their pleasure with a direct prose quotation. Oinomaos and the Scholiast on Aristeides report L63 in direct prose, and Apollodoros' indirect quotation may be a direct quotation transformed; as a divine apologia L63 goes easily into direct prose. Only Oinomaos reports direct poetic forms for L62 and L64, each expressed in a single verse. They were probably invented no earlier than the fifth century.

The Messenian Wars (Q13-21)

According to the legend the Heraklids divided their conquests into three parts, and Argos went to Temenos, Lakedaimon to Aristodemos' sons, and Messenia to Kresphontes. So the kings of Messenia down to the Spartan conquest were reputedly Heraklids. Polyphontes' murder of Kresphontes and his two sons led to the war of Sparta upon Messenia, according to Isokrates (6.23, 31), although the war began more than three centuries after the traditional date of the Heraklids' return. The two Messenian Wars (or a war of Spartan conquest followed by Messenian insurgency) which Sparta waged in the century c. 740–640 are historical, but the story of the wars, as Pausanias (4.4–24) and others tell it, is very untrustworthy; and the Delphic oracles attached to these wars, though set within the period after 800 which we call historical in this study, are no more authentic than the Heraklid oracles and no less legendary in character.

Pausanias has the only complete account of the Messenian Wars and reports all the responses that relate to them except Q13. He drew his material from third-century sources, Myron's history and Rianos' epic poem, in which Rianos told a pro-Messenian form of the legend, developed after Epaminondas' restoration of the Messenians to their country in 370/69. Isokrates obviously employs a pro-Spartan version of the legend, since he cites Q13 and Q18 in the speech that he wrote in support of Archidamos' plea for Athenian aid to Sparta against the Boeotians and Messenians. This version justified Spartan rule over Messenia by representing Sparta's war on the Messenians as vengeance for the murdered Kresphontes. This was apparently not Ephoros' version, which may have been a pro-Messenian account that Myron and Rianos elaborated.[17]

Pausanias quotes four responses in hexameters (Q15–17, 20) and one in iambics (Q14).[18] It is not likely that Rianos invented Q15–17, since he

---

17 See H. L. Ebeling, *A Study in the Sources of the Messeniaca of Pausanias* (Baltimore, 1892); Lionel Pearson, "The Pseudo-History of Messenia and Its Authors," *Historia* 11 (1962) 397–426. Pearson (p. 412) shows that Myron's and Rianos' accounts are almost worthless as history: they followed the trend of Kleitarchos, Hegesias, Phylarchos, and Duris, who reshaped history into romance and tragedy.

18 Diodoros and Oinomaos quote Q15, the Suda quotes Q20, in the same verse form as found in Pausanias. Oinomaos has a two-verse hexameter form of Q14 as against Pausanias' five-verse iambic form; and though it has the same content as the first three lines of Pausanias' form, it is phrased differently.

dealt only with the second Messenian War, unless he wrote something about the antecedents of his theme. It is probable that Pausanias found these verses in Myron's history, although Myron certainly did not invent them: they were surely already in the tradition when he received it. Possibly they had appeared in Ephoros' history; but they surely do not belong to the early legend. It is impossible to say when they were composed: probably appropriate oracular responses were introduced as developing episodes demanded them and first expressed in indirect or direct prose—Diodoros' prose version of Q14 is partly in indirect statement. Apparently no verses were ever composed for Q13, 18, 19, and 21.

The responses, as well as Pausanias' whole narrative, have the traits of folktale and legend. The narrative is rich in manteis, portents, dreams and visions—features that are likely to reflect the pre-Delphic legend. The seers are the Messenians Tisis, Epebolos, Ophioneus, Theoklos, Mantiklos, and others unnamed; the Athenian-Messenian Lykos, Pandion's son; the Spartan Hekas; the Boeotian Bakis.[19] Tisis, a man devoted to the mantic art, was the Messenian envoy who received Q14 at Delphi. On his way back to Ithome a Spartan ambush waylaid him, but spared his life when they heard a shout from an invisible person telling them to release the oracle bearer (*chrêsmophoros*); and so he delivered the response to King Euphaes in Ithome. This was a command to sacrifice an Aipytid maiden to the underworld gods, a prescription of divine will that Tisis himself could have spoken, as Kalchas spoke the divine will that ordered the sacrifice of Iphigeneia. Or the mantis Epebolos could have been the speaker of this oracle in an early Messenian version of the sacrifice episode: for he rejected the maiden on whom the lot first fell as victim because she was not really an Aipytid; then he refused to accept Aristodemos' murder of his daughter because he had not sacrificed her to the underworld gods. In this he acted as the speaker of divine will who supervises the proper execution of that will.

Diodoros, in fact, lets us see how the Delphic Apollo succeeded the manteis in the legendary tradition. When the Messenians were despairing (at a time when dogs were howling ominously), an elder told them to pay no attention to the offhand statements of the manteis, who could not foresee the future in their own affairs; in such grave circumstances they should send someone to Delphi; and so they sent an envoy (Tisis) to Delphi, who received Q14 from the Pythia (Diodoros 8.8.1–2). The

19 Tisis: Paus. 4.9.3–4; Epebolos: 4.9.5, 8; Ophioneus: 4.13.3; Theoklos: 4.16.1, 5, 20.1–3, 21.2–3, 5, 10; Mantiklos: 4.21.2,12; anonymous seers: 4.12.4; Lykos: 4.20.4; Hekas: 4.16.1, 21.7, 12; Bakis: 4.27.4.

elder's admonition is a device for introducing the Delphic Oracle into the story of the wars, a pro-Delphian effort to enhance the Oracle's reputation. By the fifth century Delphi had a significant role in the legends of Thebes, the house of Atreus, the Heraklids, the Mermnads of Lydia; and so it could hardly be that the Pythian Apollo had had nothing to say to the Messenians and their Spartan conquerors in the course of their wars.

Q16 is a conditioned prediction: the Messenians will lose Ithome when the two emerge from their hidden covert, and this will happen when necessity comes to the changed in nature. The condition was fulfilled when the mantis Ophioneus, who, born blind, had acquired vision, lost his sight again. Then the mantis Theoklos understood the meaning of Apollo's oracle. We notice that Ophioneus' blindness followed upon a series of portents and a dream (Pausanias 4.13.1–3): the bronze image of Artemis dropped its shield; the rams that Aristodemos was about to sacrifice butted each other violently and killed themselves at the very altar; all the dogs gathered in one place, howled all night, and then went off together to the Spartan camp. And Aristodemos had an ominous dream: he was armed and ready to enter battle, and the victim's entrails lay before him on the altar, when the daughter whom he had killed appeared, dressed in black—gashes visible on her throat and breast— swept the entrails from the table, and took her father's weapons from him, putting a gold crown and a white cloak on him instead. This was a portent of Aristodemos' death, since crowns and white cloaks were the funeral dress of the Messenians' illustrious dead. Immediately thereafter Aristodemos heard the news of Ophioneus' second blindness, another portent of defeat and death. In the pre-Delphic legend it was either the blind Ophioneus or another skilled mantis who interpreted the portents and the dream (though that is pretty clear without a mantis). When the Delphic version of the legend was developed, the Ophioneus episode provided some narrator with the opportunity of inventing a conditioned prediction in verse which obscurely foretells loss of the city when the seer becomes blind. The failure of the Messenian manteis to interpret Q16 serves the same purpose as the elder's recommendation against manteis in Diodoros' account of Q14: Apollo at Delphi has knowledge that the seers lack; and so his place in the legend is justified, even if his prophecies are too unintelligible to benefit the Messenians.

A prophecy of the same kind as Q13–21 remained unversified and unattached to Delphi. The Messenians possessed *chrêsmoi* of Lykos, Pandion's son, an exiled Athenian who came to Messenia and founded the Andanian mysteries of Demeter and Kora (thus is an Eleusinian origin asserted for them). When Eira's fall was near in the second war, Aristo-menes recalled an oracle of Lykos, which concerned the secret talisman of the Messenians: if they should lose it, a flood would cover their land forever; if they should preserve it, they would some day recover their country. Therefore they buried the talisman on Mount Ithome. It may be that this particular prophecy was not invented until after the Messenians recovered their country about 370; but the episode reveals that the oracles of Lykos were a factor in the legend. The talisman prophecy is similar in content and manner to Q15–17, 20, which likewise indicate strange means of victory or signs of defeat. Rianos' source had not converted the Lykos *chrêsmos* to a Delphic pronouncement; and it may be that other responses which Myron or Rianos called Delphic had in other versions been identi-fied as oracles of Lykos.

There was also a verse-oracle of Bakis on the restoration of Messenia; it purported to be a prediction of the battle of Leuktra, when the flower of Sparta would perish and Messene would be inhabited again (Pausanias 4.27.4), obviously composed after 370 and attributed to Bakis. Pausanias also found another verse of Bakis, obscure enough, which he interpreted as a prediction of the fall of Eira. The verse mentions Messene, overcome by *patagos* and *krounoi*, in reference to the terrific thunderstorm that accompanied the fall of Eira (Pausanias 4.20.7–21.9). Though the predic-tion of restoration must be a fourth-century production, and the other verse cannot be dated (we can only say that Pausanias found it in a corpus of oracles ascribed to Bakis), it is apparent that Bakis as well as the Delphic Apollo had at some point entered the Messenian legend as speaker of prophecies.

As Aristodemos had a prophetic dream, so did a Messenian peasant girl, who dreamt that wolves carried a bound and clawless lion to her family's field, and that she not only freed the lion but also found his claws and restored them to him. The next day Cretan archers who had captured Aristomenes carried him bound into the field, and she fulfilled the dream by releasing him and restoring his sword to him (Pausanias 4.19.5–6). This dream vision is expressed in the same kind of metaphor as Q16.

On the Spartan side Hekas interpreted signs and gave instructions to his fellow-citizens. In the thunderstorm on the night when the Spartans made their final assault on Eira he pointed out that the lightning was on the Spartan right and therefore favorable; and he advised the Spartan commanders to let Aristomenes and his men go through their lines in safety when they abandoned Eira.

The Messenian and Spartan seers have significant names. Lykos suggests Apollo Lykeios or Zeus Lykaios, both prominent in the Peloponnesos. Hekas suggests Hekatos, epithet of Apollo, and probably the name of a once distinct god, companion of Hekate, who became identified with Apollo as Hekate did with Artemis.[20] Theoklos, "God-famed," was a descendant of Eumantis, "Good Prophet," who belonged to the Eleian Iamids, a famous mantic family. Eumantis accompanied the Heraklid Kresphontes to Messenia, as Hekas' ancestor accompanied the Heraklid Aristodemos to Lakonia. Theoklos' son Mantiklos, "Famous Prophet," also important in Messenian legend, is a form of Herakles. According to Pausanias (4.23.10), when Mantiklos had moved to Sicily with refugee Messenians after the war, he founded a sanctuary of Herakles, known thereafter as Herakles Mantiklos. Ophioneus has an alternative form of the name of Ophion, a primordial being, sometimes called Titan or Giant (see Fontenrose 1959; 230–237), related to Python; and so he is likely to be in origin a snake-daimon of mantic powers.

It is evident that the Delphic Oracle is a needless encumbrance in a legend that is already loaded with seers and portents. As if to complicate matters still more, the Pythia in Q19 bade Aristomenes go to Trophonios at Lebadeia for his lost shield. And visions of the Dioskuroi and Helen appeared at critical moments to thwart the Messenians. The mantis Theoklos told Aristomenes not to pursue fleeing Spartans past a wild pear tree on the plain, because he saw the Dioskuroi sitting on it (Pausanias 4.16.5); Aristomenes did not heed him and lost his shield that day. Later when Aristomenes made a foray into Sparta itself, phantoms of Helen and the Dioskuroi turned him back (Pausanias 4.16.9). The whole story as we know it from Pausanias, Isokrates, and others turns on prophecies, oracular commands, dreams, and portents; nearly every event fulfills a prediction or has an ominous consequence.

NARRATIVE ORACLES INVENTED AS DELPHIC RESPONSES

In the narratives just reviewed oracles that were originally non-Delphic acquired a Delphic attribution, at least in some versions. In these narratives the oracles are central or at least very important; there would really be no story without them (a curse or a god's command, which is

---

20 Paus. 4.16.1 introduces Hekas as descendant of the seer who came with the Heraklid Aristodemos' sons to Sparta. All manuscripts have ὁμώνυμος ῾Εκάτου, "homonym of Hekatos," so that Hekatos would be the ancestor's name; but Bekker emended this to ῞Εκα τοῦ, giving the ancestor exactly the same name.

also a pronouncement on the future, is sometimes substituted for an oracle).

There are other narratives that in themselves require no prophecies or other divine communications; but in transmitting and elaborating them storytellers may have recourse to an oracle or develop an episode that requires one; and this oracle may be called Delphic from the start, if it entered the story in the archaic period or later. Or a tale like the Oedipus legend, which begins with a prophecy, may acquire an additional oracle called Delphic from the first. And some quasi-historical—or pseudo-historical—narratives set within the centuries after 800 may contain oracles called Delphic when first told. So in both traditional legends, when told in the historical period, and in later narratives, storytellers and writers introduced oracles as pronouncements of the Delphic god.

Orestes (L7–8)

In contrast to the primary oracle of the Oedipus legend (L17) the oracles of the Orestes legend were Delphic from the first. Whereas the tale of Oedipus requires an oracle at the outset, the Orestes tale has no need of any and did not originally have any.[21] In several passages the Odyssey gives us the whole story and makes no mention of any divine pronouncement that Orestes must avenge his father.[22] Orestes, aware of his filial duty, returned to Argos and killed his father's murderer Aigisthos, who is the villain in the Odyssey: it was Aigisthos who seduced Clytemnestra to his bed and to betrayal of her husband, and the Odyssey emphasizes his role. Clytemnestra's part as his accomplice is hardly mentioned (Odyssey 11.410; and she killed Kassandra, 11.421–423); and Orestes' deed of matricide is no more than implied (3.309–310): the object of his vengeance was Aigisthos. Between the Odyssey and Aeschylus' Oresteia the emphasis of the legend had shifted from the killing of Aigisthos to the killing of Clytemnestra. The new emphasis brought Orestes' dilemma into the story. His decision to kill his mother needed a divine sanction, and since the legend had reached this point after the Delphic

---

21 It is possible that in the original legend Agamemnon's ghost told Orestes to avenge his father, as the ghost of Hamlet's father told Hamlet. For the relation of the Orestes and Hamlet legends to each other see Gilbert Murray, "Hamlet and Orestes," *Proc. Brit. Acad.* (1914) 389–412. Compare the Alkmaion legend: Amphiaraos ordered Alkmaion and his brother to murder Eriphyle. Osiris' ghost appeared to Horos for the same purpose; Plut. *Mor.* 358bc. So the Orestes legend may offer another example of how a non-oracular speech may be converted into an oracle.

22 Od. 1.29–43, 298–300; 3.193–198, 234–310; 4.514–547; 11.387–464; 13.383–384; 24.19–22, 95–97.

sanctuary had won prestige, he got his sanction from the Pythian Apollo. It was probably Delphi itself, or Delphians, who introduced the episode of Orestes' consultation at Delphi, when he received the divine command to kill his mother (L7), essentially the legend as Aeschylus received it (see Defradas 1954: 160–204). The Delphians used this legend to present their Apollo as highest *exêgêtês*, interpreter of human and divine law.

Delphi's interest in the Atreid legend had already begun before Stesichoros wrote his *Oresteia*; for his Orestes, it appears, received a bow from Apollo for warding off the Erinyes (frag. 40 Page). This is apparently the Delphic Apollo. Whether Stesichoros' Apollo gave Orestes an oracular command as well we cannot know; but it may be that Euripides, whose Orestes received both a bow and a response from the Delphic Apollo (*Or.* 268–270), drew his version from Stesichoros, who in turn drew upon the obscure poet Xanthos, perhaps the author of the first literary version of the Delphic Orestes legend; but we know almost nothing more about his poem than its subject.[23]

Pindar does not mention the Delphic Oracle when he touches on the Orestes legend in *Pythian* 11.15–37. He is not, of course, telling the whole story, but he knows of Orestes' sojourn at Strophios' house in Kirra (Krisa) and joins him in friendship with Pylades. The *Odyssey* (3.307) has Orestes return to Mycenae from Athens, presumably the scene of his boyhood exile. The episode of sojourn at Kirra, if not a by-product of Delphic consultation, made Orestes' Delphic visit plausible: if he lived for eight years in the very polis of the Delphic Oracle, he could conveniently and appropriately consult the Delphic god before returning to Mycenae or Argos and get the god's sanction for the awful deed of matricide.[24]

So the Delphic Oracle had surely entered the legend before Aeschylus' time, though his *Choephoroi* and *Eumenides* have the earliest extant references to L7 and L8. Sophocles, Euripides, and later writers follow Aeschylus in having Orestes receive his sanction for matricide from Delphi. Aeschylus alone has an elaborate response for L7 (*Ch.* 270–296); the rest confine themselves to the simple injunction and, except Sophocles, emphasize the matricide.

In the legend known to Xanthos and Stesichoros it is probable that Orestes went back to Delphi after the matricide only for purification. Aeschylus probably invented L8, Apollo's command that Orestes go to

---

23 See C. M. Bowra, *Greek Lyric Poetry from Alcman to Simonides*, 2d ed., (Oxford: Clarendon Press, 1961) 112–118.

24 On a Phocian Orestes who precedes the Argive Orestes at Krisa see Fontenrose 1960a: 227.

Athens for trial, which we should consider a response though irregular in mode of delivery. It is necessary to Aeschylus' complication of the plot, in which Orestes must not only receive purification from Apollo, but also stand trial before the Areopagus court in Athens.[25] The few later notices and the red-figured vase-paintings of Orestes and Erinyes at Delphi are all derived from Aeschylus' *Eumenides*.

L7 never had a direct-verse form and probably never a direct-prose form either (at least fixed in writing). The only direct form of L8 is the trimeter speech of *Eumenides* 64–88 that Aeschylus composed for Apollo.

Oedipus (L18)

Sophocles' *Oedipus the King* has made the prediction spoken to Oedipus, that he was destined to kill his father and marry his mother, about as well known as that in which Laios received a warning against his unborn child (L17). But whereas the prophecy spoken to Laios belongs to the story from its beginnings and was certainly not Delphic at first, the prophecy spoken to Oedipus is not an original feature and appears to have been attributed to Delphi from its inception. Every source explicitly attributes L18 to Delphi with the exception of the Second Vatican Mythographer (230), who surely had Delphi in mind when he wrote ivit (Oedipus) ad templum ut quaereret: "he went to the temple to ask." All later writers who quote the oracle directly or indirectly are obviously dependent on Sophocles' version of the legend. Apollodoros and Zenobios prefix a warning to the prediction of patricide and incestuous marriage: Oedipus should not return to his native land; but although Sophocles does not express this prohibition as part of the response, it can be inferred from verses 794–797, where Oedipus says that on hearing Apollo's response he took care not to go back to Corinth. Yet we cannot suppose that Sophocles invented this response; for he did not invent Oedipus' visit to Delphi, nor did he first place Oedipus' encounter with Laios at the *Schistê Hodos* of Phokis, which would not be a probable scene of meeting before Delphi had entered the story.[26]

L18 is always quoted indirectly, as in Sophocles' *Oedipus*, with the unimportant exception of a late Argumentum of Aeschylus' *Seven Against Thebes*, which expresses it in direct prose.

---

25 Aeschylus apparently combines the Delphic legend with an Athenian legend in which Orestes went back to Athens for acquittal, an *aition* of the Areopagus court. On divine and demonic forces in the *Oresteia* see Fontenrose 1971: 84–85, 87, 88, 98–104.

26 The earliest scene of the patricide was in Boeotia, probably at Potniai near Thebes. See Robert, *Oidipus* 80–93. Notice Nic. Dam. 8J: Oedipus went to Orchomenos for horses and met Laios on the way somewhere in Boeotia.

Croesus (Q99–103)

Perhaps the best known of all Delphic oracles are those which the Pythia spoke to Croesus, especially Q99 and Q100. So well has Herodotos' Lydian history impressed them on the minds of readers and scholars that they have established themselves as typical Delphic responses. Yet most contemporary authorities no longer consider these responses genuine. Clearly much of the Lydian history is pseudo-historical narrative. We cannot be sure of much besides the rule of a Mermnad dynasty in Lydia in the seventh and sixth centuries, Croesus' dedications at Delphi and elsewhere, the war of Lydians and Persians, the fall of Sardis, and probably Croesus' alliance with Sparta. On Herodotos' sources of his Lydian history much has been written.[27] Clearly Herodotos owed much to Delphic informants, but he probably drew also on Lydian, Asian Greek, Athenian, and Lacedaemonian sources as well, both oral and written.

This material Herodotos organized in tragic form: the story of Croesus illustrates the progress of *olbos* through *koros* to *hybris* and *atê*. Croesus, the richest man in the world, had more wealth (*olbos*) than any man needs, and he deemed himself the most fortunate of men (*koros*, satiety). He revealed arrogance (*hybris*) in his meeting with Solon, the first episode (if we pursue the dramatic analogy, the earlier Mermnad history from Gyges to Alyattes is prologue). In the second episode a warning misfortune came to Croesus in the death of his son Atys. Nevertheless he decided to check the rise of Cyrus, and wanting divine assurance of victory tested the Oracles to discover the most reliable. He found Delphi to be alone truthful (Q99) with the exception of Amphiaraos in Thebes, who also responded satisfactorily to his question. Then when Croesus asked at Delphi whether he should take the field against the Persians, the Pythia replied with Q100: if he should make war on the Persians he would destroy a great kingdom. He made war and his own kingdom was destroyed (*atê*).[28]

Chronologically it is barely possible that Solon could have met Croesus as king, but the episode is surely unhistorical: it comes from the tradition of the Seven Wise Men. The tale of Atys and Adrastos is the myth of Attis and Kybele historicized; and Croesus on the pyre appears to

---

27 See Oeri 1899: 7–17; Panitz 1935: 45–49; Defradas 1954: 208–228; Crahay 1956: 182–207; Parke 1956: 126–140.

28 The final episode ends with Apollo's rescue of Croesus from the pyre (*deus ex machina*); and in the *exodos* Croesus rebukes the Delphic Oracle and is rebuked in turn (Q103).

represent the Anatolian god Sandon, who dies in the fire. It is unlikely that Croesus survived the fall of Sardis (see Bakchylides 3.23–62) as in Herodotos' narrative.

The five Delphic oracles have the same function as the oracles of ancient legends, especially those that appear in tragedies based on the legends: they are steps in the story or drama, veiled warnings to the powerful and arrogant man and at the same time incitements to doom. None is like any historical response in mode or content, except that Herodotos' version of Q100 contains a second clause which advises Croesus to ally himself with the strongest Hellenes. This clause may arise from an actual response by which Croesus was advised to ally himself with Lakedaimon. Since Croesus unquestionably made rich offerings to the Delphic Apollo, he may very well have consulted the Oracle. Surely the Pythia would have named Lakedaimon in response to his question on an alliance, since that was obviously the strongest Greek state in Croesus' time and surely well known to him as such; but she would not have phrased her reply so indecisively, as though several Greek states might contend for the rank of mightiest. In any case, there is no historical example of a reply in this form. It is really more likely that Croesus himself decided on a Lacedaemonian alliance, and if he went to Delphi at all, he did so to get a sanction of the alliance (it is unlikely that he asked for a sanction of his Persian campaign).

Not too much should be inferred from Croesus' offerings at Delphi. He made rich offerings to several prestigious Greek sanctuaries, apparently with no other purpose than to win the good will of the Greek states. Herodotos mentions offerings that Croesus made to Delphi, Amphiaraos, Didyma, and Ephesos, and he probably made them elsewhere. At Didyma (Branchidai), says Herodotos (1.92.2), Croesus made offerings equal in amount and quantity to those that he made at Delphi; and yet in Herodotos' narrative Didyma failed Croesus' test of Oracles.

Herodotos' history appears to be the source of all later notices of the Croesus oracles except that of Nicolaus of Damascus, whose source is probably Xanthos' Lydian history. Nicolaus tells a story of Croesus on the pyre which differs in several details from Herodotos' version. Yet it is essentially the same story: in both versions the Pythian Apollo had spoken Q100 to Croesus; Cyrus put Croesus on a pyre after taking Sardis; Apollo sent a rainstorm to save Croesus from the flames; and Croesus asked Cyrus to let him send chains to Apollo at Delphi and rebuke the god (Q103). So the pyre story with its antecedents was already current in Greek oral and written tradition in the fifth century, and both Herodotos and Xanthos incorporated it in their histories. To this nuclear narrative Herodotos added other tales that the Croesus tradition brought him.

Q99

The test oracle is no more likely to be genuine than Q92, Q239, and L155. In Q92 Glaukos dared to ask Apollo whether he might perjure himself for gain; in Q99 Croesus tested the veracity of Apollo himself, speaker of Zeus's will. Neither Greek nor Lydian would have been so presumptuous and impious. The story of the test both enhances Delphi's glory and builds up Croesus' hybris, starting him on his road to doom (*atê*). It puts Croesus in the same class as the Aesopic rogue who tried to deceive the Pythia (L155), or as Daphidas, who tried to make the Delphic Apollo look ridiculous (Q239); they, like Croesus, were testing the Delphic Oracle. Though Apollo in Q103 makes no point of Croesus' test, in Xenophon's *Cyropaedia* (7.2.17) Croesus grants that his test of Apollo's Oracle was an impious act.

The theme of Apolline omniscience recurs in L172. Expressions of knowledge and quantity in terms of sand and the measures of the sea were proverbial. Hesiod has δείξω δή τοι μέτρα πολυφλοίσβοιο θαλάσσης: "I shall show you the measures of the roaring sea."[29] The verses of Q99 suggest creation for another purpose, perhaps a riddle, and subsequent adoption or adaptation to service in the Croesus legend as Apollo's answer to the test question.

Q100

Herodotos quotes this response indirectly, ἢν στρατεύηται ἐπὶ Πέρσας μεγάλην ἀρχήν μιν καταλύσειν: "if he marches against the Persians he will destroy a great kingdom." Later authors, beginning with Aristotle (*Rhet.* 1407a), quote an hexameter verse, Κροῖσος ῞Αλυν διαβὰς μεγάλην ἀρχὴν καταλύσει: "Croesus, having crossed the Halys, will destroy a great kingdom." It is expressed in the third person, an unusual form in reference to the consultant even when the response is spoken to his envoys or agents (notice Q101, 102). Those scholars who suppose that all responses must have had a verse form (see Parke 1956: 133) believe that this was the form in which Herodotos knew Q100, though he did not choose to quote it directly. This is improbable; more likely this response had only an indirect form in the oral tradition (though an occasional narrator

---

29 OD 648. See Pind. *Pyth.* 9.44–49, where Chiron describes Apollo's omniscience, especially ὅσσα τε χθὼν ἠρινὰ φύλλ' ἀναπέμπει χὠπόσαι / ἐν θαλάσσᾳ καὶ ποταμοῖς ψάμαθοι [οἶσθα] (46–47). See Crahay 1956: 193, who also points out the echo in Q99's third verse of Homeric Hymn 4.48.

might choose to express it in direct prose). By Herodotos' time verse forms had been devised for Q99, 101, 102, but not for Q100 and Q103.

Q100 is often cited as a typical example of Delphi's clever ambiguities: whatever the outcome, it is said, the Oracle will be proved right. This is to say that every war must be decisive, which is obviously far from true: Croesus' campaign could have ended without destruction of either kingdom. Hence Q100 is clearly a *post eventum* composition.

Q101

Croesus' third response is introduced with *All' hotan* (But when), a characteristic opening of traditional oracles, especially chresmologic productions, as we shall see in chapter 6. It was spoken after the fall of Astyages (550 B.C.), when Cyrus became king of all Iran. If we accept the narrative as history, it must have been spoken about 547. Yet Apollo tells Croesus that his kingdom will endure until the Medes have a mule for king, which appears to say that this will happen in the future, if it is going to happen at all. Furthermore *Lyde podabre* (tenderfooted Lydian) suits the condition of Lydians under Persian domination in the fifth century rather than the warrior Lydians of the Mermnad kingdom.[30]

Q102

Herodotos tells us plainly that Q101 was the second oracle that Croesus received after his test. He then takes the story through to the fall of Sardis. Only in his account of the fall does he mention Q102, when Croesus' mute son cried out and saved his father; for Croesus, having consulted Delphi about a cure for his son's malady, was told that he should not want to hear his son's voice, who would first speak on an evil day. For a consistent narrative this consultation would have to be later than Q101, that is, probably in the year preceding the fall of Sardis, and thus fulfilled soon after it was spoken. Croesus would have received this fairly plain warning of disaster in the midst of his preparations for invading the Persian dominions. Hence Q102 seems unconnected with Q99–101 and more fittingly spoken years before the fall of Sardis. We would suppose that Croesus would have taken measures for his son's cure soon after the death of Atys; so probably Q102 came to Herodotos from a different source.

Q103

The theme of divine *apologia* following upon a consultant's rebuke of Apollo for having misled him occurs in L63, spoken to the Heraklids.

---

30 See Crahay 1956: 199–201; on Q102 see 186–188.

As in the Heraklid legend, so in the Croesus tale the consultant receives a series of oracles which he misunderstands. After disaster he reproaches Apollo, who then makes his defense, explaining his previous responses, in the form of a response spoken by the Pythia. The Heraklids, however, achieve final success thereafter; for Croesus all is lost.

The Croesus legend had several versions; the legend was built on oracles; and the oracles were called Delphic from the start (though the possibility of a Didymaean version must not be ruled out). Although some later writers do not specify Delphi, most name Apollo as oracle-speaker, surely meaning the Delphic Apollo; and the few who are less specific surely intend a Delphic oracle.

Lykurgos (Q7)

Since it is probable that the Delphic Oracle sanctioned the so-called Lycurgan constitutional reforms of Sparta (Q8), perhaps sometime in the seventh century, the legend of the lawgiver Lykurgos, including response Q7, must have been formed somewhat later. As Eduard Meyer pointed out, the only thing about Lykurgos that the sources agree upon is that the Spartans worshiped him as a god. He had a sanctuary (*hieron*) in Sparta and received annual sacrifices. He was an old Laconian god, the Wolf-worker, probably related to the Arcadian Lykaon and Zeus Lykaios.[31] Meyer suggested that Q7 was the Delphic sanction of the cult of Lykurgos as a god in Sparta. More likely the Spartan cult of Lykurgos antedates the Delphic oracular establishment. Moreover the form and content are not those in which sanctions were expressed.

---

31 See Herod. 1.65; Strabo 8.5.5, p. 366; Paus. 3.16.6; Plut. *Lyk.* 1. On Lykurgos as god see Eduard Meyer, *Forschungen zur alten Geschichte* (Halle, 1892) 1.269–283; H. Jean-maire, *Couroi et Courètes* (Lille: Bibliothèque Universitaire, 1939) 582–588; A. H. M. Jones, *Sparta* (Oxford: Blackwell, 1967) 5–7. Some historians still believe in an historical Lykurgos; see H. Michell, *Sparta* (Cambridge Univ. Press, 1952) 19–25; G. L. Huxley, *Early Sparta* (Cambridge, Mass.: Harvard Univ. Press, 1962) 40–43; W. den Boer, *Laconian Studies* (Amsterdam: North-Holland Publ. Co., 1954) 154 note 1. K. M. T. Chrimes assumes the historicity of Lykurgos in her argument on his date in *Ancient Sparta* (Manchester Univ. Press, 1949) 305–347; see den Boer, *op. cit.* 104–126. The so-called Olympic discus on which the names of Lykurgos and Iphitos were inscribed as founders of the Olympic truce along with the rules of the games is a weak support for an historical Lykurgos who would be a contemporary of Iphitos around 776; Iphitos is himself a shadowy figure. For the discus see Aristotle frag. 533 Rose *ap.* Plut. *Lyc.* 1; Phlegon *Ol.* 1.4; Paus. 5.20.1. The discus does not survive; we do not know what kind of letters were inscribed on it; and in any case it could not have been inscribed in 776 or thereabouts—there was no writing then—and probably not before 700 at the earliest. The names of Lykurgos and Iphitos were inscribed on the discus (perhaps later than the rules) to support the tradition that they were the founders. Again we may see the lawgiver god: he devised the Olympic laws as well as Sparta's. His son was Eukosmos, according to Paus. 3.16.6.; i.e., the god was father of the constitution.

The hexameter oracle itself points to Lykurgos' divine character in the third and fourth verses. In Herodotos' story, as soon as Lykurgos entered the megaron of the temple, and before he could ask his question, the Pythia greeted him with Q7. The spontaneous response is characteristic of Legendary oracles. As L41 begins with the statement that Hesiod, dear to the Muses, is entering Apollo's temple, Q7 begins with an address to Lykurgos in the second person: "Lykurgos, dear to Zeus and all the Olympians, you have come to my rich temple." Besides this greeting the verse response has no more to express than the god's uncertainty whether to address Lykurgos as god or man. There is no message, if the four verses that Herodotos quotes are the whole response. It may well be that its lack of message caused someone to add the two hexameters that Diodoros quotes; but they amount to no more than a statement that Apollo will give Sparta the finest constitution of any city's. In Diodoros' account Lykurgos received Q9 as his constitutional response in a separate consultation; and that is of little use to a would-be lawgiver, who is merely advised to guide his people on the road that leads through courage and concord to the house of freedom, and to avoid the road that leads through strife and ruin to the house of slavery—after that Lykurgos might well go to Crete to find the laws that he needed (see Herodotos 1.65.4).

Kypselos (Q59–61)

In Herodotos' account (5.92) of the meeting of the Peloponnesian states to hear Sparta's proposal that the Peisistratids be restored to Athens, the Corinthian Sosikles spoke against restoration. In his speech he recounted the origins of the Kypselid dynasty at Corinth, quoting Q59–61 as part of the story. The speech is fictitious and the narrative mingles Corinthian legend with history.[32] It is the source of all later notices of the Kypselos legend and of the oracles quoted in it, except apparently that of Nicolaus of Damascus, who has details not mentioned in Herodotos' story and perhaps drawn from Hellanikos or Androtion. But Nicolaus does not quote the verses: his indirect quotation of Q60 is an interpretation of it rather than an accurate report of its content; and all that he says about Q61 is that Kypselos received a favorable response (*sympherousan phêmên*).

In truth the three responses show the traits of Legendary oracles. All

---

32 See Crahay 1956: 234–246; Parke 1956: 115–120. Parke recognizes the *post eventum* character of Q59–60, spoken to Eetion, but he thinks them "forged" in Kypselos' lifetime, and he is ready to accept Q61 as genuine, except the third line. See also W. G. Forrest, *The Emergence of Greek Democracy* (London: Weidenfeld and Nicolson, 1966) 111, 121–122.

three are prophecies and two are obscurely phrased (mode E3).³³ The obscurities are plays on the name of Eetion, Kypselos' father, said to be from Petra (hence eagle and stone). Moreover Q59 is a spontaneous response, and so apparently is Q61. In Q61 Kypselos is greeted in the same words as is Hesiod in L41, Ὄλβιος οὗτος ἀνὴρ ὃς ἐμὸν δόμον ἐσκαταβαίνει (ἀμφιπολεύει, L41: "Blessed is this man who enters my house"); and the second line in both begins with the visitor's name; then both continue with a prediction of great fame followed by final doom for either the consultant or his descendants. It is a formula of narrative prophecies.

Q59 and Q61 were obviously invented as Delphic responses. Q60, however, probably was an anonymous oracle. Only in the Anthology is it labeled Delphic. Herodotos says only that it had come to the Bakchiads' knowledge at an earlier time (some indefinite time before Eetion received Q59); and Nicolaus says the same thing. The first two verses are a riddle, which no doubt antedates the Kypselid legend; and it does not fit the situation very well.

Adventitious Oracles

Although the Orestes legend had no oracle to begin with, L7 and L8 were introduced into it as Delphic pronouncements. Some other ancient legends require no oracles in their basic plots and were originally told without them; later in the course of their transmission they became embellished with prophecies or oracular commands, which were not considered Delphic at first, but which eventually acquired a Delphic attribution in some versions. Such are the legends of Alkmaion (L38–40), Herakles (L107–114, 119–120), and the Trojan War (L1, 56, 98–100, 122). In the earliest Alkmaion legend it was Amphiaraos himself who before his death ordered his sons to kill their mother and to make war on Thebes.³⁴ In the Herakles legend it was first Eurystheus himself who ordered the hero to perform labors for him; then Zeus entered the story to ordain the labors and also Herakles' servitude to Omphale.³⁵ And we have seen that in the legends of the Trojan War, as they appear in the Homeric poems,

---

33 Herodotos also calls Q61 *amphidexion*, though the three verses quoted are clear enough, so that How *ad loc.* interprets the adjective as "two-edged," in that it indicates success for Kypselos, but an end to the dynasty thereafter.

34 Apollod. 3.6.2; Diod. 4.65.6; Hyg. *Fab.* 73; cf. the prophecy of the dead Amphiaraos, predicting victory of the Epigonoi and the death of Adrastos' son, Pind. *Pyth.* 8.39–56.

35 The labors: Od. 11.622; Diod. 4.10.7. Servitude to Omphale: Soph. *Trach.* 248–257; Pherekydes 3.82bJ *ap.* Schol. *in* Od. 21.22; Serv. auct. *Aen.* 8.299.

seers like Kalchas made the necessary predictions and revelations (all of which are elaborations of the story and unnecessary to the basic legend). Agamemnon's consultation of Pytho (L1), mentioned in the Odyssey (8.78–81), is unique, and indicates an early appearance of the Delphic Oracle in the Trojan legend, though it cannot have occurred much earlier than 700. In the Iliad Agamemnon as commander gathers his forces at Aulis on his own authority, making sacrifices to the gods and giving heed to omens and to Kalchas.

Quasi-Historical responses are much less likely than Legendary responses to find their way into established tales that initially had no need of oracles, since most tales of that kind are the old legends of prehistoric times. A legendary or pseudo-historical tale that began after 800 was not so likely to acquire an oracular episode if it began without one. Still, some of these later tales are old legends or folktales transformed, and there are some into which oracles were introduced.

In a speech before the Athenians, King Leotychidas of Sparta told the story of Glaukos, Epikydes' son, and Herodotos' report of it (6.86) is the source of all later references to it and to response Q92. The story is plainly a fable: Herodotos has the king introduce it with the words "We Spartans say (*legomen*) that there lived in Lakedaimon three generations ago Glaukos, Epikydes' son." And in concluding his story the king says that the whole family of Glaukos had died out in Sparta and that there was no longer any house there identified with him.[36] Glaukos is plainly a fictitious person, and the story is a variant of a widespread tale ordinarily told as we find it in Conon 38 and Pseudo-Herodotos (*ap.* Stob. *Flor.* 3.28.21). In both accounts there is an Ionian depositor, either Archetimos of Erythrai, who leaves gold with Kydios of Tenedos (Pseudo-Herodotos), or an unnamed Milesian (as in Leotychidas' tale), who leaves gold with a banker in Tauromenion (Conon).[37] The receiver at first denies the deposit, just as Glaukos denies it, and then attempts a trick whereby he will return the deposit and the depositor will reject it: he puts the gold inside a hollow fennel stalk, which he seals and hands to the depositor. The trick fails when the depositor throws the stalk to the

---

36 Yet Parke 1956: 380–382 considers Glaukos and the response historical: "That a Spartan, Glaucus, did make such an inquiry and receive this verse response can be taken as certain"; but it is not clear why it must be so taken. See also Dempsey 1918: 137–138. On the story as apologue see Crahay 1956: 97–99; cf. Panitz 1955: 71. Surely no Greek would ever have asked such a question at Delphi, and no man who intended to forswear himself would thus reveal his intention.

37 The receiver's name *Kydios* is probably the original of or a variation on the name *Epikydes* of the receiver's father in Herod. 6.86.

ground in anger and breaks it open, revealing the gold. In Herodotos' tale Glaukos' consultation of Delphi, asking whether he might forswear himself for gain, replaces the attempted trick. Then the moral is pointed when after a response—which, though affirmative, predicts that Horkos' son will pursue the perjurer until his whole house has perished—Glaukos asks forgiveness and is told that the intention is equivalent to the deed. And Glaukos' line came to an end. The new moral imposed upon the tale suits the change from hollowed fennel stalk to Delphic consultation.

The verse oracle is based on Hesiod's *Works and Days* 213–341 and owes much of its phrasing to it, as Crahay points out. The seventh verse is *Works* 285 without change; the personification of Horkos comes from *Works* 219; the doom of the perjurer's family is announced in *Works* 284; and *Works* 322 is the source of Glaukos' question.

The preceding pages illustrate the various ways in which oracles were introduced into tales, how they were transmitted and attributed, how they acquired Delphic attributions, and how they were quoted. The predictions and divine commands of oral narrative acquired a Delphic attribution in transmission, sometimes infrequently (L27), sometimes in several versions, so that the Delphic label became established in literary tradition (L17, 60–67; Q13–21). In some instances a Delphic response replaced a different narrative device (Q92) or was introduced for a definite purpose into a story that began without oracles (L7–8, Q7); or, if a story had an oracle to start with, Delphic oracles were added for new episodes, as in the Oedipus legend (L18–21). Or Delphic responses were invented with the original story as integral parts of it (Q59, 61, 99–103).

We have no verse form for several oracles discussed in this chapter, and probably they never had a verse form: their only direct form might be the variable prose statement of a narrator, or as L8, the trimeter speech of a dramatic poet. The others received at some point an hexameter expression.

CHAPTER

Questionable Responses

In the foregoing chapters many responses classed as Quasi-Historical have been shown to be not authentic (or at best questionable). They are transparently folkloric in character; and for many the Delphic attribution is rather casual, an accident of tradition. We must now consider a number of questionable Quasi-Historical responses, most of them well-known from the pages of Herodotos or Plutarch or Pausanias; oracles which many historians and classicists would not want to reject, so familiar have they become as examples of typical Delphic oracles.

THE CYRENAIC ORACLES

Herodotos (4.150–164) reports eight of ten responses on the foundation and early history of Cyrene (Q45–51, 118–120). He distinguishes two versions of the foundation legend, putting Q45 and Q46 in the Theraean version, Q47–50 in the Cyrenaic; Q118 and Q119 appear in his account of Cyrene's early history.

None of these responses is likely to be genuine. Only Q46 and Q48 might be considered to be derived from an actual Delphic sanction of a Theraean colonial enterprise in Libya; but as they stand they are part of a dubious narrative. According to Herodotos Q46 followed upon seven rainless years, in which all trees withered, a god-sent punishment of the Theraeans for having ignored Q45. Droughts have certainly occurred in Greece, but it is unlikely that the driest year has not had some rain. And if a single season (October–May) ever went by without any rain at all, a city would have consulted an Oracle then to discover the cause or find out what to do, and would not have let seven years go by without doing anything. A seven-year drought is a folktale motive, and so is the sending of it for a divine punishment. Q48 likewise followed upon misfortunes resulting from Battos' neglect of Q47; and Q48 was also disobeyed after a half-hearted attempt to send a colony to Libya. The records of certainly genuine responses show no instance of disobedience; this is also a folkloristic feature.

Q49 is an example of oracular rebuke to the consultant, unattested among Historical responses; it is like L57, 141, 176, and Q26, which point the morals of fables. All Quasi-Historical oracles which contain a rebuke are at best dubious (Q26, 30, 92, 103, 112; cf. Didyma 6C). Q50 is the statement that whoever goes to Libya too late for the division of land will regret it. This was spoken to all Hellenes who came, no matter what their questions were (cf. L89). This resembles the authentic Q124, "Free Athens," spoken to every Spartan enquirer; but it is said that Kleisthenes bribed the Pythia to do this. It was nothing that the Pythia would otherwise be likely to do.

Q118 has the features of lame king and god-appointed savior. Battos III was lame, and when he came to the throne, the Cyrenaeans consulted Delphi about the best thing to do in the circumstances. The Pythia told them to send to Mantinea for an arbitrator. The theme of lame king appears in Pausanias' version (7.2.1) of the Medon-Neileus legend (L68–69): Medon was a lame king, and Neileus refused to remain in Athens as his subject after losing the kingship to him. It appears also in Q163, predicting disaster if Sparta should have a lame king. This was not really a Delphic response, but taken from the chresmologue Diopeithes' oracle collection (pp. 148–150) in an attempt to keep Agesilaos from the throne. The theme of the god-appointed man whom the consulting city should summon for its salvation appears in Q18, 53, 54, instructing Sparta to summon Tyrtaios, Terpander, and Thaletas. In response to Q118 the Mantineians sent Demonax as lawgiver to Cyrene.

Q47 was spoken to the founder of Cyrene, whose true name was Aristotle of Thera, in response to his inquiry on his speech defect; and the response assumes that he was already called Battos. Likewise in one version of Q45 Grinnos inquired about his son Battos' speech. But *Battos* is probably a Libyan title that kings of Cyrene assumed and that Greeks identified with their word *battos*, "stammerer"; hence the story of Battos' speech defect. The founder could not have had this name until he had established himself in Cyrene.

The inescapable or enforced divine command appears in Q45–49. The Theraeans and Battos neglected the god's command or carried it out imperfectly, but were finally forced to found a colony in Libya. The legend of L73 is similar: the Aeolians neglected the divine command to sail to farthest Mysia, according to Demon. As in the Battos story the god spoke the same command several times to Kometes and then in the next generation to Penthilos, who obeyed it and settled his Aeolians on the Mysian coast. When the Boeotians failed to follow Apollo's command to found a city in the Pontic land sacred to Herakles, they suffered losses in war; then the god repeated his command (Q94–95). Similar is Q227, spoken to Ptolemy when he ignored the instructions of his dream vision to fetch an image of Sarapis from Sinope.

Like spontaneous response, irrelevant response is a feature of narrative consultations; that is, the Pythia does not answer the question asked, but tells the enquirer something else. In Q45 Grinnos asking about other matters (Herodotos), and in Q47 Battos asking about his speech defect, are told only to colonize Libya (except in Diodoros' version of Q47). Likewise Oedipus, asking who his true parents were, was told with apparent irrelevance that he should not go back to his native land; else he would kill his father and marry his mother (L18). Other examples of irrelevant response are L60, 99; Q41, 249, 250, 268.

Dynastic decline or termination is a theme that Q119 and Q120 have in common with Q61, spoken to Kypselos of Corinth on his sons and grandsons, and with Q245, spoken to Attalos I of Pergamon on his grandsons and great-grandsons. Similar is Q96, spoken to the Lydians on Gyges' kingship. Q119 also has the distinctive sign, ambiguously expressed, that will mark the end of someone's prosperity or security: Arkesilaos III must not fire the oven that he finds full of jars (p. 61). In L75 the Boeotians will lose their country when they see white ravens. This very sign of white ravens (in L163 indicating the right site for colonists) appears in a variant legend of Arkesilaos III: the appearance of a white raven was an ominous portent for his reign, according to an anonymous prophecy (Herakleides *Rep.* 4.4).

The whole history of early Cyrene as told by Herodotos and others is a fabric of legend. The responses may have been suggested by an original Delphic sanction of the colonial enterprise; more likely they have their origins purely in legendary tradition. According to Callimachus (*Hymn* 2.66) Apollo in raven form guided Battos when he came to Libya. Here may be the germ of Apollo's oracular role in the story.

The Cyrenaic legend began in several oral traditions: we have already noticed Theraean (Q45–46) and Cyrenaic (Q47–50) versions. Q51, reported by Menekles, belongs to still another version. Herodotos probably took his Cyrenaic narrative from a written source, a chronicle composed in Cyrene and fitted with "Delphic" oracles. For Q47, 49, 50, and probably Q119 (for which Herodotos' prose version shows traces of hexameters) verses were composed, or perhaps adapted from other compositions. Q50 does not look as if it were originally meant to be an oracle.[1]

THE TEGEAN ORACLES

Apparently all later sources derive their information about the Spartan-Tegean War and the three responses attached to it (Q88–90) from Herodotos directly or indirectly. Hence, although some sources introduce one or more of the three without reference to Delphi, they obviously have the Delphic Apollo in mind as speaker. Three writers, however, who quote a single line of Q88 show a different tradition. Polyainos (1.8) tells about a stratagem of the Arcadian king Elnes and ends his story by quoting line 4 of Q88 as the conclusion of an unspecified *logion*. Two Scholiasts quote the second verse without reference to the Tegean War, but in illustration of the earliest Arcadians' way of life: "there are many acorn-eating men in Arcadia"; both call it an oracular response, but only one ascribes it to Delphi.[2] Their manner of quoting the line suggests a proverb. Likewise the first three words, Ἀρκαδίην μ' αἰτεῖς, "you ask me for Arcadia," are listed in paroemiographers and quoted elsewhere as a proverbial saying without reference to an oracle.[3]

Q88 is the same kind of response as Q100 and many others, the apparent promise of victory that turns out to be a prediction of defeat; the Spartans, like Croesus, were too ready to assume a favorable meaning. The first three lines of Q90 are a riddle adapted to the narrative (p. 81); the final two were added to fit the riddle as an oracle to the tale. Even so the final three words Τεγέης ἐπιτάρροθος ἔσσῃ do not properly have the

---

1 See Crahay 1956: 110–133; Oeri 1935: 20–28; Defradas 1954: 245–253; Ludolf Malten, *Kyrene: Sagengeschichtliche und historische Untersuchungen* (Berlin: Weidmann, 1911) 196–201. A fourth-century B.C. inscription of Cyrene (*SEG* 9.3 = Meiggs-Lewis, *Greek Historical Inscriptions* 5) offers evidence of the Cyrenaean tradition and may point to a chronicle. It alludes to Q47, mentioning Apollo but not Delphi, and quotes what purports to be the pact between Thera and the colonists. The authenticity of the pact is questionable, but see L. H. Jeffery, "The Pact of the First Settlers at Cyrene," *Historia* 10 (1961) 139–147.

2 Scholl. on Lyk. 482 and on Aesch. *Prom.* 450.

3 Diogen. 2.69; Apost. 3.83; see PW, p. 15.

meaning required, but the opposite, "You will be helper of Tegea," and one suspects that they were devised for a rather different story.

Probably Q88 belongs to an earlier Tegean tale of the war; then Spartans, to enhance national pride, devised the tale of finding Orestes' bones and the two responses Q89–90 required for it, leading to Spartan victory. But that victory is questionable: Herodotos does not tell us explicitly that the Spartans took Tegea, and it does not appear that they did so, although Sparta acquired hegemony over Arcadia as over most of the Peloponnesos. Spartans could hardly have been in possession of Tegea at any point before the later fifth century if the Tegeans showed the Spartan chains on the walls of Athena Alea's temple in Herodotos' time (1.66.4).

In itself Q89 could stand as a genuine response, since it merely prescribes instituting a hero cult of Orestes at Sparta as a condition of success in war. It is, however, too much a necessary step in the story; this response must be spoken so that the Spartans can ask, "Where are Orestes' bones?" and be given the riddle of Q90, which leads to Liches at the blacksmith shop. If the Delphic Oracle ever directed the Spartans to establish Orestes' tomb or *hêrôon* at Sparta, the response would either be a sanction of a Spartan initiative or a Delphic instruction designed to fill a gap in the cults of Sparta (at some point Dorian Sparta began to appropriate the pre-Dorian Atreids as her own; see H. T. Wade-Gery, *CAH* 3.566). It would probably not be expressed as a command to bring Orestes' bones to Sparta, but in the manner of H23, 44, 49, 60, (cf. H37), a simple direction to establish the cult. In any case the Spartans would be prepared to supply the necessary bones for the tomb.

THE WOODEN WALL

The two famous responses spoken to Athens on Xerxes' invasion (Q146–147) offer special problems. They lie close to the border of Historical and Quasi-Historical, since they were reputedly spoken in 481/80, and it is Herodotos who reports them. Whatever the date of his birth, which is uncertain (p. 8, note 10), Herodotos seems to scholars too close to the events of 480 to allow any doubt about the authenticity of these responses. He lived many years in Athens when events of the Persian Wars were still vivid in men's memories, and he talked to older men who had lived through Xerxes' invasion. So in general historians and commentators have accepted these oracles as unquestionably true pronouncements of the Pythia. Parke says, ". . . there can be no doubt that we have here the original utterances of Delphi before the event."[4] It is not likely, one may suppose, that forty years after Salamis anyone could successfully circulate these oracles as Delphic, if they were not; for elder Athenians would presumably have known that they were false.

Yet we have to recognize that these two oracles are very unlike any Historical responses and are very like Legendary and unauthentic Quasi-Historical responses. (1) Each consists of twelve hexameter verses, very long for a genuine Delphic response (even longer than most unauthentic verse responses). (2) Q147 is expressed mainly in mode E3, unclear predic-diction: Zeus will grant Athens an invincible wooden wall, and Salamis will lose (or destroy) many children of men at sowing time or harvest. A minor mode of Q146 is E2, clear prediction—the invader will destroy Athens and other towns—a mode almost absent from Historical responses. (3) Apparently Q146 is a spontaneous utterance. Herodotos says that when the Athenian envoys, having performed the customary rites (*ta nomizomena*) about the sanctuary, seated themselves in the megaron, the Pythia spoke her twelve verses. He can hardly mean to include the asking of their question among the preliminaries; and surely questions were not asked before entry into the megaron. Only among Legendary and non-genuine Quasi-Historical oracles do we find spontaneous responses and absence of questions. Again, the question of Q147 is in request form, equally unhistorical. (4) The envoys, receiving Q146 with dismay, were advised by the Delphian Timon to renew the consultation. They did so and received Q147. Herodotos does not inform us whether they made their second consultation on the same day or the next. They could hardly have waited a whole month, a consideration that must be taken into account: for those who consider Q146–147 genuine are also likely to believe that monthly (or even yearly) consultations were the rule in 481/480—they are forced to suppose that Q147 was spoken on the same day. If it was spoken immediately after Q146, this was in effect a compound consultation like those of Q47, 140, 250, 268; L42, 63, 64, 69, 73. Histori-cal consultations show only single question and response. (5) Not only is the long poetic form suspect, but so are the specific content and manner of expression, which closely resemble the Croesus oracles Q101 and Q103. Q146 like Q101 counsels flight before an invader (this is contingent advice in Q101): there will be nothing for the consultant to do but give up and

4 Parke 1956: 170; see How and Wells 1912: 2.181–182; A. Hauvette, *Hérodote historien des guerres médiques* (Paris, 1894) 322–328; N. G. L. Hammond, *A History of Greece to 322 B.C.* (Oxford: Clarendon Press, 1959) 223; C. Hignett, *Xerxes' Invasion of Greece* (Oxford: Clarendon Press, 1963) 441–445.

run. And as in Q103 Apollo pleads with the Moirai to avert Croesus' doom and succeeds in gaining from them a concession of three more years for Croesus, so in Q147 Athena pleads with Zeus to avert Athens' doom and gains from him the concession of a wooden wall, which will remain untaken. No Historical response advises threatened people to take flight (cf. H17), and none offers information on Olympian affairs. (6) Q146 begins *Ô meleoi* ("O wretched men"), which is a common opening of Bakid, Sibylline, and other traditional oracles (pp. 155, 171). In fact, Tzetzes (*Chil.* 9.812) attributes the whole first verse of Q146 to Bakis.[5]

It may seem impossible that these oracles can have been entirely manufactured after the fact, although they show so many dubious features. If they be rejected as completely unhistorical, then the whole story of Themistokles' interpretation of Q147 (that the wooden walls were ships) has to be removed from history, and to do so creates a greater difficulty: how did the story arise and how did it become accepted as true forty years later? It looks as though there had been an oracle on a wooden wall and that Themistokles interpreted it in accordance with his policy of building a strong navy and depending on it.

Crahay (1956: 295–304) sees but one oracle in two parts of twelve verses each, which Themistokles either, in the manner of Kleisthenes and Kleomenes (Q124, 137), induced the Pythia to speak, having composed the verses beforehand; or, in the period when the Persians had cut off access to Delphi, circulated as Delphic oracles, knowing that if all turned out well Delphi would not disown them. He emphasizes the extent to which Themistokles relied upon reported portents to further his own strategy; and it is very likely that he manufactured many of these prodigies.[6]

This is to suppose that the oracles were spoken or composed in the summer of 480, in agreement with most historians, although Herodotos plainly places the Athenian consultation before the assembly of the Hellenic allies at the Isthmos in the fall of 481. It has seemed to scholars that the verses reflect the Persian advance after Thermopylai and their approach to Athens. Yet those who consider these to be genuine Delphic pronouncements must then face the problem of Athenian access to Delphi and must allow sufficient time before the battle of Salamis for the state

---

5 Q146 has a three-part structure (see pp. 177–181), in which the message component is interrupted by a long explication: salutation (line 1), message (1–2), explication (3–11), message (12). Q147 also has three parts, of which the explication occurs at two points: explication (1–2), assertion of mantic authority (3), explication (4–5), message (6–12).

6 See Herod. 8.41.2–3, 55, 65; Plut. *Them.* 10.

envoys to go to Delphi, have two consultations, and return to Athens, and for the debate on the interpretation of "wooden wall" that followed the envoys' return. If one supposes that the Oracle was open only on the seventh of the month (or only on the seventh Bysios, which throws the consultation back to early March at latest, long before Thermopylai), the problem becomes still more complex—but obviously Herodotos' narrative supposes much more frequent consultations. It must be that if there was a consultation Herodotos' indication of the time is about right; it had to take place several months before Salamis.

Herodotos' narrative is the source of all the numerous later notices of these responses except one. Aelian, citing Aristotle and Philochoros, says,

μετοικιζομένων γὰρ τῶν Ἀθηναίων ἐς τὰς ναῦς ἡνίκα τοῦ χρόνου ὁ Πέρσης τὸν μέγαν πόλεμον ἐπὶ τὴν Ἑλλάδα ἐξῆψε, καὶ ἔλεγον οἱ χρησμοὶ λῷον εἶναι τοῖς Ἀθηναίοις τὴν μὲν πατρίδα ἀπολιπεῖν ἐπιβῆναι δὲ τῶν τριήρων, . . .

[NA 12.35]

"The Athenians moved into the ships when the Persian kindled the great war against Hellas, and the oracles said that it was better for the Athenians to leave their country and embark on the triremes, . . ."

The time of the *chrêsmoi* is uncertain, since the indications are here confused: they could have appeared when Xerxes began the war or when the Athenians had abandoned the city or at any point in between. We cannot know how completely or accurately Aelian reports Aristotle and Philochoros, but it seems evident that they refer to Q147, if not also to Q146. The formulaic λῷον εἶναι τοῖς Ἀθηναίοις, "it is better for the Athenians," presumes a question in the same form; observe too the unspecified plural *chrêsmoi*. It is conceivable that the Athenians under Themistokles' leadership consulted several Oracles, asking a divine sanction for abandoning the city and relying on their fleet. The same form of question would have been asked at each: "Is it better that . . . ?" And the answer of each would be expressed in the same terms. The consultations could have been made as early as the fall of 481, since the Athenians knew then that the Persian forces were on the move and would come with a great navy. But this supposition does not account for the debate on the wooden wall. The debate in Herodotos' narrative follows upon the receipt of Q147 as he reports it. We must suppose his story and the two responses built up from the conventional kind of response that Aristotle and Philochoros reported: that the "wooden wall" phrase either was used in such a response or came from a chresmologue's oracle attributed to Delphi (see pp. 159, 165); and that the two verse oracles were composed some time after Salamis.[7]

It is very possible that Herodotos' story was developed in thirty or forty years and accepted as truth even by his elder contemporaries. We do not in fact have any record of how Herodotos' narrative was received or of any objections that his contemporaries may have made. We hardly appreciate the great difference between his time and ours in the reporting of events, the preservation of records, the means of communication, the general state of knowledge. The Greeks had almost none of our facilities in communications and records: there was nothing of what we call media; there was little in the way of archives. We scarcely realize how much they depended on oral reports and how ready men were to believe what they were told.[8]

Actually the authenticity of Q146–147 has no greater foundation on grounds of nearness to Herodotos' lifetime than have other responses that he records for the 481–479 period, i.e., Q144, 145, 149, 152, 153, spoken to the Argives, Cretans, Delphians, and Spartans. Of these Parke (1956: 167–168, 172–174) does not hesitate to reject Q149 (Delphians), 152 and 153 (Spartans). Crahay (156: 304–325) shows conclusively that none can be genuine. The defender of the authenticity of Q146–147 may argue that Athenian conditions of public information and record were much superior to those elsewhere, and that it would not be so easy there to attribute responses falsely to Delphi in one generation.[9] But what about Q149, said to be spoken by Apollo to the Delphians themselves? And yet the story and the response cannot be authentic (Fontenrose 1960a: 198–205). So we must conclude that these two responses are dubious at best; if authentic they are extraordinary and unusual pronouncements of the Delphic Oracle.

---

7 Crahay 1956: 301–302 would have the verses composed, though not just as we have them, in the summer of 480, including the two final verses of Q147 addressed to Salamis. Notice that in Herodotos' account chresmologues played a part in the interpretation of Q147.

8 If around 440 Herodotos was told that these verses were spoken by the Pythia at Delphi, or if anyone doubted his statement that they were, how could he verify their authenticity? There were probably no records kept at Delphi; and the Delphians generally accepted any oracle as Delphic that was said to have been.

9 How (How and Wells 1912: 2.181–182) makes the argument: "The authenticity of the first oracle [Q146] is proved by the fact that no one would later have invented gloomy predictions and advice falsified by the event, as well as by the adaptation in Aesch. Pers. 83f." But what is false? The Persians took all mainland Attica; they burned the city, including the gods' temples. As for Pers. 84–86 it is more likely that Aeschylus' lines suggested line 6 of Q146 than that the response suggested these phrases to Aeschylus. On Q152–153 see Hignett, op. cit. 439–440.

THE TOMB OF PAUSANIAS

Nobody, so far as I know, has questioned the authenticity of Q174, which may be taken as no more than a direction to place the regent Pausanias' tomb in the *protemenisma* of Athena Chalkioikos' temenos in Sparta and to set up two bronze images of him. Yet there are several features of the response and story that raise doubts. (1) Although the direction to transfer Pausanias' tomb to the place where he died is clear enough in Thucydides' account, the second direction is obscure, namely that the Spartans should return two bodies instead of one to the goddess. Diodoros, depending probably on Ephoros, expresses the first direction somewhat obscurely in his version: they should restore her suppliant to the goddess. This response, says Diodoros, the Spartans considered impossible of performance and finally hit upon the substitution of two images. (2) According to Diodoros, the Lacedaemonians came to Delphi to ask a response on other matters, but the god told them to restore her suppliant to the goddess. As we have seen, it is a characteristic of legendary and pseudo-historical consultations that the Pythia's reply ignores the questions asked. (3) A direction to establish a hero cult is common enough. In most cases the cult would be observed at an existing grave; in special cases a new grave would have to be made and the hero's remains (or what passed for them) be brought from elsewhere. But an oracular order to move a man's grave to the place where he died is strange and unprecedented among Historical responses. It has the flavor of legend about it.

Thucydides does not tell the whole story of Pausanias' death and burial as it was told among the folk. He limits his information to what he considers to be true history. And it may be that the tale of Pausanias' ghost had not yet arisen, but it is likely that it lies behind Thucydides' words, καὶ ὡς ἄγος αὐτοῖς ὂν τὸ πεπραγμένον ("and as the event had brought pollution on them"). Aristodemos reports the response, attributed only to "the god," as an instruction to appease the daimones of Pausanias. Plutarch's version is similar: an anonymous oracle instructed Sparta to appease Pausanias' ghost (*psychê*), and the city sent for psychagogues from Italy to exorcise the *eidôlon* (Plutarch *Mor.* 560ef; *Hom. Mel.* 1). Pseudo-Themistokles (*Epist.* 4) appears to have this tradition, since he speaks of an avenging spirit (*palamnaios*, *alitêrios*) "to be dismissed by bronze statues according to the god's oracle to the Spartans on Pausanias." The author Pausanias, however, tells of a somewhat different spirit, an Epidotes, whose function was to avert the wrath of Zeus Hikesios, directed not against the Spartans but against the regent Pausanias himself for his murder of the Byzantine maid Kleonike, which brought an *agos* on him;

and though he tried to remove this curse by consulting Arcadian psychagogues, he failed to rid himself of it. In accordance with a Delphic oracle
the Spartans made the bronze statues and instituted worship of Epidotes
(Pausanias 3.17.7–9).

What we have, then, is a tale of the ghost or avenging daimon of
Pausanias haunting Athena's temple and troubling the Spartans until they
took measures through an oracle or necromancers or both to rid themselves of the spirit. It is a variant of the avenging spirit tale told of the hero-
athletes (Fontenrose 1968: 76–79, 85). After Pausanias' victory at Plataia
and his service to the state as regent, the ephors punished him for wrongful
acts done at Byzantium. Pausanias then conspired with the king of Persia
and attempted to promote a helot rebellion. The Spartans recalled Pausanias, charged him with Medism and treason, and put him in prison (compare Euthykles, Q168). Later, after being freed because of lack of evidence
against him, Pausanias took refuge in Athena's temenos when the ephors
proceeded against him once more on discovering good evidence of his
guilt, and shut himself in a hut within the precinct (the athlete Kleomedes
also took refuge in a temple of Athena and enclosed himself in a chest,
Q166). The Spartans starved him, then moved him outside the sanctuary
to die, and buried him in unconsecrated ground. Plague (or Pausanias'
ghost) afflicted Sparta, leading to the oracular response, which prescribed
the site of Pausanias' tomb and the two bronze images (i.e., the return of
two bodies) as appeasement of his avenging spirit. The story of Pausanias
parallels in every feature the hero-athlete tale.

The story starts from true history, Pausanias' activities after 479, his
troubles with his own city, and probably his death as suppliant in Athena's
sanctuary. And two bronze statues of him were seen by the author Pausanias, who mentions no tomb—besides Thucydides only Nepos mentions
Pausanias' grave. Any other facts are conjectural: it is possible that after
Pausanias' death a ghost scare came upon the Spartans. In any case here
were the materials with which to frame a story on a well-known pattern.
And we can now understand the meaning which the grave and the statues
assumed in the tale: they were the devices by which the ghost was laid.
Aktaion's ghost was laid by burning the remains of his body and chaining
a bronze image of him to a rock (L138). Jason's sons, after being stoned to
death, afflicted the Corinthians and were appeased at oracular command
(L35) by annual sacrifices (presumably at their grave) and by an image of
Deima (Terror; compare Epidotes). When famine came upon the Locrians
for mutilating the statue of Euthykles, the Delphic Oracle commanded
them to honor the offended image (Q168); and thereafter the Locrians

erected an altar for the worship of Euthykles and honored his image equally with Zeus's. Hesychios informs us ($E4750$) that Epidotes is a name of Zeus in Lakedaimon; and probably this Zeus was identified with the Epidotes, averter of Pausanias' *agos*, his avenging daimon. Perhaps the story began as an *aition* of the two statues of Pausanias that stood beside Athena's altar. The Delphic Oracle entered the story very soon: for Thucydides attributes the response to Delphi about fifty years after Pausanias' death; though perhaps Delphi was not present in the story to begin with: manteis and psychagogues would be enough. It may be that the Delphic Oracle sanctioned a Spartan proposal to place Pausanias' grave at the entrance of Athena's temenos and to set up the statues by the altar; but if so it was not Q174 in any of its versions that the Pythia spoke to them.

THE LOCRIAN MAIDENS

Much has been written in the past century about the Locrian maidens, and most scholars accept as fact the testimony of ancient writers that from some indefinite early date the Opuntian Locrians sent two maidens every year, or periodically, to the temple of Athena in Troy, where they served the goddess by performing the menial tasks of sweeping and washing the temple. The *aition* is a typical legend of offended deity: Aias Oileus' son offended Athena when he raped Kassandra in her temple, dragging his victim from Athena's image, which she had clasped. Not satisfied with Aias' death at sea on the Achaean fleet's return Athena sent a plague on the Locrian land in the third year after Troy's fall, whereupon the Locrians received an oracle (L157) which instructed them to send two maidens to serve Athena in order to propitiate her.[10] This oracle is nowhere identified as Delphic; and only Aelian says that Apollo spoke it; whereas, according to Annaeus Placidus, it was Athena who gave the order *per oraculum*.

---

10 See Aen. Tact. 31.24; Timaios 566.146J *ap.* Schol. vet. *in* Lyc. 1155 = *ap.* Tzetz. *in* Lyc. 1141; Callim. *Aitia* 1.35 Pf. *ap.* Schol. A *in* Il. 13.66; Lyk. 1141–1173 with Schol. vet. and Tzetzes; Polyb. 12.5.7; Strabo 13.1.40, pp. 600–601; Ael. frag. 47; Annaeus Placidus *ap.* Serv. auct. *Aen.* 1.41; Apollod. epit. 6.20–22; Iambl. *Pyth.* 8.42; A. Wilhelm, "Die lokrische Mädcheninschrift," *Jahr. Oest. Arch. Inst.* 14 (1911) 163–256 (inscription, 168–169); Walter Leaf, *Troy: A Study in Homeric Geography* (London: Macmillan, 1912) 126–144; Lewis Farnell, *Greek Hero Cults and Ideas of Immortality* (Oxford: Clarendon Press, 1921) 294–305; A. Momigliano, "The Locrian Maidens and the Date of Lycophron's *Alexandra*," *CQ* 39 (1945) 49–53; Parke 1956: 326–329; G. L. Huxley, "Troy VIII and the Lokrian Maidens," *Ancient Society and Institutions: Studies Presented to Victor Ehrenberg* . . . (New York: Barnes and Noble, 1967) 147–164.

According to Aelian (as fragment 47 is reconstructed), the Locrians ceased after a long time to send the maiden tribute. Then a disease came upon their women, causing them to bear crippled and monstrous infants. The Locrians went to Delphi, but the god in wrath refused them a response; they insisted and finally received a reply which is not quoted but which pointed out their omission (Q232). The Locrians then submitted to Antigonos the decision concerning which Locrian city should send the tribute. Antigonos told them to select the city by lot. Thereupon presumably the Locrians resumed the sending of the maidens, but had again ceased to do so without apparent mishap before Plutarch's time (*Mor.* 557c). The Antigonos mentioned is generally supposed to be Gonatas, so that the Locrian omission and Q232 must be dated to the early third century B.C.

Nobody, except Farnell, accepts the beginning of the story as historically true—Aias' rape of Kassandra, L157, and the initiation of the maiden tribute soon after Troy's fall—but scholars are almost unanimous in accepting the reality of the maiden tribute over several centuries and its renewal in the third century at the behest of the Delphic Oracle after an interval of neglect. We are asked to believe that every year (or at intervals) the Locrians sent two maidens across the sea to Ilion to spend perhaps the rest of their lives in menial service to the goddess, subject to various indignities. As some sources inform us, they had to land on the Trojan shore at night and make their way secretly to Athena's temple; for the Trojans were on the watch for them, to intercept and kill them. Once the maidens reached the temple they were safe. As the goddess' charwomen each wore a single chiton and went barefoot with uncovered and shorn head. Obviously they had to remain unmarried. When they died they were given no burial rites; their bodies were burnt and the ashes cast into the sea.

But there is hardly a detail on which the sources are consistent. Some say that the tribute was annual (Strabo, Aelian, Annaeus Placidus); others seem to say that when a girl died the Locrians sent a successor (Timaios, Apollodoros, Lykophron and Scholiast).[11] According to Annaeus Placidus, only one maiden was sent, and she was sent to be sacrificed. A Scholiast (on Lykophron 1159) says that after renewing the

---

11 One gathers from Aelian (*ap.* Sud. K908) that when the Locrians stopped sending the maidens, those who had last been sent grew old in Troy, since no successors came. This implies that their predecessors did not serve to old age. Tzetzes (on Lyk. 1141) says that after sending maidens for a time, the Locrians began to send one-year-old girl babes with their nurses. This is probably his misunderstanding of παρθένους ἐνιαυσιαίας in Schol. vet. meaning "maidens sent annually."

tribute the Locrians sent one maiden; but otherwise the sources, which with one doubtful exception are from the third century and later, report two maidens or refer to them in the plural. This Scholiast is the only source besides Aelian to report cessation and renewal of the tribute, but does not mention Q232; furthermore he says that L157 did not fix a term for the tribute; other sources report a thousand-year term (Timaios, Apollodoros, Iamblichos, Tzetzes). Only Lykophron and his commentators tell us about the Trojans' attempt to kill the girls, though Aeneas Tacticus (or his interpolator) mentions the Trojans' watch to prevent the maidens from reaching Athena's temple (and Apollodoros says that the Trojans chased them); but, he adds, the maidens always succeeded in getting through safely. In fact only a Scholiast on Lykophron (1159) reports the actual killing of a maiden, whereupon the Locrians refused to send any more girls. But according to Timaios the thousand years had expired, so that the Locrians' obligation was ended; and he mentions no renewal of the custom. One gathers from Lykophron and Timaios that none of the girls received burial from the Trojans; but Tzetzes limits this indignity to the girls whom the Trojans killed.

According to Polybios the maidens were chosen from the hundred noble families of the Locrians; and Lykophron's list of Locrian towns points to a distribution of the burden over all eastern Lokris. But Aelian speaks of an attempt to assign the obligation of furnishing the maidens to one city only, which Antigonos told them to select by lot. A third-century inscription (see note 10 under A. Wilhelm) indicates that Naryka volunteered to be the city in conjunction with the family of Aianteioi; and Annaeus Placidus says that the one maiden sent was chosen from Aias' family. We might suppose that after renewal the Aianteioi of Naryka assumed the duty of sending one maiden instead of two; but against that supposition is the fact that the inscription definitely refers to two maidens.

Generally the beginning of the tribute is placed soon after the fall of Troy. Strabo, however, depending on Demetrios of Skepsis, dates it to the period of Persian domination. Polybios seems to say that the hundred families from whom the girls were selected by lot were designated for this purpose before the settlement of Italian Locri, i.e., before 700.

Thus the evidence for the tribute of the Locrian maidens is very much confused. Timaios and Callimachus appear to have had the whole story in some form; Lykophron has thirty-three lines on it; and later writers are dependent on them directly or indirectly. Polybios has no more than a single sentence stating that the girls were chosen from the hundred houses, and he does not mention Q232. He tells the reader that members of the hundred families took part in the settlement of Locri, where their descendants were highly esteemed, that the families therefore antedated the colony; and that the maidens sent to Ilion were selected from them. This information he probably took from Timaios, who simply supposed that the tribute had been sent from a very early date. In fact the evidence for the custom as described above is untrustworthy. Callimachus and Lykophron were not writing history; Timaios was often uncritical and liked to rationalize myths, and we have only a brief notice of his testimony. Furthermore no source antedates the third century. For the passage found in the text of Aeneas Tacticus' *Poliorketika* (31.24), a work written before 350, is probably no exception: that passage, which simply cites the Trojans' failure to keep the Locrian maidens from entering Ilion as an example of the difficulty of preventing planned intrusions, is apparently a later interpolation. It is bracketed by editors Hercher and Hug, and is certainly out of place: it has little to do with the topic under discussion in chapter 31, which is the passing of secret messages into a besieged city. Hence it is very likely to have been written in the third century or later and interpolated in Aeneas' text.

Scholars find evidence for the maiden tribute in the aforementioned inscription from Naryka in Opuntian Lokris (which Wilhelm dates 270–240). It does not really tell us much, and the little information that it yields contradicts the literary sources. On condition of receiving certain privileges and immunities, with which most of the inscription is concerned, the Aianteioi and the city of Naryka "have undertaken [*anedexanto*] the maidens [*koras*]," interpreted as their undertaking the obligation of providing the girls for the tribute. The Locrians undertake to give *tropheia* to the girls' parents and fifteen minas to each of the girls for dress (*kosmos*) and food until a specified time, probably their marriage (here the end of the line is lost). That is, the maidens receive rewards and support as if chosen to an honored position, and presumably they will get married. Later a provision is made for some legal process affecting the maidens who have served: τοῖν κόραιν ἐπιδικῆσαι τοῖν πρόσθ[ε]ν κὰτ τὸ δυ[νατὸν---], which appears to mean that the Locrians are to free the previously chosen girls from their service. One other article stipulates that the people of Naryka shall not give boys as hostages for the girls if they are unwilling to do so. This is of a piece with other provisions of the treaty which establish the inviolability of the persons and property of Aianteioi and citizens of Naryka in their relations with other Locrians: hostages will not be expected of them as a guarantee that they will fulfill their part of the bargain. The clause has been interpreted to mean that the boys would be hostages for the fulfillment of the obligation undertaken by the Aianteioi and Naryka. Yet, if we knew nothing otherwise about the Locrian maidens we would suppose that the hypothetical hostages would be given by Naryka for maidens whom they had received.[12] In fact, we would, if otherwise ignorant, understand *anedexanto* of the first line as "received." There is nothing in the visible text inconsistent with our reading the compact as an agreement of Naryka and the Aianteioi to receive two maidens from the Locrians for an unstated purpose.

In Physkos, a few miles from Naryka, there was a temple of Athena Ilias. This is very likely the temple which the maidens served for a period, having entered upon their duties after taking part in a dramatic ritual of installation. The "Trojans" who tried to prevent their arrival were Locrian men enacting the part of Kassandra's offended countrymen. We may suppose that the girls set out from Naryka with guides; the "Trojans" pretended to look for them—perhaps there were enactments of interceptions and narrow escapes; but the guards always failed and the girls always reached their destination. The report of the dramatized acts was taken by men in distant parts of Greece, who never saw the ritual, to be an account of actual events.[13] But could not the conjectured ritual drama have been enacted at Ilion itself? The Ilion of historical times was a Greek city and its inhabitants were Hellenes, though in the accounts of the Locrian maidens they have identified themselves with the ancient Trojans and are eager to punish Aias' people.[14] Yet it is difficult to believe that the Locrians sent two high-born maidens a long distance across the sea every year for a ritual and sacred service of Athena in expiation of a prehistoric crime. It is simpler to suppose that these sacred acts occurred in the Ilian Athena's cult at Physkos.[15] One clause of the treaty requires all the Locrians to make sacrifice to Lokris Aianteia in Naryka.

---

12 See line 15, [Λοκροῖς Ναρυκαί]ους παῖδας ὁμήρους μὴ δόμεν ἀέκοντας ἐν τὰς κόρας.

13 There are several instances of dramatic rituals or ritual dramas misunderstood as real events: the sacrifice of the eldest Athamantid (Fontenrose 1948: 161 with note 89); the dolphin rider (Fontenrose 1951: 143 note 78); the succession combat of the King of the Woods at Nemi (Fontenrose 1966: 39–44).

14 Strabo 13.1.40, p. 600, may be taken as evidence that the maidens actually came to Ilion: "The present-day Ilians say that the city was not completely destroyed by the Achaeans nor was ever wiped out. The Locrian maidens in any case (*goun*), starting a little later, were sent yearly." But the second sentence may not be meant as an Ilian argument for the continuity of the city; it is more likely Strabo's own statement of an argument for an uninterrupted city of Troy; but Strabo himself did not accept it.

15 It may be that the very cult and temple of Athena Ilias were founded at Physkos at this time to provide an Ilion for the ritual and service.

When did these observances begin? It could only be after the Trojan legend-cycle had been diffused throughout Greece, probably after 700 (Aias' rape of Kassandra was narrated in the *Iliûpersis*), when noble Greek families began to claim descent from Achaean heroes and to commemorate events of the Trojan War. The Aianteioi of Lokris were a clan that claimed descent from the Locrian hero Aias, Oileus' son, just as there were Aiakids and Heraklids in historical times. At some point they reflected on their supposed ancestor's crime and concluded that they should make a ritual expiation of it; and they induced all the Opuntian Locrians to share the guilt and atonement. This is likely to have occurred in the early third century, not long before the inscription of the treaty. This is the time of Callimachus, Lykophron, and Timaios, who probably wrote about it in the last decade of his life (270–260).

The evidence for the ritual is concentrated in the third century. Later sources are dependent on that, and there is nothing earlier (unless the Aeneas Tacticus passage is genuine). Apparently the so-called renewal of the rite was really its institution; that is, the foundation was represented as a restoration after a lapse. So the whole story of the thousand-year tribute beginning three years after Aias' rape of Kassandra is the aetiological myth of the dramatic ritual instituted around 270. This consideration brings us to Aelian's testimony, which is the only evidence that we have for Q232 and, except a Scholiast on Lykophron, for a renewal of the maiden tribute after a lapse. Fragment 47 of Aelian's lost works was made up by Hercher from seven entries in the Suda. The passage is incomplete; there are serious gaps in the account, and we cannot be sure that the parts really belong together or come from Aelian. The first sentence (Suda *Π*3092) reports L157, calling for two maidens every year until the goddess is appeased. The second (*K*908) reports that the maidens grew old in Troy, since their successors did not arrive (scholars refer this to the lapse). The third (*E*1015) says that the women (unspecified) bore crippled infants (*empêra*) and monsters (*terata*); and the men, completely forgetting their transgressions (τῶν τετολμημένων σφίσι λήθην καταχέαντες—an odd phrase) came to Delphi. The fourth (*K*2162) reports that the Oracle would not receive them, since the god was angry at them; but when they insisted on finding out the cause of the wrath, he at last spoke. The fifth (*Π*2918) is a brief statement that he (presumably the god) reminds (*propherei*) them of their omission concerning the maidens; there is no text of the oracle, direct or indirect. The final two entries (*A*2417 = *E*3257, *E*3852) concern the referral to Antigonos.

Without the final two entries we would suppose that the whole story referred to legendary times. If we grant that the first five really belong together and that 3–5 refer to the Locrian maidens, we appear to have a story in which the first maidens sent had no successors; then came the births of crippled and misshapen infants as punishment for the omission, followed by consultation of Delphi and a response that seems to be not much later than L157. The "transgressions" (*tetolmêmena*) of the third entry (*E*1015), however, would ordinarily mean positive acts rather than an omission; and in the fourth (*K*2162) the god who is angry at the consultants is the oracle-speaker, Apollo—if this sentence really follows the third entry. However that may be, we notice the legendary character of the story: all the women bear defective infants; nobody remembers the offense committed; Delphi is consulted, and Apollo reveals the offense and directs a remedy for it.

In conclusion we may not only declare Q232 not genuine, but ask whether it has any right even to unauthentic Quasi-Historical status. There could have been a Delphic sanction of the Locrian rite around 270, but we hear nothing of it; it is not what Aelian (or the Suda) is talking about.

COLONIZATION ORACLES

Delphi has received much credit from both ancient and modern writers for oracles on colony founding in the great period of Greek colonization from 750 to about 500 (see Parke 1956: 49–51). And, true enough, there are about fifty oracles called Delphic on colonial settlements and city-founding: they tell the consultants where to go, often in obscure or riddling terms, and sometimes initiate the project. Some of these oracles are assigned to the legendary period, but others purport to be the Delphic Apollo's actual response to a colony founder (*oikistês*) in the historical period of colonizing Italy, Sicily, Libya, and the Euxine regions. Yet in spite of Delphi's reputation for colonizing and the wealth of surviving oracles on this subject, a very small number have passed the scrutiny of critical historians. Parke and Wormell admit fewer than twenty to their lists of historical oracles, but accept fewer than ten as genuine and give qualified approval to most of these. We have already looked at the Cyrenaic responses; now we shall consider several that purport to be the foundation oracles of western colonies and one on the foundation of Abdera on the Thracian coast.

Q27

Earliest, if genuine, is the oracle spoken to Archias, leader of the Corinthians who founded Syracuse:

'Ορτυγίη τις κεῖται ἐν ἠεροειδέι πόντῳ
Θρινακίης καθύπερθεν ἵν' Ἀλφειοῦ στόμα βλύζει
μισγόμενον πηγαῖσιν ἐυρρείτης Ἀρεθούσης.[16]

The verses indicate the site of Syracuse clearly enough by reference to the isle of Ortygia and the spring Arethusa, whose waters, according to ancient folklore, were those of the Alpheios River rising after its passage under the sea from Elis. Parke (1956: 67) believes these three verses to be only part of a longer oracle; but they are sufficient to define the place and could be accepted as authentic, if it is true that in its earliest years (around 735–733) the Delphic Oracle was consulted on colonial projects and responded with verses of this kind rather than with a sanction of the usual form. The opening, *Ortygiê tis*, is a variation upon the traditional opening, *Esti tis* (pp. 172–174), "There is a certain Ortygia," followed by a precise indication of the site. Furthermore, since the islet and spring probably received their names from the Greek settlers, the verses are likely to have been composed after the foundation of Syracuse.

Pausanias alone quotes these verses, and he makes the only mention of Q27, unless Diodoros (5.3.5) refers to it vaguely, when he says that the harbor isle was named Ortygia after Artemis Ortygia by oracles (*chrêsmoi*) and men. It belongs to a different story from Q31, spoken to both Archias and Myskellos, founder of Croton, when they consulted Delphi on their proposed colonies: the god asked them to choose wealth or health; Archias chose wealth and was directed to Syracuse; Myskellos chose health and received Croton. This response is disqualified at once, since Croton was founded a quarter-century after Syracuse; it belongs to a kind of fable, meant to explicate a proverbial expression. According to Pseudo-Plutarch (*Mor.* 773ab), Archias was one of the Corinthian envoys who consulted an unspecified Oracle when drought and plague befell Corinth after the Bakchiads' killing of Aktaion, and who were told to punish the murderers (PW 398), i.e., to expel the Bakchiads. Archias, therefore, did not go back to Corinth, but sailed to Sicily and founded Syracuse. Other sources do not mention any oracle in connection with the foundation of Syracuse (see Thucydides 6.3.2).

The verses of Q27 probably came to Pausanias directly or indirectly

---

16 For translation of oracles quoted see the Catalogue.

from one of the historians of Sicily, Hippys of Rhegium or Antiochos of Syracuse or, less likely, Philistos of Syracuse. These men apparently began their histories with traditional accounts of city foundations and the island's early days; e.g., Antiochos and Philistos began theirs from the legend of Minos, Daidalos, and Kokalos.

Q28–30

Diodoros quotes three verse-oracles spoken by the Pythian Apollo to Myskellos of Achaean Rype on the founding of Croton. Myskellos came to Delphi because his wife had borne no children, and the god told him,

> Μύσκελλε βραχύνωτε φιλεῖ σ' ἑκάεργος Ἀπόλλων
> καὶ γενεὰν δώσει· τόδε δὲ πρότερόν σε κελεύει
> οἰκῆσαί σε Κρότωνα μέγαν καλαῖς ἐν ἀρούραις.

[Q28]

It is a recurrent characteristic of narrative oracles not to answer the question but to tell the consultant something else (see Q41, 45, 47; L18). Here Apollo does promise progeny, but in a subordinate message; his main purpose is to tell Myskellos to found Croton. The whole expression and construction, moreover, are characteristic of narrative oracles: the salutation with statement of Apollo's affection; the assertion of mantic authority, enclosing the minor message and followed by the principal message.

Myskellos did not know where Croton was and asked Apollo, who replied in a six-verse oracle (Q29), directing him to the right country. When Myskellos reached the appointed land he found the site of Sybaris more attractive and wanted to settle there, but received a rebuking oracle that told him to accept the gift that the god gave him (Q30). No source attributes this to Delphi; and it seems absurd to suppose that Myskellos would go all the way back to Delphi from Italy in order to ask his question. The only reason to call Q30 Delphic is that Diodoros ascribes Q28–29 to the Pythia, though he alone does so. Like Q31 it points the moral of a fable or parable; it is designed to illustrate the maxim. The oracular rebuke is found only in moral tales (cf. Q92).

The identical vocative of the salutations in Q28 and Q30, Μύσκελλε βραχύνωτε ("short-backed Myskellos"), also betrays the narrative character of these oracles. In no Historical response do we find a consultant addressed with an unflattering adjective, an allusion to a physical, mental, or personal characteristic, or to a defect. Compare Q101, Λυδὲ ποδαβρέ ("tenderfooted Lydian"); Q102, μέγα νήπιε Κροῖσε ("big fool Croesus"); Q182, Ἀρκάδες Ἀζᾶνες βαλανηφάγοι ("acorn-eating Arcadian Azanes").

Our sources found these oracles in the histories of Antiochos and Hippys, although Diodoros may have taken them directly from Timaios. Strabo cites Antiochos (555.10J) for Q28 and Q30; Zenobios cites Hippys (554.1J) for Q30; Strabo and Zenobios do not mention Delphi or even Apollo, and so we cannot be sure whether Antiochos and Hippys did so. In any case they told the foundation legend of Croton as true history. Parke (1956: 69–70) rejects these three oracles as "forgeries"; the term is misleading, since the versifier surely had no intention of passing a spurious oracle as truly Delphic; he was simply making verse oracles for a narrative. At any rate the case for authenticity is weak.

Q34–35

As Diodoros tells the story, the Epeunaktai or Partheniai of Sparta, under Phalanthos, deciding to leave their city (or perhaps being requested to leave), went to Delphi to ask for Sikyonia. The Pythia replied in six verses, beginning "Fair is the land between Corinth and Sikyon, but you will not settle there." She directed them instead to Satyrion and Tarentum, "where a goat kisses the briny swell, dipping the tip of his hoary beard;" there they should build Tarentum (Q34). They did not understand the response and asked for clarification. The Pythia then replied: "I grant you Satyrion and Tarentum to live in and to be a plague to the Iapygians" (Q35).

The first line of Q34 is a proverb (p. 86). The opening motif is that of Q88: the Pythia refuses the land desired and offers something else; but the Spartans were deceived by Q88 and failed, whereas Phalanthos and his men successfully founded Tarentum when they had come upon the indicated sign.

Diodoros is likely to be dependent on Antiochos (555.13J), who told the story of the Partheniai's revolt; but in Strabo's paraphrase only Q35 is mentioned. It is very likely, however, that Antiochos had both oracles, and that Strabo has abbreviated the Delphic consultation, quoting only the informative response. Strabo does not mention Delphi in his summary of Antiochos' account; but since Diodoros expressly attributes these responses to Delphi, we may believe that this attribution came to him from Antiochos directly or indirectly.

Since Q35 is fairly straightforward—Apollo simply says that he grants the enquirers Satyrion and Tarentum as a place to settle and be a plague to the Iapygians—the response could be taken as a genuine Delphic command or sanction versified at a later time. But again, as with Q27, to take it so would mean that would-be colonists were accustomed to refer their projects to Delphi in the eighth century. It seems unlikely that Delphi had as yet acquired enough reputation to be consulted on a colonial project from distant Sparta. Furthermore Q35 belongs to the same story as Q34 and the shadowy founder Phalanthos; and the second line after *oikêsai* surely represents nothing that would have appeared in a command or sanction.

Quite another tradition is evident in Q36, in which Phalanthos is told to found his city where he sees rain falling from a clear sky (p. 69). Parke rejects Q36 as "obviously spurious" (1956: 71–73), but is inclined to find an authentic oracle behind Q34–35 combined. They are, however, hardly more entitled to our trust than Q36. Parke supposes the oracle given to the settlers under some other leader than Phalanthos, who he grants is a mythical figure. Phalanthos is, in fact, a form of the dolphin-rider Palaimon (see Fontenrose 1951: 144).

Q40

Diodoros quotes the verse response spoken to Antiphemos and Entimos on the foundation of Gela (c. 690 B.C.). Parke (1956: 65, 67) considers it to be one of the two responses on Sicilian colonies most likely to be authentic; the other is Q27. It is true that the response merely instructs the founders to go to Sicily, found a city at the mouth of the Gela River, and call it Gela. But again we must ask whether a Rhodian and Cretan were likely to go to Delphi for consultation on a colonial project so early in the seventh century. Furthermore, though the Pythia indicates the site clearly, her instruction to name the city Gela after the river arouses suspicion. Generally settlers named a city at the time of settlement; hence the verses were probably composed after the fact and were incorporated in the foundation legend—or one version of it—which Hippys or Antiochos then adopted for his Sicilian history as a true account of Gela's origins.

In another version, perhaps also reported by one of the same historians, the consultants were Antiphemos and Lakios, brothers, who went to Delphi and received no response to their inquiry; instead the Pythia told Lakios to sail to the sunrise. Thereupon Antiphemos laughed, and the Pythia told him to sail to the sunset and found a city (Q41), which was named Gela after his laughter (*gelôs*): thus Aristainetos, an otherwise unknown historian, tells the story. The other sources do not mention Lakios. The earliest, Theopompos (322GH), does not mention Delphi, and the oracle merely tells Antiphemos that he will found a city; he laughed, because founding a city had been far from his expectations. We know

Theopompos' testimony only from some verses of Tzetzes quoted by the Scholiast on Thucydides (6.4.3); and it may be that he is not reliably reported. Q41 is obviously spurious: it belongs to an anecdote that plays upon the city's name.

In still another account (Zenobios 1.54) Antiphemos and Entimos were told by an anonymous oracle to beware of the four-eared. They paid no attention to it and were killed by the bandit Phoinix, called the four-eared (*tetraôtos*). Although Q40 lacks the folktale character of this oracle and of Q41, it nevertheless comes out of the same kind of material, the legends that grew up around the founding of Greek cities overseas.

Q43

According to Plutarch, Timesias of Klazomenai, founder of Abdera on the Thracian coast of the Aegean (c. 650 B.C.), received an oracle on his colony: Σμῆνα μελισσάων τάχα τοι καὶ σφῆκες ἔσονται, "Swarms of bees will soon be wasps for you." Plutarch does not make clear whether this is the whole oracle or only one line of it; he also does not specify Delphi as the place where it was spoken; and it is unlikely that a man from Klazomenai would have gone to Delphi for an oracle, especially in the seventh century, rather than to Didyma or another Asian Oracle. Herodotos (1.168) informs us that Timesias, after founding Abdera, was driven out by hostile Thracians; but the later Teian settlers honored him as a hero (probably as *oikistês*). He mentions no oracle. Parke (1956: 61) thinks that Q43 was never spoken from the tripod, but invented by Delphians to impress the Teians with their god's foreknowledge as demonstrated in the first founding of the city; but this seems improbable. The verse is a proverb and certainly not composed as an oracle. At some point it was introduced into the legend of Abdera's beginnings as an obscure prediction of Timesias' experience with the native Thracians.

The only Historical Delphic oracles on the founding of a colony are H6, which sanctioned the Spartans' decision to establish a colony in Trachinia, and H14, which sanctioned the Parians' colony on Pharos. H6 was spoken in 426 and H14 after 385, long after the colonization era. There is no oracle on the founding of an overseas colony that is at all likely to be genuinely Delphic; and indeed it is unlikely that Delphi was active before 600 in either directing or sanctioning colonies. It was the stories of city-founding, developed by poets and logographers, who wrote *ktiseis* of cities, that introduced oracles which directed the founders, often in obscure language. Oracles became a convention of these kinds of composition, and often they were attributed to Delphi, but by no means always. Generally the *ktiseis* were based, at least in part, on oral tradition, into which oracles had already entered as narrative features. Hence it is these legends and the compositions based on them that brought Delphi the reputation which it had in Hellenistic and Roman times of having played an important role in colonization.[17] No doubt the Delphians did nothing to discourage this acquired reputation.

Certainly emigrants sought the will or favor of the gods when they left their old homes and built new cities in distant and unfamiliar lands. Generally a band of colonists had a mantis in their company, as Lampon among the Athenians who founded Thurii; and the earliest colonists were probably content with the usual forms of divination. If in the pre-classical period they ever went to Delphi or Didyma for divine approval, we have no certain record of it; the "Delphic" oracles reviewed above are not evidence for sanctions of this kind.[18]

Moreover, if we look into the evidence for Delphi's colonizing reputation, we find that it was not really extensive or definite. Perhaps Cicero has contributed most to that reputation in the rhetorical question that he asks at the beginning of De divinatione (1.1.3): quam vero Graecia coloniam misit in Aeoliam, Ioniam, Asiam, Siciliam, Italiam sine Pythio aut Dodonaeo aut Hammonis oraculo?: "What colony did Greece send to Aeolia, Ionia, Asia, Sicily, Italy, without Pythian or Dodonaean or Hammon's oracle?" The Delphic Oracle is one of three, and Cicero could have added Didyma and others. There is only one response on overseas colonies, obviously legendary, attributed to Dodona in extant literature.[19] There is none at all for Ammon. It is not very likely that either had anything much to do with colonization, so that Cicero's remark hardly establishes a prominent role for Delphi in that respect. Callimachus (Hymn 2.55–57) says only that Apollo delights in city-founding and directs the founders; he does not mention Delphi. According to Menander Rhetor (3.17, p. 442 Spengel), Apollo sent forth colonies from Delphi and Miletos (Didyma) to Libya, the Hellespont, and all Asia. Pompeius Trogus (Justin 8.2.11) refers only to Apollo and restricts his activity to Athenians;

---

17 See Callim. *Hymn* 2.55–57; Cic. *Div.* 1.1.3; Pease 1917. For opposing views of Delphi's role in colonization see Defradas 1954: 233–238, 256–257; Forrest 1957.

18 It may be that the Milesians who colonized the Black Sea coasts sought approval of their projects from Apollo at Didyma. A decree of the Milesian colony Apollonia-on-Ryndakos (*Milet* 1.3.155) gives Apollo Didymeus credit for leading the colonists' host against the Propontic natives; see Fontenrose 1933: 234–236.

19 Steph. Byz. 197 Mein. It is like Q41 in that one of the consultants is told to sail to the sunrise, the other to the sunset. Another "Dodonaean" oracle concerns the founding of Corinth: Schol. vet. on Pind. *Nem.* 7.105 (155). See Parke 1967a: 129–131, 179.

but there were few Athenian colonies. No ancient writer attests a unique Delphic role in promoting colonies. Delphi's modern reputation for advising colonists arises from scholars' reading too much into the passages cited and from accepting foundation legends and the spurious oracles in them as historically sound.

Chresmologues and Oracle Collections

ORACLES VARIOUSLY ASCRIBED

Pausanias' narrative of the Messenian Wars, as we have seen, is filled with oracles, visions, and omens. Some of the oracles were attributed to Delphi in Pausanias' sources; others remained the utterances of Messenian and Spartan seers, who in the early legend probably spoke all of them and interpreted the dreams and portents as well; still others were reputedly taken from the oracles of Lykos and Bakis, that is, from oracle collections attributed to these shadowy *chrêsmologoi*, who supposedly lived in archaic or earlier times.[1] We have noticed too that some other oracles are not firmly attached to Delphi and that a seer enters the tradition. Still others that received a Delphic attribution came from oracle collections.

Q204

According to the story, oracles of Bakis led Epaminondas to restore the Messenians to their own country, and Pausanias quotes two verses

---

1 The two-verse oracle of Bakis at Paus. 4.27.4 is a fourth-century production as probably are the "Delphic" verse-oracles on the Messenian Wars. The oracle of Lykos (Paus. 4.20.4; see p. 106) on the Messenian talisman is also a fourth-century production, but is not quoted directly.

which predict both Spartan defeat at Leuktra and the resettlement of Messene:

Καὶ τότε δὴ Σπάρτης μὲν ἀπ᾽ ἀγλαὸν ἄνθος ὀλεῖται
Μεσσήνη δ᾽ αὖτις οἰκήσεται ἤματα πάντα.

[Pausanias 4.27.4]

Then the glorious flower of Sparta will perish, and Messene will again be inhabited for all days.

This is apparently a fragment of a larger oracle. As I shall make clear later, the phrase *kai tote dê* introduces the main message of Bakid and other oracles after a preceding clause of two or more verses, introduced by *All' ho(po)tan*, which defines the time or occasion of fulfillment. Epaminondas also dreamed that the hero Kaukon, founder of the Andanian mysteries of Demeter and Kora, came to him in the dress of a hierophant and, after assuring him of continued military glory, told him to restore their country and cities to the Messenians, now that the Dioskuroi had removed their wrath from them.[2] Then Kaukon came to the Argive general Epiteles in a dream and told him that he should dig between a yew and a myrtle that he would find growing on Mount Ithome and rescue the old woman, as she was suffering from her confinement in her bronze prison and was about to expire. Epiteles found the place and uncovered a bronze hydria, in which he found a tin scroll that contained the *teletê* of the Great Goddesses; this was the Messenian talisman which Aristomenes had buried there nearly three centuries earlier in accordance with the oracles of Lykos.

Thus the story of Messenian restoration is as much permeated with prophecies and portents as the narrative of the earlier wars, to which it forms a sequel in Pausanias' *Messeniaka*. In addition to the dreams mentioned, the priest of Herakles in Sicilian Messene dreamed that Zeus invited Herakles Mantiklos to be his guest at Ithome; and the Messenian Komon dreamed that he had sexual union with his dead mother and that the act revived her.

In his *Boiotika* Pausanias returns to Epaminondas and Leuktra. There he quotes Q204, reputedly spoken at Delphi in the sixth century to the Thessalians, when they made war on Boeotian Thespiai and were unable to take the Thespian fortress called Keressos:

Λεῦκτρά τέ μοι σκιόεντα μέλει καὶ Ἀλήσιον οὖδας,
καί μοι τὼ Σκεδάσου μέλετον δυσπενθέε κούρα.
ἔνθα μάχη πολύδακρος ἐπέρχεται· οὐδέ τις αὐτὴν

---

2 For the Dioskuroi's wrath and its cause see Paus. 4.27.1–3. For the whole story of the dreams and the restoration of Messenia see 4.26–27.

φράσσεται ἀνθρώπων πρὶν κούριον ἀγλαὸν ἥβην
5   Δωριέες ὀλέσωσ᾽ ὅταν αἴσιμον ἦμαρ ἐπέλθῃ.
τουτάκι δ᾽ ἔστι Κερησσὸς ἁλώσιμος, ἄλλοτε δ᾽ οὐχί.³

[Pausanias 9.14.3]

That is, Keressos could not be taken until the Spartans had been defeated at the tomb of Skedasos' daughters. If we remove the last line, the message is the same as that of the incomplete Bakid oracle on Leuktra, and similarly expressed: the Spartans will lose their splendid youth (Q204: πρὶν κούριον ἀγλαὸν ἥβην / Δωριέες ὀλέσωσ[ι]; Bakis: Σπάρτης μὲν ἀπ᾽ ἀγλαὸν ἄνθος ὀλεῖται). But Bakis links Spartan defeat at Leuktra to the restoration of Messenia; Q204 links it to the tomb of Skedasos' daughters.

On or beside the battlefield of Leuktra was a tomb (or tombs) of the Leuktrides, the site of a hero-cult. The story told was that the Leuktrides were the daughters of Skedasos, a resident of Leuktra, or of Leuktros and Skedasos (Diodoros).⁴ Their number varies: Q204 mentions two, as does Pseudo-Plutarch; Nonnos Abbas has three, and others leave the number indefinite. Likewise the young Spartans of the story are two or three or indefinite in number. Sometime before the Thessalian war on Thespiai (according to Pausanias; Plutarch says long before the battle of Leuktra) these Spartans, who stayed overnight at Skedasos' house, raped his daughters in his absence. Thereupon either the Spartans killed the girls or the girls killed themselves. Skedasos, having sought satisfaction from the Spartan authorities in vain, cursed the Spartans and then committed suicide over his daughters' grave (probably the fourth-century tomb was also supposed to hold Skedasos' body). Consequently the Spartans met defeat when they fought the Thebans on the plain of Leuktra beside the tomb.

We cannot say when the verses that Pausanias quotes for Q204 were composed; he may have taken them from Ephoros or some other fourth-century historian. In any case the substance of this oracle was circulating around Greece soon after the battle. Xenophon reports a *chrêsmos* according to which the Lacedaemonians were fated to be defeated at the place where the maidens' tomb was situated; this is the substance of the verse response except for the final line on Keressos. Xenophon does not tell us who spoke this oracle. According to Diodoros, whose source was probably Ephoros, Theban chresmologues told Epaminondas that the

---

3 For translations of "Delphic" oracles quoted in this chapter and the next see the Catalogue.

4 For the legend see Xen. *Hell.* 6.4.7; Diod. 15.54; Plut. *Pelop.* 20.3–4; Ps.-Plut. *Mor.* 773b–774d; Paus. 9.13.5; Nonnos Abbas 10, p. 992 Migne = Apost. 15.53.

Lacedaemonians were doomed to meet defeat near the tomb of the daughters of Leuktros and Skedasos, essentially the oracle as Xenophon reports it. According to Plutarch (*Pelop.* 21.1), it was Pelopidas who received an oracle before the battle: he dreamed that he saw Skedasos' daughters weeping at their tombs and cursing the Spartans; he saw Skedasos too, who told him that he would defeat the enemy if he should sacrifice a blonde virgin to the maidens. The demand was satisfied when a young sorrel mare virtually offered herself as victim. According to Pseudo-Plutarch (see note 4), Skedasos told the dreaming Pelopidas that the Lacedaemonians would pay the penalty to him and his daughters at Leuktra; and that the Thebans should sacrifice a white colt beside the maidens' tomb on the day before battle. The Spartans also received oracles that they were destined to be defeated at Leuktra. According to Diodoros, the Spartan renegade Leandrios revealed an ancient oracle (*palaion logion*) that the Spartans would lose their hegemony when defeated at Leuktra by the Thebans. According to Plutarch, *chrêsmoi kai logia* came to the Spartans warning them to beware of *Leuktrikon mênima*, but they didn't know which Leuktra or Leuktron was meant, since there were three places so named, one of them on the Laconian coast, another near Arcadian Megalopolis. Herein we may perceive a tale of *avertisse-ment incompris*: the Spartans supposed that the oracle meant a place familiar to them and took care to avoid battle there; then unwittingly they engaged the Thebans at Boeotian Leuktra.

So an oracle reputedly forecasting Spartan defeat at Leuktra was current in Greek tradition from about 371 on, in several versions, variously ascribed to Bakis, to chresmologues, to the ghost of Skedasos appearing in Pelopidas' dream (compare Kaukon's ghost that appeared in Epaminondas' dream), and to the Delphic Oracle. Delphi is connected only with the six-verse form that Pausanias reports, reputedly spoken to the Thessalians on Keressos. Why the Thessalians are brought in is unclear. It was the Thebans under Epaminondas who took Thespiai with Keressos shortly after Leuktra. The final verse on Keressos may be an addition to an already complete oracle. In any case it is evident that the Delphic shrine is only casually connected with the oracular tradition of Leuktra, and that Q204 cannot be a genuine Delphic response. It is more likely to be originally an oracle of Bakis.

Q163

After the death of King Agis of Sparta in 399 his son Leotychidas and his brother Agesilaos disputed the succession. In support of Leotychidas the chresmologue Diopeithes produced an oracle of Apollo which warned the Spartans against a lame kingship (*cholê basileia*): Leotychidas' partisans meant thus to exclude Agesilaos, who was lame in one leg. But Lysander, who supported Agesilaos, cleverly countered the move by interpreting the oracle to mean not physical lameness, but illegitimacy, a non-Heraklid king; for Leotychidas' opponents maintained that he was not truly Agis' son. Lysander's interpretation prevailed, and Agesilaos became king (Xenophon *Hell.* 3.3.1–3).

Xenophon says only that it was a *chrêsmos* of Apollo that Diopeithes produced, presumably from a Spartan oracle collection. It was not a response made to a Spartan consultation in which they referred the succession question to the Delphic Apollo. Xenophon mentions no consultation, and Pausanias (3.8.10) expressly tells us that Lakedaimon did not refer the dispute to Delphi. But Pausanias labels the response Delphic, presumably as a direction spoken to the Spartans at an earlier time. Besides Pausanias, only Pompeius Trogus clearly attributes Q163 to Delphi.

Pausanias quotes a four-verse oracle, and so does Plutarch three times:

Φράζεο δὴ Σπάρτη, καίπερ μεγάλαυχος ἐοῦσα,
μὴ σέθεν ἀρτίποδος βλάστῃ χωλὴ βασιλεία.
δηρὸν γὰρ μόχθοι σε κατασχήσουσιν ἄελπτοι
φθισίβροτόν τ' ἐπὶ κῦμα κυλινδομένου πολέμοιο.

Nowhere is Plutarch more explicit than to indicate "the god" as speaker. But one of the three works in which he quotes it is his *De Pythiae oraculis*; and since he generally quotes Pythian oracles in his Delphic dialogues, unless he indicates a different provenance, we may infer that he considered this to be a Pythian pronouncement. Still, we cannot be entirely sure of this. His interlocutor Boethos has just referred to Sibyls and Bakides, who broadcast general predictions of catastrophes, some of which are bound to occur. Sarapion replies that Boethos is right about such predictions of future events in general terms; but when the prophecy specifies the manner, time, antecedent and attendant circumstances, of a predicted event, which comes to pass as predicted, then it cannot be a conjectural statement but evidence of foreknowledge; and Sarapion thereupon quotes Q163, followed by Q238 (p. 161), saying no more than that it was a prophecy made beforehand.[5] Moreover Plutarch's group of interlocutors are at the moment beside the Sibyl's rock.

---

5 Plutarch's Sarapion must believe that Lysander's interpretation of Q163 was wrong; since he cites it as an example of true prediction, specifying manner, time, and circumstances, of when under the lame King Agesilaos the Spartans lost their supremacy to the Thebans at Leuktra. See Flacelière 1937: 161 note 32; Plut. *Ages.* 30.1.

Only Diodoros, quoting the content indirectly, does not connect Q163 with the succession dispute of 399. At a debate in Sparta, he tells us, about 475, following the formation of the Delian League under Athenian leadership, the speakers recalled an ancient oracle (*archaia manteia*) in which the god told them to take measures not to have a leadership that was lame; and they interpreted the condition as fulfilled in Sparta's present situation, when she was powerful on land only and not on the sea. Even if we question Diodoros' historical accuracy for this period and doubt that this oracle was known at that time, his notice is additional evidence that Q163 did not come from Delphi at any time, but belonged to a Spartan oracle collection, perhaps to an official collection kept in the Spartan archives.

Worthy of notice is the role of Diopeithes the chresmologue, who brought this oracle forward in support of Leotychidas. As we shall see, the chresmologues had a great deal to do with the oracular tradition and literature. Q163 begins with *Phrazeo dê*, a conventional opening of chresmologues' oracles. Oracles from such collections often found their way into official collections.

Q180

The proverbial phrase, "an eagle in clouds" (αἰετὸς ἐν νεφέλῃσι), appears in the final verse of Q180. The Scholiast on Aristophanes' *Knights* (1013) quotes a three-verse oracle:

> Εὔδαιμον πτολίεθρον Ἀθηναίης ἀγελείης
> πολλὰ ἰδὸν καὶ πολλὰ παθὸν καὶ πολλὰ μογῆσαν,
> αἰετὸς ἐν νεφέλῃσι γενήσεται ἤματα πάντα.

Blessed city of Athena that have seen and suffered much, you will become an eagle in clouds for all days.

The Scholiast calls it a *chrêsmos* only without further specification. He is explaining the words of Demos, who, after asking Kleon and the Sausage-Seller to read their oracles to him, adds that he especially wants to hear "how I shall become an eagle in clouds" (1013). Previously Demos has heard only Kleon's oracles (61), which Kleon has just said are oracles of Bakis (1003); and Demosthenes has earlier informed Nikias that Kleon keeps oracles of Bakis (123–124). And not long thereafter Kleon obliges Demos with a winged *chrêsmos*, αἰετὸς ὡς γίγνει καὶ πάσης γῆς βασιλεύσεις (1087): "how you become an eagle and will rule all earth." Again in the *Birds* a chresmologue comes to Cloudcuckootown with oracles of Bakis (962, 970), among which occurs the clause, αἰετὸς ἐν νεφέλῃσι γενήσεαι (978): "you will become an eagle in clouds." These are admittedly mock oracles of Aristophanes' invention, but he clearly did not invent this phrase: he knew it as part of a reputedly Bakid oracle that circulated among Athenians in the later fifth century.

Nowhere is Q180 firmly attached to Delphi. Zenobios, quoting only the proverbial phrase, calls it a *chrêsmos*. The nearest to Delphic attribution occurs in Aristeides' reference to it, when he says that "the god" (*ho theos*) has called Athens an eagle in clouds in comparison with other cities.[6] This is the second of two oracles in honor of Athens that Aristeides cites as pronouncements of the city's *exêgêtês patrôos*, "ancestral exegete," whom he earlier (112) defined as Apollon Pythios. So for Aristeides the god who called Athens an eagle in clouds is obviously Apollo; but he may not mean precisely the Apollo of Delphi, since by "ancestral exegete" he may mean no more than Apollo as prophetic god, who inspired Bakis, the Sibyl, and all seers who spoke in his name.

The phrase probably went into proverbial usage from the oracular tradition. It appears, slightly altered to αἰετὸς ἐν νεφέεσσι, in an oracle which Plutarch (*Dem.* 19.1) attributes to the Sibyl. In fact, eagles and lions are favorite symbols of oracular literature, as in Q60, Αἰετὸς ἐν πέτρῃσι κύει τέξει δὲ λέοντα; where "eagle on rocks" appears to be a conscious alteration of "eagle in clouds."

The verses of Q180 show another favorite opening of traditional oracles (by which I mean oracles found in oracle collections and popular narratives, or that floated in popular tradition, anonymous or attributed to Apollo or to a famous seer; in short, all oracles never actually spoken at an oracular seat), namely the hailing of a person or people or city as blessed, *eudaimôn* or *olbios* in the proper form.

Q229

Only Ovid attributes to Delphi the oracle that summoned the cult of Aesculapius to Rome in 293 B.C., when a plague gripped the city. This is definitely a false ascription. Livy says that the Romans consulted the Sibylline Books, which instructed them to bring Aesculapius to Rome from Epidauros. Valerius Maximus confirms Livy and reports what is probably the whole content of the oracle, that unless this should be done, the Romans could not recover their former healthy condition. Ovid reports

---

6 See Parke 1956: 185 and PW 121, p. 54, whose argument is that Aristeides' context, "if it can be trusted," proves this to be a genuine Delphic oracle and not from a collection attributed to Bakis. Aristeides' attribution, if it is Delphic, cannot be trusted, since he accepted uncritically the traditional attributions of oracles that he cites.

the Delphic response in Latin verses, in which the Romans were told to go on to Epidauros and summon Apollo's son, because they had need of him rather than of Apollo for their woes.

Parke (1956: 274; PW 353, p. 143) supposes that consultation of the Sibylline Books was followed by consultation of Delphi, which Livy probably reported in his eleventh book. This is what happened in 205, when envoys whom the Romans, in obedience to a Sibylline oracle, had sent to fetch the Idaean Mother from Phrygia, received Q237 at Delphi, having stopped there on the way to Pessinûs. Yet, on that occasion, as Livy and others tell us, it was the Sibylline oracle alone which instructed the Romans to bring the Mother to Rome; from their consultation at Delphi they learned how to accomplish their purpose through the good offices of King Attalos of Pergamon. The circumstances of Q229 are not the same: Ovid's Pythian Apollo speaks essentially the same command as the Sibylline oracle, to bring Aesculapius to Rome from Epidauros in order to end the plague. Valerius Maximus mentions no subsequent confirmation at Delphi; and Ovid mentions no antecedent Sibylline oracle. Whether by intention or faulty memory Ovid put the Sibylline order in the Pythia's mouth. In doing so he did nothing unusual in oracular transmission. Whoever the reported original speaker, or whatever the origin of an oracle, it was likely to be attributed to other speakers and origins as it circulated.[7]

SEERS AND CHRESMOLOGUES

The four oracles just reviewed received various attributions in transmission. Attribution to Delphi seems to be late, rare, and almost casual, an assumption of the writer or his source that the speaker was Apollo at Delphi. Three of them belong to the swarm of oracles that circulated through the Greek cities in the fifth and fourth centuries. Whatever the ultimate origin of these oracles, they found their way into oracle collections, which were represented as the pronouncements of Apollo or of a famous mantis of the past, Bakis or the Sibyl or, less often, some other.

The oracles in circulation were statements or commands relevant, or interpreted as relevant, to contemporary events and crises. At the begin-

---

7 Other Roman and Italian oracles may have a Sibylline origin, whether in the Roman collection or in popular tradition. Q183, the proverbial "Do not move Camarina" (p. 85) is found among the *Oracula Sibyllina*, which, though not the Roman books—and very late— may nevertheless indicate a Sibylline connection. Q228, supposedly spoken to the Romans in a Samnite war, and attributed by Pliny to the Pythian Apollo, may be originally Sibylline.

ning of the Peloponnesian War, says Thucydides (2.8.2), many oracles (*logia*) were spoken and many chresmologues "sang" in both belligerent and neutral cities. When Archidamos first invaded Athens with a Spartan army the chresmologues "sang" all sorts of oracles (2.21.3). After the plague began, the elder Athenians recalled an ancient hexameter verse, a prophecy that there would come a Doric war and a plague with it (2.54.2). Thucydides himself heard prophecies throughout the war that it would last thrice nine years (5.26.4). After the Sicilian disaster the Athenians felt great wrath against the chresmologues and manteis who had encouraged them to suppose that they would take Sicily (8.1.1). Herodotos too speaks of *logia* that Themistokles cited in argument with Eurybiades before the battle of Salamis, according to which the Athenians were destined to settle Italian Siris (Herodotos 8.62.2).

The populace either received these oracles on pathways of rumor or heard them from chresmologues. Whatever the manner of transmission nearly all were ultimately the pronouncements of chresmologues, whether their own inspired utterances or, more often, extracts from the oracle books in their keeping. These oraclemongers had great prestige and influence throughout the archaic and classical periods. From the late fifth century, it appears, they lost repute among the more educated and less credulous Athenians: the comic poets, for example, lampooned them as charlatans. Nevertheless it is clear, even from the comedies, that they retained the confidence of most Athenians; and it is probable that among other Greeks they lost little if any prestige at any time. Certainly they continued to ply their trade and to prosper in it.[8]

Chrêsmologos and *mantis* are overlapping terms for a speaker of oracles. Bakis, Hierokles, and Lampon are identified by either title.[9] But the mantis as diviner, interpreter of omens and dreams, is not likely to be called a *chrêsmologos*; and the man who did not speak oracles through direct inspiration from a god, but possessed a collection or book of oracles that a god or former mantis had reputedly spoken was not called mantis but only *chrêsmologos*. The *logos* suffix appears to reflect either of the two meanings of *legein*, "speak" or "gather," so that a *chrêsmologos* may be either an oracle-speaker, on the analogy of *pseudologos*; or an oracle-collector, on the analogy of *anthologos*, *karpologos*, *chrysologos*.

---

8 On chresmologues and manteis see Clem. Alex. *Strom.* 1.131–135, 397–400P; Cic. *Div.* 1.43.95; Bouché-Leclercq 1880: 2.93–226; Latte 1939: 850–852; Oliver 1950: 1–17; Nilsson 1951: 130–142.

9 See Thuc. 8.1.1; Aristophanes *Pax* 1046–1047 and Schol. vet. on 1046; Schol. vet. on Aristoph. *Eq.* 123, *Aves* 521; Paus. 1.34.4, 10.12.1.

The chresmologues made their livings as mantic experts, either providing or interpreting oracles on demand. Many won fame and prestige;
some attained official positions as exegetes. Many wandered about, ac-
quiring reputations in more than one city. For example, Diopeithes, who
in 399 revealed Q163 to the Spartans in support of Leotychidas, had
earlier been influential in Athens, where he attracted Aristophanes' invi-
dious notice.[10] Aristophanes' comedies provide our best, most plentiful,
and most intimate information about chresmologues and their activities.
He lets us see them at work in Athens, their practices and claims as they
plied their trade. There is comic exaggeration in his picture, but as in all
great comedy, it is exaggeration of the truth. Among the *alazones* of the
Birds who plague Peisthetairos after his foundation of Cloudcuckootown
appears a chresmologue, who comes with an oracle of Bakis that refers,
he says, directly to the new city. He ignores Peisthetairos' reluctance to
hear it and begins,

Ἀλλ' ὅταν οἰκήσουσι λύκοι πολιαί τε κορῶναι
ἐν ταὐτῷ τὸ μεταξὺ Κορίνθου καὶ Σικυῶνος

[967–968]

But when wolves and hoary crows shall dwell together between Corinth
and Sikyon . . .

The rest is self-serving: the founder should make sacrifice to Pandora
(Earth), and should give a cloak, new sandals, a bowl, and a handful of
cooked entrails to the prophet of Bakis' verses who first appears; if he
does so he will become an eagle in the clouds. Peisthetairos counters with
an oracle of Apollo which comically reverses the chresmologue's Bakid
oracle: when an uninvited impostor disturbs sacrificers and wants to eat
entrails, they should give him a beating without mercy, even if he be
Lampon or great Diopeithes (*Birds* 959–991).

The mock oracle of Bakis is given verisimilitude with the frequent
Bakid opening *All' hotan*, which Peisthetairos' Apolline oracle counters
with the equivalent *autar epên*. The Bakid verses contain two oracular
tags, the eagle in clouds and "the [land] between Corinth and Sikyon."
The latter is employed for the first verse of Q34, Καλόν τοι τὸ μεταξὺ
Κορίνθου καὶ Σικυῶνος, attached to the foundation legend of Tarentum.[11] Originally the verse on Corinth and Sikyon was no more relevant
to Q34 than to the oracle of Aristophanes' chresmologue, who explains that

---

10 Aristoph. *Eq.* 1084–1085, *Vesp.* 380, *Aves* 988 with Schol. vet.; Plut. *Per.* 32.
11 The message of Q34 begins with verse 3 (see Diodoros' version). I believe that the
first two verses came from, or were adapted from, a Bakid oracle.

"Corinth" is Bakis' riddle for the air. Somewhat altered, the same verse appears in an oracle spoken to Aesop.[12] It appears that this expression, varied according to circumstances, was a floating oracle fragment of the later fifth century, attributed to Bakis or to Apollo.

In the *Peace* (1043–1126) the chresmologue Hierokles appears at Trygaios' sacrifice to Eirene in now peaceful Athens. When he has learned the purpose of the sacrifice he begins to recite an oracle, Ὦ μέλεοι θνητοὶ καὶ νήπιοι (1063): "O wretched and foolish mortals." The introductory *Ô meleoi* appears elsewhere in oracles of Bakis and the Sibyl. Hierokles professes to be reciting an oracle of Bakis:

> Εἰ γὰρ μὴ νύμφαι γε θεαὶ Βάκιν ἐξαπάτασκον
> μηδὲ Βάκις θνητοὺς μηδ᾽ αὖ νύμφαι Βάκιν αὐτὸν
> Τr. Ἐξώλης ἀπόλοι᾽ εἰ μὴ παύσαιο βακίζων.
>
> [1070–1072; cf. 1119]

For if the nymphs did not deceive Bakis, nor Bakis mortals, nor the nymphs Bakis himself—Trygaios. Be damned, if you don't stop Bakizing.

His oracle, often interrupted, expresses an objection to making peace at this time, and not "until a wolf marries a ewe"; the condition precedent is expressed in a proverbial metaphor. His speech incorporates two more proverbial expressions, "You will never make the crab walk straight," and "You will never make the rough *echinos* (hedgehog or urchin) smooth." We have already observed proverbial expressions in the Bakid oracle of the *Birds'* chresmologue. Recourse to proverbs, we have seen, is characteristic of traditional oracles.

Trygaios counters Hierokles with a *chrêsmos* which he attributes to Homer, and Hierokles replies that the Sibyl did not speak it (1095; cf. 1116). Trygaios then quotes two verses from the Iliad (9.63–64). Hierokles now recites, Φράζεο δὴ μή πώς σε δόλῳ φρένας ἐξαπατήσας/ἰκτῖνος μάρψῃ (1099–1100): "Take care that a kite doesn't beguile you and grab you," in which we observe again a favorite opening of Bakid and other traditional oracles.

Hierokles was a real chresmologue, prominent in Athens in the later fifth century, whither he came from Oreos in Euboea (*Peace* 1047, 1125); so that he appears to be, like Diopeithes, a wandering practitioner of his art, or at least not resident all his life in one city (Latte 1939: 852). He is

---

12 See p. 86 and Athen. 5.219a; Aristeides *Or.* 49, pp. 493–494; Schol. vet. on Aristoph. *Aves* 968 (who seem to suppose that this was Aristophanes' model); Suda Ει337.

mentioned in a treaty between Athens and Chalkis in 446/5: he was to choose three men to assist him in making the treaty-confirming sacrifices for Chalkis in accordance with the oracles.[13]

In the Apolline oracle which Peisthetairos recites to the chresmologue (*Birds* 983–988), Lampon is coupled with Diopeithes; neither should be spared a severe beating if he should turn out to be the uninvited impostor. Earlier in the play Peisthetairos refers to Lampon's habit of swearing by the goose whenever he said something deceitful, as an example of oaths sworn by birds instead of gods (521). Besides this oath and Lampon's gluttony—the object of comic poets' jibes—only two events of his life are reported. When he was shown a ram of single horn, he interpreted the prodigy to mean that power in Athens, then divided between Perikles and Thucydides, would settle on just one of them, on him in whose presence the sign had occurred (presumably Perikles). Anaxagoras cut the ram's head open and revealed the physical cause of the phenomenon; yet Thucydides soon after went into exile, and Lampon won acclaim as a true prophet (Plutarch *Perikles* 6.2). More important was Lampon's participation in the Athenian colonization of Thurii in 444/3 as head mantis, apparently with the official title of exegete. He and his staff of manteis were known thereafter as *Thûriomanteis*. According to an Aristophanic Scholiast (on *Clouds* 332) he produced many oracles about the colony.[14]

It could have been Lampon who composed Q186 on drinking water in measure and eating bread without measure. Diodoros mentions no consultation, saying only that the colonists, whose leaders were Lampon and Xenokritos, received an oracle from Apollo. It is possible that Lampon devised the oracle with full knowledge of the country around Sybaris-Thurii, availing himself of the riddle or proverbial phrase about water in measure (p. 81).

Aristophanes also mentions the seer Stilbides. In the *Peace* (1026–1032), just before the appearance of Hierokles, Trygaios begins preparations for sacrifice and asks the chorus whether he is not laying the wood down like a mantis; and in the next speech he substitutes the name *Stilbides* for *mantis*. According to the Scholiast, Stilbides was a celebrated seer of the kind who expounded old oracles, which may mean that he was an official exegete or that he carried his own collection. He accompanied the Athenians to Sicily as the mantis whom Nikias trusted most, and he

---

13 IG I².39.63–66. He was also a butt of the comic poet Eupolis; see Schol. vet. on Aristoph. *Pax* 1046.

14 See Diod. 12.10.4–6; Phot. *Lex.* 1.282 Naber; Schol. vet. and rec. on Aristoph. *Nub.* 332, *Aves* 988. Lampon was ridiculed by other comic poets, Kratinos, Lysippos, and Kallias; see Athen. 8.344ef. The Scholiasts call Lampon both mantis and chresmologue.

died there, leaving Nikias without a skilled mantis at a critical time.[15]

Aristophanes lets us see chresmologues most intimately, though in an unfavorable light. Herodotos too has much to say about chresmologues and manteis who were active from fifty to one hundred years before Aristophanes began writing his comedies. He mentions the Athenian *chrêsmologoi*, apparently the city's official interpreters, who interpreted Q147 as predicting an Athenian defeat in a naval battle at Salamis, but were proved wrong in the event and to be less skillful interpreters of the god's words than Themistokles (7.142.3–143.1).

The most revealing information about chresmologic practice is found in Herodotos' account of Onomakritos (7.6.3–5), Athenian chresmologue and arranger (*diathetês*) of the oracles of Musaios. He had reputation and influence as a friend of the Peisistratids; but Hipparchos expelled him from Athens for inserting into the oracles of Musaios a spurious prophecy that the islands off Lemnos would disappear into the sea. Later the exiled Peisistratids, now reconciled with him, took him with them to Xerxes' court at Susa, where he read some of his oracles, omitting those that were unfavorable to the Persians and revealing only those that promised Xerxes success in the proposed invasion of Greece—for example, a prophecy that a Persian, leading the march, was destined to bridge the Hellespont. Pausanias (1.22.7) believed that a verse on the gift of flying that Musaios received from Boreas was an invention of Onomakritos, and that the only genuine composition of Musaios was a hymn to Demeter. Christian writers asserted that all the oracles and poems of Musaios and Orpheus were Onomakritos' compositions.[16]

Another chresmologue who supported the Peisistratids was Amphilytos the Acarnanian, who encouraged Peisistratos in his successful attempt to seize Athens and establish his third tyranny with the verses:

Ἔρριπται δ' ὁ βόλος, τὸ δὲ δίκτυον ἐκπεπέτασται,
θύννοι δ' οἰμήσουσι σεληναίης διὰ νυκτός.

[Herodotos 1.62.4]

The cast is made, the net is spread, and the tuna will leap on a moonlit night.[17]

---

15 Philochoros 328.135J *ap.* Schol. vet. *in* Aristoph. *Pac.* 1031; Plut. *Nik.* 23. The comic poet Eupolis also noticed Stilbides, Schol. *loc. cit.* Aristophanes also mentions Eurykles, an *engastrumythos* (belly-speaker, ventriloquist); see *Vesp.* 1018–1020; also Schol. vet. on 1019; Plato *Soph.* 252c and Schol. vet.; Hesych. E7133; Suda E45. Eurykles was a python (see p. 196, note 1) rather than a chresmologue and none of his oracles is reported.

16 Clem. Alex. *Strom.* 1.131, 397P; Eus. *PE* 10.11, p. 495d; Suda O654. On verses attributed to Onomakritos see Paus. 8.31.3, 37.5; 9.35.5.

17 The first line is like Q213 in manner of expression. It has the same metrical pattern; and both begin with a perfect middle-passive third person singular followed by a particle and definite noun subject.

Plato joins Amphilytos with Bakis and the Sibyl as *chrêsmôdos* (*Theag.* 124d). He calls him a fellow-countryman (*hêmedapos*), and Clement calls him Athenian (*Strom.* 1.132, 398P), probably because of his role in the restoration of Peisistratos. He is an example of the wandering chresmologue, born and reared in Akarnania, later establishing himself in Athens and winning prestige in that city.

Not only were oracles of Bakis and Musaios fulfilled at the battle of Salamis, says Herodotos, but also an oracle spoken by the Athenian chresmologue Lysistratos many years before the battle: Κωλιάδες δὲ γυναῖκες ἐρετμοῖσι φρύξουσι (8.96.2): "and the women of Kolias will use oars for their roasting." This was fulfilled when a wind carried the wreckage of ships sunk in the battle to Cape Kolias.

In 510 or a little earlier Antichares of Eleon in Boeotia, said to be Bakis' birthplace, advised the Spartan Dorieus to settle Herakleia in Sicily, citing an oracle of Laios. Antichares was apparently a chresmologue who carried a book of oracles which he called *Laiou chrêsmoi*. These could be oracles spoken to Laios, spoken by Laios, or collected by Laios, who must be the Theban king, father of Oedipus. When Dorieus had received this advice from Antichares, he went to Delphi to ask Apollo whether he would take the country to which he was setting out, and received an affirmative answer (Q121). It is possible that Dorieus sought confirmation from Delphi of the oracle that Antichares spoke; but it is unlikely that he received an unqualified prediction that he would take Herakleia or any city (notice how Dorieus' question is phrased, and the disputed story that Sybaris was the city that he took). One rather suspects that two attributions of a single oracle are combined in Herodotos' narrative: it was an "oracle of Laios" which became attributed to Delphi as Q121.[18]

THE ORACLE COLLECTIONS

As Antichares possessed oracles of Laios, other chresmologues carried books of oracles attributed to famous seers of former times (only the Laios oracles may bear the name of someone who was not a seer; and that is uncertain). Many chresmologues carried oracles of Bakis, of which there were certainly many collections. Hierokles in Aristophanes' *Peace* and the chresmologue in the *Birds* claimed to have oracles that Bakis once

---

18 See Herod. 5.43. Parallel to Antichares' oracle and Q121 are the *logia* cited by Themistokles (Herod. 8.62.2); see p. 153. Other seers mentioned by Herodotos are the Acarnanian Megistias, present with the Spartans at Thermopylai (7.219.1, 221); the Iamid Teisamenos (9.33.1; Paus. 3.11.6–8; see Q160); the Iamid Kallias (5.44.2–45.2); Euenios of Apollonia and his son Deiphonos (9.92–95).

spoke. In the *Knights* Kleon is in effect a chresmologue who possesses a collection of Bakis' oracles, which help him to keep Demos under his control (109–143, 195–210, 960–1096), The Sausage-Seller challenges him with oracles of Glanis, "Bakis' elder brother" (1003–1004), and the two engage in an oracle-reciting contest, in which Glanis' oracles prove superior; for Demos takes the Sausage-Seller as his steward in place of Kleon. As comic oracles these are burlesque exaggerations of the "genuine" oracles of Bakis in circulation; otherwise they would have no comic effect. The first that Kleon reads allows us insight into the constituents of such oracle collections: it begins,

> Φράζευ 'Ερεχθείδη λογίων ὁδὸν ἥν σοι Ἀπόλλων
> ἴαχεν ἐξ ἀδύτοιο διὰ τριπόδων ἐριτίμων.
>
> [1015–1016]

Erechtheus' son, observe the path of oracles which Apollo has proclaimed to you from the adyton through his esteemed tripods.

If Kleon had not said that his were oracles of Bakis we would say that this purported to be a Delphic response. Kleon's Bakis appears to inform his auditor that not only did he receive this message from Apollo, but from Apollo at Delphi. The two verses quoted are not Aristophanes' invention (see Q3, 259; L11, 50); the comedy is in the four verses which follow, to which this opening lends a mock solemnity. The chresmologues gathered all sorts of oracular verses, some composed in the Pythian Apollo's name; hence the conflicting attributions of some oracles, reported as from Bakis or from the Delphic Apollo or from some other source.

We hear of one Bakis and of several Bakides. The Bakis usually referred to is the Boeotian from Eleon, whom the nymphs had inspired. According to some authorities there were three chresmologues called Bakis, of whom the Boeotian was oldest. The other two were Attic and Locrian; or, according to Philetas of Ephesos, the third was Arcadian from Kaphye, also called Kydas and Aletes. Or there were two Bakides, one Boeotian, the other Athenian or Arcadian.[19] It seems probable, as some scholars have thought, that *Bakis* was not a proper name but a title that prophets assumed in the archaic period. In any case, we can be sure that most oracles of Bakis current in the fifth century and later had not

---

19 Boeotian Bakis: Theopompos 78GH; Paus. 10.12.11; Cic. *Div.* 1.18.34. Three Bakides: Schol. vet. on Aristoph. *Eq.* 123; Philetas *ap.* Schol. vet. *in* Aristoph. *Pac.* 1071, *Aves* 962 = *ap.* Sud. B47. Two Bakides: Clem. Alex. *Strom.* 1.132, 398P; Schol. vet. on Aristoph. *Eq.* 123. Bakis and the nymphs: Aristoph. *Pax* 1070–1071; Paus. 4.27.4, 10.12.11. See Bouché-Leclercq 1880: 2.105–107. According to Schol. on *Pax* 1071 and Suda, Peisistratos was called Bakis.

been spoken by anyone called Bakis who lived in Boeotia or elsewhere in the distant past. Those men who carried oracles of Bakis dealt with them as did Onomakritos with oracles of Musaios.

A Bakis was, in fact, a male Sibyl. Some writers refer to one Sibyl, others to several Sibyls, as many as ten.[20] The comic Hierokles at first says that he speaks oracles of Bakis; then after Trygaios has recited an oracle of Apollo, Hierokles says that he does not recognize it, because the Sibyl didn't speak it (Aristophanes *Peace* 1095; cf. 1116), as though his own oracles had been spoken by Bakis or Sibyl indifferently. Sibyls and Bakides are often lumped together as terms designating the inspired seers and seeresses of early times.[21]

The Erythraean Sibyl, whose name was Herophile, corresponds to the Boeotian Bakis as the person usually meant when a Sibyl is mentioned; but in an Italian or Roman context it is the Cumaean Sibyl that is commonly meant. The Sibyl of Cumae was also called Herophile (as well as Amaltheia, Demo, Demophile, Deiphobe, Taraxandra, Melankraira), as were the Sibyls of Marpessos, Delphi, and others—who were also given other names—for the several Sibyls merge with one another.

The Sibyl of Delphi, also called Daphne, Artemis, and perhaps Manto (Diodoros 4.66.5–6), cannot be clearly distinguished from the Erythraean, Marpessan, Samian, and Colophonian Sibyls. She was born before the Trojan War, says Pausanias (10.12.2), and predicted that Helen would grow up to bring war upon Asia and Europe and to cause the fall of Ilion. According to Plutarch (*Mor.* 398c), she was the first Sibyl and came from Helikon, having been reared by the Muses (as the nymphs inspired Bakis). The Delphian Sibyl should not be confused with the Pythia: she is a wholly legendary figure, who was said to have come to Delphi, apparently at the time of the Trojan War or soon thereafter; and to have spoken her oracles from a rock which both Plutarch and Pausanias saw below Apollo's temple, next to the *bouleutêrion*, now identified with a rock just below the polygonal wall (see Map, fig. 1, no. 24).

Plutarch's Diogenianos adduces a Sibylline prophecy of the eruption of Vesuvius in A.D. 79 (near Cumae and Dicaearchia; *Mor.* 398e), a graphic

---

20 On Sibyls see Herakleitos 92DK *ap.* Plut. *Mor.* 397a (earliest notice); Plato *Phaedr.* 244b and Schol. vet.; Chrysippos *ap.* Schol. vet. *in Phaedr.* 244b; Plut. *Mor.* 398c–399a; Ael. *VH* 12.35; Paus. 10.12; Clem. Alex. *Strom.* 1.108, 384P; Suda Σ354–362; Firm. Lact. *Div. inst.* 1.6.7–16 (quoting Varro in 7–12); Isid. *Orig.* 8.8.3; Schol. vet. on Aristoph. *Eq.* 61, *Aves* 962; Bouché-Leclercq 1880: 2.133–214; Kurfess 1951: 5–22.

21 Plato *Theag.* 124d; Cic. *Div.* 1.18.34; Plut. *Mor.* 399a; Lucian *Per.* 29–30; Clem. Alex. *Strom.* 1.132, 399P; Schol. vet. on Aristoph. *Eq.* 902.

prediction of outbursts of fire, seethings of the sea, hurlings of rocks and flames, and destruction of cities. It is just after the conversation about the Sibyl, which concludes with a reference to Bakides as well, that Sarapion quotes Q163 and immediately thereafter Q238:

> Ἀλλ' ὁπότε Τρώων γενεὰ καθύπερθε γένηται
> Φοινίκων ἐν ἀγῶνι, τότ' ἔσσεται ἔργα ἄπιστα·
> πόντος μὲν λάμψει πῦρ ἄσπετον, ἐκ δὲ κεραυνῶν
> πρηστῆρες μὲν ἄνω διὰ κύματος ἀίξουσιν
> 5 ἄμμιγα σὺν πέτρᾳ, ἡ δὲ στηρίξεται αὐτοῦ
> οὐ φατὸς ἀνθρώποις νῆσος· καὶ χείρονες ἄνδρες
> χερσὶ βιησάμενοι τὸν κρείσσονα νικήσουσι.

This obviously *post eventum* prophecy refers to an eruption and earthquake in the bay of Thera, an old crater, in 196 B.C., a few years after the Roman defeat of Carthage and very soon after the Roman and Aetolian defeat of Philip V of Macedon at Kynoskephalai. It is essentially the same prediction as the Sibylline prophecy just mentioned (which is not quoted in verse): eruptions of fire, upheavals of rocks and flame through the water; lines 3–5 could serve both. There was apparently a Sibylline prophecy of volcanic eruption that could be fitted with varying introductions and conclusions to specific occasions.

Q238 is mentioned nowhere else, and, as with Q163, Plutarch does not explicitly attribute it to the Pythia; it is in his treatise on her oracles that he quotes it.[22] It has a characteristic opening of Bakid and Sibylline oracles, *All' hopote*, introducing a condition precedent, an event that will herald the predicted event. No Historical Delphic oracles are predictions of natural catastrophes.

There were many collections of Sibylline oracles. Most well known are the Sibylline Books of Rome, acquired at an early date, although the story of how King Tarquin bought them from the Sibyl of Cumae is pure legend.[23] As we have already noticed, the Sibylline oracle which directed the Romans to institute a cult of Aesculapius was attributed by Ovid to the Delphic Oracle (Q229). The Roman collection was never fixed; oracles were interpolated from various sources at many times. Fire destroyed the books then present in the Capitol in 83 B.C.; but a new

---

22 Probably Poseidonios' treatise on fate is Plutarch's source of Q238; see Flacelière 1937: 161 note 33.
23 Dion Hal. *Ant. Rom.* 4.62; Pliny *NH* 13.13.88; Bouché-Leclercq 1880: 2.187–190.

collection was made. Oracles reputedly Sibylline were gathered from everywhere under conditions which allowed entry to many that were obviously not in the earlier collection and whose authenticity was questioned.[24] Surely the contents of unofficial Sibylline collections of chresmologues fluctuated even more.

Onomakritos, we have noticed, kept a collection of oracles of Musaios. According to Herodotos, an oracle of Musaios, as well as oracles of Bakis and Lysistratos, was fulfilled in the battle of Salamis; and another oracle of Musaios, similar to verses of Bakis which Herodotos quotes, predicted the Persian defeat at Plataia. The name of Musaios is always closely associated with that of Orpheus, and we hear of *chrêsmoi* of Orpheus too; in fact, those that Onomakritos kept were sometimes called oracles of Orpheus. The verses attributed to Orpheus and Musaios included both prophecies and ritual directions; in reference to these verses the term *chrêsmos* has a broad meaning. According to Aristophanes' Aeschylus in the *Frogs*, Orpheus taught *teletai*, Musaios taught remedies and oracles. According to Plato's *Protagoras*, Orpheus and Musaios and their company produced *teletai* and *chrêsmôdiai*; and in the *Republic* Adeimantos describes the mendicant priests (*agyrtai*) and manteis who go from one rich man's door to another's with books of Musaios and Orpheus.[25]

Another oracle book bore the name of Abaris, the Hyperborean shaman. According to the legend, the whole world was afflicted with plague or famine or both. An Apolline oracle (Q79) informed all men that their woes would end if the Athenians should offer pre-plowing sacrifices (*proêrosia*) in their behalf. Abaris came from his northern land to Hellas in response to this oracle and made sacrifices to Apollo. It was then, according to the Scholiast on Aristophanes' *Knights* (729) that Abaris wrote down the oracles called *chrêsmoi* of Abaris and sometimes *chrêsmoi Skythinoi*. Most of these were probably ritual prescriptions. Abaris was one of the *iatromanteis*, like Aristeas of Prokonnesos; and he was said to have traveled over the earth carrying Apollo's golden arrow, offering healing and purification. Hence we may suppose that Q79 came originally from the oracles of Abaris. Only an Aristophanic Scholiast and Libanios clearly attribute

---

24 Suet. *Aug.* 31.1; Tac. *Ann.* 6.12; G. Wissowa, *Religion und Kultus der Römer* (Munich: Beck, 1912) 536–537; P. Boyancé, *Études sur la religion romaine* (Rome: École Française de Rome, 1972) 354. See Fontenrose 1939: 444–449 on the secular oracle (Phlegon *Macr.* 4; Zosim. *Nov. hist.* 2.6), which may have been composed as late as 200–204.

25 Musaios' oracles: Herod. 7.6.3–5, 8.96.2, 9.43.2. *Chrêsmoi* of Orpheus: Suda *O*654; Kern, *Orph. frag.* 332, 333. Orpheus and Musaios: Plat. *Prot.* 316d, *Rep.* 364b–365a; Aristoph. *Ran.* 1032–1033. See Bouché-Leclercq 1880: 2.109–116; Linforth 1941: 67–97; Oliver 1950: 6–8.

it to the Delphic Apollo. Aristeides attributes it along with Q180 to the *exêgêtês patrôos* of Athens, apparently meaning the Pythian Apollo; and the Scholiast on Aristeides apparently accepts this attribution when he says that "the god" spoke this oracle. Lykurgos, our earliest authority, says only that Apollo was speaker; and this is consistent with the story that Abaris gathered Apolline oracles.[26] Q79 belongs to the foundation legend of the Athenian *Proêrosia*, offered in behalf of all Hellenes. This sacrifice appears to be an ancient institution, which probably antedates the Delphic Oracle and Abaris (or the time when he is supposed to have lived).

Pausanias mentions an exegete, Iophon of Knossos, who had a collection of oracles in hexameter verse, which he said Amphiaraos had spoken to the seven Argive chieftains in their war on Thebes. Iophon is otherwise unknown and undatable.[27] There also appear to have been oracles of Mopsos in circulation; Clement cites anonymous authorities who said (*phasi*) that Battos of Cyrene had put them together.[28] Compilations of oracles were apparently also made in the names of other legendary or semi-legendary seers of the distant past. A Scholiast mentions poems of Euklos the chresmologue, a Cypriote. As famous chresmologues of old Pausanias names Cypriote Euklos, Athenian Musaios and Lykos, Pandion's son, and Boeotian Bakis. Euklos, says Pausanias, predicted the Persian invasion of Hellas before Bakis did so; and he quotes verses of Euklos which predicted Homer's birth.[29] We may suspect that L80 on Homer's birthplace and death came from such an oracle collection; for most sources do not mention Delphi or even Apollo; moreover the two versions of L80 in verse indicate a fluctuating text.

All these oracles had authority as statements reputedly spoken by a god to or through a seer. The god was most often supposed to be Apollo: the Sibyls, for example, were generally assumed to speak in his name.[30] In Aristophanes' *Knights* (1002-1096, 1229-1240) Kleon professes to have oracles of Bakis, but he also considers them to be Apollo's statements.

---

26 On Abaris see Herod. 4.36; Lykurgos *ap.* Harp., p. 2 Dind.; Schol. vet. on Aristoph. *Eq.* 729; Suda *A*18; Bouché-Leclercq 1880: 2.117–119.

27 Paus. 1.34.4. I interpret Pausanias thus, "Iophon the Cnossian of the exegetes produced oracles in hexameter, saying that Amphiaraos had spoken them to the Argives, etc." But Bouché-Leclercq (1880: 2.225 with note 1) understands him to mean that Iophon produced oracles of the exegetes, saying that Amphiaraos had spoken one of them. Pausanias' text, if correct, must mean that Iophon attributed all the oracles to Amphiaraos.

28 Clem. Alex. *Strom.* 1.133, 399P: Φασὶ δὲ τὴν Μόψου καλουμένην μαντικὴν συντάξαι τὸν Κυρηναῖον Βάττον, . . .

29 Paus. 10.12.11, 14.6, 24.3; Schol. vet. on Plato *Hipp. M.* 295a.

30 Paus. 10.12; Diod. 4.66.5–6; Virg. *Aen.* 6.9–101. See Cic. *Har. resp.* 9.18: (maiores) fatorum veteres praedictiones Apollinis vatum libris . . . contineri putaverunt.

According to Theopompos (78GH) it was Apollo who sent Bakis to purify the Spartan women of their madness. That Bakis was Apollo's minister may appear inconsistent with the tradition noticed earlier that Bakis received his inspiration from the nymphs; but probably most Greeks would easily accept both statements. In the *Birds* Peisthetairos responds to the chresmologue's oracle of Bakis with an oracle of Apollo ("which I copied down from Apollo," *Birds* 982), naming no seer who had received it. This is a comic scene, but it offers evidence of oracle collections that bore only Apollo's name.

Athens, Sparta, and other city-states appear to have kept books of oracles in their archives. When Kleomenes of Sparta helped the Alkmeonids end the Peisistratid tyranny in 510, he took possession of the Peisistratid oracle collection that he found in the temple (probably Athena's) on the Acropolis and carried it back to Sparta (Herodotos 5.90.2). From these oracles the Spartans learned that they were destined to suffer many disasters from the Athenians. Herodotos does not name a god or seer for the Peisistratid collection. They were surely not the oracles of Musaios which the Peisistratid henchman Onomakritos had in his keeping: for this appears to have been Onomakritos' own collection, and, furthermore, Hippias knew that some were Onomakritos' forgeries. Peisistratos himself had the nickname of Bakis (see note 19); but this does not mean that he kept oracles of Bakis; and if the Acropolis collection consisted of Bakis' oracles, Herodotos would almost certainly have mentioned the name. The Peisistratid collection was composed either of oracles gathered from many sources or of oracles reputedly spoken by Apollo at Delphi and other oracular shrines.

The Spartan kings also kept a collection of Delphic oracles. Each king, Herodotos informs us, appointed two officers called Pythioi; the four Pythioi went as the state's envoys (*theopropoi*) to consult the Delphic Oracle and to bring back the Pythia's responses. The kings kept these oracles, and the Pythioi also had knowledge of their contents; and it is very likely that the Pythioi were delegated to be custodians of the collection.[31] In it were the oracles given to Lykurgos on the laws; these oracles

---

[31] Herod. 6.57.2, 4; Cic. *Div.* 1.43.95; Suda Π3078; Bouché-Leclercq 1880: 2.217–218. It is possible that the official *exégêtai Pythochrêstai* of Athens kept the Athenian oracle books as part of the sacred traditions and laws with which they were charged; see Bouché-Leclercq 2.216–217 and Oliver 1950: 6–17, who believes that the official exegetes of the fourth century succeeded the *chrêsmologoi* of the fifth. But there is no evidence that the city exegetes had anything to do with oracles. It is true that a chresmologue like Lampon may be called an exegete, but the term is not confined to officials who held the title. See Herbert Bloch, "The Exegetes of Athens and the Prytaneion Decree," *AJPh* 74 (1953) 407–418.

Pausanias, exiled Spartan king, published in 395 (Strabo 8.5.5, p. 366). They surely included Q8, probably genuine (in its simplest form), but also some unauthentic Delphic oracles. Plutarch (*Mor.* 1116f) refers to the oracle about Lykurgos in the oldest Spartan archives (*anagraphai*); and that can only be Q7. Like the Sibylline Books of Rome such oracle books of the Greek cities suffered many accretions of oracles, which the keepers, receiving them in oral tradition, thought to be genuine pronouncements made in earlier times (or which they sometimes inserted for political reasons). Q163, which Diopeithes cited against Agesilaos in 399, appears to come from a Spartan oracle collection, perhaps the state's. There was the *palaion logion* known to the Spartans concerning a defeat at Leuktra. It may well be that several of the "Delphic" responses which concern Sparta were drawn from the official collection and were not spoken at Delphi.

We know little about the Spartan and Athenian oracle collections, and next to nothing about those of other Greek cities. So far as we know, the Delphians kept no record of oracles spoken; and it is surprising how few are mentioned in Delphic inscriptions. We are best informed about the Roman books of Sibylline oracles, already discussed. These differ from Greek-city collections, which were meant to be the accumulated responses of gods spoken at oracular seats like Delphi and Dodona; but the Sibylline Books of Rome, as the term indicates, were a collection of oracles supposedly spoken by a famous Sibyl.

There were many oracle collections in the ancient world, both private and public, and there were many oracles that circulated orally. These oracles were variously attributed, and attributions of a single oracle shifted from one reporter to another. Often enough an oracle that one person had attributed to Bakis another attributed to the Sibyl and another to the Delphic Apollo. And the contents of collections constantly changed. Bouché-Leclercq (1880: 2.142) states the process admirably: "Les tenants des chresmologues et sibylles . . . firent circuler des prédictions versifiées dont le recueil, sans cesse grossi par des apports anonymes, finit par constituer une attestation suffisante." There was a good deal of pious fraud in the gathering and keeping of oracle collections; and there was a good deal of credulity and superstition in the popular acceptance of circulating oracles. If a chresmologue said that an oracle came from Apollo at Delphi, his auditors were likely to believe him. Thus a Delphic label became attached to many chresmologic oracles.

CHAPTER

The Conventions and Structure of
Traditional Oracles in Verse

OPENING FORMULAE OF TRADITIONAL VERSE ORACLES

In the last chapter I pointed to several formulae of Bakid and other chresmologic oracles that also occur in responses which some writers, ancient and modern, have assumed to be Delphic. For example Q238 begins *All' hopote* (But when), picked up by *tot(e)* (then) at the beginning of the main clause. The second oracle of Bakis that we encounter in Greek literature (Herodotos 8.77) begins Ἀλλ' ὅταν Ἀρτέμιδος χρυσαόρου ἱερὸν ἀκτὴν / νηυσὶ γεφυρώσωσι . . . (see below, p. 185), expressing the condition of fulfillment, a definition of the time when an enemy will come in ships and destroy Athens, which is followed by a prediction of victory. This prediction has two parts, a specific prediction of victory and a more general prediction of the consequences of victory: then Zeus and Victory will restore freedom to Hellas. The second part is introduced with *tote*. More usually *kai tote dê* (just then) picks up *All' hopotan / hotan / hopote*, placed immediately after the conditional relative clause at the beginning of the prediction or direction that is the main message of the oracle.

Pausanias quotes a Bakid warning to Thebes concerning the tomb of Amphion and Zethos:

Ἀλλ' ὁπόταν Τιθορεὺς Ἀμφίονί τε Ζήθῳ τε
χύτλα καὶ εὐχωλὰς μειλίγματ' ἐνὶ χθονὶ χεύῃ

. . . .

καὶ τότε δὴ πεφύλαξο πόλει κακὸν οὐκ ἀλαπαδνὸν
ἐρχόμενον . . .

[9.17.5]

The whole message is that if, when the sun is in Taurus, the Tithoreans come to pour libations and make prayers to the twins, and take earth from the tomb and carry it to Phokos' tomb in Tithorea, the Thebans will have a bad harvest. Hence the Thebans kept watch over the tomb at that time. This oracle, then, is the *aition* of a Theban rite or custom, evidence that ritual prescriptions of this kind, as well as predictions, appear among the Bakid oracles.[1]

When a comic poet or satirist composed an oracle of Bakis, he employed the conventional formulae of the oracles that were believed to be genuine utterances of Bakis. In Aristophanes' *Birds* (967–968) the chresmologue begins his oracle with *All' hotan*, though no *tote* introduces the apodosis. In this comic oracle, ritual prescription is combined with prediction. In the *Knights* (197–201) Demosthenes reads an oracle which predicts Kleon's fall and the Sausage-Seller's succession. He tells the Seller that the gods have spoken the oracle, which he has taken from Kleon's collection of oracles of Bakis (*Knights* 123–124, 1003). It begins, Ἀλλ' ὁπόταν μάρψῃ βυρσαίετος ἀγκυλοχήλης . . . ("But when a leather eagle of crooked claws seizes . . ."), followed by *dê tote* introducing the conclusion.[2]

In the *Life's End of Peregrinos* (29) Lucian quotes an oracle which Theagenes, Peregrinos' companion, declared to be a genuine pronouncement of the Sibyl:

Ἀλλ' ὁπόταν Πρωτεὺς Κυνικῶν ὄχ' ἄριστος ἁπάντων
Ζηνὸς ἐριγδούπου τέμενος κάτα πῦρ ἀνακαύσας
ἐς φλόγα πηδήσας ἔλθῃ ἐς μακρὸν Ὄλυμπον
δὴ τότε πάντας ὁμῶς οἳ ἀρούρης καρπὸν ἔδουσι
νυκτιπόλον τιμᾶν κέλομαι ἥρωα μέγιστον
σύνθρονον Ἡφαίστῳ καὶ Ἡρακλῆι ἄνακτι.

---

1 See p. 146 for the Bakid prediction of the battle of Leuktra, incompletely quoted at Paus. 4.27.4.

2 See also *Lys.* 770–776, an anonymous *chrêsmos* which Lysistrata reads to the women, and which begins *All' hopotan*, predicting success for them if they leave their husbands.

But when Proteus, best of all Cynics, having kindled a fire in Zeus's temenos, leaps into the flame and goes to high Olympos, then do I command all men alike who eat earth's fruit to honor the greatest hero, night-roamer, enthroned beside Hephaistos and Lord Herakles.[3]

Though put forth seriously as a genuine Sibylline oracle, this is just as much a counterfeit as Aristophanes' oracles of Bakis or Lucian's own Bakid oracle with which he counters Theagenes' Sibylline:

Ἀλλ' ὁπόταν Κυνικὸς πολυώνυμος ἐς φλόγα πολλὴν
πηδήσῃ δόξης ὑπ' ἐρινύι θυμὸν ὀρινθείς,
δὴ τότε τοὺς ἄλλους κυναλώπεκας οἵ οἱ ἕπονται
μιμεῖσθαι χρὴ πότμον ἀποιχομένοιο λύκοιο.

But when the Cynic of many names leaps into a great flame, stirred in spirit by the Erinys of glory, then all the dog-foxes who follow him should imitate the fate of the departed wolf.

In five more verses "Bakis" instructs the Achaeans to stone any cowardly disciple who refuses to leap into the flame after his master (Peregrinos Proteus), so that he may not continue enriching himself at their expense (Lucian means Theagenes in particular). This mock Bakid oracle, we notice, is a parody of the preceding Sibylline oracle, particularly in the first three lines, which have not only the correlatives *All' hopotan . . . dê tote*, but also much of the same vocabulary.[4] It is truly Aristophanic in content and tone and has the same purpose as the oracles with which Peisthetairos and Trygaios respond to intruding chresmologues: the gods ordain punishment for mountebanks.

In this passage from the *Peregrinos* no difference can be discerned between Bakid and Sibylline oracles in their conventions and formulae. The oracle from the Sibylline Books of Rome that reputedly authorized the *Ludi Saeculares* of 17 B.C., Augustus' famous celebration, begins *All' hopotan*, which lacks a following *kai tote dê* or equivalent.[5]

Four "Delphic" responses begin with *All' hotan* or variation followed

---

3 Peregrinos Proteus, in fact, received a cult after his death in Mysian Parion; there his image gave oracles, according to Athenag. *Leg. pro Christ.* 26. Some of these oracles and perhaps some of Peregrinos' own sayings may have entered the late oracle collections, as the oracles of Alexander of Abonuteichos also may have done. See Buresch 1880: 80; Nilsson 1961: 525; E. R. Dodds, *Pagan and Christian in an Age of Anxiety* (Cambridge Univ. Press, 1965) 59–63.

4 Notice *Kynikos < Kynikon; es phloga . . . pêdêsêi < es phloga pêdêsas; Hêphaistoio < Hêphaistôi*.

5 Zosim. 2.6; Phlegon *Macr.* 4. The *Oracula Sibyllina* (Kurfess 1951) show approximately twenty examples of prophecies (or paragraphs) which begin with *All' hotan / hopotan*; e.g., 1.319, 2.6, 3.97, 5.155, 8.50, 11.47, sometimes followed by *dê tote*, sometimes not.

by *kai tote dê* or variation. We have already noticed Q238. Another is Q101, in which the formula is admirably suited to the Macduff theme: "But when [*All' hotan*] the Medes have a mule as king, then is the time [*kai tote*], Lydian, for you to flee. . . ." Q114 belongs to the moral tale of Siphnos' fall: "But when [*All' hotan*] white *prytaneia* and a white-browed *agora* appear in Siphnos, at that time [*tote dê*] there will be need of an intelligent man. . . ." The fourth is the epicene oracle, Q134, spoken to the Argives, in which the final four of nine verses are addressed to Miletos; and only a common prediction of woe for both cities unites the two parts. The first three of the five verses addressed to Argos are:

Ἀλλ' ὅταν ἡ θήλεια τὸν ἄρσενα νικήσασα
ἐξελάσῃ καὶ κῦδος ἐν Ἀργείοισιν ἄρηται,
πολλὰς Ἀργείων ἀμφιδρυφέας τότε θήσει.

Here the main clause contains *tote* alone, but is not introduced by it. The more usual *kai tote dê* appears, however, at the beginning of the second section, addressed to Miletos:

καὶ τότε δὴ Μίλητε κακῶν ἐπιμήχανε ἔργων
πολλοῖσιν δεῖπνόν τε καὶ ἀγλαὰ δῶρα γενήσῃ . . .

It is much as though the events in Argos will be the condition precedent to the events forecast for Miletos. In fact, these nine verses never appear together as one oracle in any source. Herodotos quotes each part in a different chapter; and he alone informs us that they belong together in a single response. Pausanias and the Suda show only the first three verses quoted above and attach them to the story of Telesilla (p. 71). Since Herodotos does not mention Telesilla, his history is probably not their source. Tzetzes, citing Herodotos, quotes the Milesian section only. In the Anthology the two parts appear as separate oracles. The response as a whole is obscure and cannot be easily explained in relation to either Argive or Milesian events of the early fifth century. It is furthermore unlikely that even in an unauthentic response the Pythia would be represented as addressing anyone but a consultant.[6] What we appear to have in Q134 are two extracts from oracles of Bakis or some other collection.[7]

---

6 On the difficulties of the epicene oracle see J. Bury, "The Epicene Oracle Concerning Argos and Miletus," *Klio* 2 (1902) 14–25; J. Wells, "Some Points as to the Chronology of the Reign of Cleomenes I," *JHS* 25 (1905) 195; How and Wells 1912: 2.70–71, 94–95; Crahay 1956: 172–179. Bury, How, and PW 84 accept it as genuine. But we must suppose two oracles, one spoken to Milesians; and there is no example of a Milesian consultation at Delphi, even in the period 494–334 when Didyma was apparently inactive; see Fontenrose 1933: 21–23.

7 See p. 173, and also Crahay 1956: 173–174 on the hypothesis that this oracle comes from a ritual poem on aetiological legends: Q134, lines 1–5, concerns the Argive Hybristika.

Like chresmologic oracles that we have seen, they could be applied after the fact to any suitable event; notice Pausanias' interpretation of a Bakid verse as a prediction of the fall of Eira. Herodotos' informant or source had combined one oracle (lines 1–5) with the second part of another (the *kai tote dê* portion, lines 6–9) for a reason that eludes us and attributed the whole to the Delphic Oracle.[8]

The *All' hotan / hopotan* opening introduces conditioned commands and conditioned predictions, modes B and F, and occasionally a conditioned prohibition (which occurs so rarely that I have not distinguished it as a separate category from C1 and C2). Ordinarily in "Delphic" responses the condition is expressed without an introductory adversative conjunction in an ordinary vivid-future conditional clause, as Q20, *Eute tragos pinêsi*; Q122, *eut' an dê* (in third line) picked up by *tênika*; L51, *entha d' an.*[9]

Another frequent opening is *Phrazou / Phrazeu / Phrazeo*, usually in the meaning "Beware," "Take heed," but sometimes "Notice." In Herodotos' first mention of Bakis he quotes a two-verse oracle:

Φράζεο βαρβαρόφωνος ὅταν ζύγον εἰς ἅλα βάλλῃ
βύβλινον Εὐβοίης ἀπέχειν πολυμηκάδας αἶγας.

[8.20.2]

Take care, when the foreigner casts a paper yoke into the sea, to remove bleating goats from Euboea.

This was interpreted as a warning to the Euboeans; but, says Herodotos, they had disregarded it until disaster came upon them, apparently supposing that a paper yoke was absurd (the *zygon byblinon* means Xerxes' papyrus cables used for his bridge over the Hellespont) and casting it into the sea equally so. But the Euboeans' disregard probably means that they had never heard this oracle at all; it is a *post eventum* prophecy.

To Aristophanes' mock oracle, beginning *Phrazeu Erechtheidê*, the Sausage-Seller replies with an oracle of Glanis, "Bakis' elder brother," which begins the same way: Φράζευ 'Ερεχθείδη κύνα Κέρβερον ἀνδραποδίστην (*Knights* 1030): "Beware of the Kerberos dog, the enslaver," mocking Kleon's oracle of Bakis much as Lucian's oracle of Bakis mocks Theagenes' Sibylline oracle. Again in the *Peace*, after Trygaios has

---

8 Aristophanes' fictional Delphic oracle, F1 (*Vesp.* 158–160), expressed indirectly, reflects the formula discussed: Philokleon says that the god once told him at Delphi, ὅταν τις ἐκφύγῃ μ' ἀποσκλῆναι τότε. See also Peisthetairos' Apolline oracle (*Aves* 983–988), which begins *autar epên*, a variation of the usual opening formula.

9 For the correlative *prin / prosthen . . . prin* see Q16, 71; for other means see Q204; L11, 27, 166.

responded to Hierokles' Bakid oracle with Homeric verses, Hierokles begins anew with Φράζεο δὴ μή πώς σε (1099; see below, p. 176). The oracle on the lame kingship of Sparta, Q163, produced by Diopeithes in support of Leotychidas, begins Φράζεο δὴ Σπάρτη (see p. 149). Among the Legendary responses *Phrazeo* introduces three (L11, 50, 100; cf. L69, where *phrazeu* follows a vocative). Again, in Q34 *phrazou* occurs as second word in the third line, introducing the positive command after a denial. In Q16, a Messenian oracle, the opening statement, "Heaven grants you glory in war," is followed by ἀλλ᾽ ἀπάταισι | φράζου μὴ Σπάρτης δόλιος λόχος ἐχθρὸς ἀνέλθῃ, where *phrazou mê* begins the second verse and follows the second word in the sentence.[10]

Tzetzes quotes the verse, ῏Ω μέλεοι τί καθῆσθε; λιπὼν φεῦγ᾽ ἔσχατα γαίης, as an oracle of Bakis. It is the first verse of Q146, which the Pythia spoke to the Athenians after Xerxes had begun his march upon Hellas, according to Herodotos. This opening, *Ô meleoi* ("O wretches"), is also characteristic of Bakid and Sibylline oracles. For example, the oracle of the Sibyl who appears upon the scene after Cyrus has put Croesus on the funeral pyre in Nicolaus' version of the story (68J) begins, ῏Ω μέλεοι τί σπεύδεθ᾽ ἃ μὴ θέμις: "O wretches, why are you hurrying [to do] what is unlawful?" Here too the exclamation introduces a question, in which the meaning of the verb is the counterpart of that in Q146: "Why are you hurrying? Stop," as against "Why are you sitting? Run away." So the mock oracle of Bakis which Hierokles speaks in the *Peace* (1063–1068) begins, "O wretched (*Ô meleoi*) mortals and foolish" (p. 155), and like Nicolaus' Sibylline oracle continues with admonition of the auditors that their act is offending the gods.

The foregoing oracles address wretched and unfortunate auditors. Others greet the auditors as happy and fortunate, as already noticed in Q180 (p. 150), *Eudaimon ptoliethron*, which also begins Q68; in both the city is Athens. The usual adjective, the first word of the first line, is a form of *olbios* or *eudaimôn*. This is the opening of several Quasi-Historical

---

10 Probably forms of *phrazesthai* employed in other responses are suggested by this conventional opening, as in the oracle of Glanis (Aristoph. *Eq.* 1067), where Αἰγείδη φράσσαι κυναλώπεκα differs little from Φράζευ ᾽Ερεχθείδη κύνα Κέρβερον (*Eq.* 1030); and compare Q16 for a warning against trickery. In Q31 and Q203 after salutation and restatement of the question, the third line begins the message with *all᾽ age dê phrazesth(e)*. Q60, beginning with the favorite eagle-lion metaphor has *eu phrazesthe* in the third verse, followed by vocative *Korinthioi* "who dwell around fair Peirene and Corinth of beetling brow," perhaps in allusion to the "land between Corinth and Sikyon." In F11 *phrazesth᾽ ô Delphoi* begins the second line. In Livy's quotation of Q202 in direct Latin prose *phrazou* is rendered *cave*: Romane aquam Albinam cave lacu contineri, cave in mare manare suo flumine sinas. Cf. L77.

and Legendary responses, Ὄλβιος οὗτος ἀνὴρ ὃς ἐμὸν δόμον εἰσκαταβ-
αίνει (ἀμφιπολεύει), are the words with which Apollo greets Kypselos in
Q61 and Hesiod in L41; and the name begins the second verse of each.
Homer was greeted more equivocally in one version of L80, Ὄλβιε καὶ
δύσδαιμον. The Megarians who were to found Byzantion were told,
Ὄλβιοι οἳ κείνην πόλιν ἀνέρες οἰκήσουσιν (Q44). The Sybarites in their
days of prosperity are suitably addressed: Εὐδαίμων Συβαρῖτα πανευδ-
αίμων (Q122). In two others the initial Eudaimōn describes not the hearers
but third persons, Chariton and Melanippos, plotters against Phalaris (Q85),
or the Corinthian (Q242). Q258 shows a variation: olbio- replaces eu- as
prefix to daimōn in the compound adjective, which is placed at the end of
the verse, describing an obscure philosopher, Themistokles: Ἐσθλὸς
ἀνὴρ μακάρεσσι τετιμένος ὀλβιοδαίμων.[11]

The "fortunate" opening does not appear in any known Bakid
oracle nor in any Sibylline oracle outside of the late Judaeo-Christian
Sibylline collection; but the absence means little in view of the few
surviving oracles explicitly attributed to Bakis or, in pre-Christian
centuries, to the Sibyl (about twenty altogether, including oracles from
the Sibylline Books of Rome). Among the Oracula Sibyllina, however,
we find Ὄλβιοι ἀνθρώπων κεῖνοι κατὰ γαῖαν ἔσονται (4.24): "Blessed
will be those men on earth." These late oracles follow the conventions of
earlier Sibylline verses: the content may be Jewish or Christian, but the
diction, mannerisms, and formulae are much the same.

Another favorite beginning of traditional oracles is Esti or Eisin,
meaning "There is/are," Esti often followed by tis. The mock oracle of
Bakis which Kleon reads to Demos in the Knights begins,

> Ἔστι γυνὴ τέξει δὲ λέονθ᾽ ἱεραῖς ἐν Ἀθήναις
> ὃς περὶ τοῦ δήμου πολλοῖς κώνωψι μαχεῖται.
>
> [1037–1038]

There is a woman and she will bear a lion in holy Athens, who will fight
many gnats for the people.

The effect of Esti in the opening verse is to call attention to a woman
destined to bear a lion; then follows the relative pronoun hos, referring
in this oracle to the woman's child, the lion. In L166,

> Ἔστι τις ἐν τεμένει Γλαύκου γένος ἄλκιμος ἀνὴρ
> ὅς γ᾽ ὑμῖν πρώτιστ᾽ ἐπιέξεται ἀντιβολήσας,

---

11 Responses without these adjectives, but declaring the consultant dear to the gods
are Q7 (Lykurgos), Q28 (Myskellos). Cf. Q56. For the woeful greeting some lines of Or.
Sib. begin aiai soi, e.g., 3.303, 319, 323.

the first verse declares the presence of a Glaukid in the temenos, and the relative clause of the second verse tells the Magnesians that he will be the first to meet them. If *Esti tis* calls attention to a city or land, *entha* (where) introduces the defining clause, as in Q90:

> Ἔστι τις Ἀρκαδίης Τεγέη λευρῷ ἐνὶ χώρῳ
> ἔνθ' ἄνεμοι πνείουσι δύω κρατερῆς ὑπ' ἀνάγκης.

Then relative *entha* is picked up by demonstrative *entha* (there) in the fourth line. Similar to Q90, and probably affected by it, is Q192, in which Mantineans are likewise instructed to bring a hero's bones, those of Arkas, from a place in Arcadia: Ἔστι δὲ Μαιναλίη δυσχείμερος ἔνθα τε κεῖται / Ἀρκάς, ... In the six verses *entha* occurs three times, the demonstrative being repeated. Here *de* replaces *tis*; hence Parke (1956: 198) supposes that one or more verses preceded. But if Q192 was taken from an oracle book, the *de* is easily explained. In the *Oracula Sibyllina* there occurs the verse, Ἔστι δέ τις φύλη βασιλήϊος ἧς γένος ἔσται... (3.288), "And there is a royal nation from which will be a progeny...." This begins a new topic, really a new prophecy, but is joined to the preceding verses and continues an account of the Hebrew nation.[12] Herein, I believe, lies an explanation of some verse oracles which begin with the conjunctions *alla* and *de*, as though something had gone before. They introduce verses taken from an oracle book that was produced by a single poet or compiler, who either composed several distinct oracles or arranged and modified oracles previously composed, and conceived of the book as one long poem. The *All' hotan* opening in particular suggests a preceding prophecy or direction.

The plural *Eisin* occurs in Q9, one of the responses supposedly spoken to Lykurgos on the Spartan constitution, Εἰσὶν ὁδοὶ δύο, "There are two roads," which are then distinguished by *hê men ... hê de*, as the roads of freedom and slavery.

None of the Historical verse responses begins with any of these opening formulae. Only H66 might be considered an exception. The first verse is the statement, "Apollo who dwells at Delphi has said this to the Athenians." The second verse then begins with *Estin soi*: "You have a sanctuary of Demeter Chloiê and blessed Kourê before the *propylaion* on

---

12 The section on the Hebrews begins *Esti polis*: "There is an ancient city on earth, Ur of the Chaldees, from which (*ex hês dê*) is a nation of very righteous men" (*Or. Sib.* 3.218–219). Another *Esti de* occurs in 1.261: "And there is among the Phrygians on the black continent a steep high mountain, and its name is Ararat"; here no *entha* or relative pronoun follows. For future *estai (de)* or *essetai*, "there will be," see *Or. Sib.* 4.67, 83, 97; 5.130, 344, 361.

the acropolis, where (*hou*) all the people celebrate Glaukôpis Athena, where (*hou*) the ear of holy wheat first grew." The pronouncement itself, therefore, has the opening with *Estin*, indicating the existence of a place, further defined in the "where" clauses. This oracle was inscribed on stone, perhaps in the reign of Hadrian, i.e., it was delivered about A.D. 125, perhaps later. As we shall see, almost all the surviving Historical Delphic oracles in verse date from the second century A.D. and later; and it is not surprising that a Delphic response of that period should adopt a mannerism of traditional oracles.

Oracular poets might be expected, like epic poets, to avail themselves of formulaic phrases, especially if they were composing verses orally. Hence we may see no more in the recurrent opening phrases than a convenient employment of hexameter tags. The fact is that these phrases are extremely rare in epic, and some do not occur at all. Iliad 2.811 begins *esti de tis*, introducing the hill Batieia. Two speeches in the last book of the Odyssey begin with the vocative *Olbie* (24.36, 192, Achilles and Odysseus). The adjective *olbios* begins the verse and sentence on the happy lot of the Eleusinian initiate in the Homeric Hymn to Demeter (2.480). None of these verses is prophetic. In any case, whether these are epic expressions or not, they occur with sufficient frequency to be considered conventional openings of traditional oracular compositions, both chresmologic and "Delphic."

THE STRUCTURE OF TRADITIONAL VERSE ORACLES

What we begin to perceive in our review of characteristic openings is a conventional technique of composing oracular poems. The oracular poet employed the formulae, devices, and diction of his fellows and predecessors, as well as a number of structural patterns, which are fairly constant and at the same time flexible. In a short oracle of one to three verses the structure is bound to be less complex than in a longer oracle. For example the Battos oracle, Q47, is expressed in two verses as Herodotos reports it:

> Βάττ' ἐπὶ φώνην ἦλθες· ἄναξ δέ σε Φοῖβος Ἀπόλλων
> ἐς Λιβύην πέμπει μηλοτρόφον οἰκιστῆρα.

Here we observe a salutation (A) expressed in the single vocative *Batt(e)*; a brief restatement of Battos' question (B) in an allusion to his problem; the god's reference to himself as speaker of oracles (C); the message (E), in effect a command, though expressed in statement form.[13] Thus four components of an oracular poem are packed into two hexameter verses. To these verses (the second being altered after the caesura) seven are added in the version that Diodoros quotes: they add a prediction that the Libyans will attack Battos and his men (verses 4–5) and a command to pray to Zeus, Athena, and Apollo (5–7); then the god repeats his prediction of Battos' kingship in Libya (7–9), an elaboration (F) of his message in confirmation of it. The oracle ends with a second reference of the god to himself, ἄγει δέ σε Φοῖβος Ἀπόλλων (9). This conclusion repeats the third component (C); the prediction and second command are additions to the message (E).

The same components may be clearly seen in L164, the first of four verse oracles attached to the foundation legend of Magnesia-on-Maeander:

> "Ἤλθετε Μάγνητες Κρήτης ἀπόνοσφι τραπέν[τες,]
> οἰωνὸμ πτερύγεσσι σὺν ἀργεννῆσιν ἰδόντες
> [ἐ]γ μέλανος, καὶ θαῦμα καταθνητοῖσιν ἐφάνθη,
> [κ]αὶ δίζησθε πάτρην εἰ λώιόν ἐστιν ἱκέσθαι.
> 5 ἀλλὰ χρεὼγ γαίης ἀπ[ὸ π]ατρίδος ἄλλοθι νεῖσθα[ι·]
> πατρὶ δ' ἐμῷ καὶ ἐμοὶ [καὶ] συγγόνῳ ᾧδε μ[ελ]ήσει
> μήτι χερειοτέραμ βῶλ[ο]μ Μ[ά]γνητα δάσασθαι
> χώρας ἧς Πηνειὸς ἔχει κα[ὶ] Πήλιον αἰπύ.

This response begins with a more elaborate salutation (A): the god addresses the consultants with the vocative *Magnêtes*, which he modifies with participial phrases and introduces with a second-person plural verb to express the circumstances of their consultation; the salutation thus merges in the second verse with a restatement of the question (B) preceded by reference to the phenomenon that provoked the question, the appearance of a white raven (2–4). Here the poet restates the precise question, using almost the formula of Historical sanctions, *ei lôion estin*—but, as in the Battos legend and others, the god has other plans; in the message (E) he directs the Magnesians elsewhere (5). There follows the god's statement of his mantic authority (C): Apollo, Zeus, and Artemis will be concerned for the Magnesians' welfare (6), a concern that Apollo expresses in an explication or elaboration of the message (F): the Magnesians will acquire lands no worse (meaning better) than those that they possessed in Thessaly (6–8).

The verse form of the Kadmos oracle, L11, which probably came to

---

13 The letters A–F that I employ here refer to the components of oracular poetry defined below (see pp. 177–180).

our sources from Mnaseas' collection of Delphic oracles, shows every component at least once except a restatement of the question.[14] It is an eighteen-verse composition that begins, Φράζεο δή μοι μῦθον Ἀγήνορος ἔκγονε Κάδμε, where the familiar opening expresses the god's admonition to heed his words, one way of expressing his mantic authority (C), also alluded to in his reference to Kadmos' presence in Pytho at the end of verse 2. The salutation (A) is made in the first verse and also in the very last words, *olbie Kadme*, a conventional opening phrase employed to close the poem. The message (E) is complex and spread through the whole composition: the god tells Kadmos to rise early, leave Pytho, and take the road through the Phlegyans and Phokis (2–4), until he reaches the herd of Pelagon, where he should take a cow that has a white crescent on each flank (4–8). This is an expression of a condition precedent (D): when Kadmos comes upon such a cow, he must take her as the guide of his course. Then the god makes a clarifying statement (F): "And I shall tell you a very clear sign and it won't escape you" (10), to introduce a second condition precedent (D, where the cow reclines, 11–12) to the final commands: sacrifice the cow to Earth and found a city on the hilltop, after killing Ares' guardian (13–16). The final verses contain an elaborative prediction (F) of future fame and immortal marriage (i.e., with Harmonia), the result of carrying out the god's prescriptions.

Hierokles' oracle of Bakis in the *Peace* (1063–1086) has the same components as L11 in a different order. The salutation (A) is necessarily first, since it is partly a conventional opening, Ὦ μέλεοι θνητοὶ καὶ νήπιοι. The next four lines are a compound-complex relative clause dependent on this vocative, which gives the reason (F) for calling the listeners wretched and foolish (1064–1065, 1067–1068). Then Hierokles' Bakis states his mantic authority (C): "If the goddess nymphs have not deceived Bakis, nor Bakis mortal men, nor the nymphs Bakis himself . . ." (1070–1071). The message follows (E): "It was not the gods' will to free Peace yet" (1073). This is repeated in a *gar*-clause, formally a reason for the message (F): the gods don't yet want them to cease war (1075–1076)—here Hierokles indicates the condition precedent (D) in a *prin*-clause—"until a wolf weds a sheep." There follows a repetition of the message (1078–1080); finally Hierokles, justifying his oracular message to Trygaios, but still speaking in hexameters, pronounces two *gnômai* (F; see p. 155).

---

14 But that appears in Nonnos' pseudo-direct version; twice (*Dion.* 4.294–295) the god says, μαστεύεις τινὰ ταῦρον . . .

In the 38-line secular oracle of the Sibylline Books (see note 5), though probably late, the same components appear in a still different order. An oracle which begins *All' hopotan* must express the condition precedent first (D): "But when the longest span of life for men is reached, fulfilling a cycle of 110 years ..." (1–2). Then the Roman is told to remember the instructions given him (3–4): this is the Sibyl's assertion of mantic authority (C), and it includes the salutation (A), the simple vocative *Rômaie*; the admonition is repeated near the end (36). Then in 32 lines the message (E) is stated, a series of detailed commands for the celebration of the *Ludi Saeculares*. They are interrupted by a reason (F) for sacrificing to Zeus in the daytime and not at night (13–14). The composition ends in an elaborative prophecy (F) of perpetual sovereignty over Italy and Latium.

The analysis of these five verse-oracles reveals six components of oracular poetry. Very few oracles contain all six, and a short oracle may have only the message.

A. Salutation. This may be a simple one-word vocative or a vocative modified by adjectives or relative clauses extending sometimes over two or three verses. Often the god or seer characterizes the addressee(s) by reference to his / their country or city: in Q3 Apollo addresses the Peloponnesians,

> Ὦ γῆς ἀκρόπολιν πάσης Πελοπηίδα κλεινὴν
> ναίοντες πρέσβεις τε βροτῶν πάντων καὶ ἄριστοι.

The salutation is not necessarily in the second person. The *Olbios / Eudaimôn* openings are often in the third person. In Q61 and L41 the god greets Kypselos and Hesiod as each enters the temple with "Ολβιος οὗτος ἀνὴρ ὃς κτλ. Occasionally the person saluted is absent; the Pythia, directing the consultants to the site of Byzantion, says, "Happy the men who will settle that city of the Thracian coast" (Q44). In oracles represented as spoken by Apollo at Delphi, Didyma, or another oracular seat, the salutation is almost always made to the consultant or to the city that he represents; in oracles of Bakis and the Sibyl it is made to the seer's actual or intended audience, or it may be an apostrophe to someone absent.

B. Restatement of the question. In many verse-responses the god restates the question or problem within the first three verses, not as in Historical sanctions, where the message merely restates the question in approval, but as a preliminary to stating the message. This may be a fairly precise repetition of the question with necessary changes of person, as in L164, quoted above. Relatively frequent is the formula, "You have come to ask," as in Q31, ἦλθετ᾽ ἐρησόμενοι Φοῖβον τίνα γαῖαν ἵκησθε (cf. Q182, 203, 259; L171). Sometimes the restatement is less precise and may be just an allusion to the subject of the question, as in Q47, "Battos, you have come for [cure of your] voice" (cf. Q88, L80). The question may be implied in a statement or direction that is not ostensibly a restatement of it, as in Q102 (to Croesus), μὴ βούλευ πολύευκτον ἰὴν ἀνὰ δώματ᾽ ἀκούειν / παιδὸς φθεγγομένου, which is the essence of the message (cf. Q51, 188; L101). This component is found almost entirely in oracles reputedly spoken at oracular seats, since it presupposes a questioner. It does not appear in any extant chresmologic oracles, although it is conceivable that Bakis or the Sibyl could be supposed to address a questioner. The single non-Apolline example that I have encountered occurs in an oracle of Alexander of Abonuteichos, who begins, Δίζεαι ὅστις . . . ("You want to know who is secretly lying with your wife") in response to the question of a cuckold husband (Lucian *Alex.* 50; cf. L5, 40, 80, 164; F13).

C. *Assertion of Mantic Authority.* The oracle-speaker has several modes of asserting his credentials, the authority or sanction with which or under which he speaks; and he may employ more than one mode in a single pronouncement. For example, Q29 begins, Αὐτός σοι φράζει ἑκατήβολος· ἀλλὰ συνίει, addressed to Myskellos, founder of Croton: in the first clause the Pythia informs him that Apollo himself is speaker of the message (cf. Q47 above); in the second she bids him understand or heed it. The *ipse dixit* statement is all that we have of L176, Ταῦτά τοι ἐκ τρίποδος τοῦ Δελφικοῦ ἔφρασε Φοῖβος. One of Kleon's Bakid oracles, like Q29, combines *ipse dixit* with an admonition to heed the oracle: "Observe, Athenian, the path of oracles which Apollo has proclaimed from the adyton through his esteemed tripods," followed in the next verse by *ekeleus(e)* (*Knights* 1015–1016), a further expression of Apolline authority (cf. L11). Sometimes Apollo speaks the admonition in his own person, as in Q80, Πείθου ἐμοῖσι λόγοισιν· ἄκρον λάβε καὶ μέσον ἕξεις, a one-verse response consisting solely of admonition and message. More indirectly the god may say that the matter at issue is his concern, as in Q204. Again, as in some Apolline oracles, the god reminds an auditor that he has come to the oracular seat, as in Q61 and L41, "Happy is this man who enters my house," and in Q7, "You have come, O Lykurgos, to my rich temple." The foregoing oracles invoke Apollo's authority in one way or another; but in Q17 the Pythia refers to Zeus's will: Ζεὺς γὰρ ἔνευσ᾽ οὕτως (cf. L17, 165); and so does the Sibyl when she tells the Delphians, ἦλθον ἐγὼ χρήσουσα Διὸς νόον αἰγιόχοιο (Clement *Strom.* 1.108, 384P): "I have come to reveal the will of aegis-bearing Zeus," which adapts a common form of component B as seen in Q31 and others cited above. Or, as in L165, the auditors may be told that Zeus or the gods grant them good fortune or success. Occasionally the speaker is content with declaring that the message is predestined, as in L166.

D. *Condition Precedent.* This component is the determinant of modes B and F, since it expresses the sign of fulfillment, the time of action or critical event. It is usually expressed in some kind of conditional or conditional-relative clause or in an "until"-clause, since "X will occur when Y happens" (e.g., Q101) may also be expressed as "X will not occur until Y happens," well illustrated in the Birnam Wood prophecy of *Macbeth* (cf. Q16, 204). It may be expressed in a participial phrase or in a statement (cf. L165).

E. *Message.* This is the core of the oracle: the modes of chapter I are functions of the message, and the topics are message contents. It may be indicative: a prediction of the future or a statement about past, present, or future. Or it may be jussive: a command, recommendation, or prohibition.

F. *Explication.* Often the oracle-speaker adds or inserts statements to justify or clarify or expand his message, or occasionally some other component, e.g., his mode of salutation. This may be a simple reason, introduced with *gar* or *epei*, as in Q20, σχεδόθεν γὰρ ὄλεθρος, "When a goat [*tragos*] drinks the water of Neda, I no longer protect Messene; for doom is near." Croesus was told that it would be better for him if his son should never be able to talk, αὐδήσει γὰρ ἐν ἤματι πρῶτον ἀνόλβῳ (Q102). Q92(A), a seven-verse response, is mostly devoted to explication: the god bids Glaukos swear a false oath for immediate gain, ἐπεὶ θανατός γε καὶ εὔορκον μένει ἄνδρα; then he takes four more verses to expand upon his answer, describing the nameless son of Horkos who brings destruction upon the perjurer's whole family. The reason may be added without a conjunction: "Do you ask me for Arcadia? It's a big thing to ask for (B). I won't give it to you (C). There are many acorn-eating men in Arcadia to prevent you (F)"; the message (E) follows, what the god will grant instead (Q88).

It may be the purpose of the message that justifies it. Lucian's oracle of Bakis (*Peregrinos* 30) orders the stoning of any disciple of Peregrinos who escapes the fire, "so that he may not, being cold, try to warm himself with speech, filling his purse by making many loans in Patrai." To Apollo at Didyma is attributed an oracle on Pan, which concludes with an order to worship Artemis "that she may become your helper" (Didyma 38).

The reason given Glaukos in Q92(A), "since death awaits an oath-keeping man too" is gnomic in content. In a number of oracles the message is capped with an aphorism. L22 (= Q247), spoken to Theseus on statecraft, ends ἀσκὸς γὰρ ἐν οἴδματι ποντοπορεύσει. The *gar* indicates that the *gnômê* is given as a reason; but Q51, in which Battos is told to leave Thera and go to the continent (Libya) ends in an aphorism without causal conjunction as a moralizing conclusion to the direction given: οἷά τ᾽ ἀνὴρ ἔρξει, τοῖον τέλος αὐτὸν ἱκάνει (cf. Q144).

Finally, the oracle-speaker may elaborate his message with the intention of clarifying, defining, or expanding it. Apollo directs the Magnesians to the Pamphylian land beyond Mount Mykale in the first four verses of L165, and then employs four verses, a full half of the response, for further definition of the place and a promise of victory and glory from Zeus if they conduct themselves rightly. Such final promises of future victory or prosperity—when the question has not been how to obtain it—cannot be considered an expression of the message: they are more like expressions of purpose, meant to add conviction to the message (cf. Q47, longer form; L164, 167). The chresmologue's oracle of Bakis in the *Birds* (977–979) and the anonymous oracle of *Lysistrata* (774–776) end with warnings on the advantages of obedience and the disadvantages of disobedience. Most of the fourteen verses of Q3 are devoted to an explanatory elaboration. After salutation (A) of the Peloponnesians (1–2), who have come to ask about ending a plague and famine, the god tells them (C) to heed his oracle. Then he tells them that Zeus is angry because they have neglected the Olympian festival which he ordained; thereupon Apollo sketches the history of the festival, mentioning the three founders—Peisos, Pelops, Herakles; and returns to Zeus's wrath (F, 4–13). Finally, only in the last verse and the end of the preceding (13–14), Apollo states his message (E), advice to allay Zeus's wrath by renewing the festival.

Any one of these six components may merge with another. For example, an assertion of mantic authority (C) may be stated as a reason for or corroboration of the message (F): "for this is Zeus's will" (Q17). The line between the message (E) and elaboration of it, which is one form of explication (F), cannot always be drawn easily (cf. Q47, longer form). There are sometimes ambiguities of this kind; but almost everything said in the verse oracles which survive can be classified under these six components—almost nothing can be considered purely expletive, as distinct from elaborative or explicative. Of course, an oracle should have a message, and some short oracles are confined to that (e.g., Q27, 43, 90). The other components are not essential, though each may be expected as a fitting accompaniment to the message. What we must notice is the conventional and formulary nature of these components as they are expressed in oracles, and of the manner in which they are fitted together in the structure of an oracle. It is this structure that distinguishes oracular verse from other kinds of poetry; and though a component (especially A, D, F) may appear in other genres, it usually has a distinctive appearance when used in an oracular poem.

Few verse oracles contain five or six components. Very many, if not most, are constructed of three or four components. This means thirty-five possible combinations of three or four components, regardless of the order in which they appear, and forty-two possible combinations of three to six components. Since with one or two apparent exceptions all have a message, there are twenty-six possible combinations with component E. In fact, only five appear ten or more times among the traditional oracles under study ("Delphic," "Didymaean," chresmologic): ABEF, ACE, ACEF, AEF, DEF. Three others appear from five to seven times: ABCEF, ADE, CEF.

The simple commands, prohibitions, and warnings (modes A and C) expressed in verse are likely to preface message and explication with salutation and restatement of the question (ABEF) or salutation and assertion of mantic authority (ACEF) or salutation with both restatement and assertion (ABCEF). In the first of these combinations the salutation may be omitted (BEF, not frequent); in the second either the authoritative statement or the explication may be omitted (ACE, AEF). Other combinations occur, but are rare, at least among surviving oracular commands. A good example of oracular command in verse is Q203, spoken to the Achaeans when they laid siege to Aetolian Phanai:

> Γῆς Πέλοπος ναέται καὶ Ἀχαιίδος οἳ ποτὶ Πυθὼ
> ἤλθετε πευσόμενοι ὥς κε πτολίεθρον ἕλητε,
> ἀλλ᾽ ἄγε δὴ φράζεσθε λάχος πόσον ἦμαρ ἕκαστον
> λαῶν πινόντων ῥύεται πόλιν, ἡ δὲ πέπωκεν·
> οὕτω γάρ κεν ἕλοιτε Φάναν πυργήρεα κώμην.

The salutation (A) ends in a relative clause which at once becomes something more than a description of the Achaean consultants: the god lightly alludes to his mantic authority (C) by reminding the Achaeans that they have come to Pytho for an oracle, and completes the clause with a future participle expressing purpose, which introduces a restatement of their question (B), "to inquire how you can take the town." Then Apollo speaks his message (E), an obscure command (mode A3: the Achaeans do not understand it at first), introducing it with ἀλλ' ἄγε δὴ φράζεσθε (also used in Q31), an epic phrase which recalls the characteristic opening with *Phrazou dé*. In the final verse the god states the reason (F) for his command, marking it with *gar*, although it is the tautological kind of reason often used: "for that is the way for you to take the city." Here five components (ACBEF) are employed in as many verses.

But usually in commands and prohibitions (B) or (C) is omitted. Q182, a ten-verse response, begins much as Q203 does:

> Ἀρκάδες Ἀζᾶνες βαλανηφάγοι οἳ Φιγάλειαν
> νάσσασθ' ἱππολοχοῦς Δηοῦς κρυπτήριον ἄντρον,
> ἥκετε πευσόμενοι λιμοῦ λύσιν ἀλγινόεντος
> μοῦνοι δὶς νομάδες, μοῦνοι πάλιν ἀγριοδαῖται.

Here too a descriptive clause depends upon the opening vocative phrase (A), but without any allusion to Pytho or to the oracle-speaker; it refers, as in some other oracles, to the homeland of the consultants and is entirely part of the salutation. Moreover this clause does not include the restatement of the question (B); whereas in Q203 the expression "you have come to inquire" belongs to the relative clause, in Q182 it is the main verb (plus participle) of the first sentence; and it introduces not an indirect question but a noun phrase indicating the subject of inquiry. In Q182, moreover, the god returns to salutation: the fourth verse, consisting of two phrases descriptive of the Arcadian visitors, can be directly attached to the first two verses (have 3 and 4 been shifted?). There follows without conjunction a statement of the reason for famine (F): Demeter is angry because they have slighted her (5–7). The message (E) concludes the response: to avert worse famine the Arcadians must appease the goddess with due honors (8–10). The sequence is A/B/AFE.

Prohibitions usually show the same or similar structures: e.g., Q102:

> Λυδὲ γένος πολλῶν βασιλεῦ μέγα νήπιε Κροῖσε
> μὴ βούλευ πολύευκτον ἰὴν ἄνα δώματ' ἀκούειν
> παιδὸς φθεγγομένου. τὸ δέ τοι πολὺ λώιον ἀμφὶς
> ἔμμεναι· αὐδήσει γὰρ ἐν ἤματι πρῶτον ἀνόλβῳ.

The salutation (A), both honorific and depreciatory, is followed by a prohibition (E) in which Croesus is told to give up his desire and which thus restates his question (B). There follows a positive statement of the prohibitory message (E): "It is better that it be far away from you," and finally the reason (F). The sequence is AE/B/EF.[15]

---

15 For the common jussive structures see also Q3, 4, 28, 47, 51, 92, 144, 148, 188, 243, 246; L17, 22, 29, 41, 53, 55, 100, 147, 164, 167, 171; F13; Aristoph. *Eq.* 1015–1020 ("Bakis"); Didyma 37.

Most simple predictions (mode E) and statements on past or present events (mode D) that are composed of three or more components show the same five combinations that are most frequent among commands and prohibitions. Q61, a three-verse oracle (if complete) is like Q203 in its opening, but lacks an explication (and in a spontaneous response there can be no restatement of the queston):

> Ὄλβιος οὗτος ἀνὴρ ὃς ἐμὸν δόμον ἐσκαταβαίνει
> Κύψελος Ἠετίδης βασιλεὺς κλειτοῖο Κορίνθου
> αὐτὸς καὶ παῖδες, παίδων γε μὲν οὐκέτι παῖδες.

The whole oracle is a single sentence of third-person salutation (A), which becomes a reminder of the god's mantic authority (C) in the relative clause and a message in the third verse (E). The clause, "Who enters my house," has the same effect as "who have come to Pytho" in Q203: it reminds Kypselos that he stands in Apollo's temple where true oracles are spoken. Then *autos kai paides*, which appears to continue the complimentary statement about Kypselos, joins with the introductory *Olbios houtos anêr* to become a prediction of prosperity for Kypselos and his sons, continued in the final half-line, a noun phrase expressing a third subject of the sentence and introducing a negative of the predicate: "yourself and your sons [will be prosperous; your] grandsons no longer [will be]."

Q259, a 23-verse oracle, shows the same components as Q203 and also has a similar opening:

> Ὦ ζαθέης γεγαῶτες Ἐριχθονίοιο γενέθλης
> ἔτλητ᾽ ἐλθέμεναι καὶ ἐμὴν ἐρεείνεμεν ὀμφὴν
> ὅππως δῃωθῇ περικαλλέος ἔδρανα σηκοῦ.
> κλῦτε δαφνηρεφέων μυχάτων ἄπο θέσκελον ὀμφήν.

The salutation (A), as in Q182, introduces the statement which reminds the consultants that they have come to Apollo's Oracle; here, however, there is no mention of oracular seat or temple: rather the god explicitly refers to his mantic power: "You have ventured to come and ask for my response"; and the assertion of authority (C) is reinforced in the fourth verse with a "straight from the tripod" (*ipse dico*) statement. In between the two parts of component C the god restates the question (B). Thereupon the Athenians are told why Zeus's lightning struck their temple of Apollo, and then are bid endure the Moirai's designs; the whole message (E) fills fifteen verses (5–19). The response concludes with the reason (F), stated in two sentences introduced with *gar*: Zeus allows the Moirai to have their way—wherein a final allusion to the god's mantic authority is perceptible, since Apollo as oracle-speaker knows the will of Zeus and the Moirai. The sequence is AC/B/CEF/C.[16]

Combinations of components CEF are somewhat more frequent among predictions than among jussive oracles. A good example is Q15, spoken to the Spartans in the Messenian-War legend:

> Οὔ σε μάχης μόνον ἔργ᾽ ἐφέπειν χερὶ Φοῖβος ἄνωγεν,
> ἀλλ᾽ ἀπάτῃ μὲν ἔχει γαῖαν Μεσσηνίδα λαός,
> ταῖς δ᾽ αὐταῖς τέχναισιν ἁλώσεται αἶσπερ ὑπῆρξεν.

The Pythia first presents herself as speaking for Apollo (C): "It is not Phoebus' will that you wage war by combat alone." The adversative *alla* introduces a compound *men . . . de* sentence; the *men*-clause introduces the reason (F): "the Messenians took their land by deceit"; the *de*-clause states the message (E): "it will be taken by the same arts." A Sibylline oracle (Phlegon *Macr.* 4), though twenty-two verses long, has the same basic structure; it is the Erythraean Sibyl's prophecy of the destiny of her own soul and body after the end of her thousand-year life: despite her sorrows in life as Apollo's seeress, her soul and body will become the sources of every kind of divination among men. In the first eight lines she dwells upon the mantic inspiration (C) that comes to her from Apollo (unhappy though it be): the rest is prophecy of her afterlife (E), interrupted by two *gar*-sentences stating the reason (F) why her body lies unburied on earth (15–17). This oracle is a poet's composition, conceived as the Sibyl's soliloquy and organized according to the conventions of oracular poetry.[17]

The condition precedent (D), a necessary constituent of conditioned commands (mode B) and conditioned predictions (mode F), rarely occurs among oracles expressed in other modes (usually it occurs in mode C, otherwise when B or F is a subordinate mode). Most frequent are the combinations ADE(F) and (C)DEF (the four-component compositions being less frequent); that is, the condition-message complex (DE) is accompanied by a salutation or an explication. All other combinations with component D are rare.

---

16 Several predictions are composed of only salutation and message (AE): Q59, 60, 159, 245, 249. For the combinations A(B)EF and ACE(F) see also Q147, 196, 230; L80, 88, 108; and three Sibylline oracles (Nic. Dam. 68J; Clem. Alex. *Strom.* 1.108, 384P; Zosim. 2.37).

17 Other examples of CEF predictions are F9 (combined prediction and command) and Lucian *Alex.* 40. For CEF jussive oracles see Q123, Didyma 41.

The conditioned command with salutation is well illustrated in Q101:

Ἀλλ' ὅταν ἡμίονος βασιλεὺς Μήδοισι γένηται
καὶ τότε Λυδὲ ποδαβρὲ πολυψήφιδα παρ' Ἕρμον
φεύγειν μηδὲ μένειν μηδ' αἰδεῖσθαι κακὸς εἶναι.

The familiar *All' hotan* introduces the condition precedent (D), which expresses the Macduff theme; *kai tote*, marking the conclusion, is immediately followed by the pejorative vocative *Lyde podabre* (A), introducing the god's command (E), expressed in three infinitives (two with *mê* are technically prohibitions, but simply repeat the command in negative terms: "run away and don't stay").[18]

The oracle of Bakis quoted by Herodotos (8.77) also places the condition first with *All' hotan*:

Ἀλλ' ὅταν Ἀρτέμιδος χρυσαόρου ἱερὸν ἀκτὴν
νηυσὶ γεφυρώσωσι καὶ εἰναλίην Κυνόσουραν
ἐλπίδι μαινομένη λιπαρὰς πέρσαντες Ἀθήνας,
δῖα Δίκη σβέσσει κρατερὸν Κόρον Ὕβριος υἱὸν
5   δεινὸν μαιμώοντα, δοκεῦντ' ἄνα πάντα πιθέσθαι.
χαλκὸς γὰρ χαλκῷ συμμίξεται αἵματι δ' Ἄρης
πόντον φοινίξει. τότ' ἐλεύθερον Ἑλλάδος ἦμαρ
εὐρύοπα Κρονίδης ἐπάγει καὶ πότνια Νίκη.

[8.77]

But when they bridge the shore of Artemis Chrysaor and seaside Kynosura, with mad hope destroying bright Athens, noble Justice will quench mighty Insolence, dread furious child of Transgression, thinking to subdue the world. For bronze will mingle with bronze, and Ares will redden the sea. Then far-seeing Zeus and Lady Victory will bring on Hellas' day of freedom.

The condition precedent (D, verses 1–3) is followed immediately by the prediction (E) of victory (4–5). Then a formal reason (F) is expressed with *gar* (6–7), hardly more than an elaboration of the prediction. Finally with *tot(e)* the prediction is repeated in different form: Bakis reveals Zeus's design, thus suggesting that he speaks under the god's authority (C). The sequence is DEFE/C.

Q17, a Messenian oracle, shows a similar structure:

Τοῖς τρίποδας περὶ βωμὸν Ἰθωμάτᾳ Διὶ πρώτοις
στήσασιν δεκάδων ἀριθμὸν δὶς πέντε δίδωσι
σὺν κύδει πολέμου γαῖαν Μεσσηνίδα δαίμων·
Ζεὺς γὰρ ἔνευσ' οὕτως. ἀπάτη δέ σε πρόσθε τίθησιν,
5   ἤ τ' ὀπίσω τίσις ἐστ' οὐδ' ἂν θεὸν ἐξαπατώῃς.
ἔρδ' ὅπῃ τὸ χρεών· ἄτη δ' ἄλλοισι πρὸ ἄλλων.

---

18 For ADE(F) see also Q6, 44, 122, 134, 139, 212; Aristoph. *Aves* 967–979 ("Bakis").

The condition precedent (D) is expressed in a participial phrase, followed by the prediction (E): "Whoever first place a hundred tripods around Zeus Ithomatas' altar, to them heaven grants the Messenian land with victory." The hint of divine authority in "heaven grants" is corroborated in "for Zeus has so willed" (C/F). Then comes more prediction, followed by admonition (4–6). The oracle ends with a gnomic expression (F), "some come to ruin before others." The sequence is DEC/FEF.[19]

Such are the structures of oracular poetry. It has conventions of content and conventions of poetic expression, patterns and formulae both flexible and fixed. These are due in part to the genre itself, in part to the meter employed. Since dactylic hexameter was the epic meter, we may expect to find epic echoes in verse oracles. In those quoted or discussed above we may observe several compositional formulae of epic origin: Ὀλύμπια δώματ' ἔχουσι (Q7), σχεδόθεν γὰρ ὄλεθρος (Q20), ἄναξ δέ σε Φοῖβος Ἀπόλλων (Q47), κατέχει φυσίζοος αἶα (Q90), μέγα νήπιε Κροῖσε (Q102), ὥς ποτέ τις ἐρέει (Q134), (οὐ γὰρ) θέσφατόν ἐστι (Q188), ἀλλ' ἄγε δὴ φράζεσθε (Q203). Hendess points out many more in his *Oracula Graeca* (1877; see also McLeod 1961).

THE CHARACTERISTICS OF AUTHENTIC VERSE RESPONSES

That verse oracles attributed to the Delphic Apollo are composed under the same conventions and show the same kinds of structure and formulae as the chresmologic and narrative oracles does not in itself prove, or even imply, that they are not genuine pronouncements of the Pythia. It may be argued that this correspondence is only to be expected, since, if the Delphians delivered responses in verse, they would follow the conventions of oracular verse, especially in oral and spontaneous verse composition. We may even maintain the essential truth of the ancient belief that the Pythia or the first Delphic prophet invented hexameter verse; that is, that the first verse oracles were genuine pronouncements of the Pythia in a form devised by the Delphic priesthood, and that the inventors of chresmologic and narrative oracles adopted the Delphic form. The problem of authenticity, of course, must be settled on other grounds; and all the Quasi-Historical oracles discussed so far in this chapter are unauthentic or at best questionable for other reasons than their verse form. But if authentic Delphic oracles do not conform or rarely conform closely

---

19 For (C)DEF see also Q16, 20, 33, 34, 238; L51, 166; and three Bakid oracles (Aristoph. *Eq.* 197–201, Lucian *Per.* 30; Paus. 9.17.5).

to the traditional patterns of oracular verse, then the circumstance that a "Delphic" oracle has a traditional verse form may contribute to a judgement against its authenticity. The question of the genuine conventions, if any, of Delphic verse must rest upon an examination of the Historical and presumably genuine verse responses.

We have the texts of only seven Historical verse oracles. This number excludes the spurious verse forms of H3 and H17, the unauthentic H55, and the fragmentary H56. To these seven may be added three Quasi-Historical verse responses that appear to be genuine. We must look carefully at the texts of these ten responses.

H28

> Αὐδῶ ᾽Ερεχθείδῃσιν ὅσοι Πανδίονος ἄστυ
> ναίετε καὶ πατρίοισι νόμοις ἰθύνεθ᾽ ἑορτὰς
> μεμνῆσθαι Βάκχοιο καὶ εὐρυχόρους κατ᾽ ἀγυιὰς
> ἱστάναι ὡραίων Βρομίῳ χάριν ἄμμιγα πάντας
> καὶ κνισᾶν βωμοῖσι κάρη στεφάνοις πυκάσαντας.

There follow further directions in prose for sacrifices to the gods and for other religious acts. The prose sentences may in fact be another response; for before the reading of this oracle to document his argument, Demosthenes makes a statement that the Athenians worship Dionysos with dance and song "not only in accordance with the laws on the Dionysia, but also according to the oracles, in all of which you will find directions to the city, both from Delphi and from Dodona, to set up choral dances, etc. Now take the oracles themselves and read them." So we cannot be sure whether Demosthenes has one or two oracles read, nor are we sure that the verses were spoken at Delphi. In any case the content is unexceptionable and appears to be a versification of cult directions that would usually be expressed in prose. In the first two words ("I declare to the Athenians") we may see a faint assertion of mantic authority (C). There follows a salutation (A) of the kind found in traditional oracles: the god refers to the consultants' city and customs. The last three lines consist of the message (E), directions for worship of the same kind as the following prose directions. There are no epic phrases, although the first two verses have a vaguely epic cast.

In summary, H28 may be called a conventional verse response in that it is in no way aberrant; yet it is colorless and hardly typical. Furthermore its authenticity is questionable; I have classified it as Historical on a tentative assumption that Demosthenes was offering a response spoken not long before (PW place it in their sixth period, 373–300). He can be understood in that fashion; and it may be that he had the oracle read to his auditors because they had not yet heard it. In fact, he says nothing about the time of utterance, but speaks only of oracles from Delphi and Dodona, probably kept in the state archives. Although commonplace in content (cult directions) H28 appears to order the establishment of Dionysos' cult in Athens; and it is strange that a fourth-century response instructs the Athenians to offer fruits and make sacrifices on altars to Dionysos. H28 may be the composition that purported to be the divine order directing the introduction of Dionysos' cult to Athens (and the first Athenian cult of Dionysos was probably too early for a Delphic sanction). So it may have lain in the Athenian archives for a long time before 348 B.C. (although it was surely not composed before the fifth century).

H63

"Ἅπαντα τἀναγκαῖα συγχώρει θεός.

Plutarch's Theon says that this was spoken "a short time ago," which I have taken at face value; but such phrases are often used vaguely and may cover a good deal of time. Apparently Plutarch himself did not witness this consultation. The response is a gnomic utterance (see p. 87 note 62) in iambic trimeter; and all trimeter responses are suspect.[20] This line may have been taken from a tragedy.

H65

"Ἄγνωστον μ' ἔρεαι γενεὴν καὶ πατρίδα γαῖαν
ἀμβροσίου Σειρῆνος. ἕδος δ' Ἰθακήσιός ἐστιν,
Τηλέμαχος δὲ πατὴρ καὶ Νεστορέη Ἐπικάστη
μήτηρ, ἥ μιν ἔτικτε βροτῶν πολὺ πάνσοφον ἄνδρα.

A restatement of the question (B) is followed by the answer (E), a two-component composition. There are epic resonances, especially in the first and fourth verses, as befits a response on Homer. Moreover, it is possible that this response was designed to please the consultant, Emperor Hadrian, who asked, "Whence was Homer and whose son?" by responding with his own intuition—well known, we may suppose, to the Delphians—that Homer was an Ithacan, son of Telemachos and Epikaste. It was obviously the final redactor who introduced Hadrian's consultation and the response into the *Certamen*, which in its extant form is dated in the Antonine period. The date of the consultation, if Hadrian inquired in person, must be 125–130. It is probable that the consultation occurred within the

20 On the spuriousness of iambic responses see Pomtow 1881; but Parke 1945 believes that Delphi sometimes employed iambic verse in prohibitions and denials (e.g. Q112).

redactor's lifetime, and for this reason I have classified H65 as Historical; but he may have been born later, and we don't know exactly when he produced his edition of the *Certamen*: the Antonine period covers fifty-five years. Moreover how trustworthy is the *Certamen* as a source for even recent events? May not the story be a bit of upper-class folklore, an anecdote that circulated in learned Antonine coteries? So again, we cannot be sure that we have an authentic Delphic response before us.

H66

> Φοῖβος Ἀθηναίοις Δελφοὺς ναίων τάδε [εἶπεν·]
> "Εστιν σοι παρ' ἄκρας πόλεως παρὰ [τὸν προπύλαιον]
> οὗ λαὸς σύμπας κλήιζει γλαυκώ[πιδ' Ἀθήνην,]
> Δήμητρος Χλοίης ἱερὸν Κούρ[ης τε μακαίρας,]
> οὗ πρῶτον στάχυς εὐξή[θη ζειῶν ἱεράων] . . .

These verses were inscribed in Athens. There are nine more lines, but too few words are visible on the stone for reconstruction; there is mention of *aparchai*, and the final words are [λώι]ον ἔσται, which indicate a sanction (mode A2). We have already noticed the first verse: the sentence of introduction that would ordinarily precede quotation of an oracle has been versified as the first line of the response and serves as an assertion of mantic authority (C). The verses which follow define (F) the locale of whatever rites are prescribed (E) in the last seven lines. There can be no doubt that this is a genuine Delphic oracle of the second century A.D., probably from Hadrian's time. The structure CFE is not uncommon, and it contains some formulaic expressions: we have noticed *Estin soi*; *glaukôpid' Athênê* might be expected in this response; and *Delphous naiôn* looks like a poetic tag. The content, however, is unlike that of most traditional oracles: it consists of ritual prescriptions put into verse. The verse alone distinguishes it from such prose compositions as H29, which begins Συμφέρει Ἀθηναίοις περὶ τοῦ σημείου τοῦ ἐν τῷ οὐρανῷ γενομένου θύοντας καλλιερεῖν Διὶ Ὑπάτῳ κτλ., where we perceive the components BE.

H67

> "Ενθα μακροῖσι χρόνοισι σεβάσμιος εἴθισεν αἰὼν
> λουτροῖσιν χρῆσθαι τετιημένα σώματα γήρως,
> οὗ χόρον ἱστᾶσιν κοῦραι θαλάμων ἀμύητοι
> εὐρύθμως λωτοῖο πρὸς εὔφθογγομ μέλος ἡδύ,
> θηλοπρεποῦς Φωτὸς μελάθροις "Ηραν προσεβάζου.

These verses appear in an inscription of the late second century A.D. found in the old Latmic Gulf region. It may be an inscription of Magnesia-on-Maeander, which sometimes consulted Delphi (see H45), so that a case can be made for Delphic provenance of the oracle. But there is no indication in the context that it is Delphic, and I am inclined to think that it is not. The response has a superficial appearance of obscurity owing to the periphrastic language in which it is expressed; but its meaning is really very clear: it consists only of the message: the consultants should worship Hera (probably found a sanctuary) at the eunuch's house, situated by the old men's baths and the girls' orchestra. On the whole, it is rather unlike the traditional oracles in manner and phrasing.[21]

H68

> Χειλιετὲς μήνειμα πάτρης Διὸς ἐξαναλύσας
> μειλιχίη Σεισίχθονι ἐν ἄλσει βωμὸν ἐνείρας
> θύεο, μὴ διερεύνω μ' ὦ πόλις, Εἰναλίῳ νῦν
> ἐννομίην Κρονίδη, φοιβῇ χερὶ δὲ ἀρητῆρος,
> 5   πυρῶν καὶ καρπῶν τ' ἐπιδράγματα πάντα· καλείσθω
> ἀσφάλιος τεμενοῦχος ἀπότροπος ἵππιος ἀργής·
> ὧδε πόλις δὲ ὑμνεῖτε δεδραγμένον εἶφι βεβῶτα
> οὗ τε βάθρῳ κύκνειον ὅσοι γέρας ἀμφιπένεσθε
> ἐν χόρῳ εὖ αἰνεῖν Σεισίχθονα καὶ Δία ΜΕΙΛΑΞ.

This response was inscribed at Tralles around A.D. 250; the caption reads, "Oracle of the Pythian given to Kleitosthenes the priest of Zeus on the safety of the city." It is mostly message (E), a series of commands for ritual acts in Poseidon's worship.[22] In the third verse μὴ διερεύνω μ(ε) appears to be an odd way of saying "Don't question me," i.e., "Obey me," and so may be taken as a mild assertion of mantic authority (C). Then comes a weak salutation in ὁ polis, repeated in polis of the seventh verse. The ritual commands are expressed in the manner of H28 and H66;

---

21 One would like to have the whole inscription. Just before the verses there appear the final words of the preceding text "—saying to her, 'Appease Hera.' 'Where [or What] [Hera] shall [he/she?] appease?' The god replied, . . ." Either there was an earlier oracle or this was a bipartite consultation, of which we have no Historical example. The prose fragment looks like narrative conversation. The inscription may have recorded the foundation legend of Hera's cult at Magnesia or elsewhere.

22 PW 471 read *exanelysas*, aorist indicative, in the first verse, as in the first publication, BCH 5 (1881) 340, which makes no good sense. I accept Ziebarth's *exanalysas*, aorist participle, expressing an act identical with that expressed in the main verb: the act of sacrifice is that which expiates Zeus's wrath. Whether the stone showed *A* or *E* as fifth letter, the participle was obviously meant. The verses are badly written, sometimes unintelligible: the syntax is poor (notice *de* after a vocative in verse 7, and otiose *de* and *te* in 4, 5, 8); and there are lapidary's mistakes, one of which, I believe, is *patrès* for *patros* in verse 1, otherwise *patrès* must be taken with *exanalysas*, which elsewhere governs accusative of the object liberated and genitive of the oppressing object.

and the final two verses resemble H67 in their manner of specifying the scene of worship: "At whose altar, all you who have the task of worshipful song, praise Poseidon and Zeus in chorus." There are no oracular formulae or epic phrases in this composition.

These miserable verses are explicitly labeled "Oracle of the Pythian," and, if so, reveal a sad decline in the god's poetic art, in keeping with the general decline of Oracles in the third century. Yet one wonders whether this is really a product of the Delphian priesthood. It is quite possible that "the Pythian" is merely a way of designating Apollo as supposed speaker. In a contemporary poem inscribed at Didyma, the god who spoke oracles in the Didymeion, who is celebrated in the poem for renewing the sacred spring in a time of need (the Goths' attack in A.D. 263), is called the Pythian.[23] So H68 may be a made-to-order oracle: Kleitosthenes engaged a poet to compose the verses, having perhaps first obtained a sanction at Didyma or Klaros or some other nearby sanctuary of his proposed foundation or renewal of Poseidon's cult in Tralles; or perhaps, he got approval not only of his project but also of ready-made verses to express the god's intention, much as I suppose Amelios did for H69.

H69

Amelios' long-winded hymn to Plotinos, presented as Apollo's oracle (but not clearly the Pythian Apollo's), need not be quoted in full. It begins,

> Ἄμβροτα φορμίζειν ἀναβάλλομαι ὕμνον ἀοιδῆς
> ἀμφ᾽ ἀγανοῖο φίλοιο μελιχροτάταισιν ὑφαίνων
> φωναῖς εὐφήμου κιθάρης χρύσεῳ ὑπὸ πλήκτρῳ.

Then Apollo summons the Muses to join him in his song, ὕμμι καὶ ἐν μέσσαισιν ἐγὼ Φοῖβος βαθυχαίτης (10). The first ten verses are taken up with this hymnal assertion of mantic authority (C), in which the god presents himself as bard rather than prophet. Then Plotinos, the subject of inquiry, receives the salutation (A), δαῖμον ἄνερ τὸ πάροιθεν, which fills three verses (11–13) and foreshadows the message (E), which reveals Plotinos' divine destiny in thirty-five verses (14–48), all spoken in the second person and addressed to Plotinos. This part is broken into a statement on the pure abode to which Plotinos has gone (component E; verses 14–18); a passage on his inspired life in the flesh, when he saw the beatific vision (F; 19–32); a statement on his present residence in Elysion

23 Theodor Wiegand, "Achter vorläufiger Bericht über Ausgrabungen in Milet und Didyma," *Abh. Akad. Berlin* (1924) 22.

(E; 33–35); and a description of this paradise in conventional terms (F; 36–48), which includes another salutation, ὁ *makar* (A; 46). Then the hymn concludes,

> στήσωμεν μολπήν τε χοροῦ τ' εὐδίνεα κύκλον
> Πλωτίνου Μοῦσαι πολυγηθέες, αὐτὰρ ἐμεῖο
> χρυσείη κιθάρῃ τόσσον φράσεν εὐαίωνι
>
> [49–51]

a return to the initial assertion of authority (C). The verses contain no purely oracular formulae, but are expressed in epic language throughout and filled with Homeric echoes, as the first verse and phrases like *all' age* (8), *kai tote men* (19), *nyn d' hote dē* (33), attest. It is a very atypical response.

Q12

> Εἴ κεν ἐπικτήτου μοίρης λάχος Ἀπόλλωνι
> ἥμισυ δάσσωνται, πολὺ λώιον ἔσσεται αὐτοῖς.

This is unexceptionable in form and content, merely the versification of a sanction: the Spartans asked whether they should divide certain acquired land with Apollo and received an affirmative reply. Our only source, however, is Oinomaos' essay against Oracles; he objects that Apollo refers to himself in the third person, and he asks, "What other Apollo do you mean?" Furthermore, according to Oinomaos, the consultants were the Spartan kings Charilaos and Archelaos, who reigned between 775 and 750, which is very early for a genuine Delphic oracle; but it may have been received at a later time and credited in Spartan or literary tradition to an earlier time.[24] If it was spoken in the eighth century, it may be the earliest genuine verse oracle (and perhaps the earliest genuine oracle, but Q8 could be earlier) that we have. If authentic, it indicates an early Delphic practice of expressing sanctions and simple commands in two or three verses which merely put the typical prose formula, as expressed in H2, 38, 45, as nearly as possible into hexameters. It is perhaps the kind of response that lies behind the tradition that verse oracles were spoken at Delphi and other oracular seats. Only the simple message is economically conveyed; there are no other components nor any formula other than a verse rendition, *poly lôion essetai*, of the ordinary sanction formula.

---

24 See Parke 1956: 93, PW 539. Parke is very dubious about the authenticity of Q12, and PW relegate it to "Oracles of Quite Uncertain Date," in the subsection on "religious cults," among legendary and doubtful responses. Yet it is more likely to be genuine than most Q responses that Parke accepts without question.

Q69

Ἀρχηγοὺς χώρας θυσίαις ἥρωας ἐνοίκους
ἵλασο τοὺς κόλποις Ἀσωπιὰς ἀμφικαλύπτει,
οἳ φθίμενοι δέρκονται ἐς ἥλιον δύνοντα.

My tentative conclusion with respect to Q12 tends to be supported by Q69, reputedly spoken to Solon. It is somewhat more poetic in diction, but contains the simple direction to propitiate the heroes buried on Salamis. Plutarch connects it with the story of Solon's acquisition of Salamis: how Solon went by night to the island, then in Megarian hands, and made sacrifice to the heroes Periphemos and Kychreus, thus assuring success in his purpose of taking Salamis. The verses themselves suggest no such story: they are a simple direction to worship heroes.[25] It appears that a genuine Delphic verse-oracle, which may really be later than Solon's time, was fitted to a pseudo-historical narrative of the winning of Salamis for Athens.

Q148

Ὦ Δελφοὶ λίσσεσθ' ἀνέμους καὶ λώϊον ἔσται.

This verse is quoted by Clement of Alexandria. Herodotos reports the response indirectly: καί σφι ἐχρήσθη ἀνέμοισι εὔχεσθαι· μεγάλους γὰρ τούτους ἔσεσθαι τῇ Ἑλλάδι συμμάχους: "and they were told to pray to the Winds; for they would be great allies for Hellas." From this Parke and Wormell (PW 96) construct a second verse: Ἑλλάδι γὰρ μεγάλοι ποτὲ σύμμαχοι οὗτοι ἔσονται. In any case, salutation, message, and explication (AEF) are visible in this short response.[26] Clement's verse may well be authentic; it is no more than the versification of an ordinary command or sanction to pray to specified deities, to which a reason was added, probably versified too (cf. H7, 27).

It is surprising that of seven Historical verse oracles, six are very late, spoken between about A.D. 100 and 300, if the indications of date are accepted at face value. Only H28 is early, supposedly spoken in the

---

25 The third verse is nothing more than a definition of heroes; but the storytellers made it into a support of the Athenian claim, saying that the Megarians buried their dead facing east. Hereas of Megara, however, said that the Megarian dead faced west too; and in fact this was the universal Greek custom; see Plut. *Solon* 9. Parke (1956: 110) rejects this oracle, apparently because of the story attached to it, and places it among "Fictitious Oracles of the Sixth Period" 373–300 (PW 326).

26 How and Wells (1912: 2.209) point out an hexameter line in Herodotos' narrative (ἐξαγγείλαντες ... κατέθεντο) just after his notice of Q148. If the phenomenon is not accidental, it may mean that Herodotos' source was either a narrative poem or a commemorative inscription in verse; either probably quoted the response.

fourth century B.C. It is also noteworthy that some question can be raised about the authenticity or the Delphic provenance of all except H66. Four are not certainly Delphic (H28, 67, 68, 69). Four are not certainly contemporary with the extant record or its author, and so may not be properly classed as Historical responses in the sense defined (H28, 63, 65, 67), and in truth may be traditional narrative oracles, never spoken anywhere. H65 is recorded in a questionable source. Yet, as far as content goes, all seven may be accepted as authentic responses, spoken either at Delphi or another established Oracle.

The evidence, then, points to few responses in verse before the second century A.D., and to a considerable increase in authentic verse oracles thereafter. The evidence from Didyma confirms this impression; of eight verse oracles, all recorded in inscriptions, six belong to the second and third centuries A.D. (Didyma 27–32); the other two are 14, 15, inscribed in 228/7. From Klaros all the genuine oracles that survive are late and mostly in verse. This frequency of late verse oracles might be interpreted as a return to the practice of responding in verse, if it could be proved that many verse oracles were spoken at Delphi or Didyma in earlier times. Rather the authentic records show prose statements, usually stereotyped, and very few verse responses at any time before A.D. 100. The reason for the increase was likely to be the influence of Plutarch's essay "On the Pythia's Not Speaking Verse Oracles at the Present Time." Plutarch and his contemporaries accepted the literary and folk tradition about Delphi, supposing that the practice of speaking verse oracles had lapsed. Probably the Delphic authorities read his treatise and were aroused by it to attempt more verse oracles: more attractive responses, they believed, would help enhance and renew the Oracle's prestige.

Whatever the intentions of their authors, these late verse-oracles, whether spoken at Delphi or elsewhere, are uniformly bad. The poets obviously wanted to produce verses like those of the oracles which they read in literature or received from tradition, and to do so on short notice. Having models before them they were aware, if vaguely, of the conventions, structures, formulae, and diction of oracular verse. But they lacked competence and skill. They barely succeed in versifying the message, and add little if anything to it. H66, the most competently composed in what we can see of it, has a simple CFE structure; H68 barely manages to show an ACE structure in which the salutation and an admonition to heed the god's words are almost casually inserted. Only the long H69 shows a complex structure, which can be outlined as $C^1A^1E/F/E/FA^2C^2$ (ring composition); but it is really a hymn posing as an oracle.

In contrast to the late Historical compositions the three Quasi-Historical verse responses are early productions; the latest is dated 480 B.C. They are also different in character, simple responses expressed in competent verses; they express sanction or command in economical phrases of poetic diction; and they have their own sanction formula, observable in Q12 and Q148, *lôion estai/essetai*. The poets apparently made no attempt to imitate the oracles of popular tradition and chresmologues' collections. They confined themselves to the simple message, as in prose oracles; a vocative may be added, as in Q148, to fill out a verse. Hardly different is H28, the only surviving Historical verse response of pre-imperial date. Besides an elaborate two-verse salutation of conventional character it is confined to simple cult directions. Of the late Historical verse-oracles H66, which alone is a certainly authentic pronouncement of Delphi, has this simple character (though it is long), and it ends with *lôion estai*. The late verse oracles from Didyma (27–32) seem to continue the ancient practice of putting simple messages into verse, although the poets sometimes attempt elegant expression. From Klaros, however, after A.D. 100 come long pretentious oracles, similar to the late Sibylline compositions.

Alexander of Abonuteichos, establishing a new Oracle after Plutarch's time, spoke responses in verse, apparently attempting to adhere to the literary and popular tradition of what verse-oracles should be. His compositions are mediocre at best and not much like the authentic verse responses of earlier times; his pronouncements are nearer to the traditional oracles in diction and content, although he seldom attempted a complex structure.[27]

Authentic verse oracles, therefore, differ in style and content from the traditional oracles of folk narrative, poetry, chresmologues' compositions, and oracle collections. They are simple in structure, short, mainly confined to the message, not much embellished with formulae—the main formulaic expression being derived from prose responses—and not strongly epic in diction or manner. But traditional oracles are a genre of poetry. The original compositions of this kind purported to be the pronouncements of seers, who were also poets; in time such compositions were attached to Apollo at Delphi or Didyma or some other sanctuary. That is why the composer of a traditional oracle did not usually imitate genuine Delphic verse oracles.

---

27 Lucian *Alex.* gives us almost all the information that we have about Alexander and his Oracle at Abonuteichos in Paphlagonia.

CHAPTER

The Mantic Session

What happened at Delphi in an oracular session, when a consultant asked a question and received a response? Writers on Greek religion and civilization still tell their readers essentially what Farnell told his in 1907:

> ... the Pythoness ascended into the tripod, and, filled with the divine afflatus which at least the later ages believed to ascend in vapour from a fissure in the ground, burst forth into wild utterance, which was probably some kind of articulate speech, and which the [*Hosioi*], the "holy ones," who with the prophet sat around the tripod, knew well how to interpret. ... What was essential to Delphic divination, then, was the frenzy of the Pythoness and the sounds which she uttered in this state which were interpreted by the [*Hosioi*] and the "prophet" according to some conventional code of their own.[1]

The Pythia mounted the tripod, priests and *Hosioi* attended her—otherwise this account is wholly fanciful. There was no vapor and no chasm:

---

1 Farnell 1907: 189. See Bouché-Leclercq 1880: 3.96–97; Dempsey 1918: 54–55; Poulsen 1920: 23–24; Flacelière 1938: 104–105, 1965: 50–52; Parke 1956: 33, 1967b: 82–84. Farnell still used the term "Pythoness" for the Pythia, as had been customary down to the end of the nineteenth century. No ancient writer refers to the Delphic priestess as Pythoness; in fact, the only occurrence of the word *pythonissa* that I can find is in the Vulgate at Chron. 10.13 to designate the sorceress whom Saul consulted (where the Hebrew has simply the masculine *'ôbh*). The term *pythôn* was applied in late antiquity to an *engastrimythos* like Eurykles (Plut. *Mor.* 414e). No pythons of this kind are ever connected with Delphi.

the Pythia experienced no frenzy that caused her to shout wild and unintelligible words; she spoke quite clearly and directly to the consultant without need of the prophet's mediation.[2] We know almost nothing about what happened in the consultation of the Oracle; but such evidence as we have destroys the conventional modern picture of the Pythia's activity as Farnell expresses it. Greek and Latin authors tell us little or nothing about the mantic process at Delphi; one or two who describe a séance are wholly untrustworthy. In fact very few authors whose works have come down to us ever consulted the Delphic Oracle or witnessed a consultation; many of them never visited Delphi. And Plutarch, who as priest of the Delphic Apollo did witness consultations and hear responses spoken, tells us very little about the procedures of the Delphic Oracle.[3] He says nothing about vapors, toxic or other, nothing about a frenzy or trance of the Pythia, nothing about wild or incoherent speech from the Pythia's mouth, except in one passage—a report of an exceptional consultation (H72) that vitiates rather than confirms the modern rationalistic description as expressed by Farnell.

CHASM AND VAPORS

Plutarch mentions *pneumata*, *dynameis*, *anathymiaseis*, and *atmoi* which affect the Pythia, inducing the *enthousiasmos* under which she speaks Apollo's oracles. These currents and exhalations are obviously not vapors; they are nothing visible nor otherwise perceptible to the senses, but entirely theoretical: Plutarch's Lamprias thus explains the mantic inspiration of the god's ministrants at oracular temples, relying upon Aristotelian and Stoic theories about the powers of earth.[4] These emanations from earth are physical causes of the same breed as the influences of stars and planets that astrologers postulate. This is clear from the argument in *De defectu oraculorum* (*Mor.* 432c–438d) in which the speakers do not agree on the causes of the Pythia's inspiration, and in which the earth-exhalation theory is opposed to the demonic (although Lamprias tries to reconcile them). Plainly Ammonios and other participants are unaware of any

2 On Delphic mantic procedures and the Pythia's activity see Bouché-Leclercq 1880: 3.84–102; Oppé 1904; Flacelière 1938, 1965: 39–54; Latte 1940; Parke 1939: 18–38, 1940a, 1956: 17–41, 1967b: 72–88; Will 1942; Amandry 1950; Delcourt 1955: 44–108; Fauth 1963: 523–539; Whittaker 1965: 21–28; Nilsson 1967: 170–174.

3 For Plutarch's priesthood and other offices at Delphi see SIG 829A, 843; Plut. *Mor.* 792f, 700e.

4 See Will 1942; Amandry 1950: 216–225; cf. Flacelière 1947: 20–21, 38–87. The Stoic nature of Lamprias' arguments (though it has Aristotelian sources) is evident from its agreement with Quintus Cicero's argument in Cic. *Div.* 1.19.38, 1.36.79, 1.50.115.

perceptible exhalations, not to mention vapors. Furthermore Lamprias cannot say how the mantic current flows from earth, whether through air by itself or mingled with water (i.e., rising in springs and presumably present in the water that the Pythia drank, *Mor.* 432d); nor can he say how it affects the human soul (432f–433a). Lamprias conjectures that earth's exhalations can change place, lose force, or disappear altogether; like some modern scholars he resorts to earthquakes, excessive rains, and landslides for an explanation of their waning or disappearance (434bc). These conjectures were not verifiable by observation on the spot; if there had been visible vapors their presence or absence would have been noticed at once and could not be a subject of debate.

As Ammonios points out (435a–d), if exhalations produced the Pythia's inspiration, why then did the Delphian priests pour cold water over the sacrificial goat to learn from the victim's shuddering or failure to shudder whether oracles would be spoken that day? For the exhalations, if present, would produce the mantic enthusiasm whether the victim shuddered or not. Furthermore the exhalations would affect anyone that breathed them, and not only the Pythia—exactly as in the old foundation myth that Diodoros tells (16.26.2–4) and to which Ammonios alludes: the herdsman who first came upon the site received mantic inspiration, and his goats were inspired to gambol and to utter strange bleats; and likewise everyone who came to the spot thereafter received the inspiration, until the Delphians devised the office of Pythia. Diodoros, we should notice, says nothing about *pneumata* or exhalations of any kind, although his story obviously assumes some power inherent in the place; and Ammonios uses only the term *dynamis* in reference to the myth.

Plutarch's Lamprias argues that the exhalations are sometimes strong, sometimes weak, indicating again that one could not really feel them. Or rather usually could not: for in support of his argument he points to a phenomenon that the god's ministers and many visitors had witnessed— as they had informed him; he does not seem to have experienced it himself (and this may mean that Plutarch had not): "Not often nor regularly, but occasionally and fortuitously, the room in which they seat the god's consultants is filled with a fragrance and breeze [*pneumatos*], as if the adyton were sending forth the essences of the sweetest and most expensive perfumes from a spring" (*Mor.* 437c). Obviously this fragrant breeze had nothing to do with the Pythia's activity; i.e., her mounting the tripod did not depend on its presence. It did not occur often or regularly; when it came, it did so unexpectedly. Above all, it had no toxic effect—else the consultants would be affected—and was the opposite of "mephitic." Will (1942: 175) and Amandry (1950: 222) look upon the reported fragrance as a purely subjective phenomenon: a sweet smell is associated with divinity. It may be that occasionally drafts within the temple carried the fragrance of incense or of flowers to the consultants' room (see Euripides *Ion* 89–90), where ordinarily one would perceive no such scent.

Much later, in his dialogue on the Pythia's oracles, Plutarch barely mentions *pneumata*, and then only to dismiss the possibility that their disappearance caused the failure of the Pythia's poetic powers (*Mor.* 402b). He says nothing anywhere about toxic or "mephitic" properties in the conjectured *pneumata*. In fact, "mephitic gas" as a Delphic phenomenon appears to be entirely a modern fantasy. Strabo mentions only a *pneuma enthousiastikon* that causes the Pythia to speak oracles when she sits on the tripod; Pseudo-Longinus refers to an *atmos entheos* that affects her; according to Iamblichos it is a fiery *pneuma* that arises from earth to envelop the Pythia in radiance. In the Pseudo-Aristotelian *De mundo* the *pneumata* which arise from outlets at Delphi and Lebadeia make their recipients enthusiastic; and probably the Pseudo-Aristotle's source of information was also the elder Pliny's, who refers to an intoxicating exhalation (*exhalatione temulenti*) which issues from the earth at certain sites, of which Delphi is an example, and causes oracle-speaking. Contrary to Iamblichos' fiery *pneuma* it is in Pompeius Trogus' account of the Delphic Oracle a cold blast that produces madness (*vecordia*) in the minds of the seers. A current of that sort, like Pliny's, might well be called toxic; and Valerius Maximus speaks of *divini spiritus haustus pestifer* that comes over the Pythia when she descends deep within the oracular cave.[5] Only in Valerius' *pestifer* do we have an adjective that might be translated "mephitic"; but he uses it in reference to the story of Appius Claudius' consultation at Delphi in 48 B.C. (Q249) that Lucan so graphically describes (*BC* 5.123–224), when, as the story goes, the Pythia, forced to receive Apollo's inspiration at an unpropitious time, died soon afterwards. Valerius, or rather the source common to his narrative and Lucan's, wants to account for the Pythia's misfortune on this occasion: Appius forced her to descend into the inmost part of the cave, where she would receive sure oracles; but the malignancy of the *spiritus* increases with the depth of the cave and the truth of the oracles received there.

---

5 Strabo 9.3.5, p. 419; Ps.-Long. 13.2; Ps.-Aristotle *Mund.* 395b; Iambl. *Myst.* 3.11; Pompeius Trogus/Justin 24.6.9; Pliny *NH* 2.95.208; Val. Max. 1.8.10. See also Dion Cass. 62.14.2; Cic. *locc. cit.* (note 4) and 2.57.117; John Chrys. *Ep. I ad Cor. Hom.* 29.1, p. 242 Migne; Origen *Cels.* 3.25, 7.3; Schol. vet. on Aristoph. *Plut.* 39.

No writer mentioned, except Plutarch, appears to have had first-hand knowledge of Delphi; Strabo introduces his remarks on Delphi with "they say" (*phasi*). No source mentions anything like a gas or visible vapor issuing from the earth; what Pliny and Valerius Maximus mention are exhalations or air currents with perceptible effects. And almost none mentions a chasm or fissure in the earth, the indispensable source of the "mephitic vapor" in modern accounts of the Delphic Oracle. Several authors—but none earlier than Lykophron—speak of a cave (*antron, spêlaion, specus, caverna,* etc.). Strabo refers to anonymous informants (*phasi*) who told him that the *manteion* was a hollow deep cave with a narrow mouth, whence arose a *pneuma enthousiastikon*; he may mean a perpendicular shaft or a cave sloping gradually downward. For Lucan and Valerius Maximus the cave seems to slope downwards below or behind the temple's adyton; the Pythia descends into it and roams about it.[6] In fact, this cave is the adyton in Lucan's conception of Apollo's temple.[7] No gases or vapors issue from it; the *spiritus* which Lucan twice mentions (*BC* 5.132, 165) is that *numen* with which Delphi's rock is instinct. Moreover when Phemonoe, the Pythia, finally enters the cave and utters a response, Apollo has taken possession of her person. For Pliny the inebriating exhalations issue from oracular caves (*fatidici specus*) at Delphi and elsewhere. Several authors who mention a cave at Delphi without reference to exhalations of any kind appear to mean no more than the adyton.[8]

The first mention of a chasm appears in Diodoros' version of the aforementioned myth, in which a herdsman, whom Plutarch calls Koretas, and his goats happened upon a chasm and at once began to behave strangely. Diodoros calls it *chasma*; saying that it brought mantic enthusiasm to anyone who approached it and looked into it. A Scholiast calls it *chaos*, telling essentially the same story and not mentioning any exhalations (see note 25). Plutarch and Pausanias refer to the story without mention of a chasm, although Plutarch may imply it in his use of the verb *empiptein* twice in the aorist participle (*empesontos, empesonta*): either

---

6 See Lucan *BC* 5.169–170: bacchatur demens aliena per antrum / colla ferens. Obviously Lucan has no clear plan of adyton and cave in mind. Aside from 169 Lucan refers to *antra* or *cavernae*. In two verses he uses *hiatus*, once singular (131), once plural (82), obviously not meaning a cleft or fissure but the cave or its entrance; in 131 *hiatus* (*muto Parnasos hiatu*) has *fauces* as synonym in 133 (*seu spiritus illas / destituit fauces*).

7 See *BC* 5.84–85: sacris se condidit antris / incubuitque adyto...; 146: illa pavens adyti penetrale remoti...; 169–171: bacchatur... per antrum / ... per inania templi...

8 Lyk. 207–208; Ovid *Met.* 3.14 (cf. 15.634–636); Sen. *H. Oet.* 1475; Stat. *Theb.* 1.492, 3.474, 3.611–613, 8.175–176; Sil. It. 12.321–323, 337; Claudian 2.14, 28.29–34; Nonn. *Dion.* 4.289, 9.270–274; Serv. *Aen.* 3.92; Oros. *Hist.* 6.15.11; Prud. *Apoth.* 438.

Koretas fell in or he merely chanced upon the spot where the mantic force could affect him. The latter interpretation is more probable; for not only does Plutarch's Lamprias mention nothing that the herdsman fell into, but in the first instance he follows the participle (empesontes) with kata tychên: "happening on [the dynamis] by chance" rather than "falling into it by chance" (Mor. 433c); and in the second his participle governs the genitive of dynamis: "first happening on the dynamis of the place" rather than "first falling into [it]" (Mor. 435d). The second interpretation is supported by Pausanias' notice of the story: ἤκουσα δὲ καὶ ὡς ἄνδρες ποιμαίνοντες ἐπιτύχοιεν τῷ μαντείῳ καὶ ἔνθεοί τε ἐγένετο ὑπὸ τοῦ ἀτμοῦ καὶ ἐμαντεύσαντο ἐξ Ἀπόλλωνος (10.5.7): "I have heard that shepherds happened on the Oracle and became inspired from the exhalation and spoke oracles from Apollo." Here an atmos is mentioned, but no chasm.[9] Themistios briefly alludes to the shepherd on Parnassos who was seized by the mantic pneuma from Castalia (Or. 4, p. 53a). It is probable that Pausanias and Themistios, or their sources, have converted the dynamis of the myth into an air current or exhalation; and it is also probable that the chasm was absent from one version of the myth, which may have been the Delphic version, since Plutarch's Lamprias, who mentions no chasm (although he was then sitting only about ninety meters up slope from the temple adyton), names the most learned Delphians as his informants about the Koretas story (Mor. 433cd, 435d).

Outside of the myth we hardly ever hear about a chasm. The Pseudo-Longinus mentions a fissure under the Delphian tripod whence comes an atmos entheos like emanations that issue from sacred stomia (13.2). Pompeius Trogus says essentially the same thing (24.6.9): from a deep foramen rises a cold blast. Others mention a chasm without mention of exhalations: Apollodoros says that Python tried to keep Apollo from approaching the chasm (1.4.1). According to a Scholiast (on Lyk. 1419), there is a great chaos at the tripod, whence arise oracles from Hades; and Palaiphatos (50) puts the tripod over the chasm. The hiatus terrae at which Lactantius Placidus places the scene of Delphic oracle-speaking (in Cirrha ... hiatus terrae est ubi responsa Delphica dabantur, Theb. 8.331: "in Kirra ... there is an aperture of earth where Delphic responses are given") may indicate a cave, as in Lucan's account, rather than a chasm or fissure. Likewise those who mention a stomion as the source of mantic pneumata

---

9 Paus. 10.5.12 says that the early bronze temple fell into a chasm and was melted in fire. This is a purely mythical event, and the chasm meant could be the Pleistos gorge. Notice that Pausanias' verb for "fall in" here is espiptein.

at Delphi may mean a cave or simply a vent; the word can hardly mean a chasm or cleft.[10]

There is no consistency among those sources that refer to caves or chasms and to exhalations and air currents at Delphi. The exhalations were theoretical constructions, and so was the cave or chasm whence they arose; for once physical currents are conceived, the next step is to assume an underground chamber for them to arise from. The same phenomena were alleged for other Oracles which we know very well did not have them. The author of De mundo alleges stomia and pneumata for both Delphi and Lebadeia; but Pausanias' eyewitness account of oracular consultation at Lebadeia does not confirm him: there was an underground chamber (called chasma, but artificially constructed) at Lebadeia, but no natural cave or fissure, and no exhalation (9.39.4–13). Prudentius, rejoicing in the cessation of Oracles, mentions first the lapse of Delphi and the Sibylline Books and then Dodona: perdidit insanos mendax Dodona vapores (Apoth. 441), "lying Dodona has lost its mad vapors;" but he is simply transferring the false Delphic tradition to Dodona.

Not only is the late evidence inconsistent; but it also offers no good evidence for the presence at Delphi of a chasm or cave from which toxic gases, or any kind of gases or vapors, arose to envelop the Pythia, seated on a tripod over the aperture, and to induce in her a mantic frenzy or trance. No writer earlier than the third century B.C. who has much to say about Delphi—Aeschylus, Euripides, Pindar, Herodotos, all of whom were well acquainted with Delphi—makes any mention of chasm or gases or even pneumata. Pausanias, who visited Delphi in the Antonine period and studied its topography, has nothing to say about such phenomena (aside from his allusion to the atmos in the Koretas myth). In fact Pausanias attributes the Pythia's inspiration to the waters of the spring Kassotis, which, he says, go underground after leaving the fountain house and rise again in the adyton (10.24.7). As is well known, the geological and archaeological exploration of the temple site carried on by the French School of Athens since 1892 has revealed no chasm, cave, or exhalations of

---

10 Ps.-Aristotle Mund. 395b; Dion Cass. 62.14.2; Iambl. Myst. 3.11; Lucian Nero 10; Origen Cels. 3.25, 7.3, who speaks of stomion of Castalia. A stomion is properly a mouth, a small opening; for Ps.-Aristotle and Iamblichos it may mean the vent whence underground pneumata escape. Surely Aeschylus does not mean either oracular cave or chasm at Ch. 807–808, τὸ δὲ καλῶς κτίμενον ὦ μέγα ναίων / στόμιον, meaning Apollo. His stomion is a synonym of mychos, as is evident some lines later (953–954): τάπερ ὁ Λόξιας ὁ Παρνασίας / μέγαν ἔχων μυχὸν χθονὸς . . . , i.e., it means the adyton, exactly as some writers use antron, etc. (see note 8); and they probably did not mean that the adyton was constructed as an artificial cave. See also Eum. 39, 180, for mychos used of the Delphic adyton.

any kind.[11] Nor is it likely that there could be such phenomena at Delphi. The rock there is limestone and schist, as in most of Greece; it is not volcanic country, in which fumes and vapors, toxic and non-toxic, might be found rising from the ground. And would not such fumes kill or at least harm the Pythia? Do any volcanic gases have merely an inebriating effect? Caves and sinkholes are frequent in limestone country, but nothing of the sort is found beneath or near Apollo's temple at Delphi, nor anywhere within a mile of it.[12]

There is no reality whatever behind the vapors and chasm. The oracular-cave tradition is probably derived from the myth of Apollo's combat with the serpent Python, who lived in a cave. That was originally the Corycian Cave, several miles above Delphi, near Lykoreia, where the Delphoi lived before moving down the mountain to Pytho (Fontenrose 1959: 409–419). There are no caves at Pytho, nothing nearer than Sybaris, a perpendicular limestone sink, far down Papadhia Creek, near its junction with the Pleistos; the Castalian gorge is the only feature at Pytho that is at all suitable for Python's lair.

Since we have no real evidence for chasm and exhalations, and none at all for gases and vapors, we have no need to suppose that the Delphians produced these phenomena artificially. Thus we can dismiss all theories such as Holland's about smoke rising through a vent in the adyton floor from a fire lighted in a basement room (the cave).[13] These are efforts to explain phenomena that exist in modern fancy rather than in ancient reality. Certainly no ancient writer mentions anything like smoke, and the elusive and fitful fragrance which is mentioned could hardly have come from burning laurel leaves and barley meal.

---

11 See Oppé 1904; Bourguet 1914: 249, 1925: 22; Courby 1915: 66; Poulsen 1920: 24; Will 1942; Amandry 1950: 219–220; Roux 1976: 110–117, 154–157. But Flacelière (1938: 105–106, 1965: 48) still holds to a chasm and vapors, having recourse to earthquakes and slides to explain its disappearance—impossible, however; for so large a chasm, a source of vapors or fumes or air currents, could not be obliterated without a trace.

12 From my first visits to Delphi in 1935–36 I have heard that vapors were sometimes seen coming from clefts in rocks on the west side of the modern village around the site of the modern tourist hotel, probably half a mile west of Apollo's temple. These rocks were removed for the making of a new road some years ago. The rocks had a few small cracks in them; the vapors, if genuine, had no special property and were probably produced by temperature changes. See report of Sp. Marinatos' talk, *Hestia* (January 23, 1959). In any case that is not where the ancient Delphians built their temple of Apollo; nor do the phenomena suit the ancient fancies of chasm and currents nor the modern fancies of mephitic fumes.

13 See Holland 1933; his reconstruction of Delphic procedure is further vitiated by the role which he has the omphalos play in it; for his omphalos is that *proskynitarion* cupola which the French excavators mistook for the true omphalos until Bousquet (1951) discovered the truth. See Fontenrose 1959: 375 note 13, 377 note 17.

THE PYTHIA'S ECSTASY

Even more firmly established than the chasm and vapors in the modern stereotype of a mantic session at Delphi is the Pythia's frenzy or trance: those who are willing to give up the gases cling to the frenzy. Yet, as Amandry (1950: 41–56) has shown, there is no reliable evidence in ancient literature or art for a frenzied and raving Pythia: the conception of the Pythia's madness, found in a few late writers, has its origin in Plato's conception of prophetic *mania* (*Phaedrus* 244a–245c, 265ab), based on the word play *mantikê/manikê* and parallel to telestic, poetic, and amorous *mania*. And *mania* means transport, rapture, inspiration, ecstasy, not insanity, frenzy, delirium, hysteria: the Pythia no more takes leave of her senses or enters into violent emotional outbursts than, as a rule, do poets or lovers in the inspiration and emotion which they experience. The Greek word *mania* was translated into Latin as *insania* or *vecordia* in Plato's meaning as in others, so that Lucan and other poets described a mad and raving Pythia.

The Homeric epics and Hesiod do not mention the Pythia at all in their rare allusions to Delphi, nor do the Homeric Hymns, including the Hymn to Apollo, which contains the earliest version that we have of Apollo's foundation of the Delphic Oracle. The Pythia is first mentioned by Theognis (807–808, who alludes to her as *hiereia* at Pytho); and she next appears in the *Eumenides* of Aeschylus, in which she speaks the prologue. There she prays to Delphic deities before entering the temple to give responses to consultants. In these lines she speaks calmly, though she is about to begin her mantic duties. After entering the adyton she immediately returns in great fright, because she has found the adyton filled with Erinyes surrounding the suppliant Orestes (L8)—a sight such as she had never seen before at Delphi. Her emotional excitement is extraordinary and has nothing to do with mantic inspiration.

Herodotos, telling of many men's visits to Delphi, both historical and unhistorical, always represents the Pythia as speaking directly to the consultant, sanely and articulately, if often ambiguously, without any indication of unusual excitement. He would certainly grant that she spoke under Apollo's inspiration; but so far as his narrative goes, nobody would ever suspect that the Pythia was frenzied or hysterical. The Codrus-painter, who shows Aigeus before the Pythia (L4), confirms the impression that we get from Herodotos. The Pythia, called Themis, sits calmly on the tripod and speaks to Aigeus (fig. 2).

Euripides' *Ion* gives us more information about a Delphic consultation

FIGURE 2. Aigeus before the Pythia called Themis (L4). Codrus Painter, Vulci Cup, Berlin Mus. 2538, reproduced from Eduard Gerhard, *Auserlesene griechischen Vasenbilder*, vol. 4, no. 328; Berlin, 1858.

than any other source before Plutarch's Delphic dialogues. All that we learn about the Pythia's behavior is contained in verses 91–93:

θάσσει δὲ γυνὴ τρίποδα ζάθεον
Δελφὶς ἀείδουσ' Ἕλλησι βοὰς
ἃς ἂν Ἀπόλλων κελαδήσῃ.

Here scholars have seen evidence of the Pythia's frenzy, in which she utters "wild cries" (A. S. Way) or "frenzied utterances" (M. A. Bayfield). But all that Ion says is, "And the Delphian woman is seated on the holy tripod, singing to Hellenes cries (*boai*) that Apollo sounds." Poetically *boê* may mean loud speech or song.[14] And Ion says only that the Pythia "sings"; the "cries" are Apollo's that she alone hears. In any case we may expect the Pythia to raise her voice under inspiration, perhaps loud enough for Ion to hear her from the temple steps—although he really does not say that he hears her: he simply knows what she is doing at the moment. Ion rejoices in the dawn and the beginning of daily religious activity: "The rising sun's rays are striking Parnassos' peaks; the smoke of myrrh rises to Phoebus' roof; and the Pythia is sitting on her tripod, speaking Apollo's oracles to Hellenes": he means no more than that. Though the Pythia herself appears as a character in the play, nothing is said anywhere about mantic frenzy or wild, unintelligible cries; when she appears at 1320, she has just left her tripod seat, but shows no signs of frenzy; she speaks rationally and normally, perhaps with some excitement, but that is caused by the events on stage.

Strabo, so often cited for the chasm and exhalations (9.3.5, p. 419), says only that the Pythia, sitting on the tripod over the chasm, receives the *pneuma enthousiastikon* and speaks oracles in verse and prose. If Plutarch, who must have attended many oracular sessions at Delphi, plainly said that the Pythia went into a frenzy and raved, we would have to accept his report as fact. But he says no such thing; in fact, he says just the opposite. He attributes the Pythia's inspiration to the god's impulse: Apollo moves her to speak, but she speaks with her own voice, and each Pythia according to her native endowments. The god does not speak with the Pythia's vocal chords and lips: Apollo puts the visions in her mind and a light in her soul that causes her to see the future; and she reveals the visions in her own words. As the sun makes use of the moon in reflecting light, so Apollo makes use of the Pythia in speaking oracles. Plutarch's Lamprias expressly rejects the notion that the god possesses the body of the

---

14 See Il. 18.495, Pind. *Ol.* 3.8, *Pyth.* 10.39, for the *boê* of flutes and lyres. See Eur. *El.* 879, *IT* 1386.

Pythia as a python (divining spirit) takes possession of a prophet's body.[15]

Thus does Plutarch destroy the whole theory of mediumship and possession, though some modern scholars still advance it. As Dodds expresses it: ". . . the god entered into [the Pythia] and used her vocal organs as they were his own, exactly as the so-called 'control' does in modern spirit-mediumship; that is why Apollo's Delphic utterances are always couched in the first person, never in the third."[16] On the contrary, we have seen that several Delphic oracles, whether genuine or not, are expressed in the third person (see H29, 63, 66; Q12, 15, 16, 28–31, 47, 51, 76, 103, 119, 263; and many responses make no allusion to Apollo in either person). Rohde and others have believed that the Dionysiac cult, which had an important place in Delphic worship, affected Apollo's cult and Oracle, so that the Pythia became possessed of the god in the manner of a maenad (that is, the maenad considered her frenzy the god's possession of her, and so did the Pythia.) As Latte shows very clearly, Dionysiac ecstasy had nothing to do with prophecy; that is Plato's telestic mania. The Pythia's inspiration is not Dionysiac, but thoroughly Apolline in nature, i.e., mantic.[17]

Parke supposes some Dionysiac influence on Delphic procedure, but does not emphasize it. He appears to accept the mediumship theory in a modified way, explaining the alleged frenzy as "a self-induced hypnosis. Her conscious ego became submerged, and a dissociated personality spoke in answer to enquiries. Later she would recover normal consciousness in a somewhat exhausted condition. . . ." (1956: 39). In this state, of course, she gave utterance to "the confused and disjointed remarks of a hypnotized woman," upon which the prophets exercised their imaginations "to reduce them to the form of a response." Hypnosis does not usually produce confused and disjointed speech; in any case nothing in any reliable source supports this hypnotic interpretation.[18]

---

15 Plut. *Mor.* 397bc, 404, 414e.

16 Dodds 1951: 70. See Dodds 70–74; Rohde 1925: 287–291. Much earlier Bouché-Leclercq suggested Dionysiac influence on Apollo's cult (1880: 3.88–89). See also Parke 1956: 12–13.

17 Latte 1940; see Amandry 1950: 42, 196–200. On telestic mania see Linforth 1946.

18 Parke 1956: 36–40, 1967b: 79–80, 84. He says that "the Pythia was often known to succumb to the toil," but what evidence is there besides the unusual circumstances of H72 and Lucan's fictitious account of Q249? For the hypnotic trance Parke can only adduce the proverb Ἐν ὅλμῳ εὐνάσω, "I shall make my bed on a *holmos*." Zen. 3.63 cites the superstition that those who sleep on a *holmos* (a round flat stone or mortar) become *mantikoi*, but he does not mention Delphi. He does not say "the *holmos*": it is a general superstitious belief that any *holmos* has that property. In any case this is not evidence of an hypnotic state in anyone; the Pythia did not sleep on the *holmos*; and the hypnotic trance is something quite different from frenzy or madness.

The one record that we have of an hysterical and incoherent Pythia, though often cited, far from confirming these widely held assumptions of the Pythia's delirious and irrational state, directly contradicts them. Plutarch's Lamprias tells his company about foreign envoys who had come some time before to consult the Pythia. When the priests poured cold water on the goat victim to find out whether the day was propitious for speaking oracles, the animal remained unmoved. His shuddering was the sign needed, and the priests in their zeal to please the visitors kept drenching the goat until he was forced to shudder. As a result the Pythia was reluctant to perform her office:

κατέβη μὲν εἰς τὸ μαντεῖον ὥς φασιν ἄκουσα καὶ ἀπρόθυμος, εὐθὺς δὲ περὶ τὰς πρώτας ἀποκρίσεις ἦν καταφανὴς τῇ τραχύτητι τῆς φωνῆς οὐκ ἀναφέρουσα δίκην νεὼς ἐπειγομένης ἀλάλου καὶ κακοῦ πνεύματος οὖσα πλήρης· τέλος δὲ παντάπασιν ἐκταραχθεῖσα καὶ μετὰ κραυγῆς ἀσήμου καὶ φοβερᾶς φερομένη πρὸς τὴν ἔξοδον ἔρριψεν ἑαυτὴν . . .

[*Mor.* 438b = H72]

She entered the *manteion* unwillingly. At her very first remarks it became evident from the roughness of her voice that she was not in control of herself, but like a foundering ship, filled with an inarticulate and evil spirit. Finally, becoming totally hysterical, she raised an unintelligible and fearful shout and rushed for the door . . .

She then fell unconscious and died a few days later. We notice here the Pythia's rough voice, incoherent speech, loud shout, and paroxysm. The description much resembles the modern stereotype of a normal Delphic consultation. But it is obvious that matters went very wrong that day. It was a unique and unprecedented occurrence: that is Lamprias' point (Parke grants that the occasion was exceptional). But if the priests were used to interpreting the Pythia's wild and incoherent utterances, why did they not do so on this occasion?

Lamprias' argument is that the omen of the shuddering goat was improperly produced; the failure to shudder at first indicated an improper day for oracle-speaking so that the Pythia was affected. This is very likely a true story in its essentials, and we may suppose that the Pythia's alarm affected her. It is also not improbable that the Pythia was suffering at the time from some mental or nervous illness and that the event hastened her death; we know nothing about her.

Only Lucan presents a Pythia who behaves like the unfortunate woman of H72. He calls her Phemonoe, traditionally the name of the first Pythia.[19] As Lucan tells the story, Appius Claudius in 48 B.C.,

19 Strabo 9.3.5, p. 419; Paus. 10.5.7, 6.7; Eus. *Chron.* 2, p. 38 Schoene; Porph. *ap.* Stob. *Flor.* 26.21.

wanting to know the outcome of the civil war that had just begun, went
to Delphi, where the Oracle had not been in operation for several years.
Still, the priests and Pythia were on hand, and the priests forced the
reluctant Phemonoe to enter the adyton and speak a response to Appius.
At first she feigned inspiration and pretended to respond; but she betrayed
herself by her unfrenzied demeanor and calm, articulate speech. Appius
then threatened her with punishment, and so she submitted finally to the
god:

> ... tandemque potitus
> pectore Cirrhaeo non umquam plenior artus
> Phoebados inrupit Paean mentemque priorem
> expulit atque hominem toto sibi cedere jussit
> pectore. bacchatur demens aliena per antrum
> 170   colla ferens, vittasque dei Phoebeaque serta
> erectis discussa comis per inania templi
> ancipiti cervice rotat spargitque vaganti
> obstantis tripodas magnoque exaestuat igne
> iratum te Phoebe ferens.
>
> [BC 5.165-174]

Finally possessing the Delphian breast Apollo never more abundantly
invaded his priestess's body. He expelled her former mind and bade her
human nature yield her breast wholly to him. She rages madly about the
cave, her neck no longer her own; and Phoebus' bands and garlands loose
in her bristling hair, her head shaking, she circles about the temple's empty
spaces and scatters the tripods in her way; she seethes with great fury,
bearing you, Phoebus, in her rage.

This is a picture of possession, and the Pythia is merely the god's medium:
Phemonoe now has Apollo's knowledge of all times and events. She
finally finds Appius' fate "lurking among so many great men's fates";
and then,

> spumea tum primum rabies vaesana per ora
> effluit et gemitus et anhelo clara meatu
> murmura, tum maestus vastis ululatus in antris
> extremaeque sonant domita jam virgine voces.
>
> [BC 5.190-193]

Then mad frenzy flows through her foaming lips, groans and loud panting
cries; and then when the maiden was at last subdued a dismal wail and
finally words sounded in the vast caves.

Her response to Appius (Q249) is clear and coherent enough, although
ambiguous in meaning: Appius will have no part in the war, but will

have peace alone in a valley of Euboea. Appius heard her words clearly and understood them in their literal sense, not realizing that they predicted his imminent death. Phemonoe did not recover easily from her possession: her features were flushed or deathly pale; she sighed and moaned. Finally the god left her and she fell to the ground; and we gather that she died then or soon after.

Here is the reluctant Pythia forced to perform her office, wild cries, erratic behavior, flight from the adyton, fainting, and death, just as in Plutarch's story.[20] What is different, besides her articulate response, is that Lucan attributes her behavior to Apollo's possession of her, whereas Plutarch attributes the Pythia's pathological behavior to a bad *pneuma* and denies anything but divine inspiration on normal occasions. It is, in truth, mainly this passage of Lucan that has produced the usual modern notion of the Pythia's activity. Lucan is not only describing an unhistorical consultation, but he also had no knowledge of Delphi; he simply knew something of the poetic and legendary tradition. It is Aeneas' visit to the Sibyl of Cumae in *Aeneid* 6 that lies behind Lucan's account of Appius' visit to Delphi, as Amandry and others have pointed out.[21] The Sibyl receives the god within her; her color, features, and voice change; she heaves and pants, tosses wildly about: At Phoebi nondum patiens immanis in antro / bacchatur vates (*Aen.* 6.77–78), "Not yet enduring Phoebus the prophetess rages wildly in the cave" (cf. *BC* 5.169–170: bacchatur demens aliena per antrum / colla ferens . . .); the god's possession of her is an exhausting and horrendous experience. So through Lucan the Pythia of the modern stereotype is really a Sibyl, whose normal behavior under inspiration (in legend at any rate) is much like that of a Pythia who was not behaving normally.

What support remains for a violent frenzy or delirium of the Pythia? The statements of Christian fathers such as John Chrysostom (see note 5) about the Pythia's madness caused by an evil *pneuma* rising from beneath her and entering her genitals as she straddles the tripod are worthless as evidence. The sole support left for the Pythia's frenzy is the cult myth that Diodoros tells and others refer to (see note 25). In that it was a

---

20 Bayet 1946 believes that Lucan had heard about the event which Plutarch describes, and that he adapted it to Appius' consultation. Lamprias says that it happened recently and mentions the prophet Nikandros, whom Plutarch knew. The *De defectu* may have been written about 90 or even earlier. If the event occurred around 60 it would be recent enough. But it seems unlikely that Lucan had that event in mind; and it is enough, I believe, to see Virgil's Sibyl-Aeneas scene as his source.

21 See Amandry 1950: 21, 237–238. Aeneas and Sibyl: Virgil *Aen.* 6.9–158; cp. *BC* 5.166–181, 190–193, 211–218, with *Aen.* 6.46–51, 77–82, 98–102.

herdsman who was first affected by the chasm or the very earth at the site; then everyone who came there was affected—How were they affected? They foretold the future and felt an enthusiasm strong enough to cause them to leap into the chasm (in Diodoros' version). It was to prevent this danger that the Delphians appointed a young woman to be Pythia; she mounted a tripod placed over the chasm, on which she could be safely enthusiastic and speak responses. The main effect of the enthusiasm that the herdsman and others felt on the spot was the ability to foresee future events; the feature of overenthusiastic persons who leaped into the chasm is meant only as an *aition* of the institution of the Pythia, and, in Diodoros' version at least, cannot be separated from the non-existent chasm.

Of course, the Pythia represented the god Apollo, and she went through a process of receiving his inspiration. She would show herself inspired, enthusiastic; her emotion would affect her utterance, just as an actress in the role of Medea or Clytemnestra or Lady Macbeth does not speak in her normal voice, but suits her utterance to the role she plays. After all, she was a Delphian woman chosen from all others to speak for Apollo; she felt the meaning and sanctity of her office. She would certainly make the consultation a dramatic occasion; for the speaking of oracles was above all a dramatic ritual. After a session on the tripod, according to Plutarch (*Mor.* 759b), the Pythia feels calm and peaceful.[22] It is the same kind of feeling, he says, that a warrior feels after battle or that a bacchant or corybant feels after the dance; it is a return to normal calm after excitement, not a return to sanity after madness or frenzy or delirium. The Pythia experienced enthusiasm, but not an uncontrolled and irrational frenzy. Confusion arises from translating *mania* as "madness" or "insanity," since these words immediately connote a pathological

---

22 Flacelière 1950: 308 cites *Mor.* 759ab and 763a against Amandry's view of the Pythia's ecstasy, which I accept essentially. Neither passage implies a delirious state of the Pythia when on the tripod. What Plutarch (if he is the author of the *Amatorius*) is presenting here explicitly is the doctrine of *Phaedr.* 244a–245c, 265ab: there is an unhealthy *mania* produced from the body, and a healthy *mania*, the *enthousiastikon pathos*, which is a participation in divine power. This can have violent manifestations, but it means every sort of excitement, rapture, inspiration—poetic, telestic, mantic, and amatory. After quotation of Sappho's famous ode (31 Voigt) Plutarch asks whether those physical and emotional effects of love passion are not plainly *theolêpsia*, and continues, τί τοσοῦτον ἡ Πυθία πέπονθεν ἁψαμένη τοῦ τρίποδος (*Mor.* 763a). This implies that the Pythia does not manifest so much emotional excitement as the lover. Plutarch then asks whether the flute and *tympanon* and the music of the Mother's rites have aroused the devotee so much (as amatory passion has the lover). Presumably the *orgia* carried devotees to much more violent transports than the more subdued inspiration that I suppose for the Pythia; but notice that in Plutarch's passage we simply have the sequence of amatory, mantic, and telestic *mania*. Each is a different kind. All are beneficent: e.g., telestic *mania* is a remedy for unhealthy *mania*.

condition—derangement, raving, erratic behavior—usually the word calls up the symptoms of manic-depressive insanity. There has been talk of the Pythia's hypnotic trance (see note 18); but in the prevailing conception of her frenzy she is manic in the psychotic sense of the word. Yet *mania*, especially as Plato and Plutarch use the word, means a high state of emotion and comprehends all kinds of transport, enthusiasm, and inspiration.

The Speaking of Responses

If we dispose of the Pythia's frenzy, we dispose also of her incoherent babbling. Farnell grants "some kind of articulate speech," though it is "wild utterance." Dempsey and others (see note 1) speak of her incoherent cries. In this view the attendant priests or prophets had to make an intelligible answer out of her babblings, and they had a code for doing so. But there is very little evidence for this view. All records of responses that mention the Pythia represent her speaking directly and clearly to the inquirer, as Amandry has emphasized (1950: 120–121). Notice Q7, as Herodotos tells the story (1.65.2): as soon as Lykurgos entered the *megaron* the Pythia addressed him in hexameter verse: "You have come, Lykurgos, to my rich temple,..." (cf. Herodotos 5.92b.2). When Croesus' envoys entered the *megaron* to ask the question that would put the Pythian Apollo to the test, the Pythia answered them directly in five lines of verse (Herodotos 1.47.2 = Q99). When, after the Pythia's response, a consultant asks another question or makes a statement about it, the Pythia immediately makes an intelligent reply, as in Q92, when Glaukos, reminded of the perjurer's harsh fate, asked forgiveness, and the Pythia replied that to tempt the god was equivalent to the deed (Herodotos 6.86c.2). These are probably unauthentic oracles; but all testimony is the same: the Pythia herself always replies in articulate speech, verse or prose. Some authors of our sources, notably Plutarch and probably Herodotos, knew Delphic procedures; and the manner in which they present the conduct of a consultation must be reliable.

The records of Historical responses tell us very little, but nothing different. For seven (H3, 7, 9, 15, 20, 22, 41) we are told that the Pythia spoke the response. Many do not indicate a speaker, and most that do so say that Apollo or "the god" spoke. The formula in inscriptions seems to be always ὁ θεὸς (or Ἀπόλλων) ἔχρησε (H2, 19, 23, and seventeen others); only the inscription of H41 mentions the Pythia in the formula κατὰ τὰς μαντείας τῆς Πυθίας. Since the actual speaker was a human being, the formula "the god spoke" would fit either the Pythia or a male prophet as speaker. But nowhere in any kind of record is it ever said that the prophet or priest spoke the response or delivered it to the consultant.

The principal support of the conventional view is Strabo's statement:

Φασὶ ... ὑπερκεῖσθαι δὲ τοῦ στομίου τρίποδα ὑψηλὸν ἐφ᾽ ὃν τήν Πυθίαν ἀναβαίνουσαν, δεχομένην τὸ πνεῦμα ἀποθεσπίζειν ἔμμετρά τε καὶ ἄμετρα· ἐντείνειν δὲ καὶ ταῦτα εἰς μέτρον ποιητάς τινας ὑπουργοῦντας τῷ ἱερῷ.

[9.3.5, p. 419]

They say that over the opening is set a high tripod on which the Pythia mounts, receives the *pneuma*, and speaks oracles in both verse and prose; and these too are put into verse by certain poets who work for the sanctuary.

Strabo says plainly that the Pythia herself speaks all responses, whether in verse or prose; and that poets who serve the cult put the prose responses into verse—this seems to mean all the prose pronouncements, but can be taken to mean some of them. Strabo does not say that these poets were the priests. But if he wanted to inform the reader that the priests or *Hosioi* put the prose oracles into verse, would he say it in this way? Would he not say explicitly that the priests and cult attendants put the prose utterances into verse? And it is the prose oracles only that the poets versify; and they do not do so because the Pythia's utterances are incoherent and unintelligible.

Strabo is making the same reference as Plutarch, when his Theon accounts for the change (which he assumes to have taken place) from verse to prose expression at Delphi:

πολλῶν δ᾽ ἦν ἀκούειν ὅτι ποιητικοί τινες ἄνδρες ἐκδεχόμενοι τὰς φωνὰς καὶ ὑπολαμβάνοντες ἐπικάθηνται περὶ τὸ χρηστήριον, ἔπη καὶ μέτρα καὶ ῥυθμοὺς οἷον ἀγγεῖα τοῖς χρησμοῖς ἐκ τοῦ προστυχόντος περιπλέκοντες. Ὀνομάκριτοι δ᾽ ἐκεῖνοι καὶ Πρόδικοι καὶ Κιναίθωνες ὅσην αἰτίαν ἠνέγκαντο τῶν χρησμῶν ὡς τραγῳδίαν αὐτοῖς καὶ ὄγκον οὐδὲν δεομένοις προσθέντες ἐῶ λέγειν ...

[*Mor.* 407b]

We used to hear many men say that certain versifiers would sit around the Oracle, listening to and taking in the words, weaving hexameters and metres and rhythms extemporaneously as vessels for the oracles. How much responsibility those men, Onomakritoi and Prodikoi and Kinaithones, bore for the oracles, for having added tragic expression and pomposity to statements that didn't need them, I leave unsaid ...

Theon is not speaking of a contemporary practice, but of what has been said to be a former practice: many men used to say so (does the past tense mean that nobody says so any more?). The "poetic men" were not priests or temple attendants of any kind: they were men engaged in versifying oracles of their own volition, men like Onomakritos, Prodikos, and Kinaithon. Onomakritos, we have seen, wrote oracles of Musaios; the other two are early epic poets, authors of the *Minyas* (Prodikos) and of five Cyclic epics, the *Little Iliad* among them (Kinaithon).[23] It is not clear where they sat: *chrêstêrion* may mean the whole sanctuary or just the adyton of the temple—probably the latter, since they listened for the Pythia's words. Did they sit in the adyton or outside the door in the cella? In any case they were not the priests and *Hosioi* who attended the Pythia; and the words suggest that they overheard the Pythia's speech.

At any rate, it is these men whom some persons held responsible for the obscurities and ambiguities of verse oracles. Theon argues that the Pythia now speaks clearly in prose because that is what contemporary men want; they look with suspicion on metaphors and riddles and ambiguities and therefore find fault with high-flown poetic language. In earlier times, he says, men revered the unfamiliar; they liked indirection, circumlocution, grandiloquent expression, and they wanted oracles expressed in such language. Later they began to find fault with the obscurities of poetic expression and demanded plain, clear, unadorned speech in oracles; and some blamed the aforesaid "poetic men" for the obscure and periphrastic expression of responses (*Mor.* 406f–407c). Theon's argument thus runs directly counter to the accepted notion of attendants' versifying the Pythia's incoherencies. It is poetic expression, says Theon, that transformed the Pythia's clear responses into unclear and unintelligible forms.

Immediately after the quoted passage Theon says, "Most disrepute has come upon the poetic art from the vulgar wandering soothsayers who beg around the shrines of the Mother and Sarapis, who compose oracles of their own or take them by lot from collections [*grammateia*] for slaves and women, who are chiefly attracted by the verses and the poetic language" (407c). These are contemporary chresmologues, simply a meaner

---

23 The second and third poets' names are uncertain: the manuscripts of *Pyth. or.* show *prodotai* and *kinesônes*, i.e., "betrayers" and "meddlers" or "alterers" ("who are going to alter," if this is a corruption of *kinêsontes*). These terms would have some point in Plutarch's argument: the poetasters misrepresent the oracles that they versify. The appropriateness of Prodikos and Kinaithon is not clear: it may be that they composed oracles for their epics. See *Mor.* 407c. See also McLeod 1961, who believes that oral bards practised at Delphi; he accepts dubious responses as authentic.

variety of men like Onomakritos, to whom the alleged versifiers of Delphi are assimilated. These poets (if real and not purely hypothetical) were much more like chresmologues than consecrated attendants of the Pythia. Were there really men at Delphi who earned their livelihood by putting the Pythia's prose responses into verse? Or does Theon's versifier tradition dimly reflect the activities and practices of chresmologues who gathered collections of verse oracles and called them Delphic (p. 159)?

Only Strabo and Plutarch mention these Delphic poets. And neither's remarks can be taken as good evidence of their actual presence at Delphi in former times. They were perhaps solely hypothetical, serving the same purpose as the modern theory of the prophet-Pythia relationship: they were meant to account for the verse form of oracles, a problem to some ancients as to modern scholars. The ancients, of course, accepted all the traditional oracles of legend and poetry as authentic. If these traditional oracles, or most of them, were never spoken by the Pythia in any sense, the proportions of the problem are greatly reduced.

The cult myths hardly support the view that prophets really composed the responses. In the Homeric Hymn to Apollo the god brings Cretans to Pytho and installs them as his priests:

> Κρῆτες ἀπὸ Κνωσοῦ Μινωίου, οἵ ῥά τ᾽ ἄνακτι
> ἱερά τε ῥέζουσι καὶ ἀγγέλλουσι θέμιστας
> Φοίβου Ἀπόλλωνος χρυσαόρου, ὅττι κεν εἴπῃ
> χρείων ἐκ δάφνης γυάλων ὑπὸ Παρνησοῖο.
>
> [393-396]

Cretans from Minoan Knossos, who make sacrifices to the Lord and report *themistes* of Phoebus Apollo Chrysaor, whatever he says when he speaks from the bay tree under Parnassos' dells.

Since the Hymn does not mention the Pythia, it may reflect an early period when male prophets received Apollo's inspiration. But the poet may be speaking generally and imprecisely, meaning simply that the priests have something to do with the delivery of responses. At any rate these verses offer feeble support to the conventional view and cannot be pressed very hard in its service.

The poetess Boio, contrary to the Hymn, told how Hyperboreans came to Delphi and founded the Oracle; and among their leaders were Pagasos, Aguieus, and the poet Olen, who became Apollo's first speaker of oracles and inventor of hexameter verse. But, says Pausanias, who cites Boio, this is the only indication of a male speaker: in all other traditions only women speak the oracles. Here again the evidence, such as it is, shows only an original male prophet succeeded by the Pythia and not a Pythia who speaks on a tripod and a prophet who announces the message orally or in writing to the enquirer. Furthermore Olen is really a Delian figure: he came to Delos from Lykia and first sang hexameters there. Boio's story has a Delian myth transferred to Delphi.[24]

In the myth of the mantic chasm the herdsman Koretas spoke oracles when inspired on the oracular site; then other men were mantically affected in the same place. After a time the office of Pythia was instituted, and she alone thereafter received the inspiration.[25] This, as has been observed, is obviously an *aition* of the Pythia institution, and the myth expressly excludes any male oracle-speakers after the first Pythia was installed. It offers no support whatever to the theory of prophet as framer of the oracle and the person who spoke it or gave it to the consultant. Rather it tells us plainly that the person who received the earth's mantic *dynamis* was the oracle-speaker: men who happened upon the site received the inspiration at first and spoke oracles which their hearers understood at once; then the Pythia replaced them as inspiration-receiver and oracle-speaker.

Euripides' Ion may be understood to indicate a male oracle-speaker when he tells Kreusa that she cannot expect to receive the oracle she wants:

> Οὐκ ἔστιν ὅστις σοι προφητεύσει τάδε.
> ἐν τοῖς γὰρ αὐτοῦ δώμασιν κακὸς φανεὶς
> Φοῖβος δικαίως τὸν θεμιστεύοντά σοι
> δράσειεν ἄν τι πῆμα.

> [Ion 369–372]

These words must be understood in their context. Earlier (333–335) Ion offers Kreusa his help in her desire to have a response from Apollo: he will be her *proxenos*. Later Xuthos appears on the scene and asks, τίς προφητεύει θεοῦ (413), "Who speaks for the god?" Ion replies, "I do outside, but inside others have the duty, noble Delphians." In a broad sense of the term the humblest servant of Apollo is his *prophêtês*. In 369–372, after Ion has learned what Kreusa wants to ask (about the god's child, born of an illicit love), he says, "There is nobody who will help you to such a response as this. For if Apollo should look bad in his own houses, he would justly do some harm to the person who performs the mantic

---

24 Boio *ap.* Paus. 10.5.7–8. Olen on Delos: Herod. 4.35.3; Call. *Hymn* 4.304–305; Paus. 1.18.5, 5.7.8, 8.21.3, 9.27.2; Laidlaw 1933: 12.

25 Diod. 16.26.1–4; Plut. *Mor.* 433cd, 435d; Paus. 10.5.7; Schol. vet. on Eur. *Or.* 165; Themist. *Or.* 4, p. 53a.

office for you." Here *themisteuonta* repeats the meaning of *prophêteusei*: the verbs are synonyms in this meaning as in others. The genders are masculine: Ion refers to all who preside over and assist in the mantic rites of a consultation; and he means not only Delphi but all Oracles of Apollo. In this interpretation of the lines I have assumed that Kreusa would ask the question herself, needing only a Delphic sponsor, who would be Ion. It is also possible that Kreusa as a woman cannot ask the question herself, but must do so through a Delphian *proxenos*, a priest or other servant of the temple, who would refuse to put her question to the god (this somewhat changes the meaning of *prophêteusei*).[26] Either interpretation raises an interesting observation. Ion appears to say that Apollo would speak the truth if the question should be put, even though the response would be discreditable to himself, and would then punish his agent for forcing him to reveal the truth.

In every account of a consultation we are told that the enquirer spoke directly to the Pythia (or to the god) and that then the Pythia (or the god) responded directly to him. Nowhere are we told that the priest-prophet informed the enquirer of the god's response, except when the actual enquirer was not himself present but had sent one or more envoys. Then the priest copied the response and sealed the copy within an envelope, which he delivered to the envoys. In some instances the absent enquirer did not want the envoys to know the oral response by putting the question themselves and hearing the answer. Then he or they (if a city government) submitted a written question. This is the meaning of the late and scanty evidence about written questions and sealed replies.[27] It has nothing

---

26 Plut. *Mor.* 385c cites a Delphic law that no woman may approach the *chrêstêrion*. This would seem to be confirmed by *Ion* 222, when in responding to the Athenian maidservants' question whether it is *themis* for them to enter the temple (? *gyala*) Ion says, *Ou themis*. But after their question about the omphalos, he tells them how it is lawful for them to enter the adyton: "If you have offered a cake before the temple, wanting to ask Phoebus a question, go to the altar; and don't go into the interior (*mychon*) without sacrificing sheep"; i.e., you must sacrifice sheep at the altar before entering the temple. See Legrand 1901: 47–48. Kreusa tells Ion that she has come to consult the Oracle: "[I have come] wanting to learn a secret oracle from Phoebus," and Ion says, Λέγοις ἄν· ἡμεῖς τἆλλα προξενήσομεν (335), i.e., Ion will act as her *proxenos*, which may mean that she would need some Delphian minister to ask the question for her. But all consultants seem to have needed a Delphian *proxenos*, though only as a sponsor, not to ask the questions and receive the answers for them. It may be that Ion means only that he will help her get a secret response. See Legrand 1901; Amandry 1950: 111 note 4. A fifth-century vase-painting may show a woman consultant; Amandry 66, pl. 1.3 = *CVA*, France 12, Louvre 8, 37.4–6.

27 According to Zen. 6.11, citing Aristeides (see also Suda *T*154; Apost. 16.20), the consultant received the response under seal and was warned that if he broke the seal before the appointed day he would be subject to one of three penalties. This, if valid, can only be true of emissaries. Schol. vet. on Aristoph. *Pl.* 39 is the only evidence for written questions;

to do with the normal consultation when the enquirer appeared in person.[28]

It is clear that priests and *Hosioi* attended the Pythia when she sat upon the tripod. There were two priests (*hiereis*), at least after 200 B.C., appointed for life.[29] The title *prophêtês* never appears in Delphic inscriptions, although Herodotos, Plutarch, and Aelian refer to one or more prophets at Delphi.[30] It is probable that *hiereus* and *prophêtês* are two titles for the same office, the former being the official designation in the administration of the Delphic sanctuary. The title *prophêtês*, then, is either an unofficial title that non-Delphians used after the analogy of usage at other oracular shrines, such as Didyma, or, more probably, was the designation of the *hiereus* who presided at an oracular session—it may be that the two priests took turns in attendance (see Halliday 1928: 60) or that if both attended, the senior in length of service presided. Plutarch refers to his contemporary Nikandros once as *hiereus* (*Mor.* 386b) and again as *prophêtês* (438b), precisely with reference to his attendance at a consultation (H72).

The *prophêtês* is the man who speaks for the god. The title may be applied to the mantis himself, as the Pythia calls Apollo *prophêtês* of father Zeus in Aeschylus' *Eumenides* (19). Pindar speaks of Teiresias as *prophêtês* (*Nem.* 1.60). The Pythia is often called *prophêtis* (e.g., Euripides *Ion* 42, 321). The priest of Apollo at Didyma had the title *prophêtês* (Fontenrose 1933: 94–112), but it is uncertain whether this annual magistrate was himself receiver of divine inspiration or not, since there is some evidence, though dubious, of a woman (*gynê chrêsmôdos*, Iamblichos *Myst.* 3.11) who actually spoke Apollo's will (Fontenrose 1933: 121–125). In most instances a *prophêtês* is not himself a mantis; he is the god's representative, a man who oversees and administers an oracular session. The priest-prophet who attended the Pythia presided over the mantic session at Delphi, answering

the inquirers wrote their questions on tablets and then held them out to the Pythia, who made an appropriate answer to each (this, by the way, would surely mean that the enquirers could see the Pythia). This is certainly not Delphic procedure; the Scholiast's source may have Dodona or another place in mind. If this had been the practice at Delphi, one would expect that excavators would have found such tablets as at Dodona; but as yet none has turned up. See Amandry 1959: 149. In H21 Athens submitted written questions in two sealed urns, and the Pythia was asked only to indicate the urn which held the god's response. This is a very special case.

28 For the conventional view of the prophet as reporter of the oracle see Parke 1940a; Whittaker 1965: 26, 31.

29 The two priests are named in numerous Delphic inscriptions of manumissions: *SGDI* 1684–2342; see Daux 1936a: 187–209, 1943: 49–95. On the Delphic priesthood see Parke 1940a.

30 Herod. 8.36.2–37.1; Plut. *Mor.* 292d, 438b; Ael. *NA* 10.26; cf. Eur. *Ion* 369, 413.

all questions except the question put to the Pythia as the god's mouth-piece. He probably put the Pythia's response in writing and delivered a copy to the messengers of absent enquirers; he reported the response to anyone who had a right to know it; sometimes, perhaps, he announced it publicly when there was no need to keep it secret.[31]

The *Delphôn aristês* (noble Delphians) who attended the Pythia, according to Ion, were the priests and *Hosioi*. There were five *Hosioi*, appointed for life, according to Plutarch (*Mor.* 292d): they assisted the priest-prophets in the performance of the rites and in all religious duties, e.g., in the sprinkling of the victim with cold water to find out whether the god was propitious for speaking oracles that day (*Mor.* 437a). It appears that not all five were present at every consultation: at the abortive session of H72, when the Pythia suffered some kind of seizure, the prophet Nikandros and those of the *Hosioi* who were present, says Plutarch (*Mor.* 438b), fled from the room. Out of two priests and five *Hosioi* perhaps four attended the Pythia at each session, one priest designated prophet for the occasion and three *Hosioi*. But probably the whole college could be present if all seven members wished to be.[32]

Clearly it was the Pythia who spoke the oracles in Apollo's name; the priests and *Hosioi* performed all other duties. But did the Pythia confine herself to speech? Did she practice any sort of divinatory rite, such as the drawing of lots? There has been much speculation about a lot Oracle at Delphi, since some late authorities tell about lots or pebbles that were kept in a bowl on the tripod and which leaped when a consultant asked his question; others mention an ancient lot Oracle on Parnassos.[33] Much has

---

31 Thus we may interpret Schol. A on Il. 16.235: προφήτας γὰρ λέγουσι τοὺς περὶ τὰ χρηστήρια ἀσχολουμένους καὶ τὰς μαντείας τὰς γινομένας ὑπὸ τῶν ἱερέων ἐκφέροντας. Here the prophets appear to be distinguished from the priests. And is it that they report the oracles in subordination to the priests or the oracles spoken by the priests (or under the priests' supervision)? In any case the statement is general, meant to explicate the poet's *hypophêtai*, a designation of the Selloi of Dodona.

32 The *Hosioi* were apparently chosen from certain reputable Delphian families, since they were said to be descendants of Deukalion; see Plut. *Mor.* 292d and the *Delphôn aristês* of Eur. *Ion* 416. They made a secret sacrifice to Dionysos in Apollo's temple on the occasion of the Thuiades' awakening of Dionysos Liknites; Plut. *Mor.* 365a. They were, however, primarily ministers of Apollo, as Plutarch makes clear (*Mor.* 292d, 437a, 438b) and several Delphic inscriptions which name *Hosioi*: e.g., FD 3.2.118; 3.3.297, 300, 302; BCH 20 (1896) 719; 49 (1925) 83, 86.

33 Mantic *psêphoi*: Nonn. Abb. *Narr.* 2.20, p. 1045 Migne 36; Kosmas *Carm. Greg.* pp. 610–611 Migne 38; Suda Π3137. Lot Oracle: Philochoros 328.195J *ap.* Zen. 5.75; Call. *Hymn* 2.45 and Schol.; Hesych. Θ743; Steph. Byz. 317–318 Mein.; see Fontenrose 1959: 427–431. On bones of Dionysos or Python in the tripod basin see Call. frag. 643 Pf.; Hyg. *Fab.* 140.5; Clem. Alex. *Protr.* 2.18, 15P; Serv. auct. *Aen.* 3.360; EM 255. See Fontenrose 374–376; Holland 1933: 201–207. Figure 2 shows the Pythia holding a bowl; and Apollo or

been made of the verb *anairein* (take up), used from Herodotos' time on, as a verb of oracular speech at Delphi.[34] This verb seems suitable for Q96 (Herod. 1.13), in which Apollo confirms Gyges as king of Lydia: this could be a yes-or-no proposition, and so could H3, as Plato's Socrates reports it in the *Apology* (21a): ἀνεῖλεν οὖν ἡ Πυθία μηδένα σοφώτερον εἶναι, the question being, "Is anyone wiser than Socrates?" In H11, Xenophon uses *aneilen* twice (*Anab.* 3.1.6,8) to say that Apollo told him to which gods he should offer sacrifice; and a lot could have been drawn to select the divine name or names. But Herodotos also uses this verb for Apollo's pronouncements of Q109, 144, 160, the content of which could not have been easily produced by lot drawing. Q144 is a three-verse response introduced by *anelein*, advising Argos not to enter the war against the Persians (Herodotos 7.148.3); lots could decide the question whether or not to enter, but could not produce the verses or their content. In Q160 the Pythia told (*aneile*, Herodotos 9.33.2) Teisamenos, inquiring on another matter, that he would win the five greatest contests. Q109 (Herodotos 6.34.2) contains mode B in its first-met form.

Yet the verb *anairein* may have acquired the broader meaning of "speak oracularly" from a former practice of divination by lot, or from some continued use of lots in the mantic rites at Delphi; if so, it acquires the meaning "proclaim" or "ordain" for introducing oral responses from its primary meaning of "take up" (a lot). The verb *anairein* introduces eight Historical responses: H3, 4, 5, 10, 11, 12, 21 (Androtion), 27, two of which have the *lôion kai ameinon* formula in response to a question framed in the same words; three others indicate approval of proposed policies or plans (H4, 5, 12); and the remaining two (H3, 10) are responses that a drawing of lots could have produced.

The evidence for a lot Oracle at Delphi has so impressed Amandry that he infers two kinds of oracles delivered at Delphi.[35] There was the divinatory rite, in which the Pythia drew lots, and the prophetic rite, a grander operation, in which the Pythia spoke in verse or prose—but in this rite too she may have made some show of drawing a lot from the bowl. Prophetic sessions were held only on the official consultation days, perhaps the seventh of the month; but the divinatory rite was accessible

a woman holds a bowl on vase-paintings and other art works described by Amandry 1950: 67–77, pls I-VI.

34 Notice the use of *klêroun* for Apollo's oracular speech at Eur. *Ion* 907–910: ὅστ' ὀμφὰν κληροῖς.

35 Amandry 1950: 29–36, 84–85, 232–233; see Parke 1956: 18–19; Whittaker 1965: 27–28. Earlier Robbins 1916 had emphasized the lot Oracle at Delphi and posited two kinds of oracles delivered there. See Fontenrose 1952.

on any day that was not *apophras* (when the temple was closed to all oracular business), provided that the preliminary rites, such as the sprinkling of the victim, were favorable. Thus Amandry's suggestion of two oracular rites also provides an answer to the thorny question of the frequency of consultation days.

Amandry's solution is ingenious and at first sight looks plausible. It suits very well the kind of question and answer that occurs among the Historical oracles, especially those recorded in inscriptions, wherein the question "Is it better that I/we do X?" demands the answer Yes or No and is answered in every instance in the same terms, "It is better..." But if Amandry is right we should expect some negative replies. We have few surviving records of this question and answer; but in every instance the reply to such a question is affirmative. Only four show the question *lôion kai ameinon esti* or equivalent with affirmative answer, usually expressed in the words of the question: H5, 25, 54, 61. But in seven others an affirmative response expressed in the "It is better that/to" formula or equivalent implies the question, "Is it better that/to?": H2, 19, 27, 45, 47, 66, 74. For H33 we have the question, "Is it better that" without the answer, which is lost; but the question, "Is it better that we make larger and finer dresses for Artemis, Demeter, and Kore?" must have received an affirmative reply. In H36 the reply "It is better to" is made to the question "What is better [*lôion kai ameinon*] for me and my sons to do?" This may not be a Delphic response; and the use of the formula in a question of this kind is unprecedented among responses attributed to Delphi; yet the sanction formula of the answer is positively expressed. Perhaps someone may point to H21 as an example of a negative reply to the formulaic question. If we had only the testimony of Philochoros and Androtion, as quoted by Didymos, "It is better not to work the sacred land," we would have to grant a negative answer in this instance to the formulaic question. But we have the inscription of the Athenian decision to submit the question to the Delphic Oracle, in which the method of making the inquiry is prescribed. Two questions were inscribed on tin plates and sealed in vases, and the Pythia would be asked to indicate which vase contained the words according to which the Athenians should act. Both vases contain a question phrased, "Is it better and more good [i.e., *lôion kai ameinon esti*] for the demos of the Athenians...?"; one continues with "that the *basileus* let for rent lands of the sacred *orgas* [to get income] for the building of a portico and repair of the goddesses' sanctuary?", the other with "to leave unworked the lands now uncultivated within the sacred *orgas*?" The latter is the message contained in the vase that the Pythia indicated. She could have drawn lots to choose; but her answer is an affirmative reply to the question contained in the vase indicated. That there are fourteen affirmative replies to this formulaic question, and no negative replies, among extant records leads to the conclusion that it was used for requesting a sanction, and that the sanction was always granted.

Amandry points to Q125, in which the Pythia chose ten tribal eponyms from a hundred names of traditional heroes (archêgetai) that Kleisthenes submitted to her. Aristotle uses the verb aneilen; but, as we have seen, this often means merely the speaking of an oracle. Neither Aristotle nor any other source tells us that Kleisthenes submitted a hundred names on lots; he may have presented a list of written names; it is also possible that he submitted a hundred names orally. Yet even if Kleisthenes presented the Pythia with an urn containing a hundred disks or slips inscribed with names, asking her to draw ten, no general practice is indicated: this was a special device on a single occasion. The only parallel is the legendary L162: the Thessalians sent lots to Delphi inscribed with names of men nominated for the kingship, and Aleuas' uncle secretly inserted the name of his nephew. The Pythia picked Aleuas' lot; but his father objected that Aleuas' name had not been entered and made a second inquiry; the Pythia replied in a verse, "I mean the redhead whom Archedike bore," i.e., Aleuas. Obviously the submission of names on lots was a device occasionally employed for consulting the Delphic Oracle; and H21 is evidence for the presenting of choices to the Pythia. However, this evidence does not suit Amandry's hypothesis of the divinatory rite; for H21, L162, and Q125 (if it involves lots at all) show lots brought to Delphi by the inquirers, whereas the evidence for a lot Oracle indicates the use of pebbles (psêphoi) in the tripod basin.

Finally, Amandry lays much emphasis upon a phrase in an inscribed treaty between Delphi and Skiathos about 350–340, which defines amounts in staters and obols that citizens of Skiathos will be charged at Delphi in the performance of their religious obligations. After clauses which prescribe charges for pelanos (the cake-offering required as a preliminary to consultation) and victim's hide—really fees paid in lieu of the offerings—the next provision reads αἴ κ᾽ ἐπὶ φρυκτὼ παρίηι, τὸ μὲν δαμόσιον στ[α]-τῆ[ρ]α αἰ[γιναῖον, τὸ δὲ ἴδιον . . .]; then after a break of one line, τῷ θεω [ι χρηστήρ?]ιον ἐπὶ [τὰν τράπ]εζαν αἶγα κ[αλλι]στεύοντα κα[ὶ τ]ἄλλα ἱερὰ καττὰ [π]άτρια. None of this is very clear, not to mention the incompleteness of the text. Amandry sees in phryktô the two beans or lots used in the divinatory rite—for *phryktos* is the word used in L162 for the Thessalian lots presented to the Pythia—and interprets as follows: "If [a citizen of Skiathos] appears for the consultation by two beans, the charge will be one Aeginetan stater for a public matter, [a smaller amount] for a private matter. [If he wants to consult the oracle, he will consecrate?] to the god [as a preliminary sacrifice] on the table a choice goat and the other sacred offerings according to custom."[36] Sokołowski, however, takes *phryktô* to be sacrificial cakes like the *eilytai* offered to Trophonios at Lebadeia. He also suggests that the word is dative singular with iota omitted, so that the clause would mean, "If he comes forward (to consult the Oracle) after having made a preliminary sacrifice of a *phryktos*." We should notice that everything else in the surviving portion of the treaty concerns charges for sacrificial cakes and victims. If we interpret *phryktô* as accusative dual, we may translate, "If he comes for the sacrifice of two cakes," realizing that the rest of the sentence is lost and that the meaning of this clause must remain obscure; for we know almost nothing about the details of daily worship at Delphi. The text of the following clause is very incomplete, and the reading *chrêstêrion* is at best uncertain; if correct, it ought to have the meaning which it has at *Ion* 419, "victim," specifically the goat victim offered as a sacrifice preliminary to consulting the oracle. Hence this treaty offers weak support for the hypothesis of a special divinatory rite.

As far as the evidence shows, there was only one kind of mantic rite and session at Delphi. The Pythia gave her answer directly and orally to the consultant without any intermediaries or interpreters, unless she was called upon to draw a lot or point to an urn, when she probably accompanied her act with speech. She would certainly have had no difficulty in speaking most of the Historical responses: all that she had to do was to repeat the words of the question when sanctioning a proposal, and to name the gods that the consultant should worship if he asked what he should do for success in his undertaking.

There remains only the problem of verse oracles; for the Pythia did speak in verse sometimes, probably oftener in the later period than earlier (pp. 186–195). Did she spontaneously compose hexameters herself? It may be that some Pythias who had skill at manipulating verse formulae would often do so; and that less confident Pythias confined themselves to prose.

---

36 Inscription, *BCH* 63 (1939) 184 = Amandry 1950: 245, no. XVI. See Amandry 1939, 1950: 32–33, 107–110: Sokołowski 1949.

Or did the priest-prophet or some *Hosioi*, having knowledge of the question beforehand, frame verses for her reply? There is not the slightest evidence of this; we know from all testimony that the consultant put his question directly to the Pythia and received his answer at once. But an enquirer might let a Delphian know his question before submitting it to the Pythia. For example, King Kleomenes of Sparta induced Kobon, an influential Delphian, to persuade the Pythia to give a response denying Demaratos' legitimacy to the Spartans (Q137). If Kleisthenes and Pleistoanax suborned the Pythia (Q124, H7), they or their Delphian friends were obviously able to speak with her before the consultations. In the instances of bribery the Pythia was instructed what to reply; but probably none of these responses was put into verse (H7 may have been).

The Pythia may sometimes have had previous knowledge of the question and have had time to prepare verses in reply; or a priest or other person may have had time to prepare them for her or to assist her in composing them. But we really have little right to offer such a conjecture as even possibly true. We know almost nothing about the matter—little more than that the Pythia heard the question and made a response.

THE MANTIC RITUAL

The argument of the foregoing pages almost completely invalidates Farnell's picture of the Pythia at work (p. 196). The Pythia was not seized with a frenzy; she spoke coherently, and it was she, not the prophets, who gave the response in final form to the enquirer. We know little about the mantic rite itself. All that we know with some certainty is that the Pythia prepared herself by bathing in the waters of the Castalian spring; and she probably drank water from this spring too.[37] She burned bay leaves and barley meal on an altar before mounting the tripod (Plutarch *Mor.* 397a). When she was seated upon the tripod, she wore a bay-leaf crown and apparently held a bay sprig in her hand, shaking it on occasion.[38] Probably on first taking her seat she drank water from the spring Kassotis, which rose on the slope above the temple (see Pouilloux and Roux 1963: 79–101); for this water had a place in the mantic rite, being piped or carried into the adyton; and from it the Pythia was believed to draw her

37 Bathing: Schol. vet. on Eur. *Phoen.* 224; cf. Ps.-Kallisthenes 36 Raabe; Iambl. *Myst.* 3.11. Drinking: Lucian *Bis acc.* 1; Oinomaos *ap.* Eus. *PE* 5.28, p. 224a; Greg. Naz. *Or.* 39.5, p. 340 Migne.

38 Call. *Iambi* 4.26–27; Lucan *BC* 5.142–144; Nonn. *Dion.* 9.270–274; Schol. vet. on Aristoph. *Plut.* 39. For shaking bay see Aristoph. *Plut.* 213 and Schol. vet.; Aristonoos' hymn, *FD* 3.2.191.9–10; Lucan *BC* 5.154–155.

inspiration (Pausanias 10.24.7). It is much more doubtful that she chewed bay leaves—although this is an article of Delphic belief that some scholars firmly hold. This belief is based almost entirely on Lucian's *Bis accusatus* (1), though he does not definitely connect the practice of bay-leaf chewing with Delphi. Lucian humorously describes Apollo's frantic rush from one Oracle to another to answer enquirers who demand his responses: he hurries from Delphi to Kolophon to Xanthos to Klaros (which is the same as Kolophon) to Delos (where there was no Oracle) to Branchidai (Didyma), "in short wherever the promantis, having drunk the holy water, chewed the bay, and shaken the tripod, bids him be present." This can hardly be taken seriously, and it is obvious that these three acts were not performed at all the shrines mentioned. The only other possible evidence comes from Oinomaos, who, addressing the Delphic Apollo, taunts him for telling consultants in a response what human beings had often learned from sages who had not chewed the bay or drunk the water of Castalia. This too is a generalizing statement, and the participles used are of masculine gender. Oinomaos and Lucian were contemporaries, both Cynics of a sort, who perhaps drew upon a common source, a Cynic composition that disparaged oracle-speakers in general, imputing to them nonsensical practices as pretended means of inducing inspiration.[39]

The most certain statement about Delphic procedure is that the Pythia sat upon a tripod when under the god's inspiration she spoke his oracles. The seat on which she sat was called *holmos*, defined as a round stone or a bowl-shaped object; i.e., it was a hollow seat (fig. 2).[40] It occupied the tripod neck, which would ordinarily hold a cauldron or kettle. But we hear of a bowl (*phialê*) on or by the tripod in connection with the lots: if the information is reliable, we cannot know just where it was placed in relation to the *holmos*. The tripod was perhaps three to four feet high, to judge from vase-paintings (and the sources speak of it as a high seat); at any rate the Pythia had to mount it.

Just where the tripod stood in the adyton; where the inquirers sat in relation to the Pythia and the priests; whether there was an underground chamber to which the Pythia descended (and which may be the reality behind the *antron* that some writers mention), or whether she sat on the

---

39 No other ancient statement on bay's mantic properties makes reference to Delphi: Lyk. 6 (Kassandra) and Schol. vet.; Tib. 2.5.63–64 (Sibyl); Juvenal 7.19 (the poet). It was an article of ancient folklore that seers and poets received inspiration from chewing bay leaves.

40 See Eur. *Ion* 91–92, 1320–1323; Xen. *Apol.* 12; Diod. 16.26.5; Lucr. 1.739; Strabo 9.3.5, p. 419; Poll. *Onom.* 10.81; Iambl. *Myst.* 3.11; Suda Π3137; Schol. vet. on Eur. *Or.* 165; Schol. vet. on Aristoph. *Eq.* 1016 and *Plut.* 9, 39.

same level as the consultants, and if so, whether they could see her or not—
all these questions have been much debated, but we have no need to go
into them deeply since they hardly affect the issues raised in this book.[41]
There is nothing in the evidence to show conclusively that the Pythia was
separated from enquirers so that they could not see her during the session.
In all records of consultations the consultant not only speaks directly to
the Pythia, but appears to look at her too; at least it is never said that he
could not see her, and the reader is likely to suppose that he could. As
soon as Lykurgos (Q7) and Eetion (Q59) entered the *megaron* the Pythia
addressed them, as Herodotos tells the stories; and most likely if the
Pythia could see them as they entered, they could see her (these are not
genuine responses, but Herodotos and his informants knew how consultations were conducted). Furthermore in Q125, which is genuine, the
Pythia perhaps had to draw names from a vase or other vessel presented
to her; and in the legend of L162 she definitely drew a name from the
phryktoi presented to her. How could this be managed if the consultants
could not confront her with the lot container or list of names?[42]

The principal evidence invoked for a separation of the Pythia from
the consultants is Plutarch's account of H72 (*Mor.* 438b), the unfortunate
session in which the Pythia was overcome with some emotional sickness.
When she began to speak, says Plutarch, it was evident from the roughness of her voice that something was wrong with her. Does this justify us
in supposing that the consultants and attendants could not see her as well
as hear her? Plutarch is remarking only upon the extraordinary quality of
her voice. Then with a shriek she rushed from the tripod and flung herself
at the door, so frightening the prophet, *Hosioi*, and the foreign emissaries
present that they fled from the room. They returned immediately and
picked her up (she had fallen before reaching the door). If she was in a
separate room or a closed-off compartment, and if the door was between
her position and the consultants' room, how could the prophet and
others present see her running toward the door (if this was simply an
open passage, then they could see the Pythia sitting on the tripod, and the
supposed division of the adyton into two rooms would have no point)?
It looks as if they became frightened both from hearing and seeing her;
when she ran toward the door, they rushed out ahead of her; that is, they
had been sitting between the Pythia and the door. They left the room

---

41 See Courby 1915: 59–69; Flacelière 1938: 80–105; Roux 1976: 101–110.

42 Again in H21 the reader gets the impression that the Pythia will look at the two vases
presented to her by the Athenians, although it is true that she could answer the question,
which vase contained the proper course for the Athenians to take, without looking at the
vases.

(= adyton) and the Pythia did not, and it was to this room that they returned and found her on the floor.[43]

Courby and Holland supposed that the Pythia descended to a basement room (the *antron*); Flacelière wants a lower level, and the same level, for both Pythia and consultants.[44] They rely on the verbs *katabainein*, *katienai*, *katerchesthai*, and others meaning "go down," which Plutarch uses of both the Pythia and consultants on their entering the temple or adyton for an oracular session.[45] This is not very cogent evidence, since verbs of motion compounded with *kata* may mean "return," "come to land," "enter a contest," or simply "come to," "reach." Therefore Plutarch may mean simply that the Pythia and consultants enter upon the scene of operations, the mantic arena, the object of her office and their visit. Or these words may mean "go down" to the temple from the town, much of which was situated higher up the slope. For when Alexander came to Delphi for an oracle (Q216) on a non-oracular day (*apophras*), and the Pythia refused to appear at his summons, he went up (*anabas*, *Alex.* 14.4), says Plutarch, and dragged her to the temple.[46] Plutarch's use of "go up" and "go down" in reference to the Pythia may reveal his intimate acquaintance with Delphi as resident and priest. Most writers on consultations use verbs that mean just "enter" and "leave" (*eisbainein*, *eisienai*, *eiserchesthai*)—for example, Herodotos of Lykurgos, Croesus' envoys, and the Athenian envoys who received Q146 and Q147, and Euripides of the Pythia and Xuthos.[47]

It makes little difference to our central problem—what sort of

---

43 It is just before this passage that Plutarch mentions the fragrance which sometimes pervades the room (*oikos*) in which the consultants sat. In the usual interpretation the *pneuma* carries the fragrance "from the adyton as source" (i.e., a source in the adyton); we can also interpret Plutarch's words as "filled with a fragrance and *pneuma*, as if the adyton were sending forth essences of the finest perfumes from a spring." Neither interpretation demands that we separate the *oikos* from the adyton whence the fragrance rises. Or if we do so take it, nothing prevents our interpreting the *oikos* as a waiting room in the cella, just outside the adyton door (understanding adyton as the whole rear room behind the west wall of the cella—if there was such a wall), where consultants awaited their turns to enter the adyton and speak to the Pythia. On the *oikos* see Courby 1915: 63–64; Roux 1976: 132–136, 148–149.

44 Courby 1915: 64–66; Holland 1933; Flacelière 1938: 95–100. We have to keep in mind too that Plutarch knew the fourth-century temple, which may have had a different plan from the sixth-century temple, which Herodotos knew, and from the seventh-century temple.

45 Pythia: Plut. *Mor.* 397a, 408c, 438b; Val. Max. 1.8.10; Oros. *Hist.* 6.15.11, where the verb *descendere* probably indicates belief in an oracular cave. Consultants: Plut. *Mor.* 407d, *Timol.* 8.2. Cf. Hom. Hymn 3.443 concerning Apollo's entering the adyton.

46 Inscriptions mention the Pythia's house: FD 3.5.50, III 2 (= SIG 251); SIG 823A.

47 Herod. 1.47.2, 65.2; 7.140.1, 141.1; Eur. *Ion* 42, 69–70, 418.

responses were actually spoken at Delphi—just where the Pythia sat, and whether or not the consultants could see her; but the conclusion to which I incline and with which the evidence is in accord—that the consultants could see the Pythia—supports other conclusions to which we have come: the Pythia spoke directly and coherently to the consultants with a simple, clear response, generally in prose.

Other questions about the mantic rite are peripheral: the preparations of the Pythia, priests and consultants; preliminary sacrifices; fees and other charges; frequency of consultation days—these matters may be left to a study of Apollo's Delphic cult as a chapter in a book on the cults of Delphi.

ADDENDUM

Procedures of Other Oracles

Other Apolline Oracles appear to have been similar to Delphi in methods and operations. It is uncertain whether a man or woman spoke for Apollo at Didyma. Presumably this person received the god's message as at Delphi—but in truth we know nothing of mantic operations at Didyma. Patara and Argos had prophetesses; at Klaros and Ptoon a man spoke the god's words. We know little about the Apolline Oracles at Abai, Tegyra, the Theban Ismenion, and elsewhere; but there is no evidence that they differed in this respect. At an Oracle of Apollo the seer received inspiration. We hear occasionally of lots, as at Delphi, or of incubation.[48] But men generally believed that Apollo in some manner informed his agent directly.

Fifty-four responses attributed to Didyma (see Catalogue of Responses of Didyma, pp. 417–429), not counting a few fragments. Thirty-one of these are Historical and show the same characteristics as the Historical responses of Delphi. Only among the remainder do we find extraordinary responses. There are few extant responses attributed to the other Apolline Oracles; and among them too the Historical responses show no extraordinary character (on responses of Klaros see p. 237). So the evidence for all Apolline Oracles has essentially the same character: all ambiguous responses and spectacular predictions are at best questionable, and the well-attested responses are commonplace.

Aside from the Apolline Oracles it is difficult to find an established and permanent inspiration Oracle anywhere at any time, past or present; exceptions are very dubious. In the ancient Aegean world we find only the Thracian Oracle of Dionysos among the Satric Bessoi, where, according to Herodotos (7.111.2), a woman promantis spoke oracles in the manner of the Pythia at

---

48 See Herod. 1.182.2; Latte 1939: 840, 1940: 13–15; Amandry 1950: 36 note 1.

Delphi. He adds "and nothing more intricate [*poikiloteron*]," apparently meaning no more complex than the Pythia's methods and responses. It seems that Herodotos is dismissing what he considered to be false notions current among Greeks about the Bessoi's Oracle of Dionysos; but it is uncertain whether he himself had firsthand knowledge of it. This was probably a healing Oracle like the sanctuary of Dionysos at Amphikleia in Phokis, where a male promantis served the god. There, says Pausanias (10.33.11), Dionysos healed the towns-people and their neighbors through dreams; the priest as promantis spoke oracles under the god's influence. It was an incubation Oracle like those of Asklepios and Amphiaraos.

All non-Apolline Oracles in Hellas made use of divinatory devices or of incubation. At Zeus's Oracle of Dodona the priestess drew lots and perhaps interpreted signs; at Olympia the Iamids inspected the entrails and hides of victims sacrificed on Zeus's great altar. At the oasis of Siwa in the Sahara the priests of Ammon, identified with Zeus, interpreted the movements of the god's image carried in procession. These various devices yielded Yes/No answers or made choices.[49]

If we look elsewhere in the ancient world we find no example of an estab-lished inspiration Oracle like the Delphic and other Apolline establishments. In Egypt, Italy, and elsewhere we find only sign Oracles, lot Oracles, and occa-sionally dream Oracles or *psychomanteia*. The so-called Oracle of Ishtar at Arbela near Nineveh did not resemble Delphi: there was no single prophetess who spoke; the recorded pronouncements are addresses to kings, conventional eulogies and hymns; and the same kinds of pronouncements were spoken in the name of Asshur and other deities.[50]

Nothing much like the Delphic Oracle appears in any contemporary society, nor in fact anywhere since ancient times. Divinatory devices are wide-spread; for example, the Ifa divination of the Yoruba in Nigeria, a manipulation of palm nuts or a divining chain for the selection of a previously composed oracular text; or the poison Oracle of the Azande of the Nile-Congo divide, in which the death or survival of poisoned chickens provides Yes/No answers.[51] Yoruba diviners practise Ifa divination at the house of Ifa in every village. Diviners do not operate the poison Oracle: anyone may do so except the person who wants information from it; and the site of operations is a clearing in the bush.

Inspired seers are common enough, but they are more like the chresmo-logues, independent operators unattached to a single site or establishment. Diffi-cult to find is a single person, like the Pythia, in a permanent office receiving

49 See Parke 1967a; Bouché-Leclercq 1880: 2.277-360; Amandry 1950: 176-179.

50 Guillaume 1938: 42-47; Stephen Langdon, *Tammuz and Ishtar* (Oxford: Clarendon Press, 1914) 124-147; Morris Jastrow, *The Religion of Babylonia and Assyria* (Boston 1898) 341-349.

51 See Bascom 1969; Evans-Pritchard 1937. The Yoruba divining methods may also be used to produce Yes/No answers.

inspiration at a fixed site, like Delphi. C. R. Whittaker (1965) believes that something like the Delphic Oracle is perceptible in the Oracle(s) of Mwari in the Matopo Hills of Mashonaland in southern Rhodesia. He depends on others' reports; even so, his account shows little resemblance between Mwari's Oracle and Delphi. More recently M. L. Daneel has not only visited shrines of Mwari but has also consulted the Oracle at Mt SaShe and heard the Voice of Mwari.[52] There are in fact several Oracles of Mwari, high god of the Shona, who speaks from caves. At least three caves in the mountains around the village of Wirirani at Matonjeni serve as oracular shrines (Daneel 1970: 41); each is kept by different servants of the god.

Led by the high priest, Daneel went to the cave of Mt SaShe in January 1967 with the Gutu messenger, who wanted to consult Mwari on the Gutu chieftainship succession and report the response to his people at Gutu. The consultation took place at night. Fifty yards from the cave they took off their shoes, approached the seated high priestess and her attendant, and sat down beside them with their backs to the cave. They then greeted Mwari by clapping their hands and loudly calling him by his praise names. The Gutu messenger then presented himself in a speech of thirteen sentences, in which he barely alluded to the business on which he had come. In this speech he mentioned Daneel's gifts to the god, which were then passed to the mouth of the cave. There followed a conversation between the Voice and the Gutu messenger, then another between the Voice and Daneel.

In theory it is Mwari himself who speaks from within the cave. In reality it is a member of the priestly family, at Daneel's visit a woman, who slipped into the cave unseen before the consultants arrived and then returned to the village a half hour after the others (Daneel 1970: 42, 80). She acted much as any Shona spirit-medium; only her spirit was Mwari, and no one could watch her undergo possession or see her as she spoke; whereas villagers gather about a spirit-medium in his possessed state and can see his face as they address him.[53]

In the whole conversation with the Gutu messenger and Daneel the Voice made no predictions and said nothing ambiguously. In fact, everything said was very clear, and also commonplace. The Voice principally complained of the young Shona who adopt European ways and of the quarreling at Gutu, and was otherwise rather discursive; but finally answered the messenger's question, saying that an elder should become chief at Gutu (Gutu did not heed this and elected a younger man). Other pronouncements of the Voice that Daneel reports secondhand do not differ essentially from this; he reports no predictions

---

52 Daneel 1970: see especially 76–81. Michael Gelfand has visited the cave at Dula rock, but did not hear the Voice; see *An African's Religion: The Spirit of Nyajena* (Cape Town, Wynberg, Johannesburg: Juta, 1966) 33–42.

53 See M. Gelfand, *Shona Religion* (Cape Town, Wynberg, Johannesburg: Juta, 1962) 31–32, 46–50. According to Daneel 1970: 77 the Voice of Mwari as spoken by the medium was "high pitched as if in a trance."

or ambiguous speeches. Most consultations amount to petitions for rain; but the Voice may be presented with tribal problems such as succession to chieftainships (Daneel 1970: 26, 34). The attendant priests may interpret Mwari's words to the questioner, but that is only because of difference in dialects used: the priest puts Mwari's words into the questioner's dialect and also interprets the questioner's words for Mwari. Mwari's words are clear in his language.

The consultation of Shona spirit-mediums goes much the same way, except that one can see the medium. The medium becomes possessed at night. The would-be consulters waiting outside then enter his hut and clap hands as they sit down. The medium is attended by an acolyte. The visitors ask questions on personal and tribal matters. In a séance that Michael Gelfand attended, the spirit, like Mwari, complained about Europeans and contemporary conditions, and made commonplace and discursive answers to questions.[54] There were no predictions, no ambiguities.

The Oracle of Mwari, therefore, has very little resemblance to the Delphic Oracle in its procedures. The content of responses may be similar in that they contain religious and political directions; but Mwari is mostly concerned with answering requests for rain. The manner of response, however, is very different; whereas the historical Pythia seldom replied in more than one sentence, and to the point, Mwari's Voice is discursive and inclined to conversation.

This survey of oracular establishments, ancient and modern, reveals that inspiration Oracles of the Apolline kind have been and are rare. The Pythia institution at Delphi (and its equivalent at other Apolline Oracles) appears to be unique. The pronouncements of other Oracles tend to confirm our conclusion about genuine Delphic responses, that they were generally commonplace statements or commands. Nowhere do we find extraordinary predictions, nowhere ambiguous statements or commands. Likewise we find no analogy for a frenzied Pythia that babbled incoherent words interpreted by priests.

The Shona mediums undergo possession and enter into a kind of trance, although their behavior is not frenzied and their utterances are clear and coherent. Possession and trance are shamanistic phenomena. Shamans may enter into a kind of frenzy, but as a rule they do not speak incoherently or unclearly. And they are more concerned with magic and healing than with prophecy.[55] Moreover the shaman is an independent operator, not the holder of a permanent mantic office at an oracular establishment. The only possible exception is the shamanlike priest of the state Oracle of Nechung Gompa monastery near Drepung in Tibet. Like other Tibetan oracle-priests he becomes possessed and

---

54 Gelfand, *Shona Religion* 48–50.

55 On shamanism see Henry N. Michael, editor, *Studies in Siberian Shamanism* (Arctic Institute of North America, Univ. of Toronto Press, 1963); M. A. Czaplicka, *Aboriginal Siberia* (Oxford: Clarendon Press, 1914) 166–255; Mircea Eliade, *Shamanism* (New York: Pantheon Books, 1964); Jane Belo, *Trance in Bali* (New York: Columbia Univ. Press, 1960); René Nebesky-Wojkowitz, *Oracles and Demons of Tibet* (The Hague: Mouton, 1956).

enters into a frenzy. But his utterances are clear and not spectacular: he generally gives advice on governmental problems.[56]

In any case the Pythia was not a shaman; so much is clear from the evidence that we have and especially from Plutarch's testimony. There were shamans in Hellas in the archaic period, the *iatromanteis* (physician-seers), men like Abaris, Aristeas, and Hermotimos (Dodds 1951: 140–146). It may be that their practices had some influence on the operations of Bakides and Sibyls. We have already seen that Lucan cast the Pythia in a Sibylline role and that he is largely responsible for the conventional view of the Pythia as frenzied and possessed. But the Delphic Oracle was definitely not a shamanistic institution.

---

56 On Tibetan oracle-priests and Nechung Gompa see Nebesky-Wojkowitz, *Oracles and Demons of Tibet* 409–466, 544–552.

Conclusion

The results of this study demand a rejection as non-genuine of almost all responses said to have been spoken in the first three centuries of the Delphic Oracle, roughly 750–450. Many readers will object to such wholesale dismissal. Although they must grant that the evidence after 450—when the Historical responses (those attested in contemporary records) were spoken—shows that the Pythia generally spoke simple commands and sanctions on religious matters, still, they will ask, might not the Pythia have spoken a different kind of response in the earlier centuries, ambiguous and predictive verse oracles such as those that appear in the pages of Herodotos? They will point to the lack of contemporary records for the earlier period in contrast to the later, so that, they will say, we cannot know that a Pythia of earlier times delivered the same kind of responses as a later Pythia. Their question may be given a multiform answer.

1. The argument comes to this: we should believe that remarkable responses were spoken in the period for which we have no contemporary evidence, but were not spoken in the period for which we have such evidence. That is, stories can be believed about ill-documented ages that are not credible if told about well-documented ages.

2. We have contemporary records in two Milesian inscriptions of sixth-century Apolline responses spoken at Didyma. One is probably

earlier than 550; and Rehm was surely correct in believing that it records an oracular response. It is a fragmentary inscription, from which we learn that the god has decreed or approved a law whose content is lost; if one obeys, λῷον καὶ ἄμεινον ἔσται ("it will be better and more good," the exact Delphic formula of sanctions), and if one does not, the contrary (Didyma 4). It was probably a cult law, but we cannot be sure. The other inscription, which Rehm dates late in the century, records a response which contains laws for a cult of Herakles (Didyma 7). The first part bans women from the sanctuary: then follow regulations on sacrifices. Thus contemporary evidence of early Apolline oracles, though scanty, does not support the objectors' argument.

3. The extraordinary Quasi-Historical responses allegedly spoken in the early period have exactly the same character as those allegedly spoken after 450, when we have contemporary records. The oracles concerned with Croesus, Tegea, the Kypselids, Cyrene, have the same features as those supposedly spoken to Philip, Alexander, Pyrros, Appius Claudius, and Julian.[1] Moreover they are very like Legendary responses.

4. To accept the early Quasi-Historical oracles as authentic means that we must suppose present at Delphi before 450 a kind of mantic talent and sagacity that cannot be paralleled in any other time or country, nor in Greece itself, except that other Apolline Oracles were credited with the same faculties.

5. The authority for most early Quasi-Historical responses is untrustworthy. With few exceptions those first attested after the fifth century are questionable on several grounds.

The issue in effect reduces itself to the trustworthiness of the Delphic oracles that Herodotos reports; readers want to believe his stories of remarkable oracles. Crahay (1956) has carefully studied all the oracles that Herodotos quotes or reports and has come to the conclusion that most are not authentic, at least in the form in which Herodotos reports them. If anyone objects (see Nilsson 1958: 247) that the form of an unauthentic response must be like that of genuine oracles (since it would be modeled on them), I can only reply that this was definitely not the case in ancient Greece. Narrative oracles take the forms established in narrative and chresmologic tradition, not the form of demonstrably genuine responses. It was on this tradition that Herodotos and his sources drew.

The question will certainly be asked (I have already encountered it),

---

[1] Perhaps some scholars still accept these as genuine, but they have to grant that contemporary records for the later centuries do not show these kinds of responses.

"Why were the Greeks so content with the responses that they received from Delphi when tradition led them to expect more extraordinary responses?" In the first place we do not know that they were content; we simply encounter no objections to authentic oracles in extant literature: we find only Oinomaos' objections, mainly to the oracles of tradition. In the second place we have the hard fact of the Historical responses: these are what clients actually received. Apparently a consultant simply accepted the reply given as that which Apollo wanted to give him. It was, moreover, often the reply that he expected, as when Xenophon asked to what god to make sacrifice in order to fare well on his journey into Asia and received the reply "to Zeus the King" (H11). And in the third place is it not true everywhere that the oracles and prophecies of story are more marvelous than those actually spoken, whether by individual seers and fortune-tellers or at oracular establishments? This is evident among the Shona, to whom the Voice of Mwari speaks such oracles as we noticed at the end of chapter 7. But in the Shona myths and legends we find more spectacular oracles. In the legend of the spirit Chaminuka the spirit voice forecast that the Matabele would overcome and subject the Varozvi (which naturally came to pass). In another legend the spirit Vanyagwau predicted that his medium and her husband would become rich; and they unexpectedly became rich soon afterward.[2] Why are the Shona content with what the Voice and the spirit-mediums tell them when they have more spectacular oracles in their tradition?

To our knowledge no one before Plutarch seems to have noticed any discrepancy between report and actuality with respect to Delphic responses. And Plutarch thought that the difference between prosaic contemporary responses and the extraordinary responses of tradition was due to a decline of the Delphic and other Oracles. Like everyone else he supposed that the oracles of tradition had really been spoken from the tripod; he believed that all the oracles reported by Herodotos, Ephoros, Timaios, Theopompos, Atthidographers, and others were genuine. But in the words of the Irish bull, the Delphic Oracle not only wasn't what it used to be: what was more, it never was. The Pythia had never spoken any other kind of response than what she was speaking in Plutarch's time.

Responses in verse were always rare. Plutarch's Theon points out that numerous prose oracles were spoken in past centuries (*Mor.* 403). Significant is his reference to Theopompos' rebuke (307 GH) of certain

_____

2 Michael Gelfand, *Shona Ritual* (Cape Town, Wynberg, Johannesburg: Juta, 1959) 13–14, 30–32, 46–47. Extraordinary oracles are reported for Dodona, but could not have been spoken there; see Paus. 7.25.1, 10.12.10; Strabo 6.1.5, p. 256.

men who maintained that the Pythia did not speak in verse; but when Theopompos tried to refute them he could find very few contemporary verse oracles. From this we perceive that in the fourth century B.C. a learned man like Theopompos supposed that the contemporary Pythia was speaking in verse when she seldom or never did so, and that there were some men at the time who observed that she did not. It must be the same for the ambiguities and marvelous predictions as for the verse: most men thought that the contemporary Pythia was speaking the kind of oracles transmitted in the narrative and chresmologic traditions.

Ambiguity is an article of Delphic belief. So another question is sure to be asked: How did the Delphic Oracle acquire its reputation for ambiguity if no ambiguous responses were ever spoken there? The truth is that this reputation is wholly modern: Delphi had no such reputation in antiquity. Herodotos quotes ambiguous and obscure oracles, but never says that ambiguity was a Delphic characteristic. Euripides' *Ion* makes no reference to ambiguities.[3] Plutarch tells us that the Pythia speaks clearly; his Theon (*Mor.* 407bc) holds attendant poets responsible for the obscurities of past responses, i.e., the traditional oracles that he thought genuine; and in them it is not so much ambiguity that he is talking about as the use of periphrases and kennings, the conventional expressions of poetry. Only occasionally, he says (*Mor.* 407 c–e), the earlier Oracle employed ambiguity deliberately, and then only to conceal the message from others than the recipient (though in many stories it is the recipient who did not understand the message).

Only very late do we find any reference to customary Delphic ambiguity: there is little besides two passages of Lucian. In *Zeus Tragodos* (28) Momos tells Apollo that he does not speak clear oracles, but is usually indirect (*loxos*), enigmatic, and imprecise.[4] In *Dialogues of the*

---

3 In Aesch. *Ag.* 1254–1255, when Kassandra tells the Chorus that she has been speaking Greek, they reply, Καὶ γὰρ τὰ πυθόκραντα· δυσμαθῆ δ' ὅμως, generally taken as "So do the Pythian oracles; yet they are hard to understand." But this does not take account of *gar*, always "for." Literally Kassandra says, "And yet I understand Greek well"; the Chorus reply, "(Yes,) for (you understand) the Pythian [i.e., Apollo's] statements; but they are nevertheless hard to understand." J. S. Blackie translates, "Thou speakest Apollo's words: true, but obscure." The Chorus mean not Delphic oracles but Kassandra's prophecies; "Pythian" is simply "Apolline" by metonymy. Notice that L7 and L8, the Delphic oracles of the *Oresteia*, are very clear in meaning.

4 Perhaps the defenders of Delphic ambiguity will point to Apollo's name *Loxias*, relying upon the derivation of it from *loxos*—"oblique," "indirect." It is especially used for the Delphic god in poetry. It is not, however, a common name for him, and the etymology is probably false. It is a Stoic etymology, found in Cornutus 32. Plutarch (*Mor.* 511b) accepts it; but the point he makes is that the Pythian Apollo is concise and brief in speech and is

Gods (16.1) Hera says that Apollo deceives his clients with indirect (*loxa*) and equivocal answers at Delphi, Klaros, and Didyma.[5] Obviously Lucian has in mind the famous oracles of literature and tradition. Almost the only Historical response to which late authors refer is H3 on Socrates' wisdom (which is not ambiguous); they commonly quote or cite the Oedipus and Croesus oracles and others of the same kind as typical pronouncements of the Delphic Apollo.

For example, Oinomaos in his attack on the oracular Apollo cites Legendary and dubious Quasi-Historical responses almost exclusively, most of them well known from Herodotos, other historians, and poets. He points to particular ambiguities and obscurities in these oracles, but never says that the Delphic Apollo has a reputation for ambiguity or is commonly ambiguous. He censures Apollo's Oracles, especially Delphi, for deceit, poor advice, nonsensical statements, utter worthlessness, qualities which he found in all the god's responses, clear or obscure. Someone, however, may point to the oracles that Oinomaos himself received from Klaros as examples of unclear responses that are certainly genuine. Those are three verse responses in trochaic trimeters (*ap.* Eus. *PE* 5.22–23, pp. 214a–215b). The first (beginning with *Estin*) informed Oinomaos that "There is in the land of Trachis a garden of Herakles, full blooming, well watered, where fruit is gathered every day without diminishing." Oinomaos does not tell us what his question was; but he interpreted the response as foretelling a prosperous reward for his labors. Then—and this is significant—he learned that the same response had been given to Kallistratos, a Pontic merchant. Later when Oinomaos asked for a teacher of wisdom he received a meaningless two-verse response; and a third oracle was equally worthless for his purpose. It is not ambiguity that Oinomaos censures in these three oracles: each could be clear enough in a context, though expressed in poetic language; it is irrelevance and worthlessness. It looks as though these oracles were selected by lot or drawn from a stock of prepared written texts and delivered in that form. The consultant then had to figure out the application of the verses to his problem as in Ifa divination. This supposition suits the procedure that Tacitus describes (*Annals* 2.54): the prophet at Klaros entered a *specus* after hearing only the number and names of the consultants, and then delivered

---

called Loxias because he shuns garrulity rather than obscurity. This derivation has no more value than another Stoic interpretation: Apollo, identified with Helios, is called Loxias because of his course on the ecliptic; Kleanthes, frag. 542 von Arnim *ap.* Macr. *Sat.* 1.17.31 (who also cites Oinopides). More likely Loxias is related to *legein* or to Sanskrit *laksh-*; see *RE* 13.1533.

5 See also Dion Chrys. 10.23; Ps.-Liban. *Decl.* 51.18.

verse responses to questions that had been silently asked.[6] The little
evidence otherwise available about Klaros does not indicate an aleatory
method, but is not inconsistent with it. There are only two other Clarian
oracles extant that are certainly genuine, both in iambic or trochaic verse
and fairly contemporary with Oinomaos' oracles; they could be texts
selected by chance, but it is possible that varied methods were employed
at Klaros or that changes of procedure occurred.[7]

It was not a reputation for ambiguity that Delphic Apollo had, but
for truth-telling. Quintus Cicero, as speaker in Marcus Cicero's dialogue
on divination, lauds Delphi's record for truth over centuries, and says
nothing about ambiguities.[8]

The famous dictum of Herakleitos—ʿΟ ἄναξ οὗ τὸ μαντεῖόν ἐστι
τὸ ἐν Δελφοῖς οὔτε λέγει οὔτε κρύπτει ἀλλὰ σημαίνει: "The lord to
whom the Oracle at Delphi belongs neither tells nor conceals but indicates" (frag. 93DK *ap.* Plut. *Mor.* 404d)—has strangely been taken to refer
to the Delphic god's ambiguities, without regard to the context in which
Plutarch quotes Herakleitos.[9] His Theon is making the point that the
Pythia reflects Apollo's voice as the moon reflects sunlight. It is her voice
that consultants hear; the god does not speak to them, but makes his
thoughts and intentions known through the Pythia's body and soul: that
is, through her he indicates his meaning. The verb *sēmainein* well suits the
directions and sanctions that the Pythia usually spoke.

Tradition helped build the Delphic Oracle's prestige. Yet the tradition
had to arise from the reality of the Delphic Oracle and its actual responses.
Men went there from the Oracle's foundation to receive advice and
sanctions, believing in the sanctity of the place and in Apollo's special
authority when he spoke there through the Pythia. The site itself inspired
the belief; the tradition and Delphic propaganda promoted it.

---

6 There are, however, grave difficulties about Tacitus' passage on Germanicus' consultation. He concludes: et ferebatur Germanico per ambages, ut mos oraculis, maturum
exitum cecinisse. Notice *ferebatur*; moreover *ambages* may mean just such an irrelevant
response as Oinomaos received, which could with effort be interpreted to foretell an early
death; and perhaps the interpretation was made after Germanicus' death. Notice Tacitus'
words: [sacerdos] edit responsa . . .; he does not say that he spoke them. The account of this
consultation probably reached Tacitus in distorted form. On procedures of Klaros see also
Iambl. *Myst.* 3.11.

7 See Buresch 1889: 10–11, 47 (II = Aristeides Or. 25.312).

8 Cic. *Div.* 1.19.37–38; see also Liban. *Decl.* 41.20.

9 See Parke 1956: 40 with note 100; Delcourt 1955: 103; Amandry 1950: 178 note 3,
suggests a reference to a Delphic lot Oracle, since *sēmainei* is the verb used to introduce
oracles of Dodona.

What effect or influence did Delphi have upon the Greek states? If we look through genuine responses we must say that it had no direct and active influence upon them; it took no initiatives in Greek affairs: Delphi did not send Sparta to war against Athens—Sparta was already determined to make war and sought Delphic confirmation (H5). When the Pythia told all Spartan clients to free Athens (Q124) she was telling them what the Athenian Kleisthenes had paid her to tell them. Even in the narrative tradition the Delphic Apollo makes little attempt to affect the policies of cities; he simply speaks the truth when asked for it. The Greek states valued Delphic sanctions for their enterprises and laws, and above all for their cult laws and institutions. Remember that the Platonic Socrates would leave the regulation of religious institutions in the ideal republic to Apollo at Delphi.

ADDENDUM

Pp. 233–234. An early sixth-century B.C. inscription (*DI* 11), very fragmentary, found at Didyma in the nineteenth century, but now lost, apparently recorded a response. The word *lêistoi* is visible, taken as "pirates" (who are assumed to be the consultants); but that should be *lêistai*. There follows, "And the god said, 'It is right to do as (your) fathers.'" This may be the whole response (Mode D1, Topic 3j). If this is a response of Apollo Didymeus, it further confirms the commonplace character of archaic responses for which we have contemporary evidence: it is no more extraordinary than Didyma 4 and 7.

Catalogue of Delphic Responses

The Catalogue is divided into four parts: I, Historical Responses; II, Quasi-Historical Responses; III, Legendary Responses; IV, Fictional Responses. These terms are defined in the Introduction, pp. 7–9. The responses are numbered separately in each category; and each number is preceded by H, Q, L, F, according to the classification (as they are cited in the text and notes): H1–75, Q1–268, L1–176, F1–16.

Each entry is headed by its letter-number symbol, which is followed by the PW number in parentheses. Then for H and Q responses the date or approximate date of utterance is given. If the response is judged unauthentic the date is enclosed in brackets and followed by the phrase "Not genuine." A few Q responses are designated "Doubtful," "Possibly genuine," "Probably genuine," or otherwise qualified. All L and F responses are understood to be not genuine.

After the heading (first line) the Consultant (C) is indicated, then the Occasion (Occ.), the Question (Q), and the Response (R). The response is expressed in English paraphrase or summary, from which unessential details and phrases are omitted. The PW corpus has the original texts of all but fifteen: H30, 32, 44, 49, 51, 72, 74; Q24, 79, 120, 268; L36; F10, 15, 16.

The letters (A), (B), in parentheses indicate the parts of a double response, in which there was a second question and answer. The only tripartite response recorded is Q268, where (C) indicates the third part. Numerals in parentheses—(1), (2), (3)—indicate differing versions of a response.

The response is followed by an indication of mode and topic (for explanation see chapter 1, pp. 13–20, 24–26). Symbols of subordinate modes and topics are placed in parentheses.

Below the response the source or sources are cited; it is my hope that all ancient and medieval notices are included, no matter how insignificant. The citations follow headings which indicate whether or not the source explicitly attributes the response to Delphi. The heading *Delphi* introduces citations of sources that make this attribution. The heading *NP* (No Place) introduces citations of sources that name no oracular centre. Under *NP* the subheading "Apollo" indicates sources that name Apollo as the speaker without specifying the Delphic Apollo. "The god" indicates sources in which only "the god" is designated as speaker without specifying the deity. "Oracle" indicates sources which inform the reader only that an oracle was spoken. *OP* (Other Place or Person) indicates non-Delphic ascriptions; and the alleged Oracle or seer (Dodona, Bakis, etc.) follows as a subheading. I assume that a Scholiast or commentator makes the same attribution as the writer on whose work he is commenting; for example, a Scholiast may say only that "the god" spoke, or merely that an oracle was spoken, when the writer has specified Delphi or Apollo. Likewise if a later writer indicates an earlier as his source, I assume that he makes the same attribution as the earlier writer. But in some instances the Scholiast or later writer may be more specific than his authority.

Under the heading *Delphi* and under each subdivision of *NP* and *OP* the citations are classified according to whether they represent direct or indirect quotation of the response or merely inform us that it was spoken. "Direct," followed by "Verse" or "Prose," introduces citations of direct quotation. "Verse" alone means dactylic hexameter; other kinds of verse are specified. "Pseudo-Direct," followed by "Verse" or "Prose," introduces citations of direct quotation which do not purport to be the god's actual words, but which are a literary rendering of them. These include (1) the directly quoted responses of drama and other poetry which are obviously the poet's composition, framed to fit his metre (see e.g., L8, 17); and (2) direct quotations in Latin, translations of the original utterances. All direct quotations of F responses are classed as "Direct"; from the fictional point of view these were the god's words. "Indirect" introduces citations of sources that quote the response indirectly. "Testimony" introduces citations of sources that refer to the response without quoting it; knowledge of the response's content must be inferred from the context, which in some instances is not informative. A citation is sometimes followed by a citation or citations in parentheses, less precise references to the response in the work cited. Following citation of direct quotation a parenthetic citation indicates indirect quotation or testimony; following citation of indirect quotation it indicates testimony.

If the first citation, when more than one is listed, does not indicate the earliest source, then the earliest source is marked by an asterisk. A heading *Comment* follows the citations of most responses, including references indexing relevant pages of the text, and for some, explanatory remarks and discussion that are more conveniently placed there than in the text or notes.

The H and Q responses are arranged only in rough chronological order: the first are the earliest, and each period follows in sequence. When I have come upon a previously overlooked response I have added it at the end of the group. For nothing would have been gained by renumbering many responses, which would have entailed extensive text revision and risk of error. The Legendary responses are very roughly arranged according to their appearance in ancient literature; but there are many exceptions: in particular, responses pertaining to the same legend are likely to be juxtaposed.

The Catalogue lists 535 responses. Most of these are responses that at least one source has explicitly attributed to the Delphic Oracle. But included are a number for which such attribution is lacking. Since they are usually assumed to be Delphic and with a few exceptions appear in the PW corpus, I have been willing to include them in the Catalogue. The PW corpus contains 615 entries. Fifteen of my 535 do not appear in it, so that 95 PW entries are not included in the Catalogue. PW often give a later version of a response its own number; e.g., PW142, 374, 481, 501, are all versions of L11, the oracle spoken to Kadmos. Or PW sometimes take the two parts of a double response as two responses; e.g., PW 4–5 = Q58. This reduction accounts in part for the different totals. The remainder, over one-half, of the excluded PW entries are responses that for various reasons I have rejected from the Catalogue.

PW130 and 475 I consider to be oracles of Didyma (though not genuine). PW400 and 522, spoken to Milesians, could be Didymaean too; they are surely not meant to be Delphic. PW263 is expressly assigned to Dodona by Demosthenes 19.297; and the Delphic Apollo is too uncertainly one of "all the gods" who agree with Zeus and Dione.

PW135 expresses, I believe, not the specific words of an oracle, but a phrase from several oracles. PW151 is merely Oedipus' reference to oracles which Ismene reported to him in his exile: there is no content indicated, no ascription to Delphi, and no indication that the Oedipus legend contained other oracles than L17–21, or that Ismene's act is anything other than Sophocles' invention. PW213 says no more than that Helen's parents awaited a Delphic oracle—i.e., intended to consult Delphi at the proper time in the future—and no fulfillment is mentioned: the only response which Tyndareos received concerning Helen is L126 (= PW530). PW320, 393–395, 398, 407, 413, 558, 571, 577, are either pseudepigrapha or too uncertainly Delphic. PW196 is Ino's false response: the story is that Ino bribed the envoy to bring back a false response, the content of which she gave him, and to say that he had received it at Delphi (or some unnamed shrine); there is nothing in any source to indicate that the words were spoken by a suborned Pythia. PW184–186 are not responses: Neoptolemos-Pyrros went to Delphi to demand satisfaction from Apollo for killing Achilles or to atone for his misconduct on his earlier visit; that is, he did not go there to consult the Oracle, and no response was given him. Or he went with the intention of consulting about Hermione's barrenness, but never asked his question: in all versions of the story he was murdered at Delphi by either Orestes or the priest Machaireus (see Fontenrose 1960a: 212–213). PW478 should not be considered a Delphic oracle simply on the ground that Ovid in poetic language says that Atlas learned his destiny from Themis Parnasia (*Met.* 4. 643); divine beings like Atlas do not consult the Delphic Oracle, if one excepts Aphrodite and the Charities in F5 (= PW 500), which is purely Themistios' fiction. PW 167 is not a reference to an actual or supposed oracle, but only to a hypothetical question and response.

I omit PW582–590, which are single-word fragments of responses, and also PW257 and 528 as fragments. I also omit all the *dubia et pseudepigrapha* in PW's Appendix, 591–615, with the exceptions of 600–602.

I. Historical Responses

H1 (PW123). c. 440-430.

C. Athenians.

Occ. and Q. Not stated.

R. The persons specified shall receive public maintenance in the prytaneion.

Mode A2, Topic 2b

Delphi. Testimony—Inscription of Athens, *IG* 1². 77 = Oliver 1950: 13, lines 7-11.

    Comment: The text is mutilated and the exact sense unclear. On the inscription see Oliver 1950: 139-141; Wesley E. Thompson, "The Prytaneion Decree," *AJPh* 92 (1971) 226-237. There can be little doubt that the inscription means the Delphic Apollo, who, if not definitely mentioned in a missing part of the inscription, is surely meant in lines 9-10 as the interpreter of *nomima* for Athens. The reference seems to be to an oracle that approved public maintenance for certain categories of persons, and I have therefore classified the mode as A2; if not that, it was a simple command (A1). We cannot be sure that this was a recent response.

H2 (PW124). 430-420.

C. Athens.

Occ. Apparently a wish to honor the deities mentioned.

Q. Probably whether it is better to perform the sacred acts indicated in R.

R. It is better to put on the goddess's *peplos* and to sacrifice and make first offerings to the
    Moirai, Zeus Moiragetes, Ge . . . [the inscription breaks off here].

Mode A2, Topic 1b

Delphi. Indirect—Inscription of Athens, *IG* 1². 80.10-12.

    Comment: See pp. 192, 212, 221.

The text of the response is incomplete. A sanction beginning *lôion kai ameinon* almost certainly is spoken in answer to a question phrased in the same formula.

H3 (PW134, 420). Before 430 B.C.?
C. Chairephon, Athenian.
Occ. Desire for divine assurance of Socrates' great wisdom.
Q. Is anyone wiser than Socrates?
R. (1) No one is wiser (Plato). (2) No man is freer or juster or more sensible than Socrates (Xenophon).
Mode D1, Topic 3j
Delphi. Indirect—(1) Plato *Apol.* 21a–c (23a, 28e–29a, 30a). Ath. 5.218e. (2) Xen. *Apol.* 14. Ath. 5.218ef.

Testimony—Plut. *Mor.* 1116ef. Aristeides 13.189–190, 46.211. Paus. 1.22.8. Jul. *Or.* 2.79a, 7.238d. Olymp. on Plato *Gorg.* 26.18. Ps.-Socr. *Epist.* 15.1.
NP. Indirect—Apollo: Cic. *Acad.* 1.4.16; *Sen.* 21.78.

Testimony—Apollo: Cic. *Am.* 2.7, 10; 4.13. Ovid *Tr.* 5.12.15. Max. Tyr. 3.3, 13.9, 39.5.
R. (3) (Spurious form). Sophocles is wise, Euripides wiser, but of all men Socrates is wisest.
Mode D1, (Topic 3g)
Delphi. Direct, Verse (iambic trimeter)—Apollon. Molon *ap.* Schol. vet. *in* Aristoph. *Nub.* 144. Schol. Arethas on Plato *Apol.* 21a. Incomplete—Lucian *Am.* 48. Diog. Laert. 2.5.37. Origen *Cels.* 7.6, pp. 697–698. Liban. *Decl.* 2.27 (1.99–101, 178). Schol. on Aristeides 13.189, p. 326 Dind., 46.211, p. 643 Dind. Schol. on Lucian *Herm.* 15.
Indirect—Galen *Protr.* 9.22. Vitr. *Arch.* 3, praef. 1. Tert. *Apol.* 46.5.
Testimony—Pliny *NH* 7.31.118, 7.34.120, 34.12.26. Lucian *Herm.* 15; *Rhet. pr.* 13. Tert. *An.* 1. Liban. *Epist.* 1488.3. Schol. on Lucian *Am.* 23.
NP. Direct, Verse (iambic trimeter), Incomplete—Apollo: Porph. *Plot.* 22. *Theosophia, Chrêsmoi tôn Hell. theôn* 62. Oracle: Justin Martyr *Coh. ad Gr.* 36, p. 32S.
Indirect—Apollo: Val. Max. 3.4 ext. 1. Dion Chrys. 55.8. The god: Chor. Gaz. 32.135.
Testimony—Apollo: Dion Chrys. 13.30.

Comment: See pp. 8, 17, 26, 32, 34, 36–37, 187, 212, 220, 237.

There can be no doubt that all the writers under *NP* knew that this response was Delphic, but they do not explicitly refer it to Delphi.

Although Cicero's indirect form is "Socrates is wisest of all men," he is no doubt not referring to the spurious verses but to Plato's *Apology*, where Socrates himself at first took the Pythia to mean that he was wisest of men. The verses express the common misunderstanding.

It is often difficult to tell whether a Testimony refers to version (1) or to (3). If the superlative is used and the date is A.D. I am inclined to refer the notice to (3).

In the first chapter I express my misgivings about the genuineness of this response. A number of scholars have questioned it. K. Joël sees a pious fiction of the Socratic school modeled on the legend of the Seven Wise Men: *Der echte und der Xenophontische Sokrates* II (Berlin 1901) 772–775. For an opposing view see Legrand 1903.

H4 (PW136). 433 B.C.

C. Epidamnians.

Occ. Korkyra's refusal to help them against the attacks of the exiled aristocrats and their foreign allies.

Q. Should they hand the city over to the Corinthians, its founders, and try to get help from them?

R. They should hand it over and make the Corinthians their leaders.

Mode A2, Topic 2d

Delphi. Indirect—Thuc. 1.25.1.

> Comment: See pp. 14, 38, 220.

Since the response appears to repeat the words of the question, I have classified the mode as A2, a sanction. The question was probably put in the "Is it better for us to. . . .?" formula.

H5 (PW137). 431 B.C.

C. Spartans.

Occ. Athenian breach of truce.

Q. Is it better for them to make war on Athens?

R. If they fight with all their strength, victory will be theirs; and Apollo himself will assist them, invited or uninvited.

Mode A1 (E1), Topic 2e

Delphi. Indirect—Thuc. 1.118.3, 123.1; 2.54.4. Plut. *Mor.* 403b. Philostr. *Vit. Soph.* 1.5.575.

NP. Direct, Prose—The god: Suda *A*899.

> Testimony—The god: Jul. *Or.* 8.250c.

> Comment: See pp. 33, 37, 43, 220, 221, 239.

The form of the question suggests that the Pythia actually spoke a sanction, which Thucydides has expressed in mode A1; the message is essentially a command, "Fight with all your strength in order to have victory." But whether sanction or command, the Pythia added the promise of Apollo's help, expressing the Delphians' partisanship for the Spartans.

H6 (PW159). 426 B.C.

C. Spartans.

Occ. Decision to found a colony in Trachinia.

Q. Should they found the colony?

R. They should do so.

Mode A2, Topic 2c

Delphi. Testimony—Thuc. 3.92.5.

> Comment: See p. 142.

For the reason for classifying this as mode A2 see the *Comment* under H4.

H7 (PW160). 427 B.C.

C. Spartans.

Occ. All consultations of Spartans.

Q. Any.

R. They must bring back the seed of Zeus's demigod son from the foreign land to their own; otherwise they will plow with a silver plowshare.

Mode A1 (E1), Topic 2a (3j)

Delphi. Indirect—Thuc. 5.16.2. Plut. Mor. 403b.

NP. Indirect—Apollo: cf. App. Prov. 1.39.

   Comment: See pp. 37, 87 note 62, 212, 224.

   This is like Q124 and Q137 in that it is charged that someone bribed the Pythia to make the pronouncement. Like Q124 it was spoken to each Spartan who came to consult the god, whatever the question that he asked.

H8 (PW162). 421 B.C.

C. Athens.

Occ. Misfortunes in battles.

Q. Not stated.

R. Restore the Delians to Delos.

Mode A2, Topic 2d

Delphi. Testimony—Thuc. 5.32.1.

   Comment: It is probable that Athenian misfortunes suggested restoration of the Delians, and that the Athenians asked whether it was better to do so.

H9 (PW164). 421–415.

C. Athenians and allies, probably on more than one occasion.

Occ. and Q. Not stated.

R. Offer the fruits of the harvest to the two goddesses [Demeter and Kore].

Mode A1, Topic 1b

Delphi. Indirect—Isokr. Or. 4.31.

   Testimony—*Inscription of Athens, IG 1². 76 = Michel 71 = SIG 83, lines 4–8, 25–26, 32–34.

   Comment: The inscription specifies at least one-sixth of a medimnos for every 100 medimnoi of barley and at least one-twelfth of a medimnos for every 100 medimnoi of wheat; but whether this was ordered in the oracle or was specified by the Athenian assembly as the way of executing the command is not clear. Isokrates does not include this in his indirect form. See Q79 Comment.

H10 (PW165). c. 420 B.C.

C. Athens.

Occ. and Q. Not stated.

R. Apollo is exegete for the Athenians.

Mode D1, Topic 1d

Delphi. Indirect—Inscription of Athens, *IG* I². 78.4–5.

    Comment: See p. 220.

The instructions contained in this decree about sacrifice of an ox to Apollo, adornment of a chair for the god in the prytaneion, and distribution of sacrificial meat to the citizens may be part of the oracle, but what remains of the inscription does not make that clear. See Oliver 1950: 139, I2.

H11 (PW172). 401 B.C.

C. Xenophon.

Occ. Proxenos' invitation to accompany him on Cyrus' expedition.

Q. To what god should he sacrifice and pray to make his intended journey successful, to fare well upon it, and to return in safety.

R. He should sacrifice to Zeus Basileus.

Mode A1, Topic 1b

Delphi. Testimony—Xen. *Anab.* 3.1.5–8, 6.1.22. Cic. *Div.* 1.54.122. Diog. Laert. 2.50.

    Comment: See pp. 43, 220, 235.

H12 (PW174). 394 B.C.

C. Xenophon.

Occ. Megabyzos returned to Xenophon the deposit of money pledged to Artemis that Xenophon had left with him in Ephesos.

Q. Not stated.

R. Buy for Artemis the indicated estate [at Skillûs on the Selinûs River].

Mode A1, Topic 1a

Delphi. Testimony—Xen. *Anab.* 5.3.7. Strabo 8.7.5, p. 387.

    Comment: See pp. 32, 220.

H13 (PW175). 388 B.C.

C. King Agesipolis of Sparta.

Occ. Argive proposal of a truce when the Spartans are about to invade.

Q. Is it sanctioned [*hosion*] not to accept the Argive truce, which they offer not at a proper time but whenever the Spartans intend to invade?

R. It is sanctioned not to accept a truce unjustly offered.

Mode D1, Topic 1d

Delphi. Indirect—Xen. *Hell.* 4.7.2.

    Testimony—Aristotle *Rhet.* 1398b. Plut. *Mor.* 191b, 209a.

    Comment: See pp. 17, 18.

H14 (PW177). After 385 B.C.

C. Parians.

Occ. Sending out a colony.

Q. Not stated.

R. Found a colony on the island of Pharos in the Adriatic.

Mode A2, Topic 2c
NP. Testimony—Oracle: Diod. 15.13.4.
> Comment: See p. 142.
> The only reason for calling this Delphic is that H56 was spoken at Delphi.

H15 (PW178). After 383 B.C.
C. Klazomenai and Kyme.
Occ. Dispute over possession of Leuke.
Q. Which city does the god choose to be possessor of Leuke?
R. Let that city which is first to make sacrifice in Leuke have it. On the day agreed upon each party must start from its own city at sunrise.
Mode A1, Topic 1b (2d)
Delphi. Indirect—Diod. 15.18.2.
> Comment: See pp. 16, 38, 212.

H16 (PW182). After 373 B.C.
C. Ionian League.
Occ. Transfer of the Panionia to a safe place near Ephesos.
Q. Not stated.
R. They should take *aphidrymata* from their ancient and ancestral altars at Helike in Achaia.
Mode A2, Topic 1a
Delphi. Indirect—Diod. 15.49.1.
> Comment: This is essentially part of a sanction of the transfer of the Panionia.

H17 (PW256). 370 B.C.
C. Delphians.
Occ. Jason of Pherai's intention of presiding at the Pythian games and consequent threat to the sacred treasury.
Q. What should we do if Jason takes the god's money?
R. Do not trouble yourselves; this will concern me [Aelian].
Mode E1 (C1), Topic 1d (3j)
Delphi. Direct, Verse (iambic trimeter)—Zen. Athôos 29 = E. Miller, *Mélanges*, p. 352.
> Indirect—*Xen. Hell. 6.4.30.
NP. Indirect—The god: Ael. frag. 52 *ap.* Sud. Δ836.
> Comment: See pp. 19, 38, 87 note 62, 187.
> Zen. Athôos 29 quotes the similar Q231, supposedly spoken on the occasion of the Gauls' invasion, as spoken in response to the question on Jason's threat. This is nearly a century earlier than Q231; but compare Q149, in which, at the time of the Persian invasion, Apollo says that he is capable of protecting his own. Xenophon is contemporary to Jason's threat, but reports only the statement ὅτι αὐτῷ μελήσει, "that it will concern him [Apollo]," and introduces it with λέγεται δὲ ἐπερομένων τῶν Δελφῶν τί χρὴ ποιεῖν . . . ἀποκρίνασθαι τὸν θεὸν κτλ. It is no more than a report that has reached Xenophon, and he does not vouch for the consultation himself.

The response is unusual for an Historical oracle. It fits into the tradition already established that Apollo will protect his own shrine from its enemies. See Fontenrose 1960a: 198–205. It may be that on this occasion the Pythia spoke the response that tradition demanded.

H18 (PW259). c. 356 B.C.
C. Kallistratos, Athenian.
Occ. Exile following flight from a death sentence.
Q. Not stated.
R. If he goes to Athens, he will obtain the laws.
Mode E1, Topic 2b.
Delphi. Indirect—Lykurgos Leokr. 93.
    Comment: See pp. 19, 67 note 15.
    Kallistratos apparently asked the question "Shall I receive the benefit of the laws if I return to Athens?" The Pythia replied that he would; and he was put to death after his return. This can be taken as I have explained it in chapter 1: a simple affirmative answer into which a double meaning was later read. But I confess to some doubts about its authenticity. Lykurgos spoke against Leokrates in 330. Kallistratos died in 356. Lykurgos introduces the oracle with "What elder does not remember and what younger man has not heard of Kallistratos . . . ?" Over a quarter century has gone by, and in this time a pseudo-historical tale could easily have grown up about Kallistratos' end.

H19 (PW260). 356 B.C.
C. Chalcidians and King Philip of Macedon.
Occ. Treaty of alliance between Chalkidike and Philip.
Q. Probably whether it is better that they conclude this alliance.
R. It is better that they become friends and allies according to the terms agreed upon.
    They should make sacrifice to Zeus Teleos and Hypatos, Apollo Prostaterios, Artemis
    Orthosia, and Hermes; and pray that the alliance may be successful, and give thank-
    offerings and gifts to Apollo at Pytho.
Mode A2 (A1), Topic 2d (1b)
Delphi. Indirect—Inscription of Olynthos, Tod, Greek Historical Inscriptions 2.158 =
    TAPhA 65.105, lines 12–16.
    Comment: See pp. 14, 212, 221.
    In this response the directions for sacrifice and prayer appear to be added to the sanction that was requested.

H20 (PW261). After 355 B.C.
C. Philomelos, Phocian chief.
Occ. Third Sacred War.
Q. None asked; he intended to ask about the conduct of the war.
R. He may do as he wishes.
Mode D1, Topic 3j

Delphi. Indirect—Diod. 16.27.1 (25.3).

> *Comment:* See pp. 38, 39, 53, 212, 315, 339.

This was not really a response from the tripod, but a remark that the Pythia made when Philomelos was compelling her against her will to speak from the tripod. I have included it among H responses on the supposition that Diodoros found it in Ephoros' history, probably in book 30, added by Demophilos. It may be no more than the association of an oracular anecdote with Philomelos, made soon after the supposed event, as later it was associated with Alexander; see Q216. Here too there are more than 25 years from the event to the time when Demophilos recorded it, if he did: Diodoros may have found the story in a later work.

H21 (PW262). 352/1.

C. Athenians.

Occ. Question of letting lands within the Eleusinian *orgas*.

Q. On a tin plate they inscribed the question, "Is it better for the demos of the Athenians that the *basileus* let the lands now unworked within the sacred *orgas* for the building of a portico and repair of the goddesses' sanctuary?" On another they inscribed the question, "Is it better for the demos of the Athenians that the lands now unworked within the boundaries of the sacred *orgas* be left unworked for the goddesses?" They put one plate (taking care not to know which) into a gold hydria and the other into a silver hydria, which they sealed and which their envoys showed to the Pythia and asked: Should the Athenians act according to the words in the gold hydria or according to those in the silver hydria?

R. It is better for them that the lands be left unworked.

Mode C1, Topic 1d

Delphi. Testimony—Inscription of Eleusis, *IG* 2². 204 = Michel 674 = *SIG* 204.

NP. Indirect—The god: Androtion 324.30J *ap.* Did. *Phil.* 14.46–47. Philochoros 328.155J *ap.* Did. *Phil.* 13.55–56.

> *Comment:* See pp. 17, 37, 38, 40, 43, 220, 221, 222, 226 note 42.

H22 (PW265). c. 340 B.C.

C. Unknown.

Occ. Prodigies at the time of Philip's entry into the war against Amphissa.

Q. Not stated.

R. Dire responses [*deina manteumata*] favorable to Philip.

Mode?, Topic 2d

Delphi. Testimony—Aischines 3.130. Cic. *Div.* 2.57.118. Plut. *Dem.* 19.1, 20.1.

> *Comment:* Plutarch alludes to several responses, the character of which cannot be more precisely known; but his *manteumata* may be a generalizing plural. This report can only be included as one response.

H23 (PW277). Before 320 B.C.

C. Halieis.

Occ. A sacred snake of Asklepios was carried unobserved in the wagon which brought Thersandros, uncured of consumption, back from Epidauros to Halieis, where the snake cured him.

Q. What should they do: take the snake back to Epidauros or let him stay where he is?

R. They should let the snake stay there, found a temenos of Asklepios, make an image of him, and place it in the sanctuary.

Mode A1, Topic 1a

Delphi. Indirect—Inscription of Epidauros, *IG* 4². 122 = *SIG* 1169 = Edelstein 1945: T423, sect. xxxiii.

> *Comment:* See pp. 32–33, 38, 212.

It is pure assumption to suppose that Thersandros' experience occurred not long before the inscription was made. The inscription is a long record of Asklepios' cures. It gives no indication of when Thersandros visited Epidauros or when Halieis consulted Delphi. This account looks very much like the foundation myth of Asklepios' sanctuary at Halieis; but that could have occurred in the fourth century, following upon the fame that the Epidauros sanctuary had acquired in the fifth century. To be on the safe side I have considered this near-contemporary evidence.

H24 (PW278) c. 350 B.C.

C. Athenians.

Occ. and Q. Probably Demon's proposal as indicated in *R*.

R. They should dedicate Demon's house and garden to Asklepios and make Demon priest of Asklepios.

Mode A2, Topic 1a

NP. Indirect—The god: Inscription of Athens, *IG* 2². 4969 = Michel 840 = *SIG* 1005 = Edelstein 1945: T729.

H25 (PW279). 338–335.

C. Isyllos the poet.

Occ. Composition of a paean in honor of Apollo.

Q. Is it better that he inscribe the paean?

R. It is better for both present and future that he inscribe the paean.

Mode A2, Topic 1b

Delphi. Indirect—Inscription of Epidauros, *IG* 4². 128 = Edelstein 1945: T594, lines 35–36.

> *Comment:* See pp. 35, 37, 221.

H26 (PW280). c. 325 B.C.

C. Cyrene.

Occ. Adoption of a code of ritual regulations.

Q. Not stated.

R. They should use purifications, consecrations, and religious services forever while living in Libya. The code follows.

Mode A2, Topic 1d

NP. Indirect—Apollo: Inscription of Cyrene, *SEG* 9.72.

> *Comment:* See p. 14.

The code is expressed in direct prose, but is surely not part of the response as such: the Pythia approved it, but did not read it from the tripod. Probably the code was presented to the Pythia with the question, "Is it better for the Cyrenaeans to adopt this code?"

H27 (PW281). Fourth century B.C.

C. Acharnians or Athenians.

Occ. Erection of altars of Athena and Ares.

Q. Probably whether it is better for the demos of the Acharnians to construct the altars mentioned in *R.*

R. It is better for the demos of the Acharnians and the demos of the Athenians to construct the altars of Ares and Athena Areia, that the Acharnians and Athenians may have reverent relations with the gods.

Mode A2, Topic 1a

Delphi. Indirect—Inscription of Acharnai, L. Robert, *Études épigraphiques et philologiques* (Paris: Champion, 1938) p. 294, lines 5–10.

> *Comment:* See pp. 220, 221.

H28 (PW282). Before 348 B.C.

C. Athenians.

Occ. Consideration of the welfare and prosperity of the state.

Q. Not stated.

R. Remember Bakchos and in the streets set up a seasonable chorus for Bromios and make burnt offerings on the altars with garlands on your heads. For health sacrifice and pray to Zeus Hypatos, Herakles, Apollon Prostaterios; for good fortune to Apollon Aguieus, Leto, Artemis, and set up mixing bowls and dances along the streets, and wear garlands after the ancestral custom; to all Olympian gods and goddesses, raising your right arms, make offerings.

Mode A1, Topic 1b

Delphi. Direct, Verse and Prose—Dem. 21.52 (54–55).

OP. Dodona? Dem. 21.52.

> *Comment:* See pp. 187–188, 190, 193, 194.

There may be two oracles here, one in verse, the other in prose, one from Delphi the other from Dodona. The heading is *Manteiai*, but that is not Demosthenes' insertion. He introduces the quotation with mention of oracles from Delphi and Dodona. The first part on the worship of Bakchos is in verse; the following directions for sacrifice to various gods are in prose. There is no indication of how long before 348 this response was spoken.

H29 (PW283). Before 340.

C. Athenians.

Occ. A portent that appeared in the sky.

Q. What shall the Athenians do, or to what god shall they sacrifice or pray, for better consequences from the portent?

R. It is to the Athenians' advantage with respect to the sign that appeared in the sky to make sacrifice to Zeus Hypatos, Athena Hypata, Herakles, Apollon Soter, and to send offerings to the Amphioneis. For good fortune sacrifice to Apollon Agueius, Leto, Artemis, and fill the streets with sacrificial smoke and set up bowls and dances, and wear garlands after the ancestral custom. To all Olympian gods and goddesses, raising your arms, make thank-offerings after the ancestral custom. Sacrifice and make offerings to the Hero Archegetas after whom you are named, according to the ancestral custom. On the proper day kinsmen should fulfill their duties to the dead as is customary.

Mode A1, Topic 1b

Delphi. Direct, Prose—Dem. 43.66.

Indirect, Incomplete—Poll. *Onom.* 1.28.

Comment: See pp. 33, 189, 207. As with H28 we cannot tell how long before the oration this response was spoken.

H30. 330 B.C.

C. Athens.

Occ. Probably a proposal to honor Pluto.

Q. Not stated.

R. They should spread the couch for Pluto and adorn the table.

Mode A2, Topic 1b

NP. Testimony—The god: Inscriptions of Athens, *IG* 2². 1933 = Michel 857 = *SIG* 1022, lines 1–3; *IG* 2². 1934.3–6. *IG* 2². 1935.4–6.

Comment: This is as likely to be Delphic as H24 and H33 from similar Athenian inscriptions, which PW include among Delphic responses.

H31 (PW284). 344/3.

C. Amphictiony.

Occ. and Q. Not stated.

R. The Amphictions must complete the work [temple?] quickly so that suppliants may be received in the proper month; they must have this hymn recited to the Hellenes at the yearly Theoxenia and offer sacrifice with supplications of all Hellas. At the quinquennial Pythian festival they must make sacrifice to Bakchos and institute a choral contest, set up an image of Bakchos by the golden lions, and prepare a fitting grotto for him.

Mode A2, Topic 1b

Delphi. Indirect—Philodamos *Hymn*, inscription of Delphi, Diehl 2.255 = *BCH* 51 (1927) 467–468, lines 105–108, 110–114, 131–134, 136–140.

Comment: In the verses cited Philodamos indicates a recent oracle given to the Amphictions, probably a sanction for a special occasion (perhaps the completion of the temple), with increased honors for Dionysos. Philodamos was engaged to compose the hymn for the occasion. See H32.

H32 (See PW p. 116 *ad* 284). 344/3.

C. Philodamos of Skarpheia.

Occ. Composition of a hymn to Dionysos for the Amphictions.

Q. Not stated; probably a request for a sanction.

R. It is better for him to publish the hymn.

Mode A2, Topic 1b

Delphi. Testimony—Inscription of Delphi, Diehl 2.257 = *SGDI* 2742 = *SIG* 270, lines 6–8.

   Comment: See p. 35; H31.

   The prose appendix to Philodamos' hymn recording a Delphic decree in Philodamos' (and his brothers') honor, is fragmentary, but the *manteia* alluded to is surely a sanction that the poet sought for the publication or inscription of his hymn. His question must be the same as that which Isyllos asked (H25).

H33 (PW285). 335/4.

C. Athenians.

Occ. Proposal to improve the dress and adornments (*kosmoi*) of the goddesses.

Q. Is it better for the demos of the Athenians to make the holy dress and adornments larger and finer for Artemis or to leave it as it now is? Is it better to make the holy dress larger and finer for Demeter and Kore or to leave it as it now is? Should the same thing be done in the other sanctuaries . . . [the inscription breaks off here]?

R. [The response does not appear in the visible inscription but is certainly as follows] It is better to make the dress and adornments of these deities larger and finer.

Mode A2, Topic 1b

NP. Testimony—The god: Inscription of Athens, *IG* 2^2. 333.24–29.

   Comment: See pp. 37, 221.

   Although the question is put alternatively, it is without doubt a request for a sanction of their decision to improve the deities' *kosmoi*. It is inconceivable that the response should be to leave them as they are, or that it would be inscribed if it were against improvement.

H34 (PW334). c. 360 B.C.

C. A husband.

Occ. Desire for children.

Q. Not stated.

R. He will have a child and should offer hair.

Mode E2 (A1), Topic 3a (1b)

Delphi. Indirect—Inscription of Delphi, *FD* 3.1.560 = *BCH* 80 (1956) 550, line 3.

   Comment: See pp. 19, 25.

H35 (PW330). c. 275 B.C.

C. Amphictiony?

Occ. Decision to establish an agonistic festival, the Soteria, after victory over the Gauls.

Q. Not stated.

R. They should make sacrifices to the gods worthily . . . [other parts lost].
Mode A2, Topic 1a
Delphi. Testimony—Inscription of Delphi, *FD* 3.1.483.4–5.
 Comment: Probably the response sanctioned the establishment of the festival.

H36 (PW335). c. 250 B.C. ?
C. Poseidonios of Halikarnassos.
Occ. Concern for welfare of his family.
Q. What is better for him and his sons and daughters to do?
R. It will be better for them to worship Zeus Patroos, Apollo lord of Telmessos, Moirai,
    the Mother of Gods, Agathos Daimon of Poseidonios and Gorgis, as their ancestors
    did; it will be better for them if they continue to perform these rites.
Mode A2, Topic 1b
NP. Indirect—Apollo: Inscription of Halikarnassos, *AGIBM* 896 = *Rev. Phil.* 15 (1941)
    15.
 Comment: See pp. 38, 221.
    The response is in sanction form, although the question asked is "What is better to
do?" The question nevertheless contains the sanction formula, "better and more good."
It may well be that Poseidonios got this response from an Asian oracle, perhaps Didyma.
The Apollo of Telmessos is mentioned in the text; but the Telmessoi whom Croesus
consulted (Herod. 1.78.2–3; cf. 1.84.3), a family or guild of seers, were probably Lycian;
and the Telmessos referred to is probably the Carian city. There seems to be no evidence
for an Oracle of Apollo at the Carian Telmessos; see Georges Daux, *Rev. Phil.*, *loc. cit.*

H37 (PW336). c. 250 B.C.
C., *Occ., and* Q. Not stated.
R. Artemidoros is an immortal hero.
Mode D1, Topic 1a
Delphi. Indirect—Inscription of Thera, *IG* 12.3.863 = 1349.
 Comment: The inscription is composed of two hexameter verses, which express the
response indirectly. As expressed by the poet, the response may represent an original
command to honor Artemidoros as a hero.

H38 (PW341). Early third century B.C.
C. Kyzikos.
Occ. Foundation of the Soteria festival for Kora Soteira.
Q. Probably whether it is better to proclaim the sanctity of the city and the goddess'
    festival.
R. Since the Cyzicenes have first performed the sacrifice and the Soteria well and properly
    for Kora Soteira, it is better for them to proclaim the sanctity [*asylia*] of the city
    according to the oracles and to sacrifice to the goddess.
Mode A2, Topic 1d
Delphi. Indirect—Inscription of Delphi, *FD* 3.3.342.   Inscription of Delos, *IG* 11.4.1298
    = Michel 852 = *SIG* 1158, lines 2–10.

H39 (PW342). Second century B.C.
C. Kyzikos.
Occ. Decision to honor certain gods.
Q. Probably whether it is better to do so.
R. It is better for the Cyzicenes to sacrifice to Poseidon Asphaleios, Ge, and [other gods whose names are lost].
Mode A2, Topic 1b
Delphi. Indirect—Inscription of Delphi, FD 3.3.343 = SGDI 2970, lines 3–7.

H40 (PW343). Second century B.C.
C. Kyzikos.
Occ. Probably a decision to honor gods.
Q. Probably a request for a sanction.
R. A religious sanction or direction.
Mode A2, Topic 1d
NP. Indirect—Apollo: Inscription of Delphi, FD 3.3.344.
   Comment: The inscription is mostly lost, but the surviving letters clearly show that the god's response had the same kind of content as H38 and H39.

H41 (PW344). c. 250 B.C.
C. Tenos.
Occ. Decision to declare Poseidon's sanctuary an asylum.
Q. Not stated.
R. They should sanctify the image and temple of Poseidon [Tacitus].
Mode A2, Topic 1d
Delphi. Testimony—Inscriptions of Tenos, IG 12.5.802.4–6; 868.19–20, 29.
NP. Indirect—Apollo: Tac. Ann. 3.63.3.

H42 (PW345). 246 or 242 B.C.
C. Smyrna.
Occ. Decision to declare the city and Aphrodite Stratonike's sanctuary inviolable (asylon).
Q. Probably whether it is better that they should do so.
R. The city of Smyrna and sanctuary of Aphrodite Stratonike should have right of asylum.
Mode A2, Topic 1d
Delphi. Testimony—Inscription of Delphi, OGIS 228 = SGDI 2733 = Michel 258, lines 3–6.
NP. Testimony—Apollo: Tac. Ann. 3.63.3.

H43 (PW346). 210–200.
C. Antiocheia of Chrysaoreis.
Occ. Decision to declare the city inviolable (asylon).
Q. Probably whether it is better that they should do so.

R. The city of Antiocheia should be inviolable and sacred to Zeus Chrysaoreus and Apollon Isotimos.

Mode A2, Topic 1d

Delphi. Testimony—Inscription of Delphi, *OGIS* 234 = *SGDI* 2529, lines 16–25.

    Comment: On H41–43 see pp. 14, 212.

H44. Before 250 B.C.

C. Erythrai.

Occ. and Q. Not stated.

R. They should establish cults of Aphrodite, Demeter and Kore, Dionysos, and [another god whose name has disappeared].

Mode A1, Topic 1a

Delphi. Testimony—Inscription of Erythrai, *SIG* 1014 = *SGDI* 5692 = Michel 839, lines 2, 74, 89–90, 145, 160.

    Comment: There are probably four responses indicated here. All the inscription shows is the name of each deity in the genitive (the inscription concerns sale of priesthoods) followed by the epithet *Pythochrêstou*, indicating apparently that the Pythian Apollo ordered establishment of the cult. But to count four instances of mode A1 and topic 1a would appear to give them too high a count in the figures of chapter 1, inasmuch as we know nothing more about the responses than that they were spoken. Hence it is better to err on the cautious side and to put this down as one response.

    There is no indication of how long these cults were established before the inscription was made. But since there can be little question that the Delphic Oracle really directed the founding of these cults, it is safe to consider this Historical. And although we have no indication of content apart from the epithets, we can have little doubt that the response (or each response) was much like Historical responses on the establishment of cults or festivals, e.g., H23, 24, 27, 45. It was either a command or a sanction.

H45 (PW347). 221/0.

C. Magnesia-on-Maeander.

Occ. Decision to establish a quinquennial isopythian festival in honor of Artemis Leukophryene following upon an epiphany of the goddess.

Q. Is it better to establish this festival and declare the city inviolable [*asylon*]?

R. It is better for them to worship Apollon Pythios and Artemis Leukophryene and to recognize that the city and country of the Magnesians are inviolable. The prizes of the games should be crowns [*agônes stephanitai*].

Mode A2, Topic 1a (1d)

Delphi. Indirect—Inscriptions of Magnesia-on-Maeander, *IM* 16 (= *SIG* 557). 7–10; 31.16–19; 32.11–14; 36 (= *SIG* 558). 11–13; 38 (= *SIG* 559). 6–8; 39.6–9; 43.8–10; 45.9–12; 46 (= *SIG* 560). 17–19; 52.7–10; 53.4–6; 54.14–16; 56.8–11; 63.3–6.

    Testimony—Inscriptions of Magnesia-on-Maeander, *IM* 23.9–13; 33. 10–14; 34.11–14, 19–20; 35.23–24; 37.14–20, 29–30; 41.9–12; 42.14–16; 44.5–8, 35–36; 48.9–11, 16–17; 58.18–19; 61.24–29, 38–39; 62.1–6, 27–32; 71.10–18; 72.31–33; 79.3–5, 10–11,

17–18; 85.5–9, 17–18; 87.7–10. Inscription of Delphi, *BCH* 77 (1953) 169, lines 32–33.

Comment: See pp. 14, 190, 192, 221; L163–167.

Aside from *IM* 16 all the inscriptions cited are decrees of cities accepting the Magnesian proclamation. Some do not mention Delphi, but obviously had the Magnesian decree as shown in *IM* 16 before them.

H46 (PW348). 201 B.C.
C. Teos.
Occ. Decision to declare the city and country inviolable (*asylon*).
Q. Probably whether it is better to do so.
R. The city and country of Teos should be sacred and inviolable.
Mode A2, Topic 1d
Delphi. Testimony—Inscription of Malla in Crete, *ICr.* 1.19.2 = *SGDI* 5184, lines 7–9.
  Comment: See p. 14.
  Teos received the same sanction from Didyma; cf. Didyma 20.

H47 (PW351). c. 210–200.
C. Eretrians.
Occ. Certain legislation voted by the demos.
Q. On approval of the legislation.
R. It is good and to the city's advantage to adopt these measures.
Mode A2, Topic 2b
NP. Indirect—The god: Inscription of Eretria, *IG* 12.9.213.3–4.
  Comment: See pp. 14, 221.

The restoration εἰς Δελφοὺς is very probable in line 2 of the inscription, but we cannot be certain. The nature of the legislation is lost with the no longer visible letters.

H48 (PW354). 216 B.C.
C. Rome.
Occ. Outbreak of Second Punic War, and early defeats.
Q. With what prayers and supplications can we please the gods, and what will be the outcome of such great disasters?
R. Make sacrifice to Zeus and other gods; if you do this you will be in better shape, the republic will advance more according to your wishes, and the Roman people will be victorious in the war. Out of your income send a gift to Apollon Pythios for preserving your republic and honor him from the spoils; and keep licentiousness away from you.
Mode A1 (E1), Topic 1b (2e)
Delphi. Pseudo-Direct, Prose (Latin)—Fabius Pictor *ap.* Liv. 23.11.1–3 (22.57.5).
  Pseudo-Direct, Verse (Latin)—Sil. It. 12.324–336.
  Indirect—Zon. *Hist.* 9.3, p. 422a.
  Testimony—Plut. *Fab. Max.* 18.3. App. *Hann.* 5.27.
  Comment: See p. 38.

Silius Italicus makes some changes of content in his poetic version, but Livy reports the exact content as given above. Fabius Pictor was the envoy sent to Delphi and he read the response to the senate which Livy quotes in the Latin translation that is presumably Fabius' own.

H49. c. 210–200.
C. Anthister association of Thera?
Occ. and Q. Not stated.
R. They should worship Anthister.
Mode A1, Topic 1a
Delphi. Testimony—Inscription of Thera, IG 12.3.329.

Comment: As with H44 the inscription reports only the epithet Pythochrêstos, which here follows the name Anthister, probably an epithet of Dionysos (or possibly a hero), both in the genitive. A koinon bore his name; and such associations are likely to be Dionysiac, as those of H51, 52. How long the association (or the city of Thera) received the response before the date of the inscription cannot be said.

H50 (PW426). c. 177 B.C.
C. Rhodian garrison on Tenos.
Occ. and Q. Not stated.
R. They should make offerings to Zeus Soter, Athena Soteira, Poseidon Asphaleios, Artemis Orthosia, Herakles, Ares, Athena Areia, Enyo, Enyalios, Nike.
Mode A1, Topic 1b
Delphi. Testimony—Inscription of Tenos, IG 12.5.913.9–14.

H51. 176/5.
C. Dionysios, member of Dionysiast society of Piraeus.
Occ. and Q. Not stated.
R. Have an image of Dionysos made and set up for the orgeônes.
Mode A1, Topic 1b
NP. Testimony—The god: Inscription of Piraeus, IG 2². 1326 = Michel 986, lines 16–18.

H52 (PW349). Before 167 B.C.
C. Dionysiast society of Ionia and Hellespont.
Occ. and Q. Not stated.
R. The Dionysiac artists must have rights of asylum [asylia] and security [asphaleia] in war and peace for contests at festivals of Apollon Pythios, Heliconian Muses, and Herakles, in Delphi at the Pythian festival and Soteria, in Thespiai at the Museia, in Thebes at the Herakleia.
Mode A2, Topic 1d
Delphi. Testimony—Inscription of Teos, IG 11.4.1061 = Michel 1015, lines 17–20. Inscription of Delphi, FD 3.2.70a = SIG 705, line 27.

H53 (PW340). c. 240 B.C.

C. King Dropion of Paiones.

Occ. and Q. Not stated.

R. He should dedicate a statue of his grandfather [?] Audoleon to Apollon Pythios.

Mode A2, Topic 1b

Delphi. Testimony—Inscription of Delphi, BCH 76 (1952) 136.

Comment: The inscription has only kata chrêsmon, but since Dropion dedicated the statue to the Pythian Apollo, and since this is a Delphic inscription, we can be fairly sure that the response was spoken at Delphi.

H54 (PW427). c. 110–100.

C. Timotheos of Anaphe.

Occ. Decision to build a temple of Aphrodite.

Q. Is it better that he ask the city for a place of his choosing in the sanctuary of Apollo Asgelatas or in the sanctuary of Asklepios on which to build a temple of Aphrodite?

R. He should ask for a place in the sanctuary of Apollo, and when the temple is completed the city's decree and the oracle and the expense should be inscribed on a stone stele.

Mode A1, Topic 1a

NP. Indirect—The god: Inscription of Anaphe, IG 12.3.248 = Michel 853 = SIG 977, lines 29–32.

Comment: See pp. 38, 43, 221.

H55 (PW428). [190 B.C.] Not genuine.

C. Romans.

Occ. Appearance after Glabrio's victory over Antiochos at Thermopylai of Buplagos' ghost speaking prophetic verses against Glabrio.

Q. What should we do?

R. Restrain yourself, Roman, and let justice endure, lest Pallas bring a mightier war upon you and empty your marketplaces and you return home with loss of much wealth.

Mode C1, Topic 2e (3j)

Delphi. Direct, Verse—Antisthenes the Peripatetic ap. Phleg. Mir. 3.5.

Comment: See pp. 17, 33, 187.

Although the Roman operations in northern Greece around 190 apparently occurred in the lifetime of Antisthenes, from whom Phlegon seems to have taken all Mir. 3.5, we cannot consider this response authentic—although we have to classify it as Historical under our definition. PW consider it spurious (see Parke 1956: 276–277); as they say, it is an anti-Roman, pro-Aetolian fiction; but it probably was not made so early as 190/89.

H56 (PW429). c. 180 B.C.

C. Parians.

Occ. Embassy from the Parian colony of Pharos with a request.

Q. To what god or goddess shall the demos of the Parians sacrifice in order to keep the city and the country from harm, or to prosper in other places?

R. They should send Praxiepes to the west . . . [the rest of the response, in which the deities to whom they should sacrifice are named, has disappeared].

Mode A1, Topic 1b

Delphi. Direct, Verse—Inscription of Pharos, *IG* 12, suppl. 200 = *CIG* 1837b and vol. 2, p. 985 = *BCH* 59 (1935) 490, lines 24–26.

   Comment: Only the beginnings of the first two verses and four letters of the third remain. But the nature of the response is evident from the question asked.

H57 (PW432). Before 128 B.C.

C. Athenians.

Occ. and Q. Not stated.

R. They should send the Pythaid procession to Delphi to make sacrifice there every eight years, after observing the sign of lightning when looking towards Harma.

Mode A2, Topic 1b

Delphi. Testimony—Inscriptions of Delphi: *FD* 3.2.47 = *SIG* 698A, lines 5–6. *FD* 3.2.48 = *SIG* 711L = Daux 1936a: 566, line 8. *FD* 3.2.50 = *SIG* 699, lines 3, 11. *FD* 3.2.54 = Daux 1936a: 557, lines 6–8. Strabo 9.2.11, p. 404. Eust. *Il.* 2.499, p. 266.

   Comment: There was probably a renewal at this time of an older oracle authorizing the Pythais, which had gone unobserved for a long time.

H58 (PW437). c. 37/6.

C. Genos of Gephyraioi, Athens.

Occ. Appointment of Diotimos Diodoros' son to the office of Buzyges and priest of Zeus.

Q. About the Buzyges and priest of Zeus at Palladion, Diotimos Diodoros' son of the deme Halai.

R. Diotimos is qualified to be Buzyges and priest of Zeus.

Mode A2, Topic 1d

Delphi. Testimony—Inscription of Athens, *IG* 2². 1096 = *Hesperia* 9 (1940) 86, no. 17.

   Comment: The response is lost but can be inferred from the context.

H59 (PW457). Reign of Augustus.

C. Priest and Buzyges of Zeus at Palladion.

Occ. and Q. Not stated.

R. He ought to prepare another seat for Pallas at his own expense.

Mode A2, Topic 1b

Delphi. Indirect—Inscriptions of Athens, *IG* 2². 3177, 3178.

H60 (PW459). First or second century A.D.

C. Parians.

Occ. and Q. Not stated.

R. Found a cult of Asklepios Soter.

Mode A1, Topic 1a

NP. Testimony—The god: Inscription of Paros, *IG* 12.5.155.

   Comment: If the restoration of Πυθίου at the beginning of line 4 is correct, this is a Delphic response.

H61 (PW460). First century A.D.

C. and Occ. Not stated.

Q. Is it better to . . . [the content is fragmentary and unintelligible]?

R. (Probably) It is better to do so. [Something is said about going *Pytheiade,* "to the Pythian games." Most of the text has disappeared.]

Mode A2, Topic 1b

Delphi. Indirect—Inscription of Delphi, *SGDI* 2971.

   Comment: See p. 221.

H62 (PW462). c. A.D. 85.

C. Dion Chrysostomos.

Occ. Exile.

Q. On his course of life.

R. He should continue to do what he is doing zealously as an excellent and beneficial occupation, until he reaches the end of the earth.

Mode A1, Topic 3d.

Delphi. Direct, Prose, partly Indirect—Dion Chrys. 13.9.

   Comment: See pp. 15 note 4, 26; Parke 1956: 408–409.

H63 (PW464). c. 50–100?

C. Priest of Herakles Misogynos in Phokis.

Occ. When drunk he had intercourse with a woman, thus violating a tabu of his priesthood.

Q. Is there any forgiveness or absolution for my offense?

R. God forgives all uncontrollable acts.

Mode D1, Topic 1d (3j)

Delphi. Direct, Verse (iambic trimeter)—Plut. *Mor.* 404a.

   Comment: See pp. 87 note 62, 188, 194, 207.

H64 (PW458). First century A.D.

C. Athenians.

Occ. and Q. Not stated.

R. They should send envoys to Delphi for the ox-face sacrifice [*bouprôros thysia*] of the Dodecad.

Mode A2, Topic 1b

Delphi: Testimony—Inscription of Delphi, *FD* 3.2.66.14–19.

H65 (PW465). Reign of Hadrian.

C. Emperor Hadrian.

Occ. Desire to know Homer's birthplace and parents.

Q. Whence was Homer, and whose son was he?

R. His residence was Ithaca; Telemachos was his father and Epikaste Nestor's daughter was his mother, who bore him to be a very wise man.

Mode D1, Topic 3a

Delphi. Direct, Verse—*Cert. Hom. Hes.* 37–40 Allen. Anth. Pal. 14.102.

> *Comment:* See pp. 18, 25, 36, 188–189, 194.

H66 (PW466). c. A.D. 125.

C. Athenians.

Occ. and Q. Not stated.

R. In the sanctuary of Demeter Chloie and Kore, beside the propylaion on the acropolis, where the grain first grew, it will be better to . . . [the rest is lost or mutilated].

Mode, A2, Topic 1a

Delphi. Direct, Verse—Inscription of Athens, *IG* 2². 5006.

> *Comment:* See pp. 173–174, 189, 190, 194, 195, 207, 221.

H67 (PW467). c. 190–200.

C. Unknown.

Occ. Order to appease Hera.

Q. Where shall we appease Hera?

R. Where the old men have long taken baths, and where unwed maidens dance in chorus to flute accompaniment, in the halls of the womanish man, worship Hera.

Mode A1, Topic 1b

NP. Direct, Verse—The god: Inscription found at Ssarykemer between Miletos and Magnesia-on-Maeander, *IM* 228 = *DI* 501.

> *Comment:* See pp. 15 note 4, 33, 189–190, 191, 194, 429.

> This may very well be non-Delphic, perhaps a declaration of Didyma or Klaros. Rehm and Harder (*DI*) consider it to be an oracle of Didyma.

H68 (PW471). c. A.D. 250.

C. Kleitosthenes of Tralles.

Occ. Some affliction on the land.

Q. On the salvation of the city.

R. Having expiated the thousand-year wrath of Zeus, sacrifice to Poseidon wreathing his altar, in a grove, offering wheat and fruits. Call him Asphalios, Temenuchos, Apotropos, Hippios, Arges; and praise Seisichthon and Zeus with hymns and dance.

Mode A1, Topic 1a

Delphi. Direct, Verse—Inscription of Tralles, *BCH* 5 (1881) 340 = Erich Ziebarth, *Eine Inschriftenhandschrift der Hamburger Stadtbibliothek* (Hamburg 1903) 8–9 = O. Kern, *Genethliakon Karl Robert* (Berlin: Weidmann, 1910) 99–100.

> *Comment:* See pp. 190–191, 194.

H69 (PW473). A.D. 262 or a little later.

C. Amelios, Neo-Platonist.

Occ. Death of Plotinos.

Q. Where has the soul of Plotinos gone?

R. The Muses and I sing a hymn to Plotinos. You, Plotinos, once a man, now a daimon, have left the bond of human necessity and the body and have gone to the abodes of the blessed. Even in life the gods gave you light to see visions that mortal men seldom see. Now you live among the joys of paradise where Minos, Radamanthys, Aiakos, Plato, and Pythagoras dwell.

Mode D1, Topic 3c

NP. Direct, Verse—Apollo: Porph. *Plot.* 22.

Comment: See pp. 26, 34–35, 37, 191–192, 194.

R. Summarizes the essence of a 51-verse response, which is really a hymn. In the context Porphyry refers to two Delphic responses, but does not tell us what shrine Amelios consulted.

H70 (PW601). [A.D. 384.] Not genuine.

C. Romans?

Occ. Birth of Honorius.

Q. None.

R. Honorius will have a glorious reign.

Mode E2, Topic 2a

Delphi. Testimony—Claud. 8.141–144.

Comment: See pp. 19, 33, 38, 39.

It is possible that the Delphic Oracle was still active in 384 and that it spoke something on the birth of the emperor Theodosius' son Honorius; for Theodosius did not close the pagan temples and forbid divination until 391. Yet Claudian says that it had been silent: *tibi corniger Ammon / et dudum taciti rupere silentia Delphi.* He is indulging in encomium of the young emperor Honorius on his fourth consulship (398) at the age of fourteen. At the emperor's birth all nature showed signs of his future glory (8.141–148): all diviners and seers had something to say; Ammon and Delphi broke their silence on this extraordinary occasion. It is a traditional theme—the signs on earth and in the heavens at the birth of a savior. We can only infer the content of this supposed Delphic utterance from the context: the empress gave birth, and *quae tunc documenta futuri?*

H71 (PW350). c. 200 B.C.

C. Megara.

Occ. and Q. Not stated.

R. Megara should have *asylia* as specified [a very fragmentary inscription].

Mode A2, Topic 1d

NP. Testimony—Apollo: Inscription of Megara, *IG* 7.16 = *AGIBM* 136 = L. Robert, *Ét. épigr. philol.* (see H27) 71, pt. b.

Comment: See p. 14.

The restoration of Apollo's name in the genitive before *chrêsmos* is probable. The genitive ending *-os* is visible.

H72. c. A.D. 100.
C. Envoys of a foreign land.
Occ. and Q. Not stated.
R. [Incoherent and unintelligible words finally interrupted.]
Delphi. Testimony—Plut. Mor. 438b.
    Comment: See pp. 197, 207 note 18, 208, 218, 219, 226.

H73 (PW176). After 385 B.C.
C. Tiribazos.
Occ. Contemplated revolt against Artaxerxes II.
Q. On the revolt.
R. Not recorded.
Mode?, Topic 2e (?)
Delphi. Testimony—Diod. 15.8.4.
    Comment: It is probable that Diodoros took this from Ephoros.

H74. c. 350–325.
C. Mnesiepes of Paros.
Occ. Apparently his wish to honor the indicated gods.
Q. Presumably whether it is better to carry out the religious works sanctioned in the
response.
R. It is better to erect an altar in the temenos which he is preparing and sacrifice upon it
    to the Muses, Apollon Musagetes, Mnemosyne, also to Zeus Hyperdexios, Athena
    Hyperdexia, Poseidon Asphaleios, Herakles, Artemis Eukleia, and to send thank-
    offerings to Apollo at Pytho. It is better to erect an altar in the temenos and sacrifice
    upon it to Dionysos, Nymphs, Hours, also to Apollon Prostaterios, Poseidon Aspha-
    leios, Herakles, and to send thank-offerings to Apollo at Pytho. It is better to honor
    the poet Archilochos as Mnesiepes intends.
Mode A2, Topic 1a
Delphi. Indirect—Inscription of Paros, Arch. Eph. (1952) 40 = Philologus 99 (1955) 7, col.
    2, lines 1–15.
    Comment: See p. 221.
    There may be three responses here, each beginning "It is better, . . ."; for before
each occurrence of the formula the inscription has "The god spoke an oracle [echrēse] to
Mnesiepes," so that the oracular text is twice interrupted with this introductory clause.
That the god is the Pythian Apollo seems evident from the direction in the first two parts
to send offerings to him.

H75 (PW274). 332–330.
C. Athenians.
Occ. Athenian refusal to pay the fine imposed for Kallippos' misconduct at the Olympic
    Games of 332.
Q. Not stated.

R. Apollo will not give any response to the Athenians on any matter until they pay the fine to the Eleans.

Mode C1 (E1), Topic 1d (2d)

Delphi. Indirect—Paus. 5.21.5, citing inscriptions in elegiac verse contemporary with the response.

II. Quasi-Historical Responses

Q1 (PW485). [776 B.C. or earlier.] Not genuine.
C. King Iphitos of Elis.
Occ. Civil strife and plague throughout Hellas.
Q. Request for relief from these ills.
R. Iphitos and the Eleians should renew the Olympic Games.
Mode A1, Topic 1a
Delphi. Indirect—Paus. 5.4.6.

> *Comment:* Q1 represents a different tradition from Q2–6. In Pausanias' account Iphitos alone renewed the festival after receiving this oracle. Phlegon's account joins Lykurgos and Kleosthenes with Iphitos in a plan to renew the festival, for which they sought a Delphic sanction. Q1 is spoken as prescription of a remedy for civil strife or plague. In Phlegon's version plague and famine occur as a result of neglecting Q2.

Q2 (PW486). [884–776.] Not genuine.
C. Lykurgos of Sparta, King Iphitos of Elis, Kleosthenes of Pisa.
Occ. Contemplated renewal of the Olympic festival, including games, in order to restore harmony and peace to the land.
Q. Does the god approve of their doing this?
R. It will be better for them to do so, and they should proclaim observance of a truce to the cities that want to participate in the games.
Mode A2, Topic 1a
Delphi. Indirect—Phlegon *Ol.* 1.3. Schol. vet. on Plato *Rep.* 465d.

> *Comment:* The Scholiast puts Q2 and Q6 together as a single oracle; but he either depends on Phlegon or uses the same source. On Lykurgos as founder of the Olympic Games see p. 115 note 31.

Q3 (PW487). [776 B.C. or earlier.] Not genuine.

C. Peloponnesians through Lykurgos.

Occ. Plague and famine in Peloponnesos.

Q. Grant us an end of and remedy for the plague.

R. Zeus has sent famine and plague upon you for neglecting his Olympic festival, which Peisos, Pelops, and Herakles founded. You can end the plague if you renew the festival.

Mode A1 (D1), Topic 1a

Delphi. Direct, Verse—Phlegon Ol. 1.6.

> Comment: See pp. 177, 180.

It may be that Q1 and Q3 should be one response. But for Q1 Pausanias reports strife and plague over all Hellas, only Iphitos as enquirer, and a simple direction to renew the festival. For Q3 the occasion is plague and famine coming upon the Peloponnesians for neglect of Q2; and the Peloponnesians sent Lykurgos with a delegation to inquire at Delphi. Apollo responds with a 14-verse oracle, which summarizes the history of the games, bringing together the three legendary founders—Peisos, Pelops, Herakles—a reconciliation of traditions. Hence there are enough differences to distinguish the two.

Q4 (PW488). [776 B.C.] Not genuine.

C. Peloponnesians.

Occ. Distrust of Q3.

Q. On the content of Q3.

R. Make sacrifice at Zeus's altar and believe what seers tell you.

Mode A1, Topic 1b

Delphi. Direct, Verse—Phleg. Ol. 1.7. Eus. Chron. 1.192 Schoene = Synk. 196b.

> Comment: According to this response Delphi founded the Oracle at Olympia.

Q5 (PW489). [After 776 B.C.] Not genuine.

C. Eleans.

Occ. Desire to help Spartans in the siege of Helos.

Q. Not stated.

R. Keep to your fathers' law and protect your country. Keep out of war and lead the Hellenes in friendship every fifth year.

Mode C1 (A1), Topic 2e (2d)

Delphi. Direct, Verse—Phleg. Ol. 1.9. Eus. Chron. 1.192 Schoene = Synk. 196b.

> Comment: Eusebios appears to join Q5 to Q4 in a single consultation.

Q6 (PW490–491). [756 B.C.] Not genuine.

C. King Iphitos of Elis.

Occ. Proposal to crown Olympic victors.

Q. Shall we crown the victors?

R. Do not make apples the prize of victory, but crown the victors with garlands taken from the wild-olive tree that you find strung with spider webs.

Mode B (C1), Topic 1d (3h)

Delphi. Direct, Verse—Phleg. *Ol.* 1.10.

Indirect—Schol. vet. on Plato *Rep.* 465d.

Comment: Phlegon says that the Peloponnesians sent Iphitos to the god's (house), and that the god spoke these words. Since he has definitely ascribed Q2–5 to the Delphic Apollo, there can be no doubt that he means the same god for Q6.

The initial prohibition is not the main message; Iphitos did not ask whether apples should be the prize. The main message answers the question asked, but specifies a condition, "When (or if) you find a wild-olive tree strung with spider webs, take its leaves for the victors' crowns" (mode B).

Phlegon no doubt took his origin legend of the Olympic Games from some earlier account. He may have found it and oracles Q2–6 in Aristotle's *Olympionikai* (Diog. Laert. 5.26). In this narrative Delphi is given credit for establishing the Olympic agonistic festival.

Q7 (PW29, 216) [900–775.] Not genuine.

C. Lykurgos of Sparta.

Occ. Spartans' need of better laws.

Q. None; [request for good order (Diodoros)].

R. You, Lykurgos, dear to Zeus and all the gods, enter my temple. I don't know whether to call you god or man, but I rather think god. [You have come in quest of good order. I shall give you an order such as no other city has (Diodoros).]

Mode D1 (E1), Topic 1d (2b)

Delphi. Direct, Verse—Herod. 1.65.3. Galen *Protr.* 9.22. Them. *Or.* 7.97d; 15.193c; 19.225d. Schol. on Aristeides 13.189, p. 326 Dind. [*BCH* 5 (1881) 434–435, reported by Cyriacus of Ancona as an inscription seen at Delphi in fifteenth century.] Incomplete —Plut. *Mor.* 1098a, 1103a (1116f). Chor. Gaz. 32.92. Elias *Comm. Arist.* 1, p. 7. David *Prol. Phil.* 6.133b–134a, p. 16 PAPC 18.2. Longer version—Diod. 7.12.1. Eus. *PE* 5.27, p. 222bc. Theodor. *Gr. aff. cur.* 10.140–141. Incomplete—Oinomaos *ap.* Eus. *PE* 5.28, p. 222d (6.7, p. 260d). Cf. Anth. Pal. 14.77 (PW607).

Direct, Prose—Xen. *Apol.* 15.

Indirect—Val. Max. 5.3 ext. 2. Plut. *Lyk.* 5.3. Philostr. *Vit. Ap.* 8.7. Suda Λ824.

Testimony—Aristeides 13.189. Heliod. *Aith.* 2.27.1. Liban. *Epist.* 810.2, 4; 1488.3. Them. *Or.* 19.226d. Olymp. *Gorg.* 44.1.

NP. Direct, Verse—Oracle: Anth. Pal. 14.69. Incomplete—Apollo: Max. Tyr. 23.2. Longer version—Apollo: Apost.-Arsen. 8.46a.

Testimony—The god: Dexippos/Eunapios 100.1.7J.

Comment: See pp. 115–116, 165, 178, 186, 212, 226; Crahay 1956: 150–153.

There can be no doubt that the authors cited under *NP* considered this to have been spoken at Delphi, especially since the god says, "You have come to my rich temple," which is almost certain to be taken as Apollo's at Delphi. The Anthology surely takes the four-verse version from Herodotos, although it does not list it under Pythian oracles. Apostolios probably takes his six-verse version from Eusebios or Theodoretos; these three do not complete the sixth verse.

Q8 (PW21, 217, 219–221). Early seventh century B.C.? Probably genuine in its simplest form (1).

C. Spartans [Lykurgos].

Occ. Adoption of the Lycurgan laws.

Q. (1) Is it better for Sparta to obey these laws? (Xenophon; cf. Plut. *Lyk.* 29). (2) What laws should we adopt to benefit the Spartans most? (Diodoros).

R. (1) It is better in every respect to obey these laws (Xenophon). (2) Found a sanctuary of Zeus Hellenios [*Syllanios*] and Athena Hellenia [*Syllania*]; divide the people into tribes and *ôbai*; establish a council of thirty with the rulers; hold the Apellai from time to time between Babyka and Knakion; thus introduce and withdraw measures; the citizens' assembly is sovereign (Plut. *Lyk.* 6.1; cf. Tyrtaios). (3) As long as you keep your promises and oaths and deal with one another and with foreigners justly, honoring the elders, worshipping the Tyndarids, Menelaos, and the other Spartan heroes, Zeus will protect you (Oinomaos).

Mode A2 (A1), Topic 2b (1a)

Delphi. Direct, Verse (3)—Oinomaos *ap.* Eus. *PE* 5.28, p. 223ab. Indirect—(1) Xen. *Lac. rep.* 8.5. Plut. *Lyk.* 29. Polyainos *Strat.* 1.16.1. Suda *Λ*824. (2) *Tyrtaios 4 West *ap.* Diod. 7.12.6 = *ap.* Plut. *Lyc.* 6.5. Diod. 7.12.2 (16.57.4). Plut. *Lyk.* 6.1 (13).

Testimony—Herod. 1.65.4. Paus. Lac. 582J *ap.* Strab. 8.5.5, p. 366. Plato *Leg.* 632d, 634a. Aristotle frag. 535 Rose, Ephoros 70.174J *ap.* Clem. Alex. *Strom.* 1, 422P. Polyb. 10.2.9, 11. Cic. *Div.* 1.43.96. Strabo 10.4.19, p. 482; 16.2.38, p. 762. Dion. Hal. *Ant. Rom.* 2.61.2. Pomp. Trog./Justin 3.3.10–11. Plut. *Mor.* 403c, 789e; *Ag. Cl. Gr. comp.* 2.3. Aristeides 13.192, 45.11. Paus. 3.2.4. Liban. *Or.* 64.16. Schol. on Aristeides 13.192, p. 331 Dind.

NP. Indirect—(1) The god: Nic. Dam. 56J.

Testimony—Apollo: Isyllos *Hymn*, Inscription of Epidauros, *IG* 4². 128.70–71. Val. Max. 1.2 ext 3. Max. Tyr. 23.2. Aug. *CD* 10.13.3, 12.16.1. Oracle: Suda *P*154.

Comment: See pp. 5, 56, 85, 115, 165, 192; Defradas 1954: 258–266.

Xenophon's version approximates the genuine form of the question and response. He reports that Lykurgos, after framing his laws, went to Delphi with the noblest Spartans and asked εἰ λῷον καὶ ἄμεινον εἴη τῇ Σπάρτῃ πειθομένῃ οἷς αὐτὸς ἔθηκε νόμοις; and the god replied that it would be better in every respect (τῷ πάντι ἄμεινον εἶναι) if Sparta should do so. We need only leave out Lykurgos: Sparta sent envoys to Delphi who received a response exactly like the Historical sanctions approving the newly framed laws. The two opinions which Herodotos reports, (1) that the Pythia had dictated the Spartan constitution to Lykurgos (i.e., to the Spartans), and (2) the Spartans' own assertion that they had taken their laws from Crete, are not incompatible. The Pythia merely sanctioned the constitutional reforms, however derived; she did not dictate them. A code of laws approved at Delphi was sometimes viewed as the god's pronouncement (see H26). The famous *rêtra* that Plutarch quotes, probably drawn from Aristotle's *Spartan Constitution*, is presented as Apollo's response; but Plutarch also reports the simple sanction (*Lyk.* 29).

Q8 in its simplest form as a sanction may be the earliest authentic Delphic response that we have. And we may have contemporary evidence for it in Tyrtaios' verses. If the

Lycurgan laws were adopted in the seventh century, then Tyrtaios could have been a contemporary of the event. But the dates of the reforms and of Tyrtaios are too uncertain to allow us to call this response Historical; and Tyrtaios' words may not refer to a recent event.

Q9 (PW218). [900–770.] Not genuine.
C. Lykurgos.
Occ. Receipt of Q8.
Q. What shall the rulers do to rule well and the citizens to obey?
R. There are two ways opposite to each other, one leading to the house of freedom, the other to the house of slavery. Lead the people on the road that goes through courage and harmony; avoid that which leads through strife and ruin.
Mode A1 (C1, D1), Topic 2b (3j)
Delphi. Direct, Verse—Diod. 7.12.2. Oinomaos ap. Eus. PE 5.28, p. 223cd.
      Comment: See pp. 116, 173.

Q10 (PW222). [900–750.] Not genuine.
C. Spartans or Lykurgos or Kings Alkomenes and Theopompos of Sparta.
Occ. Increase of wealth-seeking in Sparta, or desire for new laws.
Q. Not stated.
R. Love of money and nothing else will destroy Sparta.
Mode E1, Topic 3j
Delphi. Direct, Verse—Diod. 7.12.5.
      Indirect—Cic. Off. 2.22.77. Ael. VH 14.29. Liban. Prog. Vit. 5.17. Suda Δ997, Δ824.
NP. Direct, Verse—The god: *Aristotle frag. 544 Rose ap. Zen. 2.24 = ap. Schol. vet in Eur. Andr. 445. Ps.-Plut. Prov. Alex. 43, p. 1261W. Diogen. 2.36. Apost. 8.77. Oracle: Olymp. on Plato Alk. I, p. 164. Makar. 2.68. Incomplete—Oracle: Plut. Mor. 239f.
      Indirect—Oracle: Plut. Ages. 9. Paus. 9.32.10. Schol. on Aristoph. Pax 622.
      Comment: See pp. 84–85.
      Theodor Bergk took the hexameter as a line from Tyrtaios' Eunomia (frag. 3), and joined with it the distich that follows in Diod. 7.12.6, usually taken with the verses that follow (see Q8). If this is so, then Tyrtaios says that Apollo spoke this from his rich adyton, presumably to the Spartans; but I doubt that Diodoros took this from Tyrtaios: it does not sound like him.

Q11 (PW561). Before 500? Possibly genuine.
C. Spartans.
Occ. and Q. Perhaps a proposal to swear oaths by Herakles.
R. It is better to establish these oaths by Herakles.
Mode A2, Topic 1d
Delphi. Indirect—Plut. Mor. 271c.

Q12 (PW539). c. 750 B.C.? Perhaps genuine.
C. Kings Charilaos and Archelaos of Sparta.

Occ. and Q. Perhaps a proposal to allot half the acquired land to Apollo.

R. If they allot half of the acquired portion to Apollo, it will be better for them.

Mode A2, Topic 1b

Delphi. Direct, Verse—Oinomaos *ap.* Eus. *PE* 5.32, p. 226d.

> *Comment:* See pp. 192, 193, 195, 207.

As far as content goes this response is acceptable; but one may doubt whether Spartans consulted Delphi in the eighth century, in the earliest days of the Oracle, when it had not yet acquired great fame. The response is, moreover, quoted by Oinomaos, who probably took this from an oracle collection, the other contents of which were mostly not genuine oracles.

Q13 (PW296). [c. 740 B.C.] Not genuine.

C. Spartans.

Occ. Appeal of the murdered Kresphontes' sons to help them.

Q. Apparently whether they should accept the appeal.

R. They should accept the offer and help the wronged.

Mode A1, Topic 2e

Delphi. Indirect—Isokr. *Or.* 6.23, 31.

> *Comment:* See pp. 103, 104.

Q14 (PW361–362). [c. 725 B.C.] Not genuine.

C. Messenians.

Occ. Siege of Ithome in first Messenian War.

Q. On means of victory.

R. Sacrifice a maiden, chosen by lot from the Aipytids, to the underworld gods [or a maiden from another family that offers her willingly (Pausanias)].

Mode A1, Topic 1c

Delphi. Direct, Verse—Oinomaos *ap.* Eus. *PE* 5.27, p. 221d. (iambic trimeter) Paus. 4.9.4.

> Direct, Prose, partly Indirect—*Diod. 8.8.2.

> Testimony—Eus. *PE* 5.26, p. 221a.

> *Comment:* See pp. 103, 104, 105.

Q15 (PW363). [c. 725 B.C.] Not genuine.

C. Spartans.

Occ. Defeat in battle in the course of the first Messenian War.

Q. Not stated.

R. The Messenians acquired their land by trickery; it will be taken by trickery.

Mode E3, Topic 2e

Delphi. Direct, Verse—Diod. 8.13.2. Paus. 4.12.1. Oinomaos *ap.* Eus. *PE* 5.27, p. 221c.

> Testimony—Eus. *PE* 5.26, p. 221a.

> *Comment:* See pp. 103, 106, 184, 207.

Q16 (PW364). [c. 725 B.C.] Not genuine.

C. King Aristodemos of Messenia.

Occ. Spartan siege of Ithome.

Q. On the conduct of the war.

R. Beware of trickery that will bring the Spartans victory. They will take the fort when the two leave their lurking place; and the end will come when the doom comes to the changed in nature.

Mode F (C1), Topic 3h (2e)

Delphi. Direct, Verse—Paus. 4.12.4 (13.3).

> Comment: See pp. 103, 105, 106, 171, 207.

Q17 (PW365) [c. 720 B.C.] Not genuine.

C. Messenians.

Occ. War with Sparta for nearly twenty years.

Q. On victory.

R. To those who first place a hundred tripods around Zeus Ithomatas' altar the gods grant the Messenian land with victory. Deceit puts you ahead, but punishment comes after. Do as you must. Some men have ruin before others.

Mode F (A3, D1), Topic 1b (2e, 3j)

Delphi. Direct, Verse—Paus. 4.12.7, 26.4.

> Comment: See pp. 103, 106, 178, 185–186.

Q18 (PW297–299). [c. 685 B.C.] Not genuine.

Q18(A)

C. Spartans.

Occ. Second Messenian War.

Q. How can they vanquish Messenia most quickly? (Isokrates).

R. They should get a leader [or counsellor] from Athens [and make certain sacrifices (Isokrates)].

Mode A1, Topic 2e (1b)

Delphi. Indirect—Isokr. Or. 6.31. Diod. 8.27.1. Pomp. Trog./Justin 3.5.4. Paus. 4.15.6.

NP. Indirect—Apollo: Schol. vet. on Plato Leg. 629a. The god: Suda T1206. Oracle: Kallisthenes 124.24J ap. Strab. 8.4.10, p. 362.

Q18(B)

C. Messenians.

Occ. Second Messenian War.

Q. Request for salvation.

R. They receive no response because they do not make a just request.

Mode C1, Topic 3j

Delphi. Indirect—Isokr. Or. 6.31.

> Comment: See pp. 103, 104, 121.

PW297 separate Isokrates' Or. 6.31 from the other sources cited under Q18(A), which they cite as PW299. But surely when Isokrates says that Apollo told the Spartans what people to summon help from, he is referring to the command to summon a leader from Athens.

Q19 (PW367). [c. 680 B.C.] Not genuine.
C. Aristomenes, Messenian.
Occ. Loss of his shield in second Messenian War.
Q. Not stated.
R. He should go to the adyton of Trophonios in Lebadeia.
Mode A1, Topic 1b
Delphi. Testimony—Paus. 4.16.7.
    Comment: See pp. 104, 107.

Q20 (PW366). [c. 680 B.C.] Not genuine.
C. Aristomenes and Theoklos, Messenian envoys.
Occ. Defeat in battle with Spartans.
Q. On salvation.
R. When a goat drinks the water of Neda, I shall no longer preserve Messene, for destruction will be near.
Mode F, Topic 3h (2e)
Delphi. Direct, Verse—Paus. 4.20.1 (21.3, 10).
NP. Direct, Verse—Oracle: Suda T898.
    Comment: See pp. 70, 80, 81, 103 note 18, 106, 170, 179.

Q21 (PW368). [c. 665 B.C.] Not genuine.
C. King Damagetos of Ialysos.
Occ. Need of a wife.
Q. Whence should he get a wife.
R. He should take a daughter of the best man of the Hellenes.
Mode A1, Topic 3b
Delphi. Indirect—Paus. 4.24.2.
    Comment: See p. 104.
    The best man was Aristomenes the Messenian, then present at Delphi after the second Messenian War; he too consulted Apollo at this time, but Pausanias tells us that the response is not reported by his source.
    For the Messenian War oracles, Q13–21, see pp. 103–107, 119.

Q22 (PW369). Fourth century B.C. or later. Probably genuine.
C. Messenians.
Occ. and Q. Not stated.
R. They should bring Aristomenes' bones from Rhodes to Ithome.
Mode A1, Topic 1a
Delphi. Testimony—Paus. 4.32.3.

Q23 (PW483). [c. 600 B.C.] Not genuine.

C. Argives.

Occ. End of the Heraklid line.

Q. On choosing someone to be king.

R. An eagle will show them.

Mode E2, Topic 3h

Delphi. Indirect—Plut. Mor. 340c (396c).

> Comment: See p. 74.

Q24. [650–600.] Not genuine.

C. Chians.

Occ. Assassination of King Hippoklos, followed by signs of the gods' wrath.

Q.(A) Not stated.

R.(A) They should do away with Hippoklos' assassins.

Q.(B) They all killed Hippoklos.

R.(B) Then all must leave the city, if they are all guilty.

Mode A1, Topic 3f

NP. Indirect—The god: Plut. Mor. 244e.

> Comment: There is as good reason to consider this oracle "Delphic" (PW omit it) as Q135, which is nearby in Plutarch's text (245c). Neither is definitely ascribed to Delphi.

Q25 (PW412). [c. 600 B.C.] Not genuine.

C. Hegesistratos of Ephesos.

Occ. Flight from Ephesos after killing a tribesman.

Q. Where shall he settle?

R. He should settle where he sees rustics crowned with olive sprigs.

Mode B, Topic 3h

Delphi. Indirect—Pythokles 4.488M ap. Plut. Mor. 315f.

> Comment: See p. 72.

Q26 (PW1). [c. 700 B.C.] Not genuine.

C. Aigion in Achaia (or Megara).

Occ. Offering of a tithe to Apollo after victory over the Aetolians.

Q. Who are the better Hellenes?

R. Pelasgic Argos has better land, Thessaly better horses, Sparta better women; those who drink Arethusa's water are better men, but better than they are the Argives who live between Tiryns and Arcadia; and you, Aigieis [Megarians], are not third or fourth or twelfth; you are not in the reckoning.

Mode D1, Topic 3j (3i)

Delphi. Direct, Verse—Mnaseas 3.157M ap. Phot. Lex. 2.238 Nab. = ap. Sud. Υ108 = ap. Tzetz. Chil. 9.489–496, 883–890, 10.383–385. Deinias 306.6J ap. Schol. vet. in Theocr. 14.48. Incomplete—Oinomaos ap. Eus. PE 5.29, p. 224d. Ath. 7.278e. Zen. 1.48. Theodor. Gr. aff. cur. 10.141. Tzetzes Epist. 61, p. 56 Pr.; 71, p. 63 Pr. Direct, Prose—Suda Aι45.

NP. Direct, Verse—Oracle: Anth. Pal. 14.73. Incomplete—Apollo: Chor. Gaz. 29.*Th*.3. Oracle: Strabo 10.1.13, p. 449. Steph. Byz. 44 Mein. Schol. AB on Il. 2.543, B on Il. 2.761. Schol. on Aristeides 46.166, p. 548 Dind. Eust. on Dion. Per. 473.

Testimony—The god: Plato *Hipp. Maj.* 288bc. Oracle: *Ion 2.51M *ap.* Phot. *Lex.* 2.238 Nab. = *ap.* Sud. *Y*108.

Comment: See p. 121.

Mnaseas, as quoted by Photios, the Suda, and Tzetzes, had the eight-verse response in his collection of Delphic oracles. As quoted, he reads *Aigieis* in line 7. Deinias, who attributes it to Delphi, and the Anthology, which does not, have the whole response and read *Megareis* in line 7. The only verses that appear in incomplete quotations are 1–3 in whole or in part (Strabo, Oinomaos, Athenaios, Chorikios, Theodoretos, Scholiasts), usually verse 2 alone, and 7–8, one or both (Zenobios, Stephanos, Tzetzes *Epist.*). The Suda's (*A*ι45) quotation in prose seems to be a corruption of 7–8.

It is uncertain from Photios' (= Suda's) context whether Ion quoted the whole oracle. After quoting the eight verses and Mnaseas' account of the occasion and consultation, Photios merely adds, "And Ion too recounts that the oracle was given to the Aigieis." This is evidence that Ion was acquainted with line 7; and Photios implies that he knew the whole response, but does not say whether he considered it Delphic. Plato too probably knew the whole response; he alludes in the *Hippias Major* to line 2 on the fine Thessalian horses.

The final two verses, or either of them, were proverbial, several times quoted without reference to an oracle. Clement of Alexandria (*Strom.* 7, 901P) cites Theognis as the author; but his attribution is difficult to accept, since these are two hexameters, and, as far as we know, Theognis confined himself to elegiacs (and it appears impossible to convert verse 8 into a pentameter). Nevertheless Theognis may very well have employed the proverbial saying in some form. It was known to Callimachus (*Epigram* 25.6Pf.), whose allusion to it is quoted by Photios (= Suda), *loc. cit.* Callimachus and Clement refer to the Megarian version; and this was probably the name in the old proverb, although the paroemiographers agree on *Aigieis*. If Theognis put the proverb into verse (or invented the verses) the vocative *Megareis* is easily explained as his application of the *gnômê*. It would seem to be a saying that could be fitted to any people that one wanted to depreciate. See Plut. *Mor.* 682f, 730d; Alkiphron *Epist.* 3.34; Liban. *Epist.* 1516; Diogen. 1.47; Apost. 1.59.

At some point before 400 someone, perhaps Ion, substituted Aigion for Megara in a fable that illustrated the folly of vainglory. Then an eight-verse response was composed, ending with the old proverb. It is a short poem in priamel form:

> Pelasgic Argos has the better land,
> Thessaly has the better horses,
> Lakedaimon has the better women,
> Chalkis has the better men;
> Argos has better men than they;
> But you, men of Aigion (or Megara)
> aren't even in the reckoning.

The ordinary priamel (*Beispielreihe*) is meant to emphasize the final term, here Argos; then the depreciatory proverb is tacked on as an anticlimactic term, a surprise ending that suddenly shifts attention from the superior to the worthless.

Q26 belongs to a fable, which in its first form probably did not attribute the oracle to Delphi. Plato refers it only to "the god"; and it may have been anonymous for Ion. Although Mnaseas and Deinias attribute it to Delphi, the Anthology lists it among anonymous *chrêsmoi* and not among those spoken by the Pythian Apollo. In later times the fable had both a Delphic and a non-Delphic form.

Q27 (PW2). [c. 735 B.C.] Not genuine.
C. Archias of Corinth.
Occ. Proposed colony.
Q. Not stated.
R. Ortygia lies in the sea on Trinakria, where Alpheios gushes forth mingling with the spring Arethusa.
Mode D1, Topic 3i
Delphi. Direct, Verse—Paus. 5.7.3.
NP. Testimony—Oracle: Diod. 5.3.5.
> Comment: See pp. 138–139, 140, 141, 180.

Q28 (PW43). [c. 705 B.C.] Not genuine.
C. Myskellos of Ripai.
Occ. Lack of children.
Q. On birth of children.
R. Apollo loves you and will give you children. But first he commands you to settle great Croton among fair fields.
Mode A1 (E2), Topic 2c (3a)
Delphi. Direct, Verse—Diod. 8.17.1.
NP. Indirect—Apollo: Iambl. *Pyth.* 52. The god: *Antiochos 555.10J *ap.* Strab. 6.1.12, p. 262.
> Comment: See pp. 139, 140, 172 note 11, 207.

Q29 (PW44). [c. 705 B.C.] Not genuine.
C. Myskellos of Ripai.
Occ. Receipt of Q28.
Q. On whereabouts of Croton.
R. You go by Taphiassos, Chalkis, the land of Kuretes, Echinades; a wide sea is on your left: you will not miss Lacinium or Crimisa or the Aesarus River.
Mode E1 (D1), Topic 3i
Delphi. Direct, Verse—Diod. 8.17.1.
> Comment: See pp. 139, 178, 207.

Q30 (PW45). [c. 705 B.C.] Not genuine.
C. Myskellos of Ripai.

Occ. Attraction to site of Sybaris.

Q. Is it better to found Sybaris instead of Croton?

R. Asking for another place contrary to the god's will you are only asking for woes. Accept the gift that the god gives you.

Mode A1 (C1), Topic 2c (3j)

NP. Direct, Verse—The god: Antiochos 555.10 J *ap*.Strab. 6.1.12, p. 262. Oracle: Hippys 554.1J *ap*. Zen. 3.42. Diod. 8.17.2.

    Comment: See pp. 121, 139, 140, 207.

Q31 (PW229). [c. 735 B.C.] Not genuine.

C. Archias of Corinth and Myskellos of Ripai.

Occ. Proposed migrations.

Q. (A) What land should we go to?

R. (A) Choose whether you want wealth or health.

Q. (B) Archias: I want great wealth.

    Myskellos: I want health for myself and the city.

R. (B) Archias shall found Syracuse; Myskellos shall found Croton.

Mode A1, Topic 3e (2c)

Delphi. Direct, Verse (A)—Ael. frag. 346 *ap.* Sud. *A*4104, *M*1473.

    Indirect—*Strabo 6.2.4, p. 269. Steph. Byz. 592–593 Mein. (B) Eust. on Dion. Per. 369.

NP. Direct, Verse (A)—Apollo: Schol. vet. on Aristoph. *Eq.* 1091.

    Testimony—Oracle: Mant. Prov. 2.27.

    Comment: See pp. 138, 139, 171 note 10, 178, 179, 182, 207.

Q32 (PW370). [c. 740 B.C.] Not genuine.

C. Messenian exiles.

Occ. Exile from Messenia imposed by opponents.

Q. Apollo and Artemis have let this doom come upon them after assistance rendered; how can they preserve themselves in their ruin?

R. They should sail with the Chalcidians to Rhegium and thank Artemis because she saved them from destruction along with their country, which the Spartans will soon take.

Mode A1 (D1, E2), Topic 2c (1b, 2e)

NP. Indirect—Apollo: Strabo 6.1.6, p. 257.

    Comment: Delphi is very likely "the god's [shrine]," to which the fugitives sent envoys. They blame Apollo with Artemis for their difficulty, and it is Apollo who speaks to them. The story is not part of the Messenian history that Pausanias drew from Myron and Rianos (Q14–21). As a story of colony founding in Sicily it may have come to Strabo from Antiochos or Hippys.

Q33 (PW371). [c. 740 B.C.] Not genuine.

C. Chalcidian migrants.

Occ. A tenth of the Chalcidians were sent to Apollo at Delphi in time of famine.

Q. On a place to colonize.

R. Where at the mouth of the Apsia River the female weds the male, there found a city.

Mode B, Topic 3h (2c)

Delphi. Testimony—Timaios 566.43J *ap.* Strab. 6.1.6, p. 257; 9, p. 260. Antig. Karyst. 1, p. 61 West.

NP. Direct, Verse—Oracle: Diod. 8.23.2.

　Direct, Prose—Oracle: Herakl. *Rep.* 25.3.

　　Indirect—Oracle: Dion. Hal. *Ant. Rom.* 19.2.

　　　Comment: See pp. 70, 71, 80.

Apparently Timaios was the source for this account of the founding of Rhegium and the oracle that goes with it. He probably had the verses that Diodoros quotes.

Q34 (PW46). [c. 710 B.C.] Not genuine.

C. Phalanthos and Partheniai of Sparta.

Occ. Defeat in party strife and migration from Sparta.

Q. Do you grant us Sikyonia?

R. Fair is the land between Corinth and Sikyon, but you will not settle there. Look to Satyrion, the water of Taras, a harbor on the left, and the place where a goat [*tragos*] loves salt water, wetting the tip of his gray beard. There build Tarentum.

Mode B (D1), Topic 3h (2c, 3i)

Delphi. Direct, Verse—Diod. 8.21.3.

　Indirect—Dion. Hal. *Ant. Rom.* 19.1.2.

　Testimony—Plut. *Mor.* 408a.

　　Comment: See pp. 70, 80, 81, 86, 140, 141, 154, 171.

Q35 (PW47). [c. 710 B.C.] Not genuine.

C. Phalanthos and the Partheniai of Sparta.

Occ. Q34 not understood (Diodoros).

Q. On a place to settle (Antiochos).

R. I have given you Satyrion and Tarentum to live in and to be a plague to the Iapygians.

Mode A1, Topic 2c

Delphi. Direct, Verse—Diod. 8.21.3.

NP. Direct, Verse—The god: *Antiochos 555.13J *ap.* Strab. 6.3.2, p. 279.

　Comment: See pp. 140, 141.

Strabo does not mention Delphi or Apollo, but we cannot be sure that Antiochos, whom he cites for this story, did not. Strabo reports this as the oracle which Phalanthos received on where he should found a colony; he does not mention Q34, though Antiochos may have done so.

Q36 (PW525). [c. 710 B.C.] Not genuine.

C. Phalanthos (Myskellos; Suda and Scholiast).

Occ. Setting out to found a colony.

Q. Not stated.
R. Where he sees rain falling from a clear sky, he should acquire the land and found a city.
Mode B, Topic 3h (2c)
Delphi. Indirect—Paus. 10.10.6.
    Testimony—Plut. *Mor.* 408a.
NP. Indirect—Oracle: Suda *M*1473. Schol. vet. on Aristoph. *Nub.* 371.
    Comment: See pp, 69, 141.

Q37 (PW568). [700 B.C.] Not genuine.
C. Tarentines.
Occ and Q. Not stated.
R. It will be better for them to make their habitation with the majority.
Mode A3, Topic 2c
NP. Indirect—The god: Polyb. 8.28.7.
    Comment: See pp. 71, 406.
    Cf. L158. The phrase ἄμεινον καὶ λῷον ἔσεσθαι in Polybios' text may reflect oracular approval of democratic government in Tarentum; but probably the story is an *aition* for the graveyards within the walls of Tarentum. Polybios' source may be Timaios.

Q38 (PW526). [c. 700 B.C.] Not genuine.
C. Phalanthos or Tarentines.
Occ. and Q. Not stated, but concerning welfare of Tarentum.
R. They can recover their country by scattering Phalanthos' bones and ashes in the marketplace.
Mode A3, Topic 3c
Delphi. Indirect—Pomp. Trog./Justin 3.4.14.
    Comment: See p. 75 note 31.

Q39 (PW454). [c. 700 B.C.] Not genuine.
C. Leukippos of Sparta.
Occ. Migration.
Q. Where are he and his followers destined to settle?
R. They should sail to Italy and stay in the place where they stay [a] day and night on landing.
Mode B, Topic 3h (2c)
NP. Indirect—The god: Dion. Hal. *Ant. Rom.* 19.3.
    Comment: Leukippos and his fleet put in at Kallipolis, a harbor of Tarentum. Leukippos liked the country and persuaded the Tarentines to let him stay there for a day and night. When he had stayed several days, the Tarentines asked him to move on. He persuaded them that they had agreed to let him stay there as long as it was day or night. The lack of an indefinite article in Greek makes this ambiguity possible.

Q40 (PW3). [c. 690 B.C.] Not genuine.

C. Antiphemos and Entimos.

Occ. Migration.

Q. Not stated.

R. Go to Sicily and live there; build a city of Cretans and Rhodians by the mouth of the Gela River, and call it Gela.

Mode A1, Topic 2c

Delphi. Direct, Verse—Diod. 8.23.1.

NP. Testimony—Apollo: Schol. vet. on Pind. *Ol.* 2.42 /70/.

Comment: See pp. 141–142.

Q41 (PW410). [c. 690 B.C.] Not genuine.

C. Antiphemos and Lakios.

Occ. Migration.

Q. Unknown, but not answered.

R. (A) Lakios should sail to the sunrise.

R. (B) [After Antiphemos laughed] Antiphemos must found a city where the sun sets and call it Gela.

Mode A3 (A1), Topic 2c (3e)

Delphi. Indirect—Aristainetos 771.1J *ap.* Steph. Byz. 201 Mein. EM 225.

NP. Indirect—Oracle: *Theopompos 322 GH *ap.* Schol. *in* Thuc. 6.4.3.

Comment: See pp. 141–142.

Only Stephanos, citing Aristainetos, reports a double response. EM has (B) only; Theopompos, as the Scholiast reports him, has a simple prediction that Antiphemos will found a city.

Q42 (PW384). [c. 700 B.C.] Not genuine.

C. Perieres and Krataimenes.

Occ. Foundation of Drepanum.

Q. After which of the two should the colony be named?

R. They should not name it for either.

Mode C1, Topic 2c

NP. Indirect—Apollo: Callim. *Ait.* 43.78–79 Pf.

Comment: The response may not be complete. The extract closes with the statement that thenceforth the land has not called on the founder by name, perhaps meaning that there was a strange tabu on speaking either founder's name in Drepanum = Zancle = Messina (see PW); but more likely this is Callimachus' way of saying that the land does not bear a founder's name.

Q43 (PW48). [c. 653 B.C.] Not genuine.

C. Timesias of Klazomenai.

Occ. Colony foundation.

Q. Not stated.

R. Swarms of bees will soon be wasps for you.

Mode E3, Topic 3j (3h)

NP. Direct, Verse—Oracle: Plut. *Mor.* 96b.

> *Comment:* See pp. 142, 180.

About the only reason for considering this response Delphic is that Plutarch quotes it, though not in a Delphic essay. The verse was probably not invented as a response (it may be a line from a poet); and if a response at all, is probably not the whole of it.

Q44 (PW497–498). [c. 660 B.C.] Not genuine.

C. Megarians or Argives.

Occ. Migration.

Q. Not stated.

R. Blessed are they who will settle beside the Thracian coast and the mouth of Pontos [where two dog-whelps lap the sea (Hesychios)], where fish and deer graze in the same pasture. [Go as quickly as possible with plans well made (Stephanos).]

Mode F (A1, E1), Topic 3h (2c)

Delphi. Direct, Verse—Hesych. Mil. *Hist. Rom.* 6.3, 32. Steph. Byz. 189 Mein.

NP. Direct, Verse—The god: *Dion. Byz. *An. Bosp.* 17. Oracle: Georg. Kod. *Or. Const.* 1a, 5bc. Eust. on Dion. Per. 803.

> *Comment:* See pp. 71 note 24, 172, 177.

Dionysios and Eustathios report a three-verse oracle, to which Stephanos adds a fourth. Hesychios also has a four-verse oracle, in which a verse, indicating an additional sign—two dog-whelps—is inserted between the second and the third of the three-verse form. The references are to natural features, the bay Keras (deer) and the rivers Kydaros and Barbyses (whelps).

Q45 (PW37). [c. 650 B.C.] Not genuine.

C. King Grinnos of Thera.

Occ. (1) Not stated. (2) His son Battos could not talk.

Q. (1) On other matters. (2) On his son's speech and difficulties.

R. (1) He should found a city in Libya. (2) He should go to Africa and found the city of Cyrene; there Battos would recover his speech.

Mode A1, Topic 2c

Delphi. Indirect—(1) Herod. 4.150.3. (2) Pomp. Trog./Justin 13.7.2.

Q46 (PW38). [c. 640 B.C.] Not genuine.

C. Thera.

Occ. Seven-year drought.

Q. Not stated.

R. Send a colony to Libya.

Mode A1, Topic 2c

Delphi. Testimony—Herod. 4.151.1.

Q47 (PW39, 71). [c. 640 B.C.] Not genuine.

C. Aristotle-Battos of Thera.

Occ. Speech defect.

Q. (A) What will correct my speech? (Didymos, Scholiast on Pyth. 4.9, Tzetzes)

R. (A) Battos, you have come about your speech. But Apollo sends you to Libya as colonizer [to rule over Cyrene as king. The Libyans will attack you when you land there, but pray to Zeus, Athena, and Apollo, who will give you victory; you and your descendants will rule Libya; Apollo guides you (Diodoros)].

Q. (B) I came for an oracle on my speech, but you respond on other impossible matters, bidding me colonize Libya. By what means can I do so?

R. (B) The same (shorter form).

Mode A1 (E2), Topic 2c (1b, 2e)

Delphi. Direct, Verse—Herod. 4.155.3. Anth. Pal. 14.83. Schol. vet. on Pind. Pyth. 4.6/10, 9/15. Incomplete—Bekk. Anecd. 1.224.

Indirect—*Pind. Pyth. 4.6–8, 56, 61–62 (259–262; 5.62). Herakl. Rep. 4.1. Didymos ap. Schol. vet. in Pind. Pyth. 5.59/78, 60/80.

Testimony—Plut. Mor. 405b, 408a. Schol. vet. on Pind. Pyth. 4, inscr. a, 60/107.

NP. Direct, Verse—Apollo: Schol. on Callim. Hymn 2.76. Tzetz. Chil. 6.349–350. Longer version—Diod. 8.29.

Indirect—Apollo: Inscription of Cyrene, SEG 9.3 [= Meiggs-Lewis SGHI 5, line 25]. Testimony—Apollo: Schol. vet. on Aristoph. Pl. 925 [= Ps.-Eud. Viol. 226]. Schol. on Callim. Hymn 2.65. Cf. Callim. Hymn 2.65–68. Oracle: Eus. Chron. an. 1253, 8.359 Migne. Synk. 212c.

Comment: See pp. 174–175, 178, 186, 207.

Diodoros quotes a nine-verse oracle, adding seven to the two that Herodotos and others report, and changing the last part of line 2 to suit the addition.

Q48 (PW40). [c. 640 B.C.] Not genuine.

C. Thera.

Occ. Misfortunes.

Q. On the present ills.

R. They will fare better if they colonize Cyrene with Battos.

Mode A1, Topic 2c

Delphi. Indirect—Herod. 4.156.2.

Q49 (PW41). [c. 640–635.] Not genuine.

C. Battos and fellow-colonists.

Occ. No good consequences after two years on the island of Platea.

Q. We have settled in Libya and are not faring better from living there.

R. If you who have not gone there know Libya better than I, who have gone, I very much admire your wisdom.

Mode D1, Topic 3i (3j)

Delphi. Direct, Verse—Herod. 4.157.2. Plut. Mor. 408a. Anth. Pal. 14.84.

Comment: The indications of Doric dialect in these verses are confined to the introductory *Ai ty* (for *Ei sy*). Otherwise they show *êta* where Doric would have *alpha*, so that dialectal forms are mixed, at least as Herodotos reports the lines.

Q50 (PW42). [c. 550 B.C.] Not genuine.
C. Many Hellenes.
Occ. Invitation of Cyrene to all Hellenes to become fellow-citizens in Cyrene.
Q. Not stated.
R. He who goes to Libya too late for division of the land will repent thereafter.
Mode E1, Topic 2c
Delphi. Direct, Verse—Herod. 4.159.3. Anth. Pal. 14.85.

Q51 (PW416). [c. 640 B.C.] Not genuine.
C. Battos.
Occ. Expulsion with partisans from Thera in consequence of civil strife.
Q. Shall we fight to recover our country or go elsewhere and settle?
R. Leave the island and go elsewhere; the eastern continent is better for you. Obey me without guile and accept it. As a man labors, so is the result of his labor.
Mode A1 (D1), Topic 2c (3j)
Delphi. Direct, Verse—Menekles 270.6J *ap.* Schol. vet. *in* Pind. *Pyth.* 4.6/10 (*ap.* Tzetz. *in* Lyc. 886).
    Comment: On the Cyrenaic oracles, Q45–51, see pp. 120–123; Crahay 1956: 116–122.

Q52 (PW89). [c. 700 B.C.] Not genuine.
C. Megarians.
Occ. and Q. Not stated.
R. They should construct a tomb for Orsippos.
Mode A1, Topic 1a (3c)
Delphi. Testimony—Inscription of Megara, *IG* 7.52.1–2. Schol. on Thuc. 1.6.5.
    Comment: See Fontenrose 1968: 92–93.

Q53 (PW224). [c. 675 B.C.] Not genuine.
C. Spartans.
Occ. Civil strife.
Q. Not stated.
R. They will become harmonious if they summon the Lesbian bard [Terpander] and listen to his music.
Mode A1, Topic 3g (2b)
Delphi. Indirect—Schol. on Od. 3.267.
NP. Indirect—The god: *Herakl. *Rep.* 2.6. Schol. on Aristeides 46.185, p. 593 Dind. Oracle: Diod. 8.28 = Tzetz. *Chil.* 1.387–388. Phot. *Lex.* 1.418 Naber. Suda *M*701. Apost. 11.27.
    Testimony—The god: Philod. *Mus.* 4.19. Ps.-Plut. *Prov. Alex.* 110, p. 1275 W. Zen. 5.9.
    Comment: See p. 121.

Q54 (PW223). [c. 650 B.C.] Not genuine.

C. Spartans.

Occ. Civil dissension (Philodemos) or plague (Plutarch).

Q. Not stated.

R. They should summon Thaletas.

Mode A1, Topic 3g (2b)

Delphi. Indirect—Philod. Mus. 4.18.37–38.

   Testimony—Plut. Mor. 1146c.

     Comment: See p. 121; cf. Q18, 53.

Q55 (PW230). [c. 680 B.C.] Not genuine.

C. Telesikles of Paros.

Occ. and Q. Not stated.

R. Tell the Parians that I bid you found a city on the island of Aeria [Eerie].

Mode A3, Topic 2c

Delphi. Direct, Verse—Oinomaos ap. Eus. PE 6.7, p. 256b.

NP. Direct, Verse—Oracle: Steph. Byz. 307 Mein.

   Comment: Oinomaos' reference to Delphi at PE 255b seems to apply to the three quoted responses that follow. Oinomaos points out the unclarity of νήσῳ ἐν Ἑερίη, since Telesikles would have to know that Thasos was formerly called Aeria; and it was Telesikles' son, the poet Archilochos, who used this name for the island. The phrase is in fact ambiguous: it can be taken as "in an airy island," and "airy" understood as "misty" or "up in the air." Hence I have classified the mode as A3, ambiguous or unclear command.

Q56 (PW231). [c. 680 B.C.] Not genuine.

C. Telesikles of Paros.

Occ. Civic affairs and the young Archilochos' meeting with the Muses.

Q. None.

R. Immortal and famous will be that son of yours who first speaks to you when you
   disembark on your native land.

Mode F, Topic 3d (3h)

Delphi. Direct, Verse—Inscription of Paros, Arch. Eph. (1952) 41 = Philologus 99 (1955) 8, II 50–52. Incomplete—Oinomaos ap. Eus. PE 5.33, p. 227c. Theodor. Gr. aff. cur. 10.141.

NP. Direct, Verse—Oracle: Anth. Pal. 14.113.

   Indirect—Apollo: Dion Chrys. 33.12.

     Comment: See p. 172 note 11.

   The Parian inscription is dated 250–200, indicating that the verse oracle was known in the third century B.C. and was part of the local legend of Archilochos, which is told in part II, lines 20–57. The boy Archilochos met the Muses when he was taking a cow to market. They took the cow and gave him a lyre in exchange. Telesikles marveled at his son's story, and so when the Parians chose him and a fellow-citzen to go to Delphi to inquire about civic affairs, he decided to ask also about his son's experience. But when he entered the temple the Pythia addressed him spontaneously in three verses, a message which contains the motif of the first met, a form of mode F.

According to Dion, the occasion was the impending birth of a child to Telesikles' wife; but this is inconsistent with the response.

Q57 (PW232). [c. 650 B.C.] Not genuine.
C. Archilochos.
Occ. Loss of wealth in civil strife.
Q. Not stated.
R. Go to Thasos and settle the island.
Mode A1, Topic 2c
Delphi. Direct, Verse—Oinomaos ap. Eus. PE 5.31, p. 226a.

Q58 (PW4–5). [c. 640 B.C.] Not genuine.
C. Kalondas Korax.
Occ. Killing of Archilochos.
Q. (A) None.
R. (A) You killed the Muses' servant; leave the temple.
Mode C1 (D1), Topic 3f
Q. (B) I am guiltless, since I killed him in war, when I had either to kill or be killed. So do not hate me (Aelian).
R. (B) Go to Tainaron to the tomb [or house] of Tettix and appease the soul of Archilochos with libations (Plutarch, Aelian).
(Mode A1, Topic 1b)
Delphi. Direct, Verse (A)—Galen Protr. 9.23. Incomplete—*Herakl. Rep. 8.2. Origen Cels. 3.25.
Indirect—Plut. Mor. 560e. Ael. frag. 80 ap. Sud. A4112. (A) Oinomaos ap. Eus. PE 5.33, p. 228c. Liban. Decl. 1.180.
Testimony—Pliny NH 7.29.109. Liban Or. 1.74.
NP. Direct, Verse, Incomplete (A)—Apollo: Aristeides 46.293.
Indirect—Apollo: Dion Chrys. 33.12.
Comment: See p. 242.

Q59 (PW6). [c. 685 B.C.] Not genuine.
C. Eetion of Corinth.
Occ. Lack of children.
Q. None.
R. Eetion, nobody honors you, though you deserve much honor. Labda conceives and will bear a rolling stone, which will fall among monarchs and will set Corinth right.
Mode E3 (D1), Topic 3a (2a)
Delphi. Direct, Verse—Herod. 5.92b.2. Anth. Pal. 14.86. Incomplete—Oinomaos ap. Eus. PE 5.29, p. 224c.
Comment: See pp. 116–117, 119, 226.

Q60 (PW7). [Before 685 B.C.] Not genuine.

C. Bakchiads.

Occ. and Q. Not stated.

R. An eagle conceives on rocks and will bear a lion, who will destroy many men. Take notice of this, Corinthians.

Mode E3, Topic 3a (3c)

Delphi. Direct, Verse—Anth. Pal. 14.87.

NP. Direct, Verse—Oracle: *Herod. 5.92b.3.

    Indirect—Oracle: Nic. Dam. 57.2(6) J.

      Comment: See pp. 116–117, 151, 171 note 10.

Q61 (PW8). [c. 655 B.C.] Not genuine.

C. Kypselos of Corinth.

Occ. Desire to return to Corinth (Nicolaus).

Q. None?

R. Blessed is this man who enters my house, Kypselos Eetion's son, king of Corinth: his sons will be kings too, but not his grandsons.

Mode E2, Topic 2a

Delphi. Direct, Verse—Herod. 5.92e.2. Anth. Pal. 14.88. Incomplete—Oinomaos *ap.* Eus. PE 5.35, p. 233a.

    Testimony—Nic. Dam. 57.4J.

NP. Direct, Verse—The god: Dion Chrys. 37.5. Incomplete—Oracle: Apost.-Arsen. 12.65d.

    Testimony—Apollo: Chrysippos *ap.* Cic. Fat. 7.13.

      Comment: See pp. 116–117, 119, 122, 172, 177, 178, 183.

Q62 (PW9). [c. 655 B.C.] Not genuine.

C. Kypselos?

Occ. and Q. Not stated.

R. Kypselos, who will bring many woes to Corinth.

Mode E2, Topic 3g

Delphi. Direct, Verse—Oinomaos *ap.* Eus. PE 5.35, p. 235b.

    Comment: This is an isolated verse that Oinomaos quotes immediately after Q61 without any information about it. He says only that Apollo praises both tyrannicides and tyrants. This is probably not meant to be an oracular response at all but Oinomaos' own invention, intended as a satiric version of verse 2 in Q61—what Apollo should have said.

Q63 (PW10–11). [c. 625 B.C.] Not genuine.

C. Epidaurians.

Occ. Famine.

Q. (A) On this misfortune.

R. (A) It will be better for them to set up images of Damia and Auxesia.

Q. (B) Should they make them of bronze or stone?

R. (B) Neither, but of olive wood.

Mode A1, Topic 1a

Delphi. Indirect—Herod. 5.82.1-2. Schol. on Aristeides 46.187, p. 598 Dind.

Testimony—Paus. 2.30.4.

NP. Indirect—The god: Schol. on Aristeides 13.154, p. 216 Dind.

Comment: Pausanias cites Herodotos without quoting content; therefore he was aware of the Delphic attribution, though he does not mention it.

This response might be considered authentic as essentially no more than the sanction of a cult of the two goddesses; notice Herodotos' ἄμεινον συνοίσεσθαι. But the twofold consultation arouses suspicions, and so does the second question: it is odd that the Epidaurians should ask about the materials; ordinarily a person directed to set up an image would fulfill the command as he thought best; or if he wanted a sanction, he would have already decided on materials.

The purpose of the oracle is to introduce a narrative of how hostilities began between Athens and Aigina. Athens had the holiest olive trees, or, as some said, the only olive trees at the time. The latter circumstance is plainly impossible; the former demands that Epidaurians recognize the special holiness of the Athenian trees. But the Epidaurians have to be brought to Athens in order to make an agreement with the Athenians that they will bring offerings every year to Athena Polias and Erechtheus. Once the Epidaurians make and set up the images, the land produces at once—a folkloristic feature. Then, long after, the Aeginetans steal the images, the Epidaurians cease sending offerings to Athens, and so events lead to war. Notice too the madness that seized the Athenians who tried to remove the images from Aigina. The narrative seems to be a non-Aeginetan origin myth of the cult of Damia and Auxesia on Aigina. If the goddesses are really Demeter and Persephone, as the Scholiast (p. 598 Dind.) indicates, then the cults at both Epidauros and Aigina probably precede the Delphic Oracle. See Crahay 1956: 75-77.

Q64 (PW12). [c. 630 B.C.] Not genuine.

C. Kylon of Athens.

Occ. Plot to seize the acropolis of Athens.

Q. Not stated.

R. He should seize the Athenian acropolis at Zeus's greatest festival.

Mode A3, Topic 3h (2e)

Delphi. Indirect—Thuc. 1.126.4.

NP. Indirect—Oracle: Schol. vet. on Aristoph. *Eq.* 445.

Comment: See p. 68.

Q65 (PW13). 596 B.C.

C. Athenians.

Occ. Plague.

Q. Not stated.

R. They must cleanse the city.

Mode A1, Topic 2b (1d)

Delphi. Indirect—Diog. Laert. 1.10.110.

NP. Testimony—The god: *Plato *Leg.* 642d.

Comment: The outcome was that the Athenians summoned Epimenides from Crete to perform the purificatory rites. In Plato's notice Epimenides went to Athens in accordance with an oracle ten years before the Persian Wars (500 B.C.) and made certain sacrifices which the god had ordained. The god is not named, and his oracle appears to have directed the summoning of Epimenides and to have specified the sacrifices. But according to Diogenes the Pythia told the Athenians to cleanse the city, and they summoned Epimenides, who on arrival performed the rites that he considered suitable. Diogenes dates the cleansing in the forty-sixth Olympiad (596), which is more probable for Epimenides' lifetime. The response is probably genuine.

Q66 (PW14). [c. 600 B.C.] Not genuine.
C. Epimenides of Phaistos.
Occ. and Q. Inquiry into the truth of the myth about the omphalos.
R. An unclear and ambiguous reply, from which Epimenides concluded that there is no omphalos of earth or sea.
Mode D2, Topic 3j
Delphi. Testimony—Plut. *Mor.* 409f.

Comment: According to Plutarch's story, Epimenides questioned the god about the myth in which eagles or swans flying from the ends of earth met at Pytho, the site of the omphalos. Receiving an unclear answer, he expressed his conclusion in two hexameters: "For there is no mid-omphalos of either earth or sea; or if there is, it is visible to gods, invisible to mortal men." We are not informed what the god told Epimenides. Hence the mode and topic can only be conjectured from Epimenides' verses and his inquiry.

Q67 (PW15). [c. 590 B.C.] Not genuine.
C. Solon the Athenian.
Occ and Q. Not stated.
R. Sit in the middle of the ship, steering straight; you have many helpers in Athens.
Mode A1 (D1), Topic 3j (2b)
Delphi. Direct, Verse—Plut. *Solon* 14.4.

Comment: The two hexameters came to Plutarch from his source, Androtion or Hermippos, who may have taken them from a poem (probably not Solon's own) on Solon's statecraft. They may not have been meant as an oracle at first.

Q68 (PW16). [c. 590 B.C.] Not genuine.
C. Solon the Athenian.
Occ. and Q. Not stated.
R. Blessed is the city that listens to a single herald.
Mode D1, Topic 3j (2b)
NP. Direct, Verse—The god: Plut. *Mor.* 152c.

Comment: This verse, which hardly makes a complete oracle, was also probably taken from a poem, perhaps of Solon's own composition. Plutarch's Aesop quotes it at the Seven Sages' banquet and refers it only to "the god."

Q69 (PW326). c. 570 B.C. Probably genuine.

C. Solon the Athenian.

Occ. War with Megara over Salamis.

Q. Not stated.

R. Sacrifice to the chiefs of the land, the resident heroes whom Salamis covers, who in death face the sunset.

Mode A1, Topic 1b

Delphi. Direct, Verse—Plut. Solon 9.1 (cf. 10.4).

Comment: See p. 193.

The fact that Plutarch's Solon is our only authority for this means that its authenticity is not well supported. It came to Plutarch from Hermippos or perhaps directly from Androtion. In itself it is unexceptionable; but the verses may have been composed from a prose response actually spoken. Strangely PW reject Q69, though they accept Q67 and Q68. See Linforth 1919: 16–20.

Q70 (PW17). [c. 600 B.C.] Not genuine.

C. Amphictions.

Occ. Offenses of Crisaeans and Kragalidai against Apollo's sanctuary at Delphi.

Q. What punishment should they impose on the offenders?

R. They must make war on the Crisaeans and Kragalidai, day and night, pillage their country and enslave them, and dedicate the land to Apollon Pythios, Artemis, Leto, and Athena Pronaia with the condition that they neither work it nor allow anyone else to do so.

Mode A1 (C1), Topic 2e (1b, 1d)

Delphi. Indirect—Aischines 3.108 (119). Plut. Mor. 76e.

Comment: Aischines' indirect quotation shows traces of hexameters; from them PW reconstruct a two-verse response.

Since it appears fairly certain that Krisa controlled Delphi before the First Sacred War, it is unlikely that the Amphictions could have got from the Delphic Oracle a direction to make war on the Crisaeans. The oracle was obviously invented for the Amphictions to bolster the justification that they afterwards put forth for destroying Krisa and taking Delphi under their supervision. See Forrest 1956; Fontenrose 1960a: 221–222. For the traditional view see Parke 1956: 99–108. Aside from Aischines no writer on the Sacred War mentions this oracle.

Q71 (PW18). [c. 590 B.C.] Not genuine.

C. Amphictions (or Krisa, Polyainos).

Occ. Long-lasting siege of Krisa.

Q. On means or prospect of victory (Pausanias).

R. You will not take this city until Amphitrite's wave washes my temenos, sounding on the sacred shores.

Mode F, Topic 3h (2e)

Delphi. Direct, Verse—Diod. 9.16. Paus. 10.37.6. Suda *Σ*777. Interpolation at Aisch. 3. 112 (cf. 119).

Indirect—Polyainos *Strat.* 3.5.

Comment: See pp. 64–65.

As often in stories of this kind (see L49) the versions vary about who received the oracle, the attackers or defenders. According to Polyainos the Crisaeans received this response ("This city will not be taken until . . ."), but Kleisthenes of Sikyon found out about it.

Q72 (PW237). [c. 590 B.C.] Not genuine.
C. Amphictions.
Occ. Plague in their camp in First Sacred War.
Q. What should they do?
R. They should continue the war; and they will be victorious if they go to Kos and fetch stag's son along with gold to help them, and quickly, before the Crisaeans take the tripod in the adyton; otherwise the city will not be taken.
Mode A3 (A1), Topic 3e (2e, 3g)
Delphi. Indirect—Hippocratic Corpus, *Epist.* 27.13, 9.410 Littré.

Comment: The stag's son and gold turn out to be a Coan father and son named Nebros and Chryses.

Q73 (PW23). [c. 675 B.C.] Not genuine.
C. Sicyonians.
Occ. Killing of the boy victor Teletias (Plutarch).
Q. (A) Not stated.
R. (A) They will be ruled by scourge for a hundred years.
Q. (B) Who is going to do this?
R. (B) It is the first man who on their return they hear has a son born to him [and the father should make certain sacrifices to the gods (Ox. Pap.)].
Mode F (A1, E2), Topic 3h (1b, 3a, 3g)
Delphi. Indirect—Diod. 8.24. (A) Plut. *Mor.* 553a.

Testimony—(B) Ox. Pap. 1365. 1–11 = 105.2J.

Comment: The father was Andreas, a cook, and the son born was Orthagoras, first of the Orthagorid dynasty of tyrants in Sikyon that ended with Kleisthenes. Aristotle *Pol.* 1315b, on the Orthagorids, makes no mention of an oracle.

Q74 (PW24). [c. 580 B.C.] Not genuine.
C. Kleisthenes, tyrant of Sikyon.
Occ. Plan to remove the hero Adrastos' body.
Q. Should he cast Adrastos out?
R. Adrastos was king of Sikyon, but Kleisthenes is its stoner.
Mode D1, Topic 2a
Delphi. Indirect—Herod. 5.67.2.
NP. Indirect—Apollo: Dion Chrys. 3.41.

Comment: This like Q73 is an anti-Orthagorid invention. It is unlikely that the Delphic Oracle would insult such a powerful consultant as Kleisthenes. Rebukes are found only among narrative oracles. But Crahay (1956: 247–249) and Parke (1956: 121–122) believe in the authenticity of Q74.

Q75 (PW245). [c. 592 or 556 B.C.] Not genuine.
C. Anacharsis of Scythia or Chilon of Sparta.
Occ. Desire to be recognized as wisest of men.
Q. Is anyone [of the Hellenes (Diodoros)] wiser than I?
R. Myson in Chen is superior to you in wisdom.
Mode D1, Topic 3g
Delphi. Direct, Verse—Eudoxos of Knidos and Euanthes of Miletos *ap.* Diog. Laert. 1. 1.30. Diod. 9.5.2. Diog. Laert. 1.9.106–107.
   Indirect—cf. Auson. *Sept. sap.* 80–81.
   Testimony—Paus. 1.22.8.
NP. Indirect—Apollo: *Hipponax 63 West *ap.* Diog. Laert. 1.9.107. The god: Musonius *ap.* Stob. *Flor.* 56.18.
   Comment: The fragment from Hipponax does not indicate who inquired; we learn only that Apollo declared Myson wisest (*sôphronestatos*) of all men. We should not therefore consider this Historical on the ground that Hipponax, who flourished about 550, was a contemporary of Chilon and perhaps of Anacharsis, whose supposed visit to Greece occurred about 592. Hipponax, moreover, does not mention Delphi; and he appears only to know a traditional story.

Q76 (PW247–248). [c. 590 B.C.] Not genuine.
C. (1) Milesians. (2) Ionians and Coans.
Occ. Finding of a golden tripod in a catch of fish.
Q. To whom should the find be awarded? (Valerius Maximus).
R. (1) Give the tripod to the man who is first in wisdom. (2) The war between Coans and Ionians will not end until you send the golden tripod which Hephaistos made to the house of a man who in his wisdom sees both present and future.
Mode A1, Topic 3e
Delphi. Direct, Verse (both versions)—Diod. 9.3.1–2. Diog. Laert. 1.1.28, 33. Incomplete (1)—Val. Max. 4.1 ext. 7.
   Indirect—Plut. *Solon* 4.2. Schol. Ald. on Aristoph. *Eq.* 1016.
NP. Direct, Verse (1)—Apollo: Schol. vet. on Aristoph. *Pl.* 9. Apost.-Arsen. 6.93b.
   Indirect—The god: Porphyry 260.5J *ap.* Cyr. *Jul.* 1, p. 28.
   Comment: In the early legend this was probably said to be a pronouncement of Apollo at Didyma. The consultants gave the tripod to Thales, whom they found either in Didyma or in Miletos; he sent it to Pittakos, from whom it went the round of the Seven Wise Men and back to Thales, who dedicated it to Apollo Didymeus or to Apollo Delphinios of Miletos (Diog. Laert. 1.1.29).

Q77 (PW423). [c. 590 B.C.] Not genuine.
C. Chilon of Sparta (Klearchos).
Occ. Desire for knowledge.
Q. What is best for man?
R. Know thyself.
Mode A3, Topic 3j
Delphi. Direct, Prose—Aristotle frag. 3 Rose ap. Clem. Alex. Strom. 1, 351P. Klearchos
    2.317M ap. Stob. Flor. 3.21.26 = ap. Mant. Prov. 1.43. Plut. Mor. 116c. Antisthenes
    ap. Diog. Laert. 1.1.40. Porphyry ap. Stob. loc. cit. Macr. Somn. Scip. 1.9.2. Suda
    Γ334. App. Prov. 1.81. Schol. vet. on Plato Phil. 48c.
    Pseudo-Direct, Prose (Latin)—Cic. Tusc. 1.22.52 (5.25.70). Sen. Dial. 6.11.2.
    Indirect—Cic. Fin. 5.16.44; Leg. 1.22.58, 23.61.
NP. Indirect—Apollo: Dion Chrys. 4.57.
    Testimony—Apollo: cf. Schol. on Hor. AP 219.

Comment: In view of Q105, in which Apollo tells Croesus that he must know himself to live most happily, I classify this direction as A3, unclear command. For Croesus
understood it to mean knowledge of his own identity in the sense of knowing his own
name: he was Croesus. And in truth the maxim is not easy to understand. It may mean
"Know your place in the world," "Know that you are a man," "Know your true self"
(which also can be given several meanings, including the psychoanalytic), among other
possible interpretations.

Q78 (PW494). [c. 540 B.C.] Not genuine.
C. Mnesarchos of Samos.
Occ. Commercial enterprise.
Q. On a voyage to Syria.
R. The voyage will be satisfactory and profitable; his wife is already pregnant and will
    bear a son who will excel all past and living men in beauty and wisdom and will be a
    great help to mankind for the whole of life.
Mode E2, Topic 3a (3d)
Delphi. Indirect—Iambl. Pyth. 5.
    Comment: The child born was Pythagoras. Compare Q56, 159; L10.

Q79 (PW, p. 72 ad 164). [768–550.] Not genuine.
C. Hellenes and foreigners.
Occ. Plague or famine over all the world.
Q. In what way can their misfortunes end?
R. To end their trouble the Athenians must offer pre-plowing sacrifices [proêrosia] in
    their behalf [to Demeter (Suda, Scholiasts)].
Mode A1, Topic 1b
Delphi. Indirect—Aristeides 13.105, 196, and Schol., pp. 55–56, 340 Dind. Schol. vet. on
    Aristoph. Eq. 729 [= Ps.-Eud. Viol. 333].
    Testimony—Liban. Decl. 1.180.

NP. Indirect—Apollo: *Lykurgos *ap.* Harp. 2 Dind. = *ap.* Sud. *Eι* 184 (*ap.* EM 303 = *ap.* EGud. 427 Stef. = *ap.* Cram. Anecd. Ox. 2.437). The god: Schol. on Aristoph. *Pl.* 1054.

OP. Olympia. Testimony—Phot. *Lex.* 2.107 Naber. Bekker Anecd. 1.294.

Comment: See pp. 162–163.

Aristeides 13.196 attributes this response to the *exêgêtês patrôos* of Athens, whom he defines at 13.112 as Apollon Pythios.

According to the legend, as known to Lykurgos, Abaris came to Athens as envoy from the Hyperboreans in obedience to this oracle. According to Hippostratos, cited by Harpokration, Abaris came to Athens in the third or (*v.l.*) the fifty-third Olympiad, i.e., 768 or 568 B.C. The former is more likely to be the time that the legend intended. Others, according to Harpokration, dated Abaris in the 21st Olympiad, 696 B.C; but Pindar, he adds, dated him in the time of Croesus, i.e., no later than 546, which is more in harmony with 568. Pindar does not mention Abaris in *Paean* 6, where the mutilated lines 62–72 may refer to this oracle and festival; but the visible words seem rather to indicate Delphian offerings.

Oddly PW do not give this response a number in their corpus, although they refer to it and quote sources in their comment on PW164 (= H9). They think that H9 is no more than "fresh oracular authority for the custom" of offering first-fruits to the Eleusinian goddesses. But Q79 cannot be an earlier pronouncement of H9. Q79 calls for the sacrifice of *proêrosia*, H9 for the offering of first-fruits of the harvest. Q79 is addressed to all Hellenes and, according to Lykurgos, to all mankind, since the whole world was afflicted with famine or plague or both; H9 is addressed only to the Athenians and their league. Most sources of Q79 do not specify any deity as object of worship, and only the Suda and Scholiasts indicate Demeter as recipient; H9 specifies the two goddesses, i.e., Demeter and Kore. Q79 has nothing to do with Eleusis: Demeter Proerosia is a goddess of the city.

The story is a variant of the L46 legend; there a famine came over all Hellas, and an oracle directed all Hellas to go to Aiakos and ask him to supplicate the gods, or specifically Zeus, in their behalf. So in Q79 in a time of general famine (plague, *loimos*, probably came in through iotacism), the Hellenes were directed to go to Athens for mediation.

The story is the cult myth of Demeter Proerosia in Athens. The first observance of these rites occurred when all Hellas, or the world, suffered famine, and the Delphic god told those who came to him for help that the Athenians would make offerings for them. According to Aristeides the god called Athens μητρόπολις τῶν καρπῶν. The myth thus asserts an Athenian claim to be the center of Demeter worship, alluding to the Eleusinian cult, but promoting a Demeter cult in the city.

The response appears to have been labeled Delphic from the start, although two lexicographers ascribe it to an Oracle in Elis, which should be the Zeus Oracle at Olympia.

Q80 (PW25). [c. 590 B.C.] Not genuine.

C. Pellene or Aigina.

Occ. Defeat in war with Kleisthenes of Sikyon.

Q. Should we resettle our old city or build another?

R. Take the top and you will have the middle.

Mode A3, Topic 3j

Delphi. Direct, Verse—Anaxandrides Delphos 404.1J *ap.* Prov. Bodl. 207.

NP. Direct, Verse, Incomplete—The god: Zen. 1.57. Apost. 1.97.

> *Comment:* See pp. 85, 178.

Q81 (PW26). [c. 600 B.C.] Not genuine.

C. Kleotimos for his brother Prokles, tyrant of Epidauros.

Occ. Weakening of Prokles' power.

Q. On flight and change of residence.

R. Prokles will have refuge and a change of residence where he bade the Aeginetan place the basket or where the stag casts the horn.

Mode F, Topic 3h

Delphi. Indirect—Plut. *Mor.* 403d.

> *Comment:* See pp. 66–67.

Q82 (PW27). [c. 560 B.C.] Not genuine.

C. Pythagoras, tyrant of Ephesos.

Occ. Plague and famine in Ephesos, and Pythagoras' fears for himself.

Q. Request for deliverance from troubles.

R. He should erect a temple and duly bury the dead.

Mode A1, Topic 1a (3c)

Delphi. Indirect—Baton 268.3J *ap.* Ael. frag. 48 = Sud. Π3122.

> *Comment:* See pp. 76–77.

Q83 (PW28). [c. 580 B.C.] Not genuine.

C. Sicyonians.

Occ. Famine.

Q. On a remedy.

R. They will have one if Dipoinis and Skyllis finish the images of gods.

Mode A1, Topic 1b

Delphi. Indirect—Pliny *NH* 36.4.10.

Q84 (PW552). [700–500?] Not genuine.

C. Syracusans.

Occ. Plague.

Q. Not stated.

R. They must slaughter the impious man for the apotropaic gods.

Mode A3, Topic 1c

Delphi. Indirect—Dositheos 4.401M *ap.* Plut. *Mor.* 310b.

> *Comment:* Kyanippos of Syracuse made no sacrifices to Dionysos. The angry god made him drunk, and he raped his daughter Kyane. Plague came upon the city, and the

Pythian Apollo gave the Syracusans this command. No one understood the response except Kyane; she killed her father and then herself. Kyanippos and Kyane are mythical characters; the Syracusan spring Kyane enters as a nymph into the myth of Hades and Persephone as told by Ovid *Met.* 5.409–437, 464–470; Diod. 5.4.2. The only reason for classifying Q84 as Q is that the scene is given as Syracuse, and Syracusans are the consultants.

Q85 (PW327). [c. 560 B.C.] Not genuine.
C. Conspirators against Phalaris.
Occ. Arrest and torture of the friends Chariton and Melanippos and their endurance under torture.
Q. How can we attack Phalaris?
R. Spare Phalaris now. Blessed are Chariton and Melanippos, guides of divine friendship for mortal men.
Mode D1 (C1), Topic 3j (3f)
Delphi. Direct, Verse (elegiac)—Heracl. Pont. 2.200M = Ath. 13.602ab. Oinomaos *ap.* Eus. *PE* 5.35, p. 233b. Ael. *VH* 2.4.
    Comment: See p. 172.

Q86 (PW495). [c. 555 B.C.] Not genuine.
C. Citizens of Agrigentum.
Occ. Phalaris' tyranny.
Q. Not stated.
R. Phalaris will fall from power when they become better, more harmonious, and cooperative.
Mode A1, Topic 3e (2a)
NP. Indirect—Apollo: Iambl. *Pyth.* 221.
    Comment: The citizens became harmonious through Pythagoras' teachings, so that they then overthrew the tyrant.

Q87 (PW30). [659 or c. 570 B.C.] Not genuine.
C. Phigaleian exiles.
Occ. Loss of Phigalia to Sparta.
Q. On return to their country.
R. They will not succeed in returning if they try by themselves; but if they should enlist a hundred picked men from Oresthasion, they will succeed in returning, when those men die in battle.
Mode F (A1), Topic 3g (2e)
Delphi. Indirect—Paus. 8.39.4.
    Comment: The Oresthasians were willing to die in battle for the return of the Phigaleians. It may be that Oresthasians died as allies of the Arcadians against the Spartans; but the oracle must be *post eventum.* It is probable that Pausanias found it in Ariaithos' Arcadian history.

Q88 (PW31). [c. 560 B.C.] Not genuine.

C. Spartans.

Occ. Contemplated acquisition of Arcadia.

Q. Do you give us Arcadia? (Dion Chrysostomos).

R. Arcadia is too big for you to have; many acorn-eating Arcadians will keep you from taking it. But I do not deny you: I will grant you Tegea to dance in and to measure its plain with cord.

Mode E3 (C1), Topic 3i (2e)

Delphi. Direct, Verse—Herod. 1.66.2. Lepidus 838.2J ap. Steph. Byz. 610 Mein. Anth. Pal. 14.76. Incomplete—Paus. 8.1.6 (3.7.3). Schol. on Aesch. Prom. 450.
Testimony—Philostr. Vit. Soph. 1.5.575.

NP. Direct, Verse—The god: Schol. on Aristeides 46.172, p. 561 Dind. Eust. Il. 2.607, p. 301. Oracle: Diod. 9.36.2. Incomplete—The god: Dion Chrys. 17.16. Oracle: Polyainos Strat. 1.8. Alex. Rhet. Schem. 8.446 Walz. Schol. vet. on Lyk. 482. Tzetzes on Lyk. 479.

Comment: See pp. 140, 179.

Q89 (PW32). [c. 550 B.C.] Not genuine.

C. Spartans.

Occ. Defeats in the Tegean War.

Q. What gods should they propitiate to defeat the Tegeans in the war?

R. They should bring in the bones of Orestes, Agamemnon's son.

Mode A1, Topic 1a

Delphi. Indirect—Herod. 1.67.2.

NP. Indirect—Apollo: Aen. Gaz. Theophr. p. 60 Colonna.
Testimony—Oracle: Paus. 3.11.10. Pliny NH 7.16.74.
Comment: See pp. 75, 124.

Q90 (PW33). [c. 550 B.C.] Not genuine.

C. Spartans.

Occ. Failure to find Orestes' bones.

Q. In what place does Orestes lie?

R. In Tegea where two winds blow under mighty force, and blow lies on blow and woe on woe, is the grave of Agamemnon's son; if you remove him you will be defender [epitarrothos?] of Tegea.

Mode D2 (A1), Topic 3h (2e, 3c)

Delphi. Direct, Verse—Herod. 1.67.4. Diod. 9.36.3. Lepidus 838.2J ap. Steph. Byz. 610 Mein. Anth. Pal. 14.78.
Testimony—Paus. 3.3.6.

NP. Direct, Verse—The god: Schol. on Aristeides 46.172, pp. 561–562 Dind. Incomplete —Oracle: Chor. Gaz. 37.4. Suda A2733. Bekk. Anecd. 1.408.
Indirect—Apollo: Aen. Gaz. Theophr. p. 60 Colonna.

Comment: See pp. 75, 81, 173, 180, 186. On the Tegean oracles, Q88–90, see pp. 93, 123–124; Crahay 1956; 153–156.

Q91 (PW34). [550–500?] Not genuine.

C. Spartans.

Occ. and Q. Not stated.

R. They should bring the body of Tisamenos from Helike to Sparta.

Mode A1, Topic 1a

Delphi. Testimony—Paus. 7.1.8.

> *Comment:* See p. 75.

Q92 (PW35–36). [c. 550 B.C.] Not genuine.

C. Glaukos Epikydes' son of Sparta.

Occ. Request of a Milesian's sons that Glaukos return a deposit of silver that their father had left with him.

Q. (A) May I by taking oath seize the silver?

R. (A) For the moment it is more advantageous to take oath and seize the money; so swear, since death awaits the oath-keeper too. But Horkos' nameless son follows quickly after without hands and feet, until he destroys the whole family and house. An oath-keeper's family fares better afterward.

Mode A1 (D1), Topic 3e (1d, 3f)

Delphi. Direct, Verse—Herod. 6.86c.2. Anth. Pal. 14.91. Incomplete—Paus. 8.7.8 (2.18.2). Clem. Alex. *Strom.* 6, 749P. Schol. vet. on Plato *Rep.* 363d. Schol. vet. on Juv. 13.199. Eust. *Il.* 3.278, pp. 414–415. Apost.-Arsen. 2.84d. Indirect—Juv. 13.200–202.

NP. Direct, Verse, Incomplete—Apollo: Dion. Chrys. 74.15.

Q. (B) Forgive me for my words.

R. (B) To tempt the god is the same as the deed.

(Mode D1, Topic 3j)

Delphi. Indirect—Herod. 6.86c.2.

> *Comment:* See pp. 113, 118–119, 121, 179, 180, 212; Crahay 1956: 97–99.

Q93 (PW49). [c. 560 B.C.] Not genuine.

C. Phocaeans.

Occ. and Q. Not stated.

R. They should found Kyrnos.

Mode A3, Topic 1a

Delphi. Indirect—Herod. 1.167.4 (165.1).

> *Comment:* See p. 68; Crahay 1956: 138–140.

Q94 (PW401). [c. 550 B.C.] Not genuine.

C. Boeotians and Megarians.

Occ. Pestilence (Pompeius Trogus).

Q. Not stated.

R. In the Pontic land they should found a city [sacred to Herakles (Pompeius Trogus)] around the olive tree which grows on the tomb of the city-holding hero [Idmon].

Mode A1, Topic 3h (2c)

Delphi. Indirect—Pomp. Trog./Justin 16.3.4. Schol. Par. on Apollon. *Arg.* 2.845.

NP. Indirect—Apollo: *Apollon. *Arg.* 2.846–849. Schol. vet. on Apollon. *Arg.* 2.845, 848.
   Comment: See pp. 72, 122.

PW indicate Herodoros and Promathidas as sources of the scholia on Apollonios
cited under *NP* above. It is not clear, however, that the entire scholia are drawn from
these historians. The Scholiast on 2.845 limits his citation of Promathidas to the statement
that the Herakleots, not knowing that the occupant of the tomb was Idmon, called him
Agamestor, a native hero. The Scholiast on 2.848 limits his citation of Herodoros to his
statement that the tomb was in the agora. All that the scholia say about Q94 could easily
be paraphrase of *Arg.* 846–849; they add nothing to what Apollonios tells us.

No doubt the response belongs to the foundation legend of Herakleia Pontike, and
it is possible that Promathidas mentioned it. It is likely that both he and Apollonios took
their information from Ephoros, whom the Scholiast on 845 cites with anonymous
authorities for an account of the founding of Herakleia (Ephoros 70.44aJ). Pompeius
Trogus may have drawn his account from another source, since he does not mention
Megarians, and his indirect quotation contains no more than a direction to found the city;
furthermore in his version the Boeotians had to be told a second time (Q95).

It is probable that the response was attributed to the Delphic Apollo from the outset.
It is clearly a pseudo-historical response, devised after the identification of Agamestor
with Idmon. Apparently the Herakleots did not accept this identification; at this tomb
they worshiped Agamestor as a native hero. The story arose from an attempt of others to
identify the hero with the Argonaut Idmon; it was part of a widespread effort to attach
episodes of the Argonautic legend to actual places on the Euxine coasts. On both Idmon
and Agamestor as Hellenic forms of a pre-Hellenic Bithynian deity see Fontenrose 1959:
480–481.

Q95 (PW402). [c. 550 B.C.] Not genuine.
C. Boeotians.
Occ. Defeats in war with Phocians.
Q. Not stated.
R. The remedy will be the same for the war as for the pestilence [namely, to found the
   colony ordered in Q94].
Mode E1, Topic 2c
Delphi. Indirect—Pomp. Trog./Justin 16.3.6.
   Comment: See Q94, p. 122.

Q96 (PW51). [687 B.C.] Not genuine.
C. Lydians.
Occ. Gyges' usurpation.
Q. Should Gyges be king of Lydia?
R. Gyges should be king, but punishment for the Herakleidai will come upon Gyges'
   fifth descendant.
Mode A1 (E2), Topic 2a (3f)
Delphi. Indirect—Herod. 1.13.2 (91.1–3). Nic. Dam. 10J.
   Comment: See pp. 122, 220; Crahay 1956: 189–191.

Q97 (PW244). [c. 680 B.C.] Not genuine.

C. King Gyges of Lydia.

Occ. Attainment of wealth and power.

Q. Is any mortal happier than he is?

R. Aglaos of Psophis is happier.

Mode D1, Topic 3g

Delphi. Indirect—Pliny NH 7.46.151.

   Testimony—*Val. Max. 7.1.2.

NP. Indirect—The god: Musonius ap. Stob. Flor. 56.18.

Q98 (PW50). [612/11.] Not genuine.

C. Envoys of King Alyattes of Lydia.

Occ. Alyattes' malignant illness.

Q. On his illness.

R. Apollo will not answer until Alyattes restores the temple of Athena which he burned
   at Assesos in Milesia.

Mode A1 (C1), Topic 1a

Delphi. Indirect—Herod. 1.19.3.

   Comment: At 1.22.4 Herodotos says that Alyattes built two temples for Athena
Assesia instead of one. Chorikios of Gaza (2.77), who mentions no oracle, saying only
that Alyattes learned the cause of his illness, adds τῷ μὲν (νεῷ) τὸ πλημμέλημα λύων, τῷ
δὲ θεραπεύων τὸ νόσημα . . . If we put this together with Herodotos' account, we
perceive that Alyattes had to build one temple in order to receive a response on his
sickness, and that in this response he was told to build another temple to Athena. This
accounts for the two temples. See Crahay 1956: 191–193.

Q99 (PW52). [c. 550 B.C.] Not genuine.

C. Envoys of King Croesus of Lydia.

Occ. Croesus' design of testing the Oracles with a view to further inquiries.

Q. What is King Croesus of Lydia doing now?

R. I know the numbers of the sands and dimensions of the sea; I hear the dumb and the
   man who does not speak. I smell a hard-shelled tortoise boiled with lamb meat in a
   bronze pot, which has a bronze bottom and a bronze lid.

Mode D2, Topic 3h (3j)

Delphi. Direct, Verse—Herod. 1.47.3 (6.125.2). Suda K2500. [CIG 1724, reported
by Cyriacus of Ancona as an inscription seen at Delphi in fifteenth century]. Incomplete—Oinomaos ap. Eus. PE 5.21, p. 212c; 34, p. 230b (5.20, p. 211d). Philostr.
Vit. Soph. 1.481. Origen Cels. 2.9, p. 393. Eus. Contra Hier. 14. Elias Prol. 25, p. 72
PACA 18.1. Schol. vet. on Aristoph. Ach. 3. Schol. on Lucian Zeus Tr. 30.

Direct, Prose—Malalas p. 155. Kedr. p. 240.

Pseudo-Direct, Prose (Latin)—Tert. Or. 17.

Indirect—Plut. Mor. 512e. Philostr. Apollon. 6.11, p. 222. Tert. Apol. 22.10. Them. Or.
7.97c. Liban. Or. 11.169.

Testimony—Xen. *Cyr.* 7.2.17. Parian Marble A41. Lucian *Zeus Cat.* 14; *Zeus Tr.* 30; *Bis acc.* 1. Max. Tyr. 3.1b, 29.7a (cf. 11.6cd). Them. *Or.* 19.227d.

NP. Direct, Verse, Incomplete—Apollo: Aristeides 49.377. Porph. *Plot.* 22. John Chrys. *S. Bab.* 15, p. 555 Migne 50.

>   *Comment:* See pp. 111, 113, 114, 212.

Q100 (PW53). [c. 548 B.C.] Not genuine.

C. Envoys of King Croesus of Lydia.

Occ. Croesus' projected war on the Persians.

Q. Should I make war on the Persians? And with what army should I ally myself?

R. If you make war on the Persians [if you cross the Halys (verse form)], you will destroy a great realm. Find the strongest Hellenes and ally yourself with them (Herodotos).

Mode E3 (A1), Topic 2e

Delphi. Direct, Verse—Oinomaos *ap.* Eus. *PE* 5.20, p. 212b; 21, p. 212d. Max. Tyr. 5.2a, 11.2. Theodor. *Gr. aff. cur.* 10.139. Malalas p. 155. Kedr. pp. 241, 251. Suda *K*2500, *Λ*673. Thomas Mag., Schol. on Eur. *Or.* 165 = Schol. on Nic. Dam. 68J, Fontenrose 1942a: 222.

>   Indirect—*Herod. 1.53.3, 69.2, 91.4 (46.3, 75.2, 86.1). Lucian *Zeus Cat.* 14; *Zeus Tr.* 20 (43).

>   Testimony—Parian Marble A42. Nic. Dam. 68.13J. Dion Chrys. 10.26. Lucian *Alex.* 48; *Philopatris* 5; *Charon* 11. Eust. *Il.* 2.865, p. 366.

NP. Direct, Verse—Apollo: John Chrys. *S. Bab.* 16, p. 557 Migne 50. Nonnos Abbas 1.96, p. 1036 Migne 36. Kosmas p. 433 Migne 38. Elias *Pro. Cat.* 230a, p. 126 *PACA* 18.1. The god: Schol. vet. on Soph. *Trach.* 1. Oracle: Aristotle *Rhet.* 1407a. Diod. 9.31.1.

>   Pseudo-Direct, Verse (Latin)—Apollo: Cic. *Div.* 2.56.115. Oracle: Chalcid. *Tim.* 167.

>   Testimony—Apollo: Clem. Alex. *Protr.* 38P. David *Comm. Plat.* p. 27b Br.

>   *Comment:* See pp. 67, 111, 112, 113–114, 123.

Q101 (PW54). [c. 548 B.C.] Not genuine.

C. Envoys of King Croesus of Lydia.

Occ. Desire to know the future of his reign.

Q. Will my monarchy last long?

R. When a mule becomes king of the Medes, then flee to the Hermos; don't stay and don't be ashamed to be a coward.

Mode B (C1), Topic 3h (2a, 3e)

Delphi. Direct, Verse—Herod. 1.55.2 (91.5). Dion Chrys. 13.7. Incomplete—Oinomaos *ap.* Eus. *PE* 5.24, p. 218b (21, p. 213ab).

>   Indirect—Them. *Or.* 19.226d.

NP. Direct, Verse—Apollo: Schol. vet. on Plato *Rep.* 566c. Oracle: Diod. 9.31.2. Anth. Pal. 14.112. Incomplete—Oracle: Plato *Rep.* 566c. Cf. Ath. 14.630d (verse 3 quoted, but not as an oracular utterance).

>   Testimony—Oracle: Tzetzes on Hes. *OD* 45, p. 22 Heins.

>   *Comment:* See pp. 63–64, 81, 113, 114, 125, 139, 169, 179, 185.

Q102 (PW 55). [c. 550 B.C.] Not genuine.

C. Envoys of King Croesus of Lydia.

Occ. His son's dumbness.

Q. How can my son speak? (Diodoros).

R. Foolish King Croesus, do not wish to hear your son speaking in your halls. It is much better that he do not; for he will speak first on an unlucky day.

Mode C1 (E2), Topic 3h

Delphi. Direct, Verse—Herod. 1.85.2. Diod. 9.33.2. Anth. Pal. 14.79.

    Comment: See pp. 113, 114, 139, 178, 179, 182, 186.

Q103 (PW 56). [546 B.C.] Not genuine.

C. Envoys of Croesus.

Occ. Persians' defeat and capture of Croesus.

Q. Is Apollo not ashamed of having encouraged Croesus with his oracles to make war on the Persians in the belief that he would destroy Cyrus' power, from which enterprise he shall have Croesus' chains as first-fruits? And is it the custom of Hellenic gods to be unthankful?

R. Not even deity can escape destiny. Croesus has expiated a misdeed of his ancestor five generations back, who, serving a woman's guile, killed his lord and took a throne that was not his. Although Apollo wanted the fall of Sardis to happen under Croesus' sons and not in Croesus' reign, he could not persuade the Moirai; the best that he could do was to persuade them to postpone the fall of Sardis for three years. Then Apollo saved Croesus from burning. Croesus does not rightly blame the Oracle. When Apollo predicted that if Croesus made war on the Persians he would destroy a great realm he should have sent to ask whether Apollo meant Cyrus' realm or his own. Since Croesus did not understand the response properly, he must blame himself. Again he did not understand what Apollo said about a mule: Cyrus was the mule, being child of a superior Median mother and an inferior Persian father.

Mode D2, Topic 3h (2a, 2c, 3f)

Delphi. Direct, Prose—Herod. 1.91. Incomplete—Liban. Or. 25.7. Anth. Pal. 14.80.

    Testimony—Nic. Dam. 68.13J. Lucian Alex. 48.

    Comment: See pp. 114–115. On the Croesus oracles, Q99–103, see pp. 111–115; Crahay 1956; 182–202. For unspecific allusion to them see Cic. Div. 1.19.37.

Q104 (PW 249). [c. 575 B.C.?] Not genuine.

C. Croesus' envoys.

Q. (A) What should he do to have sons?

R. (A) None.

Q. (B) What should he do to have sons?

R. (B) He will have sons.

Mode E2, Topic 3a

Delphi. Indirect—Xen. Cyr. 7.2.19.

Q105 (PW 250). [c. 550 B.C.] Not genuine.

C. Croesus' envoys.

Occ. His sons' misfortunes.

Q. What should I do to live the rest of my life most happily?

R. If you know yourself you will live most happily.

Mode A3, Topic 3j

Delphi. Direct, Verse—Xen. *Cyr.* 7.2.20 (25).

    Comment: Cf. Q77, the response "Know thyself." No doubt Xenophon invented Q104 and Q105 for his Cyrus romance; they surely do not belong to the Croesus legend. They might be classified as Fictional; but they concern an historical person in a work that purports to be historical.

Q106 (PW57). [c. 550 B.C.] Not genuine.

C. Spartans.

Occ. Contemplated gilding of the face of Apollo's image at Amyklai.

Q. From whom should they buy gold?

R. They should go to Croesus the Lydian and buy gold from him.

Mode A1, Topic 3g

Delphi. Indirect—Theopompos *Phil.* 189GH.

    Comment: This is a simple direction in response to a religious question. But it is very unlikely that the Spartans would have to go to Delphi to find out that they should buy gold from Croesus. Herodotos does not mention this response.

Q107 (PW58). [c. 550 B.C.] Not genuine.

C. Delphians.

Occ. Plague after execution of Aesop.

Q. On deliverance.

R. The plague will not cease until they propitiate Aesop.

Mode A1, Topic 1a

Delphi. Indirect—*Vita Aesopi* W 142. Ox. Pap. 1800.2.55–58. Zen. 1.47.

    Testimony—*Herod. 2.134.4.

OP. Zeus. Indirect—*Vita Aesopi* G 142.

    Comment: See Fontenrose 1969a: 111–113; Crahay 1956: 84–85; Wiechers 1961.

Q108 (PW59). [c. 575 B.C.] Not genuine.

C. Aesop.

Occ. and Q. Not stated.

R. He should tell amusing tales.

Mode A1, Topic 3d

Delphi. Testimony—Avianus *Fab. praef.*

    Comment: For responses that started men upon their careers see Q208, 252.

Q109 (PW60). [c. 560 B.C.] Not genuine.

C. Dolonkoi of Thrace (or Apsinthians—Scholiast).

Occ. Difficult war with Apsinthians (or Dolonkoi).

Q. How can we escape from our difficulties? (Scholiast).

R. Take to your country as founder [*oikistês*] the man who first invites you to the hospitality of his house as you go from the temple.

Mode B, Topic 3h (2c)

Delphi. Direct, Prose—Schol. on Aristeides 46.168, p. 551 Dind.

Indirect—*Herod. 6.34.2.

    Comment: See p. 220, Q111.

Q110 (PW61). [c. 560 B.C.] Not genuine.

C. Miltiades the Elder (or Apsinthians—Scholiast).

Occ. The Dolonkoi's (or Apsinthians') request that in accordance with Q109 Miltiades become their *oikistês*.

Q. Should he do what the Dolonkoi ask him? [Is Miltiades the man you mean? (Scholiast).]

R. He should do so. [The god means Miltiades (Scholiast).]

Mode A1, Topic 2c

Delphi. Indirect—Schol. on Aristeides 46.168, p. 551 Dind.

Testimony—*Herod. 6.35.3-36.1.

    Comment: See Q111. On Q109-110 see Crahay 1956: 263-266.

Q111 (PW62). c. 560 B.C.

C. Athenians.

Occ. Plan to colonize Thracian Chersonese.

Q. Who is the best man to make leader?

R. They should appoint Miltiades commander; if they do so their enterprise will succeed.

Mode A1, Topic 2c

Delphi. Indirect—Nepos 1.3.

    Comment: This is an alternative to Q109-110 and, although Nepos is our only authority, may be accepted as authentic. It is clear and simple in mode, topic, and expression; the only reservation may be that Nepos' report is not exact, and that originally this was a sanction of an Athenian project of founding a colony in the Chersonese under Miltiades. Herodotos reports a foundation legend which includes an oracle with the theme of the first-met (Q109). His story is improbable, since it is unlikely that the Thracians would have traveled all the way from Delphi to Athens before anyone invited them into his house (and that the Pythia knew that this would happen). In the legend Q110 reflects Q111.

Q112 (PW63). [c. 545 B.C.] Not genuine.

C. Cnidians.

Occ. Continued injuries to workmen who were cutting through the Cnidian isthmus.

Q. On the cause.

R. Do not fortify or dig through the isthmus; Zeus would have made it an island if he
had wanted to.

Mode C1 (D1), Topic 2e (3j)

Delphi. Direct, Verse (iambic trimeter)—Herod. 1.174.5. Oinomaos *ap.* Eus. *PE* 5.26,
p. 220c. Anth. Pal. 14.81.

Testimony—Paus. 2.1.5.

Comment: See Crahay 1956: 327–328.

Parke (1956: 141) thinks the story that Herodotos tells credible, and finds it significant that he heard it from the Cnidians, adding, "The oracle contained nothing for
Delphi to record with pride, . . ." But surely there is nothing in this response to discredit
Delphi: why should Apollo not express Zeus's will that Knidos remain a peninsula? It
seems somewhat more discreditable to Knidos.

The feature of repeated injuries to the workmen arouses suspicion, and so does that
of sending to Delphi on this matter. Time was short; Harpagos was approaching in his
conquest of the coast. It is true that the Cnidians themselves apparently said that they
went to Delphi, although Didyma was close, a short voyage by sea up the coast. The
reason is surely because Didyma was not in operation between 494 and 334; and it was in
this period that Herodotos heard the story from the Cnidians. Around 450 they had
forgotten Didyma. But the story remains suspicious; and Didyma surely did not make
this pronouncement either.

The story was meant to explain the visible cuttings of the projected canal—Harpagos'
arrival may have stopped work on it; or perhaps the task was too big—and the Cnidians'
failure to resist the Persians. It is therefore a *post eventum* oracle, an "excuse for non-resis-
tance" (How and Wells 1912: 1.134). The prohibition of a canal could be an acceptable
answer to an inquiry whether a canal should be dug; but the gnomic content is a dubious
feature, and so is the expression in iambic trimeter. It may be a quotation from an iambic
poet's composition.

Q113 (PW64). [535–530.] Not genuine.

C. Agyllaioi.

Occ. Strange afflictions of men and beasts that passed the stoned Phocaeans' grave.

Q. How to expiate their guilt.

R. They should make sacrifices to the dead Phocaeans and hold games for them.

Mode A1, Topic 1a

Delphi. Indirect—Herod. 1.167.2.

Comment: See Fontenrose 1968: 97–98. Crahay (1956: 80–81) thinks that this response
can be genuine.

Q114 (PW65). [c. 520 B.C.] Not genuine.

C. Siphnians.

Occ. A time of prosperity.

Q. Can the present prosperity last?

R. When there are white *prytaneia* and a white agora in Siphnos, then there should be an observant man to notice a wooden company and a red herald.

Mode C2 (F), Topic 3h

Delphi. Direct, Verse—Herod. 3.57.4. Anth. Pal. 14.82.

> *Comment:* See pp. 65, 169; Crahay 1956: 258–260.

If the response clearly indicated these events as signs of an end of prosperity, the mode would have to be classified as F. As the response is expressed it must be taken as an unclear warning, C2.

Q115 (PW66). c. 520 B.C.

C. Siphnians.

Occ. and Q. Not stated.

R. They should offer at Delphi a tithe of the proceeds from the mines.

Mode A1, Topic 1b

Delphi. Indirect—Paus. 10.11.2.

> Testimony—Ael. frag. 345 *ap.* Sud. Σ511.

> *Comment:* Consequently the Siphnians built their treasury at Delphi as depository of the tithe.

Q116 (PW67). [c. 525 B.C.] Not genuine.

C. Envoys of Polykrates, tyrant of Samos.

Occ. (1) Celebration of Pythia and Delia at the same time on Delos (Epicurus). (2) Holding an agonistic festival after dedicating Reneia to the Delian Apollo (Zenobios).

Q. (1) Am I making the sacrifices at the appointed time? (2) Shall I call the games Pythia or Delia?

R. They are both Pythia and Delia for you.

Mode D2, Topic 1a (3j)

Delphi. Direct, Verse (lyric)—Epicurus *ap.* Phot. *Lex.* 2.121 Nab. = *ap.* Sud. Π3128 = *ap.* Apost. 15.9. Zen. 6.15. Suda T175.

> *Comment:* This is a proverb made into a cryptic forecast of Polykrates' death. Polykrates could not have founded the Delia festival, which was the same as the Apollonia, known to the poet of the Homeric Hymn to Apollo (3.146–164); see Roussel 1925: 27; Laidlaw 1933: 45–49. There is no record of a Pythian festival on Delos.

Q117 (PW68). [c. 510 B.C.] Not genuine.

C. Phocians.

Occ. Thessalian invasion.

Q. Let us escape the approaching danger.

R. I shall match mortal and immortal in battle; I shall give victory to both, but more to the mortal.

Mode E3, Topic 2e

Delphi. Direct, Verse—Paus. 10.1.4 (10).

> *Comment:* The Thessalians' watchword was "Athena," the Phocians' was "Phokos," ancestral hero. The Phocians won the final victory after a Thessalian success.

Q118 (PW69). [c. 550 B.C.] Not genuine.
C. Cyrenaeans.
Occ. Accession of a crippled king.
Q. In what way can they best organize the state?
R. They should bring a lawgiver from Mantineia.
Mode A1, Topic 2b
Delphi. Indirect—Herod. 4.161.2.
   Testimony—Hermippos *ap.* Heracl. Lemb. *Epit. Herm.*, Ox. Pap. 1367.19–39.
   Comment: See p. 121.

Q119 (PW70). [c. 530 B.C.] Not genuine.
C. King Arkesilaos III of Cyrene.
Occ. Gathering of an army in Samos to restore him to Cyrene.
Q. On his return.
R. Apollo grants the kingship of Cyrene to eight generations of Battiads, to four kings
   named Battos and to four named Arkesilaos. Do not attempt more than that. Be calm
   when you return. If you should find the oven full of jars, do not bake them, but send
   them on their way. But if you bake them, avoid the seagirt land; otherwise you and
   the prize bull will die together.
Mode C2 (E2), Topic 3h (2a)
Delphi. Direct, Prose—Herod. 4.163.2–3.
   Comment: See pp. 61, 207. On Q118–119 see Crahay 1956: 122–126.

Q120. [c. 550 B.C.] Not genuine.
C. King Arkesilaos II of Cyrene.
Occ. Misfortunes.
Q. Not stated.
R. The gods are angry. The later kings do not rule like the first Battos. He was adequate
   to the title of king and ruled popularly, especially keeping up the worship of the gods.
   But his successors rule ever more tyranically. They appropriate the public funds and
   neglect reverence for the gods.
Mode D1, Topic 2a (1b)
Delphi. Indirect—Diod. 8.30.1.
   Comment: This seems to be an alternative to Q119. On Q118–120 see pp. 120–123.

Q121 (PW72). [c. 510 B.C.] Not genuine.
C. Dorieus of Sparta.
Occ. Plan to found a colony of Spartans in Sicily.
Q. Will he take the land against which he is setting forth?
R. He will take it.
Mode E2, Topic 2c
Delphi. Indirect—Herod. 5.43.
   Comment: See p. 158; Crahay 1956: 142–145.

Q122 (PW73). [Before 510 B.C.] Not genuine.

C. Amyris and other envoys of Sybaris.

Occ. Concern for the city's future.

Q. Until when shall we be prosperous?

R. You will continue to feast if you continue to honor the gods, but when you reverence a mortal before a god, then war and civil strife will come upon you.

Mode F (A1), Topic 3h (1b, 2e)

Delphi. Direct, Verse—Timaios 566.50J ap. Ath. 12.520ab.

 Indirect—Suda A1684. Eust. Il. 2.595, p. 298. Diogen. 3.26, ms. C. Apost. 2.60.

NP. Direct, Verse—Oracle: Steph. Byz. 589 Mein.

   Comment: See pp. 76, 170, 172.

Q123 (PW74). [515–510]. Not genuine.

C. Sybarites.

Occ. A spring of blood gushing forth in Hera's temple after their killing of a citharode who was suppliant at Hera's altar.

Q. Not stated.

R. Leave my tripods; much blood dripping from your hands keeps you from my temple. I shall give you no response. You killed the Muses' servant at Hera's altars and did not avoid the gods' punishment. Evildoers and their children soon meet implacable justice, and woe upon woe comes upon their houses.

Mode C1 (D1), Topic 3f (1d)

Delphi. Direct, Verse—Ael. VH 3.43.

   Comment: See pp. 76, 77. Cf. Q92 for the concluding statement.

Q124 (PW79). c. 510 B.C.

C. All Spartans.

Occ. Desire to end Peisistratid tyranny; Kleisthenes induced the Pythia to give this response to all Spartan consultants, whatever their question.

Q. Any Spartan question.

R. Free Athens.

Mode A1, Topic 2e

Delphi. Direct, Prose—Nonnos Abbas 3.3, p. 1060 Migne 36. Kosmas p. 561 (567) Migne 38.

 Indirect—*Herod. 5.63.1, 6.123.2 (5.66.1, 90.1, 91.2). Aristotle Ath. Pol. 19.2, 4 = Schol. vet. on Aristoph. Lys. 1153. Plut. Mor. 860d. Schol. on Aristeides 13.120, p. 118 Dind.

   Comment: See pp. 121, 239; Crahay 1956: 165, 280–289.

   Crahay believes that Kleisthenes did not bribe the Pythia to give this response to all Spartan consultants, as the Spartans later accused him of doing. He and his family moved more subtly. They persuaded the Delphians to take an anti-tyrannical stand, circulating a new kind of political literature, "le pamphlet oraculaire," which showed how the gods through oracles had opposed despots and tyrants.

The direct-prose form of Nonnos Abbas and Kosmas is probably based on the indirect form of Herodotos and Aristotle.

Q125 (PW80). 510/9.
C. Athenians under Kleisthenes.
Occ. Need of eponyms for the ten tribes of the new constitution.
Q. Out of a hundred names presented the Pythia should select ten.
R. Name the tribes Erechtheis, Kekropis, Aigeis, Pandionis, Athamantis, Antiochis, Leontis, Oineis, Hippothontis, Aiantis.
Mode A1, Topic 2b
Delphi. Testimony—Aristotle Ath. Pol. 21.6. Aristeides 13.192, 46.215, and Schol. on 13.192, p. 331 Dind. Paus. 10.10.1. Poll. Onom. 8.110.
    Comment: See pp. 222, 226.

Q126 (PW75). [c. 530 B.C.] Not genuine.
C. Crotoniates.
Occ. Pestilence and civil strife after the forces of Croton, Metapontum, and Sybaris killed fifty suppliant youths at Athena's image and altar in Siris.
Q. Not stated.
R. The evil will cease when they placate Athena's offended deity and the souls of the murdered men.
Mode A1, Topic 1a
Delphi. Indirect—Pomp. Trog./Justin 20.2.6.
    Comment: See p. 76. Cf. Q122, 123.

Q127 (PW76). [c. 580 B.C.] Not genuine.
C. Crotoniates.
Occ. War with Locri.
Q. They wanted means of victory and a happy outcome.
R. When they vanquish the enemy with vows, then they will do so with arms.
Mode F, Topic 1b (2e)
Delphi. Indirect—Pomp. Trog./Justin 20.3.2.
    Comment: See p. 79.
    Croton vowed a tenth of the spoils, but the Locrians vowed a ninth and won the battle.

Q128 (PW77). [c. 580 B.C.] Not genuine.
C. Leonymos of Croton.
Occ. Malignant wound received in battle with Locrians.
Q. Not stated.
R. He should go to the island of Leuke, where Aias will appear to him and heal his wound.
Mode A1 (E2), Topic 3e (3g)

Delphi. Indirect—Paus. 3.19.12.

NP. Testimony—Oracle: *Conon 18.

    Comment: See pp. 78–79, Q129.

Q129 (PW78). [c. 580 B.C.] Not genuine.

C. Phormion of Croton.

Occ. Malignant wound received at Sagra.

Q. Not stated.

R. He should go to Lakedaimon, where the first man who invites him to dinner will be his physician.

Mode F (A1), Topic 3g (3e, 3h)

NP. Indirect—Oracle: Theopompos 352 GH *ap.* Sud. Φ604.

    Comment: See p. 79. On the incurable wound see Q128; L34, 120.

Q130 (PW81). [After 506 B.C.] Not genuine.

C. Thebans.

Occ. Defeat from Athenians at the Euripos.

Q. How to punish Athenians.

R. They will not have vengeance from themselves, but they should refer it to the many-voiced and ask the nearest.

Mode A3 (E2), Topic 2e (2b, 3g)

Delphi. Indirect—Herod. 5.79.1.

    Comment: See p. 71; Crahay 1956: 272–273.

Q131 (PW82). [c. 505 B.C.] Not genuine.

C. Athenians.

Occ. Contemplated war on Aigina because of Aeginetan raids on their coast.

Q. Not stated.

R. They should delay the war for thirty years and start it in the thirty-first after assigning a temenos to Aiakos; and they will be victorious. But if they attack right away, they will eventually subdue Aigina, and will suffer and do much before success.

Mode A1 (C1, E2), Topic 1a (2e)

Delphi. Indirect—Herod. 5.89.2.

    Comment: See Crahay 1956: 274–276.

Q132 (PW83). [Before 600 B.C.] Not genuine.

C. Pelasgians of Lemnos.

Occ. Barrenness of land, women, and flocks, with consequent famine.

Q. Request for deliverance from present ills.

R. They should pay the Athenians whatever penalty they demand of them.

Mode A1, Topic 2d

Delphi. Indirect—Herod. 6.139.2. Schol. on Aristeides 13.111, p. 79 Dind.

NP. Indirect—Apollo: Chor. Gaz. 17.85.

Comment: See Crahay 1956: 268–270.

The Scholiast does not mention Delphi or Apollo, but cites Herodotos, and therefore recognizes the Delphic Apollo as the speaker. No doubt Chorikios also knew this response from Herodotos.

Q132 could be considered Legendary. The time when the Pelasgians carried off Athenian women from Brauron and afterwards killed them and their children is set in the indefinite past, long before 510–500, in which decade the Athenian conquest of Lemnos took place. Yet the story probably does not contemplate an interval of more than 300 years from the crime until fulfillment of the condition which the Pelasgians imposed before they would grant the Athenians' demand (that they surrender the island); but probably intends a shorter time by "very many years after this." The oracle is connected with an historical event; it is the actual conquest that inspired invention of it. Moreover Brauron was probably not Athenian before 800.

The narrative shows the pattern of offended deity, Artemis in this instance; see pp. 76–77. But the story is peculiar in that the Pelasgians did not carry out the oracle's direction to pay the Athenians whatever penalty they asked; they put a condition on fulfillment—that whenever the Athenians should sail in one day from Athens to Lemnos before a north wind they would yield the island to them—a seeming *adynaton*; but Miltiades sailed from the Athenian Chersonese (see Q109–110) to Lemnos in a single day. In spite of the Lemnians' not really doing what the oracle demanded, the famine apparently came to an end.

Q133 (PW572). [c. 500 B.C.] Not genuine.
C. Athenians.
Occ. Plague or crop failure following upon murder of a Metragyrtes.
Q. Not stated.
R. They should appease the Mother of the Gods' wrath [or the murdered man (*NP* sources)].
Mode A1, Topic 1a
Delphi. Indirect—Jul. *Or.* 5.159b.
NP. Indirect—Oracle: Suda M1003. Phot. *Lex.* 1.422 Naber. Apost. 11.34.
    Testimony—Oracle: Suda B99. Schol. Ven. on Aristoph. *Pl.* 431.

Comment: This too should perhaps be placed among Legendary responses. Yet Nilsson, Parke, and others, who are inclined to accept it as genuine, would date it around 500 B.C.; and some scholars would place it around 430. It was probably in the late sixth century that the cult of the Asian Mother of the Gods came to Athens and that Galloi or Metragyrtai first appeared there. Julian refers to the Mother's priest as a Gallos, a term that certainly does not belong to the prehistoric period. Yet we must realize the frequency of anachronism in legends: the very presence of Delphic oracles in legends of the Bronze Age is anachronistic. The Suda and Scholiast, who have a single source (probably a lexicon), report that the Metragyrtes predicted the coming of the Mother in search of Kore. This would place the event before Demeter's visit to Eleusis. Both this tradition and Julian identify the Mother with Demeter.

The evidence is very late, not before the fourth century A.D. Julian is our earliest authority, and his text is somewhat different from the lexicographers' version. Julian's reading is "Appease the wrath of the Mother of the Gods." The other sources have "Appease the murdered man." Only Julian refers this response to the Delphic Oracle; the others merely mention a *chrêsmos*. The story is *aition* of the Athenian *Mêtrôon*; and the response was probably unattributed at first. It is the common story of offended deity. See Nilsson 1967: 630, 725–727.

Q134 (PW84). [494 B.C.] Not genuine.
C. Argives.
Occ. Concern for their city's security.
Q. Not stated.
R. When the female defeats the male and drives him out, winning glory in Argos, many Argive women will weep. In future men will say, "A terrible triple-coiled snake has perished, vanquished by the spear." Then, Miletos, deviser of wicked deeds, you will become a feast and gift for many men; your wives will wash feet for many long-haired men; and my temple at Didyma will be in others' charge.
Mode F (E3), Topic 3h (1d, 2e)
Delphi. Direct, Verse—Herod. 6.19.2, 77.2. Anth. Pal. 14.89, 90. Incomplete—(1–3) Paus. 2.20.10. (6–9) Tzetzes *Chil.* 8.3–6.
NP. Direct, Verse, Incomplete (1–3)—Oracle: Suda T260.
    Comment: See pp. 70–71, 169, 186; Crahay 1956; 172–179.
    This is the so-called epicene oracle, which Herodotos alone reports as a single response.

Q135 (PW85). [c. 520 B.C.] Not genuine.
C. Telesilla of Argos.
Occ. Sickness.
Q. On recovery of health.
R. She should serve the Muses.
Mode A1, Topic 1b
NP. Indirect—The god: Socrates of Argos 310.6J *ap.* Plut. *Mor.* 245c.

Q136 (PW86). [c. 495 B.C.] Not genuine.
C. King Kleomenes of Sparta.
Occ. War with Argos.
Q. Not stated.
R. He will take Argos.
Mode E3, Topic 2e
Delphi. Indirect—Herod. 6.76.1, 80 (82.1).
    Comment: See pp. 68, 69 note 19, 70; Crahay 1956: 169–171.

Q137 (PW87). c. 491 B.C.

C. Spartans.

Occ. Doubts about King Demaratos' legitimacy.

Q. Is Demaratos Ariston's son?

R. Demaratos is not Ariston's son.

Mode D2, Topic 3a

Delphi. Indirect—Herod. 6.66.3 (75.3).

  Testimony—Paus. 3.4.3–6.

    Comment: See pp. 56, 126, 224, 247; Crahay 1956: 163–165.

  King Kleomenes bribed the Pythia, or was accused of doing so, to give this response to the Spartan envoys. Compare Q124, about twenty years earlier, another case of alleged bribery, which also affected Kleomenes.

Q138 (PW438). [c. 510 B.C.] Not genuine.

C. Titus and Arruns as envoys of King Tarquin of Rome.

Occ. Strange portents (Livy, Zonaras) or epidemic of sickness afflicting the young and mothers in childbirth (Dionysios).

Q. What was the cause of the sickness? (Dionysios).

R. Tarquin will fall from power when a dog speaks with human voice.

Mode F, Topic 3h (2a)

Delphi. Indirect—Zon. *Hist.* 7.11, p. 332b.

  Testimony—*Livy 1.56.4–10. Dion. Hal. *Ant. Rom.* 4.69.2–3.

Q139 (PW439). [c. 510 B.C.] Not genuine.

C. Tarquins' sons and Brutus.

Occ. Desire to know who would become king.

Q. Which of us will inherit Tarquin's kingdom?

R. He who is first to kiss his mother will have the sovereignty of Rome.

Mode F, Topic 3h (2a)

Delphi. Pseudo-Direct, Prose (Latin)—Livy 1.56.10.

  Indirect—Dion. Hal. *Ant. Rom.* 4.69.3. Dion Cass. 2, frag. 11.12. Zon. *Hist.* 7.11, p. 332d. Val. Max. 7.3.2. Serv. *Aen.* 3.96. *Liber de vir. ill.* 10.2.

NP. Pseudo-Direct, Verse (Latin)—Apollo: Ovid *Fasti* 2.713–714.

  Testimony—Apollo: *Cic. *Brutus* 14.53.

Q140 (PW484). [c. 500 B.C.] Not genuine.

C. Deinomenes of Syracuse.

Occ. Concern for his sons.

Q. (A) On his sons.

R. (A) The three will rule as tyrants.

Q. (B) To their sorrow, Lord Apollo.

R. (B) He granted Deinomenes that too as an additional response.

Mode E2, Topic 2a

Delphi. Indirect—Plut. *Mor.* 403bc.

   Comment: Compare Q59–60, 225.

   Apollo accepts the *klêdôn*, the omen of the word spoken; compare H20, when the Pythia's chance word was so taken by the consultant.

Q141 (PW241). [c. 485 B.C.] Not genuine.
C. Gelon of Syracuse and Theron of Agrigentum.
Occ. Emulation in offering of hecatombs to Apollo.
Q. With which offerings was Apollo most pleased?
R. With Dokimos' barleycakes.
Mode D1, Topic 1b
Delphi. Indirect—Porph. *Abst.* 2.17.

   Comment: Compare L57–59.

   Since Dokimos was a Delphian, it is probable that Delphi was meant to be the scene of this story, though Porphyry does not mention it.

Q142 (PW90). 490 B.C.
C. Athenians.
Occ. Appearance at Marathon of a warrior in rural dress who wielded a plowshare.
Q. Not stated.
R. They should honor the hero Echetlaios.
Mode A1, Topic 1a
NP. Indirect—The god: Paus. 1.32.5.

   Comment: One would have expected Herodotos to mention this phantom warrior and the oracle in his account of Marathon, but he does not, though he mentions the appearance of Phylakos and Autonoos against the Persians at Delphi (8.38–39). Still its character and context are unimpeachable. In all ages men have seen phantom warriors fighting on their side; e.g., the angels of Mons in the First World War.

Q143 (PW91). [489 B.Ç.] Not genuine.
C. Parians.
Occ. Discovery that the *hypozakoros* Timo had helped Miltiades in his attempt on Paros.
Q. Should they kill the woman for telling the enemy how to take the city and for revealing to Miltiades sacred things forbidden to the eyes of a male?
R. They should not punish her; she was not the instigator of the wrong; but since Miltiades was fated to end badly, she had appeared to him to lead him on to his undoing.
Mode C1 (D1), Topic 3f (3c)
Delphi. Indirect—Herod. 6.135.2.

   Comment: See p. 78; Crahay: 1956: 266–268.

Q144 (PW92). [481 B.C.] Not genuine.
C. Argives.
Occ. Persian threat to Hellas.

Q. What should we do to fare best?

R. Hateful to neighbors, dear to the gods, keep your spear inside and stay on guard. Protect the head; the head will save the body.

Mode A3 (E3), Topic 2e (3j)

Delphi. Direct, Verse—Herod. 7.148.3. Anth. Pal. 14.94. Incomplete—Oinomaos *ap.* Eus. *PE* 6.7. p. 255cd.

NP. Pseudo-Direct, Verse (Latin)—Oracle: Chalcid. *Tim.* 168.

    Comment: See pp. 128, 220; Crahay 1956: 321–324.

Q145 (PW93). [481 B.C.] Not genuine.

C. Cretans.

Occ. Persian threat to Greece.

Q. Is it better for us to help Hellas?

R. Foolish men, do you complain about all the tears that Minos sent you for helping Menelaos, because the Hellenes did not help avenge his murder at Kamikos, but you helped them exact vengeance for the woman whom a foreigner carried off from Sparta?

Mode D1, Topic 2e (3f)

Delphi. Direct, Prose—Herod. 7.169.2 (171.2). Anth. Pal. 14.95.

    Comment: See p. 128; Crahay 1956: 324–325.

    As Crahay asserts, this is part of a Cretan apology for Crete's failure to help Hellas against the Persians. Some clever Cretan thought of the old legend of Minos' death in Sicily at the house of Kokalos. The meaning is "Have you not had enough punishment from Minos' anger? Do you want more?"

Q146 (PW94). 481/80. Doubtful.

C. Athenians.

Occ. Persian invasion of Hellas.

Q. None?

R. Do not stay; fly to the ends of the earth, leaving your houses and city. For the whole body is unsound; nothing is left. Fire and war destroy it. Many fortresses will be destroyed, not yours alone. Many temples will burn, and blood drips upon their roofs, presaging inevitable evil. Leave the adyton and be ready for woes.

Mode C1 (A1, E2), Topic 2e (1d)

Delphi. Direct, Verse—Herod. 7.140.2–3. Anth. Pal. 14.92. Incomplete—Oinomaos *ap.* Eus. *PE* 5.24, p. 216bc. Eus. *PE* 13.13, p. 689d. Theodor. *Gr. aff. cur.* 10.140. Testimony—Liban. *Decl.* 20.19.

NP. Direct, Verse, Incomplete—Apollo: Clem. Alex. *Strom.* 5.14, 728P.

    Indirect—The god: Suda *A*2371. Zon. *Lex.* 211 Titt.

OP. Bakis. Direct, Verse, Incomplete—Tzetzes *Chil.* 9.812.

    Comment: See Q147.

Q147 (PW95). 481/80. Doubtful.

C. Athenians.

Occ. Receipt of Q146.

Q. Give us a better oracle for our country; respect these suppliant boughs which we carry. Otherwise we shall not leave the adyton, but will stay here until we die.

R. Pallas cannot appease Zeus with her many prayers. But I shall tell you this immovable decree: all Attica will be taken, but Zeus grants Athena a wooden wall that shall alone be untaken and will help you and your children. Do not await the onset of cavalry and infantry from the continent at your ease, but turn about and leave. You will face them sometime again. O divine Salamis, you will lose many children of men either at sowing time or at harvest.

Mode E3 (A1, C1), Topic 2e (1d, 3h)

Delphi. Direct, Verse—Herod. 7.141.3–4, 142.2 (8.41.2, 51.2, 53.1). Oinomaos *ap.* Eus. *PE* 5.24, pp. 216d–218c (23, p. 215d). Anth. Pal. 14.93. Incomplete—Dion. Hal. *Ars Rhet.* 6.2. Aristeides 46. 211–213 (186) and Schol., pp. 595, 645, 649 Dind. Plut. *Mor.* 828de. Philostr. *Vit. Soph.* 1.481. Eus. *PE* 13.13, p. 689d. Theodor. *Gr. aff. cur.* 10.140. Arg. 2 Aesch. *Pers.* Schol. on Lucian *Zeus Tr.* 31, p. 69 Rabe.

Indirect—Nepos 2.6. Pomp. Trog./Justin 2.12.13. Plut. *Them.* 10. Aristeides *ad Plat.* 4 *ap.* Phot. *Bibl.* 248, p. 430 Bekk. Liban. *Or.* 15.40. Schol. on Lucian *Zeus Tr.* 20, p. 64 Rabe.

Testimony—Lucan *BC* 5.108–109. Himer. *Or.* 2.26; *Ecl.* 5.2, 12, 41. Liban. *Decl.* 9.16; 10.27, 29; 20.19. Ps.-Themistokles *Epist.* 8, p. 748 Hercher.

NP. Direct, Verse, Incomplete—Apollo: Lucian *Zeus Tr.* 20. Clem. Alex. *Strom.* 5.14, 728P. John Chrys. *S. Bab.* 16, p. 562 Migne 50. Olymp. *Alk.* I 224. Schol. vet. on Lyk. 1418 (1417). The god: Polyainos *Strat.* 1.30.1–2. Suda *A*2371. Oracle: Elias *Pr. Cat.* 230b, p. 126 *PACA* 18.1. David *Comm. Cat.* p. 27b Br. Schol. vet. on Aristoph. *Eq.* 886, 1040. Eust. *Il.* 8.97, p. 701. Tzetzes *Exeg. Il.* p. 13 Herm. Schol. on Tzetzes *Exeg. Il.* p. 142 (143) Herm.

Indirect—Apollo: Max. Tyr. 13.1 (29.7). Arg. 1 Aesch. *Pers.* Oracle: Aristotle frag. 399 Rose and Philochoros 328.116J *ap.* Ael. *NA* 12.35.

Testimony—Apollo: Lyk. 1416–1420. Lucian *Philopatris* 5. Olymp. *Gorg.* 41.12. Oracle: Paus. 1.18.2.

Comment: See pp. 124–128, 157, 171; Crahay 1956: 295–304 on Q146–147.

Q148 (PW96). 480 b.c. Possibly genuine.

C. Delphians.

Occ. Persian threat to Delphi and all Hellas.

Q. Not stated.

R. Pray to the Winds and it will be better; they will be great allies for Hellas.

Mode A1 (E1), Topic 1b (2e)

Delphi. Direct, Verse—Clem. Alex. *Strom.* 6.3, 753P.

Indirect—*Herod. 7.178.1.

Comment: See pp. 56, 193, 195; Crahay 1956: 304–308.

Clement's verse has the first part only, ending with "and it will be better" (καὶ λώιον ἔσται); the usual sanction formula is versified. This could be actual approval of a cult of the Winds at Delphi. Compare the unidentified oracle mentioned by Herodotos (7.189.1), telling the Athenians to summon their son-in-law, i.e., Boreas, as ally.

Q149 (PW97). [c. 480 B.C.] Not genuine.
C. Delphians.
Occ. Fear of Persian attack on Delphi.
Q. Should they bury the sacred treasures or remove them to another place?
R. They should not move them; Apollo is capable of protecting his own.
Mode C1 (D1), Topic 1d
Delphi. Indirect—Herod. 8.36.1.
    Comment: See pp. 128, 249; Fontenrose 1960a: 198; Crahay 1956: 333–336.

Q150 (PW98). [481/0]. Not genuine.
C. Unknown.
Occ. Persian invasion.
Q. Not stated.
R. When the Persians enter Hellas they are fated to sack the sanctuary at Delphi, and
    after doing so to be entirely destroyed.
Mode E2, Topic 2e (1d)
NP. Indirect—Oracle: Herod. 9.42.3.
    Comment: See Crahay 1956: 336–337.
    The only reason for supposing this "Delphic" is that it predicts a Persian sack of Delphi; Herodotos does not tell us that it was spoken at Delphi itself. He says that it was really directed against the Illyrians and Encheleis when they attacked Delphi in the distant past. See Fontenrose 1960a: 203–204. If so, this is really a Legendary response. Compare the oracle of Bakis that Herodotos quotes immediately after this (9.43.2). According to Herodotos, the Persians failed in their assault upon Delphi; and in fact there is no record of their sacking the place.

Q151 (PW99). [480 B.C.] Not genuine.
C. Unknown.
Occ. Persian invasion.
Q. Not stated.
R. Persian of many-colored chariot, having seen, keep your hands off [keep your hands
    from the sacred?].
Mode C1, Topic 1d
NP. Direct, Verse—Oracle: Herakl. Pont. ap. Herodian. p. 690 Lentz = ap. Choer. in
    Theod. Can. p. 163 Hilg.
    Comment: See Parke 1940b.
    PW (p. 43) suggest that this may be part of Q150 as a warning to the Persians not to plunder Delphi. The only reason for considering this verse an oracle at all is that Herakleides quoted it in his work On Oracles, and that Pollux 7.112 quotes the phrase Θετταλὲ ποικιλόδιφρε as Delphic (PW257), spoken in 370 B.C. to discourage Jason of Pherai. This phrase I have not included in the Catalogue, since it is a fragment and nothing else is known about the response.

Q152 (PW100). [481/0.] Not genuine.

C. Spartans.

Occ. Persian invasion.

Q. On the war.

R. People of Sparta, either your city is destroyed by the Persians or it is not, and Lake-daimon will mourn a dead king of the Heraklid line. For the might of bulls and lions will not stay the enemy in battle; he has Zeus's might. And I say that he will not stop until he has destroyed one of these two.

Mode F (E2), Topic 2e (3c, 3h)

Delphi. Direct, Verse—Herod. 7.220.4 (239.1). Anth. Pal. 14.96. Incomplete—Oinomaos ap. Eus. PE 5.25, p. 219b.

Indirect—Pomp. Trog./Justin 2.11.8.

Testimony—Eus. PE 5.24, p. 218c.

NP. Testimony—Oracle: Plut. Pelop. 21.3.

Comment: See pp. 77–78, 128; Crahay 1956: 308–312.

Q153 (PW101). [480 B.C.] Not genuine.

C. Spartans.

Occ. Death of King Leonidas at Thermopylai.

Q. Not stated.

R. They should ask satisfaction of Xerxes for the killing of Leonidas and accept whatever he gives them.

Mode A1, Topic 2d

Delphi. Indirect—Herod. 8.114.1 (9.64.1).

Comment: See Crahay 1956: 312–315.

According to Herodotos, when the Spartan herald asked recompense from Xerxes, the king laughed and pointed to Mardonios, saying, "Mardonios will give them [the Spartans] the satisfaction they deserve." The herald accepted the klêdôn and left: i.e., the Spartans would take Mardonios in exchange for Leonidas. Compare Q140. As Crahay points out, it is unlikely that the Spartans would have asked Xerxes to pay them a penalty in 480; moreover Xerxes would not have been in Mardonios' camp at this time, but on his way home after defeat at Salamis. The whole story has traits of folktale and fiction.

Q154 (PW102). 479 B.C. Partly genuine.

C. Athenians sent by Aristeides.

Occ. Mardonios' campaign.

Q. Not stated.

R. They should pray to Zeus, Hera Kithaironia, Pan and the nymphs Sphragitides, and sacrifice to the heroes Androkrates, Leukon, Peisandros, Damokrates, Hypsion, Aktaion, Polyeidos. They should fight the battle in their own land on the plain of Demeter Eleusinia and Kore.

Mode A1, Topic 1b (2e)

Delphi. Indirect—Plut. *Arist.* 11.3. Clem. Alex. *Protr.* 35P.

Testimony—Plut. *Mor.* 628f.

Comment: The direction to worship the named gods and heroes is probably genuine. The final direction to fight on the plain of Demeter Eleusinia and Kore looks like a *post eventum* addition, which, moreover, allows a story of how the Athenians assumed that the god meant the Eleusinian plain, and then found out that there was a shrine of Demeter Eleusinia near Plataia.

Q155 (PW103). [479 B.C.] Not genuine.

C. Mardonios, Persian general (Scholiast).

Occ. Campaign in Hellas.

Q. How can he take Hellas?

R. (1) The Dorians are destined to be driven from the Peloponnesos by the Medes and Athenians. (2) If the Athenians join the Persians, then the other Hellenes will lose the war and their country.

Mode E2, Topic 2e

Delphi. Indirect (2)—Aristeides 13.144 and Schol. p. 189 Dind.

NP. Indirect (1)—Oracle: *Herod. 8.141.1.

Comment: See Crahay 1956: 315–317.

Herodotos mentions only *logia* which the Spartans had heard. Only the Scholiast says that Mardonios received this response; he also reports that Mardonios sent to many Oracles, including Amphiaraos and Trophonios.

Q156 (PW104). 479 B.C.

C. Hellenes.

Occ. Victory at Plataia.

Q. On sacrifices.

R. They should establish an altar of Zeus Eleutherios and not make sacrifice before quenching the fire in the country as defiled by the Persians and kindling a clean fire from the common hearth at Delphi.

Mode A1, Topic 1a

Delphi. Indirect—Plut. *Arist.* 20.4.

Q157 (PW105). 480/79. Probably genuine.

C. Hellenes.

Occ. Offerings of first fruits (*akrothinia*) after victory at Salamis.

Q. Are the *akrothinia* sufficient and pleasing?

R. Those from the other Hellenes are, but not those from the Aeginetans: from them he asks the prizes (*aristeia*) of the naval battle at Salamis.

Mode D1 (A1), Topic 1b

Delphi. Indirect—Herod. 8.122 = Plut. *Mor.* 871cd.

Comment: See Crahay 1956: 331–332.

Q158 (PW106). [479 B.C.] Not genuine.

C. Themistokles.

Occ. Arrival at Delphi with offerings of Persian spoils.

Q. Shall I place the offerings inside the temple?

R. Do not put the fine ornament of Persian spoils inside my temple. Send them back home at once.

Mode C1, Topic 1b

Delphi. Direct, Verse—Paus. 10.14.5.

Comment: Herodotos does not mention this incident. Pausanias (10.19.4) saw gold Persian shields on Apollo's temple at Delphi, Athenian offerings from Marathon; hence the Delphians had no objection to receiving Persian spoils.

Q159 (PW418). [481/0.] Not genuine.

C. Mnesarchides.

Occ. and Q. Not stated.

R. You will have a son, Mnesarchides, whom all men will honor. He will rise to great fame and will wear sacred crowns.

Mode E2, Topic 3a

Delphi. Direct, Verse—Oinomaos ap. Eus. PE 5.33, p. 227cd (228c–229b).

Testimony—Eus. PE 5.32, p. 227a.

NP. Indirect—Oracle: Vit. Eur. 1.

Comment: The child was Euripides. Compare Q59, 78.

Q160 (PW107). [c. 480 B.C.] Not genuine.

C. Teisamenos, Iamid of Elis.

Occ. Desire for children.

Q. Not stated.

R. He will win the five greatest contests.

Mode E3, Topic 3e (3d)

Delphi. Indirect—Herod. 9.33.2. Paus. 3.11.6.

Comment: See p. 220; Fontenrose 1968: 94–95; Crahay 1956: 102–104.

Q161 (PW108). [c. 510 B.C.] Not genuine.

C. Apollonia in Illyria.

Occ. Famine and sterility following upon the blinding of Euenios.

Q. What is the cause of the misfortune?

R. They wrongly deprived Euenios, guard of the sacred flocks, of his eyesight. The gods had sent the wolves, and will not cease avenging Euenios until they pay him the penalty that he chooses and considers just. When that is done, the gods will give Euenios a gift that will cause many men to felicitate him.

Mode A1 (D2, E2), Topic 3f

Delphi. Indirect—Herod. 9.93.4.

Comment: See Crahay 1956: 82–84.

The Apolloniates received the same response from Dodona. Without knowing the response Euenios chose two fine farms and the best house in Apollonia. The gods gave him the gift of prophecy. He is another Teiresias, receiving the mantic gift in recompense for his blindness. The story is essentially that of offended deity; see pp. 76–77.

Q162 (PW109). [479/8.] Not genuine.
C. Polykrates of Thebes.
Occ. A rumor that Mardonios had buried a treasure on his tent site at Plataia.
Q. How may I find the money?
R. Turn every stone.
Mode A1, Topic 3e (3j)
Delphi. Direct, Verse—Zen. 5.63. Suda *Π*222 (*Π*223).
NP. Indirect—Oracle: Phot. *Lex.* 2.52 Naber. Tzetzes *Chil.* 12.788. Apost. 13.91.
   Comment: See pp. 86–87.

Q163 (PW112). [Before 478 B.C.] Not genuine.
C. Spartans.
Occ. and Q. Not stated.
R. Take care, Sparta, that from you, sound of foot, no lame kingship grow; for unexpected trials will then oppress you for a long time, including a man-killing wave of war rolling over you.
Mode C2 (F), Topic 2a (2e, 3h)
Delphi. Direct, Verse—Plut. *Mor.* 399bc; *Ages.* 3 (30); *Lys.* 22. Paus. 3.8.9.
   Testimony—Pomp. Trog./Justin 6.2.5.
NP. Indirect—Apollo: *Xen. *Hell.* 3.3.3. The god: Diod. 11.50.4.
   Comment: See pp. 121, 148–150, 154, 161, 165, 171.

Q164 (PW113). [c. 476/5.] Not genuine.
C. Athenians.
Occ. Plague (desire to take Skyros, Pausanias).
Q. (A) Not stated.
R. (A) They should bring Theseus' bones from Skyros to Athens, give them an honorable burial, and worship him as a hero [otherwise the famine will not end (Aristeides); they will not take Skyros (Pausanias)].
Q. (B) Where are the bones?
R. (B) I am sending you a guide.
Mode A1 (E1), Topic 1a (3g)
Delphi. Indirect (A)—Plut. *Thes.* 36.1; *Kimon* 8.6.
NP. Direct, Prose (B), Indirect (A)—The god: Schol. on Aristeides 46.172, p. 561 Dind. Indirect (A)—Apollo: Aen. Gaz. *Theophr.*, p. 60 Colonna. Schol. on Aristeides 46.241, p. 688 Dind. The god: Aristeides 46.241. Oracle: Paus. 3.3.7. Schol. vet. on Aristoph. *Pl.* 627.
   Testimony—Oracle: Schol. on Eur. *Hipp.* 11.
   Comment: See p. 73.

Q165 (PW116). [550–500]. Not genuine.
C. Metapontines.

Occ. Appearance of Aristeas in Metapontum bidding them found an altar of Apollo and set beside it an image of Aristeas.

Q. What was the vision of the man?

R. They should obey the vision; if they do so, they will fare better.

Mode A1, Topic 1a

Delphi. Indirect—Herod. 4.15.3. Origen *Cels.* 3.26, p. 463 (27–31, pp. 464–467 *passim*).

> *Comment:* See Crahay 1956: 73–75.
>
> Origen cites Herodotos in his notice of the response.

Q166 (PW88). [496 B.C.] Not genuine.

C. Astypalaeans.

Occ. Disappearance of Kleomedes' body from the chest in which he had locked himself.

Q. What happened to Kleomedes?

R. Latest of heroes is Kleomedes of Astypalaia; honor him with sacrifices as no longer a mortal.

Mode A1 (D2), Topic 1a

Delphi. Direct, Verse—Paus. 6.9.8. Oinomaos *ap.* Eus. *PE* 5.34, p. 230c. Socr. *Hist. eccl.* 3.23, p. 448 Migne. Theodor. *Gr. aff. cur.* 8.115; 10.141. Incomplete—*Plut. *Rom.* 28.5. Eus. *Chron. ap.* Cram. Anecd. Par. 2.154.

> Indirect—Origen *Cels.* 3.25, p. 462.
>
> *Comment:* See p. 130; Fontenrose 1968: 73–79.

Q167 (PW117). c. 470 B.C. Possibly genuine.

C. Epizephyrian Locrians.

Occ. Report that the statues of the boxer Euthymos at Locri and Olympia had been struck by lightning on the same day.

Q. Not stated.

R. Sacrifices should be made to Euthymos.

Mode A1, Topic 1a

Delphi. Indirect—Pliny *NH* 7.47.152.

> *Comment:* See Fontenrose 1968: 79–81.

We may doubt the reported prodigy or suppose it to be a rumor: the coincidence could hardly be verified. The response itself is unobjectionable and may have been occasioned simply by Euthymos' extraordinary athletic prowess.

Q168 (PW388). [Before 500 B.C. ?] Not genuine.

C. Epizephyrian Locrians.

Occ. Famine following upon ill-treatment of the athlete Euthykles.

Q. Not stated.

R. Holding the unhonored in honor you will then plow the land.

Mode A3, Topic 3j

Delphi. Direct, Verse—Oinomaos *ap.* Eus. *PE* 5.34, p. 232b.

NP. Indirect—Apollo: *Call. *Ait.* 3.84 Pf. *ap.* Dieg. I, Ox. Pap. 2212.

> *Comment:* See pp. 81–82, 84, 130; Fontenrose 1968: 74–79.

Q169 (PW118). 460 B.C. Possibly genuine.

C. Achaeans.

Occ. Failure of Achaean athletes for two centuries at Olympia.

Q. For what reason have they failed to win a crown at Olympia?

R. They should set up a statue of Oibotas at Olympia as first Achaean victor.

Mode A1, Topic 1a

Delphi. Testimony—Paus. 6.3.8; 7.17.6, 13.

    Comment: See Fontenrose 1968: 74–79.

    As for Q167 we may suppose the response authentic without believing that the occasion was that which is alleged. It is certainly not true that no Achaean had won a contest at Olympia for two centuries. More likely the Achaeans asked at this time, the 80th Olympiad, how they might have better success in the contests; or perhaps they simply sought a sanction for erecting a statue of Oibotas (but why seek it at Delphi?).

Q170 (PW389). [c. 450 B.C.] Not genuine.

C. Thasians.

Occ. Barrenness of land and famine after they threw Theagenes' image into the sea.

Q. Not stated.

R. Bring back exiles to the land and you will reap grain.

Mode A3, Topic 2b

Delphi. Direct, Verse—Oinomaos ap. Eus. PE 5.34, p. 232a.

    Indirect—*Dion Chrys, 31.97. Paus. 6.11.7. Suda N410.

    Comment: Dion says only that "the god" spoke Q170, but immediately after attributes the companion Q171 to the Pythia.

Q171 (PW390–391). [c. 450 B.C.] Not genuine.

C. Thasians.

Occ. Although they recalled exiles, the famine continued.

Q. We did as you bid us, but the gods' wrath continues.

R. You have cast out and forgotten your great athlete Theagenes [who has fallen in sands (Dion)].

Mode D2, Topic 3e

Delphi. Direct, Verse—Dion Chrys. 31.97 (elegiac distich). Paus. 6.11.8.

    Comment: On Q170–171 see Fontenrose 1968: 75–79.

Q172 (PW126). [Before 470 B.C.] Not genuine.

C. Corcyraeans.

Occ. Failure to bring in the huge schools of tuna which a lowing bull had called to their attention.

Q. Not stated.

R. They should sacrifice the bull to Poseidon.

Mode A1, Topic 1b

Delphi. Testimony—Paus. 10.9.4.

Comment: See Pouilloux and Roux 1963: 8–16.

The Corcyraeans dedicated bronze bulls at Delphi and Olympia. See Map, figure 1, no. 1.

Q173 (PW520). [c. 450 B.C.] Not genuine.

C. Eleians.

Occ. Proposal to remove the bronze Corcyraean bull of Olympia because it had accidentally caused a small boy's death.

Q. Not stated.

R. They should let the offering stay and cleanse it according to the rites which Hellenes employ for an unintentional killing.

Mode A1, Topic 1b

Delphi. Indirect—Paus. 5.27.10.

Comment: Pausanias may be reporting a story told by his Olympian guides, or he may have taken this from Polemon's work on Olympian monuments.

Q174 (PW114). [After 476 B.C.] Not genuine.

C. Spartans.

Occ. Plague following on Regent Pausanias' death (Aristodemos).

Q. On other matters (Diodoros).

R. They should move Pausanias' tomb to the place where he died. And as the event had brought pollution on them, they must restore to Athena Chalkioikos two bodies instead of one.

Mode A3, Topic 1a (1b, 3c)

Delphi. Indirect—*Thuc. 1.134.4. Diod. 11.45.8.

Testimony—Nepos 4.5. Paus. 3.17.9.

NP. Indirect—The god: Aristodemos 1.8.5, 104J. Oracle: Plut. *Mor.* 560e.

Testimony—The god: Ps.-Themistokles *Epist.* 4.

Comment: See pp. 129–131.

Q175 (PW115). [Probably before 470 B.C.] Not genuine.

C. Spartans.

Occ. and Q. Not stated.

R. They must let the suppliant of Zeus Ithomatas go free [else they will be punished (Pausanias)].

Mode A1, Topic 1d

Delphi. Indirect—Thuc. 1. 103.2. Paus. 4.24.7 (3.11.8).

Comment: According to Pausanias, the seer Teisamenos also advised the Spartans to let the revolting Messenians go unharmed from Ithome. This is probably the only true mantic pronouncement in this event. The seer may have invoked a traditional oracle as a Delphic pronouncement; for nothing is said about the time and the circumstances: it is referred to the indefinite past.

Q176 (PW315). [468/7?] Not genuine.

C. Tirynthians.

Occ. Loss of Tiryns to Argos; desire to settle elsewhere.

Q. Where will you settle us?

R. You ask where I shall settle you. I send you to . . . to have a home and be called fishermen.

Mode A1, Topic 2c

NP. Direct, Verse—The god: Ephoros 70.56J ap. Steph. Byz. 73 Mein.

　　Comment: The text, Doric, is very corrupt. Hendess 44 (1877: 41) shows Meineke's attempt to restore it. See also Jacoby's text in his comment on this Ephoros fragment (2.1, p. 57 note). Jacoby believes that the fall of Tiryns mentioned occurred at an earlier date when the Peloponnesos was under the hegemony of Argos. These Tirynthians went to the place on the coast now called Porto Cheli and founded Halieis, i.e., Fishermen.

Q177 (PW314). [c. 464 B.C.] Not genuine.

C. Spartans (Suda).

Occ. Manifestations of divine wrath.

Q. Request for healing (Suda).

R. It is the same for you to live in Delos and Kalaureia and Pytho and Tainaron.

Mode D1, Topic 3j (3i)

NP. Direct, Verse—The god: Suda A2371. Oracle: *Ephoros 70.150J ap. Strab. 8.6.14, p. 374. Paus. 2.33.2.

　　Comment: Reference to Pytho in the text is the only indication that the Pythian Apollo may have been represented as the speaker. Probably the poet did not intend these verses to be an oracle at all. Ephoros calls the verses a chrêsmos, Pausanias a logion. The Suda is vague about the circumstances of consultation.

Q178 (PW119). c. 442–440.

C. Delphians.

Occ. and Q. Not stated.

R. They should apportion to Pindar an equal share of all firstlings offered to Apollo.

Mode A1, Topic 1a

Delphi. Indirect—Paus. 9.23.3.

　　Comment: It is probable that this instituted hero-worship of Pindar at Delphi following his death in 442.

Q179 (PW120). [c. 445 B.C.] Not genuine.

C. Pindar through Boeotian envoys.

Occ. Desire for knowledge.

Q. What is best for man?

R. He himself knows, being the poet who wrote about Trophonios and Agamedes. But if he wants a test, it will soon be clear to him.

Mode D1 (E2), Topic 3c

Delphi. Indirect—Plut. *Mor.* 109ab.

OP. *Ammon.* Testimony—*Vita Ambr. Pind.* Eust. *Prooem.* 29.

Comment: The story is a form of the fable on death as the best for man. It is attached to Pindar and expressed indirectly because Pindar had told the story of Trophonios and Agamedes (L9) in a lost poem. Since Plutarch's notice of Q179 follows closely on his notice of L9, taken from Pindar and attributed to Delphi, it is fairly certain that he intends the Delphic Apollo as speaker of Q179 too.

Q180 (PW121). [c. 450 B.C.] Not genuine.

C. Athenians.

Occ. and Q. Not stated.

R. Blessed city of Athens, having suffered much, you will become an eagle in clouds forever.

Mode E3, Topic 3j

Delphi. Direct, Verse (2-line version)—Schol. on Aristeides 13.196, p. 341 Dind. Indirect—Aristeides 13.196.

NP. Direct, Verse, Incomplete—Oracle: Zen. 2.50.

OP. *Bakis.* Direct, Verse (3-line version)—Schol. vet. on Aristoph. *Eq.* 1013. Incomplete—Aristoph. *Aves* 978.

Indirect—Aristoph. *Eq.* 1013, 1087. Schol. vet. on *Eq.* 1086, *Aves* 978.

Testimony—*Aristoph. frag. 230 HG *ap.* Schol. vet. *in Eq.* 1013.

Sibyl. Direct, Verse—cf. Plut. *Dem.* 19.1.

Comment: See pp. 150–151, 163, 171.

Since Aristophanes appears to attribute this oracle to Bakis in the *Knights* and in the *Birds*, I assume that the Scholiasts make the same attribution (unexpressed) of the *chrêsmos* that they quote, and also that Aristophanes attributed it to Bakis in the *Banqueters*. He probably quoted it there too, but the fragment tells us only that he mentioned it there.

Q181 (PW122). [Probably before 490 B.C.] Not genuine.

C. Athenians.

Occ. and Q. Not stated.

R. The Pelargikon is better unused [end of a response].

Mode C1, Topic 1d

Delphi. Direct, Verse, Incomplete—Thuc. 2.17.1.

Comment: Although Thucydides is our source for this fragment of oracle, it can hardly come from a genuine response. Thucydides puts it in the indefinite past, and it is possible that he knew no more about the supposed *manteion*. It probably expresses a superstition in the form of a proverbial phrase that was at some point represented as an oracle.

Q182 (PW493). [c. 470–450.] Not genuine.

C. Phigaleians.

Occ. Barrenness of the land and famine following upon the Phigaleian failure to replace a destroyed image of Demeter Melaina.

Q. How may we be delivered from famine?

R. Arcadians of Phigaleia, Deo gave you the unique life that you lead as nomads and farmers. She, deprived of her traditional honors, will soon make you a cannibal and child-eater, unless you propitiate her wrath with public libations and adorn her cave with divine honors.

Mode A1 (D1, E1), Topic 1a (3f)

Delphi. Direct, Verse—Paus. 8.42.6.

> *Comment:* See pp. 139, 182, 183.

Q183 (PW127). [c. 500–450.] Not genuine.

C. Camarina in Sicily.

Occ. Desire to drain nearby lake.

Q. Should we drain the lake completely?

R. Do not move Camarina; it is better unmoved.

Mode C1, Topic 2b

NP. Direct, Verse—Apollo: Serv. *Aen.* 3.701. Schol. Ver. on *Aen.* 3.701. Incomplete— The god: Zen. 5.18. Suda M904. Schol. on Lucian *Pseud.* 32. Apost. 11.49. Oracle: Greg. Cypr. 3.7, Mosq. 4.41. EM 27.

Indirect—Oracle: *Virgil *Aen.* 3. 700–701. Sil. It. 14.198.

OP. Sibyl. Direct, Verse—Orac. Sib. 3.736.

> *Comment:* See pp. 85–86.

As ascribed to the Sibyl the response has a second verse, as has also Anth. Pal. 9.685 (though a different verse), which does not quote the couplet as an oracle, but as an *epigramma demonstrativum.*

Q184 (PW128). [c. 550–450?] Not genuine.

C. Lipara.

Occ. Naval warfare with Etruscans.

Q. Not stated.

R. They should fight the Etruscans with as few ships as possible.

Mode A1, Topic 2e

Delphi. Indirect—Paus. 10.16.7.

Q185 (PW129). [c. 500 B.C. ?] Not genuine.

C. Parmeniskos of Metapontum.

Occ. Loss of ability to laugh after visiting the Oracle of Trophonios.

Q. About recovering laughter.

R. Mother will give it to you at home. Honor her especially.

Mode E3 (A3), Topic 3g (1b)

Delphi. Direct, Verse—Semos 396.10J *ap.* Ath. 14. 614ab.

> *Comment:* See pp. 69–70.

Schultz (1909: 76–77, no. 116) takes the two-verse response as a riddle. Semos' story is an anecdote on the reputed effect of a visit to Trophonios—the visitor lost the ability to laugh; see Paus. 9.39.13.

Q186 (PW131). [c. 445 B.C.] Not genuine.

C. Colonizers of Thurii (Diodoros) or Sybarites.

Occ. Need of a site on which to settle (Diodoros).

Q. Not stated.

R. They should found a city in that place where they are going to dwell drinking water in measure and eating bread without measure.

Mode B, Topic 3h (2c)

NP. Direct, Verse, partly Indirect—Apollo: Diod 12.10.5. Incomplete (verse only)— The god: Zen. 5.19. Phot. *Lex.* 1.420 Naber. Suda *A*1561, *M*818. Apost. 11.31.

  Comment: See pp. 81, 156.

Only Diodoros has the full content. He alone reports the direction to found a city where the proverbial conditions will prevail; he names Apollo as speaker and attaches the response to the founding of Thurii. The paroemiographers and lexicographers have an incomplete sentence in a single verse, "drinking water in measure and eating bread without measure." Like Q183 it is never expressly attributed to the Delphic Oracle. The paroemiographic tradition attributes it to "the god," who spoke the verse to the Sybarites, apparently as a warning against their intemperate mode of life. The Crotoniates destroyed the Sybarites, who had not heeded the warning. In this version the date of the oracle would have to be earlier than 510 B.C.

Q187 (PW132). c. 433 B.C.

C. Thurians.

Occ. Civil strife.

Q. Whom should they call founder of the city?

R. Apollo himself should be considered founder.

Mode A1, Topic 1a

Delphi. Indirect—Diod. 12.35.3.

  Comment: This seems perfectly acceptable, although the question is more likely to have been, "Is it better that we call Apollo founder of the city?" That is, this was probably a sanction.

Q188 (PW133). [c. 437 B.C.] Not genuine.

C. Athenians.

Occ. Contemplated founding of a colony on the Strymon.

Q. Not stated.

R. Why, Athenians, do you again want to colonize the many-footed place? It is difficult for you without the gods. For it is not fated until you find and bring from Troy the stubble of Resos and bury him in his fatherland. Then you can win glory.

Mode A1, Topic 1a

NP. Direct, Verse—The god: Polyainos *Strat.* 6.53.

  Comment: See pp. 75, 186.

Q189 (PW125). c. 430 B.C.

C. Athenians.

Occ. Plague following outbreak of Peloponnesian War.

Q. Not stated.

R. They should set up an image of Apollo.

Mode A1, Topic 1a

Delphi. Testimony—Paus. 1.3.4.

    Comment: Compare H10, 30, 41, 51.

Q190 (PW158). 430 B.C.

C. Kleonai.

Occ. Plague.

Q. Not stated.

R. They should sacrifice a goat to the rising Helios.

Mode A1, Topic 1b

Delphi. Testimony—Paus. 10.11.5.

    Comment: Compare H9, 28, 29, 50.

Q191 (PW161). [c. 420 B.C.] Not genuine.

C. Delians.

Occ. Expulsion from Delos.

Q. (A) Not stated.

R. (A) Find the place where Apollo was born and make sacrifices there.

Q. (B) Was the god not born on our island, but somewhere else?

R. (B) A crow will show you the place.

Mode A3 (E2), Topic 1b (3h)

Delphi. Indirect—Plut. *Mor.* 412c.

Testimony—*Kallisthenes 124.11J *ap.* Steph. Byz. 611 Mein.

    Comment: See p. 73.

Q192 (PW163). [c. 420 B.C.] Not genuine.

C. Mantineians.

Occ. and Q. Not stated.

R. Mainalia is wintry, where Arkas lies, from whom you got your name; thither I bid you go with glad heart to take up Arkas and bring him back to your city where three, four, and five roads meet. There make a temenos and sacrifices for Arkas.

Mode A1, Topic 1a

Delphi. Direct, Verse—Paus. 8.9.4 (36.8).

    Comment: See p. 173.

Q193 (PW166). [416/5.] Not genuine.

C. Athenians.

Occ. Proposed war on Syracuse.

Q. Not stated.

R. They should bring the priestess of Athena from Erythrai (or Klazomenai).

Mode A3, Topic 3g (1d)
Delphi. Indirect—Plut. *Mor.* 403b; *Nik.* 13.4.

   Comment: Compare oracle of Dodona, Paus. 8.11.12; Dion Chrys. 17.17; see Q195.

Q194 (PW578). [Before 400 B.C.] Not genuine.
C. Athenians.
Occ. Desire for welfare of the city.
Q. How will they fare better?
R. If they want good men in their city, they should put the finest thing in their children's ears.
Mode A3, Topic 3h
Delphi. Indirect—Stob. *Exc.* 2.13.89, p. 401 Mein. 4, citing Dion. Chrys.
NP. Indirect—Apollo: *Dion Chrys. 32.3.

   Comment: Dion is the only authority for this response. He says that Apollo spoke it to the Athenians. Stobaeus, who cites Dion, has the Pythia as speaker. Unless Stobaeus has taken this from a lost *Chreia*, his borrowing illustrates well how a receiver of a story can change the details. Not only does Stobaeus assume, probably correctly, that Dion's Apollo is the Pythian, but he also reports an Athenian question, how may they fare better —though Dion mentions no question at 32.3, and his response implies that it was "How may we have good men in the city?" Stobaeus also phrases the response as a direction to put the finest thing in their boys' right ears, whereas Dion's form refers only to the boys' ears without specifying which (although he adds that the Athenians pierced one ear); and this fits the moral better.

   This is an oracle in a fable. The Athenians mistook the god's words and put gold earrings in their boys' ears; in their folly they did not realize that the god meant philosophy. The tale needs consultation of an oracular god; and it is probable that in the story which Dion received the Athenians went to Delphi.

Q195 (PW168). [c. 430 B.C.?] Not genuine.
C. King Archidamos of Sparta.
Occ. and Q. Not stated.
R. He should beware of Sikelia.
Mode C2, Topic 3i
Delphi. Indirect—Suda Σ389.

   Comment: See pp. 59, 68. Compare the Dodonaean oracle referred to at Paus. 8.11.12. See Q193.

Q196 (PW169). [409–405?] Not genuine.
C. Locrians.
Occ. Famine.
Q. Not stated.
R. Locrian, you have destroyed Trachis, Herakles' city, and Zeus has given you woes and will continue to give them.

Mode D1 (E2), Topic 3f (2e)

Delphi. Direct, Verse—Oinomaos *ap.* Eus. *PE* 6.7, p. 260a.

Comment: PE 254d, which heads a long extract from Oinomaos (255b–261b), indicates that all oracles quoted are attributed to the Pythian Apollo. These include Q196 and Q197. PW think that the occasion was the fall of Trachinian Herakleia to the Oetaeans in 409 and that the response is genuine (see Parke 1956: 199–200). But Xenophon (*Hell.* 1.2.18) does not mention Locrians as allies of or included among the Oetaeans who defeated the Spartans in Trachis. Oinomaos tells us nothing about the circumstances of this oracle aside from a hint of famine. The response could well be L. It is unlikely too that the Pythia would reproach consultants in this manner. The response is obviously incomplete; the message, a direction on what to do, is missing.

Q197 (PW170). [409–400?] Not genuine.

C. Oetaeans.

Occ. and Q. Not stated.

R. Oetaeans, do not hasten on in folly of mind.

Mode C1, Topic 3j

Delphi. Direct, Verse—Oinomaos *ap.* Eus. *PE* 6.7, p. 260d.

Comment: Oinomaos brings this verse into the context of Q196, and it could be part of the same response, or at least connected with the same occasion, as PW suggest. But we really know nothing about it; it appears to be just the fragment of a response.

Q198 (PW171). [404 B.C.] Not genuine.

C. Spartans.

Occ. Victory over Athens.

Q. Should they destroy Athens?

R. They should not destroy the common hearth of Hellas.

Mode C1, Topic 2e

Delphi. Indirect—Ath. 5.187d, 6.254b. Schol. on Aristeides 13.196, pp. 341–342 Dind.

NP. Indirect—The god: Ael. *VH* 4.6.

Comment: Certainly Xenophon would have mentioned this response if it were authentic. Furthermore it is unlikely that the Spartans would have asked such a question at Delphi; they would simply have destroyed the city.

Q199 (PW173). [Before 395 B.C.] Not genuine.

C. Lysander of Sparta.

Occ. and Q. Not stated.

R. I bid you beware of a sounding hoplite and of a snake, earth's deceitful son, coming behind.

Mode C2, Topic 3h (2e)

Delphi. Direct, Verse—Plut. *Lys.* 29. Incomplete—Plut. *Mor.* 408a.

Comment: See p. 61.

Q200 (PW179). [c. 390 B.C.] Not genuine.

C. Delians.

Occ. Plague.

Q. What should they do to rid themselves of the plague?

R. They should double the altar and then sacrifice on it.

Mode A1, Topic 1b

Delphi. Indirect—Vit. Plat. Anon. p. 16 Heeren.

NP. Indirect—Apollo: Vitr. Arch. 9, praef. 13. The god: *Eratosthenes ap. Theon. Smyrn.
    Util. Math. p. 2 Hiller. Plut. Mor. 386e, 579b.

    Comment: This response surely belongs to a philosophical fable. Eratosthenes, our earliest source, ascribes it only to "the god." The fact that one of Plutarch's notices occurs in his essay on the E at Delphi is the only reason for supposing that he means the Delphic god.

    One may suppose that the story grew up around a genuine response. The direction is simple enough: the god merely directs the Delians to double the size of their altar, presumably the great altar of Apollo. It could be a sanction of a Delian proposal to do so. If it is a genuine direction, it surely means no more than that, as if a person might tell another that he should have a table or cabinet twice the size of that which he has. The god's ministers had no difficult geometric problem in mind, no thought of the paradox of doubling the cube. The behest could be carried out by doubling the width.

    Although in this way we might defend the authenticity of Q200, it seems more likely to have been designed for the anecdote about Plato. The god tells the Delians that doubling their altar will end the present ills of the Delians and other Hellenes. Thinking that fairly simple to do, they soon encounter a geometric problem, because they interpret the direction literally, that the cube should be doubled, i.e., all three dimensions, doing which would make the altar eight times as large in volume. So the Delians refer the problem to Plato, who interprets the oracle as the god's direction to study geometry. Cf. Q194.

Q201 (PW180). [c. 380 B.C.] Not genuine.

C. Diogenes of Sinope.

Occ. When in charge of the mint at Sinope he was urged by his workmen to falsify coins; or, having done so, he was in flight from a criminal charge.

Q. (1) Should I do as I am urged? (2) What should I do to win great fame? (Diog. Laert. 6.2.21, Suda).

R. Debase the currency.

Mode A3, Topic 3e (3j)

Delphi. Direct, Prose—Jul. Or. 6.188ab (191b, 199b); 7.211c (238b–d). Suda Γ334. App.
    Prov. 1.81.
    Indirect—Suda Δ1144.
    Testimony—*Diog. Laert. 6.2.20, 21.

OP. Delion at Sinope. Indirect—Chrest. Strab. Geog. 12.23.

Testimony—Diog. Laert. 6.2.20.

　　Comment: See p. 70.

This is a proverb made into a response and attached to Diogenes the Cynic in a philosophical fable. Diogenes Laertios reports both versions of the question as indicated above under Q. In the second version the story takes the same form as those about Zeno and Cicero (Q224, 248).

According to the Chrestomathia of Strabo and to anonymous authorities cited by Diogenes Laertios, Diogenes received this response from Apollo's Oracle in Sinope, called the Delion. It is likely that this was the oracular site of the original story, since it was in Sinope that Diogenes encountered his problem. Later the story was brought into the tradition that related all philosophers to Delphi.

Q202 (PW440). [400–396.] Not genuine.

C. Romans.

Occ. Swellings of the Alban Lake without rain during their siege of Veii.

Q. What do the gods portend by this prodigy?

R. Veii will not be taken as long as the waters of the Alban Lake continue to overflow
　　and reach the sea (Dionysios). [Do not let the water stay in the lake; do not let it flow
　　into the sea (Livy).] But if the Romans divert the waters into other channels, so that
　　they become dissipated and never reach the sea, then Veii will soon be taken. [When
　　the war has ended send gifts to me and renew the sacred rites that have been neglected
　　(Livy).]

Mode F (A1, C1), Topic 2e (1b, 3e)

Delphi. Pseudo-Direct, Prose (Latin)—Livy 5.16.9–11 (15.3, 23.1).

　　Indirect—Dion. Hal. Ant. Rom. 12.13. Plut. Cam. 4.4–5. Val. Max. 1.6.3. Zon. Hist.
　　7.20.

　　Testimony—App. Ital. 8.1.

OP. Veientine fata. Indirect—*Cic. Div. 1.44.100.

　　Comment: See pp. 65, 171 note 10.

The sources show clearly that this oracle belongs to Roman legend, which originally assigned it to a Veientine soothsayer or to a noble Veientine deserter who revealed the fata scripta of Veii to the Romans. Cicero, our earliest source, has only the noble Veientine. Dionysios, Livy, Plutarch, and others add the Delphic oracle to the soothsayer or fata, both saying the same thing. The oracle itself is essentially in mode F, a contingent prophecy: Veii will not be taken if the overflowing waters of the Alban Lake continue to reach the sea; or, Veii will be taken when the waters no longer reach the sea—although Livy and Plutarch express it in imperative or prohibitory terms. The condition appears to be an adynaton, and no doubt was in the original story: the Veientines thought themselves secure. But the Romans dug canals and diverted the water to irrigation.

We might ask whether the conclusion of Livy's version indicates an actual ritual prescription that the Romans received from Delphi at this time (see also Plutarch), a command to repair their neglect of the Latin festival. It seems improbable that the Romans would have consulted Delphi on such matters at this early date. PW list this among legendary oracles. See Parke 1956: 267–270.

Q203 (PW181). [Before 367 B.C.] Not genuine.

C. Achaeans.

Occ. Siege of Phana in Aitolia.

Q. How may we take Phana?

R. Observe how large a portion each day protects the city as the people drink and the city is refreshed. For thus you may take the fortress of Phana.

Mode A3, Topic 2e

Delphi. Direct, Verse—Paus. 10.18.2.

   Comment: See pp. 171 note 10, 181–182, 183, 186.

   The besiegers discovered that a spring with little water, situated outside the walls, was Phana's sole water supply; and so they blocked it.

Q204 (PW254). [c. 520 B.C.] Not genuine.

C. Thessalians.

Occ. Siege of Keressos, Thespian fort.

Q. Not stated.

R. Shadowy Leuktra, the Alesian ground, and the sorrowful daughters of Skedasos are my concern. There a tearful battle will occur. And no man will see it until the Dorians lose their youth when a fateful day comes on. Then can Keressos be taken, and at no other time.

Mode F, Topic 3h (2e)

Delphi. Direct, Verse—Paus. 9.14.3.

NP. Indirect—Oracle: *Xen. Hell. 6.4.7.

OP. Chresmologues. Indirect—Diod. 15.54.1–2. Cf. Plut. Pelop. 20.7, 21.1; Ps.-Plut. Mor. 774d.

   Comment: See pp. 144–148, 178.

Q205 (PW253). 371 B.C.

C. Thebans.

Occ. Approaching battle at Leuktra.

Q. Not stated.

R. Content not recorded.

Delphi. Testimony—Paus. 4.32.5.

   Comment: The Thebans sent inquirers to the Ismenion, Ptoon, Abai, Delphi, and Trophonios. Pausanias records only Trophonios' response, telling them in verse to set up the Messenian Aristomenes' shield, then in Trophonios' temple (see Q19), as a tropaion on the battlefield beforehand. The Trophonios oracle is dubious; but it is probable that the Thebans consulted Delphi at this time.

Q206 (PW255). [Before 371 B.C.] Not genuine.

C. Spartans.

Occ. War with Thebes?

Q. Not stated.

R. The Spartans will be victorious as long as they fight in company with flute players and not against flute players.
Mode A3, Topic 2e
NP. Indirect—The god: Polyainos *Strat.* 1.10.

    Comment: All Thebans learned to play the flute; and so the Spartans lost the battle of Leuktra, when their fluteplayers did not lead them into battle, as was customary. The response purports to be a prediction of the outcome of Leuktra. It is obviously an *avertissement incompris* of narrative.

Q207 (PW258). [Before 362 B.C.] Not genuine.
C. Epaminondas of Thebes.
Occ. and Q. Not stated.
R. He should beware of *pelagos* (sea).
Mode C2, Topic 3h
Delphi. Indirect—Paus. 8.11.10.
NP. Indirect—The god: Suda *E*1949.
    Comment: See pp. 59, 68.

Q208 (PW496). [368/7.] Not genuine.
C. Aristotle.
Occ. and Q. Not stated.
R. He should engage in philosophy.
Mode A1, Topic 3d
Delphi. Indirect—*Vit. Aristot.* pp. 427, 438 Rose. Latin *Vit. Aristot.* p. 443 Rose.

    Comment: Surely Aristotle never needed this direction. The *Vita* says that he received it at the age of seventeen. It is another example of the effort to give Delphi credit for all philosophers' careers. Cf. Q201, 224, 248, 252.

Q209 (PW554). [c. 350 B.C.] Not genuine.
C. Spartans.
Occ. Baby girls born ugly in appearance.
Q. What cure can they find?
R. Through the wrath of Aphrodite recently offended this disease befell Sparta. The goddess will cease from wrath when she is honored with an image.
Mode A1 (D2), Topic 1a
Delphi. Indirect—Chor. *Gaz.* 29 arg., 16 (2–3, 90).
NP. Testimony—Oracle—*Paus. 3.18.1.

    Comment: Pausanias saw an image of Aphrodite Ambologera near the statues of Pausanias (see Q174) and says only that it was placed there *kata manteian.* According to Chorikios the Spartans engaged Praxiteles to make the image. Hence we must consider this a Q response; otherwise the nature of Chorikios' story would call for classification as L.

Q210 (PW264). [c. 350 B.C.] Not genuine.
C. Athenians.
Occ. Political issues of the Athenian state.
Q. Not stated.
R. Though the other Athenians agree, one man is opposed to the city.
Mode D2, Topic 3g
Delphi. Indirect—Plut. Phok. 8.3.

> Comment: The man was Phokion.

Q211 (PW269). [357 B.C.] Not genuine.
C. Chairon of Megalopolis for King Philip II of Macedon.
Occ. A dream in which Philip placed a seal with a lion's form impression on his wife
Olympia's belly and saw a snake stretched on the bed beside her.
Q. On meaning of the visions.
R. He should sacrifice to Ammon and worship him especially. He will lose the sight of
the eye which he put to the keyhole of his wife's door when he saw the god in snake
form lying with her.
Mode A1 (E2), Topic 1b (3f)
Delphi. Indirect—Plut. Alex. 3.1.

Q212 (PW507). [c. 340–336.] Not genuine.
C. King Philip II of Macedon.
Occ. Concern for the succession.
Q. Who will become king after me?
R. That man will rule the whole world and subdue all men with his spear who mounts
the horse Bukephalos and rides through the center of Pella.
Mode F, Topic 3g (2a)
Delphi. Direct, Prose—Ps.-Kallisthenes Alex. p. 36 Raabe.

Q213 (PW266). [337/6.] Not genuine.
C. King Philip II of Macedon.
Occ. Plan for war against Persia.
Q. Will I vanquish the king of the Persians?
R. The bull is garlanded; he comes to an end; the sacrificer is at hand.
Mode E3 (D2), Topic 1b (3c)
Delphi. Direct, Verse—Diod. 16.91.2. Paus. 8.7.6.

> Comment: See pp. 67, 157 note 17.

Q214 (PW267). [c. 340 B.C.] Not genuine.
C. King Philip II of Macedon.
Occ. and Q. Not stated.
R. He should secure his safety from the violence of a chariot.
Mode C2, Topic 3h (2e)

Delphi. Indirect—Val. Max. 1.8 ext. 9.

NP. Indirect—Oracle: *Poseidonios *ap.* Cic. *Fat.* 3.5.

OP. Trophonios. Indirect—Ael. *VH* 3.45.

    Comment: See p. 60.

    This admittedly belongs to the pseudo-history of Philip. The story is absurd in itself as Valerius Maximus tells it. Aelian reports not only the fulfillment in the chariot engraved on the assassin's sword hilt, but also another, that Philip was killed while going around the Theban lake called Harma (in that version he did not beware of the place so named).

    Cicero takes his notice of Q214 from Poseidonios without indicating a speaker. Aelian attributes it to Trophonios; and since his source is probably Poseidonios, we can be fairly certain that Trophonios was the speaker in the original story, and that faulty transmission or simple error accounts for Delphi in Valerius Maximus' version.

Q215 (PW268). [c. 350 B.C.] Not genuine.

C. King Philip II of Macedon.

Occ. and Q. Not stated.

R. Fight with silver spears and you will win everything.

Mode A3, Topic 3h (3j)

Delphi. Direct, Verse—Suda *A*3788. Makar. 2.29. Mant. Prov. 2.23.

NP. Direct, Verse—The god: *Diogen. 2.81. Apost. 3.91.

    Comment: This is a proverbial saying as the sources indicate. The oracle story refers to Philip's policy of purchasing treason or surrender when he could do so in preference to carrying on a siege.

Q216 (PW270). [335 B.C.] Not genuine.

C. Alexander the Great.

Occ. Proposed Persian campaign.

Q. None.

R. You are invincible, youth.

Mode D1, Topic 3j (2e)

Delphi. Direct, Prose—Plut. *Alex.* 14.4. Cf. Ps.-Kallisthenes *Alex.* p. 125 Raabe.

    Indirect—*Diod. 17.93.4.

    Testimony—Auson. *Idyll* 7 *dedicatio.*

NP. Testimony—Apollo: Parmenion *ap.* Anth. Pal. 7.239.

OP. Ammon. Direct, Prose—Frag. Sabb. 151.1.10J.

    Indirect—*Diod. 17.51.3 (93.4).

    Comment: See pp. 227, 251.

    This is part of the Alexander legend, which became divided between Delphic Apollo and Ammon as speaker. Diodoros' sources indicated both; but his narrative at 17.51 shows that Ammon is speaker in the original story. There the response is longer than the Pythia's brief remark as Diodoros 17.93 and Plutarch report it: Zeus through his prophet tells Alexander that he will be always *anikêtos.* Someone then attributed this statement to Delphi and assimilated the story of Alexander's visit to that of Philomelos' consultation, when he forced the Pythia to mount the tripod and she said that he had the power to do as he wished (H2o). Like Philomelos, Alexander took the Pythia's remark as Apollo's response, a *klêdôn*, though she had not yet mounted the tripod in this case. See Parke 1956: 240 and PW, p. 110 (*ad* PW270). The vocative Ô *pai* itself points to an earlier Ammon version in which Zeus addressed Alexander as his son.

Pseudo-Kallisthenes much expands the Delphic version. His text does not mention Delphi, but reports that Alexander consulted Apollo in the country of the Akraganthinoi, which would seem to mean Agrigentum (the name was already in the text before the Armenian and Ethiopic versions were made). Alexander has just come from Lokroi, which could be taken for Italian Locri, but after the consultation he heads for Thebes. Furthermore a priestess called *Phoibolalos* refuses him a consultation, and he then threatens to carry off the tripod as Herakles had done on an earlier occasion. Obviously the scene is Delphi and the text's *Akraganthinous* must be due to some strange error of transmission. Alexander seizes the tripod, whereupon there came a voice from the adyton saying, "Herakles, Alexander, did this as a god to a god; but you are mortal: do not oppose gods. For the report of your exploits has reached the gods." The prophetess then spoke: "Alexander, the god himself has given you a response, addressing you with the stronger name; for from the chasm he shouted 'Herakles Alexander.' This I predict to you, that you are destined to become stronger than anyone." The last sentence is a transformation of the earlier *Anikêtos ei*.

The short form is reported for Ammon too. The Sabbaitic fragment has Μειράκιον ἀνίκητον εἶ, "You are an invincible boy," where the vocative *pai* has become the predicate *meirakion*.

Q217 (PW271). [335 B.C. or earlier.] Not genuine.
C. Alexander the Great.
Occ and Q. Not stated.
R. A wolf will be Alexander's guide on the expedition against the Persians.
Mode E3, Topic 3h (2e)
Delphi. Indirect—Plut. *Alex.* 37.1.
NP. Indirect—Apollo: Polyainos *Strat.* 4.3.27. Oracle: *Curt. Ruf. *Alex.* 5.4.

   Comment: The wolf (*lykos*) was a Lycian (*Lykios*) guide. Arrian does not mention either the guide or the response; and Diodoros (17.68.5) tells about the guide without reference to a response. Curtius Rufus, our earliest source, who probably depends on Kleitarchos, mentions only an anonymous oracle and reports just a prophecy that the guide will be a Lycian citizen. This may be the interpretation expressed as the response.

Q218 (PW509). [334 B.C.] Not genuine.
C. Amphiktions or Hellenes.
Occ. Alexander's crossing into Asia.
Q. Not stated.
R. Honor Zeus, highest of gods, Athena Tritogeneia, and the lord [*anax*] concealed in
   mortal body, whom Zeus begat, defender of good order for men, King Alexander.

Mode A1 (D1), Topic 1a (3a)
Delphi. Direct, Verse—Socr. *Hist. eccl.* 3.23, p. 448 Migne.

Comment: The nature of the source does not allow us to put much confidence in the authenticity of this response. See Didyma 9.

Q219 (PW272). [c. 335 B.C.] Not genuine.
C. Alexander the Great.
Occ. and Q. Not stated.
R. There will be plots against him in Macedon.
Mode E2, Topic 3e (2a)
Delphi. Testimony—Pomp. Trog./Justin 12.2.3.

Comment: More than one response seems indicated by *oracula.* Trogus says only *Delphica oracula insidias in Macedonia [praedixerant].* This is in a clause subordinate to a statement that Dodona made an ominous prediction to Alexander of Epeiros of the Jerusalem Chamber kind. It is unlikely that the Pythia made any predictions of plots or dangers to Alexander.

Q220 (PW273). [335 B.C.] Not genuine.
C. Thebans.
Occ. Portents before Alexander's attack, especially a strange spider web.
Q. On meaning of the portents.
R. This is a sign that the gods show to all mortals, and especially to the Boeotians and their neighbors.
Mode D2, Topic 3h (3j)
Delphi. Direct, Verse—Diod. 17.10.3.
Comment: See pp. 82–83.
Aelian *VH* 12.57 mentions the spider-web portent, but not the oracle.

Q221 (PW508). [335 B.C.] Not genuine.
C. Thebans.
Occ. Alexander's destruction of the city.
Q. Will they ever rebuild Thebes?
R. Hermes, Alkeides, and pugilist Polydeukes, the three having contended, will restore Thebes.
Mode E3, Topic 3g
Delphi. Direct, Verse—Ps.-Kallisthenes *Alex.* pp. 133–134 Raabe.
NP. Direct, Verse—Oracle: Tzetzes *Chil.* 7.421–422.
Comment: See Fontenrose 1968: 95–97.

Q222 (PW555). Before 300 B.C.?
C. Spartans.
Occ. and Q. Not stated.
R. They should worship Eileithuia as a goddess and build her a temple.

Mode A1, Topic 1a
Delphi. Testimony—Paus. 3.17.1.

Q223 (PW419). [310 B.C.] Not genuine.
C. Herakleia-on-Pontos.
Occ. Famine.
Q. Not stated.
R. They will deliver themselves from the evil if they crown Herakleides Euthyphron's
son while he lives with a golden crown and honor him as a hero after his death.
Mode A1, Topic 1a
Delphi. Indirect—Hermippos 3.46–47M *ap.* Diog. Laert. 5.6.91. Acad. Philos. Index
Herculanensis, col. 9, p. 25 Mekler.
Comment: In the Index Πυθίον is a certain restoration; the text appears to be taken
from Hermippos. According to Hermippos, Herakleides bribed the envoys and the
Pythia to produce this response. Then Herakleides died of a stroke while receiving the
crown. This appears to be only a malicious story, perhaps Hermippos' own invention.

Q224 (PW421). [c. 315 B.C.] Not genuine.
C. Zeno of Kition.
Occ. Need of a profession.
Q. What should he do to have the best life?
R. [He will have the best life] if he can take on the color of the dead.
Mode A3, Topic 3j
Delphi. Indirect—Schol. Ven. on Aristoph. *Nub.* 144.
NP. Indirect—The god: *Hekaton and Apollonios of Tyre *ap.* Diog. Laert. 7.1.2.
Suda Aι76, Z79, Σ1313.
Comment: The Scholiast, who alone calls this Delphic, quotes a trimeter as an
example of a non-hexameter oracle. The verse, however, is expressed in the third person.
The Scholiast also says that the verse came from a comic poet. The poet was probably
repeating a common saying; the verse has a gnomic flavor, whatever its original intention. It became an oracle only when it was attached to the legend of Zeno the Stoic,
which conforms to the usual philosopher's legend: the philosopher received his first
impulse to philosophy from the Delphic Oracle; compare Q201, 208, 248, 252.

Q225 (PW275). [c. 362/1.] Not genuine.
C. Karkinos of Rhegium through Carthaginian envoys.
Occ. Ominous dreams following upon his impregnating his mistress.
Q. On the child to be born.
R. The child will be the cause of great misfortunes for the Carthaginians and for all Sicily.
Mode E2, Topic 3e
Delphi. Indirect—Diod. 19.2.3.
Comment: Compare Q140. The child was Agathokles.

Q226 (PW276). [c. 350–300.] Not genuine.

C. Apollophanes the Arcadian.

Occ. Desire to learn who was Asklepios' mother.

K. Was Asklepios born of Arsinoe, and was he a fellow-citizen of the Messenians?

R. Asklepios, born to be a great joy to all mortal men, lovely Koronis Phlegyas' daughter
  bore you after uniting in love with me in craggy Epidauros.

Mode D1, Topic 3a

Delphi. Direct, Verse—Paus. 2.26.7.

   Comment: It is more likely that the Pythia would agree that Asklepios' mother was
Arsinoe, to please the consultant, if this were a real consultation. Compare H65. The
response seems intended to depreciate the Messenians by supporting the better-known
story that Koronis was his mother. For an inscribed hymn to Asklepios as Koronis' son
with a greeting to Apollon Pythios see Rev. Arch. ser. 3, 13 (1889) 70–71 = IG 4². 4509.

Q227 (PW286). [c. 300 B.C.] Not genuine.

C. Envoys of King Ptolemy of Egypt.

Occ. Dreams of a youth who tells Ptolemy to fetch his image from Pontos.

Q. Not stated.

R. They should go and bring back the image of his father, but leave his sister's image there.

Mode A1, Topic 1a

Delphi. Indirect—Plut. Mor. 984b. Tac. Hist. 4.83.4.

   Comment: See p. 122.

Q228 (PW352). [c. 325 B.C.] Not genuine.

C. Romans.

Occ. War with Samnites.

Q. Not stated.

R. The images of the bravest and of the wisest Greek should be dedicated in a frequented
  place.

Mode A1, Topic 1a

Delphi. Indirect—Pliny NH 34.12.26.

NP. Indirect—Oracle: Plut. Numa 8.

   Comment: See p. 152 note 7.

   Pliny attributes this response to the Pythian Apollo at the time of a Samnite war
(PW suppose the second war). According to the story, the Romans, having received this
oracle, placed statues of Alkibiades and Pythagoras in the Forum. Plutarch mentions
only an unidentified chrêsmos and does not date it in any way. Pliny says that the statues
stood there until Sulla cleared the space for the Curia, so that apparently he never saw
them; thus we cannot be sure that these statues were ever set up. The response can hardly
be genuine, though Parke (1956: 271) thinks it authentic. Either this was anonymous at
first or attributed to the Sibylline Books; see Q229. It may be Pliny's own assumption
that the Pythian Apollo spoke it; and he wonders why the Senate judged Pythagoras

the wisest Greek, when the same god had already named Socrates as superior in wisdom to all men.

Q229 (PW353). [293 B.C.] Not genuine.
C. Romans.
Occ. Plague.
Q. Help our suffering state with your healing art and let the woes of the city end.
R. You should have sought from a nearer place what you seek from me. Go to the nearer place. It is not Apollo but Apollo's son that you need to diminish your woes. Go with good omens and summon my son.
Mode A1, Topic 1a
Delphi. Pseudo-Direct, Verse (Latin)—Ovid Met. 15.637–640.
    Indirect—Lact. Narr. 15.50.
OP. Sibylline Books. Indirect—*Livy 10.47.7. Val. Max. 1.8.2.
    Comment: See pp. 151–152, 161.
    Ovid has a longer text in the Latin verse of the response than do Livy and Valerius in their indirect forms, and he phrases it very differently; but he says no more than they do: he simply elaborates the simple message that the Romans should summon Aesculapius from Epidauros in order to heal the city. For example Apollo tells the Romans to go to a nearer place than Delphi though really Epidauros is farther from Rome than is Delphi. See Q237.

Q230 (PW441). [280 B.C.] Not genuine.
C. King Pyrros of Epeiros.
Occ. War with the Romans.
Q. Not stated.
R. I say, Pyrros, that you the Romans can defeat.
Mode E3, Topic 2e
Delphi. Pseudo-Direct, Verse (Latin)—Ennius ap. Cic. Div. 2.56.116. Porph. on Hor. AP 403.
    Testimony—Ennius ap. Min. Fel. Oct. 26.6. Auson. Idyll 12.10.5. Oros. Hist. 4.1.7.
NP. Pseudo-Direct, Verse (Latin)—Apollo: Liber de vir. ill. 35.2. Aug. CD 3.17.10.
    Testimony—The god: Tert. Apol. 22.10.
OP. Dodona. Indirect—Dion Cass. frag. 40.4.
    Comment: See pp. 56, 67, 83.
    The Latin verse, Aio te Aeacida Romanos vincere posse, has no Greek original, and it would be difficult to frame a Greek hexameter with the same meaning and same ambiguity. It is Ennius' invention, as Cicero makes plain (see also Minucius Felix), and not a paraphrase of any response genuine or fictitious. Ennius wanted to put Pyrros in the role of Croesus and to give him the same kind of response as Q100. All sources depend directly or indirectly on Ennius, and all are Latin with the exception of Dion Cassius, who says that Pyrros received his response at Dodona. This is probably not an independent tradition: Dion too most likely takes the story from Ennius ultimately, but as a

touch of verisimilitude has transferred the consultation to Dodona, since Pyrros as king of Epeiros would be likely to patronize home industry.

Q231 (PW329). [278 B.C.] Not genuine.
C. Delphians.
Occ. Approach of Gauls.
Q. Shall we remove the treasures, children, and women from the Oracle to the strongest neighboring cities? (Diodoros).
R. Let the offerings and everything else stay where they are at the Oracle (Diodoros). I and the white maidens will attend to this.
Mode C1 (E1), Topic 1d (3e)
Delphi. Direct, Verse (iambic trimeter), second part—Aristeides 26.339. Zen. Athôos 29 = E. Miller, Mélanges 352. App. Prov. 2.55. Suda E1060. Tzetzes Chil. 11.394. Schol. on Aristoph. Nub. 144. Incomplete—Schol. on Aristeides 46.181, p. 584 Dind. Pseudo-Direct, Verse (iambic trimeter, Latin), second part—*Cic. Div. 1.37.81. Indirect—Diod. 22.9.5. Paus. 10.22.12. Val. Max. 1.1 ext. 9. Pomp. Trog./Justin 24.7.6.
    Comment: See p. 87 note 62; Fontenrose 1960a: 191–205. Compare Q149.

Q232 (PW331). [280 B.C. ?] Not genuine.
C. Opuntian Locrians.
Occ. Crippled and monstrous children born to Locrian women.
Q. Not stated.
R. (A) The god would not give them an oracle.
R. (B) They must resume sending Locrian maidens to Troy.
Mode A1 (C1), Topic 1b
Delphi. Testimony—Ael. frag. 47 ap. Suda A2417, E1015, 3257, K2162, Π2918.
    Comment: See pp. 132, 133, 136, 137.

Q233 (PW333). [283–239.] Not genuine.
C. Astypalaeans.
Occ. Too many hares.
Q. Not stated.
R. They should raise dogs and hunt them.
Mode A1, Topic 3e
Delphi. Indirect—Hegesandros of Delphi 4.421M ap. Ath. 9.400d.
    Comment: It is unlikely that the Astypalaeans would need a Delphic oracle to tell them this.

Q234 (PW573). [After 300 B.C.] Not genuine.
C. Antiochenes.
Occ. Unspecified difficulties.
Q. Not stated.

R. The only deliverance is the removal of the gods in Cyprus to Antioch.
Mode A1, Topic 1a
Delphi. Indirect—Liban. *Or.* 11.111.

 Comment: In Libanios' story the gods, wanting to move from Cyprus to Antioch, persuade Apollo at Pytho to speak this response. The Antiochenes had exact copies of the images made and then took the true images from Cyprus, leaving the copies in their place. This response could be classed as L, if the scene were not given as Antioch, founded in 300. The story may be no more than Libanios' invention in laudation of Antioch, where the gods preferred to dwell; hence this response might also be classified as F.

Q235 (PW358). [213 B.C.] Not genuine.
C. Sicyonians.
Occ. Plan to bury Aratos within the city walls, although an ancient law forbade such burial.
Q. On this matter.
R. You plan to reward Aratos with a rite and festival for saving you. That which is oppressed by this man and that which oppresses you is an impiety of earth, sky, and sea.
Mode D2, Topic 1a (3j)
Delphi. Direct, Verse—Plut. *Arat.* 53.2.

 Comment: The verses presumably allow the Sicyonians to move Aratos' body to a grave within the city. This could be taken as a sanction of their proposal to do so; but the verse form and its obscure language are suspect.

Q236 (PW355). 207 B.C. Probably genuine.
C. M. Pomponius Matho, Q. Catius, envoys of the Romans.
Occ. Dedication of gifts made from the spoils of victory over Hasdrubal.
Q. Not stated.
R. The Roman people will soon have a victory much greater than that from whose spoils you have brought gifts.
Mode E2, Topic 2e
Delphi. Indirect—Livy 29.10.6.

 Comment: See Q237.

 Livy's source may be Fabius Pictor; see H48. The prediction was fairly safe to make at this time.

Q237 (PW356). 205 B.C.
C. Envoys of the Romans.
Occ. Sibylline oracle telling the Romans that they can drive the Carthaginians from Italy if they bring the Idaean Mother from Pessinûs.
Q. What hope does Apollo offer them and the Roman people of accomplishing the business on which they had been sent from home?
R. They will get what they are looking for through King Attalos; when they bring the goddess to Rome, they should take care that the best man in Rome receive her as his guest.

Mode E1 (A1), Topic 1d (1a, 2d)

Delphi. Indirect—Livy 29.11.6. Dion Cass. 17.57.61. Val. Max. 8.15.3. Jul. *Or.* 5.159c.

NP. Pseudo-Direct, Verse (elegiac, Latin)—Apollo: Ovid *Fasti* 4.263-264.

> *Comment:* See p. 152.

Here the finding of a Sibylline oracle is followed by a consultation of Delphi: compare Q229. The purpose, however, was not to get Delphic confirmation of the Sibylline command, but to inquire about the best means of executing it. Again Livy may have found this in Fabius Pictor.

Q238 (PW357). [Before 201 B.C.] Not genuine.

C., Occ., and Q. Not stated.

R. When a Trojan brood surpasses Phoenicians in battle, then there will be unbelievable events: the sea will shine with fire, and after thunder, waterspouts mingled with rocks will gush upward through the water, and an unknown island will fix itself firmly there; and worse men will forcefully vanquish the better.

Mode F, Topic 3h (2e)

Delphi. Direct, Verse—Plut. *Mor.* 399c.

> *Comment:* See pp. 149, 161, 166, 169.

Q239 (PW359). [c. 135 B.C.] Not genuine.

C. Daphidas (Daphnites), *grammatikos.*

Occ. Effort to deceive the Pythia (he did not own a horse).

Q. Will he find his horse?

R. He will soon find his horse [but will be thrown from it and die (Poseidonios, Valerius Maximus)].

Mode E3, Topic 3e (3c)

Delphi. Indirect—Val. Max. 1.8 ext. 8. Hesych. Mil. *Onom.* 14, 4.160M. Suda Δ99.

NP. Indirect—Oracle: *Poseidonios *ap.* Cic. *Fat.* 3.5.

> *Comment:* See pp. 60-61, 113; Fontenrose 1960b; Q240.

Q240 (PW360). [c. 135 B.C.] Not genuine.

C. Daphidas, *grammatikos.*

Occ. and Q. Not stated.

R. Beware of the breastplate [*thôrax*].

Mode C2, Topic 3h

NP. Indirect—Oracle: Strabo 14.1.39, p. 647.

> *Comment:* See p. 60; Fontenrose 1960b.

Q239-240 are variations on the Jerusalem Chamber theme and belong to two versions of the Daphidas tale, which can be distinguished as the horse version and the breastplate version. The former necessarily implicates Delphi, since it is in essence a fable about a sophist's attempt to deceive and ridicule the Delphic Oracle. The story comes from Poseidonios, as Cicero makes clear; and although Cicero does not mention Delphi he apparently had in mind the story as told by the other sources of Q139. If the execution of Daphidas occurred in 138-133, Poseidonios may have been an infant at the time, although the tale gives no indication of how long before Daphidas' death he made his alleged test of the Oracle. Hesychios and the Suda report that the response predicted he would find his horse soon—but that could mean several years in oracular language. In any case there is no good reason to classify Q239 as H.

Probably the breastplate version of Q240 is earlier than the other. It is anonymous in the only source; and all that Strabo tells us is that Daphidas had received an oracle which warned him against the *thôrax*.

Q241 (PW337). c. 200 B.C.? Perhaps genuine.
C. Methymnaeans.
Occ. A find in fishermen's nets of a head made of olive wood.
Q. Of what god or hero is the image?
R. It will be better for the people of Methymna to honor Dionysos Phallen.
Mode A2, Topic 1a
Delphi. Direct, Verse—Oinomaos *ap.* Eus. *PE.* 5.36, p. 233d. Theodor. *Gr. aff. cur.* 10.141.
Indirect—Paus. 10.19.3.
Comment: Oinomaos ridicules this verse response, as does Theodoretos. Still, there can be little objection to accepting it as a versified sanction, although it appears in company with unauthentic responses in Oinomaos' collection.

Q242 (PW424). [?] Not genuine.
C. An Asian.
Occ. Contemplated change of residence.
Q. Is it better for me to move to Corinth?
R. Blessed is Corinth, but I would be a Teneate.
Mode D1, Topic 3j
NP. Direct, Verse—Apollo: Strabo 8.6.22, p. 380.
Comment: See pp. 86, 172.
Since Apollo was worshiped in Tenea as Apollo Teneates, he may be taken as the speaker, although Strabo introduces the verse with the phrase, "the oracle given to an enquirer from Asia." The question has the form regularly used when a sanction is wanted.

Q243 (PW339). [c. 200 B.C.?] Not genuine.
C. Cretans of Phaistos, Tarra, and Dios.
Occ. and Q. Not stated.
R. I bid you offer the Pythian purification of Phoibos with reverence, that you may live prosperously in Crete and worship Zeus.
Mode A1, Topic 1b
Delphi. Direct, Verse—Oinomaos *ap.* Eus. *PE* 5.31, p. 226b.
Comment: The second verse is so phrased that it may be read as an instruction to cleanse Apollo himself (moreover the text of this response is corrupt). According to some sources Apollo received purification in Crete for his killing of Python (Fontenrose

1959: 15, 86), so that this may be an L oracle referred to the mythical time of Apollo's combat, and the speaker may be Themis at Pytho or the god of some other Oracle. But PW assign it to the 300–190 period; and that the consultants are from three specified towns gives an appearance of historicity to this response. That Oinomaos means a pronouncement of Delphic Apollo seems evident from *PE* 215c.

Q244 (PW430). 174 B.C.
C. King Perseus of Macedon.
Occ. Portents or omens observed.
Q. Not stated.
R. Not recorded.
Delphi. Testimony—Livy 41.22.5–6.

Q245 (PW431). [Before 240 B.C.] Not genuine.
C. King Attalos I of Pergamon.
Occ. Unspecified (περί τινος).
Q. None.
R. Take courage, bull-horned; you will have kingly office, and so will your grandsons, but not their sons.
Mode E2, Topic 2a
Delphi. Direct, Verse—Diod. 34/35.13. Suda A4316.
NP. Indirect—Oracle: Paus. 10.15.3.
    Comment: See p. 122.
    Pausanias refers this to a *chrêstêrion* and not to Phaennis, whose verses on Attalos he has just quoted; she called Attalos bull's son.

Q246 (PW433). [c. 95 B.C.] Not genuine.
C. Sulla.
Occ. Perhaps the appearance of Aphrodite in a dream.
Q. Not stated.
R. Kypris has given you great power in her concern for Aeneas' brood. But make yearly offerings to all the gods; do not forget them. Bring gifts to Delphi. In a town named for Aphrodite, high in the Tauros Mountains, dedicate an axe and you will receive wide rule.
Mode A1 (D1), Topic 1b (2a, 3i)
Delphi. Direct, Verse—App. *BC* 1.11.97.
    Comment: The only indication that the response is attributed to the Delphic Apollo is the injunction in it to make gifts to Delphi.

Q247 (PW434). [c. 86 B.C.] Not genuine.
C. Athenian refugees.
Occ. Sulla's harsh dealings with Athenians.
Q. Has the fated time of Athens' destruction come upon it?

R. They should not be too much troubled in spirit; a wineskin floats on the sea.
Mode C1 (D1), Topic 3j (2f)
Delphi. Testimony—Paus. 1.20.7.

Comment: This is the same as L22, spoken to Theseus. Pausanias indicates that response, but does not quote it.

Q248 (PW435). [79 B.C.] Not genuine.
C. Cicero.
Occ. Concern for his career.
Q. How will he become very famous?
R. He should make his own nature, not the opinion of the multitude, the guide of life.
Mode A1, Topic 3j
Delphi. Indirect—Plut. *Cic.* 5.1.

Comment: Cicero's silence about having received such an oracle is conclusive. Parke, who considers this response authentic, thinks that Cicero may have alluded to it in his lost *De gloria* (1956: 407–408 with note 37). But surely Cicero would have mentioned it elsewhere; it is the sort of event that he would have referred to at every opportunity. Would he not have put it into Quintus' defense of divination in *De divinatione*?

Q249 (PW436). [48 B.C.] Not genuine.
C. Appius Claudius Pulcher.
Occ. Civil war between Caesar and Pompey.
Q. What will be the outcome of the civil war?
R. This war does not concern you at all; you will possess the hollows of Euboea.
Mode E3 (D1), Topic 3i (2e)
Delphi. Pseudo-Direct, Verse (Latin)—Lucan *BC* 5.194–196.
   Pseudo-Direct, Prose (Latin)—*Val. Max. 1.8.10. Oros *Hist.* 6.15.11.
   Testimony—Arg. Lucan *BC* 5.

Comment: See pp. 66, 199, 207 note 18, 208–210.

Q250 (PW518). [A.D. 12.] Not genuine.
C. Emperor Augustus.
Occ. Concern for the succession.
Q. (A) Who will rule after me?
R. (A) [No response.]
Q. (B) Why is the Oracle silent?
R. (B) A Hebrew boy, a god who rules among the blessed, bids me leave this house and go back to Hades. So go in silence from my altars.
Mode C1 (D2), Topic 1d
Delphi. Direct, Verse—Eus. *ap.* Cedr. 1. p. 320b. Malalas pp. 231–232. Suda *A*4413.
   Nikeph. Kall. *Hist. eccl.* 1.17, p. 83.

Comment: This is the first appearance of a Christian oracle, devised to show that the Delphic Apollo foresaw the mission of Christ and the end of Oracles. Compare Q263, 268.

Q251 (PW461). [A.D. 67.] Not genuine.

C. Emperor Nero.

Occ. and Q. Not stated.

R. He should beware of the seventy-third year.

Mode C2, Topic 3h (3c)

Delphi. Indirect—Suet. Nero 40.3.

 Testimony—Cf. Dion Cass. 62.14.2.

 Comment: Galba was seventy-three years old (or in his seventy-third year).

Q252 (PW463). [c. A.D. 155.] Not genuine.

C. Galen.

Occ. and Q. Not stated.

R. He should become a physician.

Mode A1, Topic 3d

Delphi. Testimony—Sopater Prol. in Aristid. Panath. p. 740 Dind.

 Comment: See Q208. Sopater rejects this response, saying that the Delphic Oracle was not in operation at the time. This is probably untrue; nevertheless it is unlikely that Galen had to be told by an Oracle to become a physician. Parke, however, thinks this genuine (1956: 409).

Q253 (PW510). [A.D. 193.] Not genuine.

C. Romans.

Occ. Conflict of Septimius Severus, Pescennius Niger, and Clodius Albinus for the empire.

Q. Who will rule the state most advantageously?

R. Fuscus is best, Afer good, Albus worst.

Mode D1, Topic 2a

Delphi. Pseudo-Direct, Verse (Latin)—Aelius Spartianus Hist. Aug., Pesc. Nig. 8. Incomplete—Julius Capitolinus ibid., Clod. Alb. 1.4.

Q254 (PW511). [A.D. 193.] Not genuine.

C. Romans.

Occ. Same as Q253.

Q. Who will get the state?

R. The blood of Albus and Niger, living, will be poured out; he who has come from a Punic city will rule the empire.

Mode E2, Topic 2a (3c)

Delphi. Pseudo-Direct, Verse (Latin)—Aelius Spartianus Hist. Aug., Pesc. Nig. 8.

Q255 (PW512). [A.D. 193.] Not genuine.

C. Romans.

Occ. Same as Q253.

Q. Who will succeed the victor (Septimius Severus)?

R. He to whom the gods have given the name of Pius.

Mode E3, Topic 2a.

Delphi. Pseudo-Direct, Verse (Latin)—Aelius Spartianus Hist. Aug., Pesc. Nig. 8.

Q256 (PW513). [A.D. 193.] Not genuine.

C. Romans.

Occ. Same as Q253.

Q. How long will he [Severus] rule?

R. He takes to sea in twenty ships if a single boat will cross the sea.

Mode E3, Topic 3e (2a)

Delphi. Pseudo-Direct, Verse (elegiac, Latin)—Aelius Spartianus Hist. Aug., Pesc. Nig. 8.

Comment: Q253-256 were reputedly spoken one after the other in a single session. They are inventions for the Historia Augusta, a totally untrustworthy document.

Q257 (PW468). [?] Not genuine.

C. Diogenes, a father.

Occ. His son's enduring and worsening love-sickness.

Q. Will my son ever recover from his sickness?

R. Your son will cease from his love passion when he has burned out his heart in youth with Aphrodite's seductive frenzy. So be milder in temper and do not insist on forbidding him, since you accomplish the opposite of your intentions. But if you turn to gentleness, he will soon forget his passion and return to his senses.

Mode A1 (C1, E1), Topic 3e

Delphi. Direct, Verse—Ael. frag. 103 ap. Sud. Δ1145.

Comment: The story has much resemblance to episodes of romances, and the oracle could be classified as F. It is impossible to say when Aelian supposes this event to have occurred, whether in his own lifetime or earlier. Hence to assign any date is pure guesswork.

Q258 (PW469). [A.D. 228.] Not genuine.

C. Themistokles, philosopher.

Occ. and Q. Not stated.

R. A good man, fortunate, honored by the blessed gods.

Mode D1, Topic 3g

Delphi. Direct, Verse—Synk. 361b.

Comment: Probably Synkellos took this entry from Eusebios' Chronika. The verse is apparently a fragment of an oracle, if it was originally composed for an oracle at all. Since the entry is under A.D. 228, this cannot be the fourth-century Themistokles known to Libanios. Nothing is known about an earlier philosopher of that name. See p. 172.

Q259 (PW470). [?] Not genuine.

C. Athenians.

Occ. Temple of Apollo destroyed by lightning.

Q. Why was Apollo's temple destroyed?

R. Whenever roaring winds battle together with loud thunders, and around the world there is a windless chill, and the troubled sky has no vent for escape, lightning falls on earth at random. Then in the mountains beasts fly from it in fear to their deep lairs and do not stay to look upon Zeus's descending shaft. Temples of gods, tall trees, mountain peaks, and ships at sea are overwhelmed by its fiery flight. Even Poseidon's wife, Amphitrite, is often struck and retires. So you, though you are aggrieved, endure the inflexible plans of the Moirai; for Zeus has assured them that their decrees shall remain unshaken. For it was destiny that after a long time the beautiful shrine be overcome by Zeus-thrown lightnings.

Mode D1, Topic 3h (1d)

NP. Direct, Verse—Apollo: Porph. *ap.* Eus. *PE* 6.3, pp. 238d–239d. Incomplete— Apollo: Eus. *PE* 6.3, p. 240a–c. Theodor. *Gr. aff. cur.* 10.141.

Comment: See p. 183.

This response has 23 verses, the next longest after H69. It is extremely difficult to date, but probaby was thought to have occurred before Porphyry's time.

Q260 (PW521). [?] Not genuine.
C. Cappadocians.
Occ. Loss of their herds of horses.
Q. Not stated.
R. They should import horses from Agrigentum.
Mode A1, Topic 3e
Delphi. Testimony—Serv. *Aen.* 3.704.

Comment: It seems strange that the Cappadocians should need an oracle about where to get horses, and that they should receive it at Delphi. Servius is hardly a reliable source for this sort of information.

Q261 (PW474). [c. A.D. 300.] Not genuine.
C., Occ., and Q. Not stated.
R. The Syrian is inspired, the Phoenician is learned.
Mode D1, Topic 3g
Delphi. Direct, Prose—David *In Porph. Isag. prooem.* 4, *PACA* 18.2, p. 92.

Comment: The Syrian is Iamblichos, the Phoenician Porphyry. Perhaps this verse was not originally composed as an oracle.

Q262 (PW600). [A.D. 362.] Not genuine.
C. Emperor Julian.
Occ. Contemplated war on Persia.
Q. Should I take the field?
R. Now all the gods have set out to carry trophies to the banks of the wild-beast river.
   And I shall lead them, furious war-shouting Ares.
Mode E3, Topic 2e
Delphi. Direct, Verse and Prose—Theodor. *Hist. eccl.* 3.16.21. Incomplete—Theodor. *Gr. aff. cur.* 10.140.
NP. Direct, Verse and Prose—Oracle: Kedr. p. 538b.

Comment: See pp. 5, 56, 67–68, 426.

Q263 (PW476). [361/2.] Not genuine.

C. Oribasios as envoy of Emperor Julian.

Occ. Contemplated revival of Delphic Oracle.

Q. Not stated.

R. Tell the emperor that my hall has fallen to the ground. Phoibos no longer has his house nor his mantic bay nor his prophetic spring; the water has dried up.

Mode D2, Topic 1d

Delphi. Direct, Verse—Philostorgios 7, p. 77 Berlin ed., ap. Artemii Pass. 35. Kedr. 1, p. 532b.

Comment: See pp. 5, 56, 207; Q250.

Q264 (PW246). [c. 40 B.C.?] Not genuine.

C., Occ., and Q. Not stated.

R. Most happy is Pedius, who recently died for his country.

Mode D1, Topic 3g

Delphi. Indirect—Pliny NH 7.46.151.

Comment: Pliny gives this as an example of oracula velut ad castigandam hominum vanitatem deo emissa. See Q97.

Q265 (PW538). [?] Not genuine.

C. Aristinos.

Occ. Finding men afraid to associate with him on his return home from abroad after performance of his funeral rites, when he was supposed dead.

Q. I request release from the present difficulties that arise from the customary law.

R. Perform again all that a woman giving birth does on her bed, and make sacrifice to the blessed gods.

Mode A1, Topic 3a (1b)

Delphi. Direct, Verse—Plut. Mor. 265a.

Comment: This might be classified as L; but Plutarch seems to place Aristinos in historical times.

Q266 (PW549). Before 300 B.C.?

C. Spartans.

Occ. and Q. Not stated.

R. Establish a foot race of eleven Dionysiac women.

Mode A1, Topic 1d

Delphi. Testimony—Paus. 3.13.7.

Q267 (PW550). Before 300 B.C.?

C. Citizens of Alea.

Occ. and Q. Not stated.

R. They should flog women at Dionysos' festival.

Mode A1, Topic 1d

Delphi. Testimony—Paus. 8.23.1.

Q268. [c. 250 B.C. ?] Not genuine.

C. Achaeans.

Occ. Request of Philip, Attalos' brother, that the Achaeans help him against Dorias, murderess of Attalos.

Q. (A) Inform us on the matter on which we have come [whether we should help Philip against Dorias].

R. (A) After a time one will come to this earth and will become flesh without sin. By his divine decrees he will banish destruction caused by incurable passions, and he will incur the ill will of an unbelieving people and be hanged on high, condemned to death, which he will willingly endure; and he will rise from death to eternal life.

Q. (B) Cursed woman, we have asked you three times about a woman, not about a man.

R. (B) The times ahead are invincible. She and he and their companions will defeat all men.

Q. (C) Gods, why do you treat your servants thus, when they ask to win a war with a woman? Instead of one war you bring another war on us, not being immortal gods and true masters.

R. (C) The tripod turns a third turn: the prophetess is seated. A lightbringer, heaven-sent, will take away a third of this . . . fashioning a mortal body for himself. And her name is twice 76. He will destroy the queens and all our sacred worship and will deliver the prize of all fame to the highest wisdom.

Mode E2 (E3), Topic 3g (2e, 3c)

Delphi. Direct, Prose—John of Euboea Sermon, Anecdota Atheniensia, ed. A. Delatte, 1.325 = Amandry 1950: 257–258, text LXXXIX.

   Comment: pp. 122, 240, 358.

This is from an early medieval document. John of Euboea lived in the eighth century. The history is false, but appears to concern successors of Alexander. The Achaean envoys went first to the priestess Euoptia at the Castalian spring. She answered them after drinking the mantic spring water. Her first reply made them indignant and they expostulated, but her second reply was no more satisfactory. So they left Castalia and went to the temple of Athena (Pronaia). Here they interrupted the weaving of the sacred web. The priestess Xanthippe scolded them; they insulted her; and she then gave them a cryptic prophecy: "God's prince, born of a half-divine man, with invincible strength, destroys the boundless world like an egg, encompassing all men with his spear." The envoys then left Athena's temple and went to Apollo's, where an unseen speaker addressed them—response (C). I have considered the two replies of Euoptia of Castalia as responses of the Delphic Apollo, though there is no other record of anyone's receiving oracles at the Castalian spring. But I have not included Xanthippe's response, since she presumably spoke an oracle of Athena.

III. Legendary Responses

L1 (PW19).
C. Agamemnon.
Occ. Beginning of the Trojan War.
Q. On the end of the war.
R. Agamemnon will take Ilion when the best of the Achaeans quarrel.
Mode F, Topic 3h (2e)
Delphi. Indirect—Schol. on Od. 8.75, 77, 80. Eust. Od. 8.73, p. 1586. Tzetz. *Exeg. Il.*
p. 67 Herm.
    Testimony—*Odyssey 8.78–81. Strabo 9.3.2, pp. 417–418.
        Comment: See pp. 4, 20, 91, 118.

L2 (PW20, 523).
C. Manto Teiresias' daughter and Theban captives.
Occ. Arrival in Delphi as captives of the Epigonoi.
Q. Not stated.
R. Manto should marry whatever man she meets; then she and the captives should go to
    Kolophon in Ionia.
Mode B (A1), Topic 3b
Delphi. Indirect—*Epigonoi* [*Thebaid*] frag. 4, p. 116 Allen *ap.* Schol. vet. *in* Apollon. *Arg.*
    1.308. Testimony—Paus. 7.3.1–2, 9.33.2.
        Comment: PW distinguish two responses, but the sources indicate a single consulta-
tion in the legend, when Apollo spoke to Manto and the other captives of the Epigonoi.
In the *Epigonoi* fragment, which is obviously summary, Manto met Rakios on leaving
the temple, married him according to the oracular instruction, and then went to

Kolophon. The lost epic account of the response must have included a direction to go to Ionia. Pausanias is interested only in the order that the captives should go to Kolophon. See p. 15.

L3 (PW22).
C. King Aletes of Corinth.
Occ. Coming of Melas and Dorians to Corinth, wanting to settle there.
Q. Not stated.
R. In ambiguous language Apollo appeared to forbid Aletes to receive Melas, but Aletes mistook the god's meaning.
Mode C2, Topic 2d
Delphi. Testimony—Paus. 2.4.4, 5.18.8.

Comment: The content of the response is lost. Melas apparently persuaded Aletes that he had misinterpreted the oracle, and finally with reluctance Aletes accepted him as synoikos.

L4 (PW110).
C. King Aigeus of Athens.
Occ. Lack of children.
Q. How may I have children?
R. Do not open the spigot of the wineskin until you reach Athens.
Mode C2, Topic 3j (3e)
Delphi. Direct, Verse—Plut. Thes. 3.5. Apollod. 3.15.6. Schol. vet. on Eur. Med. 679. Tzetzes on Lyk. 494.
  Indirect—Eur. Med. 679, 681. Plut. Rom. 35.7.
  Testimony—*Neophron ap. Schol. vet. in Eur. Med. 666. Eur. Suppl. 6–7. Schol. vet. on Eur. Hipp. 11. Codrus Painter, Beazley ARFVP² 1269 = fig. 2.
NP. Direct, Verse—Oracle: Anth. Pal. 14.150.

Comment: See pp. 17, 204.

For Neophron's notice we have only the testimony of the Euripidean Scholiast, who does not tell us in what form Neophron quoted the response; for he must have quoted it, since he, like Euripides, had a meeting of Aigeus and Medea in Corinth. All sources have the same tradition as Euripides, and the hexameter oracle has the same content as Euripides' trimeters. It is more probable that Euripides knew the hexameter form than that it was modeled on his verses.

L5 (PW111).
C. King Erginos of Orchomenos.
Occ. On reaching old age without children.
Q. About having children.
R. Put a new tip on the old plow-tree.
Mode A3, Topic 3j (3e)
Delphi. Direct, Verse—Paus. 9.37.4. Oinomaos ap. Eus. PE 5.30, p. 225cd. Incomplete— Plut. Mor. 784b.

Comment: The direction means to take a young wife. Compare the metaphor of L4.

L6 (PW138).

C. Inachos.

Occ. Io's terrible dreams.

Q. What must he do or say to please the gods?

R. He must banish Io from house and country to wander at the ends of earth; otherwise Zeus's thunderbolt will destroy the whole family.

Mode A1 (E2), Topic 3f (3c)

Delphi. Indirect—Aesch. Prom. 665–668.

Comment: See pp. 32, 36.

L7 (PW139).

C. Orestes.

Occ. Murder of Agamemnon.

Q. How should he avenge his father's murder upon the murderers? (Sophocles).

R. He must kill his father's murderers by guile as they killed him; otherwise Apollo will visit him with terrible diseases and assaults of Erinyes; he will be homeless and friendless, forbidden participation in sacred rites, until his death. Having done the deed he must not have recourse to any hearth but Apollo's (Aeschylus).

Mode A1 (C1, E2), Topic 3f (1d, 3c)

Delphi. Indirect—Aesch. Cho. 270–296, 1031–1032, 1038–1039 (556–559, 953–956); Eum. 84, 202–205, 466–467, 595, 623–624, 799 (713–716). Soph. El. 36–37 (1425). Eur. El. 973 (87–89, 1266–1267); Or. 29–30, 269–270, 416 (162–165, 329–331, 591–599, 1666–1669). Dion Chrys. 10.27. Thomas Mag. Arg. Eur. Or.

Testimony—Eur. Andr. 1031–1035; IT 713–715. Apollod. epit. 6.25. Aristeides 46.214 and Schol. p. 650 Dind. Liban. Decl. 6.2, 11–13, 22, 45–48, 60.

NP. Indirect—Oracle: Dict. Cret. 6.3.

Comment: See pp. 13, 32, 108–110, 117, 119, 236 note 3.

The summary of the response above is taken from Aeschylus Cho. 270–296 and 1038–1039. Other indirect quotations are brief, generally limited to the instruction to kill Agamemnon's murderers or just Clytemnestra.

L8 (PW602).

C. Orestes.

Occ. Erinyes' pursuit of him for killing his mother.

Q. None.

R. I will not betray you but will protect you. Take flight. The Erinyes will pursue you everywhere, but do not falter. Go to Athens and sit as suppliant at Athena's image. There you shall stand trial. I told you to kill your mother. Remember and fear not (Aeschylus).

Mode A1 (C1, E1), Topic 3e (1b, 3i)

Delphi. Pseudo-Direct, Verse (iambic trimeter)—Aesch. Eum. 64–84, 88 (179–243, 278–283, 669).

Indirect—Eur. IT 942–944.

Testimony—Aesch. Cho. 1034–1039, 1059–1064. Aristoph. Gramm. Arg. Aesch. Eum.

Pacuvius *ap.* Serv. *Aen.* 4.473. Vat. Myth. I 147, II 202. Schol. on Aristeides 13.108, p. 68 Dind. Cf. 7 red-figured vase-paintings listed in Louis Séchan, *Études sur la tragédie grecque dans ses rapports avec la céramique* (Paris: Champion, 1926) 93–101; see J. H. Huddilston, *Greek Tragedy in the Light of Vase Paintings* (London, New York, 1898) 56–73; Beazley *ARFVP²* 1097 *bis*, 1112, 1115, 1121.

NP. Testimony—The god: Nic. Dam. 25J.

    Comment: See pp. 109–110, 117, 119, 204, 236 note 3.

    PW say that this is "not strictly an oracle at all." It is true that the Pythia does not speak this to Orestes, and that Apollo himself is speaker; but Apollo speaks in his adyton. Ordinarily the Pythia receives his voice, but in story he may choose to speak in his own person, as to Aristodikos of Kyme from the adyton of Didyma in Herod. 1.159 (Didyma 6C); see also Q268 (C); F12. When the god speaks from his adyton, whether in his own voice or in his servant's, he is speaking an oracle.

    Nor does Orestes ask a question; but notice L41, Q7, and other examples of spontaneous utterance. Apollo knows why Orestes has come; he has in fact told him to return to Delphi (L7). Orestes is in the adyton, the place of consultation, as a suppliant to ask Apollo's protection in his present suffering. The god's consultants sometimes appear as suppliants, as the Athenian envoys who received Q147.

    In legend we may expect Delphic oracles to be spoken in exceptional circumstances and extraordinary ways. Certainly L8 has more right to a place among Apollo's Delphic responses than have PW184–186 on Pyrros' dealings with Delphi. Compare L9.

L9 (PW140).

C. Agamedes and Trophonios.

Occ. Completion of Apollo's temple at Delphi.

Q. (1) Request for their pay. (2) Request for no small reward for their labor, but the best thing for man.

R. (1) Apollo will pay them on the seventh day; let them enjoy themselves meanwhile. (2) Apollo will pay them on the third day.

Mode E1 (A1), Topic 3f

Delphi. Indirect—(1) Pind. frag. 3 Bowra *ap.* Plut. *Mor.* 109a. Plut. *Mul. erud.* 7 *ap.* Stob. *Flor.* 120.23. (2) Cic. *Tusc.* 1.47.114.

    Testimony—Pind. frag. 2 Bowra *ap.* Schol. *in* Lucian. *DMort.* 10, pp. 255–256 Rabe. Eust. *Prooem.* 29.

    Comment: See pp. 19, 37, 327; Q179.

    This appears also to be Apollo's own utterance; there is no indication in the sources that the Pythia responded to the brothers' request.

L10 (PW141).

C. King Aipytos.

Occ. Euadne's pregnancy.

Q. On this event.

R. The child is Apollo's and will be a great mantis, whose lineage will never fail.

Mode E2 (D2), Topic 3d (1d, 3a)

Delphi. Testimony—Pind. *Ol.* 6.37–38, 47–51.

> *Comment:* See pp. 19, 26.
> The child was Iamos, ancestor of the Iamids of Olympia.

L11 (PW142, 374, 481, 501).

C. Kadmos.

Occ. Failure to find the missing Europa.

Q. (1) Where shall I find Europa? (2) Where shall I settle? (Ovid, Scholiasts on Euripides and Aeschylus).

R. Search no more for Europa [whom the bull of Olympos has taken for mating], but follow a cow [marked with white on both sides], and where she lies down on her right side, there found a city [after sacrificing the cow to Gaia and killing the dread guardian Ares' son. Then your fame will endure forever and you will win an immortal marriage].

Mode B (C1, E2), Topic 3h (1b, 2c, 3f)

Delphi. Direct, Verse—Schol. vet. on Eur. *Phoen.* 638. Tzetzes *Exeg. Il.*, p. 16 Herm. Incomplete—Tzetzes *Chil.* 5.819–821, 10.454–456, 12.112–114 (10.395–401). Schol. on Tzetzes *Epist.* 82 = Cramer Anecd. Ox. 3.363.

> Pseudo-Direct, Verse—Nonn. *Dion.* 4.293–306 (2.696–698, 5.1–6). (Latin) Ovid *Met.* 3.10–13.

> Indirect—Hellanikos 4.51J *ap.* Schol. A *in Il.* 2.494. Apollod. 3.4.1. Aristoph. Gramm. Arg. Eur. *Phoen.* Sen. *Oed.* 720–722. Paus. 9.12.2 (26.3). Hyg. *Fab.* 178.4. Eust. *Il.* 2.505, p. 270. Schol. vet. on Aesch. *Sept.* 486. Schol. C on Eur. *Phoen.* 638. Schol. on Lucan *BC* 5.107.

> Testimony—Ps.-Musaios *ap.* Schol. vet. *in* Apollon. *Arg.* 3.1179 [= Ps.-Eud. *Viol.* 515]. Lucan *BC* 5.106–108. Plut. *Sulla* 17.8. Stat. *Theb.* 7.663–664. Lact. Plac. *Theb.* 7.664.

NP. Indirect—Oracle: Eur. *Phoen.* 642–644.

> Testimony—Apollo: *Pind. frag. 13 Bowra *ap.* Plut. *Mor.* 397a, 1030a = *ap.* Aristid. 46.296. Apollon. *Arg.* 3.1181–1182. Serv. *Aen.* 3.88. Oracle: Diod. 4.2.1.

> *Comment:* See pp. 13, 16, 72, 74, 175–176, 242.

The above summarizes the 18-verse oracle reported by the Scholiast on Eur. *Phoen.* 638. Brackets mark off content that appears only in it. The part not parenthesized is common to the other sources.

The Kadmos legend of classical times tells of Kadmos' visit to Delphi to ask Apollo either where to find Europa or, having given up the search, where he should settle. Hence most sources plainly indicate that the Pythian Apollo spoke L11 to him; and the few that do not, including Pindar and Euripides, surely mean the same god. But the Kadmos legend must have begun before the eighth century; and so at first either Kadmos founded Thebes without any such direction or some god or seer (Teiresias, Ismenos?) instructed him directly. If a deity, it was likely to be Athena, who advised and helped Kadmos greatly in his settlement of Thebes, and to whom he sacrificed the guiding cow. See Eur.

Phoen. 666–669, Hellanikos, Apollodoros, Ovid *Met.* 3.101–103; Fontenrose 1959: 306–320.

The earliest form of the response attributed to the Delphic Apollo was probably the prose direction of a folk narrative, to follow either a cow with certain markings or the first cow met, and to settle where the cow should first recline—probably after an admonition not to seek Europa farther. The length of the hexameter version indicates a late composition, though not conclusively; cf. Q26, 146, 147. Parke (1956: 310) conjectures that it came from Mnaseas' collection; but Mnaseas surely invented nothing in his corpus, so that the hexameter version would precede his collection. The hexameters tell the story of Kadmos' founding of Thebes in the form of Apollo's directions. They look like lines from an epic poem, the same sort of thing as the 14-line response that Nonnos invented. Possibly the 18-hexameter form comes from Antimachos of Kolophon's *Thebaid* (late fifth century).

Under Testimony I include Lucan *BC* 5.106–108, where Lucan, listing the many kinds of responses that the Pythian Apollo has spoken, says, justisque benignus / saepe dedit sedem totas mutantibus urbes, / ut Tyriis . . . PW do not refer this to the Kadmos oracle but to the foundation of Gades (PW481) and refer to "commentators" without citation as so explaining Lucan's lines. The commentators are not the Scholiasts on Lucan. One Scholiast interprets the Tyrians to be the founders of Carthage under Dido; but this is certainly not Lucan's meaning. Another, cited above, says, ut Cadmus accepit jussus bovem sequi et ubi consedisset ibi conderet urbem. This is surely Lucan's meaning. The Tyrians were Kadmos and his company, forced to leave Tyre and found a new city. Lucan is likely to allude thus to a famous response known to his readers; he continues with a reference to oracles on defensive warfare, and his example is *ut Salaminiacum meminit mare*, i.e., Q147. PW cite Poseidonios 87.53J *ap.* Strab. 3.5.5, p. 169; but he mentions only an anonymous oracle given to the Tyrians who colonized Gades. No one ever supposed that Delphi had directed the founding of Phoenician colonies, Gades or Carthage or any other.

L12 (PW143).

C. King Pelias of Iolkos.

Occ. Some matter concerning his kingship.

Q. On his reign.

R. (1) He should beware of the man wearing one sandal. (2) Death awaits him from the man whom he shall see wearing one sandal while he is making sacrifice to Poseidon.

Mode C2 (F), Topic 3h (1b, 3c)

Delphi. Indirect—(1) Pind. *Pyth.* 4.75–78. Tzetzes on Lyk. 175.

NP. Indirect—(1) Apollo: Arg. Apollon. *Arg.* [= Ps.-Eud. *Viol.* 478]. The god: Apollod. 1.9.16. Zen. 2.92. Oracle: Pherekydes 3.105J *ap.* Schol. vet *in* Pind. *Pyth.* 4.75/133. Apollon. *Arg.* 1.5–7. (2) Apollo: Serv. *Ecl.* 4.34. Oracle: Hyg. *Fab.* 12.1. Lact. Plac. *Theb.* 3.516.

Testimony—Oracle: Orph. *Arg.* 55–56.

    Comment: See p. 72.

No source actually names Delphi or the Pythian Apollo, but Pindar says that this response was spoken to Pelias "by the Mother's mid omphalos," simply a periphrasis for Delphi. Tzetzes cites Pindar and so must have Delphi in mind, but is no more specific than to refer to a *chrêsmos*. Of other sources none does more than attribute the response to Apollo.

It is a theme of the Greek hero story that a father (or father equivalent) receives a prophecy of doom to come from his son, which he tries to avoid; but the doom is fulfilled nevertheless; see L17, 23. The original Jason legend, as distinct from the Argonautic legend, probably had this prophecy; and it may be Pindar who first called it Delphic.

L13 (PW144).
C. King Pelias of Iolkos.
Occ. Pelias' dream in which Phrixos told him to fetch his spirit and the golden fleece.
Q. Should he make a search?
R. He should quickly send a ship to bring Phrixos' spirit home.
Mode A1, Topic 3e
Delphi. Indirect—Pind. Pyth. 4.164. Schol. vet. on Pind. Pyth. 4.163/290.
    Testimony—Schol. vet. on Apollon. Arg. 1.414.
    Comment: It is quite possible that this response is Pindar's invention along with Pelias' dream.

L14 (PW145).
C. Tlepolemos.
Occ. Killing of his brother Likymnios.
Q. Where should he go?
R. He should sail from Argos to the seagirt land [Rhodes].
Mode A1, Topic 3i
Delphi. Indirect—Pind. Ol. 7.32-33. Schol. vet. on Pind. Ol. 7.31/56.
NP. Testimony—Oracle: Diod. 5.59.5.
    Comment: Pindar's εὐώδεος ἐξ ἀδύτου indicates plainly enough that Tlepolemos went to Delphi, and so the Scholiast interprets him.

L15 (PW146).
C. (1) Heraklids. (2) Spartans.
Occ. Attack on (1) Peloponnesos or (2) Amyklai.
Q. (1) Whom of the Hellenes should they take as allies? (2) What should they do?
R. (1) They should ally themselves with those whom their father Herakles helped. (2) If they take the Aigeidai as allies, they will win.
Mode A3, Topic 2e
Delphi. Direct, Prose (1)—Schol. on Pind. Pyth. 5.69/92.
    Indirect—(2) Schol. vet. on Pind. Isthm. 7.12/18.
    Testimony—(2) *Pind. Isthm. 7.12-15.

NP. Indirect—(1) The god: Ephoros 70.16J *ap.* Schol. vet. *in* Pind. *Pyth.* 5.76/101. (2) The god: Aristotle frag. 532 Rose *ap.* Schol. vet. *in* Pind. *Isthm.* 7.12/18.

Comment: We might distinguish two responses here, but the conclusion of both versions is alliance with the Aigeidai of Thebes after the receivers first supposed that the god meant the Aigeidai of Athens.

L16 (PW147).
C. Amphiklos.
Occ. Migration.
Q. Not stated.
R. Settle in Chios.
Mode A1, Topic 2c
Delphi. Testimony—Ion of Chios 392.1J *ap.* Paus. 7.4.9.

L17 (PW148, 372).
C. King Laios of Thebes.
Occ. Lack of a son.
Q. How may I have a son?
R. (1) If you and Jocasta have a son, he will kill you. (2) Do not beget a son; for if you do, he will kill you. (3) You will have a son, but he will kill you; Zeus fulfills the curse of Pelops, whose son you seized.
Mode C1 (E2), Topic 3c (3a)
Delphi. Direct, Verse (3)—Arg. 5 Eur. *Phoen.* Incomplete—Mnaseas 3.157M *ap.* Schol. vet. *in* Pind. *Ol.* 2.42/70.
   Pseudo-Direct, Verse (iambic trimeter), Incomplete (2)—Alex. Aphr. *Fat.* 31.98. Schol. vet. on Pind. *Ol.* 2.40/65, 43/72. Arg. Aesch. *Sept.* and Schol. on *Sept.* 745. Indirect—(1) Aristoph. *Ran.* 1185. Paus. 9.5.10. (2) Aesch. *Sept.* 748–749 (844). Diod. 4.64.1. Dion Chrys. 10.24. Schol. on Aesch. *Sept.* 844. (3) Nic. Dam. 8J.
   Testimony—*Pind. *Ol.* 2.42–44; *Paean* frag. 57 Bowra *ap.* Schol. vet. *in* Pind. *Ol.* 2.42/70. Sen. *Phoen.* 259–260. Schol. vet. on Aesch. *Sept.* 800.
NP. Direct, Verse (3)—Apollo: Arg. 3 Soph. *OT.* Arg. 6 Eur. *Phoen.* Incomplete— Oracle: Anth. Pal. 14.67.
   Pseudo-Direct, Verse (iambic trimeter) (2)—Apollo: Eur. *Phoen.* 17–20 (1598–1599). Origen *Cels.* 2.20, p. 406. (Latin) Chalcid. *Tim.* p. 244. Incomplete—Apollo: Lucian *Zeus Cat.* 13. Oinomaos *ap.* Eus. *PE* 6.7, p. 258c (259c). Alb. Plat. *Epit.* 26.2. The god: Zen. 2.68. Max. Tyr. 19.5.
   Indirect—(1) Apollo: Soph. *OT* 713–714, 853–854, 1176 (906–908). Androtion 324.62J *ap.* Schol. *in Od.* 11.271. Karneades *ap.* Cic. *Fat.* 14.33. Hyg. *Fab.* 66.1. Triclinius on Soph. *OT* 883, 916. Oracle: Lact. Plac. *Theb.* 1.61. Vat. Myth. II 230. (2) The god: Apollod. 3.5.7. (Another version) Oracle: Malalas p. 49. Kedr. p. 45. Suda Oι34.
   Testimony—Apollo: Soph. *OC* 969–970. Epict. 3.1.16. Schol. vet. on Eur. *Phoen.* 26. Oracle: Chrysippos *ap* Eus. *PE* 4.3, p. 139a. Eust. *Od.* 11.270, p. 1684 [= Ps.-Eud. *Viol.* 728].

Comment: See pp. 4, 13, 16, 37, 95, 96–100, 108, 110, 119.

Since Sophocles and Euripides attribute this response to Apollo, the Scholiasts who quote the hexameter form in the *Argumenta* may be supposed to have made the same attribution, though they mention no speaker or place.

Malalas, Kedrenos, and the Suda have a prophecy of mother-incest through confusion with L18. Nicolaus adds that to the usual prediction of patricide.

L18 (PW149).
C. Oedipus.
Occ. When troubled by a taunt that he was not Polybos' son.
Q. Who am I and whose son am I? (Arg. Aesch. *Septem*).
R. [Do not go back to your native land (Apollodoros).] You are destined to kill your father and marry your mother.
Mode E3 (C2), Topic 3e (3b, 3c)
Delphi. Direct, Prose—Arg. Aesch. *Sept.*
 Indirect—*Soph. *OT* 791–793, 994–996. Apollod. 3.5.7. Zen. 2.68. Sen. *Oed.* 20–21 (268–272, 800, 1042–1046). Arg. 5 Eur. *Phoen.* and Schol. vet. on 44, 1044.
 Testimony—Eur. *Phoen.* 32–38, 1043–1046. Soph. *OC* 87. Aristoph. Gramm. Arg. 1.3–4 Soph. *OT*. Diod. 4.64.2. Stat. *Theb.* 1.62–66. Lact. Plac. *Theb.* 1.60. Hyg. *Fab.* 67.2–3.
NP. Testimony—Oracle: Vat. Myth. II 230.
 Comment: See pp. 4, 26 note 9, 36, 95, 97, 98, 100, 110, 119, 122.

L19 (PW150, 479).
C. King Oedipus of Thebes through Kreon.
Occ. Plague in Thebes.
Q. What should I do or say to save the city?
R. Drive out the defilement of the land and do not allow it to remain unremedied. Banish or kill the murderers of Laios, who are in the land.
Mode A1 (C1), Topic 3f
Delphi. Pseudo-Direct, Verse (Latin)—Sen. *Oed.* 233–238 (217–220).
 Indirect—*Soph. *OT* 97–98, 100–101, 106–107, 110, 306–309, 475–476, 1441 (241–243, 406–407, 603–604). Aristoph. Gramm. Arg. 1.13 Soph. *OT*. Cf. Triclinius on Soph. *OT* 95.
 Comment: See pp. 32, 97, 119.

L20 (PW152).
C. Oedipus.
Occ. and Q. See *Comment*.
R. He will die when he comes to a shrine of the *semnai theai*. There he will dwell [in his tomb], a boon to those who received him, a bane to those who exiled him. The sign will be earthquake or thunder or lightning from Zeus.
Mode F, Topic 3c (1d, 3h)

Delphi. Indirect—Soph. *OC* 88–95, 1514–1515 (453–454, 665, 791–793, 1472–1473). Arg.
1 Soph. *OC.* Sall. Pyth. Arg. 4 *OC.*

NP. Indirect—Apollo: Eur. *Phoen.* 1705, 1707.

    Comment: See pp. 20, 75, 119.

    Oedipus says at *OC* 87 that Apollo spoke these words to him when he had predicted
"those many evils," i.e., as part of L18. This prophecy, however, is not part of the tradition of L18, which in *OT* too is limited to the prophecy of patricide and incest. To join
L20 to L18 is Sophocles' innovation for the *OC.*

L21 (PW153).

C. Thebes.

Occ. and Q. Not stated.

R. Both in life and death Oedipus will protect the city [but buried elsewhere will bring
    defeat].

Mode E2, Topic 3c (2e)

Delphi. Indirect—Soph. *OC* 389–390, 605 (391–415, 452–453). Schol. vet. on *OC* 354,
    388.

    Testimony—Arg. 1 and 3.7–8 Soph. *OC.*

        Comment: See pp. 75, 119.

    It is likely that L20–21 are Sophocles' own invention for *OC.*

L22 (PW154).

C. King Theseus of Athens.

Occ. A matter concerning the city.

Q. On the welfare of the city.

R. Zeus has placed the limits and control of many cities in your city. Do not be much
    troubled in spirit as you make decisions; a wineskin floats upon the sea.

Mode C1 (D1), Topic 3j (2b)

Delphi. Direct, Verse—Plut. *Thes.* 24.5.

    Testimony—Paus. 1.20.7.

        Comment: See pp. 17, 180, 349.

    The message here is the advice not to be much troubled. The rest is explication (aside
from an initial salutation, "Theseus son of Aigeus and Pittheus' daughter"); a reason
precedes, and a gnomic statement given as a reason (*gar*) concludes the response.

L23 (PW156).

C. King Akrisios of Argos.

Occ. Lack of a son.

Q. How might there be a child born in his house? (Pseudo-Euripides).

R. He will have no son, but Danae will, and her son will kill him.

Mode E2, Topic 3c (3a)

Delphi. Indirect—Pherekydes 3.10J *ap.* Schol. vet. *in* Apollon. *Arg.* 4.1091 [= Ps.-Eud.
    Viol. 40, 256, 759]. Ps.-Eur. *Danae* 11–16 = Eur. frag. 1132 *TGF.*

    Testimony—Arg. Ps.-Eur. *Danae,* p. 716 *TGF.* Clem. Alex. *Strom.* 1, 383P.

NP. Indirect—The god: Apollod. 2.4.1 (4). Zen. 1.41. Schol. AB on Il. 14.319. Oracle: Hyg. *Fab.* 63.1. Schol. on Lucian *Gall.* 13, p. 90 Rabe. Tzetzes on Lyk. 838.

    Comment: See p. 19.

Pherekydes is likely to be the ultimate source of the writers cited under *NP.* The original prophecy of the legend, however, could not have been attributed to Delphi. It is the prophecy of the Greek hero legend, also encountered in the Jason and Oedipus tales (L12, 17). Akrisios must receive a prophecy of doom about Danae's son, so that he will attempt to prevent the birth or to destroy the child; but he will fail to do so; it is the theme of prophecy fulfilled. Perhaps in the sixth or fifth century Delphi laid claim to the prediction or storytellers began to attribute it to the Delphic Oracle as a traditional source of prophecy.

The Pseudo-Euripidean *Danae* is by common consent a Byzantine production; see Nauck's comment on the fragment. Its version of the prophecy differs from that of other sources: Akrisios is told that he will have no son, because he is destined first to produce a daughter, who will bear a winged lion destined to take the throne. This is without doubt the poet's invention, constructed out of the traditional legend.

L24 (PW183).

C. Eurystheus.

Occ. and Q. Not stated.

R. His tomb will be in Athens before Athena's temple, whence he will be a friend and savior of Athens and a bitter enemy of the Heraklids when they invade again.

Mode E2, Topic 3c (2e)

NP. Testimony—Apollo: Eur. *Herakl.* 1026–1038.

    Comment: See p. 75.

L25 (PW187).

C. Delphians.

Occ. and Q. Not stated.

R. Kill Pyrros Achilles' son.

Mode A1, Topic 3f (3c)

Delphi. Indirect—Paus. 1.13.9.

    Comment: See p. 32; Fontenrose 1960a: 212.

L26 (PW188).

C. Delphians.

Occ. Killing of Pyrros (Neoptolemos) at Delphi.

Q. Not stated.

R. Neoptolemos should have his tomb in Apollo's temenos.

Mode A1, Topic 1a (3c)

Delphi. Testimony—Strabo 9.3.9, p. 421.

    Comment: Fontenrose 1960a: 191–192, 223–225.

L27 (PW189, 373).

C. King Adrastos of Argos.

Occ. Probably concern for the marriage of his daughters.

Q. Not stated.

R. When you see a lion and a boar standing at your door, having come from my sanctuary, marry your daughters to them.

Mode B, Topic 3h (3b)

Delphi. Direct, Verse—Mnaseas 3.157M ap. Schol. vet. in Eur. Phoen. 409.

NP. Indirect—Apollo: *Eur. Suppl. 140 (220–221, 832–833); Phoen. 411; Hypsipyle, Pap. Oxyrrh. 6, p. 47. Schol. on Phoen. 135; Schol. vet. on Phoen. 409. Stat. Theb. 1.395–397 (490–497). Hyg. Fab. 69.1. Vat. Myth. I 80. Oracle: Zen. 1.30. Schol. A on Il. 4.376 [= Ps.-Eud. Viol. 728]. Eust. Il. 4.380, p. 485.

    Testimony—Apollo: Schol. vet. on Eur. Phoen. 405. Oracle: Diod. 4.65.3.

OP. Mantis. Indirect—Apollod. 3.6.1.

    Comment: See pp. 72, 95–96, 119.

L28 (PW190).

C. King Xuthos of Athens.

Occ. Lack of a son.

Q. How can he become a father? (Origo GR).

R. The man who will meet Xuthus as he leaves the temple is his son.

Mode F, Topic 3a

Delphi. Indirect—Eur. Ion 70–71, 534–537, 787–788, 1533 (302–306, 1345, and passim). Origo Gentis Romanae 2.2.

    Comment: See pp. 20, 25.

L29 (PW191, 193).

C. Orestes.

Occ. Madness from Erinyes' pursuit.

Q. How may I recover from my madness and woes?

R. (1) Go to the Tauric land, take the image of Artemis, which fell from heaven into her sanctuary, and convey it to the Athenians. (2) Go to the Scythian land, where you will be caught in Artemis' temple but saved from her altar. Then go to the temple of Hestia on Mt Melantion in Syria; there you will recover sanity.

Mode A1, Topic 1a

Delphi. Direct, Prose (2)—Malalas p. 136. Kedr. pp. 234–235.

    Indirect (1)—*Eur. IT 85–92, 977–978, 1014 (711–713, 937, 1438–1441). Hyg. Fab. 120.1 (261).

    Testimony—Arg. Eur. IT.

NP. Indirect (1)—The god: Apollod. epit. 6.26. Tzetzes on Lyk. 1374. Oracle: Prob. Praef. ad Verg. Buc.

    Testimony—Oracle: Serv. Aen. 2.116; Serv. auct. Aen. 3.331.

    Comment: See p. 32; L8.

L30 (PW192).
C. Orestes.
Occ. and Q. Not stated.
R. He should move to Arcadia.
Mode A1, Topic 3i
Delphi. Testimony—Paus. 8.5.4.

L31 (PW194).
C. Teukros.
Occ. Exiled by father from Salamis.
Q. Not stated.
R. He should settle in Cyprus and call his city Salamis.
Mode A1, Topic 2c
Delphi. Testimony—Plut. Mor. 408a.
NP. Indirect—Apollo: *Eur. Helen 148–150. Hor. Carm. 1.7.29. Schol. on Hor. Carm.
   1.7.21.
   Testimony—Apollo: Serv. auct. Aen. 1.621.

L32 (PW195).
C. King Erechtheus of Athens.
Occ. Invasion of Thracians under Eumolpos.
Q. What should he do to be victorious over the enemy? (Lykurgos).
R. (1) He should sacrifice his daughter before battle (Lykurgos). (2) Someone should kill
   himself for the city (Philochoros).
Mode A1, Topic 1c
Delphi. Indirect—Lykurgos Leokr. 99. Pseudo-Demaratos 42.4J ap. Stob. Flor. 39.33.
   Testimony—Liban. Decl. 14.12.
NP. Indirect—Apollo: Philochoros 328.105J ap. Ulp. in Dem. 19.303. The god:
   Apollod. 3.15.4. Schol. on Aristeides 13.118, p. 110 Dind.
   Testimony—The god: Aristeides 13.118–119. Oracle: Varro ap. Schol. in Cic. Sest.
   21.48. Hyg. Fab. 238.2.
OP. Poseidon. Indirect—Hyg. Fab. 46.3.
   Comment: Only Philochoros has the second version. Pseudo-Demaratos specifies the
eldest daughter; others say Erechtheus' daughter or one of his daughters. According to
Apollodoros, Erechtheus sacrificed his youngest daughter and the rest killed themselves.
In Philochoros' version it was Agraulos who volunteered to be the sacrifice.
   Usually the legend, which has several versions, is told or referred to without mention
of an oracle. For example, Phanodemos (325.4J ap. Phot. Lex. 2.64 Nab. = ap. Sud.
Π668) mentions no oracle in his version. In the version of Hyginus Fab. 46, Erechtheus
had to sacrifice his daughter because the Athenians had killed Eumolpos in battle; and it
was Eumolpos' father, Neptune/Poseidon, who ordered Erechtheus to do so. At Fab.
238.2, however, Erechtheus sacrificed his daughter Chthonia ex sortibus, which may
either refer to an oracle, possibly Delphic, or mean that Erechtheus cast lots to choose the

victim daughter. In any case *Fab.* 46 is closer to the earliest form of the tale, in which a god or seer informed Erechtheus of the demanded sacrifice.

There are indications of versions in which Teiresias or Skiros, a mantis from Dodona, informed him. The fragments of Euripides' *Erechtheus* do not inform us on this point, but since Lykurgos quotes extensively from that play immediately after his quotation of L32, it might be supposed that he took his version of the response from Euripides and that Euripides considered it to be Delphic. At *Phoen.* 852–857, however, Teiresias tells Kreon that he has just come back from Athens, where he gave Erechtheus' people victory over Eumolpos in war; which statement can only mean that he spoke the prophecy of victory to the Athenians' contingent on the sacrifice of a daughter of Erechtheus. According to Pausanias 1.36.4, Skiros came from Dodona to Athens when the city was at war with the Eleusinians, and was killed in battle after founding the sanctuary of Athena Skiras, whereupon the Eleusinians buried him at the place thereafter called Skiros. The only legendary war between Athens and Eleusis is that in which Eumolpos took part as the Eleusinians' ally (see L43); this is one version of Eumolpos' war on Athens. Skiros fought for the Athenians, probably as their mantis; but he became an Eleusinian hero. Eumolpos, himself an Eleusinian hero, was a kind of seer as ancestor of the Eumolpidai and founder of the mysteries. Either Skiros or Eumolpos himself may have spoken the prophecy in some version of the legend.

L33 (PW197).
C. King Athamas.
Occ. Exile from Boeotia.
Q. Where should he settle?
R. He should settle in the place where he is entertained by wild beasts.
Mode B, Topic 3h
Delphi. Indirect—Schol. vet. on Plato *Minos* 315c.
NP. Indirect—The god: *Apollod. 1.9.2. Oracle: Tzetzes on Lyk. 22.
    Comment: See p. 16.

L34 (PW198).
C. Telephos.
Occ. Incurable wound from Achilles' spear.
Q. What is the remedy? (Hyginus).
R. (1) The wounder will heal you. (2) You will be healed if the wounder becomes physician.
Mode E2, Topic 3g
Delphi. Direct, Prose (1)—Schol. on Aristoph. *Nub.* 919.
    Indirect (2)—Liban. *Decl.* 5.9. Schol. on Dem. 18.72.
NP. Direct, Prose (1)—Apollo: Mant. Prov. 2.28. Oracle: Chariton *Chair.* 6.3. Schol. vet. and Olymp. 1.7 on Plato *Gorg.* 447b. Eust. *Il.* 1.59, p. 46 [= Ps.-Eud. *Viol.* 753, 919].
    Indirect (2)—Apollo: Apollod. epit. 3.20. Hyg. *Fab.* 101.1. Dictys Cret. 2.10. The god: Schol. A on Il. 1.59.

Testimony—Oracle: *Kypria ap. Procl. Chrest. 1, p. 104 Allen.

Comment: See p. 79.

The four sources who attribute this response to Apollo may not mean the Pythian; at least their source may not have meant him. In fragment 700 *TGF* of Euripides' *Telephos* (*ap.* Aristoph. *Eq.* 1240) someone, probably Telephos, calls on Apollon Lykios asking "What will you do to me?" It would be reasonable that Telephos in Mysia appeal to the Lycian Apollo, an oracular god, for healing of his wound. See L74.

L35 (PW199).

C. Corinthians.

Occ. (1) Plague following the Corinthians' killing of the sons of Jason and Medea. (2) Medea's killing of her sons.

Q. (1) About the plague. (2) How should they deal with the bodies of Medea's sons?

R. (1) Appease the wrath of Medea's sons. (2) Bury them in Hera's temenos and grant them heroic honors.

Mode A1, Topic 1a (3c)

Delphi. Indirect—(2) Diod. 4.55.1.

NP. Indirect—(1) The god: *Parmeniskos *ap.* Schol. vet. *in* Eur. *Med.* 264. Schol. vet. on Eur. *Med.* 1382.

Testimony—The god: Paus. 2.3.7.

Comment: See p. 130; Fontenrose 1968: 85.

L36 (cf. PW200).

C. Atreus.

Occ. Barrenness of land.

Q. Not stated.

R. Recall Thyestes to the kingdom.

Mode A1, Topic 2a

NP. Indirect—Oracle: Hyg. *Fab.* 88.5.

Comment: PW200 is not L36, but is simply the statement that Atreus' sons went to Delphi to inquire about finding Thyestes; and apparently they never consulted the Pythia, because in Delphi they found Thyestes, who had come to consult Apollo about punishing Atreus (L37); and they then seized him.

Since Atreus' sons went to Delphi to consult about Thyestes, it is likely that Atreus as king of Mycenae had consulted Delphi about the barrenness of the land; hence Hyginus probably has Delphi in mind as the scene of L36.

L37 (PW201).

C. Thyestes.

Occ. Atreus' crime against him.

Q. How will he have vengeance on his brother?

R. He must lie with his daughter and beget a son to avenge him.

Mode A1, Topic 3b (3a)

Delphi. Indirect—Schol. vet. on Eur. *Or.* 14.

   Testimony—Cf. Hyg. *Fab.* 88.8.

NP. Indirect—Apollo: Serv. *Aen.* 11.262. Oracle: Apollod. epit. 2.14. Hyg. *Fab.* 87.
   Lact. Plac. *Theb.* 1.694, 4.306. Vat. Myth. I 22, II 147.

   Testimony—Apollo: *Seneca Ag. 294. Oracle: Ps.-Orpheus 59 Kern *ap.* Athenag.
   Leg. pro Christ. 32, p. 309.

   Comment: Hyginus *Fab.* 87 is a different story from *Fab.* 88. *Fab.* 87 has the usual
story, that Thyestes received an oracle that he should lie with his daughter, and then did so.
In 88 Thyestes had aleady lain with Pelopia, and their son Aigisthos was already a youth,
when he came to Delphi to get an oracle on punishing Atreus. There he was seized by
Agamemnon and Menelaos, who had come to Delphi in quest of him (see L36, *Comment*).
Apparently he had not yet consulted the Pythia; if he had, he could only have been told
that his and Pelopia's son would avenge him.

   It is very unlikely that L37 was originally or usually attributed to Delphi. It is an
anonymous oracle for Apollodoros, Hyginus, and others. Only the Euripidean Scholiast
attributes it to the Delphic Apollo; otherwise only Servius and Seneca are as specific
as "Apollo."

L38 (PW203).
C. Epigonoi.
Occ. Plan for war on Thebes.
Q. Not stated.
R. Make war on Thebes with Alkmaion as commander.
Mode A1, Topic 2e
NP. Indirect—Apollo: Diod. 4.66.1. The god: Apollod. 3.7.2.

L39 (PW204).
C. Alkmaion.
Occ. Command of the Epigonoi against Thebes.
Q. Ought he to make an expedition against Thebes and punish his mother?
R. He should do both because of his mother's crimes against his father and himself.
Mode A2, Topic 3f (2e, 3c)
NP. Indirect—Apollo: Diod. 4.66.3.

   Testimony—Apollo: Apollod. 3.7.5.

L40 (PW202).
C. Alkmaion.
Occ. Madness and wandering caused by his mother's Erinyes (Pausanias). Barrenness in
   land of Psophis (Apollodoros).
Q. Not stated.
R. You will have no release from terrors until you find a land that did not exist when you
   killed your mother, and settle there.
Mode A3, Topic 3i
Delphi. Direct, Verse, Incomplete—Oinomaos *ap.* Eus. *PE* 6.7, p. 257a.
   Indirect—Paus. 8.24.8.

NP. Indirect—Apollo: *Thuc. 2.102.5. Schol. on Lucian *Deor. conc.* 12, p. 213 Rabe.
The god: Apollod. 3.7.5.

Comment. See p. 15.

L41 (PW206).
C. Hesiod.
Occ. Not stated.
Q. None.
R. Blessed is Hesiod, whose fame will spread over the earth; but beware of the grove of
Zeus Nemeios [Nemea (Thucydides)], where you are fated to die.
Mode C2 (E2), Topic 3c (1d)
Delphi. Direct, Verse—*Cert. Hom. Hes.* 219–223 Allen. Prokl. *Vit. Hes.* 4 = Tzetzes *Vit.
Hes.* p. 50 Wilam. Cf. Anth. Pal. 14.77 (PW607).
NP. Indirect—Oracle: *Thuc. 3.96.1.

Comment: See pp. 13, 59, 73, 117, 172, 177, 178.

The story of Hesiod's death was known to Thucydides, but he does not identify the
oracle and states its substance indirectly. It was not his practice to quote verse oracles
(except Q181), and so we cannot know whether the verse form already belonged to the
legend in his time or whether it was then attributed to Delphi. It is probably a fifth-
century production, manufactured for the legend, which simply needs an anonymous
warning of the Jerusalem Chamber kind. The first three verses are plainly modeled on
the Lykurgos oracle, Q7. This too is a spontaneous utterance; the Pythia hails Hesiod as
he enters the temple.

L42 (PW207).
C. Orchomenians.
Occ. Plague.
Q. (A) Not stated.
R. (A) They should bring Hesiod's bones from Naupaktos to Orchomenos.
Q. (B) Where in Naupaktos will they find the bones?
R. (B) A crow will show them.
Mode A1 (E2), Topic 1a (3c, 3h)
Delphi. Indirect—Paus. 9.38.3.
NP. Indirect—The god: *Ps.-Aristotle frag. 565 Rose *ap.* Schol. in Hes. OD 631.
Testimony—Oracle: *Cert. Hom. Hes.* 247–248 Allen. Plut. *Mor.* 162ef. Prokl. *Vit. Hes.*
4 = Tzetzes *Vit. Hes.* p. 51 Wilam.
Comment: See p. 73.
Pausanias alone reports L42(B).

L43 (PW208).
C. Eleusinians or Athenians.
Occ. Defeat and death of Eumolpos, who fought with the Eleusinians against Athens.
Q. Not stated.

R. Worship Eumolpos.
Mode A1, Topic 1a
Delphi. Testimony—Schol. vet. on Eur. *Phoen.* 854.
   Comment: See L32.

L44 (PW209).
C. Athens.
Occ. Plague.
Q. Not stated.
R. The city cannot be saved unless (1) Leos' daughters are sacrificed; (2) a citizen offers his
   daughters for sacrifice.
Mode A1, Topic 1c
Delphi. Indirect—(1) Ael. *VH* 12.28. (2) Schol. on Liban. *Decl.* 42.26.
NP. Indirect—(1) Oracle: Kosmas p. 577 Migne 38. (2) The god: Schol. on Aristeides
   13.119, pp. 112–113 Dind.
   Testimony—The god: *Paus. 1.5.2. Oracle: Phot. *Lex.* 1.383 Naber.
   Comment: The myth is an *aition* of the Leokoreion, a shrine of Praxithea, Theope,
and Eubule, probably a triad of daimones at first called *Leôkoroi,* "folk-cherishers,"
which became interpreted as "daughters of Leos" (see *LM* 2.1947). Then an *aition* was
invented on the model of the legend of Erechtheus' daughters (L32), a democratic counter
to the older tale: the daughters of Leos, the People, were as willing as the daughters of a
king to sacrifice themselves for the city. The story probably arose in the fifth century
and is probably taken by the sources of L44 from Atthidographers. Therefore the divine
direction which the story demands may have been a Delphic command from the first.
On the Leokoreion see Colin N. Edmonson, "The Leokoreion in Athens," *Mnemosyne*
17 (1964) 375–378.

L45 (PW210).
C. Athens.
Occ. Famine and plague.
Q. On escape from evils.
R. (1) Send boys and girls [seven of each every year (Eusebios)] to Minos as penalty for
   the wrongs done (Oinomaos). (2) Pay the penalty that Minos asks.
Mode A1, Topic 1c (3f)
Delphi. Direct, Verse (1)—Oinomaos *ap.* Eus. *PE* 5.19, p. 209cd.
   Indirect—(1) Eus. *PE* 5.18, pp. 208d–209a.
NP. Indirect—(1) Oracle: Eust. *Od.* 11.320, p. 1688. (2) Apollo: *Marmor Parium
   A19.33–34. Schol. vet. on Plato *Minos* 321a. The god: Diod. 4.61.2. Apollod. 3.15.8.
   Plut. *Thes.* 15.
   Testimony—Apollo: Serv. auct. *Aen.* 6.14.
   Comment: See p. 14.
   Since Eusebios attributes this response to the Pythian god and then quotes from
Oinomaos, who quotes an hexameter response, it is probable that he found the attribution

in Oinomaos' text. Probably all Oinomaos' oracles aside from those which he received at Klaros are "Delphic."

In the original legend, no doubt, Minos himself imposed his periodic tribute of seven youths and seven maidens on defeated Athens without any intervening oracle, which is quite unnecessary. The story occurs without oracle in Ovid *Met.* 7.456–460, 8.169–176; Paus. 1.27.10; Hyg. *Fab.* 41. Then the story was elaborated: Minos' siege went on for a long time and he prayed to Zeus for justice; Zeus sent famine and plague on Athens, forcing the city to seek an oracle; and the god consulted told them to pay the penalty that Minos demanded or that the god himself imposed. At first this was not called a Delphic oracle; perhaps Zeus was the speaker.

L46 (PW211).
C. The Hellenes.
Occ. Drought, barrenness of land, famine.
Q. How may they escape from the calamity?
R. They will have deliverance if Aiakos prays for them [to Zeus (Pausanias)].
Mode A1, Topic 1b (3g)
Delphi. Indirect—Paus. 2.29.7 (1.44.9). Clem. Alex. *Strom.* 6.4, 753P = Eus. *PE* 10.2, p. 463c.
NP. Indirect—The god: *Diod. 4.61.1. Apollod. 3.12.6.
   Comment: See pp. 14, 295.
The four sources cited express the response differently, but the content of each amounts to the statement under R. Apollodoros speaks of *chrêsmoi theôn*, as though several oracles came to the Hellenes, perhaps from manteis; and he says that the drought was caused by Pelops' crime against King Stymphalos of Arcadia. Diodoros links L46 to L45: the drought was that which Zeus sent on Attica and all Hellas in response to Minos' prayers for vengeance on Athens; then when Aiakos prayed to Zeus, the god relieved all lands of drought except Attica, so that the Athenians had to find relief through L46. Pausanias and Clement state no reason for the drought.

Isokrates 9.14 has the earliest reference to Aiakos' prayers. He mentions no oracle: when drought came on them, the Hellenes went to Aiakos and asked him to pray for them, since he was son of Zeus and renowned for piety and Zeus's favor. Such must be the original story, which is *aition* of the cult of Zeus Panellenios or Aphesios on Aigina. Then some version introduced an oracle that directed the Hellenes to go to Aiakos; and this oracle was thereafter occasionally identified as Delphic.

L47 (PW212).
C. Theseus.
Occ. Voyage to Crete as one of the youths sent to Minos.
Q. Not stated.
R. Take Aphrodite as guide and companion.
Mode A1, Topic 1b
Delphi. Indirect—Plut. *Thes.* 18.3.

L48 (PW214).

C. Athens or Xanthos.

Occ. War with Boeotians over Melainai.

Q. Not stated.

R. The black devising death for the fair will take Blacks [Melainai].

Mode E3, Topic 3c (2e, 3h)

NP. Direct, Verse—The god: Polyainos Strat. 1.19.

> Comment: See p. 20; Fontenrose 1960a: 234–236.

> Melanthos ("Black"), Athenian commander, fought in single combat with Xanthos ("Fair"), Boeotian commander, for the border village of Melainai, and killed him by a trick.

L49 (PW215).

C. Dorians or Spartans.

Occ. War on Athens.

Q. Will they take Athens?

R. (1) They will take the city if they refrain from killing the king. (2) The Athenians will win if their king is killed; [or] That side will win whose king is killed.

Mode C1 (F), Topic 3h (2e, 3c)

Delphi. Indirect—(1) Lykurgos Leokr. 84. Suda E3391. (2) Vell. Pat. 1.2.1. Val. Max. 5.6 ext. 1.

Testimony—Paus. 7.25.2. Liban. Decl. 14.12, 17.80.

NP. Indirect—(1) The god: Schol. vet. on Plato Symp. 208d. Oracle: Demon 327.22J (or Eudemos) ap. Phot. Lex. 1.223 Nab. = ap. Sud. E3391 = ap. Apost. 8.6. Conon 26. Pomp. Trog./Justin 2.6.17. Sostratos 23.2J ap. Plut. Mor. 310a = ap. Stob. Flor. 7.66. Schol. vet. on Lyk. 1378. (2) The god: Polyainos Strat. 1.18. Zen. 4.3. Schol. on Aristeides 13.119, p. 113 Dind.; 46.237, p. 685 Dind. Oracle: Cic. Tusc. 1.48.116. Serv. Ecl. 5.11 = Vat. Myth. I 161, II 189. Tzetzes Chil. 1.192–193. Schol. on Hor. Carm. 3.19.2.

Testimony—Oracle: Prokl. Rep. p. 175 Kroll.

> Comment: See pp. 17, 78.

> According to Valerius Maximus, Kodros received this oracle, saying that the war would end (victoriously for the Athenians), if he should be killed by an enemy, which is essentially the second version. In other accounts Kodros knew about the oracle, however expressed, and deliberately sought death from an enemy.

L50 (PW225, 227).

C. Karanos or Archelaos of Argos.

Occ. Contemplated colony in Macedonia.

Q. Not stated.

R. (1) Leave Argos and go to the springs of Haliakmon, and where you see goats grazing, there you and your folk should dwell. (2) Settle in Macedonia where goats lead you.

Mode B (A1), Topic 3h (2c)

Delphi. Direct, Verse (1)—Euphorion ap. Schol. in Clem. Alex. Protr. 11P.

NP. Indirect—(1) The god: Solin. 9.12. (2) Oracle: Pomp. Trog./Justin 7.1.7–8.

Testimony—Apollo: Hyg. *Fab.* 219.5. Oracle: Dion Chrys. 4.71. Synk. 1.373, 499.

Comment: See pp. 9, 72; L51.

According to Dion and Hyginus the consultants' name was Archelaos. Hyginus has *profugit ex responso Apollinis in Macedoniam capra duce*, which could be interpreted to mean that Archelaos was told to follow a goat; and Dion says that Archelaos came into Macedonia driving goats. Hence PW distinguish the Archelaos version as a separate oracle (PW227). But see Pompeius Trogus on the Karanos version: Karanos followed goats that were fleeing a severe storm and took Edessa without the inhabitants' knowing it; their attention was on the storm. Karanos then recalled an oracle by which he was commanded *ducibus capris imperium quaerere*. The verse oracle only bids him settle where he sees goats grazing (hence the city's name, Aigai); in a looser sense the goats are guides in this version too; and in version 2 they were apparently grazing when the storm (and Karanos) came upon them.

L51 (PW226).

C. Perdikkas.

Occ. Rule as king.

Q. How may I increase my power?

R. Zeus grants power over much land to the Temenids. Go to Botteis and where you see white goats with white horns sleeping, there make sacrifice to the gods and build a city.

Mode B (A1, E1), Topic 3h (1b, 2c)

Delphi. Direct, Verse—Diod. 7.16.

Testimony—Eus. *Chron.* 1, p. 227 Schoene.

Comment: See pp. 9, 72, 170.

This might be considered another version of L50 since it also concerns goats and the founding of Aigai. But the verses are quite different in expression and call for white goats sleeping, whereas L50 calls for goats grazing or leading. Different too are the occasion, question, and consultant. Still L51, in which goats are the sign as in L50, is no more than an alternative oracle on the founding of the Macedonian kingdom with Aigai/Edessa as capital. Therefore I have called L51 Legendary along with L50, although Perdikkas lived in the seventh century. He plays the same role as Karanos does in the L50 legend. Karanos is certainly a legendary figure—tenth in descent from Herakles and sixth from Temenos (Diod. 7.17), therefore traditionally dated about the tenth century. Eusebios puts him 463 years before Alexander, which would place him about 800. For our sources he belonged to the distant pre-Olympic past. Archelaos, alternative recipient of L50, is called son of Temenos (Hyg. *Fab.* 219.1), which would place him about 1100. PW place L50–51 under "mythical oracles," and nobody, I believe, considers them historical.

L52 (PW228).

C. Karystos Chiron's son.

Occ. and Q. Not stated.

R. Leave Pelion and go to Euboea, where you are destined to build a city; go and do not delay.

Mode A1, Topic 2c

Delphi. Direct, Verse—Oinomaos *ap.* Eus. *PE* 6.7, p. 255d.

NP. Direct, Verse—Oracle: Anth. Pal. 14.68.

L53 (PW233).

C. Ankaios.

Occ. Migration.

Q. Not stated.

R. Live in Samos, now called Phyllas, instead of Same (Kephalenia).

Mode A1, Topic 2c

Delphi. Direct, Verse—Iambl. *Pyth.* 2.4.

L54 (PW234).

C. Founders of Ephesos.

Occ. Difficulty in finding a place to settle.

Q. Where shall they place the city?

R. Found the city where a fish shows you and a wild boar guides you.

Mode B, Topic 3h (2c)

Delphi. Indirect—Kreophylos 417.1J *ap.* Ath. 8.361d.

> *Comment:* See p. 74.

The indirect statement of response is introduced solely with "the god" as speaker; but since the colonists dedicated a temple to Apollon Pythios, we may believe that Kreophylos meant the speaker to be Apollo at Delphi.

L55 (PW235).

C. Alkmaion.

Occ. Madness after killing his mother.

Q. How can I recover from my madness?

R. To be healed bring me the gift of that with which your mother brought death to Amphiaraos.

Mode A1, Topic 1b

Delphi. Direct, Verse—Ephoros/Demophilos 70.96J *ap.* Ath. 6.232ef.

     Indirect—Apollod. 3.7.5.

NP. Direct, Verse—Apollo: Eust. *Od.* 11.250, p. 1697 [= Ps.-Eud. *Viol.* 22].

> *Comment:* This is alternative to L40 as a direction to Alkmaion on how to recover from the madness that his mother's Erinyes caused him. After reporting L40 and Alkmaion's consequent sojourn and bigamous marriage at the Acheloos delta, Apollodoros tells of his return to Phegeus in Psophis for the purpose of recovering the necklace and robe of Harmonia (which Polyneikes had given to Eriphyle) from his wife Arsinoe, Phegeus' daughter, so that he might give them to his new wife Kalliroe Acheloos' daughter. Alkmaion told Phegeus that he had received an oracle, presumably Delphic,

that he would be cured of his madness when he took the necklace and robe to Delphi and dedicated them there. This appears to be a falsehood in Apollodoros' story; but Athenaios, citing Ephoros, and Eustathios quote a three-hexameter response in which Apollo directs Alkmaion to bring him this gift.

Ephoros/Demophilos reported the oracle in his account of the Third Sacred War. It appears that two necklaces taken by Phocian chiefs from Athena Pronaia's temple at Delphi were identified as the necklaces of Eriphyle and Helen. The oracles spoken to Alkmaion and Menelaos (L56) belong to the *aitia* of these votive offerings; hence they were attributed to Delphi at their inception.

L56 (PW236, 404).
C. Menelaos.
Occ. Beginning of war with Troy.
Q. How can I punish Alexander?
R. Bring me the necklace that Aphrodite gave Helen.
Mode A1, Topic 1b
Delphi. Direct, Verse—Ephoros/Demophilos 70.96J *ap.* Ath. 232f.
    Testimony—Demetrios Phal. 228.32J *ap.* Schol. *et* Eust. (p. 1466) *in Od.* 3.267.

L57 (PW239–240).
C. Unclear.
Occ. Sacrifices made by a rich man and a poor man at Delphi.
Q. Not stated.
R. Hermioneus pleased Apollo more when he sacrificed barley groats from his pouch with three fingers than did the Thessalian who offered gilt-horned oxen and hecatombs. [On hearing this Hermioneus emptied the remaining contents of his pouch on the altar.] He has antagonized Apollo twice as much by doing this as he pleased him before.
Mode D1, Topic 1b
Delphi. Indirect—Porphyry *Abst.* 2.15.

L58 (PW238).
C. Rich Magnesian.
Occ. Extravagant offering of a hecatomb to Apollo.
Q. Who makes the best and most pleasing gifts and sacrifices to the gods?
R. Klearchos of Methydrion in Arcadia serves the gods best of all.
Mode D1, Topic 1b
Delphi. Indirect—Theopompos 314GH *ap.* Porph. *Abst.* 2.16.

L59 (PW242–243).
C. Rich Man or Nero.
Occ. Sacrifice of hecatombs to Apollo.
Q. How has the god liked his gifts? (Hierokles).
R. What pleased me was Hermioneus' offering of spelt [incense].

Mode D1, Topic 1b

Delphi. Direct, Verse—Hierokles *In aureum carmen,* p. 421 Mullach. Sopater *Prol. in Aristid. Panath.* p. 740 Dind. Schol. on Lucian *Phal.* II 3, p. 8 Rabe.

    Comment: See pp. 18, 37, 121, on L57–59.

According to Sopater the enquirer was Nero who had been refused a response. When he asked why he received no answer, the Pythia responded with the verse on Hermioneus' offering. The introduction of Nero into the tale in place of the rich man of the other versions should not cause us to classify this response under Q. It is simply the application of an anecdote to a well-known person. For L57–59 we cannot tell when Hermioneus and Klearchos are supposed to have lived. The three belong to essentially the same story, a timeless fable or parable on the widow's-mite theme.

The Scholiast mentions only "the god" as speaker. But he is commenting on a passage which Lucian puts into the mouth of a Delphian; and the god that the speaker refers to is the Pythian Apollo.

L60 (PW287).

C. Heraklids.

Occ. and Q. Not stated.

R. No answer to question asked; they are told to go to their fatherland.

Mode A1, Topic 3i

Delphi. Indirect—Isokr. *Or.* 6.17.

NP. Testimony—Apollo: *Pind. *Pyth.* 5.69–72 and Schol. vet. on 69/92. The god: Aristeides 13.114.

    Comment: See p. 100.

L61 (PW288)

C. Hyllos Herakles' son.

Occ. Heraklids' intention of returning to their fatherland.

Q. How can they return?

R. Await the third harvest; then return.

Mode A3, Topic 3h

Delphi. Indirect—Apollod. 2.8.2.

    Comment: See pp. 15, 68, 100.

L62 (PW289).

C. Heraklids.

Occ. Preparation to invade the Peloponnesos.

Q. How may they conquer the Peloponnesos?

R. The gods give you victory if you go through the road of the narrows.

Mode A3, Topic 3h (2e)

Delphi. Indirect—Aristeides 46.215 and Schol., p. 651 Dind.

    Testimony—*Apollod. 2.8.2.

NP. Direct, Verse—Apollo: Oinomaos *ap.* Eus. *PE* 5.20, p. 210c.

Testimony—Apollo: Max. Tyr. 29.7, 35.7. Oracle: Paus. 2.7.6.

Comment: See pp. 15, 68, 103.

Oinomaos almost certainly means Apollo at Delphi as speaker of L62–64, but there is nothing explicit on the place in Eusebios' extract or in Eusebios' introductory remarks (*PE* 210a–211c). Aristeides appears to mean the same god as him who spoke to Orestes and Themistokles, i.e., Apollon Pythios; and the Scholiast attributes L63 to Delphi.

L63 (PW290).

C. King Temenos of Heraklids.

Occ. Plan to invade the Peloponnesos.

Q. (A) How may we conquer the Peloponnesos?

R. (A) Go through the road of the narrows.

Q. (B) Our fathers obeyed the same instruction when you gave it to them and met disaster.

R. (B) (1) You are yourselves the cause of your misfortunes because you misunderstood the oracles. I meant not the third harvest of the field, but the third harvest of generation; and I meant the narrows of the sea and not the Isthmos. (2) Your fathers didn't ask what narrows I meant, whether the Isthmos or the strait at Rion and Molykria.

Mode D1, Topic 3h (3i)

Delphi. Direct, Prose, partly Indirect (2)—Schol. on Aristeides 46.215, p. 652 Dind. Indirect (1)—*Apollod. 2.8.2.

NP. Direct, Prose (1)—Apollo: Oinomaos *ap.* Eus. *PE* 5.20, p. 210d.

Testimony—Oracle: Tryphon *de Trop.* 4, 8.738 Walz.

Comment: See pp. 18, 37, 114; cf. Q130.

L64 (PW291–292).

C. King Temenos of Heraklids.

Occ. Plague following on the killing of Karnos.

Q. (A) We have met misfortune [as a result of L63].

R. (A) By killing our messenger you incurred punishment.

Q. (B) What should we do? How may we appease you?

R. (B) Worship Apollo Karneios.

Mode A1 (D2), Topic 1a (3f)

Delphi. Indirect (B)—Schol. vet. on Theokr. 5.83 [= Ps.-Eud. *Viol.* 519].

NP. Direct, Verse—Apollo: Oinomaos *ap.* Eus. *PE* 5.20, p. 211a.

Comment: See pp. 36, 37, 103.

L65 (PW293).

C. King Temenos of Heraklids.

Occ. Famine and wreck of transport fleet.

Q. On the disaster.

R. This happened because of the seer who was killed. They should exile the killer for ten years and take the three-eyed as guide.

Mode A3 (A1, D2), Topic 3g (3f)
Delphi. Indirect—Apollod. 2.8.3.
NP. Indirect—Oracle: Paus. 5.3.5. Suda *T*996. Schol. on Aristeides 13.111, pp. 80, 81 Dind.
    Testimony—Oracle: *Conon 26.
      Comment: See p. 15.

    Conon says that Karnos was a *phasma* of Apollo. It is very likely that his oracle-speaker is Apollo, probably the Pythian, but his text as we have it informs us only that the Heraklids received an oracle. Apollodoros mentions only "the god" at this point, but has already established that the Heraklids consulted Delphi for the whole series of Heraklid responses.

L66 (PW294).
C. Oxylos.
Occ. Apparently the Heraklids' invasion.
Q. Not stated.
R. He should take the Pelopid as fellow-colonist [*synoikistês*].
Mode A1, Topic 2c
Delphi. Indirect—Paus. 5.4.3.

L67 (PW295).
C. Heraklids.
Occ. Contemplated conquest of Peloponnesos.
Q. Not stated.
R. They should not make war on those with whom they eat.
Mode C2, Topic 2e (3h)
NP. Indirect—Oracle: Polyainos *Strat.* 1.7. Schol. on Aristeides 13.111, pp. 80, 81 Dind.
    Comment: On the Heraklid responses Q60–67 see pp. 17, 100–103.

L68 (PW300).
C. Medon and Neileus Kodros' sons.
Occ. Death of King Kodros.
Q. Which should become king?
R. He who first makes libation when he sees *sialos* ["pig" or "olive tree"] rub *sialos* shall receive the kingship.
Mode B, Topic 3h (1b, 2a)
Delphi. Testimony—Ael. *VH* 8.5. Paus. 7.2.1.
NP. Indirect—Oracle: Schol. on Aristeides 13.110, p. 78 Dind. Tzetzes on Lyk. 1378; *Chil.* 13.101–103.
    Comment: See pp. 16, 38, 80, 121.

    The Scholiast probably means the Delphic Oracle, since Neileus afterwards goes to Delphi to verify the meaning of *sialos* (L69).

L69 (PW301).

C. Neileus Kodros' son.

Occ. Medon's interpretation of *sialos* as olive tree and consequent claim to kingship of Athens.

Q. (A) Is *sialos* the olive tree?

R. (A) Yes.

Q. (B) In what city shall I dwell?

R. (B) Consider how to drive out the wicked Carians and settle Hellenes and Ionians there.

Mode A1 (D1), Topic 2e (2c)

Delphi. Direct, Verse (B), Indirect (A)—Schol. on Aristeides 13.110, p. 78 Dind. Incomplete (B)—Tzetzes on Lyk. 1378.

NP. Testimony—Oracle: *Kleitophon 4.368M *ap.* Schol. A *in Il.* 20.404.

   Comment: See p. 121.

L70 (PW302)

C. Neileus Kodros' son.

Occ. Contemplated migration after accession of Medon to the Athenian kingship.

Q. On a place to settle.

R. (1) Sail to the golden men, carrying bronze on your shoulders and iron in your hands; your daughter will show you. (2) Settle where a maiden gives you earth moistened with water.

Mode B (A3), Topic 3h (2c)

Delphi. Direct, Verse, Incomplete (1)—Oinomaos *ap.* Eus. *PE* 5.29, p. 224cd.

   Indirect—(1) Schol. vet. on Lyk, 1378.

NP. Pseudo-Direct, Verse (political), Incomplete (1)—Oracle: Tzetzes *Chil.* 13.105.

   Indirect—(1) The god: Schol. vet. on Lyk. 1385. (2) Oracle: Schol. vet. on Lyk. 1379.

OP. Didyma or Carian Oracles (Didyma 2). Indirect—(1) Tzetzes on Lyk. 1385. (2) Tzetzes *Chil.* 13.111–112.

   Comment: L70 is alternative to L69. The golden men are mentioned only by Oinomaos and the Scholiast on Lyk. 1378. In Tzetzes' *Chiliades* Neileus received an oracle before crossing the Aegean. Then he consulted Carian Oracles after reaching Asia.

   I believe that version (2) and the second part of (1) have a common origin; but that the stories have become different: the maiden who gives Neileus moistened clay is not his daughter, who shows the place in a rather lewd way. The feature in common is the young woman who will make the sign manifest.

L71 (PW303–304).

C. Athenians.

Occ. Coming of fugitives from the Dorian invasion to Athens.

Q. What should they do about the fugitives?

R. They must settle colonies with them [under the leadership of Ion Apollo's son (Vitruvius)].

Mode A1, Topic 2c

Delphi. Indirect—Schol. on Aristeides 13.112, p. 86 Dind.

   Testimony—*Vitr. 4.1.4. Himer. *Or.* 10.5, *Or.* 28.

   Comment: The *responsa* of Vitruvius' words, quem (Iona) etiam Apollo Delphis suum filium in responsis est professus, are, I believe, the same as those referred to in *ex responsis Apollinis Delphici*, which directed the Ionian colonization. This may be, however, an imprecise allusion to L28. Although the Scholiast does not mention Delphi he is commenting on a passage in which Aristeides is dealing with the Delphic Apollo.

   The tradition of L71 is different from that of L69–70 on the settling of Ionia. The leader is Ion, and the Athenians received the response. The story may be derived from the tradition found in Euripides *Ion* 1569–1588: it was the will of Apollo or the gods that Ion's sons should colonize Asia.

L72 (PW305).

C. Hellenes or Orestes.

Occ. Plague and famine.

Q. On the present troubles.

R. The end of woes will come when descendants of Agamemnon sail to Troy, found cities, and restore the worship of the gods.

Mode A1, Topic 2c (1a)

Delphi. Indirect—Demon 327.17J *ap.* Schol. vet. *in* Eur. *Rhes.* 251.

NP. Indirect—Apollo: Schol. vet. on Lyk. 1374.

   Testimony—Apollo: Lyk. 1374–1377. Oracle: EM 37.

   Comment: According to Demon, Orestes died before he could fulfill the oracle. In the next generation L73 was given to his son Penthilos. But Lykophron seems to say that Orestes led the colonists, and his Scholiast reports that he reached Lesbos with his men, but died before he could found a city; and the command was not carried out by his descendants for a century.

L73 (PW306–307).

C. Kometes and Penthilos (separately).

Occ. Contemplated migration of Aeolians.

Q. Whither should he sail?

R. He should sail to the farthest of Mysians.

Mode A1, Topic 3i (2c)

Delphi. Indirect—Demon 327.17J *ap.* Schol. vet. *in* Eur. *Rhes.* 251. Hesych. E6742.

NP. Indirect—The god: Phot. *Lex.* 1.218 Naber. Suda E3254.

   Comment: See pp. 26, 122.

   There are in fact two consultations here, as Demon reports the story. Kometes asked the question in the second generation after Orestes (see L72), and had to ask it three times before receiving the response. He failed to act, and his son Penthilos consulted again, receiving the same answer.

   L72–73 (also L104) represent an effort to give the Delphic Apollo credit for the

Aeolian migration to the northwest coast of Asia Minor and Lesbos, as L68–71 represent a probably earlier effort to claim the Ionian migration to Asia as inspired at Delphi.

L74 (PW308, 451).
C. Telephos.
Occ. Ignorance of who his parents were.
Q. To what place should he go to find his parents?
R. (1) Sail to the farthest of Mysians. (2) Sail to Mysia to King Teuthras.
Mode A1, Topic 3i (3g)
Delphi. Indirect—(1) Schol. vet on Eur. Rhes. 251. App. Prov. 2.85. Prov. VB Zen. Athôos 34 ap. Miller. Mél. 352. (2) *Diod. 4.33.11.
    Testimony—Apollod. 3.9.1.
NP. Indirect—(1) The god: Phot. Lex. 1.218 Naber. Suda E3254. Apost. 8.1.
    Testimony—Oracle: Hyg. Fab. 100.1.
    Comment: Cf. L73. This is one of two proverbs (see L34) that have entered the Telephos legend as oracles. See L100 for another intrusion of Delphi into the legend.

L75 (PW309).
C. Boeotians.
Occ. War with Aeolians.
Q. Shall they stay in Thessaly or look for another country?
R. (1) When white ravens appear, the Boeotians will lose their country. (2) Settle where white ravens appear.
Mode F (B, C2), Topic 3h (2c)
Delphi. Indirect (1)—Demon 327.7J ap. Didym. Dem. Comm. 12.9–11.
NP. Indirect (2)—The god: Paus. Lex. ap. Eust. Od. 13.408, p. 1746. Phot. Lex. 1.215 Naber. Zen. 3.87. Schol. vet. on Aristoph. Pl. 604. Suda E3154. Apost. 7.96.
    Testimony—Oracle: Diod. 19.53.8. Schol. on Clem. Alex. Protr. 9P.
    Comment: See pp. 20, 38, 122.

L76 (PW310).
C., Occ., and Q. Not stated.
R. Widowed Arne awaits a Boeotian husband.
Mode D2, Topic 3b (3j)
NP. Direct, Verse—Oracle: Steph. Byz. 123 Mein. Eust. Il. 2.507, p. 270.
    Testimony—Apollo: *Hyg. Fab. 275.3.
    Comment: No source gives any information about the circumstances; this may not be an oracle at all, but a line from a poet or a versified proverb. Hyginus has only a notice of Apollo as founder of Arnae, which may not be a reference to an oracle. The verse, if an oracle, may refer to migration and settlement.

L77 (PW311).
C. Thessalians.

Occ. and Q. Not stated.

R. [(On Arne) Look for?] hearing of the deaf man and sight of the blind.

Mode A3, Topic 3j

Delphi. Direct, Verse—Plut. *Mor.* 432b.

 Comment: This is a fragment of verse and like L76 may not have been intended by its author as an oracle.

L78 (PW312).

C. Gephyraioi.

Occ. Arrival in Delphi as captives of Athenians offered to Apollo.

Q. Not stated.

R. For a Gephyraean man a friendly house is the best house. Follow cattle until they recline with weariness and stay there.

Mode B (D1), Topic 3h (2c, 3j)

Delphi. Direct, Verse, partly Indirect—Paus. Lex. *ap.* Eusth. *Il.* 3.222, p. 408. Incomplete—Suda Δ1395. Apost. 6.33.

 Testimony—Zen. 3.26.

 Comment: See p. 16; cf. L11.

L79 (PW313).

C. Melanthos the Messenian.

Occ. Exile.

Q. Where shall he live?

R. He should live wherever he is first honored by hosts who set feet and head before him at dinner.

Mode B, Topic 3h

Delphi. Indirect—Demon 327.1J *ap.* Ath. 3.96e.

NP. Testimony—Oracle: Conon 39.

 Comment: See p. 72 note 25.

 At Eleusis Melanthos' hosts set the feet and head of a sacrificial victim before him.

L80 (PW317–319)

C. Homer.

Occ. Ignorance of his origin.

Q. (1) What is my fatherland? (*Certamen*). (2) Who were my parents and whence? (Pseudo-Plutarch).

R. You have not a fatherland but a motherland, the island of Ios. (1) There you will die, but beware of the boys' riddle. (2) There you will die when you hear boys speak a riddle that you cannot understand. You have two lots in life, blindness and equality with the gods in life and death.

Mode D2 (C1, E2, F), Topic 3i (3c, 3h)

Delphi. Direct, Verse—(1) Paus. 10.24.2 (8.24.14, 10.7.3). Incomplete—Cert. Hom. Hes. 59–60 (321–335) Allen. (2) Oinomaos *ap.* Eus. *PE* 5.33, pp. 227d, 229cd. Incomplete—Theodor. *Gr. aff. cur.* 10.141.

NP. Direct, Verse—(1) Oracle: Steph. Byz. 334 Mein. Incomplete—The god: Aristotle frag. 76 Rose *ap.* Ps.-Plut. *Vit. Hom.* 4, p. 241 Allen. Prokl. *Chrest.* 1, p. 100 Allen. Oracle: Anth. Pal. 14.65. Schol. on Tzetzes *Exeg. Il.* p. 154 Herm. (2) The god: Ps.-Plut. *Vit. Hom.* 4, pp. 241–242 Allen. Oracle: Anth. Pal. 14.66.

Indirect—Oracle: Nonnos Abbas 1.33, p. 1004 Migne 36. Kosmas p. 526 Migne 38 [= Ps.-Eud. *Viol.* 743]. Tzetzes *Chil.* 13.652–653.

Testimony—Oracle: *Alkidamas, Mich. Pap. 2754.8–10, *TAPhA* 56.126. Antipater *ap.* Ps.-Plut. *Vit. Hom.* 4 = Anth. Plan. 16.296.5–8. Tzetzes *Exeg. Il.* p. 37 Herm.

   Comment: See pp. 18, 36, 83 note 49, 163, 172.

   The first version has three or four verses (Pausanias and Stephanos use verse 7 of the second as the first line of the first), the second has ten. The first six verses of (2) say the same thing as (1) and have the same introductory verse, which becomes the second verse in the 4-verse version of (1). The content of verses 8–10, concerning two lots in life, does not appear in (1).

   There is only one legend about the death of Homer on Ios resulting from the young fishermen's riddle; and it is more convenient to treat the prophecy that he receives as one response than as three different responses, as PW do. The reason for their having a third response is that Oinomaos has four verses of the second version separated from the rest, although he relates the two parts to each other at *PE* 229c. The other two sources of (2) have all ten verses together in one utterance.

   Most sources, whether quoting verses or not, do not refer the response to Delphi. In particular, the Anthology lists both versions under anonymous *Chrêsmoi* and not in the group attributed to the Pythian Apollo.

L81 (PW321).

C. and Occ. Not stated.

Q. None (Athenaios).

R. Drink wine full of lees, since you don't live in Anthedon or holy Hypera, where you
   would drink clear wine.

Mode A1 (D1), Topic 3j (3e)

Delphi. Direct, Verse—Aristotle frag. 596, 597 Rose *ap.* Plut. *Mor.* 295e = *ap.* Ath. 1.31bc.

NP. Direct, Verse—Oracle: Suda *A*1268. Zon. *Lex.* 127 Titt.

   Comment: See Halliday 1928: 103–106.

   This response could be considered Quasi-Historical, since nothing prevents our supposing that it was spoken any time from the eighth century to the fourth. I have classed it as Legendary because an alternative *aition* is certainly legendary, and because PW (p. 129) conjecture that the inquirer was the eponymous hero Anthes. C. and Th. Mueller (*FHG* 2.136) suggest that the oracle was spoken to Pollis of Argos, legendary king of Syracuse, whom Athenaios mentions in the immediately preceding sentences. Pollis of Argos is a shadowy figure who probably has the same legendary origin as Pollis the Pelasgian (see *LM* 3.2621–2622) and belongs to the legends of Pelasgian settlements in Sicily and Italy in prehistoric times. According to T. J. Dunbabin, *The Western Greeks* (Oxford: Clarendon Press, 1948) 93–94, no Argive king Pollis ever reigned over the Corinthian colony of Syracuse. But René Van Compernolle ("Syracuse, colonie d'Argos?," *ΚΩΚΑΛΟΣ* 12 [1966] 75–101) argues for an historical King Pollis and an Argive foundation of Syracuse. No source definitely indicates that Pollis received this response. Probably the couplet was not composed as an oracle.

L82 (PW322).
C. Kephalos.
Occ. Lack of a son.
Q. About having sons.
R. He should mate with whichever female he first meets.
Mode B, Topic 3b
NP. Indirect—The god: Aristotle frag. 504 Rose *ap.* EM 144. Herakl. *Rep.* 38.1.
    Comment: See p. 16.
    Kephalos first met a female bear, who was transformed into a woman after he impregnated her. She bore Arkeisios, grandfather of Odysseus. We have here a fragment of the Bearson myth; see Fontenrose 1959: 532–533.

L83 (PW323).
C. Lokros.
Occ. Difference with his father, causing him to gather men and leave home.
Q. On founding a colony.
R. He should found a city where he is bitten by a wooden dog.
Mode B, Topic 3h (2c)
Delphi. Indirect—Didymos *ap.* Ath. 2.70cd. Eust. *Od.* 17.315, p. 1822.
NP. Indirect—The god: Plut. *Mor.* 294e. Hesych. *K*4562.
    Comment: See p. 16.
    Lokros was scratched by a dog-briar (*kynosbaton*) thorn, and there founded Ozolian Lokris.

L84 (PW324).
C. King Aleos of Tegea.
Occ. and Q. Not stated.
R. If his daughter should have a son, the boy is fated to kill Aleos' sons.
Mode E2 (C1), Topic 3c (3a)
Delphi. Indirect—Ps.-Alkid. *Odyss. in Palam.* 4, p. 185 Bekk.

L85 (PW325).
C. Demoklos the Delphian.
Occ. and Q. Not stated.
R. Go to Miletos.
Mode A1, Topic 3i
Delphi. Testimony—Conon 33.
    Comment: Through this oracle and the story that Conon tells, the Delphic Oracle

claimed credit for the founding of Didyma; for Demoklos was the grandfather of Branchos. Strabo reports that Branchos was descended from the Delphian Machaireus (9.3.9, p. 421).

L86 (PW328).
C. Tirynthians.
Occ. An affliction that caused them to laugh too much.
Q. How to rid themselves of this habit.
R. If they sacrifice a bull to Poseidon without laughing and cast it into the sea, they will cease.
Mode A1, Topic 1b (3e)
Delphi. Indirect—Theophrastos frag. 124 Wimmer ap. Ath. 6.261d.
    Comment: See p. 32.
    The Tirynthians failed to make the sacrifice without laughing.

L87 (PW375).
C. Meleos the Pelasgian.
Occ. Need of a new home.
Q. Not stated.
R. Every land is a fatherland.
Mode D1, Topic 3j
Delphi. Direct, Prose—Mnaseas 3.157M ap. Zen. 5.74.
NP. Direct, Prose—The god: Dionysios of Chalkis 4.394M ap. Zen. 5.74.
    Comment: See p. 18.
    Mnaseas probably included this in his collection of Delphic oracles; but Dionysios' speaker is unknown, since Zenobios' speaker is "the god." Elsewhere the statement Πᾶσα γῆ πατρίς is called only a proverb. I call it a prose statement above; but it may be a fragment of an iambic or a trochaic verse.

L88 (PW376).
C. Pierians.
Occ. Plague.
Q. We want the plague to end.
R. You will pay in terrible suffering for killing Orpheus Apollo's son (Menaichmos). If you find Orpheus' head and bury it you will escape (Conon).
Mode E2 (A1), Topic 3f (3c)
Delphi. Direct, Verse—Menaichmos 131.2J ap. Schol. vet. in Pind. Pyth. 4.176/313.
NP. Indirect—Oracle: Conon 45.
    Comment: The verses from Menaichmos seem to be an incomplete oracle; they have only salutation and the reason for the plague. They must have been followed by verses which contained the instructions that Conon reports.

L89 (PW377).
C. Chance consultants.

Occ. and Q. Any.

R. Again dear Hippolytos puts out to sea.

Mode D2, Topic 3e

Delphi. Direct, Verse—Plut. *Numa* 4.5.

    Comment: Apollo loved Hippolytos of Sikyon and rejoiced whenever he saw him setting out from Sikyon to sail to Krisa; then he inspired the Pythia to speak this verse to any enquirer who happened to be present.

L90 (PW383).

C. Kydippe's father.

Occ. Kydippe's falling sick whenever she was about to be married.

Q: What god hinders my daughter's marriage?

R. Artemis heard Kydippe swear that she would marry Akontios; that oath prevents her marriage to another. So fulfill Kydippe's oath. It will be a good marriage: Akontios is a worthy youth of good family, descendant of priests of Zeus Aristaios, who pray for wind from Zeus (Callimachus).

Mode D2 (A1, E1), Topic 3b (1d)

Delphi. Direct, Prose—Aristain. *Epist.* 1.10.

    Pseudo-Direct, Verse (elegiac)—*Callim. *Ait.* 3.22–37, frag. 75 Pf.

    Indirect—Ovid *Her.* 20/21.234.

    Comment: See p. 18.

L91 (PW385).

C. Kaphyai.

Occ. Women's sickness that caused them to miscarry.

Q. Not stated.

R. They should bury the children [whom they had stoned] and sacrifice to them every year; for they had died unjustly. They should worship Artemis as the Hanged [*Apanchomenê*].

Mode A1, Topic 1a (3c)

Delphi. Indirect.—Paus. 8.23.7.

    Comment: See p. 76 note 34; cf. L35.

L92 (PW386).

C. Argives.

Occ. Plague.

Q. Why do heat and Sirius reign throughout the year (Statius)?

R. Appease Psamathe and Linos (Conon). Sacrifice to the monster [Poine-Ker] the young men who killed her (Statius).

Mode A1, Topic 1c

Delphi. Indirect—Stat. *Theb.* 1.636–637 (557–635).

NP. Indirect—Apollo: *Conon 19.

    Comment: Fontenrose 1959: 104–115; 1968: 81–83.

L93 (PW387).
C. Koroibos.
Occ. Receipt of L92.
Q. Take my life, since I alone killed the monster (Statius).
R. Do not go back to Argos, but take a tripod and carry it from the temple, and wherever
   it falls from you as you carry it on your way, there build a temple of Apollo and stay.
Mode B (C1), Topic 1a (3h)
Delphi. Indirect—Paus. 1.43.8.
   Testimony—Anth. Pal. 7.154.5–6 = Suda Δ210. Stat. Theb. 1.638–668.
NP. Testimony—Oracle: *Conon 19.
   Comment: See p. 37.
   The source of all authorities cited for L92–93 is apparently Callimachus Ait. frags.
26–31 Pf., who told the story of Koroibos and Poine.

L94 (PW396).
C. Hermochares the Athenian and the Ceians.
Occ. Disappearance of Ktesylla's body and flight of a dove from her couch.
Q. Not stated.
R. They must found a sanctuary in Iulis in the name of Aphrodite Ktesylla.
Mode A1, Topic 1a
NP. Indirect—The god: Nicander ap. Ant. Lib. 1.6.
   Comment: Since the cult of Apollon Pythios is prominent in the story, the Delphic
Oracle is probably intended, and perhaps Nicander explicitly named it. The story is
related to that of Kydippe (L90).

L95 (PW397).
C. Delphians.
Occ. Contemplated migration as a result of the ravages of Lamia Sybaris.
Q. To what land shall they go?
R. They will free themselves from this misfortune if they expose a citizen youth at
   Sybaris' cave.
Mode A1, Topic 1c
Delphi. Indirect—Nicander ap. Ant. Lib. 8.2.
   Comment: See Fontenrose 1959: 44–45, 100–105; 1968: 81–83, cf. L92–93, 121, 156.

L96 (PW399).
C. Jason.
Occ. Pelias' request that he go in quest of the golden fleece.
Q. Not stated.
R. He should sail for the fleece [gathering the best men of Hellas. Apollo will show him
   the way over the sea, if he begins with sacrifices to him. The people in whose land he
   sets up the two tripods which Apollo gives him will never be uprooted by enemies.
   The gods will make the clod thrown into the sea an island where Euphemos' descen-
   dants will live (Apollonios)].

Mode A2 (E2), Topic 3e (1b, 2c)

Delphi. Indirect—Apollon. *Arg.* 1.361–362, 413–414; 4.529, 532–533, 1750–1752 (1.209–210, 301–302). Schol. vet. on *Arg.* 4.532.

NP. Indirect—The god: Apollod. 1.9.16.

> *Comment:* See L12–13.

The original oracle of the legend spoken to Jason is simply the command or approval as Apollodoros has it. Apollonios joins to it a number of prophetic statements in different passages of the epic for his immediate narrative purpose. When the legend first took shape Jason readily undertook the quest at Pelias' suggestion and needed no oracular approval.

L97 (PW403).

C. Jason.

Occ. Intention of going after the fleece.

Q. Not stated.

R. The greatest of their band will be held back by Zeus's commands and destiny before they reach the clashing rocks.

Mode E2, Topic 3g

Delphi. Indirect—Val. Flacc. *Arg.* 3.619–621.

> *Comment:* If this were in Apollonios we could join it to L96. Valerius probably means that Jason heard this when he went to Delphi to seek approval of his quest (L96).

L98 (PW405).

C. Spartans.

Occ. Plague.

Q. On deliverance.

R. Appease the Teucrians' deities (Lykos and Chimaireus, Schol. Lyk.).

Mode A1, Topic 1b

NP. Indirect—Apollo: Eust. *Il.* 5.59, p. 521. The god: Schol. ABT on Il. 5.64. Schol. vet. and Tzetzes on Lyk. 132.

Testimony—The god: Tzetzes *Exeg. Il.*, p. 40 Herm. Oracle: *Lyk. 132–133.

> *Comment:* According to the Homeric Scholiasts, Menelaos went to Delphi after performing the rites commanded, so that the god meant here is probably the Pythian Apollo.

L99 (PW406).

C. Menelaos and Paris.

Occ. Desire for children (Menelaos) and to marry (Paris).

Q. Request for children and a wife.

R. Why do two kings, one of Trojans, the other of Achaeans, no longer in harmony, enter my house, one asking for birth of a foal, the other for a foal? What will you devise, great Zeus?

Mode D1, Topic 3j

Delphi. Direct, Verse—Schol. A on Il. 5.64. Eust. *Il.* 5.59, p. 521.

Testimony—Cf. Ps.-Alkid. *Odyss. in Palam.* 4, p. 185 Bekk.

NP. Direct, Verse—The god: Schol. BT on Il. 5.64. Oracle: Anth. Pal. 14.100. Schol. on
Il. 5.64 in Achmîm Pap., *Sitz. Akad. Berlin* (1887) 819 = *Hermes* 22 (1887) 636.

Comment: See p. 18.

According to the Homeric Scholiasts and Eustathios, when Menelaos left Troy
after performing the duties of L98, Paris accompanied him, and both consulted Delphi at
the same time, receiving L99.

L100 (PW408).

C. Agamemnon.

Occ. Beginning of Trojan War.

Q. Not stated.

R. Take care that you do not in folly enter Mysia and receive harm from a Hellene of
foreign speech. You will avoid harm if you sacrifice to Dionysos Sphaleotas the Mysian
where you first entered the temple in Pytho to hear Apollo's voice from the adyton.

Mode A1 (C1), Topic 1b (3h)

Delphi. Direct, Verse—Inscription of Delphi, *Rev. Arch.* ser. 6, 19 (1942) 119–120; 20
(1943) 21–24; *Klio* 15 (1918) 48, no. 68.

Testimony—Schol. vet. on Lyk. 204.

Comment: This is an alternative to L1 as the response that Agamemnon received
when he consulted on the projected war against Troy. See also L56, 122.

L101 (PW409).

C. Thebans (or Hellenes—Schol. Lyk. 1194).

Occ. Famine.

Q. About deliverance.

R. To live in your land with prosperity bring the bones of Hector from Asia to Thebes
and worship him as a hero [from Ophrynion in Troad to the place called *Dios gonai*
(Aristodemos)].

Mode A1, Topic 1a

NP. Direct, Verse—Oracle: Paus. 9.18.5.

Indirect—Apollo: Schol. vet. on Lyk. 1194. Oracle: Aristodemos 383.7J *ap.* Schol. AB
in *Il.* 13.1.

Testimony—Apollo: *Lyk. 1204–1211 and Schol. vet. on 1204, Tzetzes on 1208.

L102 (PW411).

C. Theseus (or Pelops—Tzetzes).

Occ. Need of a place to settle.

Q. Where shall he found a city? (Tzetzes).

R. Whenever in a foreign land he feels distressed and sad, he should found a city there
and leave some of his companions as leaders.

Mode B, Topic 2c

Delphi. Indirect—Menekrates 701.1J *ap* Plut. *Thes.* 26.5.

NP. Indirect—Oracle: Tzetzes *Exeg. Il.* p. 95 Herm.

Comment: In Menekrates' version Theseus founded Pythopolis. In Tzetzes' version Pelops founded Killa.

L103 (PW414).

C. Athenians.

Occ. Oppressive heat.

Q. Not stated.

R. For twenty days before the dog [rising of Sirius] and twenty days thereafter use Dionysos the Physician in a shady house.

Mode A1, Topic 3e (1d)

Delphi. Direct, Verse—Chamaileon *ap.* Ath. 1.22e. Oinomaos *ap.* Eus. *PE* 5.30, p. 225c. Indirect—Mnesitheos *ap.* Ath. 1.22e. Ath. 2.36b.

Comment: Like L81 this was probably not composed as an oracle.

L104 (cf. PW415).

C. Aeolian colonists.

Occ. Contemplated migration to Asia.

Q. Not stated.

R. Appoint Echelaos leader of the colony.

Mode A1, Topic 2c

Delphi. Testimony—Plut. *Mor.* 163b.

Comment: The oracle indirectly quoted at *Mor.* 163a about sacrificing a bull to Poseidon and a maiden to Amphitrite and the Nereids at Mesogaion is an oracle of Amphitrite, not of the Delphic Apollo, as PW suppose; see *Mor.* 984e. On the Aeolian migration see also L72–73.

L105 (PW422).

C. Delphians.

Occ. Chalcidians of Euboea send offerings to Delphi for Apollo and Artemis.

Q. Should they divide the offerings equally?

R. The possessions of friends are common.

Mode D1, Topic 3j

Delphi. Direct, Prose—Klearchos 2.320M *ap.* Schol. vet. *in* Plat. *Phaedr.* 279c = *ap.* Schol. vet. *in* Lys. 207c.

Comment: See p. 18.

L106 (PW425).

C. Delphians.

Occ. Detection of a visitor who managed to have himself locked overnight in a treasury with the image of a boy that attracted him and who left a garland as reward for the intercourse.

Q. Not stated.

R. Let the man go; he has made payment.

Mode A1 (D1), Topic 3f

Delphi: Indirect—Polemon 3.124M *ap.* Ath. 13.606b.

L107 (PW442, 444).

C. Herakles (or Amphitryon—Nicolaus).

Occ. Self-exile after killing Megara's children.

Q. Where shall he live?

R. [He is given the name Herakles (Apollodoros).] He must serve Eurystheus at Tiryns for twelve years and perform the labors set him; when he completes the labors he will win immortality [great fame (Nicolaus)].

Mode A1 (E2), Topic 3f

Delphi. Indirect—Diod. 4.10.7 (26.4, 38.5). Apollod. 2.4.12. Pedias. 1.1.

NP. Indirect—Oracle: Nic. Dam. 13J.

Comment: According to Nicolaus, Herakles recalled an oracle that Amphitryon had received.

L108 (PW443).

C. Herakles.

Occ. For some reason he wanted an oracle (Aelian).

Q. Not stated.

R. [Apollo answered his question and added (Aelian)] Phoibos names you Herakles; for bringing benefits to men you will have undying fame.

Mode E2, Topic 3f

Delphi. Direct, Verse—Ael. *VH* 2.32. Schol. T on Il. 14.324. Eust. *Il.* 5.395, p. 561; 14.324, p. 989.

Testimony—EGud. 247 Sturz.

NP. Direct, Verse—Apollo: Theod. Alex. *Can.* 6, p. 177g. Suda *H*477. EM 435. Tzetzes on Lyk. 663.

Testimony—Apollo: Schol. vet. on Pind. *Ol.* 6.68/115.

L109 (PW445).

C. Herakles.

Occ. Sickness after his murder of Iphitos (or of Megara's children—Hyginus, Servius auct.)

Q. How may he cleanse himself of his crime? (Hyginus).

R. (A) The god is not here and is not speaking oracles.

R. (B) [Herakles then took the tripod and started off with it: Apollo struggled with him to recover it; when Zeus separated them, Apollo gave Herakles a response (Apollodoros).] He will be cured if he is sold, serves for three years, and gives his wages to Eurytos [to Eurytos' sons (Diodoros)] in compensation for the murder.

Mode A1 (C1), Topic 3f (1d)

Delphi. Indirect—Apollod. 2.6.2. (A) Schol. vet. on Pind. *Ol*. 9.29/43. (B) Tzetzes *Chil*. 2.426–428.

Testimony—Hyg. *Fab*. 32.3. Serv. auct. *Aen*. 8.300. Ps.-Kallisthenes *Alex*. p. 125 Raabe. *NP*. Indirect—(B) Apollo: *Diod. 4.31.5.

Comment: For references to Herakles' tripod seizure without mention of an oracle see Fontenrose 1959: 401 note 50, which also has citations of the vase-paintings and other art works that depict the tripod seizure.

L110 (PW446).
C. Herakles.
Occ. After the death of Iphitos.
Q. Not stated.
R. This is another Herakles [the Tirynthian, not the Canobian (Pausanias)].
Mode D1, Topic 3j
Delphi. Direct, Verse—Paus. 10.13.8. *Klearchos 2.320M *ap*. Zen. 5.48 (trochaic).

L111 (PW447).
C. Herakles.
Occ. War on Pisa.
Q. Not stated.
R. Pisa is our father's concern, and Pytho is mine.
Mode D1, Topic 3j (1d)
Delphi. Direct, Verse—Paus. 5.3.1.
    Comment: This verse may not have originally been meant for an oracle.

L112 (PW448).
C. Herakles.
Occ. Herakles' defeat of the Dryopes and dedication of the captive people to Apollo at Delphi.
Q. Not stated.
R. The Dryopes should be taken to the Peloponnesos.
Mode A1, Topic 3i (2c)
Delphi. Testimony—Paus. 4.34.9.

L113 (PW449).
C. Herakles.
Occ. Completion of labors (no motive indicated).
Q. Not stated.
R. It is advantageous that before his translation to godhood he send a colony to Sardinia and appoint as leaders the sons whom the Thespiads bore him. The colonists will have freedom forever.
Mode A2 (E2), Topic 2c
NP. Indirect—Diod. 4.29.1; 5.15.3(1).
    Comment: See p. 15.

L114 (PW450).

C. Herakles through Likymnios and Iolaos.

Occ. Sickness from wearing the shirt of Nessos.

Q. What should he do about his sickness?

R. His men should bear Herakles in his armor to Oita and build a huge pyre beside him; Zeus will look after the rest.

Mode A1, Topic 3c

Delphi. Indirect—Diod. 4.38.3.

L115 (PW452).

C. Samians.

Occ. and Q. (209 years after the Trojan War); not stated.

R. Move to Thrace at the Troad.

Mode A1, Topic 2c

Delphi. Indirect—Apollod. 244.178J ap. Schol. A in Il. 13.12.

L116 (PW453)

C. Cretans.

Occ. A misfortune which caused some Cretans to be sent elsewhere.

Q. Request to show them a good and advantageous place for settlement (Aelian).

R. Wherever the earthborn war against them, they should stay there and build a city.

Mode B, Topic 3h (2c)

Delphi. Indirect—Ael. NA 12.5.

NP. Indirect—Apollo: Schol. A and Eust. (p. 34) on Il. 1.39. Oracle: *Kallinos ap. Strab. 13.1.48, p. 604. Serv. Aen. 3.108. Schol. vet. on Lyk. 1303. Tzetzes Exeg. Il. p. 96 Herm. Comment: See p. 16.

The Cretans founded Hamaxitos in the Troad. On that site the field mice gnawed the leather straps of their armor. This was the country of Apollo Smintheus, the mouse god. See L169. It is unlikely that Kallinos considered this oracle to be Delphic.

L117 (PW456).

C. King Kekrops of Athens.

Occ. Sudden appearance of an olive tree and a spring.

Q. What is the meaning of this prodigy and what should they do?

R. The olive tree means Athena, the water Poseidon, and it is in the citizens' power to name the city for one of the two gods.

Mode D1, Topic 1d

Delphi. Indirect—Varro ap. Aug. CD 18.9.1.

L118 (PW477).

C. Deukalion and Pyrra.

Occ. Mankind destroyed in flood.

Q. How can we restore mankind?

R. Leave the temple, veil your heads, loose your robes, and cast behind you your great mother's bones.

Mode A3, Topic 3e

Delphi (Themis). Pseudo-Direct, Verse (Latin)—Ovid *Met.* 1.381–383.

    Indirect—Lact. Plac. *Theb.* 3.560. Vat. Myth. I 189, II 73.

       Testimony—Arnob. *Adv. nat.* 5.5. Serv. auct. *Ecl.* 6.41. Lact. *Narr.* 1.7.

         Comment: See p. 15.

    This and F5 are the only responses attributed to the mythical pre-Apolline period when Themis spoke oracles at Pytho. According to Schol. AT on Iliad 16.233, Deukalion went to Zeus's Oracle in Epeiros (Dodona) after the flood and received an oracle that he and other survivors should settle there. He married the Okeanid Dodona and named the city for her.

L119 (PW480).

C. Herakles.

Occ. and Q. Not stated.

R. You will die at the hand of a dead man; this is the end of your journeys.

Mode E3, Topic 3c (3h)

Delphi and Dodona. Pseudo-Direct, Verse (iambic, Latin)—Sen. *HOet.* 1476–1478.

OP. Zeus at Dodona and elsewhere. Indirect—*Soph. *Trach.* 1160–1161.

    Comment: See pp. 20, 65, 80.

    This riddling oracle was spoken by Zeus to Herakles and later confirmed at Dodona, according to Sophocles' play. Seneca adds Delphi to Dodona, probably without authority in the tradition. It is not in the Herakles legend that he received any such message from the Delphic Apollo.

L120 (PW482).

C. Herakles.

Occ. Suffering from the Hydra's bites.

Q. Not stated.

R. He must go eastward until he reaches a river that produces an herb which resembles the Hydra; using that as an ointment for his wounds, he will heal himself.

Mode B, Topic 3h

Delphi. Indirect—Claudius Iolaus 788.1J *ap.* Steph. Byz. 59 Mein.

    Comment: See p. 79.

L121 (PW492).

C. Delphians.

Occ. March of Krios' son and his army upon Delphi.

Q. Protect us against the approaching danger.

R. Apollo will shoot his arrow at the bandit of Parnassos. Cretans will purify his hands of bloodshed, and the fame of his deed will never die.

Mode E1 (E2), Topic 2e (1d)
Delphi. Direct, Verse—Paus. 10.6.7.
   Comment: See pp. 19, 37; Fontenrose 1959: 19–21; cf. L95.

L122 (PW505).
C. Envoys of Achaeans under Achilles.
Occ. Beginning of the Trojan War.
Q. On the war.
R. The Hellenes will win and take Troy in ten years.
Mode E2, Topic 2e
Delphi. Indirect—Dares 15. Schol. vet. on Lyk. 200.
OP. *Kalchas.* Pseudo-Direct Verse—*Iliad 2.328–329. (Latin) Ovid *Met.* 12.19–21.
   Cicero *Div.* 2.30.64.
   Indirect—Apollod. epit. 3.15.
   Testimony—*Kypria ap.* Procl. *Chrest.* 1, p. 104 Allen. Lyk. 202–203.
      Comment: See pp. 19, 414.
   This is a good example of a well-known prophecy of legend, spoken by an individual seer, that in later times was sometimes said to have been spoken at Delphi. The omen of the snake and nine sparrows which appeared as the Achaeans at Aulis made sacrifice upon an altar was interpreted by Kalchas as a sign from Zeus foretelling victory in the tenth year; Iliad 2. 299–330. The Kypria, Ovid, Apollodoros, and others who refer to this event depend upon the Iliad. But Dares and the Scholiast on Lykophron make this prediction a response of Apollo at Delphi, spoken to Achilles as Agamemnon's envoy.

L123 (PW519).
C. King Romulus of Rome.
Occ. Earthquakes and civil war in Rome.
Q. Why do these things happen in my single reign?
R. If you do not associate your brother with you on the throne, Rome will not stand nor will the folk be quiet and war end.
Mode A1 (C1), Topic 2a
Delphi. Direct, Prose—Malalas p. 172.
   Comment: See p. 9.
   The traditional date of Romulus is the eighth century and consequently this response might be classed as Q. But Romulus is as legendary a figure as Theseus, and it is more appropriate to place this among L responses. It should be noticed that only Malalas attests it; he surely did not invent it, but it is doubtless a late addition to the Romulus legend.

L124 (PW524).
C. Podaleirios.
Occ. Need of a place to settle upon his return from the Trojan War.
Q. Where shall he settle?

R. He should live in that city in which he will suffer no injury if the sky falls.

Mode B, Topic 3h

Delphi. Indirect—Apollod. epit. 6.18. Tzetzes on Lyk. 1047.

    Comment: Podaleirios settled in the Carian Chersonese in a place encircled by hills.

L125 (PW527).

C. Ainianes.

Occ. Drought.

Q. Not stated.

R. Stone King Oinoklos.

Mode A1, Topic 3c

Delphi. Testimony—Plut. *Mor.* 294a, 297c.

    Comment: Plutarch does not explicitly inform us that the Ainianes consulted the Delphic Oracle. But they were living on the plain of Kirra when the drought came and they killed Oinoklos at Kirra; therefore we may reasonably infer that the legend supposes the Delphic Oracle, probably mentioned in other versions. The oracle, however, which they received in the Inachian country (294a), indicated only by mention of a *chrêsmos*, probably has no definite provenience.

L126 (PW530).

C. Spartans.

Occ. Plague.

Q. Not stated.

R. The plague will cease if every year they sacrifice a well-born maiden to the apotropaic gods.

Mode A1, Topic 1c

Delphi. Indirect—Aristodemos 22.19J *ap.* Ps.-Plut. *Mor.* 314c = *ap.* Joann. Lyd. *Mens.* p. 113 Bekk.

    Comment: The Spartans did this until Helen was chosen. An eagle then swooped down and carried off the sacrificial sword, placing it on a heifer. The Spartans thereafter sacrificed a heifer instead of a maiden.

L127 (PW531).

C. Eurysthenes and Prokles, Heraklids.

Occ. Desire to marry.

Q. With what Hellene or foreigner should they make a marriage alliance in order to marry well and prudently?

R. They should go back to Sparta on the road by which they came, and wherever they encounter the wildest animal carrying the tamest, there they should contract marriages.

Mode B, Topic 3h (3b)

Delphi. Indirect—Ael. *NA* 12.31.

    Comment: See p. 16.

L128 (PW 532).
C. A ruler of Haliartos.
Occ. Parched land without any water.
Q. How will they find water in the land?
R. He must kill whoever first meets him on his return to Haliartos.
Mode B, Topic 3h (3c)
Delphi. Indirect—Paus. 9.33.4.
> Comment: See p. 16.

Compare the Jephthah story, Judges 11.30–40. The enquirer's son Lophis was first to meet him on his return.

L129 (PW 533).
C. Athenians.
Occ. War with Amazons.
Q. Request for help against the Amazons.
R. Just before entering battle they should invoke Apollo with the cry *Hie Paian.*
Mode A1, Topic 1d
Delphi. Indirect—Macr. *Sat.* 1.17.18.

L130 (PW 534).
C. Leukippe.
Occ. Father and sister missing.
Q. Should I look for them?
R. Go over earth as my priestess and you will find them.
Mode A1, Topic 1d (3e)
Delphi. Pseudo-Direct, Prose (Latin)—Hyg. *Fab.* 190.3.

L131 (PW 535).
C. Ancient men.
Occ. Too many animals.
Q. Not stated.
R. Help the crops that are being destroyed.
Mode A1, Topic 3e
Delphi. Indirect—Plut. *Mor.* 729f.
> Comment: The beasts were eating the crops. The remedy was to kill animals and add meat to mankind's diet.

L132 (PW 541).
C. Chalkinos and Daitos.
Occ. Tenth generation after Kephalos' exile from Athens.
Q. Request for return to Athens.
R. They should make sacrifice to Apollo first at that place in Attica where they see a trireme running on land.

Mode B, Topic 1b (3h)
Delphi. Indirect—Paus. 1.37.7.
    Comment: See pp. 16, 71.

L133 (PW542–543).
C. Athens.
Occ. Plague or an epidemic of suicide by hanging among Attic maidens (Hyginus).
Q. Not stated.
R. They should make sacrifice to Ikarios, Erigone, and their dog Maira [and hang an
    effigy of a woman (Aelian frag. 88)].
Mode A1, Topic 1a
Delphi. Indirect—Ael. *NA* 7.28; frag. 88 *ap.* Sud. *Eι45.*
NP. Indirect—Apollo: Hyg. *Astr.* 2.4; *Fab.* 130.4. Prob. *Georg.* 2.385–389. Oracle: Serv.
    Georg. 2.389. Schol. on Germ. *Aratea*, p. 51 Giles. Vat. Myth. I 19, II 61.
Testimony—Oracle: Schol. AB on Il. 22.29. EM 42.
    Comment: See pp. 76 with note 34, 404, 405, 406.
    PW distinguish two oracles, separating Aelian frag. 88 and Hyginus *Fab.* from the
rest, for a command to hang the effigy. Only the fragment, however, has this as oracular
content. Hyginus mentions only the rite of *oscillatio* as a consequence of the oracular
statement that the Athenians had neglected the death of Ikarios and Erigone (Hyginus
Astr. states the oracle as a command to satisfy Erigone in order to stop the hanging epidemic). Obviously the effigy-hanging is part of the appeasement of Ikarios and Erigone;
and a command to perform the rite was included in some versions of the oracle that
demanded worship of them. See L148.

L134 (PW556).
C. Patrai.
Occ. Famine and plague.
Q. Not stated (apparently, What is the cause of the affliction?).
R. Melanippos and Komaitho are the cause; they should be sacrificed to Artemis and
    thereafter every year the most beautiful maiden and youth. They will cease doing so
    when a foreign king comes to their land bearing a foreign deity.
Mode A1 (D2, F), Topic 1c (3g)
Delphi. Indirect—Paus. 7.19.4, 6.

L135 (PW557).
C. Eurypylos.
Occ. Madness caused by looking at the image of Dionysos in the chest which he received
    from the spoil of Ilion.
Q. Not stated.
R. Wherever he comes upon men making a strange sacrifice, there he should dedicate
    the chest and stay.
Mode B, Topic 3h (1b)

Delphi. Indirect—Paus. 7.19.8.

    Comment: On L134–135 see Fontenrose 1959: 483 note 10.

L136 (PW559).

C. Athens.

Occ. Drought and crop failure.

Q. Not stated.

R. The fugitive in Crete will end these, if they punish the murderer and restore the dead [ox] at the festival at which he died; it will be better if they taste of the dead [ox].

Mode A1, Topic 1b (3f)

Delphi. Indirect—Porphyry *Abst.* 2.29.

    Comment: This response belongs to the origin myth of the Buphonia rite at the Diipoleia festival in Athens. See Jane Harrison, *Themis* (Cambridge Univ. Press, 1927) 141–148.

L137 (PW562).

C. Heraklids.

Occ. Dispute about whether to bury Alkmene, who died at Megara, in Megara or in Thebes.

Q. Where should they bury Alkmene?

R. It is better to bury Alkmene in Megara.

Mode A2, Topic 3c

Delphi. Indirect—Paus. 1.41.1.

    Comment: See p. 15.

    The form of the response suggests a question in the form, "Is it better to bury Alkmene in Megara?", a request for a sanction.

L138 (PW564).

C. Orchomenians.

Occ. Ravages of Aktaion's ghost.

Q. Not stated.

R. They should find and bury Aktaion's remains, make a bronze image of the ghost, and fasten it to a rock with an iron bond.

Mode A1, Topic 3c (3e)

Delphi. Indirect—Paus. 9.38.5.

Comment: See p. 130; Fontenrose 1968: 83–85.

L139 (PW569).

C. Boeotians.

Occ. Drought and famine.

Q. Request for an end of drought.

R. Go to Trophonios at Lebadeia and get a remedy from him.

Mode A1, Topic 3g (1a)

Delphi. Indirect—Paus. 9.40.1.

NP. Indirect—The god: Schol. vet. on Aristoph. *Nub.* 508.

Comment: With this oracle and the attached story Delphi is given credit for the founding of Trophonios' Oracle at Lebadeia. Cf. L85.

L140 (PW570).

C. King of Delphi.

Occ. Famine and plague.

Q. Not stated.

R. Appease Charila the maiden suicide.

Mode A1, Topic 1a

Delphi. Indirect—Plut. *Mor.* 293c.

Comment: See p. 76 note 34; Fontenrose 1959: 458–460.

L141 (PW575).

C. Young Man 1.

Occ. Not stated, but it is after his desertion of his two companions when attacked by robbers.

Q. Not stated.

R. You did not help your dying friend when you were at hand. I shall not answer you; leave the temple.

Mode C1 (D1), Topic 3e (1d)

Delphi. Direct, Verse—Ael. *VH* 3.44. Simpl. on Epict. *Ench.* 32.3. Olymp. on *Alk. I,* p. 115 Creuzer. Schol. vet. on Plato *Leg.* 865b. Incomplete—EM 445.

Testimony—*Epict. *Ench.* 32.3.

Comment: See pp. 17, 21.

L142 (PW576).

C. Young Man 2.

Occ. Unintentional killing of his companion when attacked by robbers.

Q. Not stated.

R. You killed your companion when defending him. His blood has not stained you; your hands are as clean as before.

Mode D1, Topic 3f

Delphi. Direct, Verse—Ael. *VH* 3.44. Simpl. on Epict. *Ench.* 32.3. Olymp. on *Alk. I,* p. 115 Creuzer. Schol. vet. on Plato *Leg.* 865b.

L143 (PW205).

C. Amphilochos.

Occ. and Q. Not stated.

R. Found a city [Amphilochian Argos].

Mode A1, Topic 2c

NP. Testimony—Apollo: Apollod. 3.7.7.

L144 (PW 529).
C. Egyptians.
Occ. Famine consequent upon failure of the Nile to rise.
Q. Not stated.
R. If the king sacrifices his daughter to the apotropaic gods, they will have good crops.
Mode A1, Topic 1c
Delphi. Indirect—Ps.-Plut. Fluv. 16.1, 1027 W.

L145 (PW 155).
C. Athens.
Occ. Plague after expulsion of Theseus.
Q. Not stated.
R. They should conciliate Theseus by putting Lykos to death.
Mode A1, Topic 3f (1b, 3c)
Delphi. Indirect—Chor. Gaz. 17.84.

L146 (PW 536).
C. Klymene's husband.
Occ. Klymene's accidental killing of a pig.
Q. Not stated.
R. Nothing needs to be done.
Mode D1, Topic 3e
Delphi. Testimony—Porphyry Abst. 2.9.

L147 (PW 537).
C. Episkopos.
Occ. Desire to sacrifice sheep.
Q. Not stated.
R. It is not lawful to kill sheep, but if a sheep nods assent after being sprinkled, you may
   sacrifice it.
Mode A1 (C1), Topic 1b
Delphi. Direct, Verse—Porphyry Abst. 2.9.
       Comment: L146–147 belong to aitia of the beginnings of animal sacrifice and of
meat-eating. Cf. L131, 136.

L148 (PW 544).
C. Athenians.
Occ. Barrenness of the land.
Q. Request for a remedy.
R. They must offer libations every year to the Aetolians whom they wrongly killed and
   celebrate the feast of Choes.
Mode A1, Topic 1a
Delphi. Indirect—Ael. frag. 73 ap. Sud. A932, X364, (E681).

NP. Testimony—The god: Zon. *Lex.* 653 Titt.

Comment: The story that Aelian told has to be pieced together from several entries in the Suda. Some Aetolians brought wine to Athens for a festival; this, it seems, was the first appearance of wine in Attica. When several Athenians drank it in large quantities and fell into a drunken stupor, the others thought them dead and killed the Aetolians. Then the land became barren, bringing consultation of Delphi. Here the Aetolian visitors take the place of Ikarios (L133); his story is *aition* of the Aiora festival, this of the Choes.

L149 (PW 547).
C. Corinthians.
Occ. After death of Pentheus.
Q. Not stated.
R. They should find that tree [from which the Bacchantes pulled Pentheus] and honor it as a god.
Mode A1, Topic 1a
Delphi. Indirect—Paus. 2.2.7.

Comment: This probably belongs to a tale of offended deity, but Pausanias tells us nothing else.

L150 (PW 548).
C. Phanes.
Occ. and Q. Not stated.
R. Take Dionysos Lysios from Thebes to Sikyon.
Mode A1, Topic 1a
Delphi. Testimony—Paus. 2.7.6.

Comment: Pausanias dates Phanes to the time of the Heraklid invasion, when Aristomachos mistook the meaning of L62. Phanes has an obviously Dionysiac name.

L151 (PW 553).
C. Naos.
Occ. and Q. Not stated.
R. Found a cult and initiation rite of Demeter Eleusinia at Pheneos.
Mode A1, Topic 1a
Delphi. Testimony—Paus. 8.15.1.

L152 (PW 560).
C. Athenians.
Occ. and Q. Not stated.
R. Honor Herakles as a god (Arrian); build temples and sacrifice to him (Aristeides).
Mode A1, Topic 1a
Delphi. Indirect—Arrian *Anab.* 4.11.7.
NP. Indirect—The god: Aristeides 5.33.

L153 (PW563)
C. (A) Demarmenos, Eretrian fisherman.
Occ. (A) Find of a skeleton in his nets.
Q. (A) Whose is the skeleton and what should he do with it?
R. (A) He should give his find to the Eleians.
C. (B) Eleians.
Occ. (B) Plague.
Q. (B) Request for relief.
R. (B) They must recover Pelops' bones.
Mode A1, Topic 1a (3c).
Delphi. Indirect—Paus. 5.13.6.

 Comment: Demarmenos and the Eleians appeared at the same mantic session. For the theme of fisherman's find see also Q76, 241, and the story of Theagenes (Q171).

L154 (PW566).
C. Tegea.
Occ. Crop failure.
Q. Not stated.
R. Mourn for Skephros.
Mode A1, Topic 1a
Delphi. Indirect—Paus. 8.53.3.

 Comment: Skephros is another example of the slain fertility spirit. His brother Leimon killed him when he was talking secretly with Apollo. He was the son of Tegeates and Maira. For another Maira connected with fertility rites see L133. Skephros was attached to the cult of Apollo Aguieus in Tegea.

L155 (PW580).
C. A bad character (kakopragmôn).
Occ. Attempt to prove the Delphic Oracle false: he held a sparrow in his hand under his cloak.
Q. Is what I hold in my hand alive or dead?
R. Stop this [or] Do as you like; the life or death of what you hold is in your power.
Mode D1 (C1), Topic 3j
Delphi. Direct, Prose—Aesop Fab. 36. Babrius 229.
 Comment: See pp. 37, 38, 113.

L156 (PW392).
C. Temesa.
Occ. Decision to abandon Temesa because of the ravages of Polites' ghost.
Q. Apparently where to go.
R. They should not leave Temesa but appease the ghost as Heros, giving him a temenos and offering him every year the most beautiful maiden as wife.
Mode A1 (C1), Topic 1c
Delphi. Indirect—Paus. 6.6.8. Suda E3510.
NP. Testimony—Oracle: *Strabo 6.1.5, p. 255.
 Comment: See Fontenrose 1959: 101–103; 1968: 79–83; cf. L92–93, 95.

L157 (PW332).

C. Locrians.

Occ. Plague.

Q. Not stated.

R. The plague will not end unless you appease Athena by sending two maidens every year to her in Ilion as penalty for Kassandra [for a thousand years (Apollodoros)].

Mode A1, Topic 1b (3f).

NP. Direct, Prose, partly Indirect—Apollo: Ael. frag. 47 ap. Sud. Π3092.

    Indirect—The god: Schol. vet. and Tzetzes on Lyk. 1141. Oracle: Apollod. epit. 6.20. Schol. vet. on Lyk. 1159.

    Testimony—The god: Iambl. Pyth. 8.42. Oracle: *Polyb. 12.5.7.

OP. Athena. Indirect—Annaeus Placidus ap. Serv. auct. Aen. 1.41.

    Comment: See pp. 131–133, 136–137; Q232.

L158 (PW567).

C. Aisymnos of Megara.

Occ. Foundation of Megarian republic.

Q. In what way will the Megarians prosper?

R. The Megarians will prosper if they consult with the majority.

Mode A3, Topic 2b

Delphi. Indirect—Paus. 1.43.3.

    Comment: See p. 71.

    Cf. Q37, the same advice given to the Tarentines, introduced by the formula ἄμεινον καὶ λῷον ἔσεσθαι, and interpreted in the same way, the majority = the dead.

L159 (PW545–546).

C. Athenians.

Occ. Plague.

Q. Not stated.

R. The only remedy is to introduce Dionysos with all honor (Schol. Aristoph.); he stayed once in Athens in the days of Ikarios.

Mode A1 (D1), Topic 1a

Delphi. Testimony—Paus. 1.2.5.

NP. Indirect—Oracle: Schol. Rav. Aristoph. Ach. 243.

    Comment: Pegasos of Eleutherai brought Dionysos' image to Athens, but the Athenians rejected it. The god in anger sent a disease that affected the men's genitals. The plague ended when they accepted Dionysos in obedience to this response. PW distinguish two oracles, calling the Scholiast's version alternative to that of Pausanias. But Pausanias says that the Delphic Oracle aided Pegasos in his introduction of Dionysos' cult to Athens by reminding the Athenians of Dionysos' sojourn among them in Ikarios' time (see L133). This is obviously a remark intended as a reason for heeding the direction for remedy indicated by the Scholiast.

L160 (PW157).

C. Spartans.

Occ. Birth of twin sons to King Aristodemos.

Q. What should they do in this situation?

R. They should consider both sons kings, but honor the older more.

Mode A1, Topic 2a

Delphi. Indirect—Herod. 6.52.5.

Testimony—Paus. 3.1.5.

Comment: This response belongs to the origin legend of the Spartan double kingship. The supposed date would be in the twelfth century B.C. See Crahay 1956: 159-160.

L161 (PW417).

C. Pelasgians under the Spartans Pollis, Delphos, and Krataidas.

Occ. Migration.

Q. Not stated.

R. When they lose the goddess and the anchor, they should cease wandering and found a city there.

Mode B, Topic 3h (2c)

Delphi. Indirect—Plut. *Mor.* 247d.

Comments: The colonists lost an image of Artemis and an anchor fluke at the Cretan Chersonese, occupied the territory, and founded Lyktos.

L162 (PW316).

C. Thessalians.

Occ. Selection of a king.

Q. (A) Names on *phryktoi* presented to Pythia.

R. (A) Aleuas [in whose name a *phryktos* had secretly been placed in the urn].

Q. (B) Did the Pythia err in choosing Aleuas?

R. (B) I mean the redhead whom Archidike bore.

Mode A1, Topic 2a

Delphi. Direct, Verse—Plut. *Mor.* 492b.

Comment: See pp. 222, 223, 226.

This response I classify as Mode A1, since it is essentially the command, "Make Aleuas king."

L163 (PW378).

C. Magnesians.

Occ. Desire to return to Magnesia after being taken captive in war.

Q. Not stated.

R. They should return when white ravens appear.

Mode B, Topic 3h

Delphi. Testimony—Inscription of Magnesia-on Maeander, *IM* 17 = Michel 855, lines 9-13.

Comment: See p. 122.

L164 (PW379).

C. Magnesian colonists.

Occ. Contemplated return to Magnesia after seeing white ravens.

Q. Is it better to go back to our own country?

R. You must sail to another country than your fatherland, to a Magnesia which is not inferior to that which Peneios and Pelion keep.

Mode A1, Topic 2c

Delphi. Direct, Verse—Inscription of Magnesia-on-Maeander, *IM* 17 = Michel 855, lines 16–23.

> *Comment:* See pp. 175, 177.

L165 (PW380).

C. Magnesian colonists.

Occ. Receipt of L164.

Q. Where shall we go and how?

R. The man that stands before the temple door will rule you and guide the way to the land of Pamphylians beyond Mount Mykale, where is the wealthy house of Mandrolytos near the Maeander. There if you defend yourselves and avoid deceit, Zeus will grant you victory and fame.

Mode F (E2), Topic 2c (3g)

Delphi. Direct, Verse—Inscription of Magnesia-on-Maeander, *IM* 17 = Michel 855, lines 28–35.

> *Comment:* That the principal mode should be considered F rather than E2 is shown by L166, which does no more than explicate L165; one or the other is really otiose. L166 is plainly a conditioned prediction: "The man who first meets you as you leave the temple will be your guide." Only the oracle identifies him, "He will be a descendant of Glaukos." L165 is essentially the same: "The man whom you will find [meet] standing at the door [as you leave] will be your guide to the Pamphylian land, etc." Cf. L28. See p. 180.

L166 (PW381).

C. Magnesian colonists.

Occ. Receipt of L165.

Q. Who and whence is the man who will guide us?

R. There is in the temenos a man of Glaukos' lineage, who will be first to meet you as you leave my temple; he will show you a fertile land.

Mode F, Topic 2c (3g)

Delphi. Direct, Verse—Inscription of Magnesia-on-Maeander, *IM* 17 = Michel 855, lines 38–41.

NP. Testimony—Oracle: *Hermesianax *ap.* Parthen. 5.6.

> *Comment:* See pp. 172–173.

L167 (PW382).

C. Leukippos.

Occ. Magnesians' proposal to him as first met to guide them.

Q. Presumably whether he should accept.

R. Go to the Pamphylian gulf and lead the Magnesian folk until you reach the cliff of Thorax, the River Amanthios, and Mount Mykale. There the Magnesians will prosper in the house of Mandrolytos, admired by their neighbors.

Mode A1 (E2), Topic 2c

Delphi. Direct, Verse—Inscription of Magnesia-on-Maeander, *IM* 17 = Michel 855, lines 46–51.

    Comment: On L163–167 see Ath. 4.173ef, citing Aristotle or Theophrastos, on the Magnesians-on-Maeander as a Delphian colony. Just how far back the legend of *IM* 17 goes cannot be said. But the verse oracles, L164–167, were probably composed around 221/0 at the time of the institution of the Leukophryenia as an agonistic festival. The inscription accompanies *IM* 16, which tells of the epiphany of Artemis Leukophryene and the foundation of the festival, and reports H45, the Delphic approval of the festival.

L168 (PW455).

C. Hellenes.

Occ. Barrenness of fields due to Apollo's wrath.

Q. Not stated.

R. They should establish musical contests for the Delphic Apollo.

Mode A1, Topic 1a

Delphi. Testimony—Varro *ap.* Aug. *CD* 18.12.2.

L169 (PW540).

C. Aeolians and Trojans.

Occ. Plague of field mice.

Q. Not stated.

R. They must sacrifice to Apollo Smintheus.

Mode A1, Topic 1b

Delphi. Indirect—Ael. *NA* 12.5.

    Comment: See L116.

L170 (PW565).

C. Spartan kings.

Occ. Theft of Palladion from Argos.

Q. On safety and keeping of the Palladion.

R. They should make one of the thieves its guardian.

Mode A1, Topic 3g (1d)

Delphi. Indirect—Plut. *Mor.* 302d.

    Comment: This oracle and its story purport to explain why the Spartan Palladion was kept in the *hêrôon* of Odysseus. See Halliday 1928: 192–194.

L171 (PW338).

C. Envoys of Magnesia-on-Maeander.

Occ. Discovery of an image of Dionysos in a plane tree broken by the wind.

Q. What does the event mean for the Magnesians and what should they do to continue living in prosperity?

R. Magnesians, defenders of my possessions, you want to know the meaning of Dionysos' appearance in a tree. He appeared as a youth, since when you founded your city you did not build temples for Dionysos. So build them now and appoint a priest. Go to Thebes and fetch Maenads of the family of Ino, Kadmos' daughter. They will give you *orgia* and rites and will establish companies [*thiasoi*] of Dionysos in the city.

Mode A1 (D1, E1), Topic 1a

Delphi. Direct, Verse—Inscription of Magnesia-on-Maeander, *IM* 215.

Comment: This is obviously part of the legend of the coming of Dionysos' worship to Magnesia, and was surely referred to the early years of the city, in spite of a possible allusion to the Gallic invasion of 278 B.C., which causes PW to suppose a third-century date for the response and to consider it genuine. Surely Dionysos' worship was established in Magnesia long before 278. The direction to bring three Maenads of Ino's family, named Kosko, Baubo, and Thettale—patently mythical—who founded the three Magnesian *thiasoi* and received tombs in select places after their deaths, assures the legendary nature of tale and response, though admittedly these oracular verses are a late composition. The response consists of twelve hexameters, cut upon eighteen lines of the inscription.

L172 (PW472).

C., Occ., and Q. Not stated.

R. Phoibos' ray spreads everywhere; it goes through hard rocks and the sea; and the multitude of stars that return to the tireless sky under wise necessity's decree do not elude it, nor do all the hosts of the dead that Tartaros has received within misty Hades; and I rejoice in pious men as much as in Olympos.

Mode D1, Topic 3j

Delphi. Direct, Verse, Incomplete—Hierokles *In aureum carmen*, p. 421 Mullach.

NP. Direct, Verse—The god: *Jul. *Frag. epist.* 299c–300a.

Comment: See p. 113.

There is little reason to classify this as Q rather than L. It appears to belong to fable, and the moral is pointed in the last line. It is impossible to assign a date for the supposed consultation. Julian quotes this after quoting oracles of Didyma (Didyma 45, 46) and may have supposed that this too was an utterance of Apollo Didymeus.

L173 (PW551).

C. Thebans.

Occ. Plague following upon the killing of Dionysos' priest.

Q. Not stated.

R. They must sacrifice a beautiful boy to Dionysos.

Mode A1, Topic 1c

Delphi. Indirect—Paus. 9.8.2.

L174 (PW551).

C. Thebans.

Occ. A few years after L173.

Q. Not stated.

R. They must substitute a goat for the boy as victim.

Mode A1, Topic 1b

Delphi. Indirect—Paus. 9.8.2.

   Comment: PW, who more usually divide responses, join this with L173 as one response. Pausanias reports both in a single passage, but definitely says that the order to substitute a goat was spoken not many years after the instruction to sacrifice a boy.

L175 (PW579).

C. A slave.

Occ. Wish to please his master.

Q. What should I do to please my master?

R. Seek and you will find.

Mode A1, Topic 3j

Delphi. Direct, Prose—Clem. Alex. *Strom.* 4.2, 565P.

L176 (PW581).

C. A bad character (*ponêros tis*).

Occ. Not stated.

Q. Many strange questions.

R. [Conclusion only] Phoibos has told you this from the Delphic tripod.

Mode D1, Topic 3j (1d)

Delphi. Direct, Verse—Zen. 6.3.

   Comment: See pp. 121, 178.

   L175 and L176 are timeless fable morals and more appropriately classified as L than Q.

IV. Fictional Responses

F1 (PW251).
C. Philokleon.
Occ. and Q. Not stated.
R. When someone escapes him then he will wither.
Mode F, Topic 3c
Delphi. Indirect—Aristoph. Vesp. 160.
   Comment: See p. 170 note 8.

F2 (PW252).
C. Chremylos.
Occ. Poverty in a righteous life, though the wicked prosper.
Q. Should his son change his ways and become a knave?
R. Whomever he first meets as he leaves the temple he should cling to and persuade to go home with him.
Mode B, Topic 3g
Delphi. Indirect—Aristoph. Pl. 41–43 (212–213). Arg. 1, 2, 3, 6.3–4 (Aristoph. Gramm.) Pl.
   Comment: Chremylos meets the blind Plutos as he leaves the temple.

F3 (PW574).
C. Aristeas and Moirichos.
Occ. Each made the other heir of all his property.
Q. Not stated. (Probably, Which would outlive the other?).
R. [Aristeas] [Moirichos] will live longer.

Mode E2, Topic 3c

Delphi. Testimony—Lucian *DMort.* 11.1.

Comment: In Lucian's anecdote the friends consulted manteis, astrologers, dream interpreters, Chaldaeans, and the Pythian Apollo; and some said Aristeas would live longer, others said Moirichos would. The Delphic answer is not specified.

F4 (PW 499).

C. Citizens of an afflicted city.

Occ. Plague.

Q. Not stated.

R. The plague will cease if the people sacrifice a citizen's son.

Mode A1, Topic 1c

Delphi. Indirect—Liban. *Decl.* 41 *tit.,* 41.10.

Comment: This is an imaginary case that Libanios has devised for his declamation. A magus' son is chosen for sacrifice; the magus promises to end the plague if they spare his son. The speech that follows is made by an opponent of the magus' proposal. The oracle is modeled on Legendary examples: L32, 44, 95, 126, 144, 156, 173.

F5 (PW 500).

C. Aphrodite and Charites.

Occ. Eros remains an infant.

Q. Find a remedy for this misfortune.

R. You don't know the child's nature. He could be born alone, but he cannot grow alone. For his growth you need Anteros. Each will grow or fail as he sees the other grow or fail.

Mode D1 (A1, E1), Topic 3a

Delphi (*Themis*). Direct, Prose—Them. *Or.* 24, p. 305ab.

Comment: This response is patently Themistios' own invention for his discourse on Eros and Anteros. It has no place in Greek mythology. Probably because his consultants are deities (the only example of this) he places the consultation in the pre-Apolline days when Themis spoke oracles. See L118.

F6 (PW 503).

C. Achaeans.

Occ. War on Troy.

Q. Not stated.

R. All must allow Palamedes to conduct sacrifice to Apollo Sminthios.

Mode A1, Topic 1b

Delphi. Indirect—Dict. Cret. 2.14.

Comment: This is Pseudo-Dictys' own invention, not an oracle of the Trojan legend, and so is better classed as F than as L.

F7 (PW 504).

C. Dictys and two others, envoys of the Cretans.

Occ. Plague of locusts in Crete.

Q. Request for a remedy.

R. The creatures will perish by divine means, and the island will soon abound in crops.

Mode E2, Topic 3h

Delphi. Indirect—Dict. Cret. 6.11.

    Comment: This like F6 is Pseudo-Dictys' invention for his narrative purpose.

F8 (PW 506).

C. Kalchas, envoy of the Trojans.

Occ. Imminent war with the Achaeans.

Q. On the kingdom and his own affairs.

R. He should go with the Argives against the Trojans and help them with his skill; and they should not leave until Troy is taken.

Mode A1, Topic 2e

Delphi. Indirect—Dares 15.

    Comment: Pseudo-Dares, like Pseudo-Dictys, has invented a Delphic consultation and response. That Kalchas was a Trojan, who became a seer for the Greeks on the Delphic Apollo's advice, is entirely Dares' fiction. His Kalchas comes to Delphi at the same time as Achilles for L122.

F9 (PW 514).

C. Kalasiris.

Occ. Silent prayer on entering Apollo's temple.

Q. None.

R. You flee destiny by leaving the Nile. I shall soon give you Egyptian land. Be my friend now.

Mode E2 (A1), Topic 3i (3j)

Delphi. Direct, Verse (elegiac)—Heliod. *Aith.* 2.26.5.

F10

C. Charikles, priest of Apollon Pythios.

Occ. Lack of children.

Q. Request for children.

R. He will be the father of a daughter and will not have her on favorable terms.

Mode E2, Topic 3a

Delphi. Indirect—Heliod. *Aith.* 2.29.3.

    Comment: Heliodoros' Charikles says that after supplicating the god many times in his childless later years the god finally spoke to him. Surely he means that the god spoke this to him as an oracular response; but PW do not include it, although they include F12, which has no more right to inclusion.

F11 (PW 515).

C. Delphians and Ainianes.

Occ. Sacrifice and prayer at the altar.

Q. None.

R. Take notice, Delphians, of her who has greatest charm but least glory, and of the goddess' son, who are leaving my temple and crossing the sea to the sun's dark soil, where they will don a prize of the best life, a white garland on dark brows.

Mode E3, Topic 3g (3f)

Delphi. Direct, Verse (elegiac)—Heliod. *Aith.* 2.35.5.

F12 (PW 516).

C. Charikles, priest of Apollon Pythios.

Occ. Sight of the unlawful in Apollo's temple.

Q. None.

R. In return for seeing what he should not have seen, he will be deprived of the sight of his dearest.

Mode E2, Topic 3f

Delphi. Indirect—Heliod. *Aith.* 4.19.3.

> *Comment:* See p. 358.

Apparently it is the god himself who speaks in his adyton immediately after Charikles has seen what is not *themis*, just as he spoke L8 to Orestes in his own voice.

F13 (PW 517).

C. Lysippos and Straton.

Occ. Disappearance of Dosikles and Rodanthe.

Q. Where have our children gone?

R. Go to the island that Cyprus-born Aphrodite possesses and you will find them alive. But marry them in their own country. Eros, Pothos, and Aphrodite have bound them with iron chains.

Mode A1 (D2), Topic 3b (3e)

Delphi. Direct, Verse—Theodor. Prodr. *Rodanthe kai Dosikles* 196–204.

F14 (PW 502).

C. Delphians.

Occ. Gathering of men to join Dionysos' army.

Q. None.

R. Not stated, perhaps a promise of victory.

Delphi. Testimony—Nonn. *Dion.* 13.131–134.

> *Comment:* This is nothing more than Nonnos' ornament for the scene: the Pythian oracular rock, the tripod, and the Castalian spring all broke forth in utterance on this occasion.

F15

C. Cretans.

Occ. and Q. Not stated.

R. A recipe for spicing wine.

Mode E1, Topic 3h

Delphi. Testimony—Palladius *De agricultura* 11.14.13–16.

Comment: Until the appearance of H. W. Parke, D. E. W. Wormell, "A neglected Delphic oracle," *Hermathena* 97 (1974) 18–20, this response had escaped my notice. It is a strange kind of response, and just what it consisted in is not clear. Palladius' recipe does not appear to be a quotation, direct or indirect, of the god's words, but follows upon the sentence, . . . item quod Cretensibus oraculum Pythii Apollinis monstrasse memoratur. Parke and Wormell believe that the oracle prescribed the injunction that a beardless boy or another ritually pure person stir the wine.

It is also difficult to classify the response. We are told only that Apollo spoke it to Cretans. It does not appear to be meant for the legendary period; yet to what historical time can it possibly refer? Palladius wrote in the fourth century A.D., i.e., he wrote this about the time that the Delphic Oracle came to an end. It is perhaps best to classify this supposed response as Fictional; it may well be an invention of an agricultural writer, Palladius' source (notice *memoratur*).

F16

C. The poet.

Occ. Not stated.

Q. What is more advantageous for us?

R. Listen, peoples, to the Delian god's advice. Be pious; fulfill your vows to the gods. Defend country, parents, children, wives; drive the enemy away. Help friends; spare the wretched. Favor the good; oppose the false. Chastise wrongdoing; brand the impious; punish adulterers. Beware of the wicked; don't trust anyone too much.

Mode A1, Topic 3j (1b, 3f)

Delphi. Pseudo-Direct, Verse (iambic sen., Latin)—Phaedrus *Fab. Aes.* 111 / app. Per. 6.6–15.

Catalogue of Responses
of Didyma

The Didymaean responses are numbered as in Fontenrose 1933: 207–229 (where the texts and their contexts are quoted from the sources), except that 24 has been changed, since on further study the former 24 proved to contain no reference to a response; and that 47–50 have been added to the former 46 responses. In 1933 I overlooked 47 and 48; and the inscriptions of 49, 50, and the present 24 had not yet been published. It is convenient otherwise to keep the numbers as I assigned them, although I would now break up 6 into two or three responses and make changes of arrangement.

1 Legendary.
C. Lyrkos.
Occ. Lack of children.
Q. Not stated.
R. He will impregnate the first woman with whom he lies after leaving the temple.
Mode F, Topic 3a
Indirect—Parthen. 1.2.

2 Legendary (cf. L70).
C. Neileus Kodros' son.
Occ. Arrival with colonists in Miletos.

Q. Where should he settle?

R. (1) His daughter will show him. (2) He should take the land where someone offers him a clod of earth.

Mode E2 (B), Topic 3g

Indirect—(1) Tzetzes on Lyk. 1385. (2) Tzetzes *Chil.* 13.111–112.

3 (PW130) Quasi-Historical, [700–650]. Not genuine.

C. Milesian aristocrats.

Occ. The god would not admit them to the Oracle when they came to inquire about portents which appeared after they had burned the Gergithai, political opponents, to death.

Q. Why are we driven away?

R. The murder of the peaceful Gergithai, the fate of the pitch-covered, and the ever-withered tree concern me.

Mode D1, Topic 3c

Direct, Verse—Herakleides Pont. *ap.* Athen. 26.524b.

4 Historical, 600–550.

C. Milesians?

Occ. and Q. Unknown.

R. [Text lost except the conclusion] It will be better for him who obeys, otherwise for him who disobeys.

Mode A1, Topic?

Direct, Prose—Inscription of Miletos, *Milet* 1.3.178.

   Comment: See p. 234.

5 Quasi-Historical, [c. 550 B.C.]. Not genuine (cf. Q99).

C. Envoys of King Croesus of Lydia.

Occ. Croesus' design of testing the Oracles.

Q. What is Croesus of Lydia doing now?

R. Unknown but incorrect.

Mode D1, Topic 3h

Testimony—Herod. 1.46–47.

6 Quasi-Historical, [545 B.C.]. Not genuine.

C. (A) Cymaeans.

Occ. (A) Mazares' demand that they surrender Paktyes.

Q. (A) What should they do to please the gods?

R. (A) Surrender Paktyes to the Persians.

Mode A1, Topic 2d

Indirect—Herod. 1. 158.1.

C. (B) Aristodikos and Cymaean envoys.

Occ. (B) Aristodikos' distrust of 6(A).

Q. (B) Paktyes the Lydian fled to us as a suppliant to escape death from the Persians. They demand that we surrender him. We fear the Persian power but have been reluctant to surrender the suppliant until we have clearly learned from you what we should do.

R. (B) Surrender Paktyes to the Persians.

Mode A1, Topic 2d

Indirect—Herod. 1.159.2 (question stated directly).

C. (C) Aristodikos.

Occ. (C) Aristodikos removed all the birds' nests from Apollo's temple.

Q. (C) (a) None.

R. (C) (a) Most unholy man, how dare you rout my suppliants from the temple?

Q. (C) (b) Do you, Lord, thus protect your suppliants, but bid the Cymaeans surrender their suppliant?

R. (C) (b) Yes, I bid you do so, so that you may more quickly perish for your impiety, and that hereafter you may not consult the Oracle about surrender of suppliants.

Mode D1, Topic 1d

Direct, Prose—Herod. 1.159.3-4.

> Comment: See pp. 121, 358.

7 Historical, c. 510 B.C.

C. Milesians?

Occ. and Q. Unknown.

R. [Regulations for the cult of Herakles (badly damaged inscription).] Women are forbidden to enter Herakles' sanctuary [?]. There shall be no eating of greens. When [?] thighs are burned place . . . beside the thighs. Sacrifice a black sheep . . . . Beside the ox bake sweet [?] . . . .

Mode A1, Topic 1b

Direct, Verse (iambic trimeter?)—Inscription of Miletos, Milet 1.3.132.

> Comment: See p. 234.

8 Quasi-Historical, [530–500]. Not genuine.

C. Carians (Cypriotes—Polykrates).

Occ. War against Persians or Ambraciotes.

Q. Shall we take the Milesians as allies?

R. Once upon a time the Milesians were valiant.

Mode D1, Topic 3j

Direct, Verse (iambic trimeter)—Demon 327.16J ap. Schol. vet. in Aristoph. Pl. 1002. Zen. 5.80. Prov. Bodl. 776. Suda H572. Schol. vet. on Aristoph. Pl. 1002, 1075; Schol. Dorv. on Pl. 1002.

> Comment: Zenobios and the Bodleian Proverbs identify this response as Didymaean. Demon and Schol. Dorv. refer it to Apollo; in the other sources it is anonymous.

9 Historical, 331 B.C. Genuine in part.

C. Milesians.

Occ. Renewal of the Oracle.

Q. Not stated.

R. Alexander is son of Zeus; he will have victory at Arbela, where Dareios will die; there will be revolution in Lakedaimon.

Mode D1 (E2), Topic 3a (2e)

Testimony—Kallisthenes 124.14aJ *ap.* Strab. 17.1.43, p. 814.

Comment: Didyma undoubtedly proclaimed Alexander son of Zeus in gratitude for his liberation of Miletos and revival of the Oracle. The specific predictions look *post eventum*; but Didyma may very well have prophesied victory for Alexander against the Persians.

10 Quasi-Historical, [before 311 B.C.]. Not genuine.

C. Seleukos.

Occ. and Q. Not stated.

R. Seleukos is king. [When he takes the Syrian kingship he should make Daphne sacred to Apollo (Libanios).]

Mode E2 (A1), Topic 2a (1a)

Indirect—Diod. 19.90.4. Liban. *Or.* 11.99.

11 Quasi-Historical, [334 B.C.]. Not genuine.

C. Seleukos.

Occ. Desire to return to Macedonia.

Q. Apparently whether he should return.

R. Do not hasten to Europe: Asia is much better for you.

Mode C1, Topic 3e

Direct, Verse—App. *Syr.* 56, 63.

12 Quasi-Historical, [334–281]. Not genuine.

C. Seleukos.

Occ. Concern about his death.

Q. Not stated.

R. You will avoid death for a long time; but if you go to Argos, then you will die before your time.

Mode E2 (C1), Topic 3c

Direct, Verse—App. *Syr.* 63.

13 Historical, 312–246.

C. Seleucid kings.

Occ. and Q. Not stated.

R. Unknown.

Testimony—Letter of Seleukos II, Inscription of Didyma, *DI* 493, lines 3–5.

Comment: Seleukos II's letter to the Milesian demos refers to oracles of Apollo Didymeus spoken in favor of his predecessors.

14 Historical, 228/7.

C. Demos of the Milesians.

Occ. Application of Drerians and Milatians from Crete for admission to the citizen body of Miletos.

Q. Is it better now and for the future to admit Drerians and Milatians to the citizenship and apportion land to them and other perquisites which Milesians share?

R. Receive helper men as settlers in your city; for it is better [the remainder of the text is damaged].

Mode A2, Topic 2d

Direct, Verse—Inscription of Miletos, Milet 1.3.33f. 11–14, 33g.1–4.

Testimony—cf. Milet 1.3.37b. 32–35.

15 Historical, 228/7.

C. Demos of the Milesians.

Occ. Application of certain Cretans for admission to the citizen body of Miletos.

Q. Is it better now and for the future to admit . . . [name lost], Philanor, So . . . , and their company to the citizenship and to apportion land to them and other perquisites which Milesians share?

R. [Text damaged: too few words visible to reconstruct the content, but apparently much the same as 14.]

Mode A2, Topic 2d

Direct, Verse—Inscription of Miletos, Milet 1.3.33g. 11–12.

Testimony—cf. Milet. 1.3.37b. 32–35.

16 Historical, 223/2.

C. Demos of the Milesians.

Occ. Application of Cretan bands for Milesian citizenship.

Q. Is it better to enroll the men in the citizen body?

R. [Lost, but undoubtedly an approval.]

Mode A2, Topic 2d

Testimony—Inscription of Miletos, Milet 1.3.36a.

17 Historical, c. 225 B.C.

C. Demos of the Milesians.

Occ. Proposal of the Skiridai on the conduct of the festival of Artemis Boulephoros Skiris.

Q. Will it be pleasing to the goddess and beneficial to the demos now and for the future to conduct the festivals of Artemis Boulephoros Skiris as the Skiridai propose or as it is now done?

R. Not stated (undoubtedly an approval of the Skiridai's proposal).

Mode A2, Topic 1d

Testimony—Inscription of Miletos, Michel 480 = Rev. Phil. 44 (1920) 290.

18 Historical, 223–187.

C. Antiochos III.

Occ. and Q. Not stated.

R. He should govern with harmony.

Mode A1, Topic 2b

Indirect—Inscription of Iasos, Michel 467.6.

 Comment: The theos archêgetês who spoke this is probably Apollo Didymeus.

19 Historical, c. 200 B.C.

C. Demos of the Milesians.

Occ. Proposal to enlarge the Didymaean agonistic festival.

Q. Not stated.

R. They should make the Didymaean games a crowned contest [agôna stephanitên] and invite the Hellenes to it; the sanctuary of Apollo should be declared sacred and inviolate.

Mode A2, Topic 1a

Testimony—Decree of Miletos, Inscription of Kos, SIG 590.

20 Historical, 201 B.C. (see H46).

C. Teos.

Occ. Decision to declare the city and country inviolable.

Q. Probably whether it is better to do so.

R. The city and country of Teos should be sacred and inviolable.

Mode A2, Topic 1d

Testimony—Inscription of Malla in Crete, ICr 1.19.2. = SGDI 5184, lines 7–9.

21 Historical, c. 180 B.C.

C. Demos of the Milesians.

Occ. Treaty with Herakleia-by-Latmos.

Q. Not stated; probably whether it is better to make the treaty.

R. It will be better that the Milesians make the treaty with the Herakleots.

Mode A2, Topic 2d

Indirect—Inscription of Miletos, Milet 1.3.150 = SIG 633 (II), line 17.

22 Historical, c. 100 B.C.

C. Lochos son of Lochos.

Occ. and Q. Not stated.

R. Dedicate it to Apollo Delios ruler of Kalymna.

Mode A1, Topic 1b

Testimony—Inscription of Kos, IC 60.

23 Historical, c. 90 B.C.

C. Pseudo-Skymnos.

Occ. Desire to visit a king of Bithynia, perhaps Nikomedes III.

Q. Probably whether he should do so.

R. He should visit the king.

Mode A1, Topic 3e

Testimony—Ps.-Skymnos *Perieg.* 55–64.

24 Historical, c. A.D. 150.

C. Alexandra, priestess of Demeter Thesmophoros.

Occ. Concern for her sacred office.

Q. From the time that she became priestess the gods have not thus given evidence of their overseership. Why is this, and is it auspicious?

R. (A) The gods accompany mortal men . . . make their will known and the honor . . . . [The following lines are damaged or missing].

R. (B) Honor the mother and daughter with sacrifices and prayers. All mankind should honor the goddess who produced grain on earth and ended men's savage way of life, when they glutted themselves on meat, especially Neileus' people. For them she establishes the rites of Deo and her daughter. Therefore with silent service, pursuing a life of tranquillity . . . [the remainder is lost].

Mode A1, Topic 1b

Direct, Verse—Inscription of Didyma, *DI* 496.

Comment: There may be two oracles here, since "The god spoke" precedes the (B) part. But no question is visible. It may have been written at the foot of side (A), but it is also possible that the text of a long verse oracle (over 16 lines) was continued on the (B) side and the continuation introduced with the repeated formula.

25 Quasi-Historical, [c. A.D. 60]. Not genuine.

C., *Occ.*, *and* Q. Not stated.

R. Apollonios is the Oracle's equal in wisdom.

Mode D1, Topic 3j

Testimony—Philostr. *Apollon.* 4.1.

26 Historical, first century A.D.

C. Cyzicenes.

Occ. and Q. Not stated.

R. Erect a statue of hipparch T. Claudius Eumenes hero.

Mode A1, Topic 1a

Testimony—Inscription of Kyzikos, *BCH* 13 (1889) 518.

27 Historical, c. A.D. 100.

C. *and Occ.* Unknown.

Q. About a gymnasium and bath (text damaged).

R. To you building with forethought . . . I shall declare this. [There are too few words visible to reveal more of the content. There is mention of an altar.]

Mode A1, Topic 1a
Direct, Verse—Inscription of Miletos, *Milet* 1.9.345.

28 Historical, c. A.D. 120.
C. Builders of the Milesian theatre.
Occ. Proposed work on the theatre.
Q. Shall the builders undertake the placing of the arches and vaults over the columns or attend to another task?
R. It is advantageous to you, entreating Pallas Tritogeneia and valiant Herakles with sacrifices, to use the building skills of an able craftsman.
Mode A2, Topic 1b
Direct, Verse—Inscription of Miletos, *Sitz. Akad. Berlin* (1904) 83.

29 Historical, c. A.D. 130.
C. Appheion Heronas of Alexandria.
Occ. Desire for good performance.
Q. Since the ancestral gods and you yourself have always stood by him in whatever work he undertakes, he therefore asks you, Lord, whether he will come off with honor as always in the *akrônycha* and the *taurodidaxia*, and whether he will do his service with honor?
R. Pray to Phoibos, Serapis, and Nemesis, who oversees athletes' races, and you will have them as helpers of your wishes.
Mode A1, Topic 1b
Direct, Verse—Inscription of Miletos, *Milet* 1.7.205a. 9–11.

30 Historical, c. A.D. 130.
C. Karpos.
Occ. A vow to Serapis.
Q. Is it pleasing to Serapis to fulfill the vow as he has chosen to make it?
R. Immortals rejoice in the benevolent honors of mortals.
Mode D1, Topic 3j
Direct, Verse—Inscription of Miletos, *Milet* 1.7.205b. 4.

31 Historical, 284–305.
C. Damianos the prophet.
Occ. Absence of an altar of Soteira Kore in the temenos.
Q. Since he sees no altar of Apollo's sister, his ancestral goddess Soteira Kore, in the altar circle of all gods in the temenos, and the circumstance grieves him as a pious man, he asks you, Lord Apollo, to tell him whether you allow him to found an altar of her daughter beside the altar of Demeter Karpophoros.
R. Give Soteira Kore the honor of an altar.
Mode A1, Topic 1a
Direct, Verse—Inscription of Didyma, *DI* 504.15–16.

32 Historical, 284–305.

C. Damianos the prophet.

Occ. Receipt of 31.

Q. Since by your oracle you have allowed him to found an altar of his ancestral goddess Soteira Kore in the altar circle beside the altar of Demeter Karpophoros, he asks you to be ordainer of her auspicious and hymnal epithet.

R. Let us always call Soteira gentle [meilichos] with mother Deo in holy song.

Mode A1, Topic 1b

Direct, Verse—Inscription of Didyma, DI 504.29–31.

33 Historical, c. A.D. 300.

C. Probably Milesians.

Occ. and Q. Not stated.

R. Erect an altar of Poseidon.

Mode A1, Topic 1a

Testimony—Inscription of Miletos, Milet 1.6.191.

34 (PW 599) Historical, A.D. 303.

C. Emperor Diocletian's envoy.

Occ. Proposed persecution of the Christians.

Q. Not stated.

R. The Christians are an impediment to the gods' truth-speaking and are causing the oracles from the tripods to be false (Pseudo-Eusebios).

Mode D1, Topic 1d

Indirect—Ps.-Eus. Vit. Const. 2.50.

Testimony—*Firm. Lact. (Lucius Caecilius) De mort. pers. 11.

Comment: Pseudo-Eusebios' indirect form, in what purports to be a letter of Constantine, is probably not genuine; moreover it seems to have been written with Delphi in mind: the writer says only that Apollo spoke the oracle from a cave and dark recess and mentions Apollo's priestess, perhaps meaning the Pythia; for it is uncertain that Didyma had a prophetess. According to Lactantius, Diocletian received from the Milesian Apollo a response hostile to the Christians. Probably Didyma approved or sanctioned the persecution when Diocletian's envoy put the question. See Henri Grégoire, "Les Chrétiens et l'oracle de Didymes," Mélanges Holleaux (Paris: Picard, 1913) 81–91, who restores DI 306 as a record of this consultation; but though the visible letters show a reference to the Christians there is no certain indication of an oracle.

35 Quasi-Historical, [c. A.D. 323]. Not genuine.

C. Emperor Licinius.

Occ. Conflict with Constantine.

Q. On the war.

R. Old man, young warriors exhaust you. Your strength is gone, and hard old age is upon you.

Mode D1, Topic 2e

Direct, Verse—Sozomen *Hist. eccl.* 1.7, p. 17.

    Comment: The response is a quotation of Iliad 8.102–103.

36 Quasi-Historical, A.D. 362. Doubtful. (cf. Q262.)

C. Emperor Julian.

Occ. Contemplated war on Persia.

Q. Should he take the field?

R. He should take the field; he will be victorious.

Mode A1, Topic 2e

Indirect—Theodor. *Hist. eccl.* 3.16.21.

    Comment: Theodoretos says that Julian sent to Delphi, Delos, Dodona, and the other Oracles. Surely Didyma is meant to be included among the others, since Julian held the office of prophet (*Epist.* 62 p. 451), probably an honorary title. It is probable that Julian as a pious convert to paganism asked all Oracles for a sanction of his proposed campaign and received it. Q262 may have been attributed to Didyma, but Julian could not have received that response at any Oracle.

37 Fictional.

C. The king, Psyche's father.

Occ. Psyche has no suitors.

Q. That the god grant marriage and a husband to Psyche.

R. Place your daughter, dressed in funeral garb, on the crag of a high mountain. Do not
    hope for a son-in-law of human kind, but a savage and deadly evil that flies everywhere,
    plaguing everything and weakening every creature with fire and iron, that Jove himself
    fears, and that terrifies gods, rivers, and the Stygian shades.

Mode A1 (C2), Topic 3b

Direct, Verse (elegiac distichs, Latin)—Apuleius *Met.* 4.33.

    Comment: The narrator informs us that Apollo spoke in Latin on this occasion.

38 Quasi-Historical, [?]. Not genuine.

C. Peasants.

Occ. Nine men found dead.

Q. What was the cause?

R. Pan, servant of Dionysos, was going through the mountains, his wand in one hand,
    his syrinx in the other. His music frightened all the woodcutters. Death would have
    taken them all, if Artemis in anger had not stopped Pan from his rage. So you must
    pray to Artemis, that she may be your helper.

Mode D1 (A1), Topic 3g

Direct, Verse—Porphyry *ap.* Eus. *PE* 5.6, p. 190bc.

Testimony—Eus. *PE* 5.6, p. 190d.

39 Quasi-Historical, [?] Not genuine.

C. *and Occ.* Unknown.

Q. Should one swear the oath that someone proposes?

R. Mother Rea cares for flutes, drums, and an effeminate company, Pallas for war, Leto's daughter for hunting wild animals with dogs over the mountains, Hera for flowing air, Deo for gathering crops of grain, Pharian Isis for passionately searching for her husband Osiris by the streams of Nile.

Mode D1, Topic 1d

    Direct, Verse—Porphyry *ap.* Eus. *PE* 5.7, p. 192a–c. Incomplete—Eus. *PE* 5. 7, p. 192cd.

    Comment: The response as quoted appears to be a priamel (cf. Q26) without the final term, which should be that Zeus cares for the oath and fidelity to it.

40 Quasi-Historical, [second or third century?]. Not genuine.

C. *and Occ.* Unknown.

Q. Perhaps about the Delphic and Clarian Oracles.

R. I shall speak of Phoibos' Oracles, Pytho and Klaros. Many Oracles with springs and exhalations have appeared on earth, and earth has swallowed them again; the passage of time has destroyed them. But Helios [i.e., Apollo] still has the holy water of Mykale at Didyma, the rock of Pytho, and rugged Klaros, mouth of the oracular voice.

Mode D1, Topic 1d

Direct, Verse—Porphyry *ap.* Eus. *PE* 5.16, pp. 204d–205a.

41 (PW475). Quasi-Historical, [second or third century?]. Not genuine.

C. Nicaeans.

Occ. and Q. Not stated.

R. The Pythian voice cannot recover. It has become faint with the long lapse of time and is locked in unoracular silence. But make ordained sacrifices to Phoibos according to custom.

Mode A1 (D1), Topic 1b

Direct, Verse—Porphyry *ap.* Eus. *PE* 5.16, p. 205a.

    Comment: On 38–41 see Fontenrose 1933: 225–226. Eusebios quotes the verses of 40 and 41 from Porphyry without the surrounding text (except for four words that introduce 41), and he does not explicitly inform us that they were spoken at Didyma. On internal evidence 40 appears to be Didymaean, and 41 follows it immediately. PW consider 41 Delphic, but it appears to say that the Pythian Oracle is silent. See Buresch 1889: 41; Haussoullier 1902: xxviii.

42 Quasi-Historical, [second or third century?]. Not genuine.

C. Unknown.

Occ. Interest in the Jewish religion.

Q. Not stated.

R. [Probably incomplete] And God the king and creator whom earth, sky, sea, the depths of Tartaros, and daimones fear.

Mode D1, Topic 1d

Direct, Verse—Firm. Lact. *De ira dei* 23.

43 Quasi-Historical, [c. A.D. 200?]. Not genuine.

C. Unknown.

Occ. Interest in Christ.

Q. Was Christ god or man?

R. He was mortal in the flesh, wise in miraculous works, but convicted by Chaldaean
   judges he was crucified and came to a bitter end.

Mode D1, Topic 3g

Direct, Verse—Firm. Lact. *Inst. div.* 4.13.

   Comment: See Q250, 268.

44 Quasi-Historical, [c. A.D. 200?]. Not genuine.

C. Polites.

Occ. Interest in immortality of the soul.

Q. Does the soul survive death or does it vanish?

R. While the soul is bound to the body, it yields to mortal ills. But when it finds release
   at the body's death, it goes entirely to the sky, always ageless, and remains forever
   whole. For this is the ordinance of divine providence.

Mode D1, Topic 1d

Direct, Verse—Firm. Lact. *Inst. div.* 7.13. *Theosophia, Chrêsmoi tôn Hell. theôn* 37.

45 Quasi-Historical, [?]. Not genuine.

C., *Occ., and* Q. Not stated.

R. All who do harm to the gods' priests and plot against their honors with impious
   calculations do not complete the whole road of life, since they have offended the
   blessed gods whose holy ministry the priests have assumed.

Mode D1, Topic 1d

Direct, Verse—Julian *Epist.* 62, 451ab; Frag. *Epist.* 297cd.

46 Quasi-Historical, [?]. Not genuine.

C., *Occ., and* Q. Not stated.

R. I shall punish all who injure my servants.

Mode E1, Topic 1d

Direct, Verse, partly Indirect—Julian *Frag. Epist.* 298a.

   Comment: It makes little difference whether 45 and 46 are classified as Q or L. Since
Julian says just before quoting 45 that Apollo first advised the Hellenes in deeds and later
(*hysteron*) in words, presumably on proper conduct toward priests, I have supposed that
he places this response within historical times.

47 Quasi-Historical, [?]. Not genuine.

C., *Occ., and* Q. Not stated.

R. I sang, and divine Homer copied.
Mode D1, Topic 3g
Direct, Verse—Synesios *Dion* 59, p. 1157 Migne.

48 Legendary.
C., Occ., and Q. Not stated.
R. Poseidon's son, prodigy of the water, loud-voiced Triton, met the ship while swimming.
Mode D2, Topic 3g
Direct, Verse—Ael. *NA.* 13.21.

49 Historical, third century A.D.
C. Simmias (?) Hermias' son.
Occ. Unknown.
Q. Is it pleasing to the god . . . ? [perhaps, to hold a festival more or less often than annually (inscription damaged)].
R. It is better to celebrate it according to ancestral custom.
Mode A2, Topic 1b
Direct, Verse—Inscription of Didyma, *DI* 499.

50 Historical, c. A.D. 200.
C. Miletos?
Occ. Need of appointing a priestess of Athena Polias.
Q. Not stated.
R. You have come concerning a priestess of Athena, born from her father's head, who looks after citadels, helps cities, and instructs craftsmen. Her priestess should be a married woman of noble family. Therefore obeying the Moirai and Pallas appoint honorable Satorneila to be priestess.
Mode A1, Topic 1d
Direct, Verse—Inscription of Miletos, *Chiron* 1 (1971) 291–292 = *Gr.-Rom.-Byz. Stud.* 14 (1973) 65.
See addenda for nos. 51–54.

DI 278, 497, 498, 500, 502, 503, 505, badly damaged inscriptions, show fragments of responses, but not enough to justify listing them here; the few letters remaining allow us no knowledge of the messages or antecedent circumstances. *DI* 501, not found at Didyma, contains a response that I have with hesitation included among Delphic responses as H67; but it could very well be Didymaean.

Correspondence of PW Numbers
with the Catalogue

X = not included in the Catalogue

PW	Cat.	PW	Cat.	PW	Cat.
1	Q26	20	L2	39	Q47
2	Q27	21	Q8	40	Q48
3	Q40	22	L3	41	Q49
4	Q58A	23	Q73	42	Q50
5	Q58B	24	Q74	43	Q28
6	Q59	25	Q80	44	Q29
7	Q60	26	Q81	45	Q30
8	Q61	27	Q82	46	Q34
9	Q62	28	Q83	47	Q35
10	Q63A	29	Q7	48	Q43
11	Q63B	30	Q87	49	Q93
12	Q64	31	Q88	50	Q98
13	Q65	32	Q89	51	Q96
14	Q66	33	Q90	52	Q99
15	Q67	34	Q91	53	Q100
16	Q68	35	Q92A	54	Q101
17	Q70	36	Q92B	55	Q102
18	Q71	37	Q45	56	Q103
19	L1	38	Q46	57	Q106

PW	Cat.	PW	Cat.	PW	Cat.
58	Q107	100	Q152	142	L11
59	Q108	101	Q153	143	L12
60	Q109	102	Q154	144	L13
61	Q110	103	Q155	145	L14
62	Q111	104	Q156	146	L15
63	Q112	105	Q157	147	L16
64	Q113	106	Q158	148	L17
65	Q114	107	Q160	149	L18
66	Q115	108	Q161	150	L19
67	Q116	109	Q162	151	X
68	Q117	110	L4	152	L20
69	Q118	111	L5	153	L21
70	Q119	112	Q163	154	L22
71	Q47	113	Q164	155	L145
72	Q121	114	Q174	156	L23
73	Q122	115	Q175	157	L160
74	Q123	116	Q165	158	Q190
75	Q126	117	Q167	159	H6
76	Q127	118	Q169	160	H7
77	Q128	119	Q178	161	Q191
78	Q129	120	Q179	162	H8
79	Q124	121	Q180	163	Q192
80	Q125	122	Q181	164	H9
81	Q130	123	H1	165	H10
82	Q131	124	H2	166	Q193
83	Q132	125	Q189	167	X
84	Q134	126	Q172	168	Q195
85	Q135	127	Q183	169	Q196
86	Q136	128	Q184	170	Q197
87	Q137	129	Q185	171	Q198
88	Q166	130	Didyma 3	172	H11
89	Q52	131	Q186	173	Q199
90	Q142	132	Q187	174	H12
91	Q143	133	Q188	175	H13
92	Q144	134	H3	176	H73
93	Q145	135	X	177	H14
94	Q146	136	H4	178	H15
95	Q147	137	H5	179	Q200
96	Q148	138	L6	180	Q201
97	Q149	139	L7	181	Q203
98	Q150	140	L9	182	H16
99	Q151	141	L10	183	L24

PW	Cat.	PW	Cat.	PW	Cat.
184	X	226	L51	268	Q215
185	X	227	L50	269	Q211
186	X	228	L52	270	Q216
187	L25	229	Q31	271	Q217
188	L26	230	Q55	272	Q219
189	L27	231	Q56	273	Q220
190	L28	232	Q57	274	H75
191	L29	233	L53	275	Q225
192	L30	234	L54	276	Q226
193	L29	235	L55	277	H23
194	L31	236	L56	278	H24
195	L32	237	Q72	279	H25
196	X	238	L58	280	H26
197	L33	239	L57	281	H27
198	L34	240	L57	282	H28
199	L35	241	Q141	283	H29
200	cf. L36	242	L59	284	H31
201	L37	243	L59	285	H33
202	L40	244	Q97	286	Q227
203	L38	245	Q75	287	L60
204	L39	246	Q264	288	L61
205	L143	247	Q76	289	L62
206	L41	248	Q76	290	L63
207	L42	249	Q104	291	L64
208	L43	250	Q105	292	L64
209	L44	251	F1	293	L65
210	L45	252	F2	294	L66
211	L46	253	Q205	295	L67
212	L47	254	Q204	296	Q13
213	X	255	Q206	297	Q18A
214	L48	256	H17	298	Q18B
215	L49	257	X	299	Q18A
216	Q7	258	Q207	300	L68
217	Q8	259	H18	301	L69
218	Q9	260	H19	302	L70
219	Q8	261	H20	303	L71
220	Q8	262	H21	304	L71
221	Q8	263	X	305	L72
222	Q10	264	Q210	306	L73
223	Q54	265	H22	307	L73
224	Q53	266	Q213	308	L74
225	L50	267	Q214	309	L75

PW	Cat.	PW	Cat.	PW	Cat.
310	L76	352	Q228	394	X
311	L77	353	Q229	395	X
312	L78	354	H48	396	L94
313	L79	355	Q236	397	L95
314	Q177	356	Q237	398	X
315	Q176	357	Q238	399	L96
316	L162	358	Q235	400	X
317	L80	359	Q239	401	Q94
318	L80	360	Q240	402	Q95
319	L80	361	Q14	403	L97
320	X	362	Q14	404	L56
321	L81	363	Q15	405	L98
322	L82	364	Q16	406	L99
323	L83	365	Q17	407	X
324	L84	366	Q20	408	L100
325	L85	367	Q19	409	L101
326	Q69	368	Q21	410	Q41
327	Q85	369	Q22	411	L102
328	L86	370	Q32	412	Q25
329	Q231	371	Q33	413	X
330	H35	372	L17	414	L103
331	Q232	373	L27	415	cf. L104
332	L157	374	L11	416	Q51
333	Q233	375	L87	417	L161
334	H34	376	L88	418	Q159
335	H36	377	L89	419	Q223
336	H37	378	L163	420	H3
337	Q241	379	L164	421	Q224
338	L171	380	L165	422	L105
339	Q243	381	L166	423	Q77
340	H53	382	L167	424	Q242
341	H38	383	L90	425	L106
342	H39	384	Q42	426	H50
343	H40	385	L91	427	H54
344	H41	386	L92	428	H55
345	H42	387	L93	429	H56
346	H43	388	Q168	430	Q244
347	H45	389	Q170	431	Q245
348	H46	390	Q171	432	H57
349	H52	391	Q171	433	Q246
350	H71	392	L156	434	Q247
351	H47	393	X	435	Q248

PW	Cat.	PW	Cat.	PW	Cat.
436	Q249	478	X	520	Q173
437	H58	479	L19	521	Q260
438	Q138	480	L119	522	X
439	Q139	481	L11	523	L2
440	Q202	482	L120	524	L124
441	Q230	483	Q23	525	Q36
442	L107	484	Q140	526	Q38
443	L108	485	Q1	527	L125
444	L107	486	Q2	528	X
445	L109	487	Q3	529	L144
446	L110	488	Q4	530	L126
447	L111	489	Q5	531	L127
448	L112	490	Q6	532	L128
449	L113	491	Q1, 6	533	L129
450	L114	492	L121	534	L130
451	L74	493	Q182	535	L131
452	L115	494	Q78	536	L146
453	L116	495	Q86	537	L147
454	Q39	496	Q208	538	Q265
455	L168	497	Q44	539	Q12
456	L117	498	Q44	540	L169
457	H59	499	F4	541	L132
458	H64	500	F5	542	L133
459	H60	501	L11	543	L133
460	H61	502	F14	544	L148
461	Q251	503	F6	545	L159
462	H62	504	F7	546	L159
463	Q252	505	L122	547	L149
464	H63	506	F8	548	L150
465	H65	507	Q212	549	Q266
466	H66	508	Q221	550	Q267
467	H67	509	Q218	551	L173–174
468	Q257	510	Q253	552	Q84
469	Q258	511	Q254	553	L151
470	Q259	512	Q255	554	Q209
471	H68	513	Q256	555	Q222
472	L172	514	F9	556	L134
473	H69	515	F11	557	L135
474	Q261	516	F12	558	X
475	Didyma 41	517	F13	559	L136
476	Q263	518	Q250	560	L152
477	L118	519	L123	561	Q11

PW	Cat.	PW	Cat.	PW	Cat.
562	L137	572	Q133	581	L176
563	L153	573	Q234	582–598	X
564	L138	574	F3	599	Didyma 34
565	L170	575	L141	600	Q262
566	L154	576	L142	601	H70
567	L158	577	X	602	L8
568	Q37	578	Q194	603	cf. L28
569	L139	579	L175	604–606	X
570	L140	580	L155	607	cf. Q7, L41
571	cf. Q79			608–615	X

Summary of Modes, Topics, Question Formulae, Occasions

So that the reader may know more easily how the figures in Chapter 1 have been computed, the Historical, Quasi-Historical, and Legendary responses assigned to each category of mode, etc., are listed here.

I. MODES

A. Simple Commands and Instructions.

A1. Clear Commands.

H5, 7, 9, 11, 12, 15, 23, 28, 29, 44, 48–51, 54, 56, 60, 62, 67, 68 (20). Subordinate: H19, 34 (2).

Q1, 3, 4, 9, 13, 14, 18A, 19, 21, 22, 24, 28, 30–32, 35, 40, 45–48, 51–54, 57, 63, 65, 67, 69, 70, 76, 79, 82, 83, 86, 89, 91, 92, 94, 96, 98, 106–108, 110, 111, 113, 115, 118, 124–126, 128, 131–133, 135, 142, 148, 153, 154, 156, 161, 162, 164–167, 169, 172, 173, 175, 176, 178, 182, 184, 187–190, 192, 200, 208, 209, 211, 218, 222, 223, 227–229, 232–234, 243, 246, 248, 252, 257, 260, 265–267 (104). Subordinate: Q5, 8, 41, 44, 58, 72, 73, 87, 90, 100, 122, 129, 146, 147, 157, 202, 237 (17).

L6–8, 13, 14, 16, 19, 25, 26, 29–32, 35–38, 42–47, 52, 53, 55, 56, 60, 64, 66, 69, 71–74, 81, 85, 86, 91, 92, 94, 95, 98, 100, 101, 103, 104, 106, 107, 109, 112, 114, 115, 123, 125, 126, 129–131, 133, 134, 136, 138–140, 143–145, 147–154, 156, 157, 159, 160, 162, 164, 167–171, 173–175 (90). Subordinate: L2, 9, 50, 51, 65, 88, 90 (7).

A2. Sanctions.

H1, 2, 4, 6, 8, 14, 16, 19, 24–27, 30–33, 35, 36, 38–43, 45–47, 52, 53, 57–59, 61, 64, 66, 71, 74 (37).

Q2, 8, 11, 12, 241 (5).

L39, 96, 113, 137 (4).

A3. Ambiguous and Obscure Commands and Instructions.

Q37, 38, 41, 55, 64, 72, 77, 80, 84, 93, 105, 130, 144, 168, 170, 174, 191, 193, 194, 201, 203, 206, 215, 224 (24). Subordinate: Q17, 185 (2).

L5, 15, 40, 61, 62, 65, 77, 118, 158 (9). Subordinate: L70 (1).

B. Conditioned Commands.

Q6, 25, 33, 34, 36, 39, 101, 109, 186 (9).

L2, 11, 27, 33, 50, 51, 54, 68, 70, 78, 79, 82, 83, 93, 102, 116, 120, 124, 127, 128, 132, 135, 161, 163 (24). Subordinate: L75 (1).

C. Prohibitions and Warnings.

C1. Clear Prohibitions and Warnings.

H21, 55, 75 (3). Subordinate: H17 (1).

Q5, 18B, 42, 58, 102, 112, 123, 143, 146, 149, 151, 158, 181, 183, 197, 198, 231, 247, 250 (19). Subordinate: Q6, 9, 16, 30, 70, 85, 88, 98, 101, 131, 147, 202, 232, 257 (14).

L17, 22, 49, 141 (4). Subordinate: L7, 8, 11, 19, 80, 84, 93, 100, 109, 123, 147, 155, 156 (13).

C2. Ambiguous and Obscure Prohibitions and Warnings.

Q114, 119, 163, 195, 199, 207, 214, 240, 251 (9).

L3, 4, 12, 41, 67 (5). Subordinate: L18, 75 (2).

D. Statements of Past or Present Fact.

D1. Commonplace Statements of Past or Present Fact.

H3, 10, 13, 20, 37, 63, 65, 69 (8).

Q7, 26, 27, 49, 68, 74, 75, 85, 97, 120, 141, 145, 157, 177, 179, 196, 216, 226, 242, 253, 258, 259, 261, 264 (24). Subordinate: Q3, 9, 17, 29, 32, 34, 51, 58, 59, 67, 92, 112, 123, 143, 149, 182, 218, 246, 247, 249 (20).

L57–59, 63, 87, 99, 105, 110, 111, 117, 142, 146, 155, 172, 176 (15). Subordinate: L22, 69, 78, 81, 106, 141, 159, 171 (8).

D2. Extraordinary and Obscure Statements of Past or Present Fact.

Q66, 90, 99, 103, 116, 137, 171, 210, 220, 235, 263 (11). Subordinate: Q161, 166, 209, 213, 250 (5).

L76, 80, 89, 90 (4). Subordinate: L10, 64, 65, 134 (4).

E. Simple Statements of Future Events.

E1. Non-Predictive Future Statements.

H17, 18 (2). Subordinate: H5, 7, 48, 75 (4).

Q10, 29, 50, 95, 237 (5). Subordinate: Q7, 44, 148, 164, 182, 231, 257 (7).

L9, 121 (2). Subordinate: L8, 90, 171 (3).

E2. Clear Predictions.

H34, 70 (2).

Q23, 61, 62, 78, 104, 121, 140, 150, 155, 159, 219, 225, 236, 245, 254, 268 (16). Subordinate: Q28, 32, 47, 73, 96, 102, 119, 128, 130, 134, 146, 152, 161, 179, 192B, 196, 211 (17).

L10, 21, 23, 24, 34, 84, 88, 97, 108, 122 (10). Subordinate: L6, 7, 11, 17, 41, 42, 51, 80, 96, 107, 113, 121, 165, 167 (14).

E3. Ambiguous and Obscure Predictions.

Q15, 43, 59, 60, 88, 100, 117, 136, 147, 160, 180, 185, 213, 217, 221, 230, 239, 249, 255, 256, 262 (21). Subordinate: Q134, 144, 268 (3).

L18, 48, 119 (3).

F. Conditioned Predictions.

Q16, 17, 20, 44, 56, 71, 73, 81, 87, 122, 127, 129, 134, 138, 139, 152, 202, 204, 212, 238 (20). Subordinate: Q114, 163 (2).

L1, 20, 28, 75, 165, 166 (6). Subordinate: L12, 49, 80, 134 (4).

II. TOPICS

1. Res Divinae.
1a. Cult Foundations.

H12, 16, 23, 24, 27, 35, 37, 44, 45, 49, 54, 60, 66, 68, 74 (15).

Q1-3, 22, 52, 63, 82, 89, 91, 93, 98, 107, 113, 116, 126, 131, 133, 142, 156, 164-167, 169, 174, 178, 182, 187-189, 192, 209, 218, 222, 223, 227-229, 234, 235, 241 (41). Subordinate: Q8, 237 (2).

L26, 29, 35, 42, 43, 64, 91, 93, 94, 101, 133, 140, 148-154, 159, 168, 171 (22). Subordinate: L72, 139 (2).

1b. Sacrifices, Offerings.

H2, 9, 11, 15, 25, 28-33, 36, 39, 48, 50, 51, 53, 56, 57, 59, 61, 64, 67 (23). Subordinate: H19, 34 (2).

Q4, 12, 17, 19, 69, 79, 83, 115, 127, 135, 141, 148, 154, 157, 158, 172, 173, 190, 191, 200, 211, 213, 232, 243, 246 (25). Subordinate: Q18A, 32, 47, 58, 70, 73, 120, 122, 174, 185, 202, 265 (12).

L46, 47, 55-59, 86, 98, 100, 132, 136, 147, 157, 169, 174 (16). Subordinate: L8, 11, 12, 51, 68, 96, 135, 145 (8).

1c. Human Sacrifices.

Q14, 84 (2).

L32, 44, 45, 92, 95, 126, 134, 144, 156, 173 (10).

1d. Religious Laws, Customs, etc.

H10, 13, 17, 21, 26, 38, 40-43, 46, 52, 58, 63, 71, 75 (16). Subordinate: H45 (1).

Q6, 7, 11, 149, 151, 175, 181, 231, 237, 250, 263, 266, 267 (13). Subordinate: Q65, 70, 92, 123, 134, 146, 147, 150, 193, 259 (10).

L117, 129, 130 (3). Subordinate: L7, 10, 20, 41, 90, 103, 109, 111, 121, 141, 170, 176 (12).

2. Res Publicae.
2a. Rulership.

H7, 70 (2).

Q61, 74, 96, 120, 140, 163, 245, 253–255 (10). Subordinate: Q59, 86, 101, 103, 119, 138, 139, 212, 219, 246, 256 (11).

L36, 123, 160, 162 (4). Subordinate: L68 (1).

2b. Legislation, Civic Welfare.

H1, 18, 47 (3).

Q8, 9, 65, 118, 125, 170, 183 (7). Subordinate: Q7, 53, 54, 67, 68, 130 (6).

L158 (1). Subordinate: L22 (1).

2c. City and Colony Foundations.

H6, 14 (2).

Q28, 30, 32, 35, 37, 40–42, 45–48, 50, 51, 55, 57, 95, 110, 111, 121, 176 (21). Subordinate: Q31, 33, 34, 36, 39, 44, 94, 109, 186 (9).

L16, 31, 52, 53, 66, 71, 72, 102, 104, 113, 115, 143, 164–167 (16). Subordinate: L11, 50, 51, 54, 69, 70, 73, 75, 78, 83, 96, 112, 116, 161 (14).

2d. Interstate Relations.

H4, 8, 19, 22 (4). Subordinate: H15, 75 (2).

Q132, 153 (2). Subordinate: Q5, 237 (2).

L3 (1).

2e. War.

H5, 55, 73 (3). Subordinate: H48 (1).

Q5, 13, 15, 18A, 70, 100, 112, 117, 124, 130, 136, 144–147, 150, 152, 155, 184, 198, 202, 203, 206, 230, 236, 262 (26). Subordinate: Q16, 17, 20, 32, 47, 64, 71, 72, 87, 88, 90, 103, 122, 127, 131, 134, 148, 154, 163, 196, 199, 204, 214, 216, 217, 238, 249, 268 (28).

L15, 38, 67, 69, 121, 122 (6). Subordinate: L1, 21, 24, 39, 48, 49, 62 (7).

3. Res Domesticae et Profanae.
3a. Birth and Origin.

H34, 65 (2).

Q59, 60, 78, 104, 137, 159, 226, 265 (8). Subordinate: Q28, 73, 218 (3).

L28 (1). Subordinate: L10, 17, 23, 37, 84 (5).

3b. Marriage and Sex Relations.

Q21 (1).

L2, 37, 76, 82, 90 (5). Subordinate: L18, 27, 127 (3).

3c. Death and Burial.

H69 (1).

Q38, 179 (2). Subordinate: Q52, 60, 82, 90, 143, 152, 174, 213, 239, 251, 254, 268 (12).

L17, 20, 21, 23, 24, 41, 48, 84, 114, 119, 125, 137, 138 (13). Subordinate: L6, 7, 12, 18, 25, 26, 35, 39, 42, 49, 80, 88, 91, 128, 145, 153 (16).

3d. Careers and Professions.

H62 (1).

Q56, 108, 208, 252 (4). Subordinate: Q78, 160 (2).

L10 (1).

3e. Actions and Events.

Q72, 76, 86, 92, 128, 160, 162, 171, 201, 219, 225, 233, 239, 256, 257, 260 (16). Subordinate: Q41, 101, 129, 202, 231 (5).

L8, 13, 18, 89, 96, 103, 118, 131, 141, 146 (10). Subordinate: L4, 5, 81, 86, 130, 138 (6).

3f. Rewards and Punishments.

Q24, 58, 123, 143, 161, 196 (6). Subordinate: Q85, 92, 96, 103, 145, 182, 211 (7).

L6, 7, 9, 19, 25, 39, 88, 106–109, 142, 145 (13). Subordinate: L11, 45, 64, 65, 136, 157 (6).

3g. Persons, Agents.

H—Subordinate: H3 (1).

Q53, 54, 62, 75, 87, 97, 106, 129, 185, 193, 210, 212, 221, 261, 264, 268 (16). Subordinate: Q72, 73, 128, 130, 164 (5).

L34, 65, 97, 139, 170 (5). Subordinate: L46, 74, 134, 165, 166 (5).

3h. Means and Signs.

Q16, 20, 23, 25, 33, 34, 36, 39, 44, 64, 71, 73, 81, 90, 94, 99, 101–103, 109, 114, 119, 122, 134, 138, 139, 186, 194, 199, 204, 207, 214, 215, 217, 220, 238, 240, 251, 259 (39). Subordinate: Q6, 43, 56, 129, 147, 152, 163, 191 (8).

L1, 11, 12, 27, 33, 49–51, 54, 61–63, 68, 70, 75, 78, 79, 83, 116, 120, 124, 127, 128, 135, 161, 163 (26). Subordinate: L20, 42, 48, 67, 80, 93, 100, 119, 132 (9).

3i. Places, Lands.

Q27, 29, 49, 88, 195, 249 (6). Subordinate: Q26, 34, 177, 246 (4).

L14, 30, 40, 60, 73, 74, 80, 85, 112 (9). Subordinate: L63 (1).

3j. Gnomic Utterances.

H3, 20 (2). Subordinate: H7, 17, 55, 63 (4).

Q10, 18B, 26, 31, 43, 66–68, 77, 80, 85, 105, 168, 177, 180, 197, 216, 224, 242, 247, 248, 258 (22). Subordinate: Q9, 17, 30, 49, 51, 92, 99, 112, 116, 144, 162, 201, 215, 220, 235 (15).

L4, 5, 22, 77, 81, 87, 99, 105, 110, 111, 155, 172, 175, 176 (14). Subordinate: L76, 78 (2).

III. QUESTION FORMULAE

1. Shall I do X?

H4, 6 (2).

Q2, 6, 13, 51, 74, 80, 92, 96, 100, 110, 143, 149, 158, 183, 198, 201, 231, 235, 262, 268A (20).

L13, 39, 75, 105, 130 (5).

2. How shall I do X?

Q18A, 63, 85, 118, 130, 155, 203 (7). Subordinate: Q47B (1).

L7, 37, 51, 56, 61–63, 118 (8).

3. How shall I have children (or become a parent)?

L4, 17, 23, 28, 82 (5).

4. What shall/should I do?

H17, 23, 55, 62, 68 (5). Subordinate: H29 (1).

Q9, 14, 32, 47, 70, 72, 79, 102, 104, 105, 109, 113, 144, 162, 182, 194, 200, 209, 224, 248 (20). Subordinate: Q8, 114, 116, 201 (4).

L19, 29, 32, 34, 35, 46, 55, 71, 86, 109, 114, 117, 128, 153A, 158, 160, 171, 175 (18). Subordinate: L15 (1).

5. What should I do or say to please the gods?

H48 (1).

L6, 64 (2).

6. Who or what is the cause of X?

Q112, 138, 161, 169, 259 (5).

L90, 92, 123 (3).

7. Who were the parents?

H65 (1).

Q137 (1).

L18, 80 (2).

8. Whom shall I (we) choose? Who should or will be chosen?

H15 (1).

Q23, 42, 76, 106, 111, 125, 187, 212, 250, 253–255 (12). Subordinate: Q100 (1).

L15, 58, 68, 127, 162, 166 (6).

9. Where shall I go or find X or settle?

H67 (1).

Q21, 25, 29, 31, 33, 35, 39, 81, 90, 164B, 176 (11).

L11, 14, 33, 42B, 54, 69, 70, 73, 74, 79, 83, 95, 102, 107, 124, 137, 165 (17).

10. Shall I succeed in X?

Q34, 88, 121, 213, 237, 239 (6).

L49 (1).

11. What is the truth about X?

H3, 13, 63, 69 (4). Subordinate: H48 (1).

Q26, 66, 73B, 75, 77, 97, 99, 101, 103, 114, 116, 122, 139, 141, 157, 165, 166, 179, 191B, 202, 211, 220, 221, 226, 241, 247, 249, 256, 257 (29). Subordinate: Q268C (1).

L59, 155 (2). Subordinate: L69A, 153A (2).

12. Requests.

Q1, 3, 18B, 82, 117, 127, 132, 147, 177, 229, 265 (11). Subordinate: Q7, 31B, 92B (3).

L9, 88, 93, 99, 116, 121, 129, 132, 139, 148, 153B (11).

13. Statements.

Q24B, 49, 140, 171 (4). Subordinate: Q47B, 58B, 268BC (3).

L—Subordinate: L63B, 64A (2).

14. Is it better for me to do X?

H2, 5, 19, 21, 25, 27, 33, 38, 39, 45, 47, 58, 61, 74 (14).

Q8, 30, 145, 243 (4).

L164 (1).

15. What is better for me to do?

H36, 54 (2).

16. To what god(s) shall I sacrifice (and pray)?

H11, 29, 56 (3).

Q89 (1).

17. No question asked.

H20, 70 (2).

Q7, 56, 58A, 59, 61, 146, 216, 245 (8).

L8, 41, 81 (3).

IV. OCCASIONS

i. Plague, famine, drought, catastrophe.

H68 (1).

Q1, 3, 33, 46, 48, 53, 54, 63, 65, 72, 79, 82–84, 94, 107, 112, 113, 126, 132, 133, 161, 164, 168, 170, 171, 174, 182, 189, 190, 196, 200, 209, 223, 229, 232, 233 (37).

L19, 35, 36, 42, 44–46, 64, 65, 72, 86, 88, 91, 92, 95, 98, 101, 103, 116, 118, 125, 126, 128, 131, 133, 134, 136, 138–140, 144, 145, 148, 153B, 154, 156, 157, 159, 168, 169, 173 (41).

ii. Sickness of an individual.

Q45, 47, 98, 102, 128, 129, 135, 175, 257 (9).

L29, 34, 40, 55, 90, 109, 114, 120, 135 (9).

iii. Exile, loss of country, captivity, need to change residence.

H18, 62 (2).

Q25, 32, 34, 51, 61, 191B (6).

L2, 3, 31, 33, 71, 78, 79, 83, 87, 107, 112, 124, 132, 161, 163, 164 (16).

iv. Crime of others.

Q70, 85, 143 (3).

L7, 37, 106, 146 (4).

v. Crime of self.

H63 (1).

Q24, 58, 73 (3).

L8, 14, 26, 93, 110, 142, 170 (7).

vi. War or *casus belli*.

H5, 8, 13, 20, 48, 73 (6).

Q5, 13–17, 18A, 18B, 20, 64, 69, 71, 80, 87–89, 95, 100, 103, 109, 117, 119, 127, 130, 131, 136, 144–152, 154, 155, 184, 193, 198, 203–206, 213, 216, 218, 228, 230, 231, 249, 262, 268 (53).

L1, 15, 32, 38, 39, 43, 48, 49, 56, 61–63, 66, 67, 75, 100, 111, 121, 122, 129 (20).

vii. Portents, prodigies.

H22, 29, 55 (3).

Q56, 76, 123, 138, 142, 165–167, 177, 202, 211, 220, 225, 227, 241, 244, 246, 259 (18).

L6, 13, 94, 117, 123, 153A, 171 (7).

viii. Problems of rulership.

    H70 (1).

    Q23, 81, 96, 101, 118, 120, 137, 139, 212, 250, 253–256 (14).

    L12, 51, 68, 69, 160, 162 (6).

ix. Welfare of city or state.

    H16, 28, 47 (3).

    Q7–10, 38, 86, 114, 122, 124, 125, 134, 183, 187, 194, 210, 221, 234, 247 (18).

    L22, 158 (2).

x. Desire or plan to found a city or colony.

    H6, 14 (2).

    Q27, 29–31, 35, 36, 39–44, 49, 50, 110, 111, 121, 176, 186, 188 (20).

    L16, 50, 53, 54, 70, 73, 102, 104, 165–167 (11).

xi. Lack of children, desire for progeny.

    H34 (1).

    Q28, 59, 104, 160 (4).

    L4, 5, 17, 23, 28, 82, 99 (7).

xii. Desire to marry.

    Q21 (1).

    L27, 127 (2).

xiii. Wife or other woman's pregnancy; desire of knowing child's future.

    Q56 (1).

    L10 (1).

xiv. Wish to know origin, who one's parents were.

    H65 (1).

    Q226 (1).

    L18, 74, 80 (3).

xv. Death of kin or friends.

    H69 (1).

    Q105, 153 (2).

    L137 (1).

xvi. Disappearance, loss.

    Q19, 57, 90, 169, 172, 260 (6).

    L11, 130 (2).

xvii. Contemplated enterprise or career.

    H11 (1).

    Q78, 162, 201, 224, 242, 248 (6).

    L47, 96, 97 (3).

xviii. Desire for reward.

    Q75, 97 (2).

    L9, 175 (2).

xix. Test of Oracle.

    Q99, 239 (2).

    L155 (1).

xx. Worship of the gods; desire to honor and please them.

H2, 12, 25, 27, 30, 32, 33, 35, 38–40, 45, 54, 67, 74 (15).

Q2, 26, 106, 116, 141, 156–158, 236, 237, 263 (11).

L57–59, 105, 147 (5).

xxi. Religious problems.

H21, 23, 24, 26, 41–43, 46, 58 (9).

Q4, 6, 66, 74, 173, 235, 265 (7).

xxii. Interstate relations.

H4, 15, 17, 19, 56, 75 (6).

xxiii. Desire for information.

H3 (1).

Q77, 92, 179 (3).

xxiv. Family welfare.

H36 (1).

Q140 (1).

Bibliography

Listed here are the books and articles cited in text and notes only by author's name and year of publication. Included are (1) books and articles on Delphi and the Delphic Oracle, (2) those on Oracles and divination elsewhere or in general, (3) others cited in more than one chapter or otherwise important for this subject. Not all works cited are listed here; those unlisted are cited in full in the appropriate note.

Aly, Wolf
 1921. Volksmärchen, Sage und Novelle bei Herodot und seinen Zeitgenossen: Eine Untersuchung über die volkstümlichen Elemente der altgriechischen Prosaerzählung. Göttingen: Vandenhoeck & Ruprecht.

Amandry, Pierre
 1939. Convention religieuse conclue entre Delphes et Skiathos. Bulletin de Correspondance Hellénique 63.183–219, pls. XLIV–XLV.
 1950. La mantique Apollinienne à Delphes: Essai sur le fonctionnement de l'Oracle. Paris: Boccard.
 1956. Les thèmes de la propagande delphique. (Review article.) Revue de Philologie 30.268–282.
 1959. Oracles, Littérature et Politique. (Review article.) Revue des Études Anciennes 61.400–413.

Bascom, William
 1969. Ifa Divination: Communication Between Gods and Men in West Africa. Bloomington, London: Indiana University Press.

Bayet, Jean
    1946. La mort de la Pythie: Lucain, Plutarque et la chronologie delphique. Mélanges dédiés à la mémoire de Felix Grat, I, 53–76. Paris: en dépôt chez Mme Pecquer-Grat.

Bouché-Leclercq, A.
    1880. Histoire de la divination dans l'antiquité, vols. 2–3. Paris.

Bourguet, Émile
    1914. Les ruines de Delphes. Paris: Fontemoing.
    1925. Delphes. Paris: Les Belles Lettres.

Bousquet, Jean.
    1951. Observations sur l' "Omphalos archaïque" de Delphes. Bulletin de Correspondance Hellénique 75.210–223.

Buresch, Karl
    1889. Klaros. Untersuchungen zum Orakelwesen des späteren Altertums. Leipzig.

Courby, F.
    1915. La terrasse du temple, fasc. 1. Fouilles de Delphes II. Paris: Fontemoing.
    1921. La terrasse du temple, fasc. 2. Fouilles de Delphes II. Paris: Boccard.

Crahay, Roland
    1956. La littérature oraculaire chez Hérodote. Bibliothèque de la Faculté de Philosophie et Lettres de l'Université de Liège CXXXVIII. Paris: Les Belles Lettres.

Daneel, M. L.
    1970. The God of the Matopo Hills: An Essay on the Mwari Cult in Rhodesia. The Hague, Paris: Mouton.

Daux, Georges
    1936a. Delphes au IIe et au Ier siècle depuis l'abaissement de l'Étolie jusqu'à la paix romaine 191–31 av. J.-C. Paris: Boccard.
    1936b. Pausanias à Delphes. Paris: Picard.
    1943. Chronologie delphique. Paris: Boccard.

Defradas, Jean
    1954. Les thèmes de la propagande delphique. Paris: Klincksieck.

Delcourt, Marie
    1955. L'Oracle de Delphes. Paris: Payot.

Dempsey, Rev. T.
    1918. The Delphic Oracle: Its Early History, Influence and Fall. Oxford: Blackwell.

Dodds, E. R.
    1951. The Greeks and the Irrational. Sather Classical Lectures, vol. 25. Berkeley, Los Angeles: University of California Press.

Edelstein, Emma J. and Ludwig
    1945. Asclepius: A Collection and Interpretation of the Testimonies. 2 vols. Baltimore: Johns Hopkins Press.

Evans-Pritchard, E. E.
    1937. Witchcraft, Oracles and Magic among the Azande. Oxford: Clarendon Press.

Farnell, Lewis Richard
    1907. The Cults of the Greek States, vol. 4. Oxford.

Fauth, Wolfgang
    1963. Pythia. *RE* 24.515–547.
Flacelière, Robert
    1937. Plutarque: Sur les oracles de la Pythie. Paris: Les Belles Lettres.
    1938. Le fonctionnement de l'oracle de Delphes au temps de Plutarque. Études d'Archéologie Grecque: Annales de l'École des Hautes Études de Gand II, 69–107, 4 pls.
    1947. Plutarque: Sur la disparition des oracles. Annales de l'Université de Lyon, ser. 3, Lettres 14. Paris: Les Belles Lettres.
    1950. Le délire de la Pythie est-il une légende? Revue des Études Anciennes 52.306–324.
    1965. Greek Oracles. Translated by Douglas Garman. London: Elek Books.
Fontenrose, Joseph
    1933. The Cults of the Milesian Didyma. Berkeley: Ph.D. dissertation, University of California.
    1939. Apollo and Sol in the Latin Poets of the First Century B.C. Transactions of the American Philological Assn 70. 439–455.
    1942a. Varia Critica. University of California Publications in Classical Philology 12.217–224. Berkeley, Los Angeles: University of California Press.
    1942b. Review of H. W. Parke, *A History of the Delphic Oracle*. American Journal of Philology 63.472–476.
    1948. The Sorrows of Ino and of Procne. Transactions of the American Philological Assn 79.125–167.
    1951. White Goddess and Syrian Goddess. University of California Publications in Semitic Philology 11.125–148. Berkeley, Los Angeles: University of California Press.
    1952. Review of P. Amandry, *La mantique Apollinienne à Delphes*. American Journal of Philology 73.445–448.
    1959. Python: A Study of Delphic Myth and Its Origins. Berkeley, Los Angeles: University of California Press.
    1960a. The Cult and Myth of Pyrros at Delphi. University of California Publications in Classical Archaeology 4.3.191–266, pls 18–19. Berkeley, Los Angeles: University of California Press.
    1960b. The Crucified Daphidas. Transactions of the American Philological Assn 91.83–99.
    1966. The Ritual Theory of Myth. Folklore Studies 18. Berkeley, Los Angeles: University of California Press.
    1968. The Hero as Athlete. California Studies in Classical Antiquity 1.73–104.
    1969a. Daulis at Delphi. California Studies in Classical Antiquity 2.107–144.
    1969b. The Spring Telphusa. Transactions of the American Philological Assn 100.119–131.
    1971. Gods and Men in the *Oresteia*. Transactions of the American Philological Assn 102.71–109.
Forrest, George
    1956. The First Sacred War. Bulletin de Correspondance Hellénique 80.33–52.
    1957. Colonisation and the Rise of Delphi. Historia 6. 160–175.

Guillaume, Alfred

    1938. Prophecy and Divination among the Hebrews and Other Semites. London: Hodder and Stoughton.

Halliday, W. R.

    1913. Greek Divination: A Study of Its Methods and Principles. London: Macmillan.

    1928. The Greek Questions of Plutarch with a New Translation and a Commentary. Oxford: Clarendon Press.

Haussoullier, B.

    1902. Études sur l'histoire de Milet et du Didymeion. Paris.

Hendess, Richard

    1877. Oracula Graeca quae apud scriptores Graecos Romanosque exstant. Dissertationes Philologicae Halenses IV 1. Halle.

Hiller von Gaertringen, F.

    1899. Geschichte von Delphi. RE 4.2520–2583 (1901).

Holland, Leicester B.

    1933. The Mantic Mechanism at Delphi. American Journal of Archaeology 37.201–214.

How, W. W.; Wells, Joseph

    1912. A Commentary on Herodotus. 2 vols. Oxford: Clarendon Press.

Kurfess, Alfons

    1951. Sibyllinische Weissagungen. Munich: Heimeran.

La Coste-Messelière, P. de

    1935. Au Musée de Delphes: Recherches sur quelques monuments archaïques et leur décor sculpté. Paris: Boccard.

Laidlaw, W. A.

    1933. A History of Delos. Oxford: Blackwell.

Latte, Kurt

    1939. Orakel. RE 18.829–866.

    1940. The Coming of the Pythia. Harvard Theological Review 33.9–18.

Legrand, Ph. E.

    1898. Quo animo Graeci praesertim v° et iv° saeculis tum in vita privata tum in publicis rebus divinationem adhibuerint. Paris.

    1901. Questions oraculaires 2. Xuthus et Créuse à Delphes. Revue des Études Grecques 14.46–70.

    1903. L'oracle rendu à Chairéphon. Mélanges Perrot, 213–222. Paris.

    1951. Prophète et Pythie à Delphes. Revue des Études Grecques 64.296–299.

Lerat, Lucien

    1961. Fouilles à Delphes, à l'est du grand sanctuaire (1950–1957). Bulletin de Correspondance Hellénique 85.316–366.

Linforth, Ivan M.

    1919. Solon the Athenian. University of California Publications in Classical Philology 6. Berkeley: University of California Press.

    1941. The Arts of Orpheus. Berkeley, Los Angeles: University of California Press.

    1946. Telestic Madness in Plato, Phaedrus 244DE. University of California Publications in Classical Philology 13.163–172. Berkeley, Los Angeles: University of California Press.

McLeod, Wallace E.
    1961. Oral Bards at Delphi. Transactions of the American Philological Assn
        92.317–325.
Myers, F. W. H.
    1883. Greek Oracles. Essays—Classical, pp. 1–105. London.
Nilsson, Martin P.
    1951. Cults, Myths, Oracles, and Politics in Ancient Greece. Lund: Gleerup.
    1958. Das Delphische Orakel in der neuesten Literatur. Historia 7.237–250.
    1961. Geschichte der griechischen Religion II: Die hellenistischen und römische
        Zeit. 2d ed. Handbuch der Altertumswissenschaft (Müller) 5:2:2. Munich:
        Beck.
    1967. Geschichte der griechischen Religion I: Die Religion Griechenlands bis auf
        die griechischen Weltherrschaft. 3d ed. Handbuch der Altertumswissenschaft
        (Müller) 5:2:1. Munich: Beck.
Oeri, Albert
    1899. De Herodoti fonte Delphico. Basel.
Ohlert, K.
    1912. Rätsel und Rätselspiele der alten Griechen. 2d ed. Berlin: Mayer & Müller.
Oliver, James H.
    1950. The Athenian Expounders of the Sacred and Ancestral Law. Baltimore:
        Johns Hopkins Press.
Oppé, A. P.
    1904. The Chasm at Delphi. Journal of Hellenic Studies 24.214–240.
Panitz, Heinz
    1935. Mythos und Orakel bei Herodot. Greifswald: Dallmeyer.
Parke, H. W.
    1938. Notes on Some Delphic Oracles. Hermathena 27.56–78.
    1939. A History of the Delphic Oracle. Oxford: Blackwell.
    1940a. A Note on the Delphic Priesthood. Classical Quarterly 34.85–89.
    1940b. An Emended Oracle. American Journal of Philology 61.78–80.
    1945. The Use of Other than Hexameter Verse in Delphic Oracles. Hermathena
        65.58–66.
    1956. [See below, Parke; Wormell.]
    1967a. The Oracles of Zeus. Oxford: Blackwell.
    1967b. Greek Oracles. London: Hutchinson.
Parke, H. W.; Wormell, D. E. W.
    1956. The Delphic Oracle I: The History. Oxford: Blackwell.
    PW. The Delphic Oracle II: The Oracular Responses. Oxford: Blackwell, 1956.
Pease, Arthur Stanley
    1917. Notes on the Delphic Oracle and Greek Colonization. Classical Philology
        12.1–20.
Pomtow, J. R.
    1881. Quaestionum de oraculis caput selectum. De oraculis quae exstant graecis
        trimetro iambico compositis. Berlin.
Pouilloux, Jean; Roux, Georges
    1963. Énigmes à Delphes. Paris: Boccard.

Poulsen, Frederik
  1920. Delphi. Translated by G. C. Richards. London: Gyldendal.
Rehm, Albert; Harder, Richard
  1958. Didyma, Zweiter Teil: Die Inschriften. Deutsches Archäologisches Institut:
    Theodor Wiegand, Didyma. Berlin: Mann.
Robbins, Frank Egleston
  1916. The Lot Oracle at Delphi. Classical Philology 11. 278–292.
Rohde, Erwin
  1925. Psyche: The Cult of Souls and Belief in Immortality among the Greeks. Trans-
    lated by W. B. Hillis from the 8th edition. London: Kegan Paul, Trench,
    Tubner; New York: Harcourt, Brace.
Roussel, Pierre
  1925. Délos. Paris: Les Belles Lettres.
Roux, Georges
  1976. Delphes: Son oracle et ses dieux. Paris: Les Belles Lettres.
Schultz, Wolfgang
  1909. Rätsel aus dem hellenischen Kulturkreise I: Die Rätselüberlieferung. Leipzig:
    Hinrichs.
  1912. Rätsel aus dem hellenischen Kulturkreise II: Erläuterungen zur Rätselüber-
    lieferung. Leipzig: Hinrichs.
Sokołowski, F.
  1949. Sur un passage de la convention Delphes-Skiathos. Mélanges Charles Picard,
    Revue Archéologique 31/32.981–984.
Whittaker, C. R.
  1965. The Delphic Oracle: Belief and Behaviour in Ancient Greece—and Africa.
    Harvard Theological Review 58.21–47.
Wiechers, Anton
  1961. Aesop in Delphi. Beiträge zur Klassischen Philologie, Heft 2. Meisenheim am
    Glan: Hain.
Will, E.
  1942. Sur la nature du pneuma delphique. Bulletin de Correspondance Hellénique
    66.161–175.

Index

Both parts of the index include the two Catalogues, for which references to the responses, consultants, occasions, questions, and sources are made by Catalogue number; references to *Comment* are made by page numbers. Responses of Didyma are designated D. References to the Catalogue follow page references; when there are several, they are preceded by *Cat.* to avoid confusion. All numbers in a series that follows a letter—H, Q, L, F, D (in that order)—are understood to be Catalogue numbers belonging to that category; a letter precedes only the first number of a series.

A. INDEX LOCORUM

This index includes (a) citations of passages that receive discussion in text or notes or are otherwise significant for the content; (b) citations of sources for responses in the Catalogue. It omits many minor, derivative, and insignificant sources listed in the Catalogue. A reader who wants to find a Croesus response (Q99–103), for example, will almost certainly look for the Herodotos passage and not for a Scholiast or lexicographer who notices it. But all sources earlier than 300 B.C. are included, and also all passages in Diodoros, Plutarch, Pausanias, and Oinomaos, except an occasional insignificant testimony.

(a) Literature

Aelian *NA* 7.28: L133; 12.5: L116, 169; 12.31: L127; 12.35: 127, 136; 13.21: D48. *VH 2.32*: L108; 2.41: Q85; 3.43: Q123; 3.44: L141, 142; 4.6: Q198; 8.5: L68; 12.28: L44; 12.57: 340; 14.29: Q10. Frags 47: 132, 133, 136–137, Q232, L157; 73: L148; 80: Q58; 88: L133; 103: Q257; 329: 89; 345: Q115; 346: Q31.

Aeneas Tacticus *Poliorkêtika 31.24*: 134.

Aeschylus *Ag. 1254–1255*: 236 n. 3. *Cho. 270–296*: 109, L7; *807–808, 953–954*: 202 n. 10; *1031–1032*: L7; *1034–1039*: L7, 8; *1059–1064*: L8. *Eum. 19*: 218; *64–88*: 110, L8; *84*: L7.

B. General Index

Tiribazos, consultant, H73
Tiryns, Tirynthians, L107. Consultant(s): 32, Q176, L86
Tisamenos, Orestes' son, cult of, 75, Q91
Tisis, seer, 104
Tithorea, 167
Titus, Roman envoy, consultant, Q138
Tlepolemos, consultant, L14
Trachinia, Trachis, 142, 237, H6, Q196
Tralles, 190, 191
Trinakria = Sicily, Q27
tripod, Delphic, 142, 159, 178, 183, 196, 199, 201, 204, 206, 211, 213, 216, 219, 222, 224, 225, 226, 251, 253, 339, 415; Q123, L109, 176; elsewhere, 186, Q17, 76; L93, 96, D34
Triton, D48
Trojan War, 4, 19, 33, 90–91, 117, 131, 132, 133, 136, 160, 413; Cat. L1, 56, 100, 115, 122, 124
Trophonios, 5, 223, Q179; Oracle of at Lebadeia, 69, 107, 320, 335; Q19, 185, L139; alternative source of Q214. Consultant: 19, 37 L9
Troy, Trojans, 131–136 passim; Cat. Q188, 232, 238; L1, 72, 98, 99, 122, 135, 157. Consultant(s): L169, F8
Trygaios, Aristophanic character, 155, 156, 160, 168, 170, 176
Twain, Mark 71
Tydeus, 72
Tyndareos, consultant, 242
Tyndarids. See Dioskuroi
Tyre, Tyrians, 360, L11
Tyrtaios, poet 121

Valerius Maximus, historian, 151, 152, 199, 200
Van Compernolle, René, 386
Vanyagwau, Shona spirit, 235
vapors, none at Delphi, 197–200, 201–203, 204, supposed, 206, 210, 213, D40
Varozvi, African people, 235
Veientine fata, alternative source of Q202
Veii, 65, Q202
verse oracles, chapter VI
Vesuvius, eruption of, 160
Victory (Nikē), goddess, 166, 185, H50
Virgilian commentators, 85
visions, 104, 107, 145, H69, Q165
Vitalis, Gerhard, 101
Voice of Mwari, 230–231, 235

Wade-Gery, H. T., 124
Way, A. S., 206
Weird Sisters, 63

Wells, Joseph, 306
White Island, 78
white maidens, Q231
Whittaker, C. R., 230
widow's mite, 41, 378
Wilhelm, A., 133, 134
Will, E., 199
Winds, worship of, 193, Q148
witch, 68
wooden wall, 124–128
Wormell, D. E. W., 7, 88, 89, 137, 416

Xanthippe, Delphic priestess, 354
Xanthos, hero, 20. Consultant; L48
Xanthos, historian, 112, 113
Xanthos, Lycian river, 225
Xanthos, poet, 109
Xenokritos, Athenian, 156
Xenophon, 34, 147, 148, 149, 220, 332. Consultant: 32, 43, 235; H11, 12
Xerxes, king of Persia, 5, 124, 127, 157, 170, 171, Q153
Xuthos, king of Athens, consultant, 20, 25, 216, 227; L28, 48

Yoruba, Nigerian people, 229
Young Men 1 and 2, consultants, L141, 142

Zeno of Kition, Stoic, consultant, Q224
Zenobios, 84, 110
Zethos, Theban hero, 167
Zeus, 116, 125, 166, 180, 183, 185, 339, 373, 397; Cat. H7; Q3, 7, 8, 112, 147, 152, 196, 259; L6, 17, 20, 22, 46, 51, 97, 99, 109, 114, 165; D9, 39; speaker of oracles, 65, 92; gives oracles at Olympia, 17, 229, 295; at Dodona, 91, 229, 242, 396, sends signs, 90; festivals, 68; in legend, 98, 99, 117, 146; Apollo speaks his will, 113, 178, 179, 184, 218; worship of, 131, 175, 177, 191, 295; H48, 68; Q4, 154, 218, 243; temenos of at Olympia, 168; priest of, 190, H58, 59; identified with Ammon, 229; alternative source of Q107. Epithets: Aphesios, 373; Aristaios, L90; Basileus (the King), 235, H11; Chrysaoreus, H43; Eleutherios, Q156; Epidotes, 131; Hegetor, 101; Hellenios Syllanios, Q8; Hikesios, 129; Hypatos, H19, 28, 29; Hyperdexios, H74; Ithomatas, 186, Q17, 175; Lykaios, 107, 115; Moiragetes, H2; Nemeios, 59, L41; panellenios, 373; Patroos, H36; Soter, H50; Teleos, H19